HOUSE OF COMMONS   SES

TRANSPORT COMMITTEE

Second Report

FUTURE OF THE RAILWAYS IN THE LIGHT OF THE GOVERNMENT'S WHITE PAPER PROPOSALS

Volume IV

Appendices to the Minutes of Evidence

Ordered by The House of Commons *to be printed*
23 April 1993

LONDON: HMSO

£28.50 net

HC 246-IV

LIST OF APPENDICES TO THE MINUTES OF EVIDENCE

Volume IV

Future Prospects for the Railway System in the Light of the Government's Proposals for Privatisation

The cost of printing and publishing this Volume is estimated by Her Majesty's Stationery Office at £43,310.

APPENDICES TO THE MINUTES OF EVIDENCE

Press Notice

"The Future Prospects for the Railway System in the light of the Government's Proposals for Privatisation"

The Transport Committee was nominated on 13 July 1992. Its membership is as follows: Mr Robert Adley MP (Chairman), Mr Jack Aspinwall MP, Mr Matthew Banks MP, Mr Peter Bottomley MP, Mr Terry Dicks MP, Mrs Gwyneth Dunwoody MP, Mr Alan Haselhurst MP, Mr Keith Hill MP, Mr John McFall MP, Mr Andrew MacKinlay MP, Mr David Marshall MP.

The Transport Committee's first inquiry is to be into **"The Future Prospects for the Railway System in the Light of the Government's Proposals for Privatisation"**. The Queen's Speech contained a commitment to increasing the role of the railways in meeting the country's transport needs. To that end the Government published a White Paper describing its plans for privatisation. The Committee invites comments on the proposals contained in the White Paper to reach it by 1 October. It would be helpful if, in addition to comments on the White Paper's proposals, submissions could address the following specific questions:

— What should be the aims and objectives of a privatised railway? What are the attractions for the private sector?

— Is there any conflict between the principle of open access and the granting of exclusive franchises?

— Who should do the strategic planning for our railways and how can different interests be co-ordinated? For example, can freight develop effectively on a primarily passenger network?

— What will be the Government's role in subsidy and investment? In what circumstances will cost-benefit appraisal be appropriate, and what criteria should be used for future rail investment?

— Railtrack, the track authority, will charge all operators "commercial" rates for track use. What principles should be used to set these charges?

— How should franchises operate so as to maximise the public interest, both for profitable and subsidised services?

— What arguments are there for switching immediately to a regime of rolling stock leasing for all operators, including BR? What are the White Paper's implications for BR's on going rolling stock investment programme?

— How is the value of stations to be assessed and what will be the relationship between a privately owned station and BR's operation of trains therefrom?

Submissions should aim at brevity but where length is unavoidable they should include an executive summary, referring to paragraphs in the main submission.

16 July 1992

APPENDIX 1

PONTEFRACT DISTRICT RAIL ACTION GROUP

Inquiry into the Future Prospects for the Railway System in the Light of the Government's Proposals for Privatisation

We are pleased to present our comments on the rail privatisation White Paper, including answers to the specific questions posed in the Committee's Press Notice of 16 July.

The Pontefract District Rail Action Group has been in existence since 1984 and seeks to represent the interests of users of the Sheffield-York, Leeds-Goole and Wakefield-Knottingley services—a mixture of West Yorkshire PTE and Regional Railways operations with varying characteristics and problems. Having seen the way in which the first two services have declined under the present Public Service Obligation mechanism, we are most concerned that the proposed franchising system should not have a similar negative impact.

We have sought, where possible, to illustrate our submission with specific reference to local conditions, given that within our area are to be found examples of most kinds of British Rail passenger services.

You are welcome to contact us if you require further information for your inquiry; in the meantime, we trust that the enclosed paper will be of assistance.

"NEW OPPORTUNTIES FOR THE RAILWAYS"

The Privatisation of British Rail

COMMENTS ON THE GOVERNMENT WHITE PAPER OF 14th JULY 1992 (Cm 2012)

GENERAL IMPRESSIONS AND OBSERVATIONS

We welcome the Government's stated determination "to see better use made of the railways" and its recognition of British Rail's greatly improved performance in recent years. At the same time, it is also a relief to note that it acknowledges there are areas where room for improvement remains. From the consumers' point of view, therefore, the test of the White Paper is in whether it sets out a coherent strategy to achieve these twin objectives of more and better services. On both counts, the result is extremely disappointing.

Such a result is inevitable, we believe, because the Government has failed to make an objective assessment of the reasons for British Rail's inability to live up to expectations. True, it is "limited by the structure of the industry in the public sector", but to then suggest that BR is "more insulated from the demands of the market than its private sector ... competitors" indicates, at best, a fundamental misunderstanding of the context in which BR operates. It does not infringe the political neutrality of our organisation to criticise the White Paper for being based on a purely dogmatic view—especially when the consequence of this is a formula which, if anything, will actually hinder development of a successful railway in the years ahead.

The partial approach adopted by the Government is well illustrated by the White Paper's selective use of evidence from abroad to support its proposals. It mentions the successful introduction of private tendered services on Swedish railways—but omits to mention that these run on infrastructure fully funded by the state. It also points to profits made by privately owned freight railways in the USA (albeit over distances which render road competition less effective)—but ignores the fact that US passenger services have only survived, and subsequently thrived, under state ownership.

Ownership of the railway is irrelevant to its performance: rather, it is the objectives; the financial and legislative framework; structure; and managerial quality which determine what it is capable of achieving. Broadly speaking, we would subscribe to the consensus view that, at present, the latter two are right, the former two wrong. Rather than seeking to change the former, the White Paper's proposals would effectively cement them more firmly into place, at the same time as upsetting an organisational and management structure which is just beginning to gel after a decade of change.

In view of this, we have to say that, in its present form, the White Paper will not achieve its stated intentions: it will lead to few genuinely new passenger travel opportunities, whilst, by fragmenting the rail network, it poses the threat of making many existing journeys a more complex operation. Nor will the economic disadvantages of rail freight be rectified.

The principal issue it fails to grasp is that the private sector will not become involved in railways unless it sees clear commerical reasons for doing so. Within the current financial and legislative framework—most notably the requirement that the railway meets its own infrastructure costs whilst the state pays for roads—many railway operations are inherently unprofitable. There is nothing in the White Paper which suggests that this will change, or that there will be any more incentive for operators to switch traffic from road to rail than at present. Indeed, we see a danger that certain proposals will actually have the opposite effect. If the Government wants private operators to grasp the "opportunities" presented in the White Paper, it must provide the conditions in which it becomes financially attractive to do so.

In summary, the White Paper is strong on "hopes" but short on the means to turn these hopes into reality. It betrays a startling misunderstanding of the way in which a modern rail systems functions; no vision of what it wants the railway to achieve; and ignores the railway's place in the wider transport market. Consequently, its effect will be, at best, minimal—at worst positively damaging.

Ironically, its one long-term benefit might arise from its probable lack of positive impact—if this persuades the Government that it will not achieve the vigorous, expanding railway it desires without substantial financial commitment. If private enterprise fails to deliver any more than the public sector, perhaps the Government will then realise that it is not any ideologically-perceived fault of the latter system which has held British Rail back, but the adverse circumstances in which the railway is forced to operate. Then, perhaps, will the measures truly necessary to enable the railway to fulfil its potential—irrespective of ownerhship—be enacted.

COMMENTS ON SPECIFIC QUESTIONS

What should be the aims and objectives of a privatised railway?
What are the attractions for the private sector?

(1) The strategic objectives of a privatised railway should be no different to those of a publicly-owned railway, notwithstanding that companies implementing these wider aims on behalf of government will, at the same time, be pursuing separate concerns of their own. In our view, the objectives of any railway should be to provide an attractive, efficient and environmentally beneficial means of transporting passengers and freight; to maximise traffic by presenting a practical, economically attractive, alternative to road transport; and to do so as part of an integrated transport network designed to meet economic, social and environmental needs on both a national and local, corporate and individual basis.

(2) The attraction of railway operation to the private sector must be as a means of earning a return on investment—it is difficult to see it doing the job properly for any other reason. However, given the inherent unprofitability of many railway operations when assessed on a purely monetary basis, it seems essential for government to take steps to make it an attractive commercial proposition if the private sector is to become involved to any meaningful degree. We will return to this theme in paragraphs (6) (8) (9) (11) to (13).

Is there any conflict between the principle of open access and the granting of exclusive franchises?

(3) It appears to us that these principles are substantially incompatible, on both commercial and subsidised services, and that to implement them in tandem will lead to either cuts on the least viable routes operated by a particular franchisee, or increases in the cost to government of providing essential passenger services.

(4) On the commercial railway, of which we will use InterCity's East Coast main line as an appropriate local example, an outside competitor successfully running trains between, say, London and Leeds, or London and Edinburgh, would inevitably abstract revenue from existing services. In order to maintain profitability, InterCity (or a successor franchisee) would need to cut costs by either reducing services on its trunk routes—thus undesirably weakening its competitive position *vis-a-vis* the new operator—or by withdrawing from the more marginal areas of its operation—in this case services to such as Bradford, Hull or Harrogate. This, of course, would represent a (possibly accelerated) continuation of the recent trend which has seen InterCity withdraw through trains from South Humberside, Shrewsbury/Telford and Blackpool.

(5) On the subsidised railway, it is possible to see a similar scenario arising. In this case we will use the group of services run by Regional Railways North Eastern as an illustration—this being the size of operation that the Government apparently intends to offer as a franchise. A franchise would presumably win the contract on the basis of running a specified level of service on all routes for a given price, with revenue from the busy Trans-Pennine and West Yorkshire urban services helping to cross-subsidise the highly unremunerative routes such as Leeds-Goole and York-Selby-Doncaster. If a successful rival operator was able to gain a share of the revenue from some of the more lucrative routes, the financial calculation on which the franchise was won would be upset, leaving two possible options, either:

(a) Cut costs—the most effective means of which is by reducing servics, with the most vulnerable being those rural routes which require the highest subsidy (a fact which, as on InterCity, BR Regional Railways has increasingly exploited in recent years), or;

(b) Maintain the existing level of service on all routes by increasing the subsidy paid to the franchisee.

Both these options appear to be contrary to the stated aims of the White Paper, and suggest that the implications of the open access concept have not been properly thought through.

Who should do the strategic planning for our railways, and how can different interests be co-ordinated? Can freight develop effectively on a primarily passenger network?

(6) Strategic rail planning should be carried out by central government on exactly the same basis as road planning—as it is in other EC countries—and should be integrated with planning for other modes of transport, land use and regional economic development. Private companies cannot be expected to consider such matters; their role, if any, should be in implementing clear strategic objectives laid down and co-ordinated by the Government. It will not be possible for the railway to fulfil its potential by any other means; indeed, we fear that if privatisation is used as a way for the Government to reduce its role in rail planning, it will lead to deteriorating services and a reduction in rail's share of the transport market.

(7) The interests of different passenger operators, and their relationship with their customers, should be co-ordinated either directly by the Government through the Department of Transport or, as envisaged in the White Paper, by an independent regulator with binding powers. Particular attention should be given to the presentation of standardised passenger information—especially the retention of a national timetable—and marketing. It is also imperative that a standard ticketing and fares structure is maintained across the network, with all tickets valid on all operators' services (subject, presumably, to existing restrictions on the use of discounted tickets).

What will be the Government's role in subsidy and investment? In what circumstances will cost-benefit appraisal be appropriate, and what criteria should be used for future rail investment?

(8) The role of government should be to provide a "level playing field" on which decisions regarding mode of transport can be taken free from artificial price distortion. This is transparently not the case at present, and represents the biggest single reason why rail currently fails to fulfil its potential, and will continue to do so post privatisation unless drastic changes are made to the proposed infrastructure funding arrangements.

(9) This implies that Railtrack's infrastructure investment and maintenance costs should be fully funded by the Government, thereby placing rail on the same footing as roads and removing the price bias which favours road use—especially for the carriage of freight. The Swedish system provides an appropriate model.

(10) On subsidy, the Government's role should be to maintain a stable level of passenger service on all lines—in contrast to the current situation under the Public Service Obligation where a constant, or increasing, level of train mileage across the network as a whole has disguised drastic reductions in service on many individual routes. To facilitate this, we would suggest that the subsidy provided should be tailored to the level of service specified, rather than, as at present, PSO grant targets being set in advance, with service levels subsequently adjusted reflect the financial support available.

(11) Cost-benefit analysis is appropriate for all infrastructure investment decisions, this being a further measure necessary to achieve the "level playing field" between road and rail. There may also be circumstances, most probably on subsidised services, where it would be an appropriate mechanism for judging the worth of

rolling stock investment. The argument that, because straight financial appraisal *can* be used on the railway, it therefore *should* be used, does not stand up to scrutiny, and distorts the market in favour of road transport.

(12) Future rail investment should be assessed on the basis of both user and non-user benefits; environmental impact; and its potential to reduce road journeys, irrespective of whether the expenditure in question can already be justified in purely financial terms. The recent announcement on capital grants for rail projects on the basis of non-user benefits is a step in the right direction, but still leave the appraisal process heavily weighted toward roads. To gain a fully representative picture when comparing the merits of investment in different transport modes, environmental, policing and accident costs should be incorporated in the analysis of road investment.

Railtrack, the track authority, will charge all operators "commercial" rates for track use, What principles should be used to set these charges?

(13) In the first instance, we share the widely-expressed doubt whether "commercial" charging for access to the rail network is sustainable in any circumstances, let alone in the context of a commitment to increase use of this network. The financial disincentives against rail use are already severe enough under the current regime of British Rail needing to simply cover its infrastructure costs; the requirement for Railtrack to earn an 8 per cent return will only worsen them, posing, we believe, not only a barrier to new entrants, but a threat to existing traffic—especially less-than-trainload freight. The recent demise of Tiger Rail and Charterail is a timely pointer to the possible effect. It is for this reason that we advocate state funding of rail infrastructure as set out in Paragraphs (8), (9), (11) and (12).

(14) Irrespective of the wider background against which track charges are set—whether they are to cover full infrastructure costs as envisaged by the White Paper, or marginal costs only as in the Swedish approach—they should be structured in such a way as to avoid placing an unfair share of the burden on any one user of a particular stretch of line.

(15) Charges should be proportional to the use a given operator makes of the network as a whole, thus allowing the maximum flexibility and avoiding the problems thrown up by the present "prime user" rule, whereby a passenger sector can be faced with full infrastructure charges despite making only minimal use of a stretch of line in comparison with other users. In some cases this system has led to the withdrawal of passenger services to avoid costs; in others it deters the introduction of new passenger services or the beneficial rerouting of existing ones because it makes it financially advantageous for a passenger sector to concentrate its services on as few lines as possible. In short, it encourages the railway to be operated as a series of individual lines rather than a network: this needs to be changed if it is to achieve its potential, especially for passenger transport.

How should franchises operate so as to maximise the public interest, both for profitable and subsidised services?

(16) In the first instance, if franchising is to work at all there will have to be a resolution of the conflict between it and the open access concept, which we identified in Paragraphs (3) to (5). This would seem to be an appropriate task for the proposed regulatory body. New entrants wishing to operate passenger trains should have to satisfy the regulator that they will not have an adverse financial impact upon existing franchised services—in effect, that they will be tapping a genuinely new market—before receiving authority to access the rail network.

(17) There also needs to be a mechanism to ensure that regionally-based franchises mesh together into a coherent national passenger network, with particular attention to connections between commercial and subsidised services, and between groups of subsidised services which are provided by different operators. It is important that InterCity services, for example, are not allowed to develop in isolation from the subsidised sectors, given that they form the backbone of the passenger network. Such tasks will, presumably, fall within the remit of the franchising authority.

(18) We are particularly pleased that the White Paper proposes that minimum service levels will be laid down in franchise specifications; this is a long overdue development, though it must be done on a line-specific basis if it is not to simply replicate the faults of the Public Service Obligation on a more regional scale. Our experience of the latter system has been to suffer a reduction in the Sheffield-York and Leeds-Goole services to the point where they are useless for all but a limited range of travel-to-work journeys, in the knowledge that this is justified by increases in frequency on routes as far apart as Northern Scotland or the West Country.

(19) It is equally important that current timetables are not automatically used as the basis for setting minimum service levels, though clearly there will be many cases where this is quite appropriate. However, given the inadequacy of such as the Leeds-Goole service (where there are no arrivals in Leeds between 08.20 and 14.57, for example), it would be wrong for these to be effectively set in stone. In these cases, the drawing up of the franchise specification should be used as an opportunity to make a fresh start in assessing what requirements a particular aservice should meet, and whether it properly does so in its present form. As well as timetabling factors, such studies should include consideration of whether a given service might better serve regional needs in a modified form, for example; by following a different route where alternatives are available; by linking with adjoining services to form through workings; or by varying stopping patterns where it overlaps other services.

(20) The process of setting franchise specifications must also include widespread consultation with local representatives. These should include local authorities; commercial, civic and community organisations; and, crucially, rail users' representatives—both the official TUCCs and independent groups with a depth of local knowledge.

What arguments are there for switching immediately to a regime of rolling stock leasing for all operators, including BR. What are the White Paper's implications for BR's ongoing rolling stock investment programme?

(21) If the White Paper's aim of increasing the number and range of services is to be achieved, then a quicker, more flexible regime of rolling stock procurement will be necessary. Furthermore, the introduction of worthwhile minimum service levels is likely to require a larger rolling stock fleet than at present if increased frequency on one line is not to be paid for by reductions on another. Leasing would be of benefit in both these circumstances, though this does not mean to say that it should replace outright purchase altogether.

(22) It is difficult to forecast how the White Paper will affect BR's rolling stock replacement programme, though the element of uncertainty it has introduced is obviously undesirable. However, the probable loss of national perspective in planning rolling stock replacement, together with a reduction of flexibility in deployment as the single BR organisation is split up, cannot be conducive to the long term stability of the replacement programme.

How is the value of stations to be assessed and what will be the relationship between a privately owned station and BR's operation of trains therefrom?

(23) The relationships between private station owners and train operators will have to be carefully monitored, and their respective responsibilities clearly defined, if the arrangement is to be in the interests of passengers. The boundaries between operational and non-operational areas of a station, for example, will need to be set out in advance of any sale. Particular attention must be given to ensuring that all existing passenger facilities are retained maintained to a proper standard, given that the revenue potential of a shop or office unit far exceeds that of the waiting room from which it might be converted. The fate of many bus stations post-privatisation is a salutary reminder of the consequence if no restrictions are placed on commercial development.

(24) The idea of private companies taking over currently neglected stations and rejuvenating them by exploiting their commercial potential is a superficially attractive notion, though given the mixed results of BR Property Board initiatives in this respect we doubt whether the new proposals will make a significant difference. Obviously, major city centre sites will be in demand, though in many cases these have already been exploited to the limit commensurate with the interests of passengers. However, the much lower interest shown in smaller town centre and suburban stations—and commercial development's failure, in many cases, to improve facilities for passengers—suggests that, as with so many of the White Paper's fond hopes, the reality will be much less exciting than the expectation.

15 September 1992

APPENDIX 2

RUSHMORE BOROUGH COUNCIL

I am writing to you in my capacity of Chairman of the Highways Committee of the Rushmore Borough Council. Matters relating to transport in Rushmore come within the responsibilities of this Committee and I am expecting members to be raising in the Committee various issues regarding the current railway "privatization" proposals. In anticipation of this a colleague on the Council has suggested that I should write to you in your capacity of Chairman of the Select Committee on Transport and in view of you known interest in railways in particular. It is also perhaps worth mentioning that Rushmore is served by the same main line as your own constituency.

One possible area of concern is that of co-ordination of timetables and bookings of separately operated rail services. One reads of the separate railway companies in earlier days going out of their way to make life difficult for customers of their rivals by refusing to arrange connections and to allow through bookings. Indeed I am told that the Settle—Carlisle line was built because the London North Western Railway made it practically impossible for Midland Railway passengers from Yorkshire to change on to LNWR trains for Scotland! This is of course an extreme situation but one would not like to see such situations arising in the future.

Another area of concern is that of cost and quality of service. Would there be an organisation comparable to, say, OFTEL, OFGAS, OFWAT, with the responsibility of overseeing the railway operators, and with the power if necessary to determine fares or withdraw franchises?

I would be most grateful for your comments on these points and indeed on any others which you think we should be considering. Any further information you can give us would be very welcome.

I am copying this letter to our local Member of Parliament, Mr Julian Critchley.

28 July 1992

APPENDIX 3

GREATER MANCHESTER TRANSPORT ACTION GROUP

Transport 2000 in Greater Manchester

British Rail: White Paper

Regarding the White Paper, the key issues are as follows.

Para. 23 says that that Railtrack will be expected to make a return on its assets. Will the assets be valued on transfer? If so, what will be the basis of valuation: historic costs, replacement costs or some other basis. Who will be responsible for the valuation; the secretary of State or Railtrack?

If it is considered that there should be a return on the value of the assets of rail infrastructure, why should this not apply for use of road infrastructure.

Para. 60 sets out the requirements for charging routine. This seems to preclude the possibility of cross subsidy for freight, InterCity and channel tunnel operations. At present, there is a considerable cross subsidy to road freight operators from other road users. If the best use, in the national economic interest, is to be made of rail infrastructure it will be essential to have charging systems for use of both road and rail infrastructure which, at least, ensure that there is fair competition between road and rail. Other factors, for example, the environment, may justify subsidy to encourage use of rail for freight.

Actually, these seem to be issues of Government policy, rather than legislation which should be clarified rightaway.

27 July 1992

APPENDIX 4

Letter to Mr Robert Adley MP House of Commons from Mr G Smith

As Chairman of the Commons Transport Committee I feel certain that you will be closely involved in the development of the BR privatisation proposals. I have no "political objections" to the proposed legislation, but do feel we passengers will be seriously disadvantaged unless some essential safeguards are built in. Could I ask that you consider these carefully?

I have written to my local MP on some immediate day to day issues and enclose a copy for your information, but the other points I have in mind are more complex and I think are part of the detailed discussion necessary. These are:

(a) Today if there is a service delay, other trains will make unscheduled calls to pick up stranded passengers. In a situation of several operators, will they be obliged to call or will they be able to say "tough luck" wait until another of your company's trains comes along as my express cannot be delayed!

(ii) There have been many examples in the past (eg Class 155 doors) when fleets of rolling stock have been withdrawn for emergency repairs and other stock has been drafted around the whole BR system to cover and provide some service. In this situation will there be some "emergency BR powers" or, again, will other operators be able to say "tough luck" if there is no service on the effected routes for possibly weeks.

(iii) In the best interests of London, most believe "Crossrail" should be built. It is proposed to use Chiltern Line services as part of this scheme. Would the private owner of the Chiltern route be able to scupper the proposal by refusing to have his services diverted? I use this as an example, not as a specific case, but it does raise the question as to whether sensible strategy should be at the mercy of local objections.

(iv) At present BR provides properly trained drivers and guards, essential to the safety of hundreds of passengers travelling at speeds up to 125 mph. How can we passengers be sure "private" train crew are properly qualified and that the trains themselves are maintained to full safety standards? Many of today's private bus operators run vehicles that are only just legal, but their potential for disaster is not so great as that of a train.

(v) I recently visited Vienna where the City has an excellent system of Underground, trams, "express trams", local railways, state and private buses. As a user it did not matter to me who owned and operated each service, but it did matter that one ticket gave overall access to the whole system—like our London Travelcard. Also, all services were co-ordinated in one timetable and map. Whoever owns what in the London area must be part of such a system. As soon as a company or two opt out, the essential system benefits are lost.

(vi) How will essential infrastructure investment be protected? Clearly a franchisee will have to pay a route user cost, but will he pay a "supplement" to, say, replace Birmingham signalling centre or a £ million maintenance bill on, perhaps, the Forth Bridge. A road user does not pay a supplement for widening the A20 for instance, as central taxation pays. Will the track authority receive similar grants from taxation? If this is not so then investment is bound to run down.

(vii) There are already indications that some bus companies are seeking to take over the local rail services in their areas. Surely this should not be allowed, in the public interest, as such acquisitions would give a <u>total public transport monopoly</u> which is surely contrary to the philosophy of privatisation.

I hope you find these thoughts useful and will consider them in your deliberations.

28 July 1992

APPENDIX 5

BOROUGH COUNCIL OF KING'S LYNN AND WEST NORFOLK

House of Commons Transport Committee Inquiry into Future Prospects for the Railway System

In connection with the above. I write to ask whether the effect of the Government's rail privatisation proposals on the development of new strategic network patterns can be examined by the Transport Committee. In particular, it is requested that the development of the Thameslink 2000 scheme be given attention.

Thameslink 2000 is supported by the Standing Conference of East Anglian Local Authorities as well as by District and County Councils in the region. The Borough Council firmly supports the scheme.

Development of the London-King's Lynn rail service lies in its incorporation into Thameslink 2000. Fundamentals, such as overall journey time improvement and procurement of suitable long distance rolling stock, are dependent upon the scheme's inherent synergy. Consequent upon these is a considerably enhanced range of through journey possibilities with attendant business and tourism marketing opportunities for the Borough Council.

It is difficult, however, to see how a franchising system based on line of route/sub-sectors can further the strategic development of Network South East as a coherent movement system for the South and East region without central direction. Put succinctly, how will the "Great Northern" company be able to combine with the "South Coast" company (and others) to develop Thameslink 2000? If the franchising system can avoid freezing the current network pattern, will the franchisees on each leg be redundant in the event of entirely new Thameslink 2000 through services being introduced?

These matters are of considerable concern to the Borough Council, which has an established record in working for the development of strategic rail and road infrastructure affecting West Norfolk. I therefore hope that the Transport Committee will be in a position to inquire into the matters raised above.

16 September 1992

APPENDIX 6

Letter from Mr P Rees (Retired Chief Civil Engineer BR Western Region.)

Comments on "New opportunities for Railways"

Paras. 8(d) and 89

A national timetable and through ticketing are not only a "benefit", they are *essential* for the proper use of the railways. Without them, many passengers will simply not bother to use the railways and will journey instead by other means. A requirement for both should be written into the Bill.

Paras. 15 and 56

"Right of access" needs very careful definition. For example, if a Franchisee is already providing the specified level of passenger service on a route, is another going to have the right to run additional services to a different timetable, always assuming that paths are available? Such would seem to be wasteful competition which might well result in a worse overall service if Franchisees are to stay in business.

Paras. 18 and 96

So long as BR specifies technical standards, there should be no problems, but if Railtrack is privatised, the "industry—wide body" would comprise representatives of the many independent parts, and thus the decision-making process would be difficult and prolonged. Railtrack should therefore either be privatised as a whole, or remain in the public sector.

Paras. 19(d) and 30

If standards of punctuality are written into franchisees' contracts it will mean in practice that their drivers will be tempted to exceed speed instructions to keep time, just as 90 per cent of HGV drivers exceed the speed limit on motorways. Sooner or later this will lead to accidents. A policing organisation will therefore be essential and I suggest that responsibility for this should be vested in Railtrack, rather than the Health and Safety Executive which is too remote from day-to-day operations. Such a requirement should be written into the Bill.

Para. 23

At present the Government seems to think that it has fulfilled its role by allowing BR to spend large sums on investment using its own or borrowed money (which BR must repay) while screwing down the BR Board with lack of sufficient money for proper maintenance of the infrastructure. In my judgement, track conditions on BR are slowly deteriorating and a day of reckoning is coming. One of the reasons for this is a serious shortfall in the extent of reballasting of continuously welded track. Another is the lack of attention to killing weeds which clog ballast and impede drainage.

It is also contrary to good environmental management to spend large sums improving stations while allowing the adjoining running track and sidings to look like untidy green carpet of weeds.

If the lack of sufficient funds for proper maintenance applied also to Railtrack, the franchising system would be likely to make matters worse for the franchisees are bound to bring pressure for reduced charges for using track and unless the Regulator is a Civil Engineer who understands the problem there may well be an unsatisfactory compromise.

It must always be remembered that the *ultimate* responsibility for track safety and the permissible speed of trains rests with BR's Civil Engineers at local level.

Paras. 86 and 87

It is most important that written into the Bill are "watertight" safeguards which compel both Railtrack and franchisees to recognise and continue the BR practice of free and concessionary travel for BR employees and retired staff who presently enjoy them. The current trend of increasing the restriction on the use of these facilities on certain trains should also be curbed. While, clearly, the requirements of fare-paying passengers must take precedence, the requirements of staff and pensioners must also be recognised.

It is also important that the BR Pension Funds' future should be clearly specified in the Bill, stating the orgainisation under which they will operate when the BR Board ceases to exist. The present level of pensions and future increases should also be safeguarded by a clause in the Bill.

Other Comments—BR Property Board

The White Paper does not seem to mention the BR Property Board and what its future will be. Its profits are currently given over largely to BR investment and it is important that this should continue, with a suitable clause written into the Bill.

Other Comments—The Freight Railway

At present freight and passenger trains use the same tracks, but it is a known fact among Permanent Way Engineers that present heavy axle-load wagons do significantly more damage to track than do high speed passenger trains. For this reason such freight trains which include wagons with axle loads up to 25 tons are usually restricted to 60 mph. If the amount of freight traffic increased, it would be even more important to retain this restriction and the frequency of track maintenance and thus the cost would also increase. The ideal solution would be to separate freight traffic on to separate tracks, but except for new routes such as the Channel Tunnel Link this is rarely possible.

The French, however, do not allow freight traffic on their TGV routes and have designed them accordingly. The quality of passenger ride on these routes is superb and beyond anything currently achieved on BR. It would detract from the appeal of BR high speed trains if the quality of ride deteriorated further due to heavy axle-load freight traffic using the same routes.

22 September 1992

APPENDIX 7

Memorandum from Mr R V Fox

"The Future Prospects for the Railway System in the light of the *Government's Proposals for Privatisation*"

The writer retired from BR service in 1979 as Services Planning Manager in the Chief Operations Manager's Department at British Rail Headquarters. Apart from war service, he spent his working life on the railways.

1. *What should be the aims and objectives of a privatised railway? What are the attractions for the private sector?*

The main *objective* of a railway built (or bought ready-made) with private finance must be to yield an income for the owners. It will therefore *aim* to provide a service which people want to buy. The attraction of a railway operation per se to the private sector will only exist, having regard to the immense capital required, if there is an equally immense reward. Since the economics of railway operation do not provide such a return, the attractions must be in some other area, such as access to large pensions funds, vide Maxwell, or in the opportunity for asset sales.

2. *Is there any conflict between the principle of open access and the granting of franchises?*

Yes, there certainly is a conflict. For a franchisee to have any hope of securing a return, he/she must be able to tailor the timing of the service to endure maximum productivity of rolling stock and train crews whilst meeting customers' requirements. A claim for access at a critical time by some other operator would undermine the utilisation of the franshisee's assets.

Members of the Transport Committee will be aware that early Railway Acts visualised "open access". For example, the Act authorising the building of the Whitby and Pickering Railway (3 William IV cap XXXV) says in section 110:

> "That all Persons shall have free liberty to pass along and to use and employ the said Railway with Carriages properly constructed as by this Act directed, upon Payment only of such Rates and Tolls as shall be demanded by the said Co."

Mr G W J Potter in his book "The History of the Whitby and Pickering Railway" (The Locomotive Publishing Co. 1906), in commenting on the Act quoted, says that "All the early railways were regarded as a type of public road or highway . . . " He goes on to say that the Railway Company usually provided the motive power. No doubt many similar Acts could be quoted. From the beginning it was the railway itself which had to arrange the timetable. Because of the diversity of users, this task cannot be delegated to franchisees. For a price of course, some special timings to meet specific priorities can be arranged. Such measures will usually be adverse on the overall economics of operation.

3. *Who should do the strategic planning for our railways and how can different interests be co-ordinated? For example, can freight develop effetively on a primarily passenger network?*

Parliament exercised a negative planning role over early railways, but even so, too many lines were built for them all to secure an adequate return on capital. In the new regime, the Railway Regulator should have a small staff for strategic planning, but this is a matter in which both the British Government and the European Community must take an interest.

Underlying rail planning, there needs to be a belief that continued unrestrained use of roads, by private cars in particular, cannot be allowed to go on ad infinitum. The populace will not freely choose to use public transport rather than the car, unless there is a quantum change in the attractiveness of the former. This is hardly feasible commercially, hence strategic planning must involve government participation.

Intensified freight operation is incompatible with short-interval regular passenger services—the old Southern Railway was able in its day to achieve better reliability than other lines by the very much lower conflict between passenger and freight services on that line.

4. *What will be the Government's role in subsidy and investment? In what circumstances will cost-benefit appraisal be appropriate, and what criteria should be used for future rail investment?*

All towns and cities have a peak-hour road congestion problem caused in the main by the use of the car for short distance travel, ie trips less than three miles. Only in urban areas is there any prospect of a railway service providing an alternative, and even this is limited. Opportunities to ameliorate this problem lie more in the encouragement of the use of buses and bicycles, and even walking, than in rail projects. Nevertheless for the major conurbations, including London, improved railways would give some hope for slowing the rate at which the environment is worsening. Reduced pollution and fewer road accidents would give significant cost-benefits.

5. *Railtrack, the track authority, will charge all operators "commercial" rates for track use. What principles should be used to set these charges?*

Charging for track use has to take account of:

(i) maximum axle weights of trains operated

(ii) the actual timing speed of the service using the track. In general, the higher the speed the higher the charge, but equally, especially slow trains would need to carry a penalty. Note that wide variations in speed are expensive because of the need for secondary lines for overtaking

(iii) number of trains passing, related to (i) and (ii)

(iv) a table of supplementary charges where special precautions have to be taken for safety or security reasons, eg movement of preserved rolling stock. Such charges could be subject to negotiation

(v) stabling charges for trains not in use should be related to the siding space set aside for this purpose and should reflect property values for the area.

So far as (v) is concerned, Railtrack might well be compensated on a cost-benefit basis, inasmuch as many road hauliers and some coach operators are able to take advantage of free overnight parking.

6. How should franchises operate so as to maximise the public interest, both for profitable and subsidised services?

Apart from the need for reliability of service, an important factor in gaining customer confidence will be some assurance of continuity of operation. Too frequent timetable changes are to be avoided, and with various franchisees there will need to be agreed dates for major changes to services. BR's 1970's aim to have one timetable a year proved too inflexible. Pre-1939, there were three major changes a year but the present twice a year regime is preferable. Because of the size of railway investment, a franchise ought to be initially for not less than five years, with a review at the end of two years. After a review, terms for an extension of the initial franchise by a further two years could be agreed.

7. What arguments are there for switching immediately to a regime of rolling stock leasing for all operators, including BR. What are the White Paper's implications for BR's on-going rolling stock investment programme?

Para. 33 of the White Paper rightly highlights the formidable investment required for a new operator who has to purchase rolling stock. It is inherent with the long life of railway coaches, and other assets, that capital outlays come in massive amounts at long intervals. Rarely is enough depreciation set aside to meet that investment, and this must be one of the reservations about handing over services with existing assets to franchisees. There is a risk that, in order to maximise current income, absolutely nothing will be put aside, that stock will not be replaced, and that after a happy (?) time running a service for ten years or so, the privatised services will fold up one by one. Such a risk seems to be a strong argument for leasing of stock as soon as possible. Pressure from customers for maintained quality would perhaps give franchisees leverage on the lessors.

8. How is the value of stations to be assessed and what will be the relationship between a privately-owned station and BR's operations of trains therefrom?

I cannot comment on the valuing of station sites, but defining a boundary between Railtrack's jurisdiction and the rest poses many legal difficulties. Will two Police forces operate on a station? There are London stations which have to be closed to prevent crush injuries when a relatively short interruption to services occurs. At Fenchurch Street, for example, prospective passengers would, in such circumstances, have to be held outside in the street during the evening peak. Public safety would demand this. For similar reasons, there could be no encroachment by station traders into defined platform areas, even though a large open space may be inviting to the uninitiated.

In BR's regime, free access to trains without ticket check has manifestly resulted in much fare evasion. It is to be hoped changes in station ownership and management would include measures to reduce such fraud.

At major terminal stations, accommodation must be available in the event of, say, a buffer stop collision, where attention can be given to injured passengers not in need of transport to hospital. Under railway ownership, ad hoc arrangements can usually be made.

14 September 1992

APPENDIX 8

Letter from Mr N Kelly to Mr Robert Adley MP

I read an entry in the "*Independent*" newspaper recently (August 27), which stated that your committee will be taking evidence from rail users regarding all aspects of travel in the area. I would be more than happy to recount my many and varied experiences as a severly disabled passenger. I am 33 years of age with a chronically unstable and extremely painful amputated right leg, a fused left ankle and foot, and a very unstable right shoulder which is prone to dislocation. I use British Rail to assist me with a number of interests and pusuits, eg photography of windmills for a proposed book that I am writing, to augment my great interest in the railway system and its trains and equipment. Until very recently BR offered a 50 per cent discount on fares "across the board", but by January 1993 that concession will cease and thereafter disabled travellers will only be allowed 35 per cent which is, in fact, a fare increase of some 16 per cent (five times the rate of inflation) to, arguably, the group that are the least able to pay. It would seem that BR have decided to jettison the concept of providing a proper public service to the disabled members of the travelling public.

Changes in policy are also noticeable in other areas of the overall service—the de-staffing of many stations is causing myself, and doubtless many others, considerable hardship particularly if there are steep flights of stairs at these un-attended venues; I use a folding bicycle instead of a wheelchair and I find it very difficult to use stairs to get from one platform to another because there is either no member of staff available, or, if there is one I am usually told in no uncertain terms that assisting me is not part of his job! Again, with no adequate space allocated on modern trains for the stowage of bicycles this presents me with further problems. Another example of inconsiderate planning is to be found at Kings Cross "Thameslink"—I defy anyone with severe mobility problems to be able to use that service at all.

I am aware that it is possible to make prior arrangements for assistance but it is very difficult for me to guarantee journey times or itineraries in advance owing to the vagaries of my condition and the side effects of my medication (ie a sudden attack of vomiting, or severe swelling of the stump which inhibits the use of my artificical leg), in which case I may have to cancel my trip totally or take a later train which may go by a different route. As I explained previously I use my bicycle which was especially bought and adapted to fit more easily into a small space, as a "wheelchair"—when I am riding it I am not putting weight on to my damaged leg, whereas if I had to walk the length of a platform, or indeed, from the ticket office to the train which I wished to catch I would never make it. I am constantly being forced to get off the machine by BR staff and BTC Police because the rules are "no bicycles". Is it not possible to have some kind of a disability badge as is used on a car? I do have such a badge for a car, but as I do not drive I have to rely on someone else when I go by car.

I have spoken several times to Mr Yummie, the BR Disabled Travel Officer, but although I think he sympathises with my problems, his hands appear to be "tied" and his teeth "drawn"! It is to be hoped that your Select Committee will be able to impress upon the Government the needs to retain the various Railcards, special concessions and facilities for people such as myself; the Secretary of State, Mr McGregor must, I feel, make it clear to the operators that these concessions must stay in place for he does not make it plain in his White Paper.

16 September 1992

APPENDIX 9

Memorandum from Mr S G Keeling on White Paper Cm 2012 July 1992

"The future prospects for the railway system in the light of the Government's proposals for privatisation".

1. *What should be the aims and objectives of a privatised railway? What are the attractions for the private sector?*

I do not believe that any private Company, which is run as a business can be altruistic. Therefore, having accepted Investor's money, the Company's first aim must be to give those investors a return (profit) on their investment. Its secondary aim, in support of the first, must be to offer an attractive package to potential customers at a price they are willing to pay. In the case of a Railway Company, such a package would need services to the places and at the times required by the customer, punctually operated, in so far as safety allows, in clean and comfortable passenger rolling stock, or in the case of freight, without loss or damage to goods in transit.

The only attraction I can see for the Private Sector is that of Advertising, and even this could rebound if the private effort fails.

2. *Is there any conflict between the principle of open access and the granting of exclusive franchises?*

Taken literally, "open access" I presume to mean anyone can enter the field of tendering for parts of the British Rail system which are opened to offer. "Exclusive Franchise" can only mean what it says—a franchise, which excludes any would be competitors. So although in the first instance the field is open, once a franchise is given—exclusively—to one competitor, it is no longer open, for the duration of the franchise given.

3. *Who should do the strategic planning for our railways and how can different interests be co-ordinated? For example, can freight develop effectively on a primarily passenger network?*

Against the background of the White Paper, which leads one to the conclusion that there could be any number of participants competing with each other, there has to be one unit to co-ordinate the conflicting wishes and aims. This has to be a Central Timing and Diagramming section, using the latest computerised methods. With programs designed to produce *the most efficient* arrangement, based on data input, the result would have to be accepted by everybody as fair and equal. With such an approach, there is no reason why freight should not develop effectively on the British Rail network.

4. *What will be the Government's role in subsidy and investment? In what circumstances will cost-benefit appraisal be appropriate and what criteria should be used for future rail investment?*

Before this can be answered, one needs to know—What weighting does the Government apply to the following factors:

(a) Environmental. Is the Government serious about this?

(b) Loss of life and injuries through transport accidents.

(c) The cost of providing and safely maintaining a railway system, as against its potential earning capacity.

(d) The costs of any available alternative system of mass transport.

(e) The importance of having a railway network for Defence needs, for mass movement of men and materials, in event of war or threat of war.

If the replies confirm that the Government considers a railway network essential to life in this country—I would suggest that this justifies TRACK AND SIGNALLING being paid for by the Taxpayer. Other costs, recoverable through charges, would begin at that point. Developments could be assessed on their contribution to easing and lowering the cost of movement.

5. *Railtrack, the authority, will charge all operators "commercial" rates for track use. What principles should be used to set these charges?*

To be "commercial"—it must pay for itself and provide funds for research and development. The costs figures should be available from BR sources now. For simplicity, it would be as well if a charge per train mile could be calculated. This might have to cover essential Light Engine mileage (enabling locomotives to move to train starting points). It is quite possible that BR has statistics to help in this calculation.

NB Net Ton Miles or Passenger Miles would not be appropriate for private operators. The operator must take his chance on the load factor—the same as any other transport operator.

6. *How should the franchisees operate so as to maximise the public interest, both for profitable and subsidised services?*

Whoever thought of franchising had better spell out what he had in mind.

To me, a franchisee must provide power, crew and rolling stock; make known his timing requirement and seek the approval of the Central Timing organisation—and then he must sell the service. All the present day and the future advertising facilities are at his diposal. The only limitation is what he can afford to spend.

For a subsidised service, I would suggest that the amount of subsidy must be defined at the time the franchise is given. The Franchisee will know what profit margin he must allow and base his charges on that.

If track charges are based on train mileage, this might give some lead as to what the subsidy should be. In the case of freight, the nature of the load carried could influence the subsidy.

The only practical example I have seen is the "Lufthansa" special coaches at Stuttgart.

7. *What arguments are there for switching immediately to a regime of rolling stock leasing for all operators, including BR What are the White Paper's implications for BR's on-going rolling stock investment programme?*

To switch immediately to rolling stock leasing entirely implies the purchase by the Government or, their take-over of all costs including maintenance, and the imposition (by agreement) of leasing charges on BR, preferably on a service by service basis. A standard charge would not be acceptable—to either BR or the customer who would ultimately be paying.

In para 33 it states, "The Government is committed to continuing investment in rolling stock but hopes to pass on to the Private Sector" . . .

So the implication is that the Government wants to get out of as much as possible as soon as possible.

8. *How is the value of stations to be assessed and what will be the relationship between a privately owned station and BR's operation of trains therefrom?*

It should be possible for BR to identify the costs of providing a station and perhaps an arbitrary figure could be calculated of its running value—say a proportion of its ticket receipts. From these figures, a net value of a kind could be assessed.

The relationship, will be rather like that of a BR locomotive and crew as at present when it operates in a Private Siding. BR does not pay for the privilege, it provides the means by which the siding can be of use. It could be held liable for damage caused by reason of negligence on the part of its employees.

In a Private Station—BR or a Franchisee would be in the same position, bound by Railway Rules and Regulations, but otherwise under the control of the Station Owner/Tenant's employees.

The attached notes have been made as I read through the White Paper and the following is a list of the paragraphs on which I have made specific comment:

Introduction; Paragraphs 5; 6; 7; 8; 9; 10; 11; 12; 13; 14; 15; 16; 17; 18; 19; 21; 22; 23; 25-33; 34-36; 37; 38; 39; 42-43; 44; 45-53; 54-55; 56-61; 62-63; 64; 65-68; 69; 70; 72; 73; 76-79; 80; 81; 82; 83; 84; 85; 86; 87; 88; 89-90; 91-94; 95-97; 98; 99; 100.

My combined opinions are given in answer to your questions, but I would add three more points:

(a) Paragraph 9 is very true, but not only must care be exercised in the pace of change, the very nature of the change requires careful debate,—by Government, Experienced Railway Operators, and Users— and each must understand the other's point of view.

(b) 'Sectorisation' requires a careful scrutiny by unbiased assessors, to establish its value.

(c) To my mind, a Railway is a geographical feature, a system to link locations geographically—for both freight and passenger movement purposes. Any move away from a geographical arrangement requires absolute justification.

THE PRIVATISATON OF BRITISH RAIL.

Analysis of the White Paper and Comments.

INTRODUCTION

Should add: 'The Railway is a costly mode of transport, especially in the UK, where it is bound by traditional regulations to preserve an exceptionally high level of safety. As such, it is unlikely ever to be able to exist unaided, for as has been shewn since nationalisation (and before) despite all efforts to reduce costs, charges have had to rise continuously and are now almost outside the range of ordinary people.'

Para. 5. '... performance is not good enough'. WHY?

1. Manpower has been reduced to the point where there is no standby cover, thus any individual failure by a key worker, whatever the cause, is likely to result in delay and/or cancellation.

2. Observance of standard safety regulations almost always causes delay to the train involved and frequently to all other trains in the locality. The application of the regulations is due in many cases to causes outside the immediate control of the operating staff, e.g. vandalism, animals on the line, suicides, communication cords pulled—these are everyday items.

In 40 years railway work, I have never known 'lack of incentive' in any way to deter me or my colleagues from making continued efforts to achieve improvement in operating performance. The job alone was our incentive. It was certainly never the pay.

Para. 6. I and most thinking railwaymen can see possible benefits in privatisation—a return to private companies. Where we may disagree is—HOW?

Para. 7. I do not think we are comparing like with like, but let us see all the details of how other countries have achieved success in private operation. Are the conditions comparable—not from what I saw in America!

ESSENTIAL REQUIREMENTS

Para. 8. (a) Safety—who is to pay for this, ultimately, the customer or the taxpayer?

(c) Note the Government agrees to pay some subsidies. Can this be taken together with quality of service?

(d) Labour made the case of Network (Nationalised) Benefits, but inter Company time tabling and ticketing arrangements existed before nationalisation.

(e) The Trade Unions will treat this pious statement with great suspicion,—and so do I.

(f) Another pious statement, I think.

Para. 9. I suppose this is a saving clause—to save somebody's skin in due course.

Para. 10. Privatisation as a single entity is not possible 'because its financial losses are too great'.

Do they really think that Privatisation can either absorb or reduce these losses (costs in fact) and still preserve the level and quality of service given now?

"Similar objections apply to the sale of BR split into purely geographical units."

Who says so? And on what grounds? The five Regions were ready made for privatisation into Companies. The reorganisations of the last 15 years have been cosmetic and adopted at a cost in morale and loyalty of staff.

Commitment to subsidies has already been made in para 8(a) above.

Para. 11. Seems to avoid cross subsidisation by allowing private operation of paying lines, and putting all subsidies into non-payers.

Para. 12. The Public will read "Fiddle" not "Flexible".

Para. 13. And that is that—regardless! "The Government has decided"—can we know who? Which Minister, on whose advice, with or without Cabinet understanding and approval?

Para. 14. FRANCHISING sounds like an IN word—it will have to be made very clear what it involves.

Para. 16. Implies a number of companies, all with a finger in the pie—but it also says that BR, the Track Authority, which will have responsibility for operating all tracks and infrastructures, and the other part which will become a residual operating company until........ When franchising is completed BR's only function will be to provide track and associated infrastructure.

If BR ultimately is only to PROVIDE the track and signalling etc., how is the control over the running of trains to be maintained? Until this point is reached, it seems that BR staff will carry out this function, and the private operators will have to provide the locomotives, rolling stock, and the traincrews. It should be understood that they will have the same problems as now, so far as the regulation and safe working of trains is concerned.

Para. 17. PURCHASE OR LEASE OF STATIONS. Will they be subject to Council Tax? If they staff them, will they collect any fee for usage?

Para. 18. "A very pious hope!"

Para. 19. (c) Management Freedom—does the proposal not mean that the Residual Rail Authorities will be trying to meet the conflicting requirements of a number of masters—the Franchisees?

(d) Clear and Enforceable Quality Standards—I cannot see that such a proviso will encourage would be Franchisees—so much is outside their control, especially punctuality.

Para. 21. "Where subsidy is required it will be provided."

This commitment seems to negate the initial philosophy to privatise. Maybe self-contained sections, such as LT&S might benefit, just as they would under a single BR organisation for the line.

Para. 22. 'Railtrack will own and control track and infrastructure and also have residual operating responsibilities for services, until they are franchised'. This needs further explanation. It may mean that these features stay as they are, if not, how and to what extent will a Franchisee be able to control his franchise in an operating sense?

Para. 23. Railtrack will not be subsidised and will be expected to make a return on its assets and charge operators etc.

This sounds like nobbling a race horse before the race!

FRANCHISING.

Paras. 25-33. Seems to be an expression of Government hopes, which are not based on practical experience nor logical thinking.

Paras. 34-36. Whoever has compiled this set of ideas is backing off here. Again "hopes" are expressed, but much less confidence.

Para. 37. European Passenger Services—they know even less about this, just a blind idea of a private development.

Para. 38. Network South East and Regional Services.—Regarded as unsaleable, so it looks as if the subsidy will continue and be give to Franchisees, who cannot lose. I presume they will be based on a percentage profit margin, which will be added to the subsidy.

Para. 39. Local Authorities. It seems that although BR and the Local Authorities are working together successfully, the Government wants to hand the task over to private venture, just to keep within their broad policy ideas.

Para. 41. The most pious hope of all! Let the bids roll in!

Paras. 42-43. It seems to me that the Government role has been one of obstruction so far.

Para. 44. By all means—if they can do better without extra cost to the customers.

FREIGHT.

Paras. 45-53. It would be a mistake to think that BR had not fought hard for a share of the freight business, so to suggest that better results can be obtained merely by handing it over to private companies is unduly simplistic.

Two features strike me (1) the actual costs will remain the same and may be higher if the benefits of scale are lost. Para. 52 says that "Railtrack will recover the costs of the freight infrastructure that remains in public hands through *user charges.*" (2) Splitting ownership will in no way mitigate the problems of handling so many trains over the chosen routes within the timescale required.

PARCELS.

Paras. 54-55. The original parcels business was huge, but in the complexity of other commitments it did not receive a fair share of investment and attention. The Collection and Delivery were costs shown to be excessive in relation to revenue, partly due to NFC machinations, and when this was discarded the business rapidly reduced to Red Star, which is unbeatable when properly carried out, and the Post Office mail, (letterpost), which has been greatly favoured over the years.

Separate private companies could focus on these two facilities—but when it comes to train movement, they would be in with the rest.

FREEDOM OF ACCESS.

Paras. 56-61. The principle of 'Freedom of Access' can be appreciated, but as acknowledged in para. 59, 'Access' only gets a train on to the rails at the starting point—thereafter, as outlined earlier in this document, it will be progressed by:

(a) Railtrack, which will control day-to-day operations through the signalling system; and

(b) 'The Residual Operating Unit'—which will continue to run the rail services until they have been franchised'.

Thus they will be exposed to the same privations as affect day-to-day working under BR.

Para. 60. Is the catch all clause of all time—which reveals the total apprehension at the base of these proposals.

Para. 61. So the government hides behind this clause. 'Await the findings', 'require an independent Regulator to ensure it operates fairly'—to whose advantage?—the investor's or the Customer's. I do not think both can have it.

MAINTENANCE DEPOTS AND STATIONS.

Paras. 62-63. Emphasis is laid on 'access'—what does it mean? Where is the safeguard to ensure that equipment is maintained to the level required even now on BR? What experience has been gained with Privately Owned wagons? I remember back in previously Privately Owned Railway days that some owners had to be chased to get repairs done.

THE REGULATOR.

Para. 64. The three main roles: each clause requires a great deal more definition, as each raises many questions. As bare principles they sound fine—but how are they to be applied, by what means? Will it involve a complaints system, where anyone who is dissatisfied can seek retribution?

Paras. 65-68. The summation of these would probably result in price increases which the traffic cannot bear.

Para. 69. There is scope here to open up a new branch of the law!

Para. 70. Is the Regulator's job designed for the existing Board Chairman, after his displacement? I shudder to think of the possibilities here.

CLOSURES.

Para. 72. No comment, but the door is kept open for further reductions.

OPERATING LICENCES

Para. 73. Prospective buyers need to read this clause very carefully . . . and 74 and 75!

SAFETY

Paras. 76–79. These paragraphs add up to no change in safety standards and leaves the last word in the hands of Railtrack, ie BR, as now.

Para. 80. BR already vets and certifies private "Operating" staff to work on BR lines, and this seems to be the same. It also applies to private locomotives and rolling stock travelling over BR lines.

Para. 81. No change—"H.M. Inspectorate will continue . . .". At present they operate through BR, a single entity able to control the whole network. What will be the position when there are numerous owners and employers?

Para. 82. Introduces a word the "Executive"—can we be more precise? What is the "body" which will certificate drivers and signalmen?

Para. 83. This is a bit nebulous. "Appropriate safety arrangements" for the future, when BR is completely defunct.

Para. 84. Was it the "Health and Safety Executive"? If so, what will be their resources? . . . a lot of displaced Operating Managers?

EMPLOYEES

Para. 85. There is no doubt that working in smaller management units, employees will more easily identify, and probably, if the management deserve it, loyalty will be restored. This, of course, reverses the course of organisation on BR, which has been followed for the last 30 years or so, in the drive for reduction in administrative costs. I think employees know too much about the business and its inherent non-profitability to invest their savings. Maybe a free share issue might win some new interest.

Para. 86. The SAFEGUARD proviso is essential to a successful changeover.

Para. 87. The Pensioners are already worried. They have seen employees in other businesses come off worse and they suspect the Government will NOT maintain its stated interest in their welfare. The reference to a "broadly" comparative scheme is not encouraging.

NETWORK BENEFITS

Para. 88. Perhaps they are—but does the electorate trust them?

TIMETABLING

Paras. 89–90. The ultimate *responsibility* for timetabling remains the *Railtrack*—does this mean free from Government interference, timetabling to the best advantage for all—NOT giving preference to one over another, because an MP has pressed for preference. Regarding paragraph 90, with all the additional conferring, will they ever get a timetable published?

TICKETING

Paras. 91–94. More pious hopes. The new owners will choose to do what is best for their individual businesses.

TECHNICAL STANDARDS AND RESEARCH

Paras. 95–97. Nothing new here—the Technicians will co-operate I think, although they never did in the last days of private enterprise. There was competition then, just think of the famous locomotive engineers.

B.T. POLICE

Para. 98. Best left as now.

THE WAY FORWARD

Para. 99. It seems that the words "by hook or by crook" have been omitted.

Para. 100. BEWARE THAT THE GOVERNMENT DOES NOT FALL IN THIS ATTEMPT!
AS A STAUNCH CONSERVATIVE AND ONE WHO REALLY KNOWS THE RAILWAY BUSINESS, I CAN SEE THE DANGER.

22 August 1992

APPENDIX 10

Letter from Mr R Watts to Mr Robert Adley MP, House of Commons

BRITISH RAIL WHITE PAPER

"NEW OPPORTUNITIES FOR THE RAILWAYS: THE PRIVATISATION OF BRITISH RAIL"

I understand that the Transport Committee is undertaking an examination of the above White Paper. In view of this I thought you might appreciate a copy of a letter that I have sent to Robert Atkins MP on this subject.

I hope you will find my comments of some use to you in examining the White Paper and its implications for the future of the national rail system. As you will see I consider the White Paper to be unclear in a number of key areas and in view of the importance of the proposals I think the Government should make its intentions much more explicit at this stage. Further, I consider the speed that the proposals look likely to be pushed through to be very unwise until the full details of how the new system might work have been properly thought through.

To Mr Robert Atkins MP, House of Commons

I have recently had the opportunity to read the White Paper "New Opportunities for the Railways: The Privatisation of British Rail" (Cm 2012 July 1992) on the Governments proposals for the future organisation of British Rail. The White Paper is very short on detail and there are a number of unanswered questions so far as the proposals are concerned which I find very disturbing in view of the speed with which a Bill is to be brought before Parliament.

The two most important unanswered questions so far as I am concerned are:

(1) how it is planned to maintain the benefits of a national railway system once franchising has taken place, and

(2) how investment will be undertaken both in the short term prior to the new system being introduced and after the new system has come in.

The White Paper lacks a vision that would have been very welcome to see in a document so fundamental to the future of the national rail system. I shall concentrate in this letter on the first point and consider how it might affect me and my family as regular users of British Rail services.

I will begin with an example of a journey that I make both for work and with my family about five times a year. The journey is from Preston to York. This is a cross country journey of about 90 miles and takes 2½ to 3 hours depending on the route used. Over the last few years British Rail's Trans Pennine services have been significantly improved with some routes having frequencies of two to three trains per hour in place of hourly services.

There are three different routes that can be used to reach York from Preston. These are:

(1) *The Copy Pit Route:* Preston, Burnley, Halifax, Leeds and York. It is necessary to change trains at Leeds.

(2) *The Diggle Route:* Preston, Manchester, Huddersfield, Leeds and York. It is necessary to change trains at Manchester. Most services on this route operate beyond Leeds to York.

(3) *The Caldervale Route:* Preston, Manchester, Todmorden, Leeds and York. As for (2) above it is necessary to change trains at Manchester and sometimes at Leeds for York.

Currently, it is possible to use services provided by both InterCity and Regional Railways. Some of the Regional Railways Services are sponsored by the West Yorkshire Passenger Transport Executive (WYPTE) whose trains operate outside its geographic area to Preston, Manchester and beyond.

Irrespective of the route or train used one ticket will cover all the services operated by both passenger businesses. It is essential that through ticketing and the inter-availability of tickets is continued when services are franchised out as proposed in the White Paper. This is one of the most important benefits passengers currently enjoy when using the national rail system. It should also be remembered that when bus deregulation was introduced ticket inter-availability between operators ended in almost all cases. I shall return to this point again later in this letter.

When I travel with my family I use the Family Railcard. This not only reduced the price of family travel but means that we use rail in preference to a car for journeys such as this. It is important that the incentive for families to travel by rail is retained when rail services are franchised. In view of the powers that the Franchising Authority is likely to have it may be worth considering making it a condition of any contract let to a franchisee that they participate in national travel discount schemes such as railcards.

In summary then the benefits for me of a national rail system are as follows:

(A) *a national timetable* ie a nationally planned timetable with connecting services and the obligation to provide a service comparable to that operating in 1988.

(B) *ticket inter-availability* ie the ability to use trains provided by more than one operator on a particular route to undertake a journey. Further British Rail's conditions of carriage allow the use of "any reasonable route" means that a journey such as that to York can be undertaken over the three lines already mentioned. This facility extends the value of ticket inter-availability and can be very useful if for any reason services on one route are disrupted by engineering work or other problems,

(C) *a national fare system,* and

(D) *national discount fares* such as railcards.

It is essential that these benefits are retained as a minimum. If there is any withdrawal of these facilities once franchising of the rail system has taken place then privatisation will not have made rail services any better for me. Indeed, it will have worsened the quality of service and would certainly reduce the number of journeys that I make by rail.

I shall now look at the above points in more detail and compare them to the statments in the White Paper:

1. *Retention of a national timetable:*

On page 2 the White Paper recognises that one of the benefits of a national rail system is a national timetable. It is important that as now a national timetable is produced providing full details of all rail services provided no matter who is operating them. This was one of the major problems with bus deregulation is that timetable information became much harder to obtain as bus operators were only willing to inform passengers of the services they provided and not of any others along the same route. This situation must not be repeated.

2. *Service frequencies*

In the absence of any statement in the White Paper the present timetable (ie 1992–93) should be taken as the minimum frequency that should apply on all routes when franchises are being prepared by the Franchising Authority. This is especially important for commuters who rely on specific services in order to get to work or educational establishment. It will also ensure that early morning and late evening services are also retained.

The White Paper says in paragraph 29 page 7 that "Franchises will...specify as appropriate the obligations placed on the operator, such as minimum frequencies"...How the Franchising Authority will decide the minimum frequency for a service is not made clear. Will it consult local authorities or consumer groups? Will it consult users of services? Clarification of this very important matter should be made by the Government in advance of the Bill.

The White Paper says that there will be no set length of time for a franchise. It would be useful to learn how services will be altered to take account of changing circumstances on a particular line. Further will these changes be discussed in advance with the bodies and people I have already mentioned? Again clarification of this point would be very welcome.

3. *Ticketing*

As I have already discussed it is essential that, irrespective of who operates a particular service or group of services that, the present inter-availability of tickets and through ticketing remains.

An example of the importance of this can be seen along the East Lancashire line. This is made up of an hourly all stations service from Preston to Colne and an approximately hourly semi fast service from Leeds which calls at the main stations on the line. This provides stations such as Blackburn and Accrington with two trains an hour to Preston and Blackpool.

It is possible that the local and semi fast services could be split between two different franchises and, therefore, two different operators. Unless operators are prepared to accept each others tickets passengers could find their choice of train severely limited.

The White Paper recognises on page 2 that one of the benefits of a national rail system is through ticketing. In paragraph 68 the White Paper says that the new Regulator will have the role to ensure that network benefits are maintained.

This is an important area that the Government needs to give further consideration to. It is essential that the Franchising Authority and the Regulator are able to ensure that all operators co-operate in providing through ticketing and also ticket inter-availability.

4. *National fare system*

The current ability to buy a ticket to any part of the British Rail system must be retained once Franchising has taken place. The White Paper is again weak on this point. On page 7 paragraph 29 it says that the Franchising Authority will set "maximum fares". What does this mean? The Regulator we are told in paragraph 69 page 15 will ensure on the one hand that network benefits are maintained, including I assume through ticketing and ticket inter-availability, and at the same time ensure that this does not give rise to anti competitive practices. How is the Regulator to decide? From the passengers point of view the former is the more important. However, it may not be the Governments and it would be helpful if the White Paper was specific on this point.

5. *National discount tickets*

The current range of national railcards ie Young Persons, Family, Senior Citizen and Disabled are retained.

There is again a case for the Franchising Authority and the Regulator having the power to make it a condition of a franchising contract that operators participate in all existing national railcard schemes.

It is not clear from the White Paper what safeguards are being considered, if any, to ensure that the consumer retains the benefits of a national rail system ie national timetable, connecting services, inter availability of tickets once privatisation takes place.

I would be pleased to receive your views on the very important points that I have raised in this letter. In view of the importance of the matter I am sending a copy of this letter to Robert Adley MP, Chairman of the House of Commons Transport Select Committee, who I know is considering the implications of the White Paper.

1 September 1992

APPENDIX 11

Letter from Mr A K Stone

'The future prospects for the Railway System in the light of the Government's proposals for Privatisation.'

In response to the invitation contained in the Press Notice dated 16 July 1992, I am submitting my comments, which I hope will be of some benefit to the Transport Committee in its deliberations.

My qualification for so doing is that I am a retired Bank Manager, who in addition to holding various managerships in the City and West End, prior to my retirement, and representing my Bank on the Baltic Exchange, has continued an active interest in financial matters to the present day. I have spent all my working life in the Money Business, highly specialised business, and even now feel that I do not know it all. I realise that BR is also a very specialised business, the running of which I know practically nothing. To float it off on to the private sector needs money. Up to now every undertaking that has been "sold" by the Government has been making profits, good profits. Well nearly all—British Steel was butchered before it came to the Money Market and is still a disaster. Good profits mean the prospect of dividends payable, and perhaps some Capital gains. In other words something coming back to the Shareholders. Money, private money, is a very serious business, unlike the money squandered by the Government and it will not be forthcoming unless there is this prospect of GAIN.

After reading the White Paper, I cannot see that the Public including the Institutions, will be putting up money for Ordinary Shares (Equity). It might just be possible to find money by way of Debentures or possibly

Preference Shares for certain parts of the Sell Off, but personally I think this too, is doubtful. In any case, if the dividends on Preference Shares and Debentures were paid, and in pre 1939 years, if my memory is correct, this was not always the case, it would only effect a decrease in profit, ie increase the Loss. If the Sell occurred, the sale should ideally be underwritten, but I can see that the shares would be left with the Underwriters and the whole thing would be a FLOP.

It is a long time since I have read such rubbish, perhaps well intentioned, as this White Paper. If the Government goes ahead wth this scheme, as detailed, it will be a disaster. There are so many facts missing, so many "ifs" and "buts". For example, to get the thing off the ground one should know what are the profit and losses for the past years. Say two decades; I suspect mostly losses, and who is going to subscribed to Losses?

My brief answers to the eight points specified in the Press Release are as follows:

(1) PROFIT and to conduct the business with this view in mind. There can only be one objective for investors, an adequate profit return on the outlay.

(2) Really a technical question. Personally I can foresee difficulties. I cannot see how you can have your cake and eat it too.

(3) We already have the Ministry of Transport, which seems the obvious home. Again the second question under this heading is technical. How does freight traffic run now? Over passenger lines? If so why cannot it continue so to run? It may not be impossible to lay down new freight track, but I would have thought is would be difficult and certainly very expensive in capital outlay.

(4) A daft question. There will continue to be losses overall and the Government will have to foot the bill if it wants any Rail System at all.

(5) If privatisation were to come about, it is to be hoped that charges for track use would be as high as can be extracted. Words like "commercial rates" mean nothing, absolutely nothing.

(6) Again one can only extract the highest rates possible.

(7) Insufficient data for a responsible answer to be given. I take it that at prestnt some rolling stock is owned by BR, and other owned by customers. This is a matter really for the Accountants to investigate and report with recommendations.

(8) How can stations, especially main line stations, be sold off? In my opinion, it simply won't wash.

Having read so far, and with the other pages which follow, I hope you will realise that I am not in favour of privatisation of British Rail at all.

NOTES ON THE WHITE PAPER.

Para. 3. "Efficiency compares well with other European Railways"...

Are we comparing like with like? We are an island, we do not cover vast distances as in France, Germany, Russia, whose railways were completely rebuilt after the war.

Para. 4. ... it is all very well to say that £1,005 million was invested in 1991. But how much was spent on Motorways? I don't suppose it was less, probably more, and no profit on Motorways either! If so much money is being spent, why isn't the end result better? I do not know, but I do know that throwing money at the problem, whether Public or Private is not going to be the means of improvement of the system.

Para. 5. "Radical changes are needed".

Perhaps they are, but I would have thought it would be better to get hold of the problem by the scruff of the neck, e.g. to bring in better and more dynamic Management and to split the undertakings into sections—one such section to be responsible for Track and Signalling, with a brief and budget, and told to produce results not just for now, but also for the future. It would take a specialised knowledge of BR to detail names for other sections, I only give Track and Signalling as an obvious example.

Para. 7. I treat the claim that Japan and Swedish Railways are profitable with reserve. I honestly believe it is impossible to operate an overall Rail System on a profit basis. We need a Railway: for freight, about the charges for which I know almost nothing, and for Passengers, where I do think there is a limit for which one can charge for a ticket. Obviously if the charge is too high, passengers will boycott the system. I think the present way of selling tickets is far too complex, there are too many different offers. It would be much better to give the present method a thorough overhaul and review to get down to something simpler.

Para. 25-33. Passenger services—Franchising.

Another watchdog Authority being set up. More bureaucracy and more expense!!!!

Para. 44. Stations.

The idea of selling or leasing could provoke all sorts of trouble. Far better to leave them alone. I know there are "shops" on stations; I think it would be a good idea to sublet Catering on Stations to an organisation that knows what it is doing, such as Forte.

Para. 54. Parcels.

Profitable, but I do not see how this could be sold and still remain within the confines of BR, using its facilities, and alongside BR Staff.

The truth of the matter is that the UK has never got to grips with BR. Pre 1939 we had four companies, which were barely coping. Rolling stock rapidly becoming outdated, little money for replacements and little or no profit. Interest payments in arrears and often no dividends. By 1945 everything needed updating. Since then despite vast sums of money being poured in, morale remains low and only part of the task has been accomplished. BR could do better.

I do not know whether there is a System in place where careful watch and record is made of what goes and is on offer, with other rail Networks on an International basis. There should be a Think Tank on this matter together with an Inspection Team to travel the network to see what goes on throughout the UK, to report to a Head Office, and to criticise local situations.

This White Paper in my view is not the answer to the problem: neither will it achieve much progress. Whoever is responsible for its contents has little idea of the realities of Commercial life and the Financial realism of today.

16 September 1992

APPENDIX 12

Letter from Dr M R Bonavia

WHITE PAPER "New Opportunities for the Railways"

Comments from Dr M R Bonavia, MA, PhD, Fellow (former Member Council) of the Chartered Institute of Transport, formerly Lecturer and examiner in transport studies, University of London, Consultant, London School of Economics, Consultant in transport organisation, Government of India and elsewhere, author of *The Economics of Transport, The Nationalisation of British Transport, The Organisation of British Railways, Twilight of British Rail?,* etc.

The White paper foresees privatisation in the following stages, not necessarily in the order below.

(1.) Establishment of Railtrack

(2.) Franchising of the entire Freight Sector

(3.) Fragmentation of passenger services (in all three Sectors) into companies of varying size for franchising

(4.) Establishment of a Franchising Authority and franchising

(5.) Establishment of the Regulator

(6.) Franchising of Railtrack

Comments on each of these steps follow, with references to paragraphs in the White Paper.

However, there is one initial and simple question, to which the White Paper gives no answer. If BR's profitable services and property income (para. 44) are removed, how can the socially-necessary services (para. 8c) be guaranteed continuance? Franchisees cannot be expected to make up the loss and will presumably look for increased levels of grant to replace the missing element of cross-subsidy. This must come either from central government (PSO) or locally (PTA/PTE). Adding to this will be the costs of two major quangos as well as the new HSE safety certification arrangements, and it seems that either the taxpayer or the rail user will have to find more money. What is the Treasury view?

Establishment of Railtrack (para. 12 and elsewhere)

No reasons or evidence are produced to support the "belief" that track and train operations should be separated. All experience in the past has tended to show that vertical integration is technically desirable because of the need for day-to-day liasion between the civil engineering and the operational aspects of railway work—totally unlike the arms-length relationship which prevails on the roads. Safety and efficiency both depend on this liasion.

This objection does not apply if the separation is purely a financial one with the franchisee or lessee accepting day-to-day maintenance responsibility. For nearly a century in France the State owned the rail infrastructure and granted leases to regional operating private railway companies. For some time a similar system prevailed in Italy, with two companies, the Mediterranean and the Adriatic, expected to compete in quality of service. But in each case this separation was found disadvantageous and was abandoned in favour of an integrated network.

The real problem of implementing the Railtrack concept will emerge with the first negotiations over charges for the use of the network. For a century or more, economists and latterly traffic costing specialists have argued over the apportionment of track costs to individual operations. BR has adopted certain conventions which are adequate for establishing the overall performance of Sectors but would not satisfy cost accountants of a keenly profit-orientated private company. The obligation placed on the Regulator (para. 65) to ensure "fairness" is quite meaningless. Clear financial performance targets will have to be set for Railtrack, and charges designed to enable these targets to be reached may be quite unacceptable to franchisees. Or is Railtrack to receive an open-ended subsidy, so that it can attract franchising?

Para. 16. seems to be in contradiction with para. 22 when it is stated that "BR's only function will be to provide track ..." and in para. 22 "Railtrack will ... control day-to-day operations through the signalling system". Signalling and overall controlling (the two functions are now largely integrated in major centres) are the heart of the operational railway. Decisions regarding priority at junctions, diversions to alternative routes, emergency working and so on are not challenged by those receiving instructions since all work for a single employer at present. When staff are working for different employers, there will be scope for endless questioning of decisions and controversial correspondence, especially when it is alleged that commercial interests have been affected.

Para. 23. "Railtrack will be responsible for timetabling" seems incompatible with the commercial freedom of franchisees. It is rather as though a manufacturer were required to design a catalogue for a competitor's products. Timetabling is a highly specialised skill and franchisees are unlikely to be satisfied with what they are offered, especially after they have been confronted with the complexity of union agreements, the diagramming of stock and trainmen's workings, the requirements for servicing cleaning and refuelling, all of which at present come within a single organisation with established procedures and disciplines.

Franchising of the Freight Sector

The White Paper states (para. 47) that British Rail will "withdraw from all involvement in rail freight operations". This seems illogical, since it is the Freight Sector that has come closest to meeting targets set by the Government.

It is also the case that in freight private enterprise has already achieved a considerable partnership with BR, for instance in private ownership of terminals, wagons (a very large investment indeed) and also locomotives. It is far from clear that firms in this field would wish to take the remaining step which consists of providing train crews, with all the commitment this would involve in selecting, training and certification of staff, together with union negotiations over pay and conditions.

The simplest way to increase private sector involvement would be through fiscal measures encouraging road-to-rail changeovers, and the creation of rail-linked forwarding and warehousing companies through tax incentives.

It is doubtful whether the large private companies engaging in trainload operations would welcome a change that obliged them to deal at first hand with a new operating company and at second hand with another body levying charges for the use of infrastructure.

Fragmentation of passenger services

There would presumably be little administrative difficulty in dividing passenger operations under separate companies if the latter were based upon the Sub-Sectors that already exist. However, adding company structures to the managerial structures now in place would obviously add to administrative overhead costs for the system as a whole; and where profit or loss for the Sub-Sector (as opposed to the Sector as a whole) came into question in cases of through ticketing, concession fares, and so on, conflict of interest could arise to the detriment of the travelling public. Again, almost certainly some Sub-Sectors companies would be franchiseable and others not; and policies might well conflict between the franchised and the non-franchised.

There is a curious statement in para. 25 that "franchises will reflect a regional or local identity". Presumably this refers to passenger services, since freight facilities must be nationwide. But local identity is already preserved on Regional Railways where there is PTE funding with distinct rolling stock liveries; Network South East is regional already; and Inter-City is essentially long-distance. What further scope exists?

A major question arises over the franchising of grant-aided "socially essential" systems. There is a pledge (para. 8c) that there will be no Beeching-type cutting down of facilities. Yet surely a guarantee committing the Government to continue such grants for at least a minimum number of years will be demanded before a franchisee will commit private capital to such a venture. But can the Department, in view of Treasury procedures, possibly give such guarantees? This will have to be clarified, but the White Paper is completely vague.

Para. 15. The right of access seems to be based on road transport analogies, where simple licensing formalities give a right of entry to the infrastructure for commercial purposes. Much more complex qualifications are needed to meet the demands of modern rail technology. Both safety and efficiency standards are involved.

Establishment of a Franchising Authority

The White Paper gives no information about the proposed composition of the Franchising Authority or the principles upon which it will be expected to work. It is presumably intended to be a temporary body, to be wound up when privatisation is complete; but the likelihood is that it will either last a very long time or be wound up with its task only partly complete. There is a strong analogy with the Road Haulage Disposals Board set up in 1953 to implement the then Conservative Government's intention to privatise long-distance road haulage. The Disposals Board was under strong pressure to show quick results and was therefore a weak seller. In consequence many hauliers who had been compensated for the compulsory acquisition of their businesses were enabled to purchase them back for substantially less than they had received in compensation. In the final event, the Board was left with a "rump" of some 10,000 vehicles without buyers and a Government decision was taken to leave them in the nationalised sector and wind up the Board after 18 months of activity.

The Disposals Board had a much less difficult task than will face the Franchising Authority, merely selling groups of vehicles with their depots, all profitable assets. Even so it was heavily criticised for hand-outs at the taxpayer's expense, and privatisation remained incomplete. History may offer a warning.

Establishment of the "Regulator"

As in the case of the Franchising Authority, the White Paper gives no details of the composition of the "Regulator" nor—even more important—about what sanctions this quango will be able to enforce if the guide-lines or instructions it issues are disregarded.

The duties outlined in para. 64 are wide-ranging but not clearly defined. They appear to include the sort of tasks formerly entrusted to the Transport Tribunal, long since abolished, and many even of those held by the Inter-State Commerce Commission in the USA This could require a large bureaucratic machine to be set up employing not merely lawyers and accountants but also railway operators.

There is conflict between para. 89 ("ultimate responsibility for the planning and operation of the timetable will remain with Railtrack") and para. 23 ("allocation of train paths will be overseen by the Regulator"). In conjunction with para. 30 ("the Franchising Authority will monitor the franchisee's performance") the possibility of overlapping and clashing responsibilities seem unlimited.

The Regulator is apparently expected to involve itself in details of operation, where friction, disputes and arbitration are considered likely to arise. At present timetabling, for instance, is carried out by BR staff accustomed to work together and responding ultimately to a single employer, even though trains of different Sectors are involved. Such harmony must be expected to end with the "Balkanisation" of the network.

Franchising of Railtrack

It is hoped ultimately to franchise Railtrack, but if the latter is to be an attractive financial proposition it must have pursued a policy of "charging what the traffic will bear" vis-à-vis the franchisees. That will obviously have had a discouraging effect on potential franchisees waiting to see how the pioneers have fared. This is yet another instance of the conflict of interests that appear inherent in the elaborate network of new companies and quangos proposed in the White Paper.

The foregoing comments should not be regarded as indicating hostility to the general principle of involving private capital in railway operations. But there are various far simpler and less costly methods of achieving this. Some, in the freight field, have been mentioned. In the passenger field, charter trains can be extended and leasing of rolling stock encouraged. Major investments in infrastructure financed by tolls analogous to those on some trunk road bridges are another possibility.

Sadly, the White Paper foreshadows a long period of unproductive managerial and legal activity, delaying physical and technical progress because of uncertainties over ownership. But it is on the loyalty and professionalism of existing railway managers that chief reliance will have to be placed for a smooth transition to the new systems envisaged by the Government. This is a strong reason for progressive rather than abrupt change, with pilot schemes in place before widespread upheavals are enforced. Even so, anxieties over personal prospects and possible redundancies are bound to reduce effectiveness at this critical stage.

The White Paper poses more questions than it answers.

18 September 1992

APPENDIX 13

MOTHERWELL DISTRICT COUNCIL

Privatisation of British Rail

I would be obliged if you would consider the following points which are of concern to my Authority. They relate to road and rail issues.

1. LEVEL OF SERVICE

While main centres of population (Glasgow, Edinburgh, London etc) are likely to retain through services I am concerned about the frequency of (InterCity) trains stopping at the less important stations, including Motherwell. I fear that Motherwell may become served only by trains which stop at West, or East Coast Main Line stations and will lose its fast services to London. There has already been a significant cut in the number of West Coast Main Line InterCity services calling at Motherwell. The emerging opportunities for employment in my area increasingly depend on our current links with Glasgow and Edinburgh.

Deregulation of bus services has shown that services on most routes at off-peak times have been reduced. Will rail services at off-peak times be reduced to such levels that it becomes unattractive to travel by train?

2. CONNECTIONS

As the services are franchised, as proposed, will connections be maintained? There is already a problem of Regional Railways services maintaining connections with late running InterCity services. My concern is that this problem will be exacerbated if services are franchised on a line, or group of lines, basis.

3. THROUGH TICKETING/COST

Through ticketing is a further point of concern. At present, a ticket can be purchased at Motherwell, or most manned stations, to anywhere on the British Rail network, whether InterCity, Regional Railways or Network South East. Will this be maintained when an array of different "operators" exist? Already, it is the case that tickets for Stagecoach services are not sold at BR stations served by their services. Additionally, I fear it will become significantly more expensive to travel over less well used lines than the same distance over busier lines. This has a bearing on the utility of the network both locally and serving the rest of the UK and Europe.

4. OPERATORS GOING INTO LIQUIDATION

I am concerned about what will happen if operators do not achieve viability.

5. MAINTENANCE

Profit motivated operators will only pay for necessary maintenance, and may refuse to pay for routine maintenance undertaken by the track authority if not specifically authorised. Litigation may result during which the track authority may withdraw certain services leading to problems of speed restrictions, safety aspects and possible partial or wholesale withdrawal of services from a route or routes.

6. INVESTMENT

The shelving of the new IC250 trains and significant signalling and track upgrading proposed for the West Coast Main Line as British Rail prepares for privatisation does not inspire confidence in the Government's commitment to the future of railways in Britain. I fear that this situation will exacerbate with privatisiation. It would require the co-operation of track authority and operator who will need to have a long-term franchise to gain finance for a major project. Previous electrification projects have had beneficial spin-offs, eg electrification of InterCity East Coast Main Line led to the introduction of Regional Railways electric services between Doncaster and Leeds and between North Berwick and Edinburgh.

The forthcoming privatisation has already led to banks refusing to finance West Yorkshire PTE for the purchase of new electric units with the result that the brand new electric service will be operated with 30 year old electric trains.

7. EUROTUNNEL

As you are aware, Motherwell is the location for Eurocentral Scotland's Eurofreight Terminal. This is a key investment on which the future economic well-being of Motherwell District depends. The generation of trade flows is but one part of the achievement of its full potential. Accessibility for passenger traffic is important and will increase in importance in future years.

8. ROAD INFRASTRUCTURE

My Authority is well placed to take advantage of developments which require ready access to the motorway system.

The future development of railfreight and the Enterprise Zone sites must achieve full potential. I am concerned that significant infrastructure investment is required now:

— To improve the junctions on the M8 and M74.

— To link the M8/M74 preferably across the Ravenscraig Site to facilitate its longer term development.

Key infrastructure investment in roads is crucial. The Lanarkshire Development Agency is currently studying these issues and information will be available soon which your committee may wish to consider.

I trust the above comments will be of assistance.

Director of Planning

8 October 1992

APPENDIX 14

TONBRIDGE & DISTRICT RAILWAY TRAVELLERS ASSOCIATION

The future prospects for the Railway System in the light of the Government's Proposals for Privatisation

My Association represents the interests of travellers who use Tonbridge, Paddock Wood and Hildenborough stations. We currently have over 60 members and are the largest commuter group in the South East. I am pleased to attach our comments on the Government's White Paper for your information.

Our response to the White Paper takes the form of (1) a general overview, (2) detailed comments on particular paragraphs, and (3) answers to the specific questions referred to in the Press Notice.

General overview

My Committee are generally sceptical about the potential benefits of privatising British Rail. Although there is much to criticise in the present railway organisation, there at least is one man ultimately in charge who is responsible for railway operational policy (though he can fairly point the finger at the Secretary of State for Transport as the source of some of his problems).

While the proposals as published have drawn back from the most dogmatic extremes which had previously been aired, the compromise, which is what it obviously is, suffers from far too many "competing" or inter-dependent authorities with axes to grind, such that no decisions of note will ever be taken. The responsibility for problems and failures will be shuffled from pillar to post, and opportunities will pass through indecision. Frankly, we believe the chosen "solution" will in practice be unworkable, with the likelihood of providing passengers with no better service than they enjoy today. The much-vaunted "holy-grail" of competition will in practice only apply at pre-franchise award stage, since the majority of rail users have only one choice of line.

The only benefit that we can identify is the removal of railway investment controls from the hand of Government, though even this is questionable since Railtrack will remain in the public sector for some time to come.

Detailed Comments (by para nos.)

Para. 1. Better use will only be made of the railways if the service required is available at an acceptable quality *and at an acceptable price,* in comparison with other modes, in particular the private car. Because of the unquantifiable externalities in the sphere of transport, such as congestion, noise and pollution, it is NOT sufficient to allow the free market to determine price levels. In the same way there will be no greater responsiveness unless customers are allowed to make their views known about the standard of service, in the widest sense, that is being provided.

Para. 2. It is perhaps a pity that some of these declared advantages are not taken full account of in the Government's present investment rules.

Para. 7. Yet we have seen only too well the demise of passenger services on the US railways since the war when they were left to fend for themselves in the private sector.

Para. 8(d). It is interesting to see that all these features are admitted to be benefits of the present system. They seem unlikely to survive the Government's over-riding competition aspirations.

Para. 9. More than any other public transport system in the South East, the public depend on the railways for reaching their place of work. The last thing that commuters will wish to face is a private railway operator going bust, like so many airlines and tour companies. What proposals will apply in the case of insolvency, or any other reason for a private railway operator to cease trading? Some form of bonding seems the minimum that should be sought.

Para. 12. It seems clear that the Government recognise that railway staff morale is likely to suffer, as yet another reorganisation takes effect.

Para. 18. It is important that there are safeguards over the future of track infrastructure. It is not impossible to envisage that a newly privatised Railtrack might consider that parts could be considered to be ripe for development.

Para. 19(a). We are not fooled. Profitability depends just as much on cutting costs as it does on increasing revenue. Even the latter can be raised by increasing prices rather than by improving patronage.

Para. 19(b). It should be noted that in many places in the South East it is the infrastructure that is the constraint to the provision of new services.

Para. 19(c). About time.

Para. 19(d). Note that there is nothing here about preserving network benefits.

Para. 23. It is not clear who is responsible for timetabling. This paragraph states firstly that Railtrack will do it. Later it says that the Regulator will allocate paths. Meanwhile paragraph 19(d) says that the Franchising Authority will specify the level of services.

Para. 28. The dead hand of Government still holds sway. What happens if franchise bids do not fall within the grant budget? Little is said about how franchises will be awarded, whether on quality or price. However, after having seen the TV franchise fiasco it is perhaps better not to know how this will work, if it ever can do.

Para. 33. The statements in this paragraph are most unrealistic. The resources and planning needed to invest in new rolling stock, with its five to ten year lead time and £ millions per unit, will surely be beyond most passenger service operators unless the franchises are substantial. It was noticeable recently that Badgerline, who had shown interest in taking over the Tilbury line, expressed doubts whether they would consider investing in new rolling stock. How can a "healthy second-hand market" be expected to develop when no-one is investing in any new?

Paras. 35–36. It is puzzling why the Government are not placing more emphasis on the sale of Inter-City. One might have thought that this business would provide a useful test-case for later sales.

Para. 37. So who of all the various authorities will decide the details of the new Euro-link? To whom will they be accountable?

Para. 38. This is interesting. We thought the aim of the Government was the imminent phasing out of subsidy for Network South East. Elections and marginal seats are far more important apparently.

Para. 42. Quite how or whether these schemes would have got off the ground under the proposed arrangements is difficult to see.

Para. 43. How will it ever be possible for Railtrack, the Franchising Authority, the Regulator and the private operator(s), not to mention any input from the Health and Safety Executive and the local station lesses; all to come to a decision about an electrification project?

Para. 44. It would lead to all sorts of interface problems if stations on a franchisee's route were leased to another private railway operator. We have already seen the daft in-fighting between NSE and InterCity about selling each other's tickets.

Para. 51. In the South East freight is a minority activity for the railway. We are concerned that, if unregulated, the European freight business will, through its powerful backers, be able to dictate to Railtrack the paths that it wishes to use at the expense of the passenger business.

Para. 56. Problems will also arise where two or more companies use the same track and delays occur. However, these probably arose pre-nationalisation so there must be precedents of a sort.

Para. 57. For the majority of passengers there will continue to be no choice. Passengers will surely have no say in the choice of franchisee?

Para. 59. Too true. These are indeed difficult issues, most of which are of the Government's own making.

Para. 66. Nothing is said about the special relationship that applies in London between BR and LT in regard to service integration, joint ticketing etc. All the discussion relates to possible monopoly abuse, with no reference to the complicated network on which London commuters depend. Will BR franchisees be expected to compete directly with an LUL service?

Para. 69. It cannot really be expected that the Regulator can perform this duty and at the same time ensure competition at every point of the system.

Para. 74. The topics on which the TUCC's can currently express their views are limited by statute. Membership would also need to be made more representative of passengers. At present a greater influence on BR management when it comes to issues like timetabling is wielded by bodies like ourselves and it is to be hoped that Travellers' Organisations will be given an opportunity to enjoy a continuing close relationship with the successor authorities.

Paras. 76–78. The more authorities there are in charge of running the system, the more the scope for "passing the buck" around for its failures. How, for instance, might the Cannon Street accident enquiry have been handled? Whose responsibility would it be to invest in ATP?

Para. 88. This is so much "pie in the sky". DTp officials have already confirmed that privatised operators may not be obliged to accept a rival company's tickets.

Response to questions raised

1. The aim of a privatised railway should be to provide the most effective service to passengers at the lowest cost. However, this is not necessarily how a privatised operator would see it. Its duty to its shareholders would be to maximise return on capital or, put another way, to maximise revenue while minimising costs. Whether following these objectives would automatically lead to a better service is problematical.

It is quite possible that some potential operators would merely see the opportunity as one of asset-stripping or property development. The necessity of running a train service would be regarded as of low priority and an inconvenience to be abandoned as soon as practically possible.

2. It is self-evident that such conflicts will arise. However, a franchise could be drawn up that was exclusive apart from the requirement to allow, for example, occasional excursions by another operator over part of the same track.

3. When the railways were formerly in private hands, Committees were set up under the auspices of the Railway Clearing House to deal with matters of mutual interest, but strategic planning only really took place in times of emergency when the Government took over railway operations.

However, with the railway system now dependent on central funding, it is essential that there is some authority that can allocate the national cake between the various transport modes. As we have stated above, it is not clear who out of the various authorities established under the proposals will then resolve any major strategic issues. The development of freight on a primarily passenger network will have to be the responsibility of Railtrack.

4. According to the White Paper, the Government will continue to meet the deficits of NSE and BR, so it will still need to take an interest in these bodies' investment decisions, as it will in those of Railtrack. Investment in infrastructure should include the use of cost-benefit analysis, which should attempt to quantify all the relevant externalities in the same way as for road schemes. Investment in rolling stock should ideally be assessed in a similar way.

5. There are a number of factors to take into account when setting "commercial" rates for track charges. Foremost is the damage sustained by individual train movements, which is a function of axle loading, speed and distance. Another is the scarcity of track capacity at peak times. (While it might be thought expedient to charge less than standard rates to freight traffic at night, this might not be popular where the traffic passed through environmentally sensitive areas.) A more likely basis is the "market" or going rate for the use of a particular line, whose value would only become apparent after the first time round.

6. Although franchises should cover the level and quality of service to be provided as suggested in the White Paper, they should also include some statement about the level of fares which can be charged. This would relate to both commercial and subsidised services.

7. As we have stated above, the problems for franchisees who wish to invest in new rolling stock are immense, particularly where this might involve a switch of traction. Rolling stock leasing would appear to be the only solution in the short term, and this would at least enable BR to complete the replacement of life-expired stock. This would also provide opportunities for the few remaining manufacturers in the rolling stock business. It is almost certain that a new franchisee would only be able to commence operations by leasing stock because of the huge capital commitment and the lead times involved.

8. The value of a station should depend on its value for those alternative uses that do not conflict with the operation of the railway. Development of stations should at all times be subservient to this, and Railtrack should be able to veto any proposals by a lessee that is likely to have an adverse effect on railway operations.

29 September 1992

APPENDIX 15

Memorandum from Mr T Hart: University of Glasgow

New Opportunities for Transport Organisation and Financing

SUMMARY

1. *Overview* Privatisation has some value but it is a mistake to regard it as the principal means of transport and environmental improvement. Roads continue to be publicly owned yet lack normal commercial pricing. Rail and bus privatisation and deregulation will fail to advance overall objectives of sustainable mobility unless accompanied by fundamental reforms in the provision and pricing of road infrastructure. For economic and environmental reasons, policy should aim towards the stabilisation of overall road traffic volumes in the period to 2010.

2. *Incentives* Policy must be adjusted to include positive incentives for rail and bus use and a more rapid introduction of road pricing with particular emphasis on *heavy lorry metering* and *Supplementary Licences for peak-period car-use* in cities and larger towns.

3. *Movement Forecasts* The existing National Road Travel Forecasts should be replaced by guideline forecasts of total movement split by mode and between longer-distance and more localised movement.

4. *Motor Taxation* By 1995, motor taxation should be split between "pure" taxation and a charge element related to paying for the costs arising from road and car use not otherwise met from direct means of pricing.

5. *Rail Track Costs* Better use of rail track should be encouraged by relieving railway operating companies of track costs in return for paying an appropriate fuel surcharge.

6. *Public Transport Investment* The slowing of rail and bus investment brought about by the uncertainties of privatisation should be avoided through the transfer to a *Transitional Support Fund for Public Transport* of at least £1.5 billion from proposed UK public investment in new roads and road widening over the next five years. 20 per cent to 25 per cent of transport fuel surcharge income should also be allocated to a *Permanent National Fund for Infrastructure Investment and Public Transport Support*.

7. *Trunk Infrastructure* Publicly owned BritRail and Britroad companies, with direct sources of track user income should be created for trunk routes from January 1995.

8. *Private Sector Finance* Policy should encourage the extended use of private finance in major projects with public spending from national sources becoming more concentrated on integrated programmes for disadvantaged areas.

9. The need for a *National Franchising Authority for rail passenger services* should be reviewed; it would encourage centralisation while conflicting with open access to the market for commercial rail services on longer-distance routes.

10. *Regional Boards,* as part of forthcoming local government reforms, should be given *planning responsibilities for non-trunk transport*—including direct income from fuel surcharges and Supplementary Licences together with decisions on spending programmes for non-trunk infrastructure and support for intra-regional public passenger transport.

11. *Regional Boards* should have power to *franchise non-trunk scheduled passenger services by any mode*, promoting overall co-ordination and greater efficiency in local spending. Four Boards are urged in Scotland, to operate from January 1995.

12. *Essential safeguards within privatising programmes*. Fears about the impact of rail privatisation should be allayed by the financing reforms outlined above and by safeguards relating to *maximun fares, national concession fares, the future rail network, timetable publication and safety*.

13. *Bus Deregulation*. To ensure the expanded role for bus and rail required for sustainable mobility, bus deregulation should be reviewed to:

(a) introduce *maximum fares for local buses* (and related concession fares) *based on the perceived costs of car use* and financed, in part, from the proceeds of Supplementary Car Licences.

(b) incorporate local bus services within the franchise arrangements proposed for passenger rail services.

(c) require service alterations to be notified at not more than two or three fixed points in the year.

NEW OPPORTUNITIES FOR TRANSPORT ORGANISATION AND FINANCING

A Comment on the White Paper on Rail Privatisation, July 1992, and on Roads, Traffic and Safety, Scottish Office, March 1992 by Tom Hart

NEW OPPORTUNITIES FOR TRANSPORT ORGANISATION AND FINANCING

A Comment on the White Paper on Rail Privatisation and the Scottish Office statement on Roads, Traffic and Safety

GENERAL COMMENT

Government now recognises that environmental targets and the future growth of both national and regional incomes require fundamental reassessment of previous views that economic growth has been closely linked with policies both permitting, and encouraging, the total movement of goods and passengers to grow faster than GNP. For the future, and particularly for the UK as the cushion of North Sea oil deflates, sustainable growth will be more dependent on keeping increases in energy-intensive and environmentally disruptive mobility below rates of economic growth. Indeed, absolute reductions in certain types of movement are seen as increasingly probable and desirable eg car traffic in inner cities, long-distance lorry traffic and lengthy trips to work.

These considerations lie behind EC and UK policies which now seek:

(a) to reduce the need for movement (via amended land use and fiscal/pricing policies)

(b) to encourage car-sharing (especially at peak periods)

(c) to encourage an increased market share for rail and bus services (and for shipping in certain instances)

(d) to encourage walking and cycling as significant and healthy modes of normal travel.

Related financial policies, reinforced by other desires to reduce expenditure from taxation and public borrowing, have also stressed the need to aviod subsidies towards additional movement and to contain public spending on transport within the disciplines of road pricing and increased reliance on bond or risk capital contributions from the private sector to major transport projects.

The central point of this comment is that the new conditions facing the UK and Scottish economy in the 21st century require a *revolution in transport organisation and financing* which is not reflected either in the *Rail White Paper* or in *Roads, Traffic and Safety*. Both of these documents remain partial statements of government policy not yet linked with overall economic and environmental objectives.

Privatisation can have some value in controlling costs and encouraging innovation but it is a mistake to regard it as the principal means of rail improvement. Indeed, this paper argues that it will lead to poorer services and network contraction unless accompanied by more fundamental reforms in the framework of transport financing and pricing.

In its introductory pages (1 to 5), *Roads, Traffic and Safety* makes some effort to discuss total transport demands but this is poorly developed and perpetuates questionable views that road-based mobility is vital for the economic future of Scotland. Unlike the emphasis of the *Rail White Paper* on financial efficiency moderated by grant-aid where economic and social objectives conflict with narrower financial criteria, *Roads,*

Traffic and Safety contains no financial assessment of Scottish roads and leans heavily on dubious cost/benefit appraisals failing to evaluate road/rail transfers.

With the important exception of large urban areas, para. 1.17 of *Roads, Traffic and Safety* sees no scope for significant transfers from road to rail and states that, even if a 50 per cent increase in rail traffic could be achieved by transfers from road, "this would only reduce road traffic by 5 per cent" (or 2 years of traffic growth at 2.5 per cent).

This statement of the unimportance of road/rail transfers is open to two serious criticisms:

(1) it understates the importance of the "exceptional" position of larger urban areas. Four-fifths of the Scottish population lives in urban conditions where EC and UK policies (including land-use policies) now anticipate long-term car traffic growth (by far the largest component in total road traffic) of not more than 1 per cent a year (UK White Paper on the Environment, 1990; EC Green Paper on the Impact of Transport on the Environment, 1992)

(2) the length of corridors from Scotland to England and continental Europe are such as to have the greatest potential for shifts from lorry, coach and car use to fully modernised rail and direct shipping services (even with a 50 per cent to 70 per cent growth in total long-distance movement to and from Scotland, by 2010, this implies that zero traffic growth is likely on roads such as the M74/M6 mainly used for long-distance trips)

In these circumstances, a doubling of long-distance rail traffic and 50 per cent increase in public transport (rail plus bus) along with increased car-sharing and moves to shorter trips within urban zones, could *stabilise both long-distance and urban road traffic volumes*. Increasingly, absolute growth in road traffic is likely to be confined to certain suburban zones, to areas of smaller town and rural growth and to longer-distance trips (under 150 miles) in more sparsely populated areas where rail does have real difficulties in increasing, or even maintaining, market share.

Cost/benefit techniques and the forcasting of both total traffic and its distribution need to be refined to remedy defects in both the *Rail White Paper* and *Roads, Traffic and Safety*. Such an approach, however, is likely to be counter-productive, bureaucratic and confusing if it is divorced from *fundamental changes in the real world of transport organisation, pricing and financing*. This also requires decisions to be taken at appropriate levels. While trunk transport and certain environmental regulations require a centralised framework, many other decisions are best taken at an intermediate level between the proposed single-tier units of local government and UK/EC levels of decision-taking. *There is a strong case for increased powers of regional decision-taking, and financial responsibility for transport and land use decisions* as part of effective arrangements for "subsidiarity".

KEY REQUIREMENTS FOR THE FUTURE TRANSPORT FRAMEWORK

Six key requirements should be incorporated in urgent legislative and administrative action to create a stablised, yet dynamic, framework related to transport's role in the 21st century. These are:

(1) Reform of National and EC Policy to remove incentives for resource intensive and environmentally destructive mobility

(2) Amended EC and UK guidelines for probable growth in total movement and its distribution

(3) A level playing field for track costs, pricing and investment

(4) Increased Regional responsibility for decisions on non-trunk transport and associated land use/environmental strategies

(5) Integrated application of franchise principles to regional transport i.e. embracing non-trunk air, ferry, bus and rail passenger services and including reform of the deregulation of local buses introduced in 1986

(6) Effective safeguards, within privatisation proposals, for:

(a) a rail route network

(b) acceptable levels of maximum fares

(c) minimum standards of discount for group travel and travel by children, students, the unemployed, elderly and disabled

(d) comprehensive timetables and through ticketing

(e) improve interchange between modes.

(f) compatible safety standards for road and rail

Neither the *Rail White Paper* nor *Roads, Traffic and Safey* give adequate attention to these issues. Modifications which could be incorporated in forthcoming legislation are outlined in the following sections. They could be fully operational by January 1995. They are also compatible with redutions in public transport financed from general taxation and related public borrowing. Major transport projects would become more reliant on private sector finance.

THE FORGOTTEN ISSUE: COMPARABLE FINANCING FOR ROAD AND RAIL

While the *Rail White Paper* proposes a move towards market forces. *Roads, traffic and Safety* leavels the road sector untouched by direct financial disciplines. At a time of incrased pressure of public spending and rising environmental concern, the level of state spending on roads is ironically being increased with no attempt to introduce equivlent pricing and investment criterial for both road and rail. Indeed, as it stands *the White Paper worsens the track cost position of rail operators compared to the competing road sector*. By seeking to maximise rail track charges (para. 23), the present proposals will encourage rail franchise holders to raise fares and trim costs when no similar pressures apply to car, lorry and bus operators. Local bus operators will continue to be virtually exempt from contribution to road costs through the rebate of Bus Fuel Duty.

Put more bluntly, the current proposals would require rail franchise holders on routes such as those to the Highlands and West Highlands to pay special "tolls" when no such tolls are levied on the greatly improved roads in these areas of light traffic. On urban and inter-urban routes, the policy would also encourage shifts from rail to road rather than vice versa. This is not compatible with the Government's own economic and environmental priorities.

The *Rail White Paper* (paras. 23 and 43) suggests that this anomaly could be eased through capital grants for new rail investment but this evades the central issue that incentives should be for shifts from car to rail (and bus) use. Full recovery of rail track costs runs counter to the economic and social case for better use of existing rail infrastructure as well as of any new routes which may be provided. The need is for *grants towards the maintenance and renewal of existing track as well as for new investment*. Such grants could be financed from motor taxation and the proceeds of road pricing. They would not require extra taxation.

The nation now needs a complementary set of government proposals to reflect, in financial terms, the full costs of road usage and to ensure direct financial returns from new trunk projects. Without realistic charges for trunk and urban road usage, the effect of the *Rail White Paper* will be an accelerated decline of rail freight and reduced investment in the Inter-City and other rail projects vital to prevent traffic moving on Britain's "free" roads creating a massive congestion and pollution legacy for the 21st century.

WHAT SHOULD BE DONE

National and EC Policy on Incentives

government should remove present incentives to car-based mobility, increased congestion costs and higher resource consumption by measures including:

—shifts from National Car Licence fees to higher Fuel Duty

—replacement of Heavy Lorry Licences with electronic metering

—supplementary road pricing in urban areas (and in some sensitive scenic and leisure areas)

—separation of the "pure tax" element in road transport taxation from charges specifically related to road and transport costs

—a linked introduction or road pricing and private finance for major commercial schemes

—full taxation of the fringe benefits of company cars

—taxation of businesses on the provision of car parking space

—a shift of tax burdens towards direct taxes on energy

"Guideline" Forecasts of Future Movement and its Distribution

Present UK national forecasts of road vehicular movement are already open to criticism for ignoring supply side constraints and failing to relate forecasts of total passenger and goods movement to modal split, load factors and road vehicular volumes. Forecasts also need to be revised in the light of "level playing field" conditions and the extension of direct pricing from the air, shipping and rail sectors into pricing for road infrastructure.

New "guideline" forecast ranges are required for:

(a) total longer-distance passenger and goods movement with probable distributions between regions and modes

(b) total "urban zone" passenger and goods movement with probable distribution by mode and by major urban regions

(c) total "smaller town and rural zone" growth in localised passenger and goods movement with probable distribution by mode and between principal rural regions.

Such forecasts will help in determining project priorities within environmental and resource constraints. They will assist in identifying where road traffic is likely to remain relatively buoyant and where the greatest potential exists for shifts to movement other than by car and lorry. *They should replace the present National (Road) Traffic Forecasts.*

Track Costs and Investment

In place of the *Rail Track Authority* seeking full recovery of track costs (less unspecifed capital grants), *rail operators should be placed in a comparable position to road operators by extending road fuel charges to rail use and relieving rail operators of track responsibilities.* If the Bus Fuel Rebate continued, local rail passenger services operators should receive a similar rebate. Where there is congestion and /or prospects of financing from the private sector, government should have power to authorise supplementary track charges on roads and railways.

Under the present rail proposals, there is also a severe danger that *road investment will proceed as planned* while *the uncertainties of privatisation will reduce immediate programmes for rail investment* below the levels essential to strengthen the equipment industry and to enlarge rail capacity to handle an increasing share of total passenger movement and longer-distance freight. Contrary to Government expectations of revival in the local bus market, bus privatisation and deregulation produced a similar dip in bus investment and continued decline in usage. Specific Government initiatives are required to accelerate the modernisation of local bus fleets and to promote "freer flow" conditions for buses.

Government should tackle this immediate problem by transferring, over the next five years, *at least £1.5 billion from the road programme to a fund available for the capital grants proposed at para. 43 of the White Paper (the appropriate proportion for Scotland could be £100 to £120 million i.e. a transfer from road to rail investment of £300 million a year between 1993 and 1997 of which £20 to £24 million might be in Scotland).* At the same time, new opportunities for private financing and road pricing could make up for part of the reduction in public road investment while also encouraging greater private interest in rail and bus sector investment. This *Transitional Capital Fund for Public Transport* could be phased out in the later 1990s as new and permanent arrangements for transport financing (outlined later in this paper) came into operation.

The combined introduction of the Rail Fuel Charge, road pricing and the proposed Public Transport *Capital Fund* would go a long way to remove unsatisfactory features of the present *Rail White Paper* and *Roads, Traffic and Safety*.

Future Financial Structures for Trunk and Regional Transport

In place of the transfer of all track costs to a *Rail Track Authority* while roads continued to be divided between the state owned trunk sector and local authority roads, it would be more effective to *separate responsibilities for trunk road and rail track from responsibilities for infrastructure serving intra-regional needs.*

Simultaneously, serious consideration should be given to introducing *direct financial disciplines for trunk and regional transport* by ending both the automatic transfer of road income to the Exchequer and the present Exchequer responsibilities for investment programmes and public transport subsidies.

A new, and more transparent, system of financing incorporating the following features could be in operation as early as 1995:

(1) The treatment of 20 per cent to 25 per cent of existing road taxation as *"pure taxation"* available for non-transport expenditure

(2) Annual re-assessment of the balance of road taxation as the charges required to cover the total costs arising from road provision and use minus any costs recovered from direct pricing

(3) Allocation of some 20 per cent to 25 per cent of road charges and rail/air fuel charges to a *National Fund for Infrastructure Investment and Public Transport Support*

(4) The transfer of trunk railways and trunk roads to new *BritRail* and *BritRoad* track authorities required to show a direct return on capital (exclusive of any capital grants)

(5) The provision of income for *BritRail* and *BritRoad* through direct receipts from trunk route fuel charges, authorised supplementary charges (as in the case of congestion or major new projects) and income from property and telecommunication wayleaves

(6) The transfer of other public road and rail infrastructure to *Regional Boards* in association with a parallel transfer of income as under (5) and of responsibility for both local transport investment and public transport support ie the proceeds of non-trunk road pricing would accrue to the Regional Boards.

These proposals would remove the present differences between road and rail pricing and financing. They would involve an internalising of costs within the transport sector and cannot be seen as easy options for additional spending on either roads or public transport. Further research on suitable road charges under (2) is desirable but is likely to confirm an aggregate under-charging of road users (especially urban and trunk route car users). An acceptable return on the road account therefore requires either *increased road fuel duties* or moves to *direct pricing*. Action on both fronts may be desirable but, for economic and equitable reasons, policy should lean towards road pricing and increased local responsibility for the use of any proceeds (as recommended in the *Joint Authorities Transport and Environment Study in Edinburgh 1991*).

Direct electronic road pricing has been technically feasible since the 1960s with recent advances providing further scope for reducing installation and maintenance costs. Because of the time required for installation and the desirablility of compatible systems within the UK and in continental Europe, extensive electronic road pricing is probably still at least 10 years distant.

On the other hand, other advances in pricing and traffic management are capable of faster implementation and have the important advantage of reducing the need for the "second best" approach of compensatory payments for reduced charges by rail and bus operators. The most important advance under this heading is likely to be the early introduction of *supplementary licences for peak-period car use* in the larger urban areas (with higher rates for inner London). This system could include weekly as well as yearly licences. Effective and economical enforcement by checking random scans of peak-period number plates against computerised lists of Supplementary Licence holders with fines ranging from a minimum of £100 to a requirement to purchase a one-year supplementary licence at three times the normal rate. Pilot schemes for supplementary licencing— eg in parts of London, Cambridge and Edinburgh—could be introduced in 1993 with a national scheme following in 1995. Net income could be subject to tax but otherwise available for local use.

Other advances possible without full electronic road pricing could include:-

a rapid introduction of *bus and light rail priority streets,* busways and bus lanes

selective closure of motorway entrances (with possible exceptions for buses, heavy lorries and multi-occupant cars) to prevent through traffic being delayed by more localised trips

introduction of *metered pricing for heavy lorries* (replacing present licences and ˙including rebates of "excess" fuel tax paid by low mileage lorries, it not being feasible to have separate rates of fuel tax for lorries and rising proportion of diesel cars)

wider use of *"fast payment" tolls* on selected stretches of existing and new road.

Such fundamental reforms would promote more responsible, and less centralised, decision taking on transport priorities within limited public funding while opening up opportunities for increased use of private finance. For example, infrastructure projects could be franchised to companies over 25 to 35 year concession periods. This would allow *payments from the proposed permanent National Fund* (reinforced by continuing elements of EC grant for integrated transport and regional development strategies) *to be concentrated on important but non-commercial projects in areas of below average income and/or higher transport maintenance costs per head of population*—a point of particular importance for the *Highlands and Islands* of Scotland.

A National Franchising Authority for Rail Passenger Services?

The Rail White Paper's proposal for a National Franchising Authority should be reviewed since it:-

(a) adds an extra layer of bureaucracy and centralisation

(b) is incompatible with proposals for open access to commercial services

(c) will lead to tension and uncertainties in relationships between PTEs and the Franchise Authority (partly recognised in para 39 of the White Paper).

Provided that Transitional Capital Grants and fuel cost supplements for infrastructure use were introduced as proposed earlier in this paper, *commercial operators would be likely to offer a greater range of unsupported passenger rail services on inter-regional routes than is presently available*. In these circumstances, the benefits of a National Rail Passenger Service Franchising Authority are not clear. Instead operators could be invited to register services which they wished to provide (including the lease of rolling stock on pre-defined terms). Initial registrations could be invited by the late spring of 1993 with an opportunity to all potential operators to review their proposals and submit final registrations by December 1993.

Services could then be introduced on a phased basis with operators having the right to review services at agreed intervals. New operators would be able to enter the market at each agreed interval while existing operators would have a similar right to vary services. Finalised proposals for summer-period services coould normally be sought by the December of the preceeding year and for winter by May. Any additional services, with regional benefits greater than expected levels of income, could be provided through tender specifications determined by Regional Boards. Prior consultation with the Rail Regulatory Authority could resolve potential pathing disputes within projected timetables.

Regional Boards

Regional Boards, with power to determine franchise specifications for intra-regional services, seem preferable to a centralised National Franchising Authority. *There is an excellent opportunity to create such Boards, with transport and land use responsibilities, as part of reforms in local government*. Rather than being heavily dependent on local taxation and central government grants, such Boards could derive their principal income from local road pricing and from road and rail fuel charges applying to non-trunk services.

In practice the Boards could receive around 50 per cent of locally arising motor taxation in return for being responsible for local transport investment and public transport support. Elements of additional funding could by available from local taxation, rail fuel charges, EC sources and the proposed Transitional and National Funds for transport (which could be administered in Scotland by the Scottish Office). The majority of funding would be based on intra-regional sources and associated with regional responsibility for decisions on expenditure. Supplementary Licences would become a significant new source of local income as well as a means of reducing congestion.

Because of the valuable role which the Regional Councils have played in transport and strategic planning, local government reorganisation in Scotland creates both the opportunity—and the need—for Regional Boards (see T. Hart, *"Getting Scottish Transport on the Right Lines: Towards Fair Financing and Regional Responsibility"*, Discussion Paper for SAPT, July, 1992). These Boards could be formed of representatives from local authorities and local Enterprise Companies (LECs) with professional executives, published accounts and rolling 5-year investment programmes.

Suitable Scottish areas, coming into operation by 1 January 1995, could be:

—Clydeside and the South-west

—Lothian and Borders

—Central, Fife, Tayside and Aberdeen

—Highlands and Islands (with part of Grampian Region)

To assist links between transport and other aspects of local planning and to improve the ability to project and publicise public passenger transport as a realistic alternative to car use, *the franchise powers of such Boards should cover all non-trunk transport, whether by bus, ferry, air or rail*. This reform would promote service co-ordination and improved interchanges, areas where the consumer interest has not been well-served by bus deregulation and very variable standards of timetable provision and interchange facilities. The financial and resource impact of this reform would also be cost-reducing.

Essential Safeguards within Privatising Frameworks

To ensure that moves towards privatisation or franchising increase the overall economic attraction of public passenger transport as an effective alternative to the higher costs of increased car use, the transport framework should ensure that:

—*Day, Weekly and Monthly Zonal Tickets* for local public transport are more widely available and priced below the marginal costs of single occupant car use

—*standard rail, ferry and bus fares* for trips over 10 miles outwith times of congestion are limited to not more than *6p per mile* (with annual revisions related to the perceived cost of single occupant car use)

—*national minimum standards of discount are introduced for group travel and travel by children, students, the unemployed, the elderly and disabled*

—*National Rail Timetables* are published by the Rail Regulatory Authority and *Regional All-mode Timetables* by the Regional Boards

—Regional Boards are required to *maintain the passenger rail network as at their date of creation for at least 10 years* (unless change is authorised after parliamentary inquiry)

—*all scheduled passenger transport service changes (by air, ferry, rail or bus) are notified at 2 or 3 fixed points in the year* (this is a necessary constraint on the timetable uncertainties of totally open access—as seen with present bus services—and of probable franchise conditions setting minimum service frequencies but leaving franchise holders free to alter times and increase frequencies out of phase with changes in adjacent and connecting services)

—*compatible standards apply to road and rail safety* (an efficient audit of rail safety is required to ensure a cost-effective approach to safety which prevents traffic transfers from safe railways to less safe roads). Reform could include *extention of the responsibilities of the Health and Safety Executive to include road safety*—an area of greater deaths and serious injuries than "in-work" occupational injuries and injuries in other parts of the transport sector.

APPENDIX Transport Finance and Future Programmes

The major share of future transport funding should be internalised within the transport sector (including the early introduction of Supplementary Car Licences in urban areas and reform of the present approach to road taxation) and with provision for increasing use of private sector finance.

Within these principles, enhanced priority for the following projects is suggested within national government, Welsh Office and Scottish Office programmes for the use of the proposed Transitional and Permanent Funds for Transport Support (with supplementary capital from EC sources):

COMMON ELEMENTS IN BRITISH PROGRAMMES

— *urban rail service and busway improvements* including funding for Light Rail, additional rail passenger rolling stock and modern buses)

— grant assistance towards *expanded passenger rail capacity and the economical introduction of higher-frequency services on inter-regional routes and on routes making a significant contribution to the quality of leisure areas* eg National Parks

— grants towards development of *inter-modal, longer-distance freight services* (making greater use of rail and shipping)

— high-speed passenger line from the Channel Tunnel *via London (Stratford) with through services to the north and west* and complemented by a Eurogauge freight bypass avoiding London (possibly routed by Guildford, Reading and Oxford)

ELEMENTS OF SPECIAL VALUE TO SCOTLAND

— *modernised port facilities,* possibly concentrated at *Rosyth,* for improved access to and from continental Europe (and including major expansion of tourist traffic by direct ferry)

— development of *West Coast Main Line south from Mossend Euroterminal as key route for inter-modal freight* to and from Europe and strategic intermodal terminals in England and Wales

— improved public transport access to *Edinburgh and Glasgow Airports (linking direct with Scottish rail network)*

— *electrification from Edinburgh to Glasgow and north to Fife and Aberdeen* (with related track up-grading and including access to Glasgow and Edinburgh Airports)

— up-grading of *East Coast Main Line* to 150/200 mph operation (with removal of present speed restrictions at Doncaster, York, Morpeth, Berwick and elsewhere) giving 2 hour timings from London to Newcastle, 3 hours to Edinburgh and 3 hours 30ms. to Glasgow and linked with increased service frequency

— modification of *West Coast Main Line* passenger services to provide improved links to Birmingham and hourly services *from Edinburgh and Glasgow to Liverpool/Manchester* (including through running to *Manchester Airport* and electrification of the "missing links" into Manchester and Liverpool).

ELEMENTS OF SPECIAL VALUE TO ENGLAND AND WALES

— projection of *integrated Channel Tunnel and trunk domestic passenger services* direct from Stratford (with Crossrail and Jubilee line connections) to the north-east and Scotland and via an improved North London line to the north-west (with a new interchange in the *Willesden* area giving convenient access to services to south Wales, the south-west and *Heathrow)*

— upgrading of *West Coast Main Line* south of Preston for 125 mph operation with *improved service frequencies* integrated with *electrification from York and Hull to Leeds, Manchester, Liverpool and Holyhead* (for Irish access). This could also include early *electrification from Skipton to Carnforth and of the West Coast Main line branches to Blackpool, Barrow and Windermere.* This would improve the accessibility by rail of both *Birmingham and Manchester Airports* (this scheme, linked with post-2000 programmes for new high-speed routes (see below) could offer better value than BR's stalled plans for 155 mph operation on the existing West Coast Line)

— improvement of existing *north-south London Crossrail* service (Thameslink)

— extension of electrified *east-west London Crossrail,* North London Line and *Heathrow* rail links to provide through, electrified services to Oxford and Newbury via Reading

— provision of a new (and electrified) route from *Cambridge via Bedford and Milton Keynes to Oxford* (also affording direct electrified access from the East Coast Main Line to *Stansted Airport* and from Norwich to Birmingham via Bury St. Edmunds, Cambridge, Milton Keynes, Coventry and *Birmingham Airport)*

POST 2000 OPTIONS

— direct passenger services from Channel Tunnel to the north-east and Scotland via Stanstead Airport and a *new high-speed relief route for the East Coast Main Line*

— new high-speed route (150/200 mph), partly based on the underused former London Paddington to Birmingham Main Line, form *Willesden to Birmingham Airport and the north-west with a potential branch from Princes Risborough to west of Swindon.* This route could relieve overloaded sections of the West Coast Main Line and of the Paddington to West and Wales Main Line, allowing frequent high-speed services to operate without delays to freight services and intermediate passenger services

— electrification of the trunk crosslinks from *Leeds/Sheffield to Plymouth via Birmingham and Bristol* and from *Reading to Bristol and South Wales.*

IMPACT ON ROAD TRAFFIC AND ROAD PROGRAMME

The programmes outlined above, together with more detailed local programmes implemented by the proposed Regional Boards, would have good prospects for *stabilising total road traffic in the crowded south-east* (with reductions in inner London and in other inner cities) while *containing overall growth elsewhere to around 20 per cent to 35 per cent* in the period to 2010 (in line with EC expectations for sustainable mobility).

The benefits would include major cuts in programmes for enlarged road capacity, substantial reallocations of public spending away from new or widened roads and reductions in the total resource and social costs of transport. The economic base of the UK would be strengthened with simultaneous cuts in congestion and improvement in the quality of the environment.

APPENDIX 16

CLYDESDALE RAIL ACTION GROUP

The Transport Committee Inquiry—Rail Privatisation

Our Group represents the 58,000 population of Clydesdale District in Southern Lanarkshire. We may only have a small voice but it seems well worthwhile our making a submission to the Select Committee. Our particular unfortunate circumstances may be relevant to the Inquiry.

Clydesdale District is well served with railways but not with railway services. Although we are most apprehensive of the means of, and motivation, for rail privatisation we must emphasise that THE STATE RAILWAY SYSTEM HAS SERVED OUR AREA VERY BADLY and that changes are undoubtedly needed.

Our submission contains:

(a) The aspects of privatisation which are of most direct concern to our area.

(b) Comments on the specific questions outlined in your press release of 16 July, although it may be that these questions were directed at larger organisations than ours. We doubt if we have been able to add to your Committee's knowledge in this section.

Clearly it is the submission in (a) we most wish the Transport Committee to consider and we would wish you to use this as our executive summary with the remainder for additional interest only.

PART A—ASPECTS OF THE WHITE PAPER MOST DIRECTLY AFFECTING CLYDESDALE

1. ONGOING UNCERTAINTY

Even at this early stage the uncertainties contained in the Bill have discouraged some Private Operator and Local Authority initiatives for improving rail transport. It is understandable that a prviate company cannot commit finance when they do not know how the track costs will be charged or even if existing transport authorities will be disbanded. Uncertainty may be unavoidable at this stage but it does appear that in the privatisation bills for other industries the changeovers were structured and guarantees given specifically to retain the confidence of private finance. Why has railway privatisation not been able to avoid these damaging uncertainties?

2. RAILTRACK AUTHORITY CHARGES

The concept of the Railtrack Authority is central to the privatisation proposals. The method of charging costs is all important and a marginal cost system of charges appears essential for all railway and road systems. If the local passenger services have to pay the full overhead costs of using, say, an InterCity line then they will simply not exist. At present they are only charged the marginal costs and some way must be found of retaining this system. A railtrack charging system which demanded the full costs per train, i.e. dividing the cake equally, would soon end up with a very much smaller cake and seriously damage the network affect to the disadvantage of the private operators.

Our interest lies in providing socially and economically necessary rural passenger services over InterCity lines, obviously where there is adequate unused capacity, which there is, and we request that the Transport Committee ensure that some method is devised of retaining this method to allow continuation of such rural services and to allow private operators to start new services. Even Doctor Richard Beeching recognised that although some services could not make a profit while paying their full share of costs and overheads the policy of discontinuing these services would just shift the costs elsewhere.

3. OPEN ACCESS—SECURITY OF PRIVATE TRAIN DEVELOPMENTS

The Privatisatioh Bill envisages completely open access and that operators would not be regulated in that if, say, 50 operators wanted to provide the same service on the same route they should be allowed to do so and "may the best man win". This could conceivably be successful on very busy routes but would prevent development on other routes. It is a fact of business that developing a new product weakens the finances of a company. Far better to let another company take the risks and development costs and then step in at the right time. It would seem that if new services are to be developed by private operators then they must have some form of security of return for a reasonable period. It is difficult to see how this should be done although in retrospect the Traffic Commission regulation of bus services in pre-war years seemed to work. It is an undeniable fact that deregulation of buses has done our area no favours at all. The capital costs for railway development are somewhat higher than for buses and a method of allowing a fair return must be found.

4. INDEPENDENT PROTECTION AND REPRESENTATION FOR THE CONSUMER

The Privatisation Bill mentions various overseeing authorities. The present authority is the independent, government appointed Transport Users Consultative Committee. Last year British Rail deliberately made one of our services (to Edinburgh) unuseable (by making the only return train leave Edinburgh before the only outward train arrived there) presumably with a view to subverting the Transport Acts by claiming at a later date that the service could be discontinued completely because no regular passengers used it and therefore there could be no hardship. The Transport Users Consultative Committee, under the Chairmanship of Mr J A Corrie, a well respected Conservative, made a Major Recommendation in their Report for 1990–91 that British Rail should make a reasonable number of Edinburgh trains stop, no doubt on the basis that the trains were running anyway and had to slow down to 15 mph to go through the station because of the junction. British Rail ignored this recommendation and actually gave the same treatment to the service to Carlisle which is now effectively unuseable.

The Secretary of State for Transport, in a reply to our letter, said he was aware of the recommendation, but thought it "not appropriate to intervene" and also that the "level of service from individual stations is a matter for the management of British Rail". It makes one wonder what is the point of the TUCC? Would Oftel or Ofgas be given the same derisory treatment and what faith can Britain have in any regulatory or users' charter authority set up under Rail Privatisation? Note that the Secretary of State includes in "level of service" what is in fact a non-service. The Transport Committee, and Parliament, must address this problem for the future. I am quite sure that Parliament, in passing the Transport Acts and setting up the Transport Users' Committees, never intended the Minister to make this interpretation in this, I would say perverse, way. In all my dealings with the railway problems, and bearing in mind that the most prominent of our supporters are businessmen and conservatives, I have not yet found one person who has any confidence in the Department of Transport where railways are concerned.

4. P.T.A.'s

Privatisation will mean some changes to the roll of the Passenger Transport Authorities. Clydesdale is in the unfortunate position of being completely outside the Public Service Obligation area and almost completely outside the Strathclyde Passenger Transport Executive Area. This is very unfortunate for us and also unfortunate for democracy that we should be in Strathclyde Region but outside the Passenger Transport Area for that Region! When the later stages of Rail Privatisation decide the roll of these authorities we would advocate that:

    (a) all areas of Britain should have the advantages of a P.T.A.,

    (b) certainly no community should be in the position of being in a local authority which has a P.T.A. but which itself is excluded from the P.T.A. Area,

    (c) that P.T.A.'s must consider services across P.T.A. Area boundaries on their own merits and not as "foreign".

5. UNFAIR COMPETITION

We cannot see privatisation of the Railways being successful if competition is unfair. Private railway operators will not invest if there is unfair competition from road transport. At present the national road system is funded entirely by the state as a "social service" and as far as we are aware there are no proposals to privatise the road system. Private investors can simply not afford to take on the "Nationalised" road transport industry, unfairly subsidised by the taxpayer. It would be literally subsidising their own competition. Perhaps privatisation of railways and privatisation of roads should take place simultaneously?

6. SAFETY

We would all want the highest safety standards for railways consistent with commercial operation and at no commercial disadvantage to competing forms of transport.

Recently there have been a spate of safety legislation for railways which fail to take into account operation over 150 years with good safety records, safety practice on other well established railways such as S.N.C.F. and the much lower safety standards imposed on competing forms of transport.

In short this adds up to unfair competition which will prevent private operation of the railways from flourishing. More details would be supplied if required.

What makes things even worse is that obvious, common sense, safety measures have been ignored because they cost money. Money which, in some well known recent cases would have saved accident costs several thousand times over.

To allow privatisation of the railways as a going concern we must have sensible safety legislation with standards not completely out of line with those in competing forms of transport.

PART B. GENERAL QUESTIONS

1. AIMS, OBJECTIVES, ATTRACTIONS?

The aim is to achieve the ultimate parliamentary duty, Freedom of the Individual, in this case the freedom of the individual to travel round his own country (even if he does not own a car). This freedom has had a low profile in recent years.

The objective is to re-establish the concept of providing a service. This concept of service has been the objective of railways in Britain and most developed countries almost since they were first invented and certainly through the Victorian years when Britain was more prosperous than at present.

The secondary objective is to provide safer, more environmentally benign and cheaper carriage of freight. Check any bunch of lorry tachograph charts to see how the road transport industry conducts itself illegally in its basis of operation.

The means are to use more private investment and management knowledge in providing service Britain clearly needs. To use private business to free the railway industry from the bean counters of anti-railway government departments.

The attractions are profits and creating an asset and technology base at a time when profitable business opportunities are few. Profits may include management and labour salaries, loan interest and leasing income in an industry which ranges from massive capital investment to the most personal and individual services.

The dis-attractions are uncertainty of trading conditions, the threat of business predators and asset strippers and the very low potential margins which result from competition with the state funded, and ill-accounted, road transport industry in all its aspects.

2. CONFLICT—OPEN ACCESS AND EXCLUSIVE FRANCHISES

There is a conflict but the two methods will have to be used and regulated in such a way as to give the best service to the customer and the Nation. The deciding factor is that the regulatory authority must have the respect of all concerned and his aim must be to bring about the best service possible and keep a long term view (trains usually last a lot longer than governments). Development of the railways must be one of the stated aims of the Regulator.

3. STRATEGIC PLANNING

No one doubts that strategic planning is necessary. British Railways Board may have the professional knowledge but for many years will be involved in commercial railway operation and cannot be impartial.

The Department of Transport command no respect or confidence as far as railways are concerned. The Department have spent the last 40 years or so generally trying to wreck the railway system, the evidence is pretty overwhelming, and it is very unlikely that they will change their ways now. The Department of Transport are essentially a roads organisation and as such cannot be expected to be impartial in the administration of a private railway system.

Perhaps the resurrection of the war time Railway Executive could be possible although they may be remembered as the authority which started the move to nationalisation in the first place. The one authority which does command respect is the Transport Users' Consultative Committee. A similar or enlarged authority, independent but appointed by Government, but not the Department of Transport, may be most capable of achieving successful railway privatisation. These committees may consist of political appointees but in recent years they have been remarkably independent, perceptive and professional and in many ways have probably represented the will of Parliament or even the Government of the day more accurately than the Department of Transport or even government Ministers!

There appears no technical reason why freight cannot operate on a primarily passenger network. Only in areas of peak commuter services does there appear to be incompatibility and these services are almost certainly not profitable. Freight services will depend on the quality of the Regulator, the concept of marginal track costing and, most of all, on introducing fair competition with road transport.

4. SUBSIDY AND INVESTMENT

Subsidy and Investment by Government will continue to be necessary on a large scale and should be at least as great as the true government subsidy to the Road Transport System. Eventually complete privatisation of roads may allow government subsidy and investment to be reduced but it is inconceivable that the rural, remote or urban commuting road systems could ever survive without extensive subsidy. Transport operation would not be possible anywhere without an element of internal cross subsidy and this should be continued and managed after rail privatisation.

We would expect that cost-benefit appraisal is appropriate in all cases. This appraisal, if properly done, takes account of the real world while strict cost accounting has to draw artificial limits. Large National economies cannot be run on a "corner shop" basis and the same is true of a national transport system. Railway investment should be on Cost-benefit as long as road investment is decided this way. When all road investment is paid for by ticket sales to road users it may be possible to reconsider rail investment but we suspect this will not come about for some time. Again private rail operators cannot compete on a basis of unfiar competition.

Cost benefit criteria for rail investment must include the total benefits and disbenefits to the Nation, including safety, environmental and strategic costs and must also consider rail alignments which could be, or have effectively been, lost forever. Note that many of these routes were lost because they were routes of "wasteful competition", a very outmoded concept indeed!

5. RAILTRACK CHARGES

Extremely complex but must alow for marginal costing. Long distance passenger rail services in the United States of America rely almost completely on marignal costing on private railtracks. Possibly experimental services should be given free, or very marginal, costing for a period. It should certainly depend on track wear so that light local trains can still operate commercially. Clearly the best time slots should cost more but should not be allocated to prevent "cost benefit" services operating necessary services.

The charging problem will depend on the quality and direction given by the Regulator. It must be the basis of "Railtrack" operation that the duty and responsibility to allow rail services to flourish, while making a financial return but not to make the maximum short term commercial return by preventing a particular rail service because they cannot match the highest payers or by discontinuing rail use altogether to use the land for other property development.

6. HOW SHOULD FRANCHISES OPERATE?

We find it difficult to address this problem even though it is at the heart of the problems in our own area of interest. We can only suggest extending the best of current practice on railways and buses.

(a) Stability

Any service must have stability, A service must run for a year or more and operators must have the financial standing to allow this. Impossible trading conditions would be taken account of by the Regulator but it would not be up to individual operators to terminate or change services unilaterally at short notice. This has been one of the main problems of bus deregualation. The fear of being stranded in remote areas, possibly in bad weather, late in the day and involving old folk or people with children. Not only is this not fair or sensible but prevents commercial success.

(b) Commercial Services

It seems reasonable to assume that any services will be relatively commercial and the operators would provide services either directly, by subcontractor or by joint arrangements with other contractors.

The problems here are providing a whole service rather than a service to cream off the best traffic at certain times. While a company may make quicker profits by operating prime time trains, passengers will be lost, and the Nation will lose cost benefit, if services do not allow for early starts, late night or Sunday trains.

Spoiling services, where an operator tries to wreck another operators services by undercutting or similar must be prevented. In other words open acccess must be regulated.

(d) Uncommercial Services

Gaps in commercial services could, or must, be filled by state funded, privately operated trains. Local authorities would appear to be best able to franchise this work to private operators very much as they do for uncommercial deregulated services. However they must have guidelines and they must have finance available. There are problems with local authority politics. A local authority may prefer to pay for better roads. A socialist type authority may provide services but decide to miss out well-off enclaves on the basis that they can use their BMW's. If the present overall road subsidy and especially the hidden subsidies to buses continue the local authority may prefer to franchise buses. Over longer distances this is counter-productive.

(e) Intermediate Services.

Many services require a length of run which takes them through several local authority areas. Co-operation by successive local authorities is not always good and may be impossible over long distances. The very breaks in a service for local authority boundaries can prevent near commercial viability. Therefore it would seem necessary that some national authority should franchise longer distance services, socially desirable and economically necessary but possibly not profitable.

(f) Operators etc could integrate bus services but be expected to maintain their train services. Rural bus services always seemed more successful when they connected with trains. We understand that government policy does not allow integrated transport.

(g) The above is very much the present InterCity, Regional Railway and P.T.A. system but presumably made fairer across the nation with the introduction of private investment and management and the hopeful elimination of the dead hand of the Department of Transport.

(h) There is still the problem of training and testing staff and the investment and provision in trains. It is clear that the deregulated bus industry is in difficulty in its bus replacement provision. The high cost of new trains is a major problem as is the construction capacity for new trains and the specialised designs available. There is a lack of suitable standard designs which could be used effectively in different parts of the network. The modern designs are not very passenger friendly although it is hoped that in this respect privatisation may improve matters. It could be that privatisation will prevent the present scandal of scrapping good trains for scrapping's sake or possibly for accountants' writing off purposes. the two for three policy etc. However in the last few years British Rail have been making a good job of eliminating surplus rolling stock which could conceivably have been used by private operators.

7. ROLLING STOCK LEASING REGIME

The problem of buying new trains, as in 6(f), lead us to say that a leasing regime should be introduced as soon as possible if the privatisation concept is serious. This does, however, mean building new, not just relabelling British Rail's present stock. It could be that a government proposal to build standard rolling stock in the early 1920's should be revived. Stock should be designed where possible for universal use with a mixture of interiors. Why, for instance, are all overhead electric EMU's in 3 or 4 car sets, nothing less? Although we would recommend an immediate start on a leasing fleet we suspect that government standard trains and massive government investment may not be exactly the way the Government see it!

The implications of the White Paper for BR's on-going rolling stock programme depend entirely on the Department of Transport and the Treasury and are therefore very bad.

8. VALUE OF PRIVATE RAILWAY STATIONS

We had worked on the principle that some stations should be "community" owned and that, rather like a bus stop or lay-by, there would be no direct monetary income, except where additional services were performed for passengers. We are concerned that main stations in City centres have a development value far in excess of their railway value. The privatisation procedure must ensure that railway stations remain primarily for railway use. Direct income from railway use depends on a true all-Britain ticket system, as attempted many years ago by the Railway Clearing House, which is probably just now becoming technically possible and which could apportion all ticket revenue to its rightful receiver no matter which trains were used or where the tickets were bought.

26 *September* 1992

APPENDIX 17

Memorandum by Professor R Glendinning

Rail Privatisation: Organisational Problems

Privatisation of all state-owned industries has naturally presented major problems but those of British Railways involve two that are, if not entirely confined to railways, apply to a much greater degree. These flow from the special characteristics of the railway industry and the degree of social obligation it is usually expected to bear.

Such problems are inherent in whatever may be the form of privatisation on which the Government have recently issued a White Paper. To implement it, however, will undoubtedly take a long time and, of course, may remain unimplemented if there is a change of government.

The first problem, viz that arising from the characteristics of railway operations, will inevitably influence the possible forms of railway organisation if in private ownership. An essential feature of railways is their use of a wide-spread and inter-related complex of staff, infrastructure (track, station and other buildings, etc.) and such other assets as rolling stock. These are used to provide countless numbers of separate services to passengers or users of freight services. For them individual charges are raised but, to an exceedingly large extent, no simple relationship exists between the use of these factors and the charges made for them. This is in great contrast with the position of manufacturing industry though, even there, the relationship which, on reasonably acceptable assumptions, enables costs to be compared with selling prices, is becoming more tenuous through increasing automation.

The staff and facilities generally at any passenger station exemplify this integrated and inter-related position, all possibly contributing to the present InterCity, Network South East or Regional passenger services. The relationship is even remote in the relatively simple case of an excursion train. Moreover for the separately managed Freight and Parcels services some staff and facilities may be used jointly with passenger services.

Where under privatisation some type of organisation would make use of the staff and facilities of another, inter-unit charging. For a highly variable use of the latter would be necessary though a commuted basis might be established with agreed arrangements for departures from normal.

Results for each of the present five Rail Businesses appear in the British Railways Annual Report but, it is important to understand, these units are not separate legal entities as they would be if privatised as such. The results are described as prepared on "management accounting" bases, ie, are not audited as they would require to be if relating to companies set up under the Companies Acts.

Such results include certain general expenses of British Railways relating to these Businesses, in varying degree. Partly at least they no doubt could be fairly directly attributed to whatever separate organisations may be set up.

For example, management expenses might largely be reflected in the separate business results of these separate organisational units and, therefore also in inter-unit charges, where appropriate.

The same situation applies particularly to depreciation, (including amortisation of infrastructure assets), somewhat surprisingly included in the accounts of British Railways under General Expenses. These would form part of inter-unit charges, particularly if one or more bodies were made responsible for the infrastructure and, of course, where other assets were jointly used.

The complex and inter-related nature of railway operation poses a *sui generis* problem. Besides the nature of the special nature of this problem there remains the other, that of public obligation, confined at present to Network South East and Regional passenger services. Government support for specific services results in reduction of the expenditure to be borne by the user, and presumably would be taken into account in any agreement with a private operator.

In this connection it should be recalled that under whatever pattern of privatisation is adopted it is intended that continental trains will be permitted to cross the Channel and run on UK lines, while it will also be open to any British company or individual to provide services on these lines. A number of possibilities have been canvassed including, for example, that of the Central Rail Group, concerned with a completely new railway. All these developments would need to be fitted into the scheme of things, the operators paying, as appropriate, for the right to operate within the present railway structure.

Some of the possible forms of organisations have been publicised. These include:—

(1) Privatisation of British Railways as one single unit.

(2) Break-up of the industry regionally, comparable in some degree with the areas covered by the pre-nationalisation main-line companies.

(3) Privatisation of the infrastructure as one unit, with private operators paying for the right to use it.

(4) Break-up of British Railways in terms of the present management units.

Naturally these possibilities could be combined in various ways.

Disposal of British Railways as one complete unit would avoid the problem of inter-unit charging, eg for the use of infrastructure or staff, etc, by other units or allocation of receipts where traffic was carried over more than one area unit. Such a possibility would require only a change of ownership and is believed to be favoured by some railwaymen, who, understandably, would see it as involving minimum disturbance to the present organisation. Against this it is argued that as one complete unit it might be less efficiently managed than if by separate operators, possibly competing with each other.

Those who recall the pre-nationalised railways and favour a form of regional organisation forget the main-line companies were far from financially successful just before World War II. This was partly due to socio-political factors, eg, in regard to fixing of rates and charges but partly also because they were not then so competently managed as today, being also bureaucratic in the extreme. Before that War they could not raise capital which had to be provided by a Railway Finance Corporation Limited, channelling finance from the banks, the security for which was underwritten by the government.

The glamour attached to the pre-war railways had, understandably, been acquired by them through technological development over more than a century, but would hardly have remained even if still in private ownership.

Conversion to a regional structure would cause very great disturbance because within each area all of the present management units are established operationally. These presumably would be broken up and reformed into "mini" organisations covering all the different types of services located within each region, inevitably losing some of the economies of scale.

It will be understood that the old main-line companies evolved only gradually over a century or more from numerous smaller units, and, after nationalisation, into the present organisation.

If different regions operated as separate legal entities their relationship to one another would have to be at "arms-length", entailing much additional work. Relationships would have to be placed on a formal basis, both for allocation of income from through running and for charging for expenditure. Prior to nationalisation, it may be recalled, receipts were allocated by the Railway Clearing House, a statutory body dissolved years ago whose work was carried out at one time by some 4,000 staff.

Doubtless the burden of allocating income and other items between areas would be greatly reduced through computerisation, but nevertheless would represent additional work.

Privatisation of the infrastucture and, separately, of operating rights would distinguish responsibility for providing and maintaining the infrastructure (possibly established on a regional basis) from that of operators competing for its use.

Naturally controls independent of operators would be necessary to ensure that, when required, paths (to use railway parlance) were available and to intervene should there be a failure to meet agreed operational and other standards.

Whatever the organisation under privatisation some safeguard against closure of part of the infrastructure merely because it became uneconomic since that would affect social obligations, would be necessary, as similarly would maintenance of the infrastructure up to a certain standard of safety.

Generally European Community policy aims at a separate body owning the whole infrastructure as in Sweden, where Banverket owns it.

Another possibility mooted is that InterCity (or any other management unit that is profitable) perhaps along with its own infrastructure should be entirely privatised.

Since this would mean charging other operators for use of the infrastructure it would be inconsistent with the arrangements for the rest of the infrastructure, not to mention Commmunity policy.

The whole situation is a complex one: these are only some of the problems that might arise in terms of the different possible forms of organisation under privatisation.

The White Paper recognises many of the difficulties mentioned above. It proposes the establishment of two bodies, one to own the infrastructure, and another to regulate in various ways its use by operators.

It processes sale of the freight and parcels services. The other rail activities are expected to be operated under franchise, regulated by one of the new authorities and making payment for use of the infrastructure.

Many feel that any change in the status of the railways should be made in the light of a national transport policy, the lack of which has regularly been the complaint of past chairmen of British Railways.

Despite their present reduced role the railways still form an important factor in the economy. Unfortunately one of the main problems for transport policy is that once railways have incurred capital expenditure, especially as regards infrastructure, it can hardly ever be used for other purposes. While obviously proposals for rail capital projects should be carefully studied because they are either funded or controlled by government, the tendency seems to be to look at their short-term impact, especially where government support or control is needed.

Most other European countries give more attention to long-term planning of capital expenditure for railways and other forms of transport so that finance, whether as compensation or as direct investment to meet social obligations, seems to be more readily forthcoming.

Since transport is an all-pervading activity, provided by a diversity of different technical means through agencies, some policy of transport co-ordination is highly desirable.

A further point is that railways are much criticised as monopolistic. If in past times they appeared to act in a high-handed manner, nevertheless even then, as a public utility, they were subject to regulation to restrict any monopolistic tendency as also to meet some degree of social obligation.

While no more monopolistic in the commonly accepted use of the term than most other providers of utility services, eg, road passenger transport, the only manner in which to reduce such monopoly as may exist would be for operators to compete for a franchise, reviewed from time to time, to provide any given service.

Privatisation would probably be most successfully achieved if one single organisation owned all the infrastructure, charging operators competing to provide services within whatever restraints, eg, to meet social obligations (for which compensation would be payable), applied. This would permit competition since, within the restraints, operators paying most for the franchise would be appointed, appointments being reviewed from time to time.

Nevertheless no matter the form of organisation adopted, unless the operational side of British Railways is privatised as one unit, a considerable amount of inter-unit charging is probable while there would be necessity for some authority to control operators, whether successors to the present British operators or continental and others allowed to use the UK lines.

Such indications of government policy as have been given suggest establishment of track and control authorities with franchising of operators.

October 1992

APPENDIX 18

COMMUNITY COUNCIL OF SHROPSHIRE

Response to "New Opportunities for the Railways"—The Privatisation of British Rail

1. We welcome publication of the White Paper in so far as it is concerned with making better use of the railways, greater responsiveness to the customer and a higher quality of service. We are, however, by no means convinced that the White Paper proposals meet these objectives. We say this for two interlinked reasons, firstly because we are not convinced that the proposals will be effective and secondly because they are not sufficiently detailed or well thought through.

2. Our views are strongly influenced by our concern for rural communities and the importance of transport to such communities. Whilst we recognise the substantial improvements which have taken place in rail services in recent years (notably through new trains and faster and more frequent services) this has by no means been the case everywhere. The loss of Shropshire's InterCity service to London made the headlines but recent timetable changes have also seen a deterioration in the services to a number of more rural stations on the Shrewsbury–Chester, Shrewsbury–Crewe and Shrewsbury–Wolverhampton lines.

3. Experience with the privatisation and deregulation of bus services does not provide any confidence that a similar formula applied to the railways will bring any benefits to rural areas. In Shropshire there has been

virtually no competition, no significant improvement to services and almost no investment in new vehicles other than some minibuses.

4. We do not oppose private sector involvement in the railways. A good deal already takes place as in the case of freight (where many wagons and some locomotives are privately owned), catering services, some booking offices at rural stations (Ludlow is a good example) and recently passenger services in the case of Stagecoach rail. In the past BR has leased rolling stock (the Class 50 locomotives were originally leased from the manufacturers) and such an approach would provide major benefits for new investment. BR's rolling stock is now obtained entirely from the private sector. This has not been without its disadvantages exemplified by the unreliability and need for numerous modifications to the Class 153/155 and Class 158 fleets and the late delivery of the latter.

5. We agree that flexible solutions would be needed to encourage private sector participation in the railways. The solutions proposed in the White Paper are, however, we believe complex and bureacratic. We have strong doubts as to whether they are even workable. The White Paper proposes to establish a track authority (Railtrack), a franchising authority, a regulator of Railtrack and operators and to continue but strengthen the role of the Health and Safety Executive. There is also a suggestion that individual stations might be sold to the private sector. The picture is further complicated by the continuing involvement of PTAs and PTEs. We do not wish to oppose this since we consider the PTA/PTE specification of services to have been successful and worthy of extention to Shire counties. The above is a complex structure for an industry which is already complex by virtue of operating on fixed tracks with varying standards of equipment and subject to a very high level of safety.

6. The White Paper skates over the very real issues of how train paths will be allocated, how timetables will be co-ordinated and how through and fully interchangeable ticketing will be ensured. Bus deregulation again does not provide any confidence in these matters.

7. Several paragraphs of the White Paper are devoted to franchising but all of this is expressed in the most general of terms with no indication of how services will actually be divided up for franchising purposes. Rail services are a complex web and the service on any given line is often a compound of two or more services which have different starting and finishing points and interlock with other services along their route. Shropshire alone has five distinct services. Rolling stock (and staff) operates on complex diagrams which also relate to location of maintenance depots. How will investment in electrification and electric trains be co-ordinated. Richard Branson's current ideas of running HST diesel sets on the recently electrified East Coast Main Line make little environmental or overall financial sense. The White Paper gives no clear indication of how the level of service will be decided. Will passengers be consulted? Frequency of trains can be important as well as reliability and punctuality.

8. We strongly agree that better use should be made of the railways but this does require an adequate level of investment. We are pleased to note the statement in paragraph 43 that "the Government is also ready to provide direct support for investment in the railway for schemes which, although not earning an adequate financial return, provide a satisfactory cost benefit return when wider benefits are taken into account". This is long overdue and could be implemented straight away thus bringing rail investment onto the same footing as road investment (and perhaps leading to electrification of the Wolverhampton to Shrewsbury line and re-instatement of the InterCity service).

9. The White Paper quotes statistics on the level of investment but these are distorted by the expenditure related to the Channel Tunnel. In the current year this amounts to half of the investment. Passengers in Shropshire remain aware of the under-investment in rolling stock which results in some services still being operated by diesel sets which are over thirty years old, other trains being cancelled because there is insufficient spare rolling stock and over crowding because trains are too short. There seems no reason to suppose that private franchisees will invest in new trains for Shropshire services and indeed the increasing age of buses running in Shropshire would suggest the opposite.

10. Rail services have we believe an important part to play in providing transport for people and goods and helping to address environmental issues. More investment is needed to achieve this and a greater private sector involvement would be welcome but this must be on the basis of retaining an integrated service with long term planning and consistency. The proposals as set out in the White Paper do not measure up to these needs. A proper policy frame work for the future of the railways is needed.

11. The publication of the White Paper has made matters worse by postponing investment projects (such as the new trains for the West Coast Main Line) and indicating that there will be yet another re-organisation of the railways just after the last (which viewed from a local perspective has had its benefits). Changes are

needed but within a framework of stability. Railways managers need to be able to concentrate on managing not re-organising. This situation is also having an adverse effect on the train construction industry.

29 September 1992

APPENDIX 19

CARLISLE CITY COUNCIL

Inquiry into the Future Prospects for the Railway System in the light of the Government's Proposals for Privatisation

Carlisle City Council believes strongly in the importance of a high quality national transport network and regards the railway system as an integral component of this network.

The West Coast Main Line is part of the country's transport backbone and is of major concern to the City Council. The Governments' proposals for privatisation will clearly affect service along the line and the future levels of investment and consequently the Council has prepared the note below which it would like to be considered as evidence by the Select Committee.

EVIDENCE TO THE TRANSPORT SELECT COMMITTEE

A CASE FOR INVESTMENT IN THE WEST COAST MAIN LINE

1.0 Whilst recognising the broad remit of the Select Committee, Carlisle City Council wishes to focus its comments solely on the future of the West Coast Main Line an issue on which the Council is involved in a lobbying movement to secure vitally needed and urgent investment.

1.1 A fast reliable, efficient and high quality West Coast Inter City service is essential to the social and economic well being of the communities served by this important transport artery.

1.2 As volumes of road traffic increase and the M1/M6 become even more congested the opportunity exists for a high quality rail service to offer a more attractive alternative form of transport. Rail transport is more energy efficient than road transport and has far less secondary environmental impacts in terms of land take, noise, and green house gas emissions.

1.3 Government regional policy pursued through measures to aid the Assisted Areas will only be effective if the regions can be reached quickly and efficiently from London. In forecasting future growth poles in Britain the Henley Centre identified the importance of executives being able to conduct a days business in London and return home the same day, while the DTI stress the importance of fast rail travel to London ($2\frac{1}{2}$ hours to London) in considering Government Department relocations. The current levels of service makes it impossible for Cumbrian businesses to attend a morning meeting in the Capital without an overnight stay or using the sleeper.

1.4 Cumbria and the Western Scottish regions served by the WCML are designated in European Community terms or "Inner Peripheral" regions. These regions are characterised by weaker economic structures due partly to the additional costs in terms of time and money on the delivery of goods and movement of labour.

1.5 As investment and commerce continues to grow in the EC "Inner Central" regions and as former Eastern European markets open up and strengthen, Cumbria's location on the edge of the Atlantica region will result in its increasing isolation and peripherality. Cumbria alone among all other regions in England has no scheduled air service.

1.6 Northbound Channel Tunnel day time trains will terminate in Manchester leaving Cumbria without a service vital for European business and tourism traffic.

2.0 For all the above reasons it is vital that the £750 million rolling stock, track, signalling and power supply improvements announced in 1991 for the WCML are carried out before privatisation if the private sector is to provide an effective service. The recent announcement by BR to put on ice plans to introduce the new 250 trains due to a lack of funding will inevitably result in the WCML service deteriorating further as the 10–15 year old rolling stock gets even older and the once state of the art signalling system becomes obsolete and failure prone.

2.1 The Central Transport Consultative Committee annual report published in August 1992 showed that a number of complaints about BR services rose by more than three and half times over the past decade with the largest number of complaints relating to punctuality. The Euston-Carlisle-Scotland services featured in three out of the five worst InterCity Services nationwide for punctuality.

2.2 Against a national average of 83.7 per cent of InterCity trains being no more than 10 minutes late, the Euston-Carlisle, Euston-Scotland (daytime) and Euston-Scotland (overnight) services registered 73 per cent, 87 per cent and 56 per cent of trains arriving on time in 1992.

2.3 The service offered on the West Coast Main Line, which was electrified more than 25 years ago, now compares badly with the East Coast where the benefits of reinvestment are clearly evident. The recent £530 million electrification of the ECML has brought about a dramatic improvement in the North East's services with the new 220 trains linking Newcastle with King's Cross in 2 hours 35 minutes compared with the fastest journey home of 3 hours 30 minutes from Carlisle to Euston.

2.4 A reduction of between 25 per cent to 30 per cent in the number of daytime trains to and from Carlisle to Euston in the 1992 summer timetable has further reduced the quality and regularity of the line compared to the ECML where Newcastle virtually has a half-hourly service to and from London.

2.5 The importance of upgrading the WCML to the business community of Carlisle can be demonstrated by the findings of two consultant studies carried out in the City in 1992. JMP Ltd. found in a survey of 91 businesses that improvements to the WCML ranked as the number one priority of all rail issues, while a PIEDA company survey revealed that rail access scored a lowly 13th out of 15 in a ranking of the most important Business Location factors affecting business development in Carlisle.

2.6 The population within approximately 10 miles of the West and ECML is around 10 million and 3.5 million respectively a ratio of 3.1 but the service level ratio is almost the reverse.

2.7 The decision to withdraw the Shrewsbury InterCity Service in May, followed by the ending of the Blackpool-London InterCity service in September 1992, a tourist destination which depends on a good quality rail service for visitors, bodes badly for the future of other connecting routes onto the WCML.

2.8 The City Council is calling on BR to implement its plans announced in January 1991 for the introduction of the next generation trains—the InterCity 250 and for major improvements to the West Coast Route. BR are asked to honour the commitment made in its launch document for the 250 which states:

"The time is now right for a major programme of investment in InterCity's West Coast route. It is the country's transport backbone, connecting London to Birmingham, Manchester, Liverpool and Glasgow by fast direct train services.

It is central to InterCity's operation and profitability, generating one third of all InterCity income. As the first route to be electrified, in the 1960's, its strategic importance has been long established.

The aim of the investment is to reduce journey times, enhance comfort and convenience and provide the highest standards of InterCity service to customers."

30 September 1992

APPENDIX 20

Comments on the White Paper's Proposals
Furness Line Action Group

The Furness Line Action Group was established in 1985 to protect, promote and improve services on the Furness and West Cumbria lines in North-West England. We are eager to support any constructive initiatives which could potentially increase utilisation of our rail infrastructure. Conversely, we are concerned as both users and user representatives about the considerable problems yet to be addressed let alone solved. Our response to the White Paper is as follows:

1. AIMS AND OBJECTIVES

The aims and objectives of a privatised railway should be to meet the transport needs of all its users especially the local community and those without access to a car. It should seek to increase utilisation of rail in an increasingly environmentally-aware age by actively encouraging a switch from road transport. Efficient operation and use of infrastructure must come before competition and choice where there is conflict. It is more important to have a train than have a choice.

We see attractions for the private sector being mainly in the areas of running additional trains to meet unsatisifed demand and in bringing local knowledge, management and promotional skills to an even greater degree than Regional Railways. However, the profit motive can conflict with these benefits, satisfying customers who provide lucrative income at the expense of the general passenger.

2. OPEN ACCESS AND EXCLUSIVE FRANCHISES

Given the objectives stated above, it is important that open access is allowed to any operator who wants to run additional trains, even if the main service is operated by one franchise. Railtrack and the Regulator would also need to play a full part in this aspect.

3. STRATEGIC PLANNING

The Government should play a fuller part in planning, given that the co-ordinating role of British Rail would diminish. It will be increasingly important that MP's, Councils, User Groups, Companies, Unions, Tourist/Development Boards and other relevant bodies are involved in the whole consultation process. Very importantly, we need to ensure we do not lag behind Continental Europe in rail planning for the future as the Channel Tunnel opens. This should also ensure that every opportunity is taken to move freight from road to rail.

4. SUBSIDY AND INVESTMENT

The Government has increased responsibility to ensure that levels of investment and subsidy are sufficient not only to support existing service levels but to renew/increase infrastructure so that rail is well placed to meet increasing demand. Current levels of investment may appear high but are in fact low when compared with our Continental neighbours who appreciate the latter point more than Britain. Privatisation must not be an excuse to cut public spending on rail transport by furtively allowing private operators to reduce services in return for lower subsidies. Investment in future rail schemes should be assessed using cost-benefit appraisals identical to those used for road transport, with environmental benefits taken into full consideration.

5. RAILTRACK CHARGES

The commercial rates for track use should not be set so high that franchisees will have to reduce operating costs to make a return. This means that the Government will have to bear much renewal cost to enable the books to balance. As renewal of infrastructure is in the interests of the Economy as a whole, this is fair. The Government does not, after all, expect the Private sector to fund roads renewal.

6. FRANCHISES AND PUBLIC INTEREST

The Franchising Authority must be fully responsible to the whole range of public bodies, including the T.U.C.C./User Groups, MPs/Councils, Tourist Boards etc in order to ensure that RAIL SERVICES ON EACH ROUTE ARE MAINTAINED AT CURRENT MINIMUM LEVELS INTO THE FUTURE. It is not good enough to assume that all Franchisees will behave in a responsible manner, when their chief aim is to maximise profit. This consultation is also imperative given that the Franchising Authority would be empowered to instigate Statutory closure procedures. A free rein must not be allowed on fares; even now British Rail are forced by P.S.O. Grants cuts to raise these by more than inflation levels each year.

7. ROLLING STOCK LEASING AND INVESTMENT

A major concern surrounding Privatisation is that of rolling stock renewal by comparatively small companies who cannot strategically plan and bulk order for the future. This barrier will encourage the use of ageing stock and the use of "healthy second hand market" suggested by the White Paper. It is likely that leasing schemes may prove too costly for less lucrative services. Overall, the public profile of the railways will suffer as it fails to make the investment necessary to compete with other forms of transport.

8. STATION SELLING-OFF

Strict conditions of sale must be laid down so operation of trains and public facilities are not affected; use should enhance the area and be subject to full Planning Permission. Stations and land must be sold off at full market value to generate maximum income which should then be re-invested in the railway, the only exception being where the new use provides a tangible attraction to patronage of the line.

9. THROUGH-TICKETING AND THE TIMETABLE

As stated in the White Paper, rail passengers currently benefit from through-ticketing and a generally unrestricted use of trains within ticket validity. The public can currently purchase Senior Citizens, Family, Students railcards valid across the Network. For leisure, there are numerous daily/weekly/fortnightly Rover tickets covering different areas of the country and boosting tourism. It is completely inadequate to hope that "passenger service operators will find it in their commercial interest to offer a range of discounted fares and travelcards". The Franchising Authority must ensure that all these are maintained centrally and decide the income attributable to each company. After all, Inter-Rail ticket income is split between participating countries AND companies on the Continent.

Through-ticketing must not be so complex as to hamper efficiency or goodwill of the public. As Railtrack will be responsible for the National Timetable, it is imperative that passengers continue to enjoy freedom of choice and are not barred from using alternate services just because another company owns the franchise!

10. INTER-CITY

We have recently seen examples of British Rail's attempts to polarise Inter-City services to a profitable core. This has removed Barrow, Blackpool, Lincoln, Shrewsbury from the Inter-City network and even threatens to halt services on the West Coast Main line north of Preston. If this is an example of short-term market forces winning over long-term strategic planning, privatisation could be a nightmare. Would road users like it if the M6 were reduced to a single carriageway north of Preston?

11. FREIGHT AND PARCELS

As freight and parcels services are sold to the Private sector, it is imperative that restrictions are placed on the operator transferring these over the road, We need to encourage more freight to transfer to rail, not throw business away.

12. SUMMARY

The White Paper is noticeably long on political "competition and free choice" rhetoric and short on detail. It raises more questions about Privatisation than it answers. This is not surprising; transport experts have been pointing out the horrendous difficulties throughout its long gestation period. Privatisation may be able to solve some of the railway's problems; it will not solve those of under-investment and under-subsidy. It is crucial that the next consultancy stage involves all the bodies mentioned above; the future of the rail network must be decided by rail users and not by politicians who may not be aware of the serious problems which could result from a rushed implementation.

For the future of the U.K. economy and its survival within Europe, there must be a reappraisal of long-term transport strategy; rail must play an increasingly important part. It is difficult to justify the introduction of resource-wasting competition at a time when the rail network is fighting for its survival. Bus Deregulation has left us with a shortage of services in rural areas and an excess in many towns and cities chasing fewer and fewer passengers. We cannot afford unbridled market forces to do the same to rail transport. Overall, it is the Government's responsibility to ensure that the railway, in whatever form, fully meets the economic, social and environmental needs of the country.

27 September 1992

APPENDIX 21

THE WHARFEDALE RAIL USERS' GROUP

Rail Privatisation White Paper

1. We have a good relationship with the West Yorkshire PTE (Metro), whose role it is to specify the level of service to be provided on local routes within the county. In the past, Metro have been responsive to suggestions from our Group and have been able to directly influence BR where necessary to improve the service.

The proposal to insert an extra level of bureaucracy, i.e. the Franchising Authority, between Metro and the service operator will result in Metro having less direct influence on the operator. This will be a retrograde step, and goes against the White Paper's stated aim (paragraph 1) of achieving "greater responsiveness to the customer".

We are also concerned that the insertion of the Franchising Authority, whose funding will presumably be a first call on revenue, will result in increased costs, and hence increased fares.

2. Investment in new electric rolling stock for use on services from Leeds and Bradford to Ilkley and Skipton is already being hampered by the prospect of privatisation. The West Yorkshire PTA has been unable to continue negotiating to lease new electric trains, in part due to the risk that the Franchising Authority may insist on another operator running the service. Uncertainties introduced as the legislation passes through parliament should not be allowed to jeopardise current investment plans.

3. The continued availability of national Railcards by all operators needs to be safeguarded. The White Paper (paragraph 94) merely expresses the opinion of the Government that operators will find it in their commercial interest to offer such facilities.

Recent experience in West Yorkshire, where Metro has been unable to persuade certain bus operators to continue accepting prepayment tickets, proves how difficult it is to achieve agreement between a number of operators.

4. Although paragraph 90 of the White Paper states that it will be the responsibility of Railtrack to produce a unified timetable for the entire network, there is no commitment that such a timetable will be available to the public in a single book, and at reasonable cost.

The timetable needs to remain operational for a minimum period of time, e.g. summer and winter periods as now. Constant timetable changes need to be avoided in order to maintain maximum customer familiarity of the service provided.

5. The White Paper makes no mention of who will be responsible for passenger information at stations. BR has gradually made improvements in this area and at most stations information about delays to services is good and appreciated by passengers. Similarly, when making enquiries about a journey, a passenger should only need to visit or phone one information centre, and not those of several operators.

6. Many journeys involve traversing more than one route and the need to maintain connections will remain important. The danger is that, with a proliferation of operating companies, the availability of connections will become more a matter of chance.

7. If stations are sold off, some operators may not be able to agree terms with the station owners regarding the fees to be paid for allowing their trains to stop. Pressures of this kind may lead to certain station stops being abandoned, or even to the building of separate stations to be served by a particular operator's trains. Passenger service requirements, rather than ownership of stations, should dictate stopping patterns.

8. We welcome the White Paper's commitment to safety as presently stated.

9. There is no mention in the White Paper about bankruptcy of franchisees. Would the services immediately be taken over so that rail travellers were not inconvenienced and would season ticket holders and others who had purchased tickets in advance be financially protected?

10. The role of the TUCCs needs to be increased so that they have more powers to influence standards of service, including the level of fares. (Similar to the present bodies which oversee British Gas and British Telecom).

27 September 1992

APPENDIX 22

LANCASHIRE COUNTY COUNCIL

The Future Prospects for the Railway System in the light of the Government's Proposals for Privatisation

SUMMARY OF RECOMMENDATIONS

1. *Question 1*

1.1 The Government should draw up a strategic rail investment plan covering a minimum ten year period which would recognise the important role that rail could fulfil in meeting its economic and environmental policy objectives.

1.2 The government should increase the level of investment in expanding the role of rail based systems.

1.3 Minimum service levels for all franchised services should be laid down that reflect the level of service in operation at the time of the publication of the White Paper.

1.4 A "level playing field" for transport investment should be created in order to enable a proper assessment to be made between competing highway and railway schemes.

1.5 The legislation must ensure that the assets currently owned by British Rail are fully protected from the possibility of short term asset stripping to the present or future detriment of the travelling public.

2. *Question 2*

2.1 The minimum level of service specified by the Franchising Authority must be no less than the level of service provided by British Rail on a line or at a station at the time of the publication of the White Paper.

2.2 The integrity of the rail network must be maintained and the network benefits that passengers currently enjoy retained as a minimum.

2.3 The Franchising Authority must make it a condition of its contracts that a franchisee cooperates in the provision of:

(i) through ticketing, the inter-availability of tickets, and network tickets, such as Rail Rovers;

(ii) national railcard schemes such as those for young persons, families, senior citizens and the disabled;

(iii) the co-ordination of timetables between different franchisees.

3. *Question 3*

3.1 The Franchising Authority should be required to consult with Local Authorities on the level of service to be provided on lines in its area.

3.2 The legislation should make clear provision for the continuation of local authority led rail schemes.

4. *Question 4*

4.1 Cost benefit analysis should be used for the assessment of all rail investment schemes in precisely the same way that it is used to assess investment in roads.

4.2 Major infrastructure schemes should not be delayed by the complex relationship likely to exist between Railtrack, the Franchising Authority, the franchisee and, where appropriate, the local authority or PTA/PTE.

4.3 The Franchising Authority must make it a contractual obligation on a franchisee that if a line is electrified during the period of a franchise that electric rolling stock will be used on it.

5. *Question 5*

5.1 Railtrack must adopt a pricing policy that enables marginal cost enhancements to passenger rail services to continue.

5.2 Railtrack should continue to charge rail freight traffic on a marginal basis for the use of the infrastructure when it is not the Prime User of a line.

6. *Question 6*

6.1 The Franchising Authority must be required to take account of quality of service factors in evaluating bids for franchises.

7. *Question 7*

7.1 The Franchising Authority should set standards for the quality and age of rolling stock in its franchises.

8. *Question 8*

8.1 The Government should consider making it a condition of purchase or lease of stations that any improvements to make a station fully accessible, or any other work required to provide adequate passenger facilities, are undertaken and financed by the purchaser/lessee within a given timescale.

8.2 Where stations are sold or leased there must be safeguards to ensure that any proposed development does not in any way interfere with its function as a railway station and that land is not disposed of or used in a manner that would prejudice future improvements to passenger facilities or the provision of park and ride.

INTRODUCTION

Lancashire County Council welcomes the opportunity to submit evidence to the House of Commons Transport Committee's inquiry into 'the future prospects for the railway system in the light of the government's proposals for privatisation'.

The format of this submission follows the questions set out in the Transport Committee's notice of this inquiry. A summary of the main conclusions and recommendations is at the front of this submission.

Q. 1. *What should be the aims and objectives of a privatised railway? What are the attractions for the private sector?*

1.1 The County Council considers that the aim of a national railway system, irrespective of ownership, is to provide a high quality service which is both affordable and meets the needs of its customers. The network must meet the transport needs of long distance, inter-urban, local and rural passengers and contribute, in appropriate circumstances, to the cost effective and environmentally effective distribution of freight.

1.2 The government has forecast that over the next 25 years road journeys by private car could rise by between 49 per cent and 80 per cent. There is growing concern at the effect this growth in traffic could have on the environment and the cost to the economy of increasing road congestion. The CBI has estimated that road congestion costs industry £15 billion per year. The rail network must, in future, play its full role in both helping relieve road congestion to the benefit of the economy and as part of an environmentally sustainable national transport policy.

1.3 The public·demand for new investment in railways has heightened in recent years. Whilst it is acknowledged that there has been a relatively high level of expenditure on railways over the last five years, much of this has been on the belated replacement of life expired assets. Investment in expanding the role of the railway has been limited to a relatively small number of "prestige" projects such as expenditure relating to the Channel Tunnel and the electrification of the East Coast Main Line. Investment is needed not only to replace life expired assets but also to meet broader aspirations. These include economic regeneration, a better environment, a reduction in road congestion and to improve the quality of rail services.

1.4 The private sector will undoubtedly be attracted to those areas of rail operation which will be profitable, including the operation of grant aided franchises. Many of the County Council's concerns regarding the potential conflict between individual private sector aspirations and the need for the rail network to play its full role in the transport needs of the nation are expanded on later in this submission.

1.5 However, the County Council is concerned that some sections of the private sector may be attracted to a privatised rail network in order to exploit potential short term gains through asset stripping. There is evidence to suggest that following the deregulation and privatisation of the bus network, there has been a certain degree of "asset stripping", for example, by closing bus stations and depots and selling off the land for non public transport related development to the detriment of the travelling public.

1.6 It is recommended that:

(a) **The Government draws up a strategic rail investment plan covering a minimum ten year period which would recognise the important role that rail could fulfil in meeting its economic and environmental policy objectives;**

(b) **the Government should increase the level of investment in expanding the role of rail based systems;**

(c) **minimum service levels for all franchised services should be laid down to reflect the level of service in operation at the time of the publication of the White Paper;**

(d) **a "level playing field" for transport investment should be created in order to enable a proper assessment to be made between competing highway and railway schemes, and;**

(e) **the legislation must ensure that the assets currently owned by British Rail are fully protected from the possibility of short term asset stripping to the present or future detriment of the travelling public;**

Q. 2. *Is there any conflict between the principal of open access and the granting of exclusive franchises?*

2.1 The principal philosophy underpinning the White Paper is the liberalisation of the network for both passenger and freight services. Once legislation has been passed it will be possible for any operator, who can satisfy the quality and safety standards, to run services anywhere on the network. It would appear likely that passenger services introduced by the private sector through open access will operate in addition to those provided through franchises awarded by the Franchising Authority.

2.2 It is appreciated that the EC is moving towards the principal of open acces for international services as set out in its Directive 91/440.

2.3 The Government also intends to provide exclusive franchises for all existing passenger services provided by British Rail. Apart from some Inter-City and Regional Railways Express services, all other franchises will almost certainly require continuing support from central government and/or Passenger Transport Authorities/Passenger Transport Executives. However, the liberalisation of the network envisaged in paragraph 2.1 above could result in services being operated in competition with those provided under franchise with possible serious financial consequences for the latter.

2.4 The White Paper suggests in paragraph 57 that "Liberalising access to the network" will "give customers wider choice and rail operators the stimulus of competition". However, unless all operators on a particular route agree to the inter-availability of their tickets then passengers will find that there choice is in fact diminished as they can only use the services provided by one operator. It is, therefore, possible that open access would increase competition between operators but diminish the choice of trains that passengers could use if ticket inter-availability is not accepted by different operators.

2.5 In paragraph 59, the White Paper recognises the many operational problems that could arise in reconciling open access to the network with franchised services. It is of considerable concern that consultants have only now been commissioned to consider the implications of this following publication of the White Paper. This fundamental issue should have been resolved before the Government announced its plans.

2.6 Under open access new entrants may consider operating "niche" services at times of the day when existing demand is known to be high. It is becoming apparent that a number of companies are already expressing an interest in operating high quality, high speed services between certain major centres on the Inter-City network. The County Council is concerned about the effect that limited or non-stop services might have on the service levels provided at some of the smaller Inter-City stations such as, in Lancashire, Lancaster. The abstraction of long distance revenue by such services may make Inter-City franchises unprofitable thus requiring Government subsidy to maintain the existing levels of service at such stations. The effect of this on parallel franchised services could be that:

(a) additional grant could be required from central government and PTEs to cover the loss of abstracted revenue;

(b) on Inter-City routes the effect of open access may make it necessary to provide grants to maintain service levels at small stations, marginal times of the day and on Sunday;

2.7 Paragraph 29 of the White Paper says that the Franchising Authority will specify the minimum frequency of service that a franchisee will have to provide. This minimum should be no less than the level of service provided by British Rail on a line or at a station prior to the publication of the White Paper.

2.8 The County Council is concerned as to how the Government intends to retain the integrity of the national passenger network once it has been split into franchises and open access has been introduced.

2.9 Paragraph 88 of the White Paper states that "The Government is concerned to ensure that, so far as possible, passengers and freight customers continue to enjoy the advantages they get from a national rail system including through ticketing, cross validity, discounted fares, and a national timetable". However, in paragraph 69 it says that the Regulator will ensure that no anti-competitive practices develop between operators whilst, at the same time, ensuring that network benefits are maintained. The White Paper does not make it clear how the current benefits will be continued except to say that, "This will be taken into account in the arrangements made for timetabling and ticketing".

2.10 It is clear that the Government would like to ensure that network benefits are maintained. However, it must state more clearly the mechanisms that will be introduced to ensure their continuation whilst at the same time preventing anti-competitive practises developing between operators.

2.11 A particular complication will be the inter-availability of tickets between different operators. At the present time many passengers not only enjoy a choice of trains but also a choice of route. It is possible that, once the network is privatised, some lines will have services provided by more than one operator. An example in Lancashire may well be the East Lancashire line which is currently served by both the local trains between Colne and Preston and the semi-fast "Roses" service between Leeds and Preston providing passengers at the major stations with a choice of two trains every hour.

2.12 It is possible that local and semi-fast services could be divided between two different franchises and, therefore, two different operators. Unless operators are prepared to accept each others tickets, passengers could have their choice of trains severely limited. This may lead to passengers making arrangements to travel other than by rail and might lead to further congestion on the roads.

2.13 Without ticket inter-availability the continuation of the present range of Rail Rovers could be jeopardised. Such tickets are available for the whole of the UK rail network or for particular areas. The loss of this facility could have an effect on the competitiveness of the tourist market.

2.14 The evidence from the deregulation of the bus industry is that through ticketing, ticket inter-availability and all-operator ticketing is not compatible with open competition. This is illustrated in Lancashire where, since deregulation, there has been a loss of ticket inter-availability between competing bus operators. At the same time one of the country's most successfull all-operator network tickets, the Red Rose Rambler, has had to be abandoned.

2.15 Arrangements will need to be made for the continuation of all of British Rail's existing national railcard schemes i.e. those for young persons, families, senior citizens and the disabled. There may well be a case for the Government to give the Regulatory Authority powers to compel operators to participate in such schemes.

2.16 Assurances also need to be given in respect of co-ordinated timetable planning. The White Paper makes no reference to any mechanism for ensuring co-ordination of services between different operators and/or different franchises. It will be particularly important to ensure continued co-ordination between longer distance and local services.

2.17 It is recommended that:

(1) **the minimum level of service specified by the Franchising Authority must be no less than the level of service provided by British Rail on a line or at a station at the time of the publication of the White Paper;**

(2) **the integrity of the rail network must be maintained and the network benefits that passengers currently enjoy retained as a minimum;**

(3) **the Franchising Authority must make it a condition of its contracts that a franchisee cooperates in the provision of:**

(i) **through ticketing, the inter-availability of tickets, and network tickets, such as Rail Rovers;**

(ii) **national railcard schemes such as those for young persons, families, senior citizens and the disabled;**

(iii) **the co-ordination of timetables between different franchisees.**

Q. 3. *Who should do the strategic planning for our railways and how can different interests be co-ordinated? For example, can freight develop effectively on a primarily passenger network?*

3.1 Under the arrangements proposed by the Government there could be considerable frustration in developing a co-ordinated strategy for the modernisation and future development of the rail system.

3.2 The White Paper suggests that Railtrack will, in the main, be responsible for promoting major investment schemes. However, what happens if Railtrack proposes that, for example, the Blackpool to Manchester line should be electrified but the franchisee wishes to continue operating a diesel service? The White Paper does not indicate how problems such as this will be resolved.

3.3 The County Council considers that for International, Inter-City and Regional Railways Express services the government should, in conjunction with British Rail and its successor bodies, develop a strategy for the progressive development and modernisation of these routes covering initially a ten year period. This should include the construction of new routes such as the Continental Main Line, between London and the Channel Tunnel, the upgrading of existing routes including electrification where appropriate and the construction of new high speed lines.

3.4 In order to assist franchisees in making bids to the Franchising Authority the tender documents should clearly set out any planned investment in the infrastructure that Railtrack is proposing. This would be particularly important if the line was to be electrified. The contract between the Franchising Authority and the franchisee should be sufficiently flexible to facilitate any changes that might be required to the operation of a service during the currency of the franchise. For example, it must be a contractual requirement that where a line is electrified the franchisee will use, in all appropriate circumstances, electric rolling stock on that line. This would help resolve the potential problem referred to in 3.2 above.

3.5 For local services, outside of PTE/PTA areas, there is considerable scope for increasing the role of County Councils in determining the level of service that is appropriate for a particular line and making the Franchising Authority aware of specific service requirements. The legislation should place a requirement on the Franchising Authority to seek the views of Local Authorites on the level of service to be provided on lines in their area.

3.6 Since 1982 on Regional Railways 127 new stations have been opened, 106 miles of track have been added to the passenger network and 70 miles of line have been electrified. The vast majority of these schemes have come about only because they have been sponsored by local authorities or the PTA/PTEs. Without the active role of local authorities the recent expansion of the network would not have taken place. There are a considerable number of local authority led schemes being considered that would considerably enhance the rail network. They include plans for further new stations and the opening or construction of new lines for passenger services, for example Leicester to Burton, Nottingham to Worksop and Blackburn to Hellifield. Such schemes might be delayed or abandoned unless there is clear provision in the legislation for Local Authority led schemes to be implemented.

3.7 Many local authority led schemes are being pursued because they assist with wider economic aims such as reducing traffic congestion and providing access to employment in areas where traditional industries have declined or disappeared.

3.8 It is disappointing that the only reference in the White Paper to the important role of local authorities in the expansion of the rail network comes in paragraph 39. This indicates a continuing role for local authorities in providing contributions for the enhancement of rail services or infrastructure in their areas.

3.9 Whilst this suggests that the many local authority led schemes can continue the White Paper contains no detail on how such schemes will be progressed given the complex relationship likely to exist between Railtrack, the Franchising Authority, franchisees and the local authority. This relationship could result in delays in progressing schemes.

3.10 The County Council considers that certain guarantees will be required before local authorities will wish to proceed with a scheme. These guarantees will include the ownership and disposal of local authority funded assets, the mechanism for ensuring their continued use and that, in the case of reopenings or service enhancements, there is a mechanism for ensuring the authority is getting value for money from franchises awarded by the Franchising Authority.

3.11 At present, Local Authorities are able to build, if they wish, safeguards into contracts entered into with British Rail before proceeding with them. The Government will need to give local authorities a guarantee that any conditions negotiated with British Rail in the period leading up to franchising will be honoured by the Franchising and Track Authorities and franchisees. This would also include any profit sharing or revenue payback agreements.

3.12 It is recommended that:

    (1) the Franchising Authority should be required to consult with Local Authorities on the level of service to be provided on lines in its area; and

    (2) the legislation should make clear provision for the continuation of local authority led rail schemes.

Q. 4. *What will be the Government's role in subsidy and investment? In what circumstances will cost-benefit appraisal be appropriate, and what criteria should be used for future rail investment?*

4.1 As stated in paragraph 1.4 above the Government will continue to have a very important role in supporting the passenger network and in directing investment to the schemes identified in its strategic plan. It is, therefore, disappointing that paragraph 42 of the White Paper does not set out a more ambitious investment programme.

4.2 The County Council has argued for some considerable time that cost-benefit analysis should be used in the assessment of rail schemes. It is not possible to capture the full benefit to the community of a rail investment scheme solely through a financial appraisal. Factors including journey time savings and environmental improvements such as reducing congestion are not included in a financial appraisal.

4.3 It is encouraging that the Government will continue to provide direct support for a rail investment scheme that does not show an adequate financial return but does provide a satisfactory cost-benefit return.

4.4 However, the County Council considers that the investment appraisal indicated in paragraph 43 is still too narrow. All rail investment schemes should be assessed using the same form of cost-benefit analysis as is used for assessing highway schemes. This would create a "level-playing field" and assist in the realisation of a balanced transport investment strategy.

4.5 The Government has yet to make it clear the full basis on which it will give grants and whether such grants will only be available to Railtrack or would include direct grants to operators, for example for the purchase or lease of new rolling stock.

4.6 At the same time the separation of responsibilities for infrastructure (Railtrack) and operation (the Franchising Authority and Franchisee) suggests that future investment projects will require complex co-ordination. The Government intends that Railtrack continues to invest to maintain and improve the network and says that investment will largely be financed from charges to operators including supported operators. Railtrack will normally take the lead responsibility for promoting major investment including electrification.

4.7 However, major schemes, such as electrification, require substantial investment in fixed infrastructure and rolling stock. Railtrack will, presumably, have to make the investment and then recoup this through higher charges to operators. This could raise fundamental difficulties, particularly in the case of electrification schemes or where line speeds are raised through improvements to the track where commercial operators or franchisees might also have to make a substantial investment in new rolling stock with a fairly lengthy pay-back period. This would normally extend far beyond the length of a particular franchise period.

4.8 As mentioned in paragraph 3.4 above it must be a contractual requirement that franchisees introduce rolling stock that realises any benefits made to the infrastructure in particular where a line is electrified. The willingness of franchisees to enter into this kind of contract will be determined by the arrangements for the transfer of assets that they have purchased or leased at the end of a franchise period.

4.9 It is recommended that:

(1) cost benefit analysis should be used for the assessment of all rail investment schemes in precisely the same way that it is used to assess investment in roads; and

(2) major infrastructure schemes should not be delayed by the complex relationship likely to exist between Railtrack, the Franchising Authority, the franchisee and, where appropriate, the local authority or PTA/PTE; and

(3) the Franchising Authority must make it a contractual obligation on a franchisee that if a line is electrified during the period of a franchise that electric rolling stock will be used on it.

Q. 5. *Railtrack, the track authority, will charge operators "commercial" rates for track use. What principles should be used to set these charges?*

5.1 The County Council considers that Railtrack should adopt a flexible charging policy.

5.2 The Government needs to ensure the continuation of service enhancements funded by local authorities and that local authorities obtain value for money in catering for specific unmet needs. This will be particularly the case where franchised service frequencies are relatively low and infrastructure cost relatively high. An inflexible charging policy could well place a disproportionately high part of the infrastructure cost onto the enhanced element of the service and make it unviable.

5.3 A particular example is the County Council's proposal to re-instate regular passenger services on the Blackburn to Hellifield line. The line is officially open to passenger services but with only an irregular service provided by British Rail during the summer months. As a consequence of the line's open status all the costs of maintaining the infrastructure are currently met by British Rail through the Public Service Obligation Grant.

5.4 The agreement which the County Council has reached with British Rail for the provision of regular services between Blackburn and Clitheroe is based on the County Council guaranteeing to meet British Rail's marginal cost of providing an enhanced service less the revenue which is earned. All infrastructure costs (other than the maintenance of the new stations) will continue to be met by British Rail through the PSO grant once the service commences.

5.5 There is a strong case, in these circumstances, for the Government to ensure that the infrastructure costs which would have been met by British Rail through the PSO grant continue to be met in full by Railtrack. This would leave the local authority to meet any shortfall between revenue earned and the marginal cost of operating the service.

5.6 Open access may provide a stimulus to the operation of new freight services. However, the success of this will depend on the charging policy adopted by Railtrack. Under the current prime user principle a freight service operating on a passenger line is only charged the marginal cost of operating on the line. Will this principle be continued by Railtrack? It is possible that any other charging policy could deter new entrants especially at a time when the road haulage industry has considerable surplus capacity and that road pricing for freight, as well as road passenger vehicles, is already charged at what is effectively marginal cost.

It is recommended that:

(1) **Railtrack must adopt a pricing policy that enables marginal cost enhancements to passenger rail services to continue.**

(2) **Railtrack should continue to charge rail freight traffic on a marginal basis for the use of the infrastructure when it is not the Prime User of a line.**

Q. 6. *How should franchises operate so as to maximise the public interest, both for profitable and subsidised services?*

6.1 The County Council considers that a flexible approach should be taken in awarding franchises.

6.2 The White Paper does not say how competing bids for franchises will be assessed other than that they will need to meet certain minimum quality standards. This raises the question of whether bids will be assessed solely on who requires the least subsidy (or, in the case of Inter City services, who makes the highest bid for the right to operate the service) or whether it would be appropriate to take other factors into account.

6.3 The County Council suggests that the Franchising Authority should give priority to franchisees that are prepared to provide a service level above the specified minimum especially where the higher service may assist in relieving road congestion and/or with the economic regeneration of an area. The age and suitability of the rolling stock operators intend to use or purchase during the life of the franchise and their overall business plan could also be taken into account.

It is recommended that:

the Franchising Authority must be required to take account of quality of service factors in evaluating bids for franchises.

Q. 7. *What arguments are there for switching immediately to a regime of rolling stock leasing for all operators, including BR. What are the White Paper's implications for BR's on-going rolling stock investment programme?*

7.1 The County Council is concerned that the White Paper already appears to have affected orders for the construction of new rolling stock. Orders for class 323 electric multiple units for the Leeds to Skipton electrification have been cancelled and the new generation InterCity 250 for the West Coast Main Line has been postponed. In other parts of the country similar problems appear to be occurring especially on Network South East. Whilst there has been significant investment in replacement rolling stock especially on Regional Railways and certain parts of Network South East there is still a considerable programme of vehicle replacement to be undertaken.

7.2 One of the consequeces of bus deregulation has been that orders for new vehicles, especially full sized single and double decker buses, has declined. At the same time the age profile of the bus fleet is continuing to rise. This will raise problems for the reliability of services as older vehicles will be required longer periods out of service for maintenance. The same situation could develop on the railways unless specified provisions is made for rolling stock standards by the Franchising Authority.

7.3 The County Council has previously argued that the replacement programme for Regional Railways services has meant that there is now insufficient rolling stock to increase capacity at times of peak travel and to expand services in order to bring about a modal transfer from road to rail. In its submission 'Congestion in Lancashire: the need for major investment in public transport', September 1991, the County Council concluded:

"... that British rail ... (should be) encouraged to come forward with additional investment proposals for diesel rolling stock. This investment would enable British Rail to enhance local services in the county and to contribute in a positive way to the reduction of urban congestion and to curb traffic growth."

7.4 The County Council is concerned that the Governments proposals could lead to a moratorium on rail investment. This is witnessed by British Rail's recent announcement that it will not be proceeding with most of the proposals to upgrade the West Coast Main Line for the foreseeable future. A moratoruium in investment will lead to loss of jobs on the rail manufacturing industry and, potentially a permanent loss of skills within the UK.

It is recommended that:

the Franchising Authority set standards for the quality and age of rolling stock in its franchises.

Q. 8. *How is the value of stations to be assessed and what will be the relationship between a privately owned station and BR's operation of trains therefrom?*

8.1 The County Council is very concerned that the proposals for the disposal of railway stations to the private sector contained in the White Paper. This could lead to asset stripping similar to that which took place to bus stations sold into the private sector following deregulation.

8.2 The interests of passengers must, at all times, be the most important consideration in determining the value of a station. The private sector will be interested in those stations where there is considerable amount of space or 'surplus' land.

8.3 It is recommended that:

(a) the Government should consider making it a condition of purchase or lease of stations that any improvements to make a station fully accessible, or any other work required to provide adequate passenger facilities, are undertaken and financed by the purchaser/lessee within a given timescale,

(b) that where stations are sold or leased there must be safeguards to ensure that any proposed development does not in any way interfere with its function as a railway station and that land is not disposed of or used in a manner that would prejudice future improvements to passenger facilities or the provisions of park and ride.

6 October 1992

APPENDIX 23

Comments on the White Paper Proposals, by John Dodgson, Reader in Economics, University of Liverpool.

INTRODUCTION

1. The proposals in the White Paper are brief, and the present comments are primarily directed at identifying the major uncertainties in the White Paper, and the main problems that may arise in implementing the Government's proposals.

Franchising passenger services

2. In terms of the proposed methods of privatisation initially under consideration (privatisation of sectors; privatisation of regional railways; a track authority with competition on the network) it appears to me that the proposal to achieve competition primarily (though not exclusively) through competition for franchises to operate passenger services for a specified period of time is a sensible one. There is extensive experience of competitive tendering for franchises in other spheres, and it clearly does increase efficiency of provision and reduce costs, though its effects on quality-of-service are rather less clear-cut.

3. The combination of franchising with the possibility of liberalised access does increase the complexity of the situation, and the uncertainty faced by potential bidders. This increased uncertainty is likely to increase the cost of subsidy to the Passenger Railway Franchising Authority as bidders build in the costs of the extra uncertainty in their bids. However, competition for successful franchisees is quite common in other areas. Successful ITV companies face competition from satellite stations and the BBC. Bus operators who win contracts to operate subsidised services on a *net* revenue basis (i.e. costs minus expected revenue) may face competition from commercial services that abstract revenue from them (though some such competition has been judged to be anti-competitive).

4. The need for access to rolling stock, as indicated in the White Paper (para. 33) is crucial. The availability and flexibility of rolling stock is one of the areas where there is a major difference between the rail and bus industries. It is important that there be an effective market for leasing the existing stock of rail vehicles, and that it is possible to shift rolling stock from line-to-line (where technical conditions, such as forms of electric traction, permit) so that a potential franchisee has as wide as possible a choice of stock for a particular service. It is also important that the existing operator is not permitted to hoard, nor prematurely scrap, stock that may be of interest to a franchisee.

5. The proposals with regard to franchising set out in the White Paper are said to be flexible (para. 26). Where franchised services are the only, or major, user of the infrastructure on which they run, I would have expected that the franchisee might prefer to take responsibility for the operation and maintenance of the track and signalling in order to secure better day-to-day control over the standard of service provided by this infrastructure. The contract would need to have conditions to ensure that the infrastructure was returned to Railtrack at the end of the contract life in a well-maintained state.

6. Competition through liberalised access (or the threat of it) with successful franchisees would keep the franchisees "on their toes", but there is also the possibility of "wasteful competition". "On the road" competition in the bus industry has sometimes led to excess capacity, with low seat occupancy. Also services have not been evenly spread through the hour, so that passengers have not always got the full benefits of extra bus frequencies. In practice though, I suspect there would only be this type of "on-the-rail" competition on a few relatively profitable rail routes: on most, if not all, former Regional Railways routes, and on many of the Network South East routes, a successful subsidised operator would not expect competition from an unsubsidised rival.

Charging for track capacity

7. This seems to me to be the issue which is at the heart of the success or failure of the Government's proposals, and about which there is most uncertainty. Railtrack is said to be self-financing (see para. 23), so a system of track charges has to be devised to cover costs. The changes also have to ensure fair access to the network and not discriminate between users. They should also provide the right signals for investment in the network or for reducing capacity in line with reductions in demand. In addition, one would expect that potential users would need to know in advance what charges they would face if they were to operate services.

8. The White Paper indicates (paras. 59 and 61) that the Government has commissioned a major consultancy study on this issue. Unfortunately, while there is a commitment in the White Paper (para. 77) to publish the advice of the study of safety to be carried out by the Health and Safety Commission, there is no such commitment to publish the results of the study of charging. This is a pity, and it is to be hoped that the Government will publish in detail the analysis of track costing and charging. Certainly I believe that your

Committee's task in assessing the *practicality* of the Government's proposals would be extremely difficult without this information.

9. It is probably not sensible to anticipate the results of the costing study. However, it is worth pointing out that simple charging systems, such as on a train-mile basis, or a train-mile-weighted-by-tonnage (or some form of axle-weight measure) basis, would not appear likely to be successful. Given the economies of route density in railway operation, such a system would mean that even if the charges were set at a level such that Railtrack's total revenue covered its costs, operators on lightly-used routes would not be covering the full costs of the infrastructure they used and would in effeçt be cross-subsidised by operators on the main trunk routes. In turn this would deter marginal users of the main trunk routes, and conflict with the Government's stated objective (para. 1) of seeing better use made of the railways. On the other hand, allocating actual track and signalling costs of a route to the actual users of that route would be extremely difficult, would lead to continual referral of disputes to the Rail Regulator, and would conflict with the need to ensure that potential railway operators would know what track and signalling costs they would face on entry. These difficulties strengthen the case for dividing the network in such a way that at least a part consists of segments that are used by only one (franchised) operator: all the track and signalling costs can then be allocated to this operator and the subsidy provided allocated accordingly (see also 5 above).

Railtrack

10. The major break with the past in the Government's proposals is to remove the vertical integration of railway operations which has been in existence since (or strictly, since shortly after) the birth of the railway industry. Clearly the White Paper recognises the need for co-ordination of services through central timetabling and through a single signalling authority. The White Paper also recognises the need for regulation of safety standards. I think that the real danger in having a separate Railtrack authority (whether it be public, as initially planned, or private) is that it may become a monopolistic organisation unresponsive to users' needs. I doubt whether a track pricing system can be devised which accurately reflects these needs, especially with regard to the need for investment in new or improved capacity. There is also the problem that "here today-gone tomorrow" franchisees will have less interest in long-term investments with a time scale well beyond the horizon of their current franchises. Further, major investment to improve high-speed rail services requires detailed co-ordination of infrastructure improvements (track or route straightening, power supply modifications, track-to-train signalling) with rolling stock improvements in the form of design and introduction of new trains. This will be difficult when a single track authority is dealing with an operator who may not survive long enough to reap the full benefits, or with competing operators using the same infrastructure. For all these reasons, I think that one of the major problems with the White Paper proposals is that they could lead to inflexibility in track capacity and (more importantly) poor quality. Your Committee might find it instructive to review the experience which Amtrak had in America in securing adequate infrastructure quality (in terms of speed of running, train pathing, and quality of ride) for its passenger trains.

11. From the Government's point-of-view, another potential danger is that track charges do not in practice generate enough revenue to cover total infrastructure costs. Increasing charging levels might also not generate enough extra revenue to cover costs if there are constraints on how capacity can be reduced (for example, through line closures). Railtrack could then end up requiring public subsidy (though see 16 below).

The role of the Director-General of Railway Regulation

12. A major role of the Director-General will be in regulating whatever track charging system is devised. I believe that, whatever charging system is devised, the mechanics of allocating railway track and signalling costs between traffics are such that the Railway Regulator will need to have considerable discrimination in interpreting those rules and in judging cost allocation disputes. Much practical experience will need to be built up on a trial-(and-error) basis. The Railway Regulation agency will also need considerable staff with rail cost allocation expertise and experience.

13. Experience with bus and airline deregulation does show that powerful operators can use unfair practices, such as predatory behaviour, to deter or destroy competition. Predatory pricing is particularly difficult to detect where operators, as in the railways, use (legitimate) price discrimination to maximise revenue from passengers. I suspect though, that the major anti-competitive activity on railways would be likely to be the prevention of access to facilities, whether they be track (existing operators could block this, even though it is provided by Railtrack, by refusing to give up train paths or securing train paths that leave little useable spare capacity), rolling stock or maintenance facilities, or stations (the White Paper discusses sale of terminals to private operators—para. 44—though some stations might be operated by franchisees and others (possibly?) by Railtrack). The Regulator will therefore need to take careful account of train pathing and timetabling procedures, station usage charges and procedures for permitting new types of rolling stock to operate. Other competition policy issues include that of whether inter-availability of tickets is to be permitted (an existing operator with a regular frequency service might justifiably claim that it should not have to accept the tickets of a competing operator with only one or two trains, because it is incurring a considerable cost to provide a regular frequency service for its own passengers, a cost which this competitor avoids).

14. In regard to consumer protection, there seems to be some overlap in the White Paper between the roles of the Railway Regulator and the Franchising Authority. The Regulator is required to "promote the interests of consumers" (para. 64), while provision of franchised passenger services will be monitored by the Franchising Authority (paras. 19 and 30).

Freight

15. The White Paper seems optimistic about the prospects for a privatised rail freight business. However it must be remembered that road haulage in Great Britain is extremely competitive, both in terms of prices, door-to-door journey time, and other aspects of service quality. General rail freight traffic (as opposed to specialised heavy haulage of coal, steel, oil, aggregates, cement and certain chemical products) has had a very chequered history with the disappearance of general wagonload traffic, the demise of BR's Speedlink network, and the recent difficulties of independent rail freight operators like Charterail and Tiger Rail. The success of future rail general freight operations will be very closely bound up with the levels of track charges. Given that freight has been treated as a marginal rail track user for costing purposes since the 1974 Railways Act, the White Paper proposals may auger increases in rail freight track and signalling costs at a time when much of the remaining general rail freight business is fighting for survival.

Cost-benefit analysis

16. One of the supposed advantages of having a separate (public) railway track authority is that road and rail are then on a more comparable basis, with both having public track authorities and private operators paying charges to use their respective networks. In view of the White Paper's suggestions that cost-benefit analysis might be used for railway infrastructure, this extends the comparability further, since cost-benefit analysis is of course the main criterion used for highway investment decisions in Britain. Railtrack could then still be required to break even (see 11 above), but this would be after receipt of capital grants from government as well as revenue from track charges to operators.

Conclusions

17. The main conclusion of these comments is that the success of the Government's proposals will be closely bound up with the success of their attempt to devise and effective charging system for track capacity. Devising an effective price system is extremely difficult given the joint nature of railway track and signalling costs, and the price mechanism has to be trusted to achieve objectives never before attempted in the formerly vertically integrated railway industry. One consequence of the failure to develop an effective pricing system could be serious distortions in long term infrastructure investment on Britain's railway network.

24 September 1992

APPENDIX 24

ORMSKIRK-PRESTON TRAVELLERS' ASSOCIATION

New Opportunities for the Railways

Preamble

1. (1) The Association was formed in 1981. Its aims are to seek the retention and improvement of services on the Ormskirk-Preston railway line in particular, and of other rail and bus services locally and nationally, and also to encourage co-ordination of bus and rail and the greater usage of public transport. Current membership is around 300 individuals, and eight corporate bodies.

(2) The Association has long held the view that the way forward to improved rail services is through a state financed rolling programme of investment, with rail related schemes such as electrification financed by Central Government on a cost benefit basis similar to that which applies for new road schemes.

(3) In the realisation that it is the firm intention of Government to introduce greater private sector involvement into the rail network, the Association feels many aspects of current operation need to be safeguarded fully within the framework of parliamentary legislation. The aspects follow, being noted to correspond with the Section noted in HMSO CM 2012, July 1992, titled "New Opportunities for the Railways".

Section 1. Proposals. British Rail

Para. 4

The Association believes that a continuation and amplification of the positive investment aspects mentioned to be the desirable way forward. These achievements could have been considerably enhanced by the application of a cost benefit financial appraisal of rail schemes similar to that which applies for road.

Para. 5

Certainly regular users know full well that the performance of the railways is not good enough, and that service quality fails to meet the public's expectations. It may well be that the industry has fewer incentives to improve its performance and has less freedom to respond to what the customer wants. The Association believes this to be the direct result of imposed financial targets, restricting the growth of worthwhile rail related schemes which fail to meet the Governments 8 per cent return.

OPTA Comment

Within the legislation the Government must ensure that finance is available for franchisees, and Railtrack to promote worthwhile schemes on a cost benefit basis similar to road schemes. Without this criteria the Association sees little scope for the private sector to promote rail infrastructure improvements.

The Essential Requirements

Network Benefits

Para. 8

The Association notes that the Government has paid particular attention to Network Benefits. Whilst there appears an implied commitment to a national timetable and through ticketing, there are further aspects which require to be enshrined within the Section. They are:

1. *Through Services*

Presently British Rail have a network of through services several examples of which are: (a) Inter City through services from Cornwall, Devon, Bristol, Gloucester, Birmingham, Manchester, Liverpool, Preston, Carlisle, Glasgow, Edinburgh and Aberdeen, and (b) Regional Railways through services Liverpool, Manchester, Sheffield, Nottingham, Peterborough, Ely, Stansted Airport, Norwich, Great Yarmouth and Ipswich. These two examples are symptomatic of many now running throughout the network.

2. *Connectional Services*

For example on a recent evening on which the undersigned was a passenger, the following events took place at Preston:-The 1725 service from London (Euston) due Preston 2005 was running 20 minutes late, then due Preston at 2025. British Rail then held the following advertised connectional services:

2020 to Lancaster, Carnforth, Grange, Ulverston and Barrow held until 2031.

2018 to Blackburn, Accrington, Burnley, Nelson and Colne held until 2030.

2021 to Burscough and Ormskirk held until 2031.

2027 to Lytham St Annes and Blackpool (South) until 2032.

OPTA Comment

Within the legislation to be introduced, the Association considers it essential that through services by whoever they may be operated, must, in the interests of a national system of through services, be not only retained but improved.

Similarly, on connectional services, having in mind the number of franchisees that may be in future involved in a similar situation to the one noted, the Association considers it essential that a similarly sensible connectional policy is mandatorily placed upon the ultimate operators of individual services. With both through and connectional services, it appears unclear as to which authority will have the co-ordinating responsibility to continue and enhance the current situation.

Section 2. Passenger Services Franchising.

Para 26.

There is no indication in the White Paper of how competing bids for franchises are to be assessed other than to meet certain minimum quality standards. This raises the question of whether the bids will be solely assessed on who requires the least subsidy (or in the case on Inter City services, who makes the highest bid for the right to operate the service) or whether it would be appropriate to take other factors into account. For example, an operator prepared to provide a service level above the specified minimum but requiring an overall higher subsidy might offer a better value for money than another operator wishing to provide the minimum service level for a lower overall subsidy. The age and suitability of the rolling stock operators intend to use or purchase during the life of the franchise and their overall business plan could also be taken into account.

OPTA Comment.

The Association considers it essential that both the Government and the Franchising Authority will need to adopt a very flexible approach in the evaluation of bids for franchises.

Para 28.

The franchising of services will be the responsibility of the Franchising Authority acting on the Government's behalf. The Government will decide on a budget grant for such services and set objectives for service levels, service quality and fares.

OPTA Comment

Within this proposal there is no stated opportunity for grass root organisations like ourselves, with detailed local knowledge to have an input into what they see as a satisfactory level of train service, service quality or fares. It is the veiw of the Association, that local input now a part of service planning, be continued and enhanced to achieve the objectives set out in the White Paper, and it must be a guarantee by Government that initial minimum service levels for each route and for each station within a franchise will be, at the very least, the existing service level provided by British Rail.

Section 7. Employees and Network Benefits.

Para 86.

The Association welcomes the commitment given that concessionary travel arrangements for existing British Rail employees, and retired staff will be safeguarded.

Paras 91, 92 and 93.

The Association believes that current ticket availability by any service between two points, should be a mandatory obligation placed upon franchisees. Tickets issued by one operator should be freely available for travel by another operator on the same route. For example locally between Leyland and Preston services are operated by through services to and from Blackpool (South), Blackpool (North), Wigan, St Helens, Liverpool, Bolton, Manchester, Stockport, Buxton, Altrincham and Chester. Under proposed franchising arrangements several franchisees may be involved in the operation of services between Preston and Leyland, and the Association considers it essential that interavailability of tickets be mandatory.

A Network Benefit now enjoyed by many members of the Association, is the various national railcard schemes. Whilst there is no obligation within the White Paper for franchisees to continue to operate the national schemes, the Association considers it essential to enshrine continuance of these concessions in awarding franchises.

Conclusion

The Association hopes the Committee will find the comments made to be useful in determining their final deliberations on the Government's White Paper. As stated previously it is considered the correct way forward would have been for an enhanced rolling programme of investment by Government. Further it is the firm belief of the Association that no discernable diversion of traffic be it passenger or freight road to rail will take place, with or without privatisation, until similar financial criteria is applied to both road and rail transport.

20th September 1992.

APPENDIX 25

· ASSOCIATION OF PRIVATE RAILWAY WAGON OWNERS

Submission to the Transport Committee from the Members of the Association of Private Rail Wagon Owners (APRO)

"The Future Prospects for the Railway System in the Light of the Government's Proposals for Privatisation"

Please accept this submission on behalf of the members of this important rail association whose names and some information on their rail wagon interests are detailed on the attached schedule.

Our members' wagon ownership represents approximately 8,500 of the estimated total of 13,200 private rail freight vehicles in working order in the United Kingdom, to be compared with 20,800 declared as owned by the British Railways Board. Because of the highly specialised and intensely capital orientated nature of the rail wagon investment, you will understand the importance of the opinions of those who currently are involved in wagon owership.

APRO is represented on the Private Wagon Federation and in addition to the comments that we make below we endorse the opinions and submission of the Private Wagon Federation to your Committee concerning this vital subject.

Whilst the Government's White Paper on the privatisation of British Rail sets out the broad principle on how the Government intends to achieve this, it is far from clear what the details of this process will be, how the mechanisms proposed would work in practice and what the implications will be for private wagon owners. We therefore would make comment of our concerns as follows:—

Infrastructure Pricing—Paras. 12, 23 and 43 of White Paper

It is widely accepted that approximately 50 per cent of a rail movements cost is attributable to pricing of the infrastructure, i.e. track, maintenance, signalling, locomotion, manning. The comparative acknowledged figure for road is 4 per cent. British Rail's 'subsidy' from the Government is recognised to be approximately 18 per cent, compared with 52 per cent for the SNCF in France and 38 per cent for the DB in Germany. It is therefore fundamental in the achievement of a level playing field with road pricing that infrastructure costing is clarified. APRO feels that the infrastructure (track, maintenance and signalling) should be supplied on a similar basis to which roads are supplied. We urge Government to consider a licensing fee for locomotives and/or wagon rolling stock, similar to the road fund licence for road vehicles.

We strongly urge the Government to prohibit British Rail from increasing their tariffs to operators and rail freight customers beyong the prevailing rate of the Retail Price Index in the interim period before the Government's intended Act of Parliament on rail privatisation. We fear that British Rail's current approach to rail customers will irretrievably drive freight from the tracks to road transport. Considering the lack of clarity on infrastructure costing this cannot be allowed to continue until the private side have full access to the railway system following the Act. APRO fear that British Rail managers are 'tidying up' rail freight sectors into business packages which they will be permitted to purchase with Government assistance (as indicated by the Secretary of State for Transport) for management buy-out opportunities.

Service Withdrawal

A number of important rail customers such as British Steel are experiencing notice of withdrawal of service by British Rail. British Rail managers declare that by 1st April next year they will have 'tidied up' non-commercial traffic. We urge the Government to prohibit British Rail from withdrawing service in the interim period before the establishment of the rail track authority.

Rolling Stock Provision—Para. 33 of White Paper

The Government's White Paper refers to public sector rolling stock being made available to the private side. APRO members would like clarification on the administration of this ambition, and guidance on how equipment will be valued, made available on an equal basis and made available to interested parties.

British Rail continues to place orders for rolling stock. APRO members are concerned that equipment with up to 25 year life expectancy is being introduced to the marketplace by British Rail managers who will not have responsibility for the effects of over supply or inappropriate supply of equipment in the future. APRO urges the Government to instruct British Rail to cease all new purchase of wagons in order that market forces may more naturally determine supply and demand.

Freight versus Passenger—Paras. 16, 23 and 51 of White Paper

APRO members are concerned that the operating speed differences between passenger and freight equipment may mean diminishing slot access for freight. We urge Government to clarify Britrack's proposed role in fairly refereeing this matter.

Provision of Private Locomotives—Para. 57 of White Paper

Open access implicitly allows provision of private locomotives for freight or passenger haulage.

APRO members urge the Government to require British Rail to issue guideline standards including a system of licensing and with a formula for manning as well as tariffication for the provision of private locomotives. Without this the Government will see no further investment in private locomotives.

Incidents—Para. 77 of White Paper

Our members are concerned about the objectivity of British Rail's investigations into Rail incidents. We recommend the responsibility is vested in the H.M. Inspecting Officer for Railways under remit from the Health & Safety Executive.

Design Approvals, Safety Standards—Para. 76 of White Paper

We recommend that rail wagon design acceptance, together with safety and maintenance standards, be regulated by an Authority independent of British Rail.

Track Routes—Paras. 53 and 71 of White Paper

APRO members are interested to know if they or their customers will be able to purchase sections of track which are only used for their customers' freight movements and whether the Section 8 grant system would embrace this type of rail investment.

Meanwhile APRO urges the Government to instruct British Rail not to dispose of any further track until the Act of Parliament is passed.

Our members seek the Government's assurance that the new Rail Authority will undertake the contractual obligations currently with the British Railways Board concerning the leasing of British Rail line to private operators for their rail services.

	No. of Wagons Owned	*Approx. Rail Freight Tonnes carried per annum*	*Rail Investment*
Tiphook Rail Ltd	2,335	not known	£71m to date
MAT Transauto Ltd	435	not known	
NACCO (UK) Ltd	207	850,000	£8.5m to date
Teesbulk Handling Ltd	27	650,000	
Silcock Express Ltd	124	not known	
Toleman Delivery Services Ltd	25	110,000	none
Cargowaggon Rail Ltd	1,015	1.5m	£66m to date
GMWDA (Waste Treatment) Ltd	50	400,000	Circa £6m
CAIB (U.K.) Ltd	3,279	not known	£27m
Kemira Ince Ltd	92	100,000	
British Alcan Primary & Recycling Ltd	43	120,000	
Marcon Topmix Ltd	35	350,000	
Carless Refining & Marketing Ltd	30	200,000	£1.5-2m
Hepworth Minerals & Chemicals Ltd	60	280,000	
	No. of Wagons Owned	*Approx. Rail Freight Tonnes carried per annum*	*Rail Investment*
British Steel Plc	356	7.5m	
Plasmor Ltd	55	170,000	20% of Group sales
E G Steele & Co Ltd	80	not known	£200k additional
Van den Berghs & Jergens Ltd	Not declared		
Charrington Fuels Ltd	Not declared		
County of Avon	17	150,000	Almost £10m

"Not known" often applicable to owners who rent to third party users.

24 September 1992

APPENDIX 26

PRIVATE WAGON FEDERATION

This submission is made on behalf of the PWF Policy Committee which represents the interests of the Federation's Members comprising Owners, Operators, Builders and Repairers of some 13,500 privately owned freight vehicles currently registered for running on BR lines.

A schedule listing the names of the companies represented by the Federation is found below.

The Private Wagon Federation is grateful for the opportunity to respond to the invitation to submit comments on the Government's proposals to Privatise British Rail.

The Private Wagon Federation represents the Builders, Repairers, Owners, Hirers and Operators of the Private account freight moved on British Railways. The Federation has five affiliated Associations, which are the Association of Wagon Builders and Repairers, the United Kingdom Petroleum Industry Association, the Chemical Industries Association, the Association of Private Railway Wagon Owners, and the Construction Materials Rail Association. There are over sixty member companies, who own a total of approximately 13,500 freight wagons, with a replacement value in excess of £750 million. Member companies generate a quarter of British Rail's annual freight revenue. The Federation is the most representative of Railfreight customers in the United Kingdom.

The problem areas expressed by our Members reflect their genuine concern for the future well being of the rail freight industry.

29 September 1992

Response by the Private Wagon Federation to the invitation to comment on the proposals contained in the Government's White Paper on "New Opportunities for the Railways—The Privatisation of British Rail"

1. INTRODUCTION

The Private Wagon Federation (PWF) represents over sixty companies who own, operate, build and maintain wagons in the UK. The member companies have investment in vehicles in excess of £750 million in replacement terms and provide significant freight revenue. They have loading and discharging equipment investments of around £1,000 million.

The members are substantial investors in the Rail Mode and have genuine concern for the future well being of the Rail Freight Industry.

2. *General Comments*

2.1 The PWF welcomes the White Paper proposals for separating Regulator, Railtrack and Operating Service Companies. This should allow for improved efficiency and an operating climate which would attract investors. The investment threshold to become a private operator should also be affordable to a wide range of interests.

2.2 The Government's intention to ultimately privatise all BR activities is clearly stated. However, the detailed process and timetable for achieving this aim are far from clear. The uncertainty of this process will discourage investment in the short term which is particularly disappointing when this coincides with the opening of the Channel Tunnel.

2.3 The terms of reference and pricing policy of Railtrack are fundamental to the success of the privatised rail system. Potential investors will need to understand how infrastructure investment needs will be identified, justified and the costs recovered from those parties benefiting from such investments. The PWF is concerned that although the possibility of direct Government support is allowed to Railtrack (section 43) which will be justified by "cost-benefit return" there is no clear statement as to how this will operate for freight traffic. The White Paper states in section 52 that all new investments for freight infrastructure will be recovered from the user. The PWF strongly recommends that wider "cost-benefit" analysis is used to support and justify infrastructure investment as is used currently to justify new road building programmes.

The provision of investment justified on the cost benefits to the whole community can only be provided from Government sources and clear provision for this should be made for freight as well as passenger traffic.

2.4 The pricing policy of Railtrack towards supply of track paths for freight traffic should take into account the different needs of high speed valuable cargoes compared with the low value, high axleload traffic. There is a danger of low value traffic switching to road if charges are based purely on track miles occupancy and do not recognise market forces.

3. *Aims and Objectives of a Privatised Freight Railway*

3.1 The creation of new opportunities for private sector involvement is welcomed but will only be forthcoming if a reasonable return on investment can be assured. Potential hidden costs relating to infrastructure and the lack of a Railtrack pricing policy are currently undermining confidence in the future of a Privatised railway system. These aspects should be addressed quickly before existing investors drift away and potential new investors lose interest.

3.2 We believe that a key aim is the retention of existing financial investment in terms of specialised wagons, equipment, manpower and expertise already contained within the private sector, together with the provision of encouragement by means of a clear "level playing field" approach which will attract further confident investment and expand the Industry.

3.3 The provision of the rail infrastructure by Railtrack in the most cost effective manner is essential. Whilst investment can be justified by cost benefit analysis and supported by the Government, the running costs of the infrastructure must be supported by the charges to the Operating Service Companies in an equitable manner. If any Operating Service Companies need Government support for social or environmental considerations then this support should be by direct help to them rather than by regulating the charges from Railtrack.

The aim of Railtrack whilst still in Government ownership should be to minimise infrastructure costs by using as many privately supplied services as possible which have been sourced from open tender. This has significantly reduced costs in recent years for supply of equipment and services to British Rail. Only when this has been vigorously followed should its transfer to Private ownership be considered. Railtrack should ideally remain as one company in private hands but with Regulator supervision as proposed in the White Paper to prevent abuse of monopoly powers. The Regulator's supervision should apply to Freight traffic.

3.4 The pricing policy of Railtrack should recognise the contribution by freight to track services primarily devoted to passengers by making charges which will ensure a contribution above the "avoidable costs" generated by the freight traffic rather than a simple "pro-rata" charging on track usage. This should also apply to limited use of passenger traffic on essentially freight only track.

4. *Open Access/Franchises*

4.1 The philosophy of open access is based on the premise that a Private Owner/Operator of acceptable freight rolling stock can access the rail system for the running of trains at agreed times for a fee paid to Railtrack(56). The granting of franchises for freight traffic would conflict with the principle of open access and is not acceptable to PWF members.

4.2 The allocation of train paths should be on a fair and equitable basis fully recognising the interests of existing users who have made considerable investments based on previous freight timetables and charging regimes. The PWF fully supports the encouragement of new railfreight or passenger traffic which should compliment rather than displace existing business.

4.3 The PWF believes that privatising the existing Trainload Freight (TLF) and Railfreight Distribution (RFD) organisations as whole entities may prevent realistic open access and prevent the entry of potential new investors. We feel it would also inhibit efficiency improvements.

4.4 Many PWF members who have long term contracts with TLF and RFD are concerned how the terms of these contracts can be fulfilled to protect their current investments. There are no details in the White Paper of how these problems will be resolved.

4.5 There is a potential of other European Railway Organisations which are currently owned and heavily subsidised by their Government's buying UK Railfreight interests offering unfair competition to UK or other private investors. The PWF recommends that investment by other state-owned railways in UK rail companies is regulated to prevent controlling interest in such companies.

5. *Railtrack/Government Role in Subsidy and Investment*

5.1 The PWF believes that the corner stone of a successful Rail Privatisation is Government's willingness to, at least initially, subsidise the costs attributable to Railtrack. With this vital feature in place the future of a rail transport freight industry can be more readily assured.

5.2 The PWF urges the Government to use cost benefit analysis based on the benefits of railfreight to the whole community to formulate a policy of investment support to Railtrack and to provide operating and investment support to Operating Service Companies.

5.3 For the benefit of the environment, the PWF strongly urges Government to protect and encourage rail borne freight traffic, which may otherwise be forced to use road transport.

5.4. The PWF recommends that when infrastructure costs on a particular line are supported by subsidised passenger services which are subsequently withdrawn as social needs change then any freight use of that line continues at the same charge until freight contracts expire or appropriate compensation for line closure is provided.

LIST OF MAJOR RAIL USERS REPRESENTED BY THE PRIVATE WAGON FEDERATION

Kemira INCE Ltd.

RMC Roadstone Ltd.

Silcock Express Ltd.

Fina (UK) Ltd.

CAIB (UK) Ltd.

Tiphook Rail Ltd.

Marcroft Engineering

W. H. Davis Ltd.

BP Oil (UK) Ltd.

E. G. Steele & Co. Ltd.

Redland Aggregates Ltd.

Total Oil Ltd.

The Distillers Co. (Carbon Dioxide) Ltd.

C. C. Crump Co.

ABB Transportation Ltd.

Toleman Delivery Services Ltd.

Plasmor Ltd.

Van den Berghs & Jergens Ltd.

Charrington Fuels Ltd.

County of Avon

MAT Transauto Ltd.

NACCO (UK) Ltd.

Teesbulk Handling Ltd.

Cargowaggon Rail Ltd.

GMWDA (Waste Treatment) Ltd.

British Alcan Primary & Recycling Ltd.

Marcon Topmix Ltd.

Careless Refining & Marketing Ltd.

Hepworth Minerals & Chemicals Ltd.

British Steel Plc.

Powell Duffryn Standard Ltd.

Bombardier Prorail Ltd.

RFS Industries Ltd.

Tarmac Roadstone Ltd.

Castle Cement Ltd.

Robert Brett Ltd.

Tilcon Ltd.

Steetley Quarry Products Ltd.

Blue Circle Industries Ltd.

EEC Quarries Ltd.

Bardon LondoN Ltd.

Chemical IndustrieS Association

CONOCO Ltd.

ELF Oil GB Ltd.

ESSO Petroleum Co. Ltd.

GULF Oil GB Ltd.

Mobil Oil Co.

MURCO Petroleum

Phillips PPL

Shell UK Oil

TEXACO Ltd.

BP Chemicals

DOW Chemicals

ICI Plc.

ICI (Chemicals & Polymers)

Roche Products

Shell Chemicals UK

UK Petroleum Industry Association

28 September 1992

APPENDIX 27

THE CYCLISTS' PUBLIC AFFAIRS GROUP

"The Future Prospects of the Railway System in the light of the Government's Proposals for Privatisation"

1. BACKGROUND

1.1 *Why are railways important?*

Railways are the most efficient and environmentally acceptable transport mode. An electric train emits only 0.2 per cent of the carbon monoxide discharged by a car per passenger kilometre.

1.2 *Why is cycle carriage important?*

Bicycles are the most efficient means of transport over short journeys. Combining bicycle use with the rail system would work towards government targets for reducing vehicle emissions and improving the health of the nation. The recent British Medical Association policy report, "Cycling Towards Health and Safety", noted the strategic importance of increased cycle use in tackling the effects of traffic congestion.

1.3 *Why hasn't this happened?*

British Rail did open the door in 1977 by providing free cycle carriage on trains. Such was the success of this policy that carriage increased by 1,200 per cent. Systematically, restrictions have been imposed that have limited cycle carriage such that, in 1984, the Harris Organisation report "Carriage of Cycles and Bulky Luggage on Trains" estimated that British Rail were losing £10m per annum through lost passenger ticket sales resulting from these restrictions.

1.4 *What is the present situation?*

New restrictions are being applied with each timetable revision. These restrictions effectively prejudice British Rail's position in the face of free competition from other transport modes.

In 1992 Scotrail banned bicycles from class 158 Sprinters at only two days notice and without any consultation. As a result of pressure from the Tourist Board, MPs, the press and cycling groups, a reversal, in part, was secured within four weeks.

1.5 *Will privatisation benefit the cyclist?*

Unlike other European countries, Britain has no comprehensive rail development plan; the Europeans are commercialising their railways successfully, and accommodate cycle carriage with minimum restrictions.

1.6 *What is the potential for a rail service meeting the diverse demands of the travelling public?*

Central to the failure of the existing British Rail service to accommodate the diverse needs of the traveller are Government investment restrictions which prevent the design of rolling stock with flexible space for the carriage of push chairs, boxes, bicycles, persons in wheel chairs or seated passengers. Only changes to the design of new rolling stock will allow the future operators of railway services to provide freedom of choice and a fully competitive mode of transport.

The Dutch "Structured Scheme of Traffic and Transport" sets out objectives to reduce noise, emmissions and road casualties. One part of the Dutch Government plan is the "Masterplan Bicycle" not only setting targets to increase bicycle use but aiming to increase railway traffic through improving the links between the bicycle and rail.

2. *Issues in Privatisation*

2.1 This section is structured, as far as is possible, to address the issues raised in the Press Notice of 16 July 1992.

2.2 *What are the aims and objectives of a privatised railway?*

2.2.1 A privatised railway should aim to provide transport choice to the travelling public. Choice must be provided by a uniform range of minimum services across all competing operators.

2.2.2 Privatised railway services should facilitate competitive efficiency between modes of transport. Competitive efficiency will be provided by investment policies which recognise the broad environmental and social costs and benefits of modal choice.

2.3 *What are the attractions for the private sector?*

2.3.1 Firstly the private sector will seek to make a return on investment.

2.3.2 One major attraction for the private sector may be to explore business opportunities not undertaken by the present operators. In Germany, Switzerland and Belgium provision of cycle hire and secure cycle parking is used to attract business to stations.

2.4 Is there any conflict between the principle of open access and the granting of exclusive franchises?

2.4.1 Exclusive franchises coupled with no reasonably convenient alternative route will result in local monopoly on many services. Service quality should reflect the needs of consumers (including those with bulky luggage ie cycles or wheelchairs) and be written into franchise contracts.

2.5 Who should do the strategic planning for our railways?

2.5.1 The railways have a major impact on our transportation systems and as such should be influenced by strategic Government planning. Targets for reducing pollution, congestion and transport casualties may all be met by attracting foot and cycle passengers on to rail services as a competitive alternative to the private motor car.

2.6 What will be the Government's role in subsidy and investment?

2.6.1 It is clear that the Government will retain a significant role in regard to investment in rolling stock. Such investment decisions will constrain the range of services provided in the future by BR or a private operator. There is an urgent need to review the investment criteria for new rolling stock, to recognise the social and commercial value in providing flexible space for bulky luggage and to take a long term view.

2.6.2 Subsidy by way of Public Service Obligation Grants will continue under franchise contracts. At present PSO grants do not recognise the role of the railways in local and regional strategy to cut vehicle pollution and congestion. PSO should, in part, be dependant upon the operator providing defined minimum levels of service for passengers with cycles or other bulky luggage.

2.7 Railtrack, the track authority, will charge all operators "commercial" rates for track use. What principles should be used to set these charges?

2.7.1 Charges by Railtrack should be based upon a set criteria reflecting the user benefits of journey times, non-user benefits of congestion and pollution relief and the cost of meeting the requirements of the franchise agreement contract.

2.8 How should franchises operate so as to maximise the public interest, both for profitable and subsidised services?

2.8.1 The franchising authority should set down in all franchise agreements a minimum standard for quality, type, frequency and timetabling of services. Whilst each franchise contract will be different in detail, key minimum standards should be uniform to all agreements. Guaranteed access for cycles to trains should be written into the forthcoming Bill.

2.9 What arguments are there for switching immediately to a regime of rolling stock leasing for all operators, including BR?

2.9.1 Leasing of rolling stock may be an essential element of attracting commercial operators to rail services. Lease of stock will allow shared development costs but will restrict the nature of the services provided by operators.

2.10 What are the White Paper's implications for BR's on-going rolling stock investment programme?

2.10.1 Clearly BR and the Government will need to re-examine the rolling stock investment programme and this is a great opportunity for change. Such a re-examination may be beneficial to customer service and to wider strategic goals. At present, designs of rolling stock fail to exploit commercial opportunities and to meet strategic objectives. The trend to remove space allocation for bulky luggage deters fare paying customers from using railway services, inconveniences the disabled community and prevents combined bicycle and train travel.

2.11 How is the value of stations to be assesed and what will be the relationship between a privately owned station and BR's operation of trains therefrom?

2.11.1 The value of stations should reflect the rail and transport related commercial opportunities for the site. For example the provision of facilities for cycle parking and hire attracts 35 per cent of all Dutch rail passengers to arrive at stations by bicycle.

2.11.2 Contracts for the sale or lease of stations should include clauses to guarantee access for passengers and their luggage for purposes of making rail journeys.

3. THE WAY FORWARD

3.1 The debate surrounding the Government's plans for the privatisation of British Rail is an opportunity to examine new approaches to Government policy towards investment in the railways.

3.2 For the forseeable future British Rail is likely to be the operator of the majority of rail services. Problems with the policy of the sector of BR towards attracting customers through provision and marketing of appropriate services can be addressed by the proposed rail regulator.

3.3 The following policy proposals are intended to highlight the opportunities to address important modal choice issues through the provision of a flexible rail service.

4. POLICY PROPOSALS OF THE CYCLISTS' PUBLIC AFFAIRS GROUP

4.1 BR should appoint an independent body to commission a demand study, based on the 1984 "Carriage of Cycles and Bulky Luggage on Trains" (Harris Organisation) report. This should be completed within one year of of the privatisation Act becoming law: the recommendations should be adopted by the Regulator to determine the minumum scope and standard of services that the Franchising Authority would require. There should be regular collection and publication of statistics on levels of bicycle carriage.

4.2 Legislation must direct the Regulator to ensure that a minimum level of service for the carriage of cycles is provided. The Regulator should include a specific person with responsibity for ensuring the needs of customers with bicycles are met. The Franchising Authority should promote, and the franchisees be contractually bound to, a policy of seamless travel.

4.3 BR, private operators and Government specifications for new passenger stock design—and refurbishment of old stock—must include flexible space for the carriage of cycles in every design. The government's continuation of the Public Service Obligation grant should be conditional, in part, on this provision.

4.4 Any Bill presented to privatise the railways should state that the Regulator is fully committed to promoting a minimum level of service for cyclists, ensuring that the Franchising Authority will require franchisees to guarantee access for cycles to trains. This will be in accordance with other EC rail operators best practices, provided at reasonable prices and with the minimum of limitations.

4.5 The Regulator should ensure that publicity—timetables, directives for staff and agents, etc.—should provide cyclists with full, accurate and widely-available information of BR and franchisees' services.

4.6 BR and franchisees' staff training must recognise that cycle carriage is added-value business. Attitude shaping should be visible, and be 'top-down' in each organisation.

4.7 Any bill presented to privatise the railways should ensure that a condition of the sale or lease of stations includes guaranteed access for passengers wishing to convey bicycles, and minimum standards for cycle parking facilities.

4.8 The principle of through ticketing should be maintained not only for passenger tickets but for reservation services including bicycle reservations.

4.9 The Government should participate in the European TCV agreement and amend legislation to allow the UK to return to a system of conveying bicycles as unaccompanied international luggage. The Regulator should ensure that operators comply with the TCV agreement.

24 September 1992

APPENDIX 28

BRITISH AIRWAYS (BA)

Submission to Transport Committee on the future for the railway system

BA welcomes the basic structure of the proposals the government has put forward for the start of the privatisation of British Rail. As BA's recent history has proved the infusion of management skills, ideas and the entrepreneurial spirit that pervades the private sector has transformed this company into the world's leading airline, renowned for its level of customer service. There is no reason why private sector involvement in rail services should not lead to more efficient, reliable services for the public as the full potential to innovate and make profits are realised.

BA are aware of the complexity of the challenge of bringing BR into the private sector and believe, as the Government have accepted in the White Paper, that a significant level of government investment in rail infrastructure must remain. BA are particularly concerned that the levels of investment by BR in both infrastructure and rolling stock do not fall during the privatisation process and that the timetables for key projects, such as Crossrail, do not slip.

BA's primary interest is in rail links which serve airports from which we operate, particularly LHR and Gatwick. BA has been an ardent supporter of the construction of the Heathrow Express link and we believe our involvement will help to improve the product, ensuring the level of service will cater for passengers' needs. A successful launch of the Heathrow Express in the private sector funded by both industry and the City will give a major boost to the Government's proposals to attract franchisees to operate BR services, and to encourage other firms to commit capital investment to the rail network.

BA also look forward to investigating the opportunity for bidding for the franchise for the Gatwick Express, where there is room for improving the level of service.

Our involvement in the Heathrow Express has led us to have some concerns about the Government's proposals which we summarise below.

1. *Ownership*

Despite funding the significant new investment in track and stations at Heathrow, it is unclear how the Heathrow Express company can exploit full economic ownership of its assets, as it has been proposed that the company will have to pay Railtrack a significant fee for access to the track between Airport Junction and Paddington. This fee will represent a significant part of the company's operating costs and as the company has no measure of control over the costs that make up this fee BA believe that the shareholders of the Heathrow Express company will not enjoy the full benefits that the risks of their share ownership should give. BA believes that if the inefficient parts of BR are not to be entrenched it is imperative that the Rail Regulator ensures strict control over Railtrack's overheads. In the medium-term the Government must continue with its proposals to allow private companies to own the key industrial assets of railways so that private operators, with a long-term commitment to the railway system, can fully exploit these assets knowing that they have complete control over costs.

2. *Track Fee*

BA accepts that the track charge will have to contain an element which will provide for the financing of infrastructure investment, in addition to the maintenance and running costs of existing assets. However, BA believe that where private companies invest significant capital in improving the network for passengers, (as is the case with the Heathrow Express) that any such capital sums should be taken into account by Railtrack and the Rail Regulator when setting the fee to be charged by Railtrack. This could either be in the form of a track fee "holiday" or in reduced annual charges.

BA also believe that service operators must have a say over how Railtrack allocates funds for capital investment spending. We believe there must be a mechanism by which franchisees can direct Railtrack to reinvest a portion of the pot of money Railtrack has received from franchisees into capital projects which the franchisee has an interest in. For instance part of the track fee that the Heathrow Express Company will pay could be reinvested in developing rail-link infrastructure at LHR.

3. *Right of Access*

Whilst BA accepts that a formal framework for regulating access to the network will need to be introduced, BA believes that in cases where private companies have created new track and infrastructure facilities, such as the Heathrow Express, that the Franchising Authority should afford these companies some protection. If private investors are to make an acceptable rate of return they may have to be awarded exclusive franchises for a closed-end period before the infrastructure reverts (at a price) to Railtrack. These franchises should allow that company to determine who else, if anyone, gains access to that route and to determine the level of charges required to compensate it for its loss of capacity on that route, should it grant access to another operator. BA therefore believe that there will be some rail services where it will not be possible to pursue the principle of "open access". BA accept that when track and infrastructure are owned by the private sector that the monopoly power of the infrastructure owner should be subject to normal regulatory control.

4. *Government investment*

In the long term BA is interested in using rail services to attract passengers to airports to help relieve congestion on the roads and to improve customer choice with regards access modes. We believe that by opening up rail links, particularly to the West and North of LHR, that it would be possible to attract a significant percentage of the 7 million domestic air passengers who use LHR (and others who currently travel to LHR by road), to travel to LHR on dedicated trains from large regional cities. As well as freeing up slots at LHR for other services for which surface transport modes were not a substitute, there would be a significant environmental cost saving.

However, if other dedicated rail links are to feed LHR directly there will need to be further significant investment in both electrification of track and of terminal facilities at LHR. BA believe that the best location for such investment will only be possible at Terminal 5 as the stations which will be built by the Heathrow Express Company at T4 and the Central Terminal Area (CTA) will only have two platforms and therefore minimal excess capacity for trains from other routes. It would be very expensive to retrofit extra platforms at CTA as well as disrupting the Paddington rail link.

If Heathrow is to compete with the likes of Charles de Gaulle, Schipol, and Frankfurt, it must have access to similar standards of integrated transport facilities.

BA are conscious that the infrastructure at Heathrow's European competitor airports have been state-funded and that the financial return on the level of investment required to provide similar services to those offered in Continental Europe may not be sufficient to attract private sector funding. We therefore believe the Government must continue to provide investment, on a partnership basis with the private sector, for infrastructure projects which ensures that there is a level playing field between the UK and its European partners.

BA welcome the Government's commitments to provide investment in infrastructure for schemes which the private sector and/or Railtrack cannot justify in terms of direct financial return but which will offer substantial cost-benefit returns to the taxpayer (e.g. less of a requirement for spending on roads, environmental cost savings, de-congestion benefits).

BA believe that if the Government is to attract a large number of franchisees it will have to continue to invest in improving rail infrastructure if franchisees are going to commit themselves to contractual obligations to run efficient and punctual services.

5. *Planning*

BA accept that Railtrack should have the lead responsibility for planning and promoting major investment in railways, in consultation with service operators and the DTp. BA believe that it is important that the DTp must maintain an active dialogue with Railtrack as decisions on other investments in the UK's transport infrastructure will inevitably impinge on railway investment decisions.

With particular regard to LHR unless the planning process is accelerated the lack of track and station capacity suggests the scope for BA to become extensively involved in rail services will be limited in the short-term.

6. *Level of fares*

The White Paper outlines that the Regulator will be given the task of controlling fares and quality of service on passenger services routes which enjoy monopoly power. BA believe there will be some routes which operate in a highly competitive environment and that the Government should follow the same principle that it advocates for freight and parcels.

The Heathrow Express, for instance, will face competition from the London Underground, coach and bus services and taxis. BA believe that there will be a large disincentive for private capital investment if on these sorts of routes the Regulator can impose maximum level of fares. BA believe that maximum level of fares should only be set on routes which are subsidised.

30 September 1992

APPENDIX 29

Letter from Mr P L Desmet

British Rail Privatisation

The privatisation of British Rail has as its greatest benefit the removal of its investment finances from the strictures necessitated by public ownership and it is important, therefore, to make the most of this opportunity. I am of the opinion that the key issue is that of funding and so I would like to submit my recent publication 'Proposed Privatisation of British Rail',* copy previously sent to Mr Robert Adley MP, to be considered as part of your written evidence. If the funding of the railways after privatisation is not right then no amount of tinkering with the current proposals is likely to bring success but, if the issue is addressed then privatisation has a fighting chance.

The creation of numerous bureaucratic organisations to oversee the franchises and rail access will in no way contribute to greater efficiency and value for money for the customer. Despite the existence of a Franchising Authority, for instance, it is very difficult to see what incentives that body can give to improve an unsatisfactory franchisee given the almost impossible task of replacing him within a reasonable period of time. The existence of various operators alongside Railtrack will lead to a lack of clear accountability and so make the Passengers Charter very difficult to sustain. The proposal to make each route a 'profit centre' for subsidy assessment purpose will end the current principal of cross-subsidy and so the subsidy required to maintain socially-necessary services, as has already happened in the bus industry, is likely to increase despite the financial improvements gained by new operators. Apart from certain exceptions, it is also difficult to see how future investment in the railways can be raised without the franchisee passing the costs on to the government.

The enclosed report* has been written on the basis that the objective-led privatisations such as the water industry have been extremely successful whilst those that lacked objectives, eg bus deregulation have not. The main question in bus and rail privatisation seems to have been 'how do we bring the private sector into the industry?' rather than 'where will the industry be in thirty years time?' It should be remembered that although

---

*Not printed

the water industry is a monopoly, many of the objectives dictated by Brussels are non-profit making environmental improvements costing many millions of pounds and so it was important at privatisation to establish the appropriate financial framework. I am sure enough expertise exists within the British Isles to address current issues such as the protection of the environment, the relief of traffic congestion and the role that the railways might play in the revitalisation of the current stagnant economy and so derive national objectives that could be enshrined in a slightly more imaginative privatisation bill. I have already worked out how every station in Scotland, Wales, the Lake District and other rural areas could be reached from London and most English cities by changing trains just once. The same principles would enable very conceivable (standard-gauge) rail journey within Great Britain to be made within three or less changes of train. These are achievable objectives provided that new rail construction, particularly in London, is planned carefully. Many of the details have only been finalised since publication and so the report merely introduces the concept.

I would draw your attention to pages 13 to 19 of the report* outlining funding arrangements which could be used by the government in its current Bill. The establishment of a Railway Savings Account and the conversion of road tax to a transport tax is recommended. The question of subsidy for the railways remains politically controversial, however, despite the attempts of successive governments the self financing railway has not been achieved and looks increasingly unlikely to become so. Although it may be possible to reduce the subsidy still further I would suggest that most of the big savings have already been made and that we are not far from the minimum level of funding. After fares British Rail currently needs approximately £1 billion per annum which it receives from various sources. It is recommended that a simple accountancy measure be undertaken at privatisation that would abolish all existing grants and subsidies and instead pay the railway all of its monies in a lump sum from the road/transport tax. If the tax were to become payable at railway stations, the railways could retain their monies before handling over the remainder to the government in a similar fashion as the post office does now; the main advantage would be the removal of the industry from the public-sector borrowing-requirement. Once the money is isolated its payment could become index-linked or, as is recommended, linked to the implementation of a national strategy disigned to alleviate traffic congestion and also designed to regulate future subsidy. It is suggested that the payment be known as standing charge and that it be increased at 5 per cent above the rate of inflation, however, because road tax currently raises some £16 billion per annum this would require an increase of less than £1 per annum on £110 tax disc for a period of say five years; a payment of £5 per annum for the relief of traffic congestion is surely good value for money.

The second means of raising money could be through the establishment of a national railway savings account. An alternative method to that suggested in the report would be for building societies and banks to administer such an account. The railway account would normally pay 1 per cent less interest than other accounts and that 1 per cent would be paid to the railways. The investor would then receive 2 per cent of gift vouchers from the railway which could be used to pay up to 50 per cent of the cost of a rail ticket including season tickets. For example £1000 invested for one year with an interest rate of 6 per cent would yield £60 whilst the railway account would pay the investor £50 in cash with £20 worth of rail vouchers; this enables the railways to receive £10 towards their agreed investment programme.

It is clear that the privatisation of British Rail can bring major benefits in the areas of private-sector management and culture and has the potential to obtain greater investment, however, the railway system is a national transport asset and this aspect is not recognised in the White Paper. Just as there is a national plan for the expansion of the road system so there should be one for the railway system too. A long-term investment plan should be formulated at privatisation and incorporated into Railtrack's investment programme. The removal of the industry from the public-sector borrowing-requirement would enable the programme to be implemented, however, the Treasury is likely to provide fierce opposition to such a removal. Nevertheless it is this which is the root of all problems and if this battle is not to be fought then any discussion on the White Paper will be inevitably trivialised. If funding does not feature prominently in the forthcoming Bill then history is likely to remember it less for the opportunities that it identified but more for those it missed.

29 September 1992

APPENDIX 30

ASSOCIATION OF TRANSPORT CO-ORDINATING OFFICERS

"The Future Prospects for the Railway System in the light of the Government's Proposals for Privatisation"

In response to the Committee's invitation for comments on the Rail White Paper I enclose a submission on behalf of the Association of transport Co-ordinating Officers (ATCO).

The Association was formed in 1974 to bring together persons whose work involved the then new County Council responsibility of public transport co-ordination. ATCO's aims centre on the provision of a better passenger transport system on a nationwide basis. Most of ATCO's work involves exchanging information between its members and with other professional bodies. The Association is now regarded as an important source of professional expertise and through its advice to the various Local Authority Associations and membership of Ministerial Working Parties is assisting in the formulation of policies and service standards.

*Not printed

The Association comprises the senior transport co-ordinating officers in all English and Welsh Counties, Scottish Regions and Passenger Transport Executives. ATCO members are thus very familiar with the challenges associated with planning and administering a passenger transport system which combines public funding and private sector operation. Also members employed by the Passenger Transport Executives have direct experience in specifying the service levels of, and monitoring the delivery of, rail services in all the conurbations and on many suburban and rural lines.

This submission addresses the specific questions contained in the Committee's Press Notice dated 16 July 1992. However I believe that there are other issues raised by the White Paper and so the submission concludes by commenting on these. In drawing together its submission the Association has had regard to the Committee's request for brevity. However, should the Committee wish any of the points to be amplified to improve clarity we would be pleased to provide supplementary details on request.

The Future Prospects for the Railway System in the light of the Governments Proposals for Privatisation

Evidence submitted to the House of Commons Transport Committee by the Association of Transport Coordinating Officers (ATCO).

INTRODUCTION

The Association of Transport Co-ordinating Officers (ATCO) represents those responsible for securing and Coordinating local authority passenger services. Through their professional duties its members are familiar with the challenges associated with planning and administering a passenger transport system which combines public funding and private sector operation.

This submission starts by addressing the specific questions contained in the Press Notice dated 16 July 1992. It then refers to two related issues raised by the White Paper which we believe are worthy of the Committee's consideration. As requested the submission aims at brevity but ATCO will be pleased to provide supplementary details should the Committee require.

Aims and Objectives

The White Paper indicates the Government's intention to improve the quality and level of use of railway services and the value for money which they offer to users. It also implies that current levels of service will be maintained or enhanced. Few would quarrel with these laudable objectives.

The aim of a private business is to maximise the financial returns to shareholders. Customer satisfaction is an important business consideration but passenger and shareholder interests do not always coincide. Considerations of national and social interest have no attraction to a private company if they detract from profitability.

One example of this potential clash of objectives is the provision of peak services. The passenger's desire to avoid overcrowding, the rail operator's wish to minimise expenditure on lightly utilised rolling stock and considerations of national and local transport policy are not easily reconciled. The practice of granting peak period commuter trains priority over freight may not be warranted in purely commercial terms.

Regulation affects the potential profit of an operator but, as recognised in the White Paper, regulatory control will be essential to protect national and consumer interests. Its effectiveness will depend on both the principle and explicit detail of the controlling mechanisms. Stability is an important factor in both business planning and customer confidence and it is in the interests of all parties for the regulatory system to be clearly understood and not subject to frequent modification or change.

Open Access

"Open access" appears suited to freight traffic, especially bulk movements which can be modified in line with changing traffic flows. The concept seems inappropriate in the passenger market which is less prone to sudden changes in travel patterns.

The White Paper accepts the need to provide a core system of franchised passenger services. This is incompatible with "open access". Bidding for a franchise requires a realistic assessment of potential revenue and an assurance that train "paths" will be available to operate the specified timetable. Introduction of an "open access" service directly affects the franchise holder's earnings, thereby weakening the core service.

It is envisaged that operators will pay for a franchise to operate profitable services. This is unlikely if they can claim "open access" without payment. Local services may be less attractive to competitors but these can include potentially profitable elements (e.g. by failing to provide additional stock to meet peak needs).

If a franchise has been realistically costed, loss of even a small proportion of revenue will have a significant effect on profit margins. An unsuccessful bidder could use "open access" to undermine a competitor's viability, thereby precipitating a new round of bidding. Such practices are not unknown among bus operators.

Recent suggestions that "open access" services should enjoy priority of timetable pathing, have preference in securing scarce high quality rolling stock or have track costs allocated on a marginal basis are incompatible with the concept of competition on an equal basis.

It is unclear if "open access" is to be accompanied by "open withdrawal" of services which compete with franchised operations.

Strategic Planning

It is imperative that rail services are treated as an integral component of an overall national transport strategy. This can only be brought about by the Government.

In the event of privatisation, determination of strategic priorities within the railway system would not be an appropriate task for the operators. "Railtrack" is also inappropriate as the provision of track and structures should be determined by the strategy rather than vice versa. The Department of Transport undertakes strategic planning of the road system but its remit is largely confined to "track". It has no direct control over traffic volume, travel costs or demand patterns.

The proposed Franchising Authority will have considerable powers to determine the pattern, frequency and cost of rail passenger services. It will be central to future investment because the franchise specifications will dictate the need for facilities and the Authority will be the body most able to modify service patterns to reflect the availability of new routes (e.g. Crossrail). It may be logical for its remit to extend to consideration of freight services, especially as the pattern of franchised passenger operations directly affects the track capacity available for freight (and vice versa). The Franchising Authority seems most suited to the role of strategic planner for rail services within an overall national transport plan.

Strategic planning for the railway cannot take place in a vacuum. The planning authority will need to maintain a degree of independence from Government and will also need to develop close links with local and regional authorities. These are already charged with strategic transport and land use planning functions and their involvement is considered essential if local accountability is to be incorporated into the rail planning process.

Subsidy and Investment

As the Government will be the source of subsidy and of investment that is not justified on purely commercial grounds, it will continue to have a central role. To date Government has defined its objectives only in terms of broad service levels and total subsidy targets. Franchising identifies subsidy more closely with individual services but will inevitably lead to greater public comparison of the relative cost of different services.

It remains to be seen whether the specified level of franchised service is designed to match anticipated expenditure demand or is scaled down to meet total expenditure targets. Highway planning largely reflects the former but is nevertheless cash constrained. Once a subsidised franchise has been let there is an ongoing commitment to fund it until expiry.

The criteria adopted for subsidy and investment, including cost/benefit appraisal, should apply equally to all modes of transport. They should be overt and open to public scrutiny. There is a case for treating all Government expenditure on transport as a single budget item rather than sub-dividing it prematurely. For example, consideration of investment in cross Pennine travel routes may be better served by considering road and rail together rather than each mode individually.

Much railway investment is already internally funded and this can continue to be the case. Improvements to track, signalling, maintenance facilities and rolling stock often result in increased earnings or reduced costs. However, loss of a vertically integrated business structure will create a need for interim funding of those large scale projects which do not produce income until completion. It is questionable whether a major route renewal or electrification could be made without Government assistance.

Rail services have an important role to play in matters of public policy. These include promotion of economic development, relief of traffic congestion and environmental considerations. Services meeting social objectives are unlikely to have a high priority for investment on purely commercial grounds. There is scope for financial input from property development but this option is not available in established areas except through taxation. There is a clear need for public funding of investment which produces social benefit or reduces overall expenditure on transport facilities.

Local and regional authorities are an important source of investment funding for rail services as part of their transport and land use strategies. Continuation of this practice will depend on their ability to influence the pattern and quality of service which their input produces.

Public investment in track, structures and safety systems can be funded either by direct grants to the track authority or by means of higher franchise payments to operators who are then able to pay increased user fees. Careful thought is needed to determine the most appropriate method.

The track authority

As envisaged in the White Paper, "Railtrack" will not only provide and maintain the track but will be responsible for allocating timetable "paths" to prospective users. Sale of "paths" to the highest bidder maximises income but creates problems in ensuring that franchise holders are able to provide the specified level of service and has a direct effect on the franchise price. The relationship between "Railtrack" and the Franchising Authority and the responsibility for allocating "paths" needs careful consideration.

Track costs will account for over 25 per cent of an operating company's expenditure but will be outside their direct control. "Railtrack" will be a monopoly supplier with almost no prospect of challenge by an alternative.

It is simplistic to say that all cost associated with operation of a service should be charged to it and costs common to two or more services shared between them. In practice this is difficult to determine and would lead to a complex recharge structure relating to frequency, speed and weight of trains run over a section of line. It would also lead to fluctuation of cost to operators as the traffic levels of others sharing common tracks varied.

There are considerable merits in the system of charging the majority of cost to the "core" service, thereby ensuring that the cost of providing fixed structures is met. Additional services provided by the "core" operator, other categories of passenger traffic and freight (or passenger services on a predominantly freight line) could then be charged marginally. Such a system could encourage use of the track by additional services. It is, however, doubtful if a system in which one operator's services meet the fixed costs whilst a direct competitor is marginally priced, constitutes fair competition. In such cases it seems reasonable for both to contribute to fixed costs.

Long term guaranteed price contracts for track use offer greater stability to the operator and to the track authority. In the case of franchised services it seems appropriate to link them with the duration of the franchise.

"Railtrack" will be expected to make track of a suitable standard available in a way that allows users to operate their committed timetables. Financial responsibility for delays, diversions etc caused by track maintenance or resulting from operators failures will need to be clearly defined.

It is suggested that fixed costs associated with electrification of a route should be charged to all users of that line, irrespective of the type of traction used on individual trains.

Franchises

Since local rail services exist to serve local needs it is essential that the Franchise Authority has a regional dimension as well as a national one. Local and regional authorities represent local communities and are responsible for local transport and planning strategies. It seems essential to involve them in preparation of the franchise specifications and to ensure that these relate directly to national objectives and local transportation plans. Determination of public interest and social necessity cannot be meaningful if imposed by remote unaccountable bodies with little knowledge of those they purport to serve.

Franchise specifications should be as explicit and detailed as possible. Experience with bus service tendering indicates that clear definition of details assists all bidders to compete on equal terms and is an essential factor in a good working relationship between the franchise holder and those monitoring operation of the franchise.

It is suggested that franchise specifications should incorporate a requirement to achieve defined minimum patronage levels. Should these not be reached due to poor performance of the operator or genuine changes in demand a new franchise should be invited.

Operation of franchise requires access to the track and other facilities needed to meet the specification. Without it the franchise is worthless. Some form of priority in allocating track capacity for franchised services seems essential if the system is to function in the interest of the passengers.

The quality of rolling stock has a direct effect on the user's perception of a service and will need clear definition in the franchise agreement. As in the bus industry, there is a risk that operators will be reluctant to invest in vehicles without a long term prospect of future returns and that old stock will be kept in service as a short term expedient.

Stability of service provision is important to users. Considerable care will be needed to allay fear of change when franchises are reviewed and to ensure that a smooth transition if operators change.

Although some franchises are purchased from the authority and others bought in by them, all carry the right and obligation to provide a specified service. The requirement to meet defined standards is equally important in both cases.

Stock leasing

Some form of stock leasing will be essential if new operators are to take over from British Rail. There is no pool of spare stock; manufacturing capacity is limited and has relatively long delivery times. Structural limitations preclude redeployment of foreign stock.

Purchase of stock on securing a franchise will require considerable investment. This must be recovered through the franchise price or fares (or both). Leasing offers a means of matching payment to earnings. Ultimately specialist leasing companies may emerge but some form of central leasing agency appears necessary during the transition from the current position

In the short term, allocation of stock to new commercial operators may lead to downgrading of service quality and journey speed in other areas. The quantity of top quality higher speed stock is limited yet this is likely to be the most sought after by new entrants.

Change of a franchised operator may lead to a requirement for replacement rolling stock, especially if the displaced company wishes to redeploy it elsewhere. This could be a formidable barrier to a new entrant. It may be appropriate for the Franchising Authority to control its own pool of stock which can be leased to operators to maintain continuity of operation. This could also allow renewal to be planned over a longer period than a single contract.

It is essential that replacement of ageing rolling stock is ongoing in order to meet passenger and safety expectations. There is, however, a risk that uncertainty over future ownership will delay present renewal, particularly when new stock is funded by regional authorities. British Rail may also find it attractive to defer renewal in the interest of short term financial targets. It is open to the Government to maintain funding of the replacement programme, thereby ensuring that manufacturing capacity remains usefully employed and that a reasonable quality fleet is available to future operators.

Stations

Unlike airports or motorway service areas, stations include track and equipment used by through services (including freight) as well as those which call. There is a case for the tracks, signals and platforms to form part of the operational railway, under the control of the track authority, with commercial activity treated separately. Determination of commercial values is relatively straightforward once the operational aspects have been separated.

Commercial activities, including development of non operational land, need not be managed by train operators although they may wish to provide their own facilities as tenants. Safeguards will be needed to ensure that passenger facilities, including the availability of information, continue to be provided at a level commensurate with the status of the station and that easy access to train services is maintained . It is essential that responsibility for the various aspects of station operation is unambiguous if customer confusion is to be avoided.

Should the operational aspects of stations be considered suitable for external ownership, safeguards will be essential to ensure that user fees do not abuse the station's position as a monopoly supplier.

There is likely to be a continuing role for local authorities in promoting and financing new local stations. Most will consist only of the basic, operational facilities but, should they prove attractive to an external operator, the interests of the sponsoring body should be protected. It would, for example, be inappropriate for a "park and ride" station car park to be used for property development.

The Closure Process

The White Paper says that "There is no reason to believe that the Government's proposals will lead to closures of services". It acknowledges, however, that the Franchising Authority may decide that a service may no longer be "socially necessary". There is no indication of how this decision will be reached or whether it will be taken before specifying a minimum timetable or when the support cost is known.

This procedure is different to the current system in which closure is precipitated by the operator. Recognition of the role of "social necessity" in the continued provision of rail services is a welcome departure from the narrow confines of the current closure procedures but it seems essential to involve the public in consideration of the effects of withdrawal of support to a service and to ensure that all aspects of such proposals are fully and openly considered.

The network effect

One of the strengths of British Rail is its ability to provide and market national coverage. Passengers can obtain timetable and cost information on an intended journey, can buy a ticket between almost any pair of stations and may use it on any train applicable to the category of fare purchased. In the event of problems en-route they can refer to a single identifiable company. Such benefits should not be lightly dismissed.

It is optimistic to claim that commercial operators will automatically choose to maintain similar facilities. This has not been the case in Manchester following replacement of local trains by Metrolink trams. Deregulation of the local bus industry has been accompanied by marked deterioration in the availability of timetable and fares information. Airline ticket interavailability, if offered at all, is restricted to higher price categories and is rarely publicised.

The franchise system offers the potential to maintain most of the present benefits. Inclusion of requirements to participate in reciprocal ticketing, to provide defined levels of information services and similar items in the franchise specification can ensure that the public and transportation benefits of national coverage are maintained. The presence of such facilities on the core system is also likely to act as an incentive for participation by any non franchised operators.

29 September 1992

APPENDIX 31

CUMBRIA COUNTY COUNCIL

The Future Prospects for the Railway System in the light of the Government's Proposals for Privatisation

The County Council's Highways and Transportation Sub-Committee considered the Government White Paper, "New Opportunities for the Railways—The Privatisation of British Rail" on 22 September 1992. I have been asked to convey the County Council's views to you.

Members were aware of the wide discussion that has been taking place on all the issues raised in the White Paper. However, they decided to concentrate on issues of particular concern to the residents of and visitors to Cumbria.

Members were primarily concerned that the level of service now operating within and to and from Cumbria should in no way be diminished as a consequence of privatisation. Indeed there are aspirations for improvements in service. As part of the County Council's submission I am enclosing copies of the document, "Moving Into the Next Century; COMMUNICATIONS in Cumbria and Beyond", published in November 1991*. The document is concerned with all modes of transport, but I would draw your attention to the rail items starting on pages 8 and 16, and in Chapter 6 (pages 35-42).

Members were pleased to note that it is intended that through ticketing facilities will be available when passengers will be using more than one private operator's train to achieve their journey. Members would also like to think that the various tickets such as the Rail Rovers and the concessionary facilities for the elderly and others will continue to be available under privatisation with some central organisation assigning the income to the various operators.

Members were also concerned that the allocation of franchises should not lead to operators choosing to provide services over what might be termed the more lucrative lengths of the line to the detriment of other sections. Take for example the service between Barrow and Preston. Some of those trains provide through services to Manchester beyond Preston and to Whitehaven beyond Barrow. Such opportunities for through travel are valued highly.

In Cumbria there is particular concern about who might operate any rail services in the future. You are possibly aware that the main bus operator in the County is Cumberland Motor Services, part of the Stagecoach Group. There have been rumours that Stagecoach are interested in operating some of the lines in Cumbria. At present Cumberland oprate some 90 per cent of registered bus mileage in the County. Members are concerned that the operation of rail services by the same bus company could lead to even greater control of public transport by one operator. You will appreciate that members are concerned that no operator should be able to exploit a monopoly situation.

Since their formation in 1974 the County Council have invested in various rail station improvements throughout Cumbria. Members are seeking assurances through the legislation that any assets in which the Council has invested will continue to be used and fully maintained, without any diminution of service and will not be disposed of by any new owner without reimbursement of the Council's investment.

Connections between different services are often affected by the late running of trains within Cumbria, particularly on the West Coast Main Line. However, British Rail do have various guidelines whereby some trains are held back in order to maintain connections or other arrangements are made, for passengers who arrive too late to get to their final destination to be conveyed by bus or taxi. The County Council suggest that the legislation will have to require arrangements to be made whereby private rail operators will have to wait or make some other provision for passengers who have been delayed.

It is noted that Railtrack will be responsible for producing a national timetable. At present both Regional Railways and InterCity produce various leaflets giving details of particular journeys between, for example, Carlisle and London. Should such services in future be operated by a series of different private operators, it is felt that such publicity setting out all the opportunities throughout the day and the week should be availble on one leaflet, and not just on a series of leaflets produced by each private operator.

At present British Rail has numerous overseas offices selling tickets and providing information of particular interest to visitors to areas like Cumbria. Members would hope that an organisation like Railtrack, responsible for timetables, would continue to provide such services in other countries.

Another issue of particular concern to members of the County Council is safety on the railways. Members have asked me to impress upon you the need to include in any legislation, requirements upon operators which will at least maintain the present safety standards on the rail system. The view has been expressed that with the privatisation of buses there has been a tendency for some operators to run buses for much longer than previously with all that that could imply for safety.

*Not printed

Concern has also been expressed for the carriage of disabled persons by rail. Members would like to think that the legislation would require somebody, if not the operator to provide the service necessary to help the disabled to make their journeys, and in particular to make connections at intermediate stations en route. It is felt that there is a need to lay down standards not only for such a service but also in respect of stations and their access by the disabled.

Finally members would like standards to be set not only for the trains on which people travel but also for the stations used by the general public. Even the smallest stations should have adequate well lit waiting space with appropriate information for travellers. Attention also needs to be given to the standards provided at larger stations for comfort, in particular where passengers may need to wait for connections, and the provision of refreshment and toilet facilities.

The above is the briefest practical resume of members' views that I can offer. But should you require any further information or explanation I am sure that members would want you to contact me immediately.

1 October 1992

APPENDIX 32

SUBMISSION BY DUMFRIES AND GALLOWAY REGIONAL COUNCIL

"The Future Prospects for the Railway System in the light of the Government's Proposals for Privatisation"

EXECUTIVE SUMMARY

This submission is made on behalf of Dumfries and Galloway Regional Council.

The submission sets out the Region's particular geographic position (1.1–1.3) and the likely impact of privatisation on investment decisions (1.4, 1.5). The submission also outlines the Council's case for upgrading of the North Channel corridor to Northern Ireland (1.6–1.7 and Appendix).

Aims and Objectives are set out in paragraphs 2.1–2.3. The primary objective of a public transport system should be to reflect the economic and social needs of the community. A second objective should be stability, whilst a third objective should be improvement in quality.

Paragraph 3.1 outlines the potential conflict between exclusive franchises and open access. Paragraphs 4.1 and 4.2 examine the need for overall responsibility for strategic planning.

The need for subsidy and investment to be considered separately is then explained. The particular problems of financing line investment on Scotland's rural railways will be acute if these are to be financed internally through franchises (5.1–5.6). This is further amplified regarding Railtrack charges (6.1).

Paragraph 7.1 explains the necessary criteria for franchising in the public interest. Paragraphs 8.1–8.2 examine the possible repercussions on new rolling stock procurement and the need for further measures. The privatisation of stations must be seen to be in the public interest (9.1).

1. INTRODUCTION

1.1 Dumfries and Galloway in south-west Scotland is a peripheral region of the United Kingdom. This fact is reflected in the designation of a significant proportion of the Region under European Community Structural Funds.

1.2 The Region has two principal interests in the future development of Britain's railways. Firstly, it is geographically and economically placed, in terms of the distances to markets, to maximise the advantages of rail travel, but the full potential for this is not currently being realised.

1.3 Secondly, the Region is geographically placed on the axis of the shortest sea crossing between Great Britain and Ireland, the North Channel crossing, and the natural transportation corridor linking the Scottish Lowlands with England and Europe. The Stranraer–Ireland route has the highest frequency of all ferry routes across the Irish Sea, and carries significantly higher volumes of passengers and road based freight traffic than other routes. Its role in serving Northern Ireland is pre-eminent but it is also of significant importance to the economy of the Irish Republic.

1.4 The postponement of British Rail's InterCity 250 project, which British Rail has linked to the current privatisation proposals, has particularly negative implications for Dumfries and Galloway and South-west Scotland.

1.5 The Council would wish to make its position clear on the future shape of the railway system.

(a) The level of quality of service, particularly on the West Coast Main Line, must be maintained at not less than that currently operating, and

(b) There must be further investment on the West Coast Main Line, both in infrastructure and rolling stock, commensurate with that on the East Coast Main Line.

2. *Comments on Specific Questions Indicated for Consideration by the Select Committee*

The following are responses to the specific questions posed in the invitation for evidence.

Aims and Objectives of a privatised railway

2.1 In essence these should be no different from a publicly owned railway, and should reflect the economic and social needs of the community served by the network, for both local and long distance travel and the movement of goods.

2.2 The most important objective should be reliability and stability in service provision whilst encouraging innovation and service development, particularly in respect of increased frequencies on routes with service development potential.

2.3 The introduction of private management systems into the railways must be designed to lead to improvements in the quality of deliverance of service. In this respect, the reference in the White Paper for a "second-hand market for rolling stock" does not indicate an emphasis on the needs of peripheral and rural areas for high quality services.

3. *Conflict Between Open Access and Exclusive Franchises*

3.1 An exclusive franchise system should bring benefits to users through greater service stability. The design of franchises for rural lines should have particular regard to providing connections at key nodal points. To permit open-access by "commercial" services on the back of such franchised operations could mean either

(a) connections would not be met on commercial services or

(b) the franchised operators would be required to move aside from their predetermined track slots, hence breaking connections, hence reducing their value to the community.

4. *Responsibility for strategic planning co-ordination*

4.1 There is a need for an overview. Many of the recent long-distance Regional Railways routes might not have emerged under a privatised regime, particularly as much services aim to provide connections across the country using more than one other service. It appears that none of the agencies proposed in the White Paper will be able to initiate new services unless these are provided commercially. For instance, the present InterCity network, which has seen a considerable contraction in its peripheral services in recent years for short-term financial reasons, should not be used as the criterion to determine a future core network. The economic and social regeneration of peripheral regions requires good quality rail services, and the reinstatement of InterCity style through services is considered essential as part of the development of regions that have lost such services.

4.2 The railways, under private operation, would require an avenue through which the community can manifest its needs and aspirations in respect of the development of rail services. There would appear to be the need for a small corporate organisation, operating under, say, a Director General of Rail Services to provide such a function.

5. *Government Role in Subsidy and Investment*

5.1 The White Paper lays particular emphasis on a general objective to control subsidy levels. The problem with the disaggregation of the rail network is that present subsidies are not on a line or service specific basis. Indeed, it is understood that the PSO does not even differentiate ScotRail from the remainder of the Regional Railways.

5.2 The rural railways in south-west Scotland are known to be in receipt of significant levels of subsidy. Cost saving measures have been made, including the introduction of new 'Sprinter' rolling stock and therefore, it is likely that, short of cutting of services, the need for subsidy has been minimised.

5.3 Without a central investment body, further investment in signalling and other measures to improve efficiency would be unlikely to take place if funding through franchises was the only mechanism; lines in south-west Scotland may not be high on the priority of the Track Authority, given their peripheral location and recent policies pursued by British Rail. If franchises are to meet investment cost they may have to operate at a higher rate. Investment in track should be free standing as, like road investment, it is of benefit to all users.

5.4 A second problem is that, while franchising will produce greater financial transparency on individual lines or groups of lines, the lack of "cross-subsidy" across the Regional Railways' network could produce a conflict between the twin aims of reducing subsidy and retaining broadly the present level of service. It is unlikely that operators of rural railways will be able to provide an improved level of service within a declining level of subsidy, particularly if improvements in infrastructure have to be funded through a charge to the Track Authority.

5.5 The Track Authority must be able to call on central funds outwith the receipts from operators to fund investment beyond cyclic repair/upgrading. There is no reason why economic/social cost benefit appraisal should not be applied to rail investment projects.

5.6 The criteria for all rail investment must be for the benefit of the community and the improvement in links between communities. There is no benefit for having a railway system for its own sake if it does not meet these objectives.

6. Railtrack Charging Policy

6.1 There have been suggestions that traffic, particularly freight, is being lost to the railways through inappropriate charging policies being applied by British Rail. The charging policy adopted by Railtrack should be clear and unambiguous and should be open to scrutiny, both by rail users and other groups, particularly where there is potential for innovation and the introduction of socially desirable services. There should be scope for such innovation on a marginal cost basis where development of services is proposed by an existing franchise operator.

7. Franchising in the Public Interest

7.1 The minimum criteria to achieve effective franchising in the public interest would appear to include,

(a) minimum levels of service with substantive quality thresholds.

(b) the design of services should reflect public needs for integration and not some arbitrary division of the system.

(c) there will be a need for a balanced approach to service frequencies, ie to avoid bunching.

(d) there would be benefits from local authority involvement in the design of franchise services, particularly if this can be achieved on a regional basis.

(e) there should be scope for service expansion in the franchise, subject to the overall needs of users and potential users being met. Flexibility is required to meet unexpected changes in economic and social activity at a local level.

(f) where there have been capital or revenue contributions from local authorities, these must be reflected in appropriate guarantees concerning continuing levels of service.

8. Rolling Stock

8.1 The immediate implications of the White Paper for new rolling stock appear to be that the recent programme of stock replacement may cease very abruptly. This could lead to a return to the conditions experienced on the railways in the 1970s and early 80s, ie, increasingly elderly and unreliable stock.

8.2 Some form of extra financial assistance to achieve phased replacement or refurbishment of rolling stock, akin to the one-time New Bus Grant, would appear appropriate. It is particularly important that rail lines that have seen recent investment do not suffer from a frozen investment policy.

9. Stations

9.1 The White Paper proposals appear targeted at larger stations in urban areas. The management of all stations requires careful assessment in respect of maintenance, marketing and appropriate staffing levels. The emphasis should be on public safety and passenger confidence.

APPENDIX

Submission to the European Commission on the Development of the West Coast Main Line and Associated Links to West Coast Ports and Towns

EXECUTIVE SUMMARY

This submission is made on behalf of local authorities and organisations in north-west England, south-west Scotland and Northern Ireland.

It sets out the main elements of the case for an appropriate upgrading of infrastructure and services on the West Coast Main Line and associated links.

The West Coast Main Line is one of three north—south rail routes between Scotland and London which developed in the 19th century. By reason of gradient and curvature the West Coast Main Line is at a general disadvantage for high-speed operation compared to the East Coast route.

Electrification of the West Coast Main Line took place in the 1960s and 1970s between London and Glasgow. Only in the 1980s was the decision taken to electrify the East Coast Main Line, a project that will be completed in 1991. With the completion of the East Coast Main Line electrification, train speeds will rise from 200 to 225kph. In contrast, train speeds on the West Coast Main Line are limited to a maximum of 175kph and at many locations are much less.

The current provision of through rail services on the West Coast Main Line between London and Glasgow and on the East Coast Main Line between London and Edinburgh of 7 and 17 trains per day, contrasts with the catchment population within 16kms of either line of 10 million and 3.7 million persons respectively.

British Rail has proposals to invest £750 million in the West Coast Main Line and plans for a new high-speed train that will operate at up to 250kph. It appears that as investment may be restricted to that part of the line south of Crewe, north-west England and south-west Scotland will see only marginal benefits in journey time.

British Rail proposals for international passenger and freight services following the opening of the Channel Tunnel in 1993 provide overnight passenger services on both West and East Coast Main Lines. The West Coast Main Line will see daytime services only as far north as Manchester; in contrast, daytime services will operate to Edinburgh on the East Coast Main Line.

The concentration of international freight terminals and proposals for freight traffic do not meet the economic needs and aspirations of north-west England, south-west Scotland and Northern Ireland.

Considerable resources have been devoted to the development of the trunk road network by Central Government. There has been a complementary rise in coach, private car and heavy goods vehicle traffic using A75 in particular, attracted by the relatively short sea crossing through Stranraer–Larne compared with other Irish Sea routes.

The pattern of rail services in south-west Scotland has seen the closure of rail lines in the 1960s and the withdrawal of InterCity services and sleeper services in the 1980s. The path of rail services to Stranraer from England is now particularly circuitous.

Northern Ireland is an Objective 1 area in the European Community, upon which emphasis has been placed on the improvement of transport links and the reduction in its peripherality. Part of Dumfries and Galloway Region is an Objective 5b area and further areas of Dumfries and Galloway and Strathclyde Regions are Objective 2 areas, as are parts of Cumbria and Lancashire.

The appropriate development of the West Coast Main Line and, in the longer term, reinstatement of a direct line to Stranraer from Dumfries, is seen as an essential element in the economic and social regeneration of these areas.

CONTENTS

1. INTRODUCTION

1.1 This submission is made on behalf of local authorities and organisations in north-west England, south-west Scotland and Northern Ireland (See Annex 1) who share common concerns regarding the lack of an appropriate strategic plan by British Rail in respect of the long distance rail network serving these areas, and in particular connecting these areas with London, the south-east of England and continental Europe via the Channel Tunnel. (See Figure 1*)

1.2 The Authorities and other commercial and community organisations who lend their support to this submission would wish to see a greater commitment on the part of the United Kingdom Government and British Rail as the trunk railway agency, to the further development of the West Coast Main Line as the preferred route between London, north-west England and western Scotland and Northern Ireland.

1.3 This submission sets out the main elements of the case for an appropriate upgrading of infrastructure and services in the West Coast Main Line corridor as part of the European Strategic rail network and seeks the support and active consideration of the European Commission in applying whatever powers may be available to achieve this objective.

* Printed page 86.

2. HISTORICAL BACKGROUND

2.1 The development of railway infrastructure and services in the broad corridor between south-east England and Scotland and Northern Ireland dates from the mid nineteenth century. Until very recent times there remained three premier routes fulfilling a strategic function in linking the Scottish Lowlands, in particular, with London and the south-east. The earliest through route had been the system of linking lines which now form the West Coast Main Line running from London northwards through Rugby, Crewe, Preston and Carlisle to Glasgow, with important loops serving Birmingham, Stoke-on-Trent, Manchester and Liverpool. (See Figure 2†)

2.2 The West Coast Main Line, being the earliest route, was routed along what has always been regarded as the natural geographical route-way between London and Lowland Scotland, following wherever possible low lying valleys but also crossing two important physical barriers at Shap, in Northern England, and Beattock, in Southern Scotland.

2.3 Following some short time after the West Coast Main Line came an alternative route running northwards from London via Peterborough, Doncaster, York, Newcastle and Edinburgh. Although for much of its length this line is a considerable distance from the North Sea, from the earliest days it has been referred to in railway terminology as the East Coast Main Line. A third route based on the Midland Railway Main Line was developed later but ceased to be used by through trains in the early 1970s and lies beyond the scope of this report.

2.4 In respect of the history of development of the East and West Coast Main Lines, a number of consistent, long-term elements are evident. Almost from the start of operations, in the mid 19th century, there developed a company rivalry in respect of the provision of high-quality rail services between London and Scotland by the two competing systems. This rivalry was accentuated in the late 19th century by the opening of several notable bridges across estuaries in eastern Scotland, which gave the East Coast Main Line some added advantage in respect of services extending north of Edinburgh to serve the industrial centres of Dundee and Aberdeen.

2.5 Even in these early days, operations on the East Coast Main Line were assisted by its general advantage in respect of potential for high speed operation in comparison to the West Coast Main Line, which, whilst providing a shorter distance between Glasgow and London, was and is hampered by its greater combination of curves and steeper gradients particularly in the section between Lancaster and Glasgow.

2.6 The modernisation and rationalisation of the British railway network which has taken place in recent decades has placed particular emphasis upon the development of long distance trunk routes including the East Coast and West Coast Main Lines. During the 1960s and early 1970s the entire route of the West Coast Main Line between London and Glasgow via Crewe and Carlisle was the subject of an electrification scheme employing an overhead wire 25 kv ac system. Whilst the major benefits of this investment accrued to British Rail in terms of reduced operating costs, there were moderate improvements in travel times and service frequency between Scotland and London as a result.

2.7 During the same period, on the East Coast Main Line, gradual improvements in train speeds were achieved by the introduction of increasingly more powerful diesel locomotives and track realignment, culminating in the 1970s in the introduction of a fleet of high-speed diesel trains capable of operating on parts of the route at speeds of 200kph. The introduction of high-speed trains on the East Coast Main Line extending as far as Aberdeen and, more recently to Inverness, has proved very successful in generating additional passenger traffic, the result also of a siginficant increase in frequency of service compared to the position in the early 1960s.

2.8 Partly because it is characterised by frequent curves, the West Coast Main Line was considered unsuitable for operation of high-speed trains based on conventional technology. The path to higher speeds appeared to lie in the introduction of the tilting Advanced Passenger Train; however after trials in the early 1980s this project was abandoned and since that time there have been only marginal improvements in running speeds on individual lengths employing conventional trains at up to 175kph. British Rail are understood to be investigating use of Italian 'Pendolino' tilting train technology.

2.9 Meanwhile the East Coast Main Line London-Edinburgh has been the subject of a large-scale electrification programme costing £306m at 1984 prices. This is due to be completed in 1991 bringing train speeds up to 225kph and could lead to reductions in travel time of the order of 20 minutes between London and Edinburgh.

2.10 A concerted campaign has been mounted to have electrification extended from Edinburgh to Aberdeen via Dundee. Through running of electric trains between London, Edinburgh and Glasgow is envisaged with the completion of Edinburgh-Carstairs electrification in 1991. There have been calls for electrification of the direct Glasgow-Edinburgh line (via Falkirk) which would permit a shorter Glasgow-London journey time than is currently possible as a consequence of the curvature of the West Coast Main Line.

---

† Printed page 87.

3. DEMAND FOR RAIL SERVICES

3.1 When considering the current level of service provided on the West Coast Main Line it is appropriate to discuss the actual and potential demand for long-distance travel in the corridor served by the line and associated links. The route serves large elements of the economic heartland of Britian as well as providing part of the most direct rail link between the south-east of England, West Midlands, north-west England and western Scotland and also much of Eire (via Holyhead) and Northern Ireland (via Stranraer and other ports).

3.2 The route complements other transport modes particularly the M1/M6/M74 motorway spine, and associated trunk links, which in its form and pattern of use represents the preferred road route between the South-East, west Midlands, north-west of England, almost the whole of Scotland and much of the northern part of Ireland (including parts of Eire).

3.3 Two important factors which dictate an improved level of service on the West Coast Main Line are (a) the relative size and economic importance of centres served by the route and (b) their relative distance in the context of needs and markets for medium-distance and long-distance rail travel, as measured by the distribution of resident population. (See Figure 3.*)

3.4 In particular, north of the Home Counties, a total of 4.4 million persons live within 16 kms of the West Coast Main Line proper (London–Glasgow). A further 5.6 million persons live within 16 kms of closely-associated loop lines serving Birmingham/West Midlands, Manchester and Liverpool. By comparison, the comparable figure for the East Coast Main Line proper (London–Edinburgh) north of the Home Counties is 2.8 million. If the main loop line to Leeds from Doncaster is included a further 0.9 million persons enter the catchment. The principal services on the West Coast Main Line therefore have a catchment population of some 10 million persons compared to only 3.7 million on the East Coast.

3.5 This brief analysis does not include areas north or west of Edinburgh or Glasgow, nor does is include other linking services from Lancashire, Cumbria and Stranraer/Northern Ireland. However it is apparent that there is a great disparity between population and service levels.

3.6 Currently, only seven trains per day are operated between Glasgow and London Euston via the West Coast Main Line although certain additional trains with origins or destinations other than in Scotland or London also use sections of the route. This is in spite of the heavy concentration of population and economic activity in the corridor which is evidenced by British Rail's own admission that one third of InterCity (long-distance) business is carried on the West Coast route and associated link lines. It should be noted that the West Coast Main Line is the principal freight route between Scotland and the remainder of Great Britain.

3.7 By comparison, the level of service between Scotland and London on the East Coast Main Line is much more frequent with 17 departures from London Kings Cross to Edunburgh Monday–Friday; two services operate through to Glasgow (Queen Street).

4. WEST COAST MAIN LINE : PROPOSED DEVELOPMENTS

4.1 The British Railways Board has announced a £750 million strategy for investment in the West Coast Main Line. The plans include a new high speed train which will operate at speeds of up to 250 kph with an intention of introducing the new train in May 1994. It is proposed that the high speed performance of the train allied with re-signalling of the route and track improvements will lead to progressive reductions in journey times. No details have yet been released as to the actual impact of this strategy on journey times on West Coast Main Line. However, it has been indicated that investment on civil engineering and signalling will be concentrated on the line south of Crewe (Weaver Junction).

4.2 Potential benefits to north-west England and southern and south-west Scotland will only be achieved by the development of the entire route to Scotland (see figure 4†). The restriction of infrastructural improvements to the section south of Crewe will principally benefit Birmingham, Manchester and Liverpool but will give only marginal time benefits to north-west England and southern Scotland. The benefits will be proportionately less for the most northerly towns and cities. (See table below).

DISTANCE, TIME AND SPEEDS : WEST AND EAST COAST MAIN LINES, 1990 AND 1996

	Distance from London (km)	Fastest times now	Fastest times 1996	Average speeds (kph) now	Average speeds (kph) 1996
Edinburgh	633 (via East Coast)	4 hrs 28 mins	4 hrs 00 mins	142	158
Glasgow	646 (via West Coast)	4 hrs 43 mins	4 hrs 15 mins	137	151
Glasgow	724 (via East Coast)	5 hrs 40 mins	4 hrs 45 mins	128	153
Carlisle	481 (via West Coast)	3 hrs 34 mins	3 hrs 03 mins	142	158
Newcastle	433 (via East Coast)	2 hrs 46 mins	2 hrs 26 mins	156	177

* Printed page 87.
† Printed page 88.

	Distance from London (km)	Fastest times now	1996	Average speeds (kph) now	1996
Preston	336 (via West Coast)	2 hrs 28 mins	1 hr 58 mins	147	171
York	303 (via East Coast)	1 hr 51 mins	1 hr 35 mins	164	192

(1996 times and speeds are estimates of likely figures on completion of presently planned improvements.)

4.3 With increasing publicity surrounding the electrification and improved frequency of faster services on the East Coast Main Line, there is a serious risk that passengers, actual and potential, will themselves treat the West Coast Main Line as a second class route. Completion of the East Coast Main Line electrification and its extension through to Glasgow will place that city more or less equidistant in time from London via either route. The attraction of new trains could well tip the balance in the user's eye in favour of the East Coast route from Glasgow. There are obvious dangers to the commercial prospect of the West Coast Main Line if there is significant abstraction of Glasgow passengers to the East Coast Main Line. Passengers from stations to the south of Glasgow have no alternative service if direct London services are curtailed in any way.

5. PROPOSED INTERNATIONAL RAIL SERVICES FOR THE UNITED KINGDOM

5.1 In December 1989 the British Railways Board announced its proposals for international rail services following the opening of the Channel Tunnel in 1993.

5.2 The proposed passenger services to northern Britain comprise a day-time service to Edinburgh via the East Coast Main Line and an overnight service to Edinburgh via the East Coast Main Line and an overnight service to Glasgow via the West Coast Main Line. Day-time services on the West Coast Main Line would operate only as far as Manchester from Paris and Brussels. The proposals indicate that the overnight service from Glasgow would stop at Carlisle, Lancaster, Preston and Crewe. The plan indicates the provision of connecting services from Northern Ireland to Glasgow, Dumfries to Carlisle, Barrow to Manchester, Blackpool to Preston and Liverpool, Eire and North Wales to Crewe.

5.3 The proposed international day-time passenger services will only operate on electrified lines. The extension of day-time services north of Manchester is restricted by the lack of a direct electrified link between Manchester and Preston. Accordingly, the strategic electrification of the Preston–Manchester line is seen as an essential pre-requisite to the further developmant of the West Coast Main Line.

5.4 The British Railways Board proposals for international rail freight services propose the setting up of major regional terminals on Merseyside, in Greater Manchester and in Strathclyde. The British Railways Board propose that a train operating centre be established at Crewe where freight trains from the north-west of England and Scotland would be combined for onward despatch to Europe. Additional terminals have been proposed by both local authorities and private developers, for example Carlisle Kingmoor in Cumbria.

5.5 There is a need to ensure that international freight services are developed to provide through services south of Crewe to continental European destinations. The economic potential of north-west England and south-west Scotland will only be acheived by the integration of further sub-regional terminals into the international network.

5.6 The Board's proposals for freight services to Ireland indicate that services to Eire will use the North Wales coast and that services to Northern Ireland would use a port in the north-west of England, probably Liverpool. The proposals indicate a daily service to Europe with an emphasis on inter-modal, train- load and trade car-carrying services. The development of international services to northern Britain will be dependent for its success upon the upgrading of existing and new links in London and the south-east England that will expedite the passage of international passenger and freight services to and from the Channel Tunnel. (See figure 5.*)

5.7 The proposed level of provision is considered to be unsatisfactory in respect of meeting the economic needs and aspirations of north-west England, south-west Scotland and Northern Ireland. The need for more comprehensive services and infrastructure had been indicated by local authorities and other organisations as part of the Channel Tunnel Act, Section 40, consultations (see Annex 3†). The current proposals do not reflect this need, particularly the limited role proposed for the West Coast Main Line.

6. ROAD AND RAIL LINKS TO SOUTH-WEST SCOTLAND AND NORTHERN IRELAND

6.1 The shortest sea crossing between Great Britain and Northern Ireland (Larne to Stranraer and Cairnryan ports) has always been an important traffic route between Northern Ireland and the mainland. The long history of rail operation of the steamer service from Stranraer, which existed as an integral part of British Rail until 1984, has until recently been an important feeder to the West Coast Main Line.

6.2 However, despite the importance of this traffic, in the 1960s the report "The Re-shaping of British Railways" under the British Railways Board Chairman, Dr Richard Beeching, proposed the closure of both lines serving Stranraer including the entire line from Dumfries via Castle Douglas and Newton Stewart to Stranraer and the 'South and West' line from Glasgow to Stranraer south of Ayr. Subsequently, the South

* Printed page 90.
† Printed page 96.

and West line from Ayr to Stranraer was maintained and remains the only rail link to Stranraer to date. A link exists between the South and West line and the Nith Valley Line between Ayr and Kilmarnock. This permitted the through operation of InterCity trains from London to Stranraer via Carlisle and Dumfries. However, the rail distance from Carlisle to Stranraer increased from 168 km to 270 km; the distance via Glasgow is some 327 km. This service comprised a day-time return service and an overnight sleeper service.

6.3 In September 1987 British Rail notified that it intended to withdraw the through Stranraer to London day-time service and to amend the route of the Stranraer to London sleeper service to operate via Glasgow. The diversion of the Stranraer to London sleeper service via Glasgow was implemented in May 1988, and the Glasgow to London sleeper service via Kilmarnock and Dumfries was withdrawn. In October 1988 the Stranraer to London through day-time service was withdrawn and replaced by a provincial service operating to Carlisle and Newcastle. In May 1990 the Stranraer to London sleeper service was also withdrawn; this service was not replaced by any other comparable service.

6.4 In addition, there has been the recent withdrawal of sleeper facilities from other stations in southern Scotland, particularly Lockerbie, although sleeper services are currently available at Carlisle and Glasgow. In Lancashire sleeper facilities are available at Preston.

6.5 The withdrawal of InterCity rail services in south-west Scotland in response to the remit of Central Government that InterCity services make an operating profit contrasts with significant funding of the Trunk Road and Motorway network in north-west England and southern Scotland.

6.6 Over the last fifteen years the Scottish Development Department has devoted considerable resources to the development of A75 trunk road between Gretna and Stranraer. The development of this route has seen, or will shortly see, the bypassing of all significant settlements and the improvement of considerable stretches of rural route as a high quality single carriageway. The A75 connects at Gretna with the A74 which links into the M6 motorway north of Carlisle which was completed as a duel three-lane road in the late 1960s.

6.7 In contrast, expenditure on local lines in south-west Scotland, Cumbria and Lancashire has been limited to the electrification of the suburban services from Glasgow as far as Ayr and the progressive introduction of modern "Sprinter" trains on Provincial services in north-west England and south-west Scotland, with some parallel increases in frequencies.

6.8 The withdrawal of InterCity services in south-west Scotland is unparalleled elsewhere in the United Kingdom. The withdrawal of these services has seen a parallel increase in the number of coach services which originate at Stranraer and serve destinations in Scotland and throughout the United Kingdom. The development of the trunk and motorway road network has seen the complementary rise in private car traffic and in heavy goods vehicle traffic which has been matched by a significant withdrawal of rail freight facilities throughout north-west England and south-west Scotland. The growth in traffic between the United Kingdom mainland and Larne is shown in the accompanying diagram (page 83). Further growth in private car traffic is anticipated on this route following the closure of the Liverpool-Belfast ferry service.

VEHICLES USING LARNE HARBOUR (TWO-WAY)

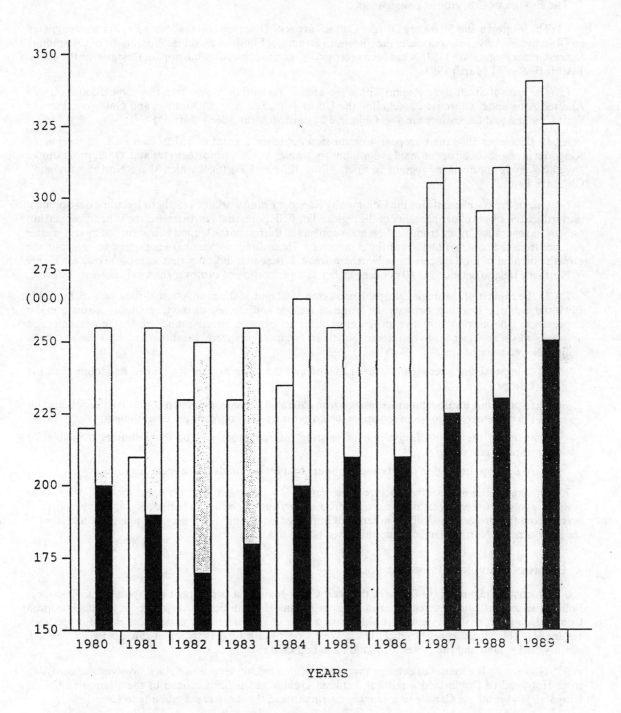

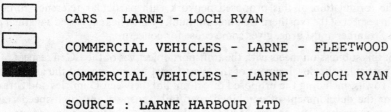

CARS - LARNE - LOCH RYAN

COMMERCIAL VEHICLES - LARNE - FLEETWOOD

COMMERCIAL VEHICLES - LARNE - LOCH RYAN

SOURCE : LARNE HARBOUR LTD
         SEALINK

7. THE EUROPEAN COMMUNITY FRAMEWORK

7.1 The Wigtown and Stewartry District Council areas of Dumfries and Galloway Region are designated an Objective 5b Asssisted Area under the European Structural Funds. A National Programme of Community Interest under Regulation 1787/84 has been accepted by the European Commission for this area for the period 1 April 1989 to 31 March 1993.

7.2 The area of Strathclyde Region within the area of the authorities making this submission is also an Assisted Area under Objective 2, including the Upper Nithsdale part of Dumfries and Galloway. Parts of West Cumbria and Lancashire are also Objective 2 Assisted Areas. (See Figure 6*)

7.3 In December 1989 the European Commission approved a grant of 137 million ECU to the United Kingdom in respect of an operational programme for transportation in Northern Ireland. Other programmes have also given approval for regions in Spain, Eire, Italy and Portugal which share Northern Ireland's Objective 1 status.

7.4 One of the key elements for the Community Support Framework for Northern Ireland's development is to reduce the effects of peripherality of the region. The CSF notes that Northern Ireland is handicapped not only by its separation by sea from markets and suppliers in the rest of the United Kingdom but by still greater distance from the continental parts of the community. These disadvantages have conspired to constrain the growth potential of local businesses in Northern Ireland. Research indicates that transport costs are higher in Northern Ireland, as much as 40 per cent higher as a proportion of turnover than in south-east England.

7.5 In the context of the single European market in 1992 and of the completion of the Channel Tunnel in 1993, the lack of a land link between the island of Ireland and the rest of the Community assumes major importance. The current objective programme aims to provide effective and efficient communication networks which are essential to counteract Northern Ireland's peripheral location. Amongst the objectives behind the programme are:

— to improve links between Northern Ireland and the other parts of the United Kingdom, Eire and Europe;

— to provide a transportation network which caters for the safe, efficient movement of people and for the movement of goods in a manner which protects and improves the environment;

— to make the most effective use of existing infrastructure and of the resources available for transportation;

— to develop the Region's ports and harbours to meet the needs of the local economy.

7.6 Of significance in the infrastructure development is a major project to connect the region's two rail systems involving the construction of a cross-harbour road and rail bridge in Belfast. Significant benefits will accrue from this project, particularly in terms of improved operational efficiency through the integration of the rail system of Northern Ireland and improved access to Larne.

8. EUROPEAN COMMUNITY TRANSPORT POLICY

8.1 Discussion regarding the future of the West Coast Main Line is pertinent in respect of EC Transport Policy and in particular, current consultations regarding draft directives on rail policy. The European Commission is proposing a network of high-speed lines linking the major urban centres of Europe. (See Figure 7†). This would appear to include the West Coast Main Line as the main route between London, north-west England and south-west Scotland including Glasgow.

8.2 However, it is a matter of concern that the indicated linking service to Belfast involves a sea crossing from Holyhead to Dublin and a rail link between Dublin and Belfast, instead of the alternative United Kingdom land route via Carlisle to Stranraer/Cairnryan and the shortest sea crossing to Larne.

8.3 The basis for the formulation of this proposed network with particular reference to consultative procedures, expecially in respect of the Northern Ireland community which has expressed a distinct preference for rail/sea services via Stranraer and Larne, gives some cause for concern.

8.4 The objectives of this submission meets with the transport objectives of the EC in respect of the needs of Europe of 1992. In particular the development of the West Coast Main Line and the associated links to West Coast Ports and Towns, including the proposed direct rail link between Dumfries and Stranraer, will create opportunities for the development of combined road/rail transport and high-speed trains in the Community's large internal market. The objectives of this submission will, if implemented, provide a vital part of the network of connections to ensure greater economic and social cohesion in the Community, improve the integration of the national rail networks of Great Britain and Northern Ireland and Eire and aid the reduction in peripherality of Northern Ireland.

---

* Printed page 91.
† Printed page 92.

9. CONCLUSION

9.1 This brief analysis has aimed at highlighting particular anomalies which appear to exist in respect of the application of rail development policies by the British Government and British Rail.

9.2 The major objectives of the inter-authority group are aimed at addressing these anomalies by achieving European Commission support for:

— recognition of the need for development of the West Coast Main Line, on at least a par with the East Coast Main Line, to fulfil its clear potential as the preferred rail route between south-east England, north-west England, south-west Scotland and Northern Ireland.

— the development of appropriate main line feeder services from areas including the Lancashire and Cumbrian coasts and south-west Scotland, with electrification of key links, especially Manchester to Preston.

— the provision of adequate access to the Channel Tunnel for through international services and dedicated interchange facilities between domestic and international services.

— the provision of high-quality linking services from Northern Ireland via Stranraer using existing infrastructure pending consideration of new lines.

— a feasibility study of the potential for reinstatement of the direct rail link between Dumfries and Stranraer as part of an EC recognised high-speed link between Northern Ireland and Europe via Channel Tunnel.

— involvement in the consultative process in respect of transport policies for Northern Ireland Objective 1 region.

EUROPEAN COMMISSION SUBMISSION

FIGURES

1. Inter-Authority Working Group Submission Area in European context.

2. Principal rail and ferry routes (Great Britain and Ireland).

3. Population with 16 kms of East and West Coast Main Line.

4. Detailed rail network in Submission Area and adjoining lines.

5. Channel Tunnel: proposed railways in the London area.

6. European Community Assisted Areas, in Submission Area.

7. Proposed European High Speed rail network.

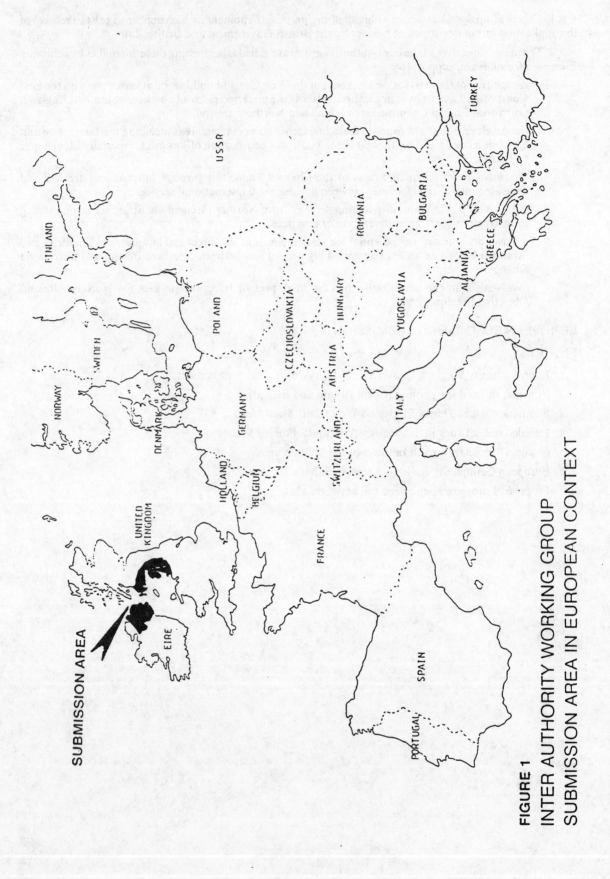

FIGURE 1
INTER AUTHORITY WORKING GROUP
SUBMISSION AREA IN EUROPEAN CONTEXT

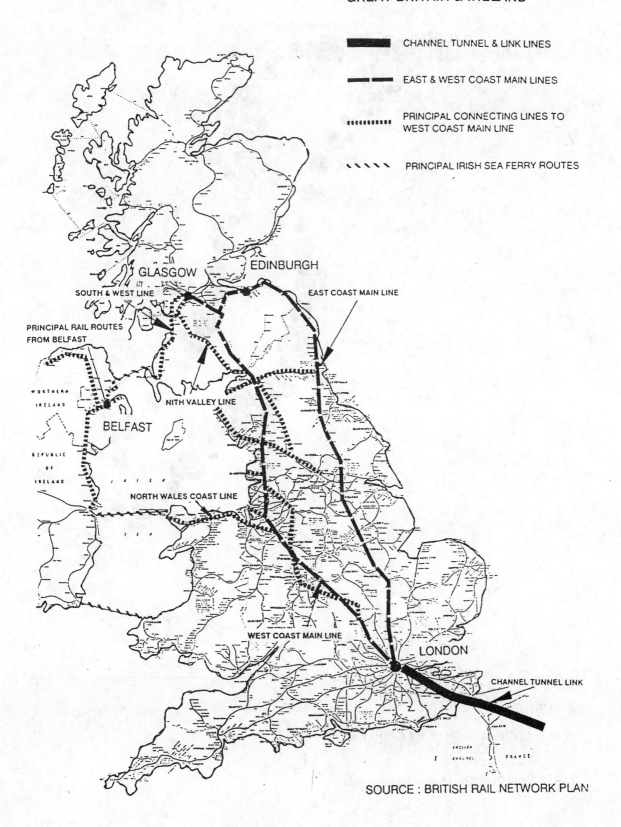

FIGURE 2
PRINCIPAL RAIL & FERRY ROUTES
GREAT BRITAIN & IRELAND

CHANNEL TUNNEL & LINK LINES

EAST & WEST COAST MAIN LINES

PRINCIPAL CONNECTING LINES TO
WEST COAST MAIN LINE

PRINCIPAL IRISH SEA FERRY ROUTES

GLASGOW

EDINBURGH

SOUTH & WEST LINE

EAST COAST MAIN LINE

PRINCIPAL RAIL ROUTES
FROM BELFAST

NITH VALLEY LINE

BELFAST

NORTH WALES COAST LINE

WEST COAST MAIN LINE

LONDON

CHANNEL TUNNEL LINK

SOURCE : BRITISH RAIL NETWORK PLAN

FIGURE 3

POPULATION WITHIN 16 KILOMETRES OF
EAST & WEST COAST MAIN LINES
(Excl. Greater London)

(1988 Registrar General's Estimates)

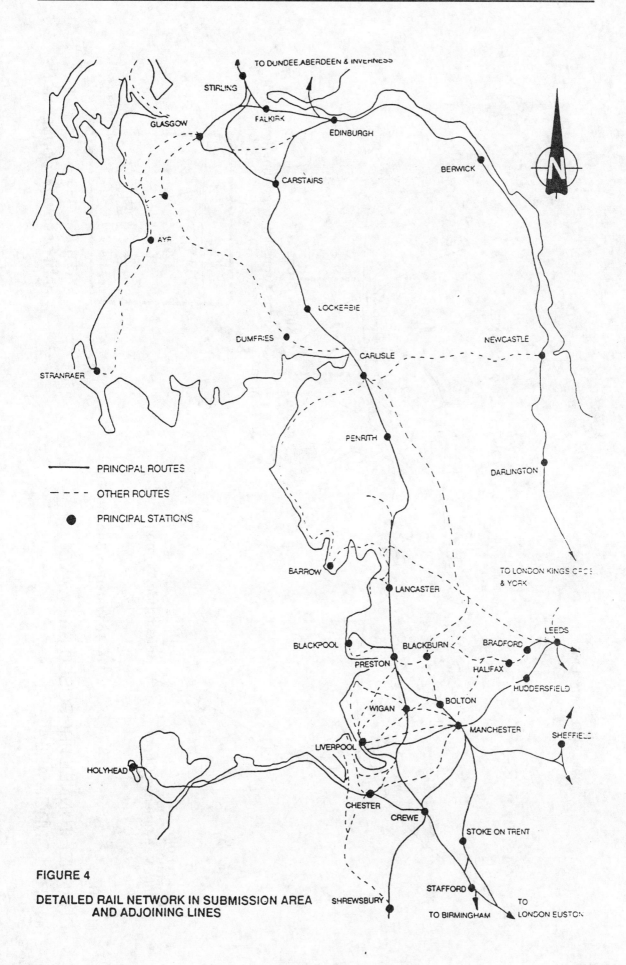

FIGURE 4

**DETAILED RAIL NETWORK IN SUBMISSION AREA
            AND ADJOINING LINES**

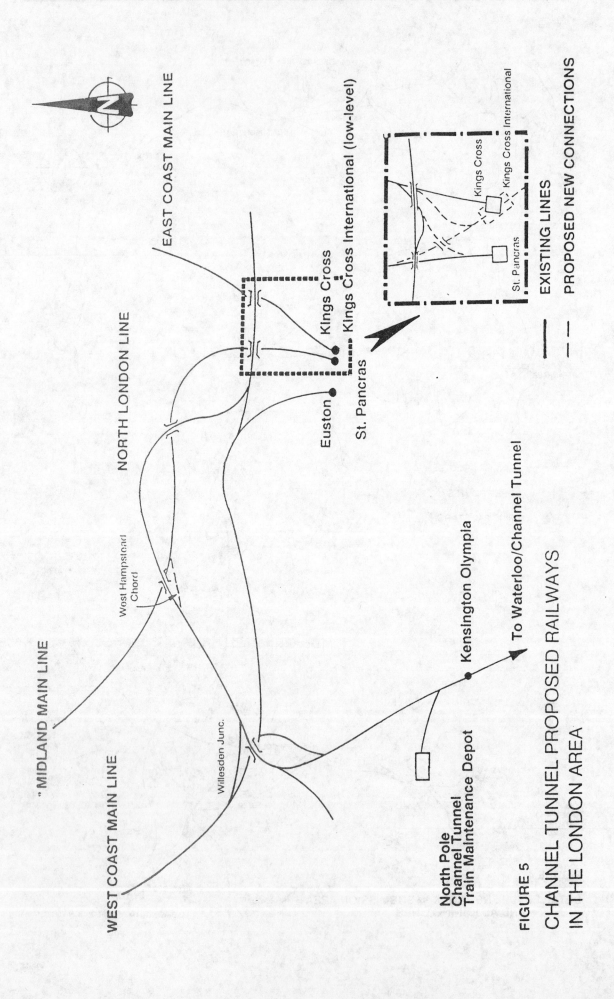

FIGURE 5

CHANNEL TUNNEL PROPOSED RAILWAYS
IN THE LONDON AREA

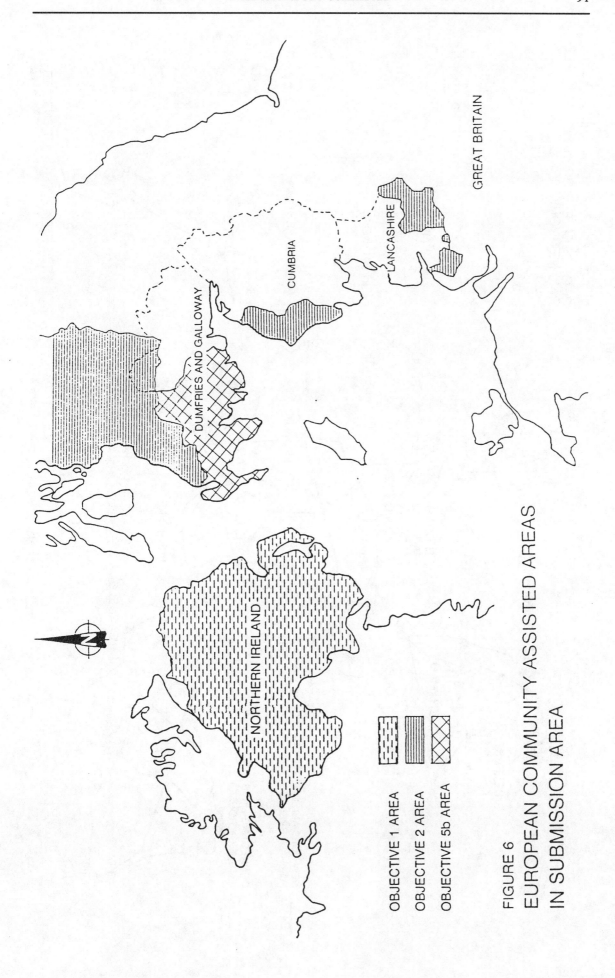

OBJECTIVE 1 AREA

OBJECTIVE 2 AREA

OBJECTIVE 5b AREA

FIGURE 6
EUROPEAN COMMUNITY ASSISTED AREAS
IN SUBMISSION AREA

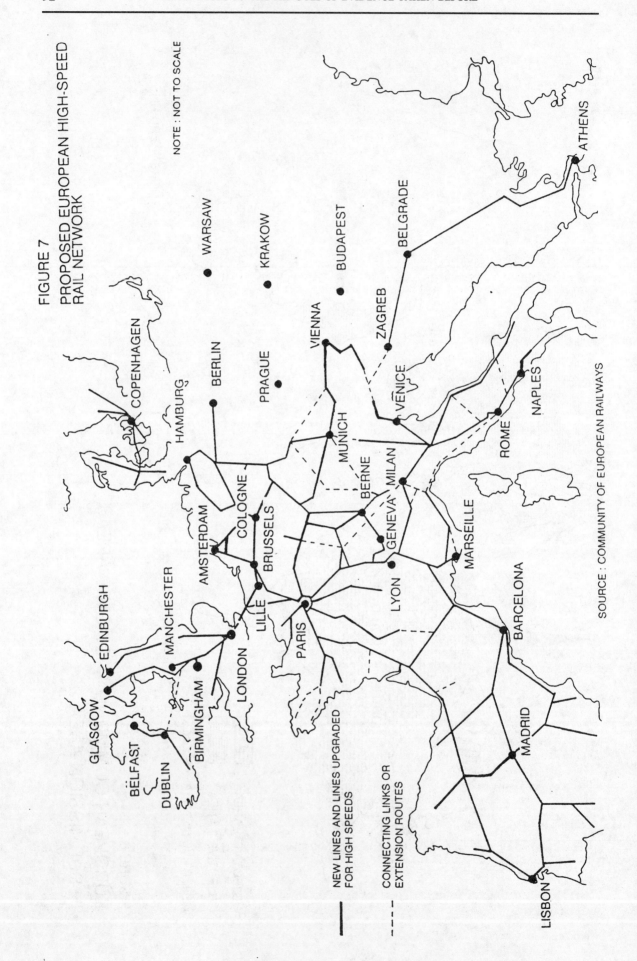

FIGURE 7
PROPOSED EUROPEAN HIGH-SPEED
RAIL NETWORK

NOTE : NOT TO SCALE

NEW LINES AND LINES UPGRADED
FOR HIGH SPEEDS

CONNECTING LINKS OR
EXTENSION ROUTES

SOURCE : COMMUNITY OF EUROPEAN RAILWAYS

Unit Load Traffic between Ireland and Great Britain Two Way

		Trailers ('000)	TEU ('000)
Northern Ireland	— Scotland	240	—
	— Holyhead/North West	148	115
	— South Wales	—	17
	— Continent (direct)	—	37
Eire	— Holyhead/North West	120	63
	— South Wales	38	35
	— Continent (direct)	6	190
TOTAL		552	457

Source: Consultants' Estimates

Note: TEU 20' Equivalent Unit

Source: PIEDA "THE IMPLICATIONS OF THE SINGLE EUROPEAN MARKET AND THE CHANNEL TUNNEL FOR RAIL LINKS TO THE NORTH WEST"

ANNEX 1

List of participant bodies

Dumfries and Galloway Regional Council

Cumbria County Council

Lancashire County Council

Annandale and Eskdale District Council

Nithsdale District Council

Stewartry District Council

Wigtown District Council

Kilmarnock and Loudoun District Council

Association of Local Authorities of Northern Ireland (also represents The General Consumer Council for Northern Ireland)

Sealink (Scotland) Limited

Larne Harbour Limited

ANNEX 2

POLICY STATEMENTS

A. *Dumfries and Galloway Regional Council*

The following policy statements from the Dumfries and Galloway Structure Plan (1984) are included in support of this submission.

POLICY TN 9

The Regional Council will encourage the transfer of Freight from Road to Rail and/or Sea Transport by:—

(a) supporting applications by industrialists for grant aid for private sidings under Section 8 of the Railway Act 1974; and

(b) encouraging the development of road/rail transfer depots in locations that have good accessibility to trunk roads and regional strategic roads.

There will be a presumption against development which would prejudice the establishment of a road to rail freight transfer facility at Airds on the disused Stranraer-Cairnryan rail link.

POLICY TN 10

The Regional Council will continue to represent to British Rail that consideration be given:—

(a) to the improvement and electrification of the Carlisle to Stranraer line via Dumfries and Kilmarnock; and

(b) to the introduction of high-speed trains on the West Coast Main Line, insofar as this is consistent with the availability and continued stopping of InterCity trains at Lockerbie and the retention of existing levels of service within the region and at connecting stations outwith the Region, particularly Carlisle.

The following policy statements, approved by the Council in 1988 are included in support of this submission.

(R1) The level of provision of InterCity and local rail services within the Region and to other areas should be commensurate with the economic and social needs of the Region. In this respect the Council would wish to see InterCity services including sleeper services provided on a similar basis to that which existed prior to May 1988, to form a basis for future expansion. In addition the development of appropriate complementary local services aimed at providing good connections with long-distance services at Carlisle, serving local needs and providing increased opportunities for through travel will be sought.

(R3) The electrification of all existing passenger-carrying lines in the region will continue to be pursued insofar as this is consistent with the strategic development of other parts of the rail network outwith the Region.

(R4) The Council will continue to press for the further development of InterCity and freight services on the West Coast Main Line with the object of maintaining its position as the preferred route between Glasgow and London.

(R5) The Nith Valley Line and Stranraer-Ayr line should be developed as a key element in the national network, with particular reference to the opportunities and needs created by the Channel Tunnel project, in addition to their role as general long-distance routes for national passenger and freight movement. The Council will co-operate with and assist British Rail in respect of the promotion of the Regional rail system for the carriage of passengers and freight.

B. *Cumbria County Council*

The following statements, from Transport Policies and Programme, 1991–92 (July 1990), are included in support of this submission.

3.2.1 The existing rail network is considered to be an essential component of the County's transport services and any reduction in its size will be strongly opposed, as will reductions in services. The County Council will continue to oppose any possible downgrading of British Rail's InterCity services on the West Coast Main Line.

3.2.2 The County Council is pressing British Rail and Central Government to improve the West Coast Main Line so that journey times are at least comparable with those on the East Coast Main Line.

3.2.3 The County Council is also pressing for the introduction of direct daytime passenger services between Cumbria and Europe from the opening of the Channel Tunnel.

The following Policy statements from the Cumbria and Lake District Joint Structure Plan (1989), are included in support of this submission:

POLICY T10

The Structure Plan Authorities will seek to maintain and improve rail services and facilities in Cumbria to support the social and economic life of the County. Particular importance will be laid on services connecting the various urban areas of the County to each other and to the major industrial and business centres of the country.

POLICY T11

The Structure Plan Authorities support the principle that heavy freight traffic should be handled by rail services wherever possible. The two authorities will therefore:

(a) consider the benefits of rail access where new industrial sites are being planned;

(b) normally permit industrial development which generates large movements of bulky and dangerous materials only on sites where this traffic can be handled by rail services;

(c) encourage the provision and improvement of facilities and services offered at public and private rail freight terminals.

C. *Lancashire County Council*

The following statements from the Draft Lancashire Structure Plan (1986) are included in support of this submission:

POLICY 48

To seek the retention and, where appropriate, the improvement of the existing rail passenger network and services including the electrification of the Blackpool-Preston-Manchester line.

POLICY 49

To provide in conjunction with British Rail:

(a) new local stations where there is sufficient demand;

(b) improvements to the appearance of, and facilities at, local and InterCity rail stations;

(c) car parking and cycle parking facilities at strategic stations to encourage "Park and Ride" where suitable land is available.

POLICY 50

(a) To seek the retention, and where appropriate, the improvement of the present freight only rail lines and ensure that the potential for increased use of all rail lines for freight is not constrained by new development.

(b) To support the transfer of bulk freight from road to rail.

D. *Association of Local Authorities of Northern Ireland*

The following statement is included in support of this submission.

The Association has participated in the Northern Ireland Passenger Working Party constituted under Section 40 of the Channel Tunnel Act 1987.

In the Working Party the Association has advanced the view that the main passenger rail link between Northern Ireland and the Channel Tunnel should be via Stranraer, Glasgow (or Kilmarnock) and Carlisle.

The Association does not favour the Dublin-Holyhead route on the basis that internal communications within the United Kingdom should not involve travel through a foreign country. An additional factor is that the rail link from Belfast (in Northern Ireland) to Dublin (in the Republic of Ireland) is continually disrupted by terrorist action particularly near the land frontier.

In the view of the Association (a) there should be a fast InterCity service from Glasgow by the West Coast route to London and the Channel Tunnel; (b) the rail service from Stranraer to Glasgow or Kilmarnock should be generally improved and should be synchronised on relevant occasions to facilitate coupling with the service to the Channel Tunnel; and (c) pressure should be brought to bear on Sealink to improve substantially the punctuality of its service on the Larne/Stranraer route.

E. *Kilmarnock and Loudoun District Council*

The following statements from the Draft District Plan are included in support of this submission.

Passenger trains from Glasgow to Carlisle and Newcastle stop at Kilmarnock. The direct Glasgow to London service no longer stops at Kilmarnock and therefore passengers travelling to London must change at Carlisle or first travel to Glasgow. There have, however, been improvements to the timetabling and frequency of trains from Kilmarnock to Glasgow. A shuttle service operates and stops at Kilmaurs, Stewarton and Dunlop.

The District Council is of the opinion that a direct overnight sleeper service to London is an important element within the package of transport and rail facilities available to residents of the District, tourists and businessmen. For this latter reason, it is also important to any strategy for improving the economy of the District. The District Council believes that the west coast London to Glasgow line should be the main rail route into Scotland and that the Nith Valley and Stranraer lines should be improved to provide a suitable service for passengers and freight.

F. *Wigtown District Council*

The following statement is included in support of this submission.

Wigtown District is in a unique geographical location which requires special consideration for enhanced transport facilities. These facilities are required, not only to further the economic and tourism potential of the District, but also because of its close proximity to Northern Ireland and the increasing traffic on the Stranraer and Cairnryan sea crossings to Larne. This traffic is liable to increase in the future due to the impending construction of a rail link between the two railway stations in Belfast City; it is anticipated that this will significantly increase the traffic through Larne Harbour.

In view of the above the District Council would wish the following to be considered, viz:

1. that the rail services between Stranraer and Dumfries/Carlisle/London be improved on a high priority basis;

2. that a direct rail link between Stranraer and Dumfries be reinstated. This would cut three hours off the present time taken to travel from Belfast to London and would encourage Channel Tunnel traffic to use this route, especially if it could be linked in the future to the West Coast line;

3. that proper facilities be constructed at Stranraer Harbour to mirror those available at Larne.

ANNEX 3

CHANNEL TUNNEL ACT 1987

SECTION 40 REGIONAL CONSULTATIONS

The following recommendations of the Working Parties and Regional Forum reflect the objectives of this submission.

Scotland

* Provide at least two direct daytime services in each direction between Glasgow and Edinburgh and the Continent from day one at reasonable times for the commencement and termination of journeys.

* Provide mixed sleeper and seated overnight services linking Glasgow and Edinburgh with Paris and Germany from day one.

* The investment criteria applied to rail infrastructure in the UK should be re-examined, since they do not take account of the wider economic and social benefits of rail investment. The full potential benefits of the Channel Tunnel may thus not be realised.

* Urgent consideration should be given to investments which would reduce journey times within the UK between Scotland and the Tunnel.

* Railfreight should maintain its objective of maximum through servicing; and a maximum number of through services should be operated south of Crewe.

* The possibility of conveying all Northern Ireland traffic rail via Stranraer should be examined.

North West and North Wales

* It is essential that the best quality through services to the Tunnel from the Region are available. The following major centres in the North West should be provided with the best levels of service that are attainable; Liverpool, Runcorn, Manchester, Stockport, Crewe, Warrington, Preston, Lancaster, Oxenholme and Carlisle. There are in addition a number of locations not on electrified routes but where a demand for through Tunnel service is likely to be considerable. These centres include Chester, Blackpool, Bolton and Manchester International Airport.

* The possibility of passengers being forced to use the (London) Euston-Waterloo underground services, during the interim period before the development of Kings Cross, is a major disincentive to market growth.

* There should be a process of continuous investment in the West Coast Main Line and a consideration of a new high-speed link, similar to the French TGV lines, to run parallel to the WCML.

* The North West is a major generator of freight traffic to the Continent. The likely volume of traffic and the distance to Continental centres suggest that some direct through services from a North West aggregation and disaggregation Node will be profitable, especially in the import direction. The addition of Scottish and Irish Traffic enhances these prospects.

Northern Ireland

* Promote the Stranraer/Scottish Route to Europe.

* Provide a guaranteed night time connection at Glasgow for Northern Ireland to and from Europe.

* Investigate the possibility of a Stranraer to Carlisle connection into the European night time service as a more reliable alternative to a Glasgow connection.

* Discuss with the UK Government and the EC ways of securing better train services in the long term from Irish Sea Ferry ports in Great Britain to European destinations.

September 1992.

APPENDIX 33

Letter from Mr E Smith

Re: "New Opportunities for the Railways" The Privatisation of British Rail Cm 2012 July 1992

I am a 1982 retired member of the BRB staff—formerly Freight Marketing Manager (Petroleum and Chemicals) at the Board, and now a member of the Retired Railway Officers Association. It was suggested at our last RRO's meeting on 7 September that individual members should send our thoughts direct to you.

1 General Comments

The foreword points out that BR makes large losses. The proposal (para 3) states, "BR has made significant improvements in recent years and its efficiency compares well with that of other European Railways". BR's productivity is among the highest of any European Railway Inter-City and Freight services operate without direct subsidy.

BR has to make do with only $\frac{1}{2}$ of the investment that European Railways have. It is not surprising that standards have fallen in recent years. BR is constantly starved of investment. Fiercely cutting back PSO grants has made matters worse. Expecting private companies to step in with their own capital investment to take over the more profitable parts will leave others in a worse position.

Cm 2012 needs to be thoroughly rethought.

2. Organisation

The Secretary of State for Transport will end up being in command of:
1. Health and Safety Commission/Executive
2. Railway Inspectorate
3. Regulator
4. Franchising Authorities
5. Residual Operating Company
6. Rail Track
7. Franchised Stations

These organisations will lead to duplication and a pyramid type structure where functions and objectives will be difficult to specify. Confusion, proliferation and rapid staff expansion will overtake any text book conceptual organisation that has been or might be envisaged.

Any White Paper should at least contain an organisation structure chart.

3. Timetables

How a combined timetable for the Public is to be achieved is anyone's guess. In 1976–79 when I was responsible for publication, 15 months elapsed from start to sale—this with few interested departments input. A multiple franchise input will complicate matters. Who will produce it?

4. Fares

The problem of fares publication, application, selling and apportionment of revenue has *always* been a particularly difficult issue. This aspect is barely touched on in the paper. Neither are claims and refunds.

5. Corporate Identity

BR has a strong "Corporate Identity" with standard station signing, directions, passenger and other information, rolling stock identity and uniforms. Staff know where they belong. Is this all to be thrown overboard? Who is to be responsible for the marketing effort and the continuation of standards?

6. Grants

No mention is made of the PSO grants nor investment flowing in from EEC funds. Do these cease? Para 14 mentions grants being given to the private sector. Will these be additional or merely a substitution?

7. Staff

Worst of all is the continuing impact upon staff and their morale. Para 12 touches on this subject. In my 43 years rising through the ranks on BR (GR, ER, LMR, BRB) I experienced the effect on continual organisational changes. I hoped that the last changes, ie Business Sector and Organising for Quality would have allowed staff and the organisation time to settle down and have a period of stability.

Now I see from the Daily Telegraph 8.9.92 that Sir Bob Reid "might alight earlier than expected". This cannot do any good for morale.

8. Staff Buy-Out

This is the only way, in my opinion, that Privatisation might succeed. The NFC is a glowing example.

9. *The effect of Economies*

BR has gone through a very difficult time over the last decade. The PSO grant has been successively cut every year. In some years BR's economies were so marked that BR was able to "turn away" grant—much to the annoyance of the Trade Unions.

The resulting economies in staff meant that the main "spine" of supervision was withdrawn. The results are very evident. My friends repeat "there was no one to collect my ticket—I could have travelled for nothing". Revenue loss is significant.

Restore supervision—this aspect is not referred to.

10. *Operations in the "field"*

Whilst it may sound desirable having several different franchised services running over the same track—how is the problem of breakdowns to be handled?

Emergencies are happening all the time = just see any Controller's log.

Who will be responsible? The White Paper is silent on this.

11 September 1992

APPENDIX 34

ANNANDALE & ESKDALE DISTRICT COUNCIL

West Coast Main Line

This Council along with a number of others in the North West of England and South West of Scotland is extremely concerned at British Rail's recent decision to delay the introduction of new rolling stock on the West Coast Main Line, believing this to be the first step in the deterioration of the services provided on that Line to the advantage of the East Coast services.

Whilst the road network on the West Coast is being currently improved (ie the construction of the M74 motorway) a large proportion of the population make use of such rail services as exist. A further deterioration in public transport would most certainly erode the quality of life within the area for which this Council is responsible. I am aware that representations are already being made to you by a number of Authorities in the North West of England and, possibly, by a number of Authorities in the South West of Scotland. This Council is represented on a Rail Forum and heartily supports that Organisation's position. I shall be pleased if you will note and report to the Select Committee this Council's concern at the current and possible future erosion of public transport services in the West of the country and at the lack of investment proposed for the future.

I do not propose with this letter to reiterate the arguments which, I am sure will be submitted by other organisaitons but merely to stress this Council's support for their attention and improvement of public rail services in the West of the country.

13 October 1992

APPENDIX 35

SUBMISSION FROM THE BRITISH TOURIST AUTHORITY AND THE ENGLISH TOURIST BOARD TO THE TRANSPORT SELECT COMMITTEE

INTRODUCTION

The British Tourist Authority (BTA) and the English Tourist Board (ETB) were established by the Development of Tourism Act 1969 and are charged under the Act with the role of advising any Minister or public body on matters relating to tourism in Great Britain as a whole (BTA), or in England (ETB). In this connection, the BTA and ETB consulted with the tourism industry on the implications of the Government White Paper, "New opportunities for the railways—the privatisation of British Rail".

We consulted a wide range of tourism interests including BTA's Development Committee which comprises representatives of all major sectors within the tourism industry; and English Regional Tourist Boards, who in turn consulted with their members who are predominantly from the small business sector. Our objective was to ensure that both the needs of domestic and incoming tourists are met by a newly privatised rail system.

It is significant that this issue has elicited more reaction than any other consultation we have undertaken in recent years, with over a hundred responses, reflecting the deep concern from many organisations that many strong and distinctive features of British Rail's service should continue to be provided by the franchised operators. These responses have been considered and summarised and form the basis of the submission.

General implications for tourism

Rail forms an essential part of business and holiday tourism. In 1991, the UK Tourism Survey showed British people took 10 million tourism trips by rail, of which 8 million were holiday tourism. This does not take into account the huge number of leisure day trips that were taken by rail. Overseas visitors are heavy users of rail services, particularly as many visitors are nervous about driving on the left. The 1991 BTA Overseas Visitor Survey showed that 49 per cent of visitors to Britain used British Rail during their stay.

We hope that the number of franchise operators will not be of the magnitude that has been suggested in the press. With large numbers it will be difficult to put together tourism promotions that are rail based, and there will be inevitable difficulties with information and ticketing (this is discussed in more detail later).

INFORMATION

At present, British Rail provides an extensive and user-friendly information service. There is a national timetable, an InterCity timetable, various regional and route-specific timetables, a network of telephone and private enquiry offices which open for very long hours and a "talking-timetable" service. The network of British Rail International offices overseas gives an essential service of information provision and ticket sales to the travel trade and to members of the public. They also act to reassure potential visitors to Britain of the ease of travel on our rail network. The White Paper does not discuss the future of this important service to visitors to Britain.

Whilst the requirement of Railtrack to produce a national timetable will help in some respects, only a portion of the enquiries made by callers relates to journey time. We feel that the role of Railtrack should be expanded to include the responsibility for full information provision, financed by mandatory contributions from the franchisees. It is essential that protection for the information service is incorporated into the final Bill.

If individuals find it difficult to make a booking, with a journey that might involve several operators, they will either travel by road or air or may not even make the journey. At the very least, restricted availability of information will cause wasted time because it will be difficult to make informed choices.

A number of issues concerning timetabling are raised immediately. Will franchisees all change timetables simultaneously? How much notice of any proposed changes will be required? What passenger or consultative committee consultation will there be? Experience with bus deregulation has shown that integrated timetables were one of the first things to disappear in a newly deregulated marketplace. PTA/Es that attempt to provide comprehesive information have found it particularly difficult to undertake this function working with several operators, all with different management systems. Operators running over common routes frequently do not show services run by other companies, resulting in the consumer having less opportunity to choose rather than the increased opportunity envisaged by the legislation.

Stations

The White Paper indicated the Government's intention to sell or lease stations to private operators. Such a move would have major implications for tourism in terms of what one may expect from the operator. There will need to be protection from operators "asset stripping" by selling parts of station premises that have been purchased. Again, the experience of bus deregulation is not reassuring in this respect. A salutary example is the bus and coach station in Southport which was sold to developers who quickly went bankrupt leaving the town without a bus and coach station. For this reason we would not favour sale of stations and would wish to see only leases offered to franchisees. We suggest the creation of an organisation analogous to BAA to manage the leasing of stations which would not inhibit commercial exploitation of sites. It should be remembered that the development of stations, notably main London termini, has contributed substantial sums which have been used for wider infrastructure development.

One large uncertainty would be the appearance and functionality of stations in the newly privatised environment. The White Paper says that the private sector would make more use of the commercial opportunities at stations, but there is a concern that the purely functional side of travel may not be adequately addressed if it were not commercially attractive. Protection must be given to ensure that passenger need is of prime consideration and that minimum service levels apply to the operation of stations as well as rail services. This is particularly true for staffing levels, about which there has been considerable anxiety recently due to safety implications.

Many stations are historic buildings and not all are listed by the DoE. We are concerned that protection is in place for this part of Britain's heritage. We would prefer to see a cohesive identity to stations externally so they are easily recognisable and we wish there to be a requirement that access from main throughfares is retained rather than allowing operators to turn over all main frontage to commercial exploitation, while retaining only side-street access to the platforms. Research has shown that the double-arrow symbol achieves extremely high levels of recognition for both domestic and overseas users.

Ticketing

There are many tickets used by both domestic and overseas visitors which allow access to parts or all of the BR system at discounted price. Over 100,000 BritRail passes are sold each year to overseas visitors and there is a wide availability of 7 and 14 day regional rover tickets which are sold to 50,000 domestic and overseas visitors each year. In addition many hundreds of thousands of day tickets valid for large regions are sold.

In London, there is extensive interchangeability of tickets with the Travelcard system for bus, underground and rail services. This interchangeability is already threatened with the proposed deregulation of London Buses. The Travelcard is vital and necessary to London for domestic and overseas visitors, plus of course, the working population of the capital.

Similarly, there is a certain amount of interchangeability of tickets in the seven Passenger Transport Executives/Authorities in England and Scotland. Already, difficulties have been encountered in these PTA/E areas where operators do not honour each other's tickets. By way of example (in a non-PTE area), the experience of Oxford is that deregulation led to major difficulties with operators not recognising each other's tickets. The phrase in the White Paper (paragraph 93), "It will be for operators to make arrangements to accept each other's tickets" is inadequate. The Bill should require operators to agree co-operative ticket deals at the time of drawing up franchise agreements.

We welcome the assurance in the White Paper that there will continue to be through ticketing which is essential to toursim. However, that is concern that where there is joint running over lines, there should be full interchangeability of tickets, recognising that supplements may be due where travellers trade up to a premium service.

The White Paper proposes that "passenger service operators find it in their commercial interest to offer a range of discounted fares and travelcards"—this does not guarantee that the valuable facility enjoyed today will continue to exist.

The existing series of discount rail cards operated by British Rail (Senior Citizen, Disabled, Family, Young Persons etc.) is important to tourism. They generate new business and encourage tourism away from the "honeypots". There value is immediately undermined if they cannot be used universally on the rail system. Although most domestic tourism is by private car, many families which do use the train are travelling on fares purchased with a Family Rail Card.

Tour operators use the ITX fare structure based on a zonal system to calculate their brochure prices. They need a central point to negotiate fares and the level of bonding required. For example one operator, Superbreak, has a £450,000 bond with British Rail. The view was expressed by one tour operator that if it became too complex to negotiate rail packages, they would switch to road.

Environmental issues

Paragraph 75 of the White Paper draws attention to the environmental benefits of rail travel. Both BTA and ETB are committed to policies of sensitive visitor management to protect the environment. The use of rail services helps restrict growth in road use and thereby congestion. The AA predicts a 15 per cent increase in car ownership between 1990 and 1995 which will place increasing pressure on the environment. It is essential that rail services remain an attractive alternative to the motor car.

Already Network SouthEast, Regional Railways and InterCity have different policies for the carriage of cycles on trains which have created problems in attempting to promote rail/cycle as a "green" holiday option. We have been receiving an increasing number of complaints about the carriage of cycles on trains. The difficulty being encountered already in this rapidly growing market is indicative of the problems that will inevitably occur in-promoting themes nationwide, or even within regions in a diverse network of franchisees.

Joint promotional schemes with British Rail are used for visitor management purposes to aid with environmental protection. Examples of such projects are the Surrey Hills Management initiative, the Devon & Cornwall Rail Project and the Tamar Valley line project. Commercial attraction is not the primary motive for such schemes; it is questionable whether franchisees would be motivated to support this type of initiative where the direct financial reward may not be great.

Rail Regulator

We see this function as a cornerstone in protection of consumers from predatory pricing or exploitation of a monopoly operation. It is essential that the Rail regulator has "teeth" to ensure that the quality of rolling stock and of every aspect of service provision meets exacting standards.

We have some anxiety concerning operation of rail routes by existing bus operators over parallel routes and feel that monopolies must be avoided at all costs.

Freight

With the current example of transfer of limestone traffic between Redmire Quarry in Yorkshire and British Steel Redcar to the roads of Wensleydale in mind, there are serious concerns that the proposed regime for the recovery of rail track costs will result in further losses of bulk freight to road. There are significant flows of such traffic in major tourism areas like Cornwall, Devon and the Peak District, where the environmental consequences of an increase in heavy road movements would be very serious.

Rural routes

Railways are a useful tool in visitor management in rural areas, by removing traffic from the roads. However, it is recognised that rural services are often not profitable. At present there is an amount of cross subsidy in rail services with the block grant system which has proved to be a strength of the system. It will be particularly difficult for the franchising to make effective judgements about services of a relatively local nature when allocating grant. The present system has allowed British Rail the flexibility to adapt the resources available to meet changing market needs. This has been done extensively, particularly in regional express services which have accounted for significant growth in provincial rail traffic.

Several organisations expressed concern that there must be a long term Government commitment to grant-aided lines when the full extent of subsidy becomes transparent. It is not clear from the White Paper how the franchising authority will respond to local social need or market demand. There was also concern that the highly expensive renewal and repair costs of viaducts, tunnels, bridges and other infrastructure would be attributed to individual lines by Railtrack thus making operation hopelessly uneconomic. Regional Railways cross subsidises its operations, but still needs £500 million of the Public Service Obligation.

London

The need for the retention of Travelcards is discussed earlier but there are other issues that are focused on London. There is already a capacity problem in the rail paths to London termini and we are concerned that the multiplicity of lines that originate and terminate in London are treated fairly. For example, there needs to be a balance in the priorities that ensures that international, long distance and suburban services compete equally and not on a basis of payment for franchises. Pricing in the London area must be coordinated.

Although it is a general point for the whole network, it is of particular importance in London that franchises are awarded on coherent groups of lines, easily comprehended by passengers. London already has a complex rail network; it should not be made more confusing for visitors.

Rolling stock

British Rail has always had a commitment to long term investment in rolling stock, track, signalling and in stations. With some of British Rail's existing stock already life-expired, we welcome the White Paper statement (paragraph 43) that the Government will provide direct support for investment taking into account the wider benefits of such investment rather than a simple cost-benefit analysis.

It is not certain that private operators would have a commitment to the provision of new rolling stock. Certainly, recent reports have shown that the average age of buses has increased substantially since deregulation of bus services. Are we to expect an increasingly ageing fleet of railway rolling stock? Obviously an operator will need to have confidence that he has an adequate period to recoup any investment in new rolling stock or other capital investment.

Disability

British Rail has a commitment to improving accessibility for disabled passengers and the White Paper says that there will be a requirement on operating companies to "have regard to the needs of passengers with mobility difficulty". The coordinated approach of British Rail has ensured major improvements in recent years, but would this process continue with a fragmented rail service? There is need for firm commitment with national criteria established.

Conclusion

The White Paper states that "services must not be disrupted by organisational change". We strongly endorse this view and urge that the necessity of ensuring that the multiplicity of issues raised by the privatisation of British Rail will mean that the Bill is not rushed and that there is adequate consultation at every stage.

13 October 1992

APPENDIX 36

YORKSHIRE AND HUMBERSIDE REGIONAL ASSOCIATION

Future Prospects for the Rail System in the light of the Government's Proposals for Privatisation

OBJECTIVES

1. **The Yorkshire and Humberside Regional Association, which represents Local Authorities in the region, believes that rail privatisation should not result in a reduction in passenger and freight services and the diversion of more traffic on to the roads. The objective for the railways should be to increase usage through higher investment and improved services and relieve road congestion in the interests of the environment.**

2. Local passenger services have an important role to play in reducing car use and easing congestion. Inter City and other longer distance passenger services are important to economic development, particularly to regions like Yorkshire and Humberside which are peripheral to the main EC growth area, and rail electrification has a major role to play in maintaining our competitive position in this respect. Freight services have the capacity to take some of the heaviest freight loads which loads which do the most environmental damage off the roads.

3. As congestion increases in urban areas and along key transport corridors, the need will become more pressing to plan all modes of transport together, especially to make the most of rail's capacity to take more traffic. Similarly rail must continue to operate as a national system with integrated ticketing and services.

4. There is some scope for making existing services and facilities more attractive. The introduction of new private services should not duplicate existing services and lead to a diversion of rolling stock and infrastructure to other purposes. The primary need of the railways is for more investment to provide better and more reliable stock and equipment and to develop the system, especially through electrification. It seems unlikely that privatisation will result in high levels of investment: bus deregulation led to a deterioration in the fleet and an increase in the average age of buses and comments reported in the press by companies who are interested in providing rail services do not suggest they are prepared to invest substantially in the system.

5. When the White Paper "New Opportunities for the Railways" was published on 14 July 1992, the Transport Secretary said he expected that broadly the national network would be maintained, that closure procedures would remain unchanged and a single timetable and compatible ticketing would continue. Commentators were, however, unable to discern whether the primary objective was to cut subsidies or to invest in a modern rail system. As the Director General of the CBI (who was supportive) put it: "It is absolutely essential that privatisation is not used as an alibi for cut-backs on much-needed investment in the rail system."

6. The Secretary of the Central Transport Consultative Committee believes that franchise companies will prefer to operate only two or three trains per day at the most profitable times on some routes. Others may not be attractive and there is clearly a danger that BR will find itself with a residue of unprofitable, subsidised lines not earning enough to support investment and a permanent target for Treasury cuts. Rural rail services, for example, needed a subsidy of £592 million in 1991.

INVESTMENTS LEVELS

7. Recent increases in rail investment have done no more than tackle some of the problems which have accumulated during years of neglect and low investment and provide for essential safety measures. Indeed, when current Channel Tunnel investment is stripped out, renewal of the rest of the network may even be falling behind once more. Even with these items included, the United Kingdom is well below levels in other advanced countries and it may even be that privatisation will take capital out of the system if proceeds from sales are taken by the Treasury.

Investment per head (£) in Railway Lines, 1991

Italy	32.8
Sweden	32.6
France	32.0
Netherlands	31.4
Germany	18.8
Belgium	12.9
Portugal	9.8
Spain	9.8
United Kingdom	5.8

8. Road and rail investment projects are assessed very differently. **Capital investment in railways seems to be regarded by the Government as a subsidy whereas road investment is accepted as essential infrastructure. This will have to change if traffic is to be attracted from road to rail. The Government should consider direct funding of the rail infrastructure to bring it into line with roads.** At present, for roads, a range of non-financial benefits are taken into account in deciding whether a scheme should be included in the programme, whereas for rail the evaluation does not recognise social benefits and an 8 per cent financial rate of return is required.

9. The Transport Minister has now announced a revised investment procedure to be introduced with rail privatisation in 1994 to tackle the road/rail investment bias. This will provide direct capital grants for those investment schemes that offer a satisfactory cost-benefit return in helping to reduce road congestion and improving rail journey times and will thus strengthen the case for some schemes. It remains to be seen what impact the system will have in practise.

10. Track and signalling will be owned and operated by a new company, Railtrack, which is likely to remain under BR control for some years, although the long term aim would be to privatise it too. Railtrack will be required to make a profit through the charges made to operators, although it will be able to apply for the above-mentioned grants. If Railtrack is to make a profit, this seems to imply heavy charges for use of the track, which would be controversial. No decision on track charges is likely to be made on this until the Coopers and Lybrand study has been completed. However, until track charges are known the full consequences of rail privatisation are impossible to predict.

FREIGHT

11. **The Association would be concerned if Railfreight charges to freight operators rise so that marginal operators, who pay less at present, are forced to use road rather than rail, thereby increasing road freight at the expense of rail.**

12. The need to modernise and improve rail services was accepted in "Roads for Prosperity", but it was stated that "even a 5 per cent increase in rail traffic would be equivalent to only 5 per cent of present day road traffic—about one years growth in recent years." This comment considerably understates the importance of rail in that it is more competitive for more environmentally damaging long-distance freight traffic.

13. Rail has the potential to take more of the heavier and most destructive loads off the roads, to the benefit of everyone. It has to be admitted, however, that present trends show no indication of this happening. Speedlink, which was set up to handle BR's wagon load business, was closed down in July 1991. Railfreight Distribution lost £118 million, equal to more than half its gross income, in 1991. The collapse of Charterail in August 1992 was disappointing. Charterail aimed to bring down handling costs by using special road trailers that could be driven straight onto wagons without special lifting equipment, thus making rail competitive over shorter distances. Operationally it was successful but financially it failed because, the company said, it could not afford to pay the level of BR charges.

14. Commenting on expected BR losses in the financial year 1991–92 in relation to privatisation, the Financial Times of 19 June 1992 predicted: "The freight losses, meanwhile, make it highly improbable that an outright buyer will be found for Railfreight Distribution. It is more likely that the private sector will 'cherry pick' the few profitable freight services, leaving the remainder to close down."

15. Rail freight users have traditionally been at a disadvantage in competing with road hauliers because the latter pay a much smaller proportion of their costs towards maintaining the roads. A lorry is charged 4 per cent of its operating costs to use the roads whereas for BR track costs represent 48 per cent of the total (although the amount charged varies over the network). After privatisation, the indications are that rail freight charges will have to rise as users are required to pay a large share of track costs.

16. **If the community is to have the environmental benefits of rail-hauled long distance freight, a more even handed approach is needed between road and rail, both in terms of allocating investment funds and charging network costs. Rail freight operators should pay annual licence fees comparable to bus and lorry operators.**

17. Yorkshire and Humberside needs to develop freight links with Europe along two axes: East-West to the Humber Ports including transpennine improvements and North-South to the Channel Tunnel, perhaps via the High Speed Link and in the longer term possibly including loading gauge improvements. Channel Tunnel—related freight depots are being established at Wakefield and Doncaster. **Privatisation must not be allowed to prejudice essential, capital intensive developments such as these.**

PASSENGER SERVICES

18. **The Association would be concerned if passenger services are reduced after privatisation and major towns and cities lose Inter City services. It seems unlikely that any income from the sale of privatised services will exceed the extra cost of (a) running the remaining services and (b) the bureaucracies which are being created.**

19. In recent years British Rail have discontinued Inter City services to a number of English towns and cities which do not lie on the Main Lines and have substituted slower and less comfortable regional services. This reduces the quality of service to residents and is a handicap in promoting economic development. In Yorkshire and Humberside there is concern for services which do not lie directly on the East Coast and

Midland Main Lines and the Grimsby/Cleethorpes InterCity service is to be discontinued. **The number of Inter City passenger services and stops must remain at least at current levels.**

20. **Rail services are an important element in traffic plans in many urban areas and the local authorities are concerned that rail privatisation should not undermine their efforts to develop co-ordinated policies to cut congestion.** In the past, inadequate levels of investment have led to old and worn out rolling stock being retained long after its useful life is over and new stock being introduced without adequate development and testing. The result has been poor performance and reliability, problems which have still not been entirely overcome. Future rail financing arrangements need to resolve this problem.

21. A shortage of resources within British Rail, notably in signalling and telecommunications, has also led to long lead times for major projects including the Leeds City west end reorganisation. Dovetailing these with Department of Transport agreement to funding has proved a major problem with the Bradford Area Electrification and these are still not completely resolved at the time of writing. **A better system is needed for approving local rail developments and ensuring that the physical and financial resources are available at the right time to avoid wasteful and unnecessary delays.**

22. **There are extensive rural areas to the north and east of the region where services seem unlikely to be attractive to private operators.** Regional Railways has come to rely increasingly on local authority support in recent years and when this has not been forthcoming, more lightly used by locally important services have been substantially cut back and/or threatened with closure. One such example is the Whitby-Middlesbrough service, which has been cut severely and no longer provides the local communities with the level of service they need. **Outside the metropolitan areas, local authorities may be small, with limited resources and have their own priorities. They will not always feel able to support services which are needed as part of a national network of inter-connecting rail services. Regional Railways must not be allowed to lean too heavily on such authorities.**

ELECTRIFICATION

23. Rail electrification should pay a key role in the development of Yorkshire and Humberside's inter-regional communications. Transpennine road links are heavily congested and improvements which are planned are palliatives rather than solutions. A study by the consultants TPA of transpennine links has recommended electrification of the Liverpool-Manchester-Huddersfield-Leeds-York route and has the support of Regional Railways. It could then be extended eastwards from Leeds through to Selby and Hull. Also recommended are faster and more frequent services on the Calder Valley route from Bradford-Halifax-Rochdale. Another study, commissioned by the Midland Main Line Consortium, has demonstrated the viability of electrifying this Sheffield-London link.

24. **From the regional point of view, rail privatisation should be assessed according to its capacity to bring forward electrification schemes like these which are needed for the regeneration of traditional industrial areas, not only in Yorkshire and Humberside but over much of the north of England.**

PLANNING

25. Rail has the potential to relieve the motorway and trunk road system of both cars and freight, but the two modes need to be planned together so that the capacity and advantages of both can be fully exploited. A relevant example here is transpennine links. Transpennine traffic continues to grow along this key corridor which is of much wider than regional importance, linking as it does the major manufacturing areas of the North West with Yorkshire and Humberside, the Humber Ports and Northern Europe. It is clear that the widening of the M62 and the A628 improvements which are already in the programme will not be sufficient. Rail clearly has a contribution to make, but the current Department of Transport study covers only roads. In the absence of a wider vision within the Department, a consortium of nine local authorities and PTEs commissioned TPA to produce a common appraisal of both road and rail options.

26. **The existing transport planning system fails to consider road, rail and other modes together as it should and rail privatisation is likely to make co-ordinated planning even more difficult.**

15 October 1992

APPENDIX 37

ROYAL NATIONAL INSTITUTE FOR THE BLIND

As the largest organisation for blind and partially sighted people in the UK, the RNIB provides services for many of the one million adults with a visual impairment serious enough for them to be registered as blind or partially sighted. Public transport is especially important for blind and partially sighted people and the railways, in particular, represent a means of independent travel when car usage, other than as a passenger is largely not an option. For this reason, RNIB has responded to the White Paper with comments that we feel are essential to ensure the transport needs of Britain's public are to be fully met.

In brief, these comments centre around the need for: adequate safety standards to be maintained throughout the new railway network to ensure that blind and partially sighted people can travel safely; the accessibility of the rail network, in terms of physical access as well as access to information; a regular and reliable service; consultation with the users of services, about the quality and type of service offered; and an adequate concessionary fare scheme applicable nationwide.

The comments of the Joint Committee on Mobility of Blind and Partially-Sighted People (JCMB) and the Royal National Institute for the Blind (RNIB).

"NEW OPPORTUNITIES FOR THE RAILWAYS
THE PRIVATISATION OF BRITISH RAIL"

Contents   *Page*

1. INTRODUCTION

1.1 The publication of the White Paper on the Privatisation of British Rail provides an opportunity to re-examine the current railway system and to ensure a higher quality of service for the public who travel by rail. Although we recognise that this has not been presented as a consultation document, the Joint Committee on Mobility of Blind and Partially-Sighted People (JCMB) and the Royal National Institute for the Blind (RNIB) welcome the opportunity to comment on the White Paper and the future of the railways in Britain.

1.2 In Britain and Northern Ireland today there are approximately 1 million adults with a visual impairment serious enough for them to be eligible for registration as blind or partially sighted. The RNIB is the largest organisation for blind and partially sighted people in the UK and provides services for blind and partially sighted people of all ages in a number of areas, including health, education, leisure, employment and training and transportation. RNIB has its own Mobility Unit, which works on behalf of visually impaired people on such issues as building design, road and streetworks and the transport and mobility of visually impaired people.

1.3 RNIB is also a member organisation of the JCMB. Established approximately 14 years ago, the JCMB is the principal organisation coordinating and representing the views of visually impaired people in a number of areas associated with mobility, including transport. Its members are: the Royal National Institute for the Blind, the Partially Sighted Society, Guide Dogs for the Blind Association, SENSE, the National Federation of the Blind, the National League of the Blind and Disabled, the Circle of Guide Dog Owners, ARROW, National Mobility Centre, the Blind Mobility Research Unit and St. Dunstan's. Associated members include British Rail, London Transport, and the Bus and Coach Council. The JCMB also has close links with the Department of Transport's Disability Unit, the Disabled Passenger's Transport Advisory Committee (DiPTAC) and the British Railways Board Advisory Group for Disabled Passengers (BRAG).

1.4 *Blind and partially sighted travellers*

Blind and partially sighted people have severe mobility problems and are less mobile than other disabled people. Indeed, figures show that approximately 52 per cent of blind and partially sighted people need help to go out, compared to 14 per cent of the disabled population in general. For this reason, blind and partially sighted people rely heavily on public transport, as car usage, other than as a passenger is not an option. A high quality and efficient public transport system is essential to meet the needs of the many blind and partially sighted people who use it and to ensure that they retain a high level of independence.

Railways are frequently used by blind and partially sighted travellers and it is important that awareness and commitment to meeting the needs of blind and partially sighted users is made.

1.5. *Summary of Key Points*

The JCMB and the RNIB believe that there are certain key principles which are of such significance, that they should be included in the substance of any legislation on the privatisation of British Rail.

These are the principles which we believe should be taken into consideration in the points made below.

—Safety of all passengers is vital and we believe that certain measures should be introduced to ensure that blind and partially sighted travellers can travel without danger.

—Services should be accessible to all passengers. This means physical accessibility to all stations as well as the accessibility of information about services. It is important that passengers are allowed a full, unrestricted and independent access into the system.

—It is also important that services are reliable and regular, offering an adequate level of service to cover essential passenger needs.

—Standards should be set in joint consultation with users and providers of the services. This includes the Franchise agreements/contracts which will determine the operation of services. It is essential that operators make provision for the needs of disabled people.

—There needs to be an adequate concessionary fare scheme for disabled people needing to travel by rail. This should be applicable nationwide and of a level sufficient to meet the financial circumstances of disabled travellers.

2. PROPOSALS

2.1 *British Rail*

Whilst we appreciate the strengths of the railways and recognise the important role that rail travel plays in our country's transportation system, we welcome the Government's commitment to improving the railways. As the White Paper points out "the railways cannot play their full role unless they give passenger and freight customers the services they expect. The key to success is a reliable, efficient operation offering high quality services to users." We welcome this commitment. However, we are concerned that the principles and practices set out in the legislation meet the needs of visually impaired users. Indeed, we recognise the need for radical changes as "Too frequently, ..., the quality of service fails to meet the travelling public's expectations" and we hope that these changes will favour a more widely accessible public transport system.

2.2. *The Essential Requirements*

Our comments are based on a number of essential requirements, some of which, we feel are vital if a high quality service for visually impaired travellers is to be maintained.

8(a) Safety

The White Paper states that the "safety of the rail network remains of paramount importance". Although some strides have been made in recent years, towards improving the management of safety on the railways, there remains considerable room for improvement.

Safety on the railways is important to all travellers. However, the existence of safety measures and safety standards is of particular importance to blind and partially sighted travellers, for whom the railways represent a particularly dangerous place. There are many steps which should be taken to ensure the safety of blind and partially sighted passengers, and which in fact, are beneficial to all travellers, offering a safe, usable and accessible railway network.

In 1989, the Secretary of State required the British Railways Board to produce an annual Safety Plan. It took two years for the first plan to emerge, and the Safety Plan for 1992 was not published until the second half of the year. In this report, accidents between trains, due to faulty signalling systems, or driving error, received a high profile. However, the most accidents to passengers in fact occur when they are boarding or leaving a train. Research recently completed indicates that approximately 35 per cent of visually impaired people who travel regularly by train have had an accident boarding or leaving a train.#

It is essential therefore that such safety precautions as platform edge warning strips (for example, a white strip along the length of the platform to indicate the edge), tactile floor markings, audible and visual warnings on trains and in stations, highlighting of stairs are used. These measures need to be specified and standardised throughout the rail network. These steps will mean that needless accidents are avoided. Other simple measures such as clear signs (especially warning signs) and the clear marking of obstructions all help to make trains and stations safer places for visually impaired people. Other improvements include clear colour contrast in trains and on stations, adequate grab rails and hand grips. These features are all important as they enable blind and partially sighted people to maximise the use of their remaining sight. Few blind people see nothing at all and many have a degree of residual vision, depending on their eye condition. They can be assisted by use of lighting, colour contrast and other features, on which low vision experts can advise.

It is essential that the Railway Inspectorate take a proactive role in setting these safety standards, not only to ensure that operators cannot operate without meeting the necessary requirements, but also to ensure that measures are standardised across the railway network.

These improvements in basic station and train design need to be made in consultation with users and experts to ensure that the railway system as a whole is fully accessible to all travellers, including blind and partially sighted people.

8(b) Quality of Service

A high quality of service for *all* passengers can only be achieved if regard is made to the needs of disabled passengers, particularly blind and partially sighted people. A fully accessible network must be accompanied by staff training. British Rail's "Passenger's Charter" published last year, made reference to increased staff training. We believe that it is essential that staff are given training in disability awareness, for example, and the correct way to guide a blind person. This would help to ensure that all disabled passengers received the help that they needed in making a journey by rail.

Although we welcome the advances made by British Rail with the special assistance service for disabled passengers, it must be recognised that this service is not ideal, nor is it entirely satisfactory. A greater level of staff awareness and a more accessible station would in many cases remove the need for such assistance.

8(c) Essential Passenger Services

We welcome the Government's commitment to the provision of vital passenger services. It should be stressed, however, that currently many services "regional and commuter" services remain inaccessible to blind and partially sighted people, for example, through the introduction of destaffed stations and the application of time restrictions on concessionary fare schemes.

Destaffed stations are of particular concern as it means that stations become virtually inaccessible to blind and partially sighted travellers. Destaffed stations represent particular dangers to blind and partially sighted people and their consequent inaccessibility is a great problem. For example, inaccessibility to a local station may for many blind and partially sighted people mean an inability to travel to work, or college, or to keep a medical appointment as rail travel represents the most important means of independent travel.

8(d) Network Benefits

The maintenance of "Network Benefits" is essential to ensure a high level of service for blind and partially sighted travellers. Without through ticketing and a national timetable, travel for visually impaired people and probably for all passengers would be even more complicated and might even discourage people from embarking on long journeys. More importantly, however, the benefits of nationally recognised concessionary fares are immeasurable and their loss would prevent many people from venturing out at all.

2.3 The Benefits of Private Sector Involvement and Liberalisation

19(a) More concern for the customers' needs

If management and employees in the private sector have greater incentives to provide the services which the consumer wants, then it is hoped that this will ensure that blind and partially sighted people receive the high standards of service which are necessary to ensure their safe and easy travel on the railways.

19(b) Competition and Ending the Monopoly

With new operators providing services, it may lead the way to blind and partially sighted people choosing their service according to the ability to provide high quality and good standards, and thus stimulating a greater awareness of the needs of disabled travellers amongst all rail operators.

19(d) Clear and Enforceable Quality Standards

The Franchising Authority will be responsible for awarding and monitoring the new franchises. It is essential that users of rail services, the travellers themselves, are consulted in the setting up of franchises. This is particularly important for disabled people as only with consultation can the needs of disabled people be properly met. We believe that consultation with local or national bodies is important before the drawing up of contracts and the Franchise Agreements.

3. PASSENGER SERVICES

3.1 Continuing Role of BR

Paragraph 22

Paragraph 22 states that "Railtrack will own the track and other infrastructure and control day to day operations ..". It is important, however, that the scope of the infrastructure is clarified. It seems clear, for example, that 'infrastructure' will include railway station platforms, but it is not clear whether this includes other parts of the railway station premises.

Station premises can be very dangerous places, particularly for blind and partially sighted people and we propose that all station premises, except the specialised area of platforms, should be covered by Department of Environment Building Regulations. This is important to ensure that the excellent work achieved in the latest Building Regulations, Part M, which makes significant advances in the design of buildings to cater for people with disabilities, including sensory disabilities, is continued. Station concourses are obviously places of frequent public use and they should be properly designed so to protect the travelling public.

3.2 Stations

Paragraph 44

Paragraph 44 states that "the Government is prepared to consider other disposal arrangements including selling and leasing [stations] provided that the interests of operators and passengers using them are protected." We believe that the selling of stations could be detrimental to the needs of public transport users, particularly disabled people, if there is not adequate control over those stations. There needs to be a degree of standardisation to ensure that visually impaired people can find their way about easily and use stations safely, wherever they are and on whatever route. For example, as mentioned in 3.1 above, all stations should comply with Department of Environment Building Regulations Part M.

4. FREEDOM OF ACCESS

Paragraphs 56 to 59

Paragraph 56 states that the Government will "establish a framework and procedures through which companies wishing to provide new railway services, who can meet necessary operational and safety standards, will have right of access to the railway network." We welcome the Government's intention to regulate access to the rail network. These "necessary operational and safety standards" should include the provision of facilities for disabled people and operators should be required to provide adequate facilities to enable visually impaired passengers to have full and unrestricted and independent access to the entire railway network.

5. REGULATION

5.1 The Regulator

The Regulator obviously has a vital role to play in the setting up and operation of the new railway network.

Paragraph 64(c)

Paragraph 64(c) states that one of the roles of the Regulator is "promoting the interests of consumers and ensuring that network benefits are maintained." We believe that the Regulator should also play a specific role in laying down provision for disabled passengers and hence making sure that the interests of *all* passengers are met.

5.2 Operating Licences

Paragraph 73

Paragraph 73 makes reference to the licence for operation which must be obtained from the Rail Regulator. We welcome the commitment to meeting the "needs of passengers with mobility handicaps". However, we are concerned that this commitment, without reference to the specific needs of disabled people, and specific reference to the particular needs of blind and partially sighted people, will be ineffective. We believe that the Regulator should be required to seek consultation with organisations of and for disabled people in order that the franchise contracts, and hence the services themselves, meet the standards of safety and quality expected by disabled passengers, as indeed by all passengers.

6. SAFETY

Paragraph 76 to 84

Safety is of paramount importance to all people travelling by rail. However, additional measures need to be taken to ensure the safety of blind and partially sighted travellers. It is essential that Railtrack and the transport operators are under obligation to provide a fully-safe signalling system and infrastructure, but also a safe operational environment for visually impaired passengers to board and leave trains at all stations and throughout the daily operational hours of individual stations.

Operators must be required to provide a safe environment on all railway premises, by taking into account measures previously detailed; for example, by bringing the design of stations and other railway premises within the scope of the Building Regulations Part M, previously mentioned (3.1).

Paragraph 77

We welcome the Government's recognition of the importance of the role played by the Health and Safety Executive (incorporating HM Railway Inspectorate) and endorsed by the Health and Safety Commission. In addition to its role set out in the White Paper, we believe that the Health and Safety Commission should also be required to take a proactive role in ensuring that:

(i) Standardisation systems for safety to which the general public are directly exposed are applied throughout the railway system.
(ii) High risk areas such as boarding and leaving trains should be highlighted and steps taken to bring about an improvement of safety standards.

(iii) Railtrack and transport operators must achieve defined targets, expressed in terms of numbers of accidents and timescale, for reducing passenger accidents.

7. EMPLOYEES AND NETWORK BENEFITS

7.1 *Network Benefits*

Paragraph 88

Network benefits are very important for blind and partially sighted people, as they make the business of rail travel much less complicated, for example, through ticketing, cross validity and a national timetable. We believe that the most important benefit to blind and partially sighted people is the current discounted fares scheme. Discounted or concessionary fares are vital as they bring otherwise expensive travel within the reach of blind and partially sighted people. This is for two reasons.

Many visually impaired people can only travel with the assistance of a companion. At the present time, they are able to do this because the visually impaired passenger and companion are allowed to travel at a 50 per cent discount each, equating to one full fare. Reduction of a discount to, say 34 per cent would result in visually impaired people paying a premium to travel, of 34 per cent in excess of the fare for an able-bodied passenger.

Many blind and partially sighted people live on very low incomes. Many are dependent on inadequate state benefits, with no specific benefit for blind and partially sighted people. This low income is compounded by the added costs associated with a disability and means that many people are unable to afford the luxuries that others take for granted. For many, necessary yet unwanted expenses are incurred; for example, it may be necessary to take taxis if a journey is too difficult by other means; or it may be necessary to have paid help to assist with household tasks which most sighted people would do themselves. Our recently published RNIB Survey* shows that 31 per cent of blind and partially sighted people had net weekly incomes of less than £70 a week and only one in ten had a weekly income of over £200 (the average weekly wage at the time the survey was conducted).

For these reasons, it is vital that there is an assurance that the current concessionary fare schemes will be safeguarded and improved rather than left to diminish in the battle for survival amongst new operators.

8. THE WAY FORWARD

RNIB and JCMB believe that there are five basic principles which could be adhered to and which would ensure the smooth passage of privatisation and which would ensure that Britain had a fully accessible railway network:

(i) Safety

Passenger safety must be paramount not only in terms of the railtrack and signalling system, but also rolling stock, platform design and overall station design.

(ii) Joint Consultation

With the multiplicity of transport between operators, there must be an effective means of joint consultation between those broadly concerned with the provision of transport, such as the individual transport operators and Railtrack and the transport users, with proper representation for people who are visually impaired. As passenger safety is likely to be a regular subject of discussion, it is also proposed that the Railways Inspectorate be involved in this consultation process.

(iii) Accessibility

The transport system must be fully accessible to disabled people, so that they may travel safely, independently and·with peace of mind. There must also be full access to information, such as timetables, train departures and fare structures, and this should be available to blind and partially sighted people in the medium of their choice. Accessibility of information, as shown by RNIB's recently published survey* is vital if blind and partially sighted people are to play their full part in society. With regards to rail travel it is essential that blind and partially sighted people have access to timetables, fare schemes and other travel information. This may only be possible if information is produced in large print, braille or tape. Whilst we welcome the advances already made by the Department of Transport's Disability Unit, we feel that the services for visually impaired people could be significantly improved. With the privatisation of rail services, provision needs to be made for accessible services for disabled people.

(iv) Service

There must be an adequate level of service, which provides visually impaired people with the means to travel to their places of employment, education, medical treatment and for reasonable social and recreational activities. Lack of accessible services leads to the exclusion of blind and partially sighted people from services and denies blind and partially sighted people the right to play their full role in society.

(v) Cost of Travel

There should be an opportunity to continue with the practice of concessionary and discount fares for visually impaired people. Concessionary fares are particularly important given the low incomes of many blind and partially sighted people.

9. CONCLUSION

The RNIB and the JCMB are both working to improve the lives of blind and partially sighted people, by ensuring better provision with society and furthering the integration of visually impaired people into the community wherever possible. As long as public transport remains inaccessible or difficult to access for blind and partially sighted people, and other disabled people, then a large proportion of society remains divided from the other. In 1990, DiPTAC identified 4.2 million people (that is 7.6 per cent of the population) as having difficulties in using public transport. It is essential that these people are considered during the privatisation of British Rail so that they may be afforded equal access to this essential public service. It is therefore necessary that the points we have raised are addressed in the basic legislation governing the privatisation of British Rail. The principles are integral to the provision of an accessible rail network. We believe that the current period of change represents an ideal time in which to reassess the transport needs of all public and to ensure that Britain has a public transport system which is fully accessible to <u>ALL.</u>

*Blind and partially sighted adults in Britain: the RNIB Survey. Volume 1. Ian Bruce, Aubrey McKennell and Errol Walker. Published by HMSO, 1991.

#Research carried out by the Cranfield Institute of Technology, 1992. Out of a sample of 230 people who travel once a week or more by train, 83 had had an accident boarding or leaving a train.

23 October 1992

APPENDIX 38

Letter from Mr A Capes

Privatisation of British Rail

From your position of some influence on the Government's thinking about the privatisation of BR, I wonder if you could suggest in the appropriate quarters that there *is* a solution to the problem of how the privatised operators could pay Railtrack for the use of the infrastructure.

It is described in my short submission to the 1988 Parliamentary Committee on rail finances, which was printed in (I think) volume 4 of the Evidence to the Committee. If you have a few moments to refer to it, I think you will find the idea it contains interesting, even though privatisation was not envisaged at the time.

Very briefly, the idea is as follow:

* Railtrack, as the national network authority, should be the *only* recipient of government subsidy to the railways.

* Operators of all rail services—passenger and freight—would be expected to run them fully commercially, although with the opportunity for local services to be supported by local authorities in exactly the same way as bus services.

* Payment by operators for use of the infrastructure would be by means of a compulsory, nationally determined *Traction Fuel Levy*. This would be a fixed amount to be paid on all diesel fuel and electricity consumed for traction purposes by the operators.The Levy could—and probably would—be set at a level well above comparable fuel tax for road vehicles.

I think you will see that this proposal has a lot to recommend it. Among the advantages would be:

— the levy would be the closest approximation possible to the novement costs imposed by different weights and speeds of trains, without resorting to charging systems of fiendish complexity and inequity. Fuel consumption, for example, increases geometrically with speed—I believe a 125mph train uses about 80 per cent more fuel than a 90mph one—which would automatically translate into payment for higher quality track and signalling for higher speeds.

— Government subsidy would be restricted to a single, clearly understandable payment with a specific purpose: to maintain a national network of rail *routes.*Government would no longer have any financial involvement in the provision of *train services*.

— There would be a huge step towards comparability between rail and road finances. The absurdity of the repair costs of a particular bridge determining a closure proposal, while a new road is proposed on the same route, would be avoided, along with a mass of other current inequities. The playing-field would be much more nearly level for investment and CoBA purposes between rail and road.

— Local authorities could realistically consider subsidy proposals for local train services, since the operating costs would be able to be clearly comparable to local buses.

— Fuel economy would become a significant factor in the design of rail traction units. This would start to recover some of the ground lost through the improvement in fuel efficiency of road vehicles in recent years. Many trains are now less efficient than a modern diesel family car at producing passenger-miles per gallon of fuel consumed.

— The Railtrack authority would have only two main sources of income: the Levy, and a single annual lump sum subsidy, which could include grants for investment in specific schemes. The Levy would be very easy to collect and account for, and the opportunities for train operators to avoid paying it would be very limited.

I do hope this idea would be useful to you. Thank you for continuing to try to get some realism and technical knowledge into the debate on the railways, to counterbalance the Government's rush towards an ideologically motivated and ill-thought-through set of intentions.

3 October 1992

APPENDIX 39

Letter from Mr D R Smith

Rail Privatisation

I understand that as Chair of the Transport Select Committee you wish to examine the issue of rail privatisation and have asked for submissions.

I have a number of concerns which I list below, but my overall concern is that the conditions for fair competition between rail and other modes of transport—particularly road—will not be created. Without fair competition the government's objectives will not be achieved and more traffic will be lost by the railways and more routes close.

The simple method to achieve a reasonable measure of fair competition would be for government to directly fund the basic infrastructure and for operators to be charged in a similar way to road users (i.e. a licence fee and/or fuel duty). Such charges would, of course, have to be comparable to those charged for use of the roads.

I would expect the total income from charging rail operators to be considerably less than infrastructure expenditure—a difference acceptable because of energy, safety and environmental benefits of rail.

There would still be occasions where the income of operators did not meet operating costs and some additional subsidy should be available to ensure these (passenger) services continue.

My other concerns are:

(1) loss of integrated services

(2) higher charges

(3) separation of stations from rest of the infrastructure

(4) reduced/slower services

(5) closure of routes

(6) inefficiency (eg the Virgin idea of using HSTs on the electrified East Coast Main Line, diverting resources from elsewhere)

(7) lack of investment

(8) failure to develop a European network

Having just read your book, "Out of Steam", I am pleased to know that you share many of these concerns and will look at the objectives of privatisation very closely indeed.

8 October 1992

APPENDIX 40

CLEVELAND COUNTY COUNCIL

Evidence to Select Committee on Transport on the Government's Rail Privatisation Proposals

What should be the aims and objectives of a privatised railway?

The aims and objectives of a privatised railway should be the same as those for any national railway system. It should meet the transport needs of the population it serves.

All developed countries depend for their success on the provision of a good transport system, including both road and rail. Rail has a number of advantages over road, it is more energy efficient and less environmentally damaging.

The "Roads for Prosperity" White paper, published in May 1989, concludes that, "effective transport is a vital element of economic growth and prosperity". It goes on to say that, "the continuing advance of our economy and society requires progressive development of the motorway and trunk road programme". The same must be true of rail, especially if we are to improve the environment by encouraging more people or goods to switch to rail from the private car or lorry, thus reducing the emission of pollutants and greenhouse gases.

What are the attractions for the private sector?

The fundamental attraction for the private sector in participating in railway operations must be their ability to make a profit. The private sector is unlikely to invest in a loss-making industry without some assurance that a return on capital can be achieved.

If the Government wishes to see competition in the provision of rail services, then it must set up a framework that both encourages competition and at the same time regularises it. Regulation is necessary to ensure efficient operations and prevent excessive profits.

Private operators are likely to be wary of operating a franchise where open access could lead to large amounts of revenue being creamed off.

Who should do the strategic planning for our railways?

The strategic planning for the railway system should be part of the strategic planning for our overall transport system including road, rail, air and water. This has to be a Government responsibility because of the need to reconcile the different interest groups. Strategic planning for rail should rest with the Government and be closely integrated with road planning.

At a more local level, local authorities should have an increased role in planning rail services. This already occurs in the metropolitan areas, where PTAs develop a local strategy and the PTEs secure local rail services through section 20 payments. This route is not currently open to shire counties, although they do have a duty to meet a need.

Section 63 of the 1988 Transport Act gives each non-metropolitan county the duty to secure services to meet requirements that would not otherwise be met.

The Government intend to allow local authorities to continue to make additional contributions. The funding of such contributions is difficult as no Standard Spending Assessment is allocated for it, the Government arguing that subsidy for rail is already paid for through PSO grant. As a result of gearing additional contributions can become very expensive indeed.

How can different interests by co-ordinated?

A rail network has a number of different constraints:

—Capacity (a function of signals)

—Speed

—Weight

Rail is unlike any other form of transport. For example, any number of buses can pass along a road, usually with the opportunity to overtake one another. Although aeroplanes are constrained at airports to slots, they can overtake one another in the sky. In contrast trains are generally required to run in continuous slots. This leads to problems with running services at different speeds along the same line. For example, freight trains are generally much slower than passenger trains, so if a mixture of passenger and freight trains are required on a line, their will be fewer overall slots. If the line is passenger only then there can be more slots, especially if the passenger trains are expresses. A freight only line is likely to be a very slow line.

In the USA where most of the rail network is owned by private freight operation, all services, including passenger services, are very slow. The slot pattern is set by the freight demand and the passenger trains are then fitted in.

An early decision will be required on the future function of each line in order to determine the slots. This implies that the entire slot pattern has to be established on the network before the services can be planned. It is not possible for a rail timetable to evolve in the same way as bus services did after de-regulation. Railway timetabling is a long-term process, which needs to be done well in advance of implementation.

What principles should Railtrack use to set charges for operators?

The key problem here relates to the cost structure of railway infrastructure which has a large fixed cost and a relatively small marginal cost for additional trains run. This, of course, is why railways with low traffic flows such as rural railways tend to be uneconomic.

It seems clear that operators using the track ought to pay at least the marginal cost of their presence; the difficulty is what contribution they ought to make towards the fixed costs. On the one hand, if they pay only marginal cost then it will clearly be impossible for Railtrack to operate without subsidy. On the other hand, there may well be traffic capable of being carried by rail where the profit over the marginal cost is only small. In this case, it would be efficient to carry the traffic because it makes a small contribution to fixed costs but might well not use rail if it had to meet an apportionment of fixed costs. This would not help anybody, because the fixed costs would not be saved but simply loaded onto another user.

This is a feature which has been central to railway economics from the earliest time. With a railway company owning the track and controlling movements, the system of charging was always based on discrimination between traffics and the principle of charging what the traffic would bear. Where a commodity was thought to be relatively insensitive to price then a higher charge was made than for commodities which were more price sensitive.

It is unlikely that such a charging system could be implemented by Railtrack as it would conflict with two basic constraints which, it is submitted would have to apply to any charging policy.

First, a potential operator would have to know in advance how much he was going to have to pay. A rail operation involves significant amounts of capital and a prospective operator would need to know in advance how much he would have to pay and would need some guarantee of reasonable stability over a number of years. It would be far too much of a risk to propose a rail operation where the allocations of fixed cost for infrastructure were not only out of the operator's control but also subject to arbitrary changes.

Secondly, if the principle of open competition is to be promoted it seems axiomatic that there should not be discrimination between operators. If two operators wanted to run trains of the same weight and speed over the same route at similar times then it seems reasonable to expect them to have to pay the same charges. But if the operators were in different markets then their surplus revenue over their operating costs other than track charges could be quite different. Hence their ability to make contributions to fixed costs would vary. If charges were set at a level which encouraged the low-margin traffic (for example an excursion train) it would not be possible to obtain much of a contribution to fixed costs from high-margin traffic (for example a Pullman type train serving a business market).

There is a strong argument for suggesting that the Government should subsidise the track rather than the actual services, charging only the marginal cost to users. This would be economically most efficient. It may also help to retain freight services (currently only contributing a marginal cost element to the fixed costs of infrastructure) or rail, rather than transferring to road.

The main advantage of this alternative method of subsidy it that it would put rail on an equal footing with that for roads, i.e. there would be "a level playing field". New road infrastructure is generally provided by central or local Government. Users do contribute through the road fund license, though tax is not hypothecated for road improvements or maintenance.

How should franchises operate to maximise the public interest?

Is there any conflict between the principle of open access and the granting of exclusive franchises?

The white paper appears to assume that it will be possible to seek franchises for the operation of blocks or rail services with cross-subsidy between individual services. Where a block of services as a whole is profitable, it is envisaged that an operator will pay for the franchise. It seems unlikely that this will be possible in practice because of the conflict with the open access for commercial services. It is difficult to see why any operator would pay for the right to run a profitable service if, under the open access policy, he could simply run it without paying. The implication is that, as was the case following bus deregulation, services on profitable routes will expand until normal profits are being made and that there will no cross-subsidy to unprofitable services.

The greatest problem from this is the loss of public control over profitable services. The routes most likely to be profitable are those that carry the greatest number of passengers and thus most likely to be key parts of the national transport system. A system of franchising allows service standards to be specified so that the services best meet national needs. But if the key services are outside the franchise system this control is lost. A service which gives the greatest profit to the operator is not necessarily that which the greatest contribution to national needs.

What will be the Government's role in subsidy and investment?

The current Government proposal that all rail subsidy should be directed through two channels. The first is grant for infrastructure, where this is considered worthwhile, and the second is through subsidy to the operators of trains through the franchising authority. The operators would pay the full cost of using the track to Railtrack who will have control over the use of track and infrastructure.

It seems clear that if railways are to continue to form part of the national and local transport network then subsidy will continue to be necessary. It also seems sensible for the reasons outlined above for that subsidy to be directed to the infrastructure rather than the operations.

In what circumstances will cost-benefit appraisal be appropriate and in what circumstances will cost-benefit appraisal be appropriate and what criteria should be used for rail investment?

Again if the Government's objective is to encourage the use of rail for passengers and freight, rather than use roads, new infrastructure investment in rail should be assessed on the same basis as roads, i.e. full cost benefit analysis including user benefits. This is normal practice in other European countries. The criteria for rail investment should be similar to that for rate, though a lower internal route of return and a longer evaluation timescale may be appropriate for rail to reflect the longer term nature of the investment.

How is the value of stations to be assessed and what will be the relationship between a privately owned station and BR's operation of trains therefrom?

Although there is little opportunity for the exploitation of stations could lead to operational problems for rail services and passengers. It could also lead to pressure for development in unsuitable locations.

23 October 1992

APPENDIX 41

BOROUGH OF GREAT YARMOUTH

General Purposes Committee

RECOMMENDED:

(i) That the following comments be made on the White Paper and referred to the Secretary of State for consideration:

(a) There is a need for District Councils as well as County Councils to have an input into service provisions, bearing in mind the more detailed local knowledge of public transport needs and requirements.

(b) In the event of services being franchised, it is recommended that the franchise operator should be required to place a surety sum with British Rail or the Government to enable British Rail to continue to operate a service should the franchisee cease to trade or go into receivership.

(c) Separation of responsibility for infrastructure maintenance and operation would lead to difficulty in implementing major investment projects such as electrification. Such projects involve high initial investment costs with the return of the investment being over a long period of time. If the period and security of the franchise is limited then the franchisee would be reluctant to make the investment.

In a similar way, the through summer Saturday trains to Great Yarmouth could be affected. These are expensive to maintain and outside the summer season have only limited use. There would, therefore, seem little prospect of a private operator running these services. In that situation, with no extra trains being available to provide additional seating capacity between Great Yarmouth and Norwich in the summer, then the only option open to a franchisee would be to limit public access by substantial fare surcharges/reservation fees which would be to the detriment of Great Yarmouth.

(d) It is essential that through ticketing is maintained, including inter-availability on all services. In addition, discount cards for the disabled and o.a.p.s. should be retained and honoured throughout the rail system.

(e) It will be necessary for robust mechanisms to be available to ensure that the interests of operators and passengers are protected in connection with the franchising of stations as well as their possible sale or lease.

(f) There is a need, if privatisation is to succeed, for all concerned, including operators and Councils and other similar organisations, to be able to establish the wider role of railways within an overall transport policy whereby the role of railways can be clearly seen. This particular issue should be addressed now before privatisation proposals are pursued much further.

(ii) That a copy of these comments be forwarded to the local Member of Parliament and his assistance sought in pursuing these with the Secretary of State.

28 October 1992

APPENDIX 42

EVIDENCE SUBMITTED BY MR R HOPE

The Future Prospects for the Railway System in the Light of the Government's Proposals for Privatisation

1. This submission deals specifically with historical and current experience of running railways in ways that relate to those set out in the Government's White Paper *New Opportunities for the Railways* published in July 1992. It does not attempt to describe the structure adopted for railways which are moving from state control towards private ownership, as in Japan and Germany, as the Committee has received evidence from others on this subject. Rather, it attempts to provide background information which is not necessarily included in factual statements from the administrations concerned.

2. My principal qualification for submitting this evidence is 21 years (1970–91) as Editor of *Railway Gazette International,* a journal which is written for and read by railway managers worldwide. I have travelled on the railways of some 70 countries, interviewed their senior executives, and kept closely in touch week by week with moves in several countries towards private ownership of railways.

3. There are actually three distinct, but interwoven, strands in the "privatisation" debate:

* the transfer of operations and assets to private companies;

* separation of managerial control of infrastructure from train operations;

* providing external operators with a legal right of access to the tracks.

All three are embodied in our own Government's proposals for British Rail. I consider them in turn, explain what experience there has been in each case, and draw conclusions.

4. But first, I must point out that the framework which is proposed for BR is entirely without precedent in the 162 years since the first vertically integrated common-carrier railway opened between Liverpool and Manchester in 1830. Neither the intricate (and sometimes devious) arrangements which existed between private companies in the last century, nor the praiseworthy efforts by governments to bring commercial pressures to bear on fossilised state-owned railways in recent years, matches remotely the extraordinary complexity of the framework now proposed in Britain.

Privatisation

5. Until the 1970s, the transfer of a national railway from state to private ownership was virtually unknown. Previously, the trend had been the other way, generally because the railways (like roads) were regarded as part of the national infrastructure which should be under government control.

6. By 1970, the only important exceptions were the USA and Canada, the latter having two competing transcontinental railways of which one was private. However, in Western Europe, Japan, and some other countries outside the communist bloc, there have always been local railways in private ownership. Usually, they serve a specific purpose such as conveying ore from a mine to a port, or commuters into Tokyo.

7. Even the US Government was forced to nationalise the huge but bankrupt Penn Central network in 1976. Long distance passenger trains, reduced to a shadow of a once-vast network, had been nationalised in 1971 under Amtrak; they ran by government directive on the tracks of private railways whose business was now confined to freight. The successful restructuring and sale into the private sector of Conrail (formerly Penn Central) in 1987 was the first major privatisation to take place, if we exclude the much smaller Alaska Railroad in 1985.

8. The example of a successful "privatisation" most frequently quoted is the break-up of Japanese Railways in April 1987. The network was split geographically into six regions that are owned and operated by independent passenger railways known collectively as the JR Group. A seventh operator, JR Freight, owns no main line track, but has access to the six passenger networks on a marginal cost basis.

9. By any reckoning, the break-up of JNR has been very successful. Staff have been shed, and the three JR Group members on the main island of Honshu have moved firmly into profit. Passenger fares have stabilised, more people are using trains, and JR Freight has reversed a long-term downward trend in tonnage carried. However, when relating the Japanese experience to Britain there are some important points to note:

9.1 Despite being required to undertake some grossly unprofitable activities, such as employing tens of thousands of ex-soldiers after World War II, building hopelessly uneconomic branch lines, carrying students at less than 10 per cent of the standard fare, and extending new high speed lines at immense cost, JNR was never allowed to write off debt. When the third world debt crisis struck a decade ago, JNR's borrowings matched those of Brazil and Mexico! Spiralling interest payments made by JNR to the Treasury were simply recycled as further loans to cover the annual deficit. The new JR Group companies were relieved of most of this debt.

9.2 In the run up to "privatisation" JNR shed about half of the 400,000 or so staff employed at the start of the 1980s. Most were simply not needed; although freight services were cut, and a few rural lines closed, JNR effectively achieved a near-doubling of productivity under the threat of privatisation.

9.3 Rail carries 35 per cent of passenger-miles in Japan, against 6 per cent in Britain and up to 12 per cent in Western Europe. The extreme density of population, with its implications for parking and road congestion, puts rail in a totally different position in Japan. Massive sunk investment in high speed inter-city and urban commuter railways allows good profits to be earned from carrying passengers, although subsidy is still required on the three smaller islands.

9.4 And finally, the former JNR railways have not actually been privatised, as all the shares are owned by government. However, it is anticipated that the three Honshu railways, at least, will be successfully floated on the stock exchange in due course.

10. Another country which has made a determined attempt to achieve privatisation is Argentina, but even here only 5,000km (15 per cent) of the network has actually been taken over by a private operator. The background here is a sprawling network that has received minimal investment in the last 40 years. Grossly over-staffed and under-used, the railways are in such poor condition that the government can credibly threaten to close down those parts which private operators refuse to take on.

11. A bidding process is under way, and it seems likely that the main lines at least will survive. Distances are long, and Argentina is a populous and productive country generating substantial freight flows for which a well managed railway could compete on a commercial basis.

12. However, all passenger services (with the exception of commuting into Buenos Aires) were to have ended on 1 August 1992; a last minute reprieve expires in December.

13. The relevance of the Argentine experience as a role model for British Rail might be considered questionable.

Separate management of infrastructure

14. Prior to 1830, railways (more properly called tramways) such as the Stockton & Darlington provided a track on which traders could haul their own wagons. As on canals, it was considered undesirable for track and vehicles to be in common ownership because this created a monopoly.

15. In 1830, with the opening almost simultaneously in the UK and US of prototypes of the railways we know today, vertical integration with infrastructure and trains under common ownership became the norm. The earlier arrangement—which was quite satisfactory for road, water and (much later) air transport—was found to be impractical on rails.

16. Essentially, there are two reasons for this. The first is that, uniquely, the rail vehicle is incapable of independent motion in two dimensions—put simply, one train cannot pass another on a single track. Thus all movement must be under central control. Secondly, there is an intimate relationship between train and track which, to a degree not found in other modes, makes them technically one system. To be effective, they must evolve and develop in close harmony.

17. In recent years, several European countries such as Switzerland have set up accounting systems which separate infrastructure costs from operations. The thinking behind this is that if the Government took responsibility for infrastructure costs, as it does on the roads, and charged a modest fee for each train, then it might be possible to run the trains on a commercial basis.

18. The EC has now required member governments to separate out infrastructure costs so that they become transparent. However, this is primarily so that open access can be implemented (see below).

19. So far, Sweden is the only country to implement fully the separation of infrastructure from train operations, although Germany plans to do so in the longer term. Since 1988, the infrastructure has been managed by Banverket (BV), and the running of trains and stations by Swedish State Railways (SJ). There have been examples of private operation of passenger and freight trains, but as yet they are peripheral. Note, however, that:—

19.1 Both BV and SJ remain under state control, so the transport minister can resolve any disputes without recourse to the courts;

19.2 No attempt is made to recover all BV's costs from the operators, nor do they contribute anything towards investment in new infrastructure. At the last count, about one-third of BV's costs were covered by operators' tolls;

19.3 The background to this development is a sharp rise in rail investment from £60m in 1988–89 to £250m in 1990–91; it is expected to run at the unprecedented levels throughout the 1990s. The objective was not to save public money, but to "sharpen up" SJ management by making its operations commercial, and at the same time allow other operators to come in. Legislation providing for open access and competition between operators is planned.

Rights of Access

20. There are numerous examples of one operator running trains over the tracks of another. It was not uncommon on the last century for a company to obtain access to a city terminus or industrial region by applying to Parliament for "running powers", if voluntary agreement could not be secured.

21. The practice continues today in North America. During the 1980s, new legislation in Canada extended rights for one railway to gain access to an industrial plant over the tracks of a competitor. The purpose is to promote competition between railway operators.

22. In urban railways, there are many examples of through running between different operators. For example, the regional express metro (RER) in Paris is a joint operation by SNCF and the city transport authority RATP. Japanese cities offer numerous examples of through running.

23. The most complex example of shared use is to be found in the Northeast Corridor, the trunk line linking Washington, New York and Boston, which passed into the control of Amtrak in 1976. Here Amtrak trains co-exist with those run by public authorities providing commuter services into the major cities; indeed, some of the services (as in Boston) are run by Amtrak under contract. Freight operators use the Northeast Corridor for access to specific industries, but they have diverted through trains to other routes where posible because of arguments over pathing, charges levied by Amtrak, and the imposition of costly safety measures such as automatic train protection which are appropriate to a busy line carrying 125 mph trains.

24. What is missing from the open access scene is any example of outright competition between passenger train operators on the same tracks. There are one or two places where varying quality is offered to meet different markets—civil servants and typists in the deathless phrase of our Minister for Public Transport. The *Venice Simplon Orient Express* is one example, but this is by voluntary agreement.

25. EC Directive 91/440 makes limited provision for state railways to form partnerships and demand right of access for passenger trains across intervening countries—say, from Italy to Spain through France. We have yet to see how this works in practice.

26. It was a heavy-handed attempt to implement of this directive by Directorate-General IV which almost resulted, earlier this year, in the failure by BR, SNCF, SNCB, NS and DB to order rolling stock for overnight trains to run through the Channel Tunnel. This episode (which is not yet resolved) illustrates graphically some of the difficulties which arise when a company wishing to operate a service of questionable profitability has to warn institutions leasing the rolling stock that it may be faced with a competitor coming in to share the available revenue. This, of course, is the franchise plus open access scenario.

Conclusions

27. There is a general move in the direction of loosening up the traditional structure whereby each country has a national railway which is under the direct control of the transport ministry. This is to be broadly welcomed, given the dismal financial performance of many state railways. It includes various moves towards private ownership and open access. Separation of infrastructure from train operations is sometimes seen as a prerequisite for open access, notably in Europe.

28. Experience suggests that head-on competition between passenger operators sharing the same tracks poses serious difficulties, and is unlkely to work in practice. However, it may be attempted in Sweden. Competition between freight operators appears to tbe easier to handle.

29. The Japanese "privatisation" has been particularly successful in raising quality, lowering fares in real terms, and reducing subsidy. Freight is doing well on a marginal-cost access basis. This could be a good model for Britian, so long as the far weaker position of BR in the transport market is compensated by robust arrangements for investment and subsidy.

30. There is very strong evidence, not least from the results of BR's latest reorganisation, that efficiency is promoted by closely integrating the management of infrastructure with commercial responsibility for train operations. Given that access is also desirable, the best way to proceed is probably to make the prime user of the infrastructure responsible for its upkeep. This does put the prime user in a dominant position, which means that the choice of prime user is essentially a political one involving consideration of social objectives.

1 November 1992

APPENDIX 43

THE AUTOMOBILE ASSOCIATION

Inquiry into British Rail Privatisation

1. INTRODUCTION

The Automobile Association represents the interests of 7.6 million members, many of whom use British Rail services to a lesser or greater extent. The Association does not wish to comment specifically on the benefits or otherwise of rail privatisation. However, the provision of park and ride at railway stations, and the security of cars parked at railway station car parks, are issues of considerable interest and concern to AA members.

2. *Park and Ride*

An essential element of local and regional transport policies is the integration of transport services to provide a flexible and efficient transportation system. The provision of park and ride facilities at railway stations is an essential element of a successful integrated transportation strategy.

Park and ride is the integration of the private car into the public transport system. It encourages car drivers to use public transport, helping to reduce traffic congestion by increasing patronage of public transport.

Many railway stations already operate car parks for rail customers. However, when British Rail is privatised, there are likely to be pressures to achieve short term financial gains by selling off land for development, including existing car parks.

The Association believes that existing car parks at railway stations should be preserved for this essential use, and that the Bill establishing the criteria for privatisation should include a clause to this effect.

3. *Car Park Security*

There are growing concerns at the level of car related crime, particularly theft of and from cars. The Home Office Police Research Group report "Preventing Car Crime in Car Parks" highlights the fact that cars parked in railway station car parks are particularly vulnerable to car theft. This is because the vehicle is often parked for long periods with arrival and departure at predictable times.

In the Fair Trading Act car parking is neither a good nor a service and therefore the driver is not entitled to consumer protection in terms of personal safety or security of the vehicle, in exchange for the parking fee charged.

The Automobile Association has joined with the Association of Chief Police Officers (ACPO) in promoting the Secure Car Park Scheme. The scheme aims to encourage car park operators to provide an optimum level of safety and security in their car parks.

The Association believes that the private operators of British Rail car parks should be encouraged to adopt the Secure Car Parks Scheme. The opportunity should be taken to impose legal requirements of the new owners of British Rail to at least be required to implement car park security measures at station car parks.

4. Conclusion

Car ownership is going to continue to increase for the rest of the decade and into the next century. Many households now totally dependent on public transport will in the future enjoy the flexibility that owning and using a car provides. This could result in a greater decline in public transport, including railway services.

If the decline in public transport is to be reversed, the private car must be integrated into public transport services through the provision of park and ride facilities. The privatisation of British Rail must not result in station car parks being developed for short term financial gains.

Users of station car parks should be assured of an optimum level of personal safety and vehicle security. The opportunity must be taken to impose this requirement on the new owners of railway station car parks.

October 1992

APPENDIX 44

Letter from Mr A J M Hulme

British Rail Privatisation

Having read the White Paper, it is somewhat sobering that the Government prays in aid American Railroads, albeit as freight operators (Para. 7). Am I not right in thinking that their Railroads have tended to operate on a day-to-day basis with no thought for the future and ever increasing freight loads, which have so damaged the track that passenger trains are unable for safety reasons to run at the speeds they attained in the fifties? It is hardly any wonder that Amtrak has so few passenger services left.

I was particulary interested in the question of ticketing arrangements raised in Wednesday's session with British Rail*, particularly interavailability. The major difficulty would seem to be accounting. If an operator suddenly found because of an accident or delay it was taking on another company's passengers, it would want some record to be made so that it could claim the value of the ticket from the first company.

The problem is worse with season tickets which cannot have coupons attached for portions of a journey since they are for unlimited use. I have been racking my brains since then to find a solution, and the answer I propose is the simplest I can think of.

I can only suggest that each franchisee should have a ticket collector on each train, and they should carry a pocket computer terminal to read a metallic strip on the season ticket; the computer terminal would enter those details and the train number onto a coupon to be inserted into the computer terminal; the passenger's entry and exit stations for that train would also be keyed in. The passenger could be asked to sign the coupon and given a copy as a safeguard against fraud.

This operation would be necessary for every ticket **not** issued on the franchisee's ticket stocks; if tickets were common to all operators it would be needed every time. The franchisee would then send in all the coupons to claim from the issuing company or central agency its rightful share of the income.

If this comes about, it is hard to see how privatisation would reduce costs, though it would certainly stimulate the computer industry!

Can I also remind you of the point made in my letter of 30 October to the Department of Transport, regarding the need for drivers to know a particular route. If different companies operate the same route, there

---

*Mins of Evid, 246-iii, 4 November 1992.

may be problems of rostering drivers employed by that company who also "know the road" for the particular journey, whereas at present all train drivers knowing the road are employed by British Rail.

6 November 1992

APPENDIX 45

HAPAG-LLOYD

What should be the aims and objectives of a privatised railway?

What are the attractions for the private sector?

Higher percentage of freight movement by rail over the congested road networks. Higher degree of flexibility in market approach, pricing and package offers. A more commercial approach to importers/exporters with a greater customer service led attitude. Should aim to create a truly effective alternative mode of transport to road which, through greater efficiency, brings cost effective results.

Main attractions for private sector, if you ignore any eventual financial benefit, would be overnight freight delivery with little or no congestion, mechanical or weather barriers. Volume business carried with minimal administration and operational backup.

Choice of operator and a real ability to match differing volumes in separate packages, matching the strengths of the customer and operator to their mutual benefit.

International Deep Sea operators like ourselves carry between 80-85 per cent of their containers within the United Kingdom by road and, therefore, the potential rail market is enormous.

How can freight traffic develop effectively in a primary passenger network?

Freight traffic, and especially maritime freight traffic runs to large degree through the night. This, we assume, is at off peak times and should not affect the passenger network timetables.

This should in fact help to hold down the track cost element for freight traffic and enable a more competitive edge.

Railtrack should be an independent organisation responsible to the Ministry of Transport, away for BR. They should be fully responsible and funded to control all track, signals, safety, property and the timetables of all freight and passenger train services.

All these items should be part of the national transport strategy along with out motorway and road networks, the funding and investment in same being of National concern. There should be no difference in the funding and investment structure of a rail or road network. To the contrary it should work hand in hand as part of a long term strategy to take in subjects such as the environment, energy control, and future developments in the transport arena.

If it were decided that an independant Railtrack organisation should charge for the track maintenance and investment on a tariffed basis then would suggest that it should:—

(a) Ensure that freight trains are discounted for off peak timetables and also minimal requirement for sophisticated signalling equipment which highspeed passenger trains must have.

(b) Such tariffs are set at a maximum utilisation figure to encourage initial usage. If set at low utilisation it will lead initially to uncompetitively high track rates and little or no support. Whatever happens the tariff must be competitive with road vehicle licencing.

If it is expected that a Railtrack authority will be self-financed, then due to our present highly competitive de-regularised road transport industry, the rail network would slowly descent into a decline looking for less and less traffic to take more and more cost.

Under what circumstances might it be possible for track and related infrastructure used only for freight to pass into private hands along with the operational part of the freight business? Could open access and effective Competition be maintained in such circumstances?

From our previous answers you will gather our preference for an independent Railtrack authority directly responsible to the MOT. We feel that to segregate or regionalise the ownership of track and track infrastructure can only lead to inefficiencies and restricted opportunities to the "customer" which in turn leads to higher tariffs and less rail usage.

Also it must be borne in mind that rail is expected to be most competitive over long distances, ie over 150 miles and hence one network for all rail activity would be pre-requisite.

How can rail compete effectively with road transport in carrying freight?

Under what circumstances is the privatisation of freight services likely to increase the attractiveness of transporting freight by rail?

To complete effectively a privatised unit must eradicate past cumbersome structures, basic inefficiencies and old practices. Result will be lower unit cots which it can then market enthusiastically on the basis of more competitive tariffs. Privatised units should develop added value services at terminals for cargo and equipment as well as a local road collection/delivery service at highly competitive prices.

Flexible rating tariffs, specifically customised for targeted cargo flows, allowing volume discounts and round trip utilisation rebates to bring rail in line with the road transport industry.

Just as the abolition of the British Road Services monopoly brought the entrepreneurial spirit to the road industry, the privatisation of BR can do the same for its rail counterpart.

As a major shipping line our investments tend to be directed towards our ships and related equipment. We tend to leave companies directly involved with the Inland Infrastructure to deal with the procurement of rolling stock, etc which we will then utilise. We find that companies directly involved in the operation, truckers, depots, terminals, know their business best and are better suited to service and maintain equipment and rolling stock.

Similar to the chassis and vehicle market in the United Kingdom there could well be a healthy leasing or mid-operator sector who could supply locomotives and rolling stock on contract or spot request.

Will private freight operators be better able to take advantage of the opportunities offered by the Channel Tunnel than BR?

A simple answer to this question is arguably yes. For all the reasons outline in our answer to question (5) we feel that a privatised rail sector would be far better equipped to seize the opportunities presented to us by the opening up of Europe via the Channel Tunnel.

However, as a deep sea operator it is unlikely we would have much requirement for the Channel Tunnel because our vessels will still call direct at main United Kingdom/Continental ports which is far more cost effective.

5 November 1992

APPENDIX 46

MIDLAND MAIN LINE CONSORTIUM

Enquiry: The Future Prospects for the Railway System in the light of the Government's Proposals for Privatisation

Derbyshire County Council, Leicestershire County Council, Northamptonshire County Council, Nottinghamshire County Council and Sheffield City Council

SUMMARY

The attached Paper is an initial response which focuses on two of the questions raised by the Members of the House of Commons Transport Committee.

Question IV

The Consortium welcomes indications given by the Government Ministers towards achieving a level playing field for both rail and road investment.

The Consortium believes that Cost Benefit analysis should always be brought into account in major rail investment schemes as applies already to road schemes.

The Consortium support the idea of making grants available to support the cost of track improvements signalling and power supply. The rail track should be "available" just as a road is available.

The question is raised as to how the benefits from rolling stock investment can be addressed bearing in mind that no such parallel investment is taken into account in road scheme justification. Subsidy should be related to train services (including individual services) not to individual operators/franchises/businesses.

The Consortium suggests that is essential for a long term strategy to be in place for rail investment which is endorsed by Government.

The Consortium believes that immediate steps are necessary to avoid an investment vacuum; the Government must take action ahead of privatisation.

The way in which track costs are to be handled is crucial to whether rail services will survive. There is a case for making direct grants and reducing reliance on service subsidy.

Question VI

Franchises should be let taking into account the wider community benefits of rail services and not solely based on financial performance.

The role and purpose of Railways should be set out.

County Councils should be formally involved in the process of determining rail service provision in the context of overall Planning and Transportation Policies.

Attention to detail on train times, ticketing, local and through service provision must apply to both profitable and subsidised services.

Criteria must be established to assess the community value of a service.

The Public Interest is only served if the wider benefits of rail travel are taken into account at every stage.

1. *The Future Prospects for the Railway System in the Light of the Governments Proposals for Privatisation*

1.1 This Consortium welcomes the Committees enquiry into the future prospects of the railway system in the light of the Governments proposals for privatisation.

1.2 The Government White Paper raises a host of questions about the future operation and development of railways on which answers need to be sought. This Consortium however would wish to draw the Committees attention to two areas of major concern, Investment and Franchising. We are therefore specifically addressing questions (iv) and (vi). In so doing we do touch upon issues raised in the light of the other questions.

2. *The Government role in subsidy and investment? In what circumstances will cost benefit approval be appropriate, and what criteria could be used for future rail investment?*

2.1 The Committee invited the Consortium to give evidence in February 1991 on the independent study into future investment on the Midland Main Line. This demonstrated that there was a financial case for electrification but also showed a much stronger case when cost benefit analysis was used in the same way that is applied to highway schemes. The Consortium has from that time pressed the Government to look more closely at the case for a level playing field between road and rail investment and for that to be applied to both urban and inter-urban services. Recent statements by Ministers that the Government is now seking such an approach to transport investment are warmly welcomed by this Consortium.

2.2 As the Committee will be aware there are a number of inconsistencies in the treatment of transport investment appraisals. Road investment takes into account user and non-user benefits, rail investment on supported services (ie Regional Railways and Network SouthEast) may take into account non-user benefits but NOT user benefits. InterCity has been precluded from taking into account any indirect benefits; investment justification relying largely on direct benefits to users which may be redeemed through increased fares. The fact that rail passengers pay a fare at the point of use has meant that British Rail has been encouraged to maximise revenue and in effect price off demand. Whilst this may make commercial sense it has the consequence of losing wider social and economic benefits.

2.3 In the Midland Main Line Study it was assumed that fares would remain at existing levels (1989) and in so doing the Financial Net Present Value (NPV) of the preferred electrification strategy was £2m at an 8 per cent rate of return. However the NPV of the social cost benefits (user and non-user) amounted to £80m. Therefore failure to secure that investment loses a very much greater benefit to the Community than the financial figures suggest. Road Schemes have always been judged on these wider benefits because there is no payment at the point of use and users do not therefore pay directly for the benefits obtained.

2.4 One of the main reasons for advocating investment in the Midland Main Line was to support economic generation in the East Midlands and Sheffield. To meet that objective it is important to ensure that both non-user benefits and user benefits are taken into account. That is why this Consortium has argued previously that it is essential to establish a mechanism for taking into account external benefits on InterCity investment—the commercial part of the passenger Railway.

2.5 It is incongruous to apply different criteria to the provision of a service by a particular business sector. For example to apply a different approach to commuter services south of Bedford to those from Northamptonshire stations simply because the former is part of Network SouthEast and the latter is served by InterCity. It is equally inconsistent to suggest that a different justification could be used for Leicester-Sheffield-Manchester service as part of a Trans-Pennine Strategy because it would be part of the supported railway (Regional Railways) compared with Leicester-Sheffield-Leeds because it is part of the commercial railway (InterCity).

2.6 Only the Government can take an overall view on transport investment. Not only should comparable criteria be used for all modes (road and rail) to establish priorities for investment but also to capture the real value of each project to the nation as a whole.

2.7 The introduction of a Track Authority would appear to open up a means of taking such benefits into account. In simple terms enhancement of the Railway could be placed on the same footing as Roads. A grant system could be established to represent the value of the investment which in turn would be reflected in lower charges to rail operators—the future users of the tracks. The Consortium recognises however that to achieve a level playing field is not that simple. The conventional approach to road schemes values three benefits namely, time savings, accident reduction and changes in vehicle operating costs. (In any assessment time savings dominate over other benefits—90 per cent in the case of trunk road schemes). Highway appraisal also rests on asumptions essentially related to the diversion and redistribution of traffic which results from a new or improved road. No account is taken as to whether such investment will itself genernate more travel demand. There is no control as such assumed over traffic volumes or travel costs.

2.8 Rail investment has not relied on any assumed growth of travel. Whilst that may be an ingredient, account is also taken of the change in demand generated by an improvement in the rail service itself, and this in turn is overridden by the direct business benefit to the railways of a particular scheme. Thus as explained above the railways have to attract more passengers to justify investment but if necessary these can be priced off to achieve a required financial rate of return. To gain an equitable basis for investment decisions and to enable proper comparisons to be made it will be essential to take a new and compatible approach to both road and rail appraisal. It needs to begin by taking a view on what would maximise the social benefit.

2.9 On road schemes national forecasts of traffic growth imply that there will be investment in new and additional vehicles but that is not something which is addressed directly as part of individual scheme appraisal. On railways the capacity to meet a given demand is not soley that of the track but also the number size and type of trains that can be run.

2.10 Rail investment has been largely driven by rolling stock replacement benefits. The Midland Main Line appraisal showed that electrification had benefits over diesel haulage which were intrinsically bound up with the means of traction and the trains formed a major part of the investment equation. Not only has the cost of new trains been a very large element but operating savings from more advanced trains has equally played a determinant part. It is not possible on a railway to assume that upgrading the track, the signalling and the power supply would by itself attract rail operators to purchase and run new trains. There would be no purpose in the Track Authority securing major improvements unless it can be assured that rail companies will be able to respond.

2.11 The Government must address the social benefit of both infrastructure and rolling stock investment.

2.12 The Midland Line Study followed conventional practice in assessing the passenger services, the Consortium is however becoming increasingly aware of the barriers towards attracting freight movement. The level playing field must apply here as well. There are social benefits in transferring freight to rail wherever possible—these are lost again because total costs fall on the user in a way does not apply to a road haulier. The method of passing on track costs is crucial. At present Railfreight services appear to pay the marginal costs of using track which is primarily provided for passenger services. Railtrack may find it necessary to change on a more overt basis. This could well be justified from the point of view of the railway as a self contained mode, however it could further disadvantage freight by rail if as many commentators suggest road hauliers do not bear the same direct cost burden of the track (namely the roads) which they use.

2.13 Subsidy is an emotive term. Some distinctions need to be drawn. If a level playing field is to be addressed then there will be public funds which should be directed towards infrastructure costs. The expenditure by Government on road construction is not seen as being as subsidy albeit that it is public expenditure. The rules should be similar for rail investment. Ideally a grant system is needed for transport infrastructure which could be applied to both rail and road projects. It does appear that the Government is thinking along these lines with grants to Railtrack, however until more is known about how that will work it is not possible to comment constructively.

2.14 The Consortium has no quarrel with the Governments position whereby subsidy as such should relate to service provision. In essence that is now the Public Service Obligation is perceived at present. That however is Business related (Regional Railways and Network South-East). Under the new regime such financial support should be service related regardless of operator. Such funding ought to reflect the value of the service provided to the Community. That may not necessarily be addressed on a network basis; essentially it ought to ensure two things, one is that the user and non-user benefits are maximised and that secondly the less tangible contribution of a rail service to the structure of a community protected. The level of subsidy and by the same token the scope for profitability on a rail service will be dictated by the level of track costs. Much depends on how that is to be handled. There is a case for grant aiding the track to make it on a par with road provision so as to ensure that the subsidy element required for a particular service is related to the day to day running costs of the service. The issue of rolling stock investment is again a matter which must be addressed in this context.

2.15 The Governments task is to set a framework which will offer a climate of confidence in which rail investment can be generated. It should be recognised that the larger part of such investment consists of renewals and upgrading the existing system. Other European countries plan rail investment with a clear cut understanding between the railways and Government on medium and long term strategies. No such Government endorsement has been forthcoming in this country. British Rails long term vision has received no such backing. In France and elsewhere investment is also related to overall quality of service objectives. In this country no such relationship has been applied. Investment projects are taken one by one with little heed to any overall coherent strategy.

2.16 One of the objectives must be to open up wider sources of finance for rail investment but it must be emphasised that that will only be achieved is there is clear Government endorsement for a programme for railway development. That also means providing a new mechanism, to replace the present External Financing Limit applied to British Railways.

2.17 The immediate challenge is to ensure that the structural changes in the Railways do not in themselves create an investment vacuum but that new criteria are established quickly to overcome the otherwise inevitable hiatus and permit investment approvals ahead of privatisation. Already short term improvement on the Midland Main Line (which at a low cost would improve the Inter-City journey times) has been deferred. It is also thought that track maintenance is being deferred and this could give rise to the service being slowed down.

3. *How should franchises operate so as to maximise the public interest, both for profitable and subsidised services.*

3.1 From the earlier part of the Paper it will be realised that this Consortium does not believe that railways stand alone as a mode of travel. That means that he public interest is best served by a railway system which behaves in a manner to maximise the benefit of its services to the whole community taking into account economic social and environmental benefits.

3.2 It is recognised that this must be achieved within justifiable limits on expenditure. It is also acknowledged that it is no easy task to effectively address how many of these benefits which do not accrue directly to the railways can be recognised in relation to any individual service or group of services. However it is vital that some attempt is made to set out criteria which can be used as a measure against which all involved can judge the value of a service.

3.3 It is necessary to determine the role and purpose of railways. At present no such definition exists and supported services appear to be somewhat arbitrarily evolved with the Public Service Obligation as the overriding parameter governing service provision. In the new regime the opportunity should be taken for rail services to be promoted in the context of the wider economic planning and transport policies. It is the Non-Metropolitan County Councils that are able to take this broader view and the facility should be established whereby they are able to include in their plans the train services they require to meet their local requirements. The County Councils in the East Midlands have already demonstrated their ability to collaborate with each other on a regional basis. The Rail Regulator and the Track Authority should be given a statutory responsibility to take into account the Lane use plans and Transportation Strategies of the County Authorities. In effect a relationship should be set up similar to that of the Metropolitan Passenger Transport Authorities.

3.4 The Public Interest is not served solely by adherence to finanical targets. It is vital that there is an affordable and reliable rail service which is both comprehensive and readily accessible to the customer. This requires attention to detail. In the East Midlands the Ivanhoe and Robin Hood Line projects are both good examples of how local rail services can be revived. Their success will depend on trains running at right times, on connections with other services, including Inter-City trains, through ticketing arrangements etc. In recent years some local services have been disadvantaged in favour of more long distance trains; it is important to keep a balance of interest. Much will depend on how track paths are allocated. Franchisees must be able to meet local requirements and be obliged to plan services in relation to other Franchises.

3.5 To encourage success it will be vital to ensure that Franchises are let for substantial periods of time, a minimum of 10 years is likely to be necessary. Certainly much larger than the three to five years applied for example to bus contracts.

21 October 1992

APPENDIX 47

ASEA BROWN BOVERI, ABB TRANSPORTATION LTD.

The Future Prospects for the Railway System in the light of the Government's Proposals for Privatisation

A. GENERAL

1. ABB Transportation Ltd. (ABB) welcomes the opportunity to respond to the Select Committee's questions about the government's plans for privatisation of the main line railway system. ABB Transportation Ltd. is a member of the Railways Industry Association (RIA) and agrees with the general remarks contained in RIA's submission to the Transport Committee*. RIA's submission necessarily takes an industry-wide viewpoint but ABB also supports RIA's specific comments in respect of rolling stock procurement. The basic situtation is set out below in two extracts from the summary of the RIA submission.

2. "i. ... The fundamental danger is that the vital need for continuing investment—in both rolling stock and track, signalling and electrification infrastructure—will be lost amid continuing political debate and

*Printed Evidence, page 258.

organsational uncertanties about the new railway administrative structures and the passage of the Rail Privatisation Bill." *(see paras 1–4, 11–13 of the RIA submission)*.

3. "iv. There are real opportunities for new private sector activity in the railway supply industry: particularly leasing of rolling stock, and the scope for large scale exeternalisation of railway maintenance and engineering functions. But even these are constrained by risks of institutional obstruction. Leasing is at risk because short franchise lives do not provide adequate guarantees to the asset owner and because of Treasury concerns about front-loading public sector expenditure with leasing provisions; private sector maintenance is critically dependent of there being no hiatus in the contractual activity as British Rail is phasesd out and Railtrack is phased in." *(see paras 9–10, 24–26 of the RIA submission)*.

B. PRESENT MARKET

4. ABB Transportation Ltd. is one of Europe's largest manufacturers and repairers of railway rolling stock and equipment. With a turnover of more than £500m, it employs some 6,000 persons at 6 locations in Derby, Crewe and York. Organisationally, the company operates as two distinct groups, Rail Vehicle and Customer Support, with further project/product centred sub-divisions.

5. Crewe Works is focused on rail vehicle maintenance, with a cost-effective organisation. Only about 50 per cent of the required orders for 1993 are place to date and any significant change of strategy by BR concerning order placement, would obviously have rapid impact.

6. Derby Works is producing the new Central Line tube trains for London Underground and a derivative design for the Waterloo & City Line. Work continues through to the end of 1994. London Underground has indicated that any order for Jubilee Line trains will be placed with GEC Alsthom, and the next major opportunity for tendering, for Northern Line trains, is not expected for some years because of public funding constraints. Meanwhile, until 1995 there is a refurbishment programme for Metropolitan Line trains. Shortage of work will appear in mid-1994.

7. York Works was totally refurbished and re-equipped during the late 1980s to meet Network SouthEast's (NSE) projected vehicle requirements through to the next century, to become the most modern integrated manufacturing site in Europe of whole vehicle production of diesel and electric multiple units and will be a centre of excellence for bodyshells. It has a maximum capacity of over 400 vehicles per year, but because of NSE cut-backs in ordering of new trains and the continuing public expenditure contraints, it is today operating at below 50 per cent of its capacity, including all types of NSE currently on order. Production of new-generation Networker vehicle for SE London and Kent continues until mid-1994. Shortage of work will appear within a year from now.

8. There are no orders to guarantee production at York Works beyond that date, even though the Networker is seen by many railway managers to offer an attractive "universal" vehicle well suited for further orders of electric communter trains, capable of running under the wires (eg on London Tilbury Southend) or on third-rail electrification (eg Kent Coast) or both (Thameslink 2000).

9. The commercial objective of ABB Transportation Ltd. is to offer a cost-effective range of vehicles for different travel markets. The vehicles are, ideally, high standardised in bogies, bodyshell and technical equipment to reduce design, construction, maintenance and operating costs, but will offer great flexibitiy in internal fixtures and fittings to meet the important differences in specification for passengers that may be sought by different operators.

10. ABB Transportation Ltd. is already competing successfully in the rail maintenance market, and supports the Government's proposals to transfer British Rail's maintenance function to the private sector.

11. ABB Transportation Ltd. believes that the present constraints on rolling stock investment, imposed because of public expenditure limitations, are highly detrimental to the vehicle supply industry in the short and longer term. The all-to-familiar British cycle of boom and bust, with the economy in servere recession with few new orders on the horizon, increases the risks currently faced:

— industry managers in Britain cannot forecast reliably how and when they may next be able to plan for production of a new fleet of trains,

— insufficient continuity of orders create the twin risks of lower morale within the workforce (many of whom are highly skilled) and a managerial deterrent to research and develop the latest technology, with the medium term risk of Britih industry becoming uncompetitive with its mainland European counterparts.

12. Clearly the present market for ABB Transportation Ltd. products in Britain is wholly within the public sector whose ability to spend in ultimately a function of Government's willingness to invest in the railway system.

13. The Government's own proposals for rail privatisation are therefore a critical factor for ABB Transportation Ltd's forward planning. It *could* be beneficial, releasing the rolling stock industry from the staightjacket of public sector funding. But *unless* the ground rules are clearly defined and are designed to assist positive decision making in a "rail" future and positive investment divisions, the onset of rail privatisation will at the very least increase the commercial uncertainties faced by ABB Tansportation Ltd., and in the worst case force the company to close plants and get rid of unique competence. As already stated, ABB agrees with

the general and specific points mady by RIA in its submission, and does not propose to duplicate those comments in its own reply to the Committee.

C. TRANSPORT COMMITTEE'S SPECIFIC QUERIES

14. We now turn to the specific questions posed in your Committee's letter of 20 October. We reply in summary form to those, in the same sequences as the questions.

Q. 15. *What are the implications for rail investment programmes of the privatisation plans and any uncertainty surrounding the future of rail services?*

16. *Greater administrative complexity:*

— on lines where modernisation is necessary for infrastructure *and* rolling stock, the greater fragmentation of railway administration and separation of responsibilities for operations and infrastructure will conflict with the need for an integrated investment getting best value from all elements of the package;

— the imposition of additional regulatory bodies will create a new source of delay for investment decision making;

— meanwhile, there is a serious risk of a moratorium on new investment while new legislation and all the new administrative structures are put in place; a 2-year investment blight will be extremely detrimental for ABB Transportation Ltd, with no "new-build" production in hand after 1994; orders for an existing or slightly modified vehicle would need to be placed by Spring 1993 to ensure continuity of production.

17. **ABB Transportation Ltd concludes that, throughout the transition period, BR must be able to purchase rolling stock according to its own normal criteria for procurement.**

18. *Franchising consequences:*

— The Franchising Authority will impose some quality requirements on successful franchisees, but the experience of the bus industry after deregulation shows that there will be strong inclination to do the minimum necessary to meet the quality standards—many analysts consider that ordering new rolling stock will be very low priority for most franchisees. For new entrants to the public transport market, they will be taking on board more than enough risk in operating the service without immediately venturing to acquire new or additional trains;

— a worst case, with a line already needing new investment but no one coming forward, might result in a vicious circle of fewer passengers and a diminishing case for new investment; which is opposite to safety, quality of service and environmental benefits which have high priority in the White Paper on rail privatisation;

— potential franchisees will wish to fix as many costs as possible; if they can lease the rolling stock, from industry, with maintenance included, this will remove a major area of uncertainty. This on the other hand calls for a sufficiently long franchise period;

— it is reasonable to conclude that in many cases, franchisees will tend to go for existing or possibly refurbished rolling stock. This would inevitably lead to a fall off in the rate of investment in new rolling stock.

19. ABB Transportation Ltd believes that there are two practical initiatives which should be agreed as a matter of urgency by Government in advance of the main legislative process for rail privatisation:

— there should be a series of strategic objectives defined for the rail system, rolled forward yearly by the Department of Transport and debated in Parliament, which will provide a focus for longer term investment priorities;

— the rules under which leasing deals for new equipment are countenanced for both public and private sector bodies must be made as attractive as possible, to kick-start a new generation of rail investment at the earliest possible date.

Q. 20. *What arguments are there for switching immediately to a regime of rolling stock leasing for all operators, including BR?*

21. *Consumer benefits:*

— The strongest argument is that it will encourage early investment in new equipment, bringing the benefits of lower operating costs and enhanced service quality and reliability for passengers. As the RIA submission states in paragraph 31, "we have to warn passengers who are waiting for their next train that none are due for delivery after mid-1994 and that, beyond that date, no trains have been ordered for the London Tilbury Southend, Kent Coast and other lines where trains are life expired".

— It has been proved that new rolling stock increases the number of passengers using the train service, eg when the Class 158 was introduce in Scotland, passenger revenues increased by + 20 per cent.

— New rolling stock designs are to the latest safety standards. No trains have yet been ordered to begin the replacement of those vehicles condemned in the recent Cannon Street rail crash report. That report also indicates that in due course all "Mark 1" types of BR rail vehicles will need to be replaced, since their structural design is inherently weaker than the modern generations of integrally-bodied vehicles.

22. ABB Transportation Ltd would be able to continue production of its Networker fleet from mid-1994 to meet the immediate need for 100 vehicles to replace those identified for urgent replacement in the Cannon Street crash report. Terms and conditions are agreed in a valid option between BR and ABB Transportation Ltd. The "universal' Networker design is fully capable of meeting future customer requirements of short and long distance commuter lines.

23. ABB Transportation Ltd therefore unreservedly supports the proposition that there should be an immediate switch to a regime of rolling stock leasing for all operators, including British Rail. But the hoped-for benefits will not be secured unless guarantees are in place for the security of assets, and unless HM Treasury rescinds its ruling that a leasing package counts fully in the first year against the public sector borrowing requirement.

24. Leasing addresses the problem of pre-delivery finance and gives cashflow benefits to the operator of the service: introducing modern vehicles into service often results in increased passenger volumes and revenucs, while the operator can match his lease repayments to the income stream.

Q. 25. *Will the British rolling stock market become more open to foreign competitors? What differences are there between British and Continental operators' rolling stock purchasing?*

26. The European Community rules on competitive tendering are already applied within Britain to new rolling stock orders, so there would at first sight be no legal change in the procurement;

— of far greater impact are the underlying administrative and political priorities attached by different European countries to their railway system: the well-documented investment record of the French, German and Dutch national railways has guaranteed a strong home market and a base on which to seek competitive orders abroad;

— British manufacturers already face an uneven playing field compared to their competitors in Europe, who benefit from supporting functions such as Eurofima and we would like to see the same benefits applied in the UK.

— the basic difference between the British and mainland European purchasing regimes is the continental railway administrations' ability to plan further ahead, eg the TGV programme in France. The result is a larger order base, permitting amortisation of railway supply industry costs over longer production runs and a greater incentive for advanced technical development.

— lack of investment during the privatisation process will undermine UK production capacity.

27. ABB Transportation Ltd supports the RIA proposals for a "Railplan" strategic framework to map— and shape—the long term objectives of the railway system in Britain.

28. In conclusion, we must thank you again for giving us this opportunity to assist your Committee's inquiry. We are preparing a detailed response to the Government's document on franchising, and should be pleased to let you have copies when it is ready, if that would also benefit your Committee.

5 November 1992

APPENDIX 48

INSTITUTION OF MECHANICAL ENGINEERS

Rail Privatisation

We are grateful for the opportunity to submit evidence to the Transport Committee on its enquiry entitled "The Future Prospects for the Railway System in the Light of the Government's Proposals for Privatisation". We are aware that responses have been made by the Railway Industry Association and by the operator (BR) so we are pleased to be able to offer this professional view from the IMechE as a learned society. This view is based on the Government's White Paper of July 1992 and the consultation document on passenger service franchises of October 1992.

IMechE seeks (in this context) to encourage the development of excellence in transport systems in general and, through its Railway Division, in rail based systems in particular. This means improving the overall quality of rail services and in particular their

— safety

— service reliability

— comfort and speed

— environmental impact

— total perceived cost

through the good offices of properly qualified and trained engineers who are encouraged to undertake "Continuing Professional Development".

The achievement of these objectives can be encouraged in both the public and private sectors by an appropriately designed commercial framework in which risk, opportunity and rewards are all recognised, measurable and controllable. The White Paper and subsequent consultation document on the franchising of passenger rail services have made progress in outlining the framework but we believe that the proposals require

— greater clarity of objectives and responsibilities

— greater simplicity in the arrangements between Rail Regulator, Franchising Authority and Franchisees

— recognition of non-user benefits of rail transport and a commitment to incorporate a proportion of these in franchising arrangements

— an undertaking from BR and Government that the planning of an investment in rolling stock, stations and route infrastructure will continue at an agreed level while the Government's proposals are progressed through Parliament

— the earliest possible establishment of Railtrack or an alternative with a view to that body taking over and developing the route infrastructure investment programme against appropriate performance incentives

— franchises of sufficient term to encourage similar long term planning and investment strategies on the part of franchisees in rolling stock and other equipment

We are particularly concerned that the present uncertainty has already created a vacuum in planning and investment. The resulting loss of quality on the railway, of the already diminished industrial base and of skilled engineers and operators will be impossible to make good in the following years if this continues, not to mention the increased difficulty in attracting top school and university leavers to this key industry.

The Institution has expressed its concern at the general level of Research and Development within UK industry and the effect of this vacuum is to reduce it further in this industry. This will affect not only short term Research and Development but will cause long term fragmentation of any output from this sector of engineering. Provision must be made, both short and long term, if UK Limited is to survive in this field.

Rail transport is a more fuel efficient and environmentally acceptable transport mode than road. This should be recognised and utilised by encouraging the development of a viable railway system operating within a co-ordinated transport policy.

October 1992

APPENDIX 49

CLYDESDALE RAIL ACTION GROUP

The Transport Committee Inquiry—Rail Privatisation

1. CONSULTATION

We had great difficulty getting to see the recent consultation paper on rail franchising.

2. STATE RAILWAYS OR PRIVATE RAILWAYS?

Our rail services (in our area) provided by the State System are extremely poor mainly due to Ministerial Directives which have interpreted Acts of Parliament in very perverse and damaging ways. Private operator franchising should improve matters but it is difficult to see private rail operators being able to compete with road transport as long as the roads are provided below cost by state funding as a social service. Their must be a level playing field and if the railways are to be privatised then the road system must also be privatised, i.e. sell off to private owners every yard of public road so that the benefits of private sector management and investment can be brought to the road transport system.

3. COMMUNITIES EXCLUDED FROM FINANCIAL SUPPORT

Rail franchising could provide a new start and it is essential that the support system for socially and economically necessary services is reviewed so that those lines excluded from support (outside the PSO or PTE areas) can be considered on their own merits. Otherwise franchising will not bring the maximum benefits.

4. SALE OF STATIONS

We can see no advantage in selling stations to the private sector. The private sector can already rent parts of stations and develop businesses and shops etc. The only reason the private sector would want to buy stations is to close the railway and sell off high value sites for profitable property development. This would mean closure of our main city termini and the British public would not stand for it which is why it was not in the election manifesto. The Act of Parliament must contain a guarantee against closure of stations for property development. However rail franchisers may want to build additional new stations which they could own outright and build to the much higher safety standards now required.

5. TIMETABLES

The timetable must continue as an ALL-STATION, ALL SYSTEM timetable with all operators contributing to the cost and guaranteeing the timetable to last for the normal specified period. Anything less would make the rail system useless for business and long distance travel and would result in major financial losses for the franchisers. It would be even worse than the drastic run down seen in the bus and coach industry. Of course the franchisers could publish their own-line timetable in addition to the national timetable . . . . just as British sub sectors do at present.

6. TICKETS

There must be through and interchangeable ticketing otherwise the system will just fall apart commercially. It was possible to achieve this 80 years ago and must be achievable now in the age of computers. Note that British Rail has been very successful at the marketing of tickets and British Rail ticket policies have been emulated on many foreign rail systems. This of course would require the continuance of the railcard, saver, cheap day and return tickets which exist for a commercial reason and which rail users will not (politically) allow franchisers to discontinue so it might as well be made clear in the Act of Parliament right from the start.

7. GOVERNMENT CONTROL

Strong government control, as in times of Victorian Values and the British Empire, is called for to protect the profits of the franchisers from petty cost cutting. It must be remembered that the first railway boom of the 1840's ran out of steam and was only revived by Government legislation for cheap fares for the working classes. The ensuing increase in passenger volume brought about the golden age of commercial railway operation in Britain.

8. REGULATOR

There must be a strong regulator with teeth. The public demands it. Railway services must not be closed without public or Parliamentary consent. At present we have the very high quality of the statutory authority for rail users, the Transport Users' Consultative Committees, well respected, with very high standards of independence, knowledge and integrity. Unfortunately British Rail and the Transport Ministers treat them with contempt. The answer is to give the TUCC's real powers.

9. PROMOTION OF COMPETITION

Your document states that one of the Regulator's duties will be to promote competition. This presumably includes the promotion of fair competition with road transport which would include provision, at State expense, of reinstatement of more customer "outlets" (stations), competitive rail routes (closed by Beeching as "duplicate routes of wasteful competition)" and new cut-offs analogous to the Dornoch Road Bridge.

10. ROLLING STOCK PROVISION

Forcing British Rail to provide rolling stock for franchisers is just too facile. It will lead to the demise of the manufacturing industry, no new building, outdated and worn out stock and ultimately either mass closure of services or fare levels increases for higher than anything we can imagine at present when, eventually, new stock has to be built abroad. Any franchiser with adequate commercial standing should be able to build his own stock or lease or buy from private industry. This policy would prevent the impending disaster of no buses in the bus industry from repeating itself on the railways.

11. CUSTOMER SERVICE

Privatisation could be a benefit to the customer but only if the Government recognises that the people want a good public transport service operating seven days a week, nearly 24 hours per day and connecting as many cities, towns, suburbs and villages as is practicable. The uneconomic "tail" must be financially supported otherwise the "tail" will get chopped off right up to the head and finally nose. The same would happen to the road system if it was not funded by the tax payer as a social service. Railways must get equal treatment whether private or public.

12. PREPARATIONS FOR U-TURNS

While privatisation could improve the railways the British People do not have complete confidence in either the motives or methods of privatisation. After the string of recent ideological disasters perpretated on the British economy and people it may be prudent to prepare a built in system for completely reversing rail privatisation should it not prove a success. Having said that we do hope that rail privatisation will be done competently and that it will be success because we badly need a change for the better.

November 1992

APPENDIX 50

Memorandum from Mr R Arnott

The Future Prospects for the Railway System in the light of the Governments Proposal for Privatisation

INTRODUCTION

My strengths lie in the operation of a railway and my answers will inevitably be influenced by my operating background from yard master/station master; district, regional and finally chief operating manager of British Railways. Nowadays with the sectorisation of BR there is no recognisable operating department. It used to carry sole responsibility for putting every class of train on to the running line, their efficient running and safety. On the old Great Western Railway the head of this department was called Superintendent of the Line, a descriptive title of his responsibilities. Privatisation will require reinstatement of the functions of the operating department.

1. *"What should be the aims and objectives of a privatised railway? What are the attractions for the private sector?*

Before the first world war there were close on thirty sizeable privately owned railway companies which in 1923 were merged into four large companies. All had the aim of making a profit and being able to pay a dividend. To achieve the aim meant providing a quality of service to compete with each other and with other forms of transport. The latter aspect became increasingly important as road transport developed in the 1930s. The same aims and objectives would be applicable today with incentives such as prestige and on-train advertising.

2. *"Is there any conflict between the principle of open access and the granting of exclusive franchises?*

There can never be open access to a railway in the sense of a car leaving a garage and joining a road because a railway can only operate as a disciplined transport mode. Franchises are the first step in the disciplined approach, ensuring that franchise holders recognise what is required in the provision of staff and rolling stock regarding paths (slots), performance and safety.

3. *"Who should do the strategic planning for our railways and how can different interests be co-ordinated? For example can freight develop effectively on a primarily passenger network?*

Strategic planning should be carried out by a section within Railtrack, maintaining close liaison with the Department of Transport to facilitate sensible overall planning of surface transport requirements, particularly where new infrastructure is required.

The particular question posed is more to do with track utilisation as it used to be organised when the operating department had full jurisdiction over the planning of all train services and their scheduling. Although there has been some track revovery, it is certainly not anything like proportionate to the massive reduction in freight traffic. Admittedly passenger trains are now faster, but this should be a challenge to improve freight rolling stock speeds and tests have been made up to 90 mph. When the volume of freight traffic was significant many freight trains had a maximum speed of 45 mph when passenger trains were running up to 100 mph. There will of course continue to be more line capacity available during the night hours.

Maybe the reinstatement or new provision of some long running loops may be shown to be necessary in long term forecasting, and this should be registered with the Department as soon as identified.

4. *What will be the Government's role in subsidy and investment? In what circumstances will cost-benefit appraisal be appropriate and what criteria should be used for future rail investment?*

I would prefer to link this question with the next one.

5. *Railtrack, the track authority, will charge all operators "commercial rates" for track use. What principles should be used to set these charges.*

In the early part of this century W. M. Ackworth said that rail charges should be based on what the traffic can bear. Putting it another way they should not be what the traffic cannot bear. The principle is still good today but circumstances are vastly different—no longer is rail the dominant surface transport mode which enabled those earlier railways to charge by a multiplicity of products and produce a total revenue made up of differing profit margins. Todays freight charges are almost exclusively on a train load basis, passenger charges by class of travel and time of day.

"Commercial charges" ought to mean charges sufficient to enable Railtrack to cover operating costs, maintenance costs and renewals. Major new works would require discussion with government on their justification. The danger of requiring commercial charges to meet the aforementioned objectives must be the possibility of frightening off potential users other than subsidised services. It is well known that a railway thrives on good track utilisation because of the level of fixed costs so it is important that fares should not dissuade people from travelling by train. There must be an element of subsidisation now for track and signalling in respect of the PSO services, and it may be necessary to increase this if full commercial charging would wreck intercity travel. Cost-benefit comes very much into the argument, after all these years there are still no established guide lines on the wider advantages of rail. One thing about privatisation would be that no longer could it be argued that rail corridors are exclusively operated and benefits exclusively enjoyed.

What must not happen is Railtrack having to permit arrears of maintenance in order "to charge what the traffic can bear."

It has happened too often in the past on BR and always leads to a deterioration in the quality of service.

6. *How should franchises operate so as to maximise the public interest, both for profitable and subsidised services?*

The profitable services should not cause any difficulty with franchise holders anxious to build on that popularity and profitability. They will ensure that their rolling stock is clean and well presented together with a good quality of on-train service and information. Subsidised services could cause a problem if franchise holders are simply content to pocket the subsidy with minimum effort to improve the quality of service or even maintain present standards. A procedure needs to be devised where improvements are costed, and subsidised if they are deemed worthwhile to attract additional passengers or at least prevent deterioration in service levels leading to loss of revenue.

7. *What arguments are there for switching immediately to a regime of rolling stock leasing for all operators including BR. What are the White Paper's implications for BR's on-going rolling stock investment programme?*

The problems which have been encountered by BR in acquiring much needed rolling stock due to the present rules certainly point to the desirability of a leasing regime being brought into operation as soon as practicable. This should also be of benefit to manufacturers in being able to plan future production on a more even basis than the present uncertainty.

Regarding the White Paper, I have only seen summaries of this in the technical journals, which did not contain any specific reference to rolling stock. However if the question relates to the philosophy of the White Paper rather than rolling stock matters *per se* then in my view this can only bring more uncertainty into the rolling stock programme which would be eased by the introduction of leasing.

8. *How is the value of stations to be assessed and what will be the relationship between a privately owned station and BR's operation of trains therefrom?*

The first part of the question is a matter for those with specialised knowledge and experience of property and valuation. Many stations occupy prime city sites and privatisation could do a lot to make them more attractive to the non-traveller, as is the case on the continent and at Gatwick airport where many Crawley residents use it for shopping. The new Liverpool Street station is a step in that direction. A completely free hand in development is of course never possible with the need not to impinge on the efficient handling of trains.

The operation of the stations however raises many interesting considerations. For a start the owners could set up ticket offices on the lines of railway travel agents, or the franchise holders could rent space there. Is there a future for ticket collectors? For many years there has been complete open access to the main line platforms at Paddington and I visualise that on-train checks will become the norm. Train indicators are now operated directly from the new signalling control centres and Railtrack must have the authority to locate these at the most effective locations on platforms. Safety used to be an important consideration at station in regard to passengers joining trains and doors being safely closed before departure, though this has had less attention in recent years with the virtual, or actual, demanning of station platforms. On the other had it can be argued that power operated doors have made the platform involvement in safety less applicable. In my view main line trains must carry sufficient on train staff for ticket checks, information, safe joining and alighting at stations, right away indication to driver. Network South-East would continue to require station checks to detect and prevent fraud.

November 1992

APPENDIX 51

G E BUSINESS SERVICES

Railway Liberalisation—Submission to the Transport Select Committee

I enclose two copies of a submission for the above Select Committee concerning the position and function of the Regulator and the potential to develop a Track Authority which could contain elements of competition within its strategic responsibilities for the operation of all rail track, both passenger and freight.

In addition I have tried to answer the questions posed in your press release of the 16 July last.

My own credentials are as follows:—

I am 49 years old and have worked in most aspects of transport for all my working life. I have a significant up-to-date working knowledge of the current issues in Regulation, specifically in the Electricity Supply Industry.

My academic qualifications include BA (Hons) Business Studies (Transport Specialisation); a Post Graduate Diploma in Transport Planning. I am currently undertaking research into Railway Regulation for a PhD at the University of Central England at Birmingham, under the supervision of Professor John Hibbs OBE. I am also a corporate Member of the Chartered Institute of Transport.

I have produced papers on the concept of Railway Privatisation commencing with a paper in the Institute Journal in January 1984. The latest paper was presented at a Public Issue Conference on Railway Privatisation on the 29 October last which drew data from both the papers submitted here.

I will be prepared to expand the themes contained here if required, and hope that your Committee may find them of interest.

M Gylee

The Future Prospects for the Railway System in the light of the Government Proposals for Privatisation

CONTENTS

Introduction

Submission to the Transport Committee

The Future Prospects for the Railway System in the Light of the Governments Proposals for Privatisation

INTRODUCTION

I have considered the prospects for the railway system under the proposed Liberalisation White Paper and enclose comments and views.

I am particularly interested in the role of the Regulatory process and feel that the White Paper is probably not the vehicle that will enable the regulatory process to operate effectively.

I have also considered the basic issue of the privatisation of the railways and suggest that an approach based on the example of the privatisation of the electricity supply industry, is both feasible and desirable.

I enclose two papers together with an Executive Summary for each. The titles are:

Regulation as a form of monitoring and control.

Characteristics of an Infrastructure Authority.

Specific Questions Answered

SPECIFIC QUESTIONS

What are the aims and objectives of a privatised railway? What are the attractions for the private sector?

— A more efficient range of service.

— a more customer orientated range of services.

— development of innovatory services geared to needs not covered by the current remit as applied to British Rail.

— the introduction of private sector financial and managerial disciplines.

— the opportunity of commercial development of inter-modal freight services (possibly on the lines of the USA after the Staggers Act).

Is there a conflict between the principle of open access and the granting of exclusive franchises?

— yes! the idea of open access (or Third Party Access) is that a series of services can be established which are fully commercially accountable. Franchising should only be an option where no competition is possible.

There are a number of ancillary issues which need to be addressed:

— there is a "logic inconsistency" between the treatment of road and rail infrastructure which favours the highway users.

— a change in the treatment of highways infrastructure will require a form of "road pricing" to be introduced.

Who should do the strategic planning for our railways and how can different interests be co-ordinated? eg: can freight develop effectively on a primary passenger network?

The Infrastructure Authority on a commercial basis but with "truly" strategic guidelines from central government (and from the EC via central government via Directive and Resolutions). The Infrastructure Authority should have sole discretion on creating policy and forward planning but its five year (or longer) business development plan must be agreed with the Regulator on a yearly rolling programme. The regulator should have an over-riding veto where the consumers interest, competition interests, or integrity of the licensed operators in at risk.

What will be the Government's role in subsidy and investment? In what circumstances will cost benefit appraisal be appropriate, and what criteria should be used for future rail investment?

The Government's supporting role should be confined to the Revenue subsidy of the relevant "operating companies". This support should also encompass the revenue implications of investment proposals by the Infrastructure Authority *which have been fully agreed by the operating companies* or groups representing those companies.

With regard to future rail investment, the position suggested above of the infrasturcture authority taking responsibility for the "forward business development plan" would set the focus on rail investment. There could be a role for government investment where, perhaps, the commercial project would need to be enhanced by additional environmental (or similar external influences which were necessary *but non-commercial* in character, eg additional costs associated with the High Speed Link to the Channel Tunnel.).

Railtrack, the track authority, will charge all operators "commercial" rates for track use. What principles should be used to set these charges?

Railtrack must have the legal obligation to "Offer Terms" to any legitimate rail service operator who has been licensed by the Regulator. The terms should be in two parts:—

(a) a composite "charge" for the "Use of the Track" and

(b) a connection charge to physically get on to the system.

The connection charge required to be paid to gain access to the system would not apply in all cases, but would apply where an operator wishes to create a new "physical" connection to the track system. Existing physical links would not have any further connection charge levied on them unless there was a physical change to the lay-out. Maintenance of the connection would be covered in the "use of track" charges.

"Use of the Track" charges are more complex. I suggest that the following general objectives and principles should be adopted:—

(a) The use of track charges should be made up of a number parameters, *perhaps;* a charge levied on all operators on a time-tabled mileage run/axle weight provision; a straight charge on all operators who run over any part of the highly utilised "core" of the track authority (perhaps based on the principle Inter-City routes); and a charge levied on all operators who wish to run to or through areas of high capacity constraint. (eg the main London terminals; Birmingham New Street etc). This charge would *not* be confined to "peak hours" but would apply where capacity was tight at any period of the day.

The point of the above suggestion is that a number of "commercial signals" could be created both with regard to the development of "innovatory" services and to direct capital investment into the areas of "high capacity constraint" on the track network.

How should franchises operate so as to maximise the public interest, both for profitable and subsidised services?

Franchises should not be offered until after the "competitive" network has been established. The distinction between *profitable* and *subsidised* will change fundamentally if a system of "road pricing" similar to the suggestions for railtrack, is introduced. The need for as wide as possible third party access should be paramount.

What arguments are there for switching immediately to a regime of rolling stock leasing for all operators, including BR? What are the White Paper's implications for BR's on-going rolling stock investment programme?

There is an overwhelming argument in favour of going for a leasing option *as well as* for the option to purchase all operating equipment. The reliance on BREL and the handful of UK equipment constructors, all building to predetermined British Rail standards, *rather than to EC and World standards is* imposing unnecessary extra costs on the UK railways and is also restricting access to markets for equipment of greater reliability. (eg: the restriction on the General Motors Freight locomotives for the Foster Yeoman aggregate trains from Somerset to Acton (in London) to a fixed maximum number. It is suggested that these locomotives from the USA are both cheaper and more reliable than the British Rail Equivalent class 58.).

The future investment policy in rolling stock by BR should now be placed temporarily, in the hands of the Regulator. The aim here is to remove the influence of British Rail over the equipment specifications and to ensure that a body with no strong ties to the traditions and "Spanish Customs" inherent in BR (like any long established organisations) looks after the forward planning for equipment in the transition period.

How is the value of stations to be assessed and what will be the relationship between a privately owned station and BR's operation of trains there-from?

I would suggest that all stations are valued on the property market as valuable real estate. Protection of the "running" areas could be achieved by excluding those areas from any sale and also ensuring that access to the running areas was secured.

The relationship between the private stations and the various operating companies can be modelled on the airport experiences with all operating companies paying agreed fees for the use of the facilities and either providing their own "station handling" facilities, or using "handling agents". Stations should be net generators of funds to the rail system.

Executive Summary

Regulation as a Form of Monitoring and Control

NEED FOR REGULATION:

A system that is currently a Monopoly Operator will not necessarily transfer easily into a fully competitive Market based operation without the introduction of a "Catalyst" to encourage the process.

There is no effective alternative system to "Regulation". The use of the powers of the Fair Trading Act 1973 and the Competition Act 1980, via the Office of Fair Trading (OFT) and the Monopolies and Mergers Commission (MMC) whilst affective in the longer term; is not a sufficient deterrent for the instant anti-competitive problem.

A Regulatory Process for the Railways:

The obvious starting point has to be to *Define the Targets* that regulation is designed to achieve[1].

"the statutory duties of the regulators include protecting the interests of producers (Licensees), of consumers (Customers) of various kinds, and of employees and third parties (eg: environment concerns). The wording varies but, for present purposes, three main objectives may be identified in the respective privatization acts:

(1) to ensure that all reasonable demands are met, and that licensees are able to finance the provision of these services;

(2) to protect the interests of consumers (customers) with respect to prices and quality of services;

(3) to enable or promote competition in the industry.

---

[1]([Beesley & Littlchild—The regulation of privatized monopolies in the United Kingdom—RAND journal of Economics Autumn 1989])

Track (Infrastructure) Authority

In regulation terms the infrastructure Authority, *as the Strategic planning company*, should a private sector Plc which is charged with the forward planning of the System over which it has control. In corporate structure terms the IA at strategic level is the *Holding Company* for the Subsidiary Tactical operations.

For the IA Subsidiaries, regulation would follow a similar format. The track operators; The Signalling and Telecommunications and Station operators would all be subject to Price Control Regulation.

Regulatory Issues

Functions of the IA and its Subsidiaries: The IA is a monopoly (or series of area monopolies) in which it has total control over the operations of Railway Companies licensed to use its tracks and associated facilities.

Proposals for Route or Station closures; or of a change of status of a route with the introduction of restrictions against classes of traffic, must be placed before the regulator for approval.

Relationship between the IA and the Operators: The prime duty of the IA subsidiaries is to *OFFER TERMS* for operating services over the chosen parts of the network. The regular would "Make a Decision" (determination) in the event of a failure to agree commercial terms. He would also need to monitor *Connection to the Network*, by the IA.

Operators:

Franchisees: The Franchise element of the British Rail Passenger Services would be treated as "Services Existing as at Vesting Day" and would be subject to Restrictive Trade Practice Registration (a section of the Rail Act 1993 S... equivalent to RTP Act 1976 s21).

Licence Conditions: In addition to the general conditions they should also contain *Full Business & Regulatory Accounts Provision; Prohibition of Cross Subsidy/Discrimination/Predatory Pricing*.

Private Companies: In addition to general conditions in the licence there should be provision for the *Full Business and Regulatory Accounts*. Provisions for Cross Subsidy and Predatory Pricing should automatically come into force once the Licensee controls more than 15 per cent of services in his operating area.

Promotion of Competition:

The promotion of Competition in all practical aspects of the provision and operation of railway services, is the prime objective.

Fair Trade & Competitive Acts 1973–1980

The employment of these items of legislation would be beneficially operated on a "Concurrent" powers basis between the Director General of Fair Trading (DGFT) and the Director General of Railway Services (DGRS).

TUCCs & Consumer Affairs

The other major aspect of the Regulators responsibility is the protection of the consumers interest and rights.

Relations to third party access and regulations:

E.C./U.K. Freedom of entry onto system; involving a "Connection & Use of Network" charging policy with the duty on the IA to quote charges.

Transit and Single Market Directives and the need to identify possible "Constraints" on the network, especially at and around the inter-connectors (eg: Channel Tunnel).

E.C. Transparency of Costs to Industry and Public Utility Tendering Directives will apply and will require that close attention will be paid to "Standards" as applied to "Construction & Use" of infrastructure and operating equipment.

Executive Summary

Characteristics of an Infrastructure Authority

Whilst the Infrastructure Authority (IA) should have the sole Strategic overview on all operational issues, the day to day operation of the Authority should be split in to the three constituent parts—Track, Signalling and Communications and Stations. Each part is capable of being tendered (or franchised) into the private sector.

The arguments also turn on the use of high technology to improve the utilization of the track, as well as to put down markers for the improved efficiency of passenger handling in a crisis by developing systems which not only inform the passengers when something goes wrong but also aids controllers in finding alternative routings, or in a major crisis, alternative forms of transport.

There is a need to ensure that some form of price control mechanism is applied to the Infrastructure Authority (as well as to all services that a] existed at "Vesting" day and b] achieve certain minimum criteria placed in the licence of new-comers.

The paper goes further into the *Clearing House* concept and also into the need to *Register all Licensed services* for billing purposes.

Other concepts are suggested, the main ones being the *Traction Committee,* as the forum for the operators and IA to agree the IA seven Year rolling investment (Business) Plan.The key concept is for the IA to be duty bound to *Offer Terms for the use of the Network.* This part of the indicator to the "market" for capital investment guidance.

Appendices
REGULATION AS A FORM OF MONITORING & CONTROL:

NEED FOR REGULATION:

A system that is currently a Monopoly Operator will not necessarily transfer easily into a fully competitive Market Based operation without the introduction of a "Catalyst" to encourage the process. The Privatisations that have taken place over the last decade or so, have tended to use a "Regulator" as the method of pulling the Ex Utilities into the Private Sector. The question has to be asked, "How successful have the regulators been?"

With all the privatized industries except Electricity, the process placed the entire structure in the private sector with little or no adjustment to its size and range of services. Eg: British Telecom; British Gas etc... With Electricity, the industry (In England & Wales) was split into three separate and distinct components; The Generators; The Transmissions system and the Distribution and Supply systems. Thus in the Electricity industry the system at the point where it went from a Utility to a series of Public Limited Companies (PLcs), went from a total monopoly to a series of competitive entities in Generation and Supply and a core Monopoly in the Transmission and Distribution systems.

At first sight it may seem that the Electricity Industry is in need of less regulation than its counterparts, but on examination the those PLcs that were created at "Vesting" ie: the date upon which the industry was placed in the private sector,have significant market influence, to the extent that they could act to prevent, or make very difficult, the entry of New companies into the Electricity Supply Industry.

In order to control the activities of the ESI., each and every company, existing or new, is obliged to be Licensed. The licenses set out the frame work within each company is to operate. The guiding principles for the industry are set out in the Electricity Act 1989 which, in common with the other Privatizations (Gas, Telecom, Water, etc.) both define the global objectives for the specific industry and set up a regulating body to ensure that the objectives are met and that the licence conditions are adhered to.

There is no effective alternative system to "Regulation". The use of the powers of the Fair Trading Act 1973 and the Competition Act 1980, via the Office of Fair Trading (OFT) and the Monopolies and Mergers Commission (MMC) whilst affective in the longer term; is not a sufficient deterrent for the instant anti-competitive problem. This issue was common in the Stage Carriage Bus service Privatisation where Predatory Pricing and other anti-competitive practices drove many "New" private stage carriage hopefuls out of the market or prevented access on reasonable terms. The problems of the Bus Privatisation process were recognised as significant where competition existed from "Day One" in their privatised state, and few Privatisations since have had the potential for active competition from Day One, until Electricity.

The Privatising of the Railway system will put in place another Ex Public Sector Monopoly which is capable of significant competition in the provision of services from day one of its new private sector state.

There is a need for Regulation under conditions of sudden and sustained competition, even as the medium to see the industry through the transition from monopoly to full commercial competition, and the Electricity Industry Model for the Regulatory Process points up some valuable insights and lessons.

A Regulatory Process for the Railways:

The obvious starting point has to be to *Define the Targets* that regulation is designed to achieve and to that end the Common Denominator identified by **[Beesley & Littlchild—The regulation of privatised monopolies in the United Kingdom—RAND journal of Economics Autumn 1989]** fits the requirements admirably:—

> *"the statutory duties of the regulators include protecting the interests of producers (Licensees), of consumers (Customers) of various kinds, and of employees and third parties (eg: environmental concerns). The wording varies but, for present purposes, three main objectives may be identified in the respective privatisation acts:—*
>
> (1) *to ensure that all reasonable demands are met, and that licensees are able to finance the provision of these services;*

(2) *to protect the interests of consumers (customers) with respect to prices and quality of service;*

(3) *to enable or promote competition in the industry.*

Strictly speaking, the duties of the regulator are not a direct obligation to achieve the stated objectives, but rather require the regulator to carry out his statutory functions in the manner which he believes is best calculated to achieve these objectives.

The three broad regulatory objectives hold true for the Railway privatisation process and are therefore put up as the "Corner-stone" of the Rail Regulatory process. Taking the post privatisation railway structure as being broadly as follows, the details of the regulatory process that will most likely be needed, can then be identified:—

A *Track (Infrastructure) Authority* subdivided into the following:-

One Strategic body that formulates "National" policies in close consultation with representatives of "Operators", Provider of the "Way", the System Control (Telecommunications and Signalling), Station/Interchange owners and the Regulator.

Three Tactical/Day to day operational bodies:—

The Owners/Franchisees of the Track; track bed and associated civil engineering

The Owners/Franchisees of the Signalling and Telecommunications systems

The Owners (and possible franchisees) of the Stations.

Franchised Train service operators.

"New" private train service operators.

Track (Infrastructure) Authority

In regulation terms the Infrastructure Authority, *as the Strategic planning company,* is a private sector Plc which is charged with the forward planning of the System over which it has control. (Whilst one IA is considered appropriate at present, it is perfectly feasible to have a number of IAs—eg: PTAs as IAs in their own areas—with the ability to interchange services between them. The interface between each IA is referred to in this paper as the Interconnector. In corporate structure terms the IA at strategic level is the *Holding Company* for the Tactical operations. It is itself a monopoly in terms of it being the only one, but as the Holding Company, its commercial competitiveness lies in the performance of its subsidiaries.

For the IA subsidiaries regulation would follow a similar format. The Track operators; The Signalling and Telecommunications and Station operators would all be subject to Price Control Regulation. This is mainly because, either franchised or purchased, the work of these bodies becomes monopolistic in character from the moment the contracts are let. In the case of the Franchise operator, conditions can be placed both in the franchise contract and in the subsequent licence to replace one franchisee with another. A private company would only be subject to the Licence conditions and would be harder to remove.

However a private company, not directly associated with the existing railway service, would probably present a more objective and inspirational view of the tasks they had chosen to perform with the result that they may be more in tune with new market requirements. Also non franchisee companies may offer significantly different, but relevant expertise, via their other non licensed interests. The diversification of interests of these companies would also spread "Risk", commercial or otherwise, and satisfy their shareholders. Regulation would apply only to the sector of the company that is directly involved with the Provision and Transmission of Railway services.

Regulatory Issues:

In line with the Titles of other Regulatory Bodies, the Railway Regulatory body should be called "OFRAIL". This, however, does not really convey the appropriate image. Therefore, *ORR Office of Railway Regulation* may be deemed more appropriate. The Regulators Title could then be—Director General Railway Services [DGRS]

From a regulatory point of view, the DGRS would confine his/her activity to the following:—

"The Provision of the Facilities exclusively for, and the operation of, Railway services, including the monitoring and control of any Restrictive Practice or Anti-Competitive practices directly related to such railway facilities and service operations".

Functions of the IA. and its Subsidiaries: The IA is a monopoly (or series of area monopolies) in which it has total control over the operations of Railway Companies licensed to use its tracks and associated facilities. Conceptually the IA. has the potential for significant competitive pressure via its subsidiaries; *The Physical Track; The Signalling & Communications & the Stations. (See Characteristics of an Infrastructure Authority).*

Because of the inability (Impossibility) to sustain competition at IA. subsidiary level on an "On Going" continuous basis (ie: Different maintenance companies constantly vying for the work on a regular basis), the licence granted to each relevant Franchisee for the day to day operation of the IA. would need to contain a *Price control* provision (RPI-X) which would prevent year-on-year price increases from tendering towards

Monopoly Pricing. This would need to be closely monitored by the Regulator who would also have full control over the annual level of "*X*" for each licensee.

The Strategic functions of the IA. would also need to be contained within a seven or 10 year rolling programme which would need to be agreed annually with the regulator and would contain a full *Costed Business Plan* submission, also each year. The agreement by all the relevant licensees, to the Strategic projections would be paramount. The plan would concern itself with achieving the maximum utilization of the Fixed Assets of the AI.; Strengthening of the Network at its "Pinch" points; development of new capital structures; introduction of new or enhanced "Traction" technology; etc . . . All developments which affected the IA. Subsidiaries and the Operating Companies would be discussed and approved in the *Traction Committee* whose duties and functions are discussed in the preceding *Characteristics of an IA*. Paper. The Regulator would be charged with protecting the Social Rail element on an interim solution basis until *Highway pricing* has been established with an *IA*. for Highways, as well as satisfying itself the no *Anti-Competitive or Restrictive Trade Practice* is distorting the debate and ultimate decision.

Proposals for Route or Station closures; or of a change of status of a route with the introduction of restrictions against certain classes of traffic, must be placed before the regulator for approval. [*Failure to approve needs to be examined from the Accounting: legal and economic view points. However, the Regulator would be expected to have unfettered discretion in such matters*.]

Relationship between the IA. and the Operators: The prime duty of the IA subsidiaries is to *OFFER TERMs* for operating services over the chosen parts of the network. In offering terms the Track Operator would act as the "Agent" for the Signalling Operator(s) so that the "Terms Offered" to operate a service would include "Use of Track" and "Use of Signalling". The payment for the "Use of Stations" would be the responsibility of the Operating Company alone. The *Bid and subsequent Offer* will be based on the Time Tabled services that the Operator wishes to run as part of his licence. Because the Routes and times may not fit exactly into the existing operating pattern the IA would be duty bound to negotiate adjustments with the operator on a strictly commercial basis.

Regulator Action: Only after the commercial discussions had failed to provide an equitable solution would the regulator be asked to "Make a Decision" (Determination) which would be binding on the parties.

The Regulator would therefore also need to monitor, and be aware of any restrictions being placed in the way of *Connection to the Network,* by the IA. Where such restrictions occurred then the licence condition covering *Connection and Use of Network* would be enforced by the regulator and, again, a *Determination* made.

OPERATORS:

Franchisees:

The Franchise element of the British Rail Passenger and Freight Services would be treated as "Services Existing as at Vesting Day" and would be subject to Restrictive Trade Practice Registration (a section the the Rail Act 1983 section . . . equivalent to RTP Act 1976 section 21). This would allow the allocation of "common" equipment such as Locomotives, Carriages etc. to all the new companies that would be created. Also, it would allow "Genuine New" companies to avail themselves of the same facilities *it they chose to*.

Licence Conditions: In addition to the general conditions also to contain *Full Business and Regulatory Accounts Provision; Prohibition of Cross Subsidy/Discrimination/Predatory Pricing*.

Separate Accounts—a definition that may be of value is contained in the PES Licence of the ESI. and is outlined below:—

The Financial year runs from 1st April to 31st March in each year.

The company divides its corporate business, both Regulated and Other into Separate Businesses, so as to be able to show the financial affairs of each separate business.

That the Separate Businesses be accounted for under the provisions of sections 222(5)b and 221 of the Companies Act 1985 (as amended and incorporated into the 1989 Companies Act).

All revenues; costs, assets and liabilities *for each Separate Business* must be kept, and be presented, in a consistent way. Any changes in presentation or interpretation will require the agreement of the Regulator.

Additional financial information, including details of *Transfers of cost/revenues* between separate businesses; *inter business loans or Parent loan guarantees,* will be required as part of a wider *Regulatory Accounts* presentation in full at the year end and in Summary at the half year.

Cross Subsidy/Predatory Pricing: There will be a provision on the Licence requiring that the *Franchise Operators* are prevented from passing costs from their rail operation business into any other *rail operation* business that they own *or* to any other *Corporate Activity whether or not it is connected with operating a rail service*. The distortion of the "Market" for rail services is totally prohibited and would be rigorously enforced by the Regulator.

Anti-Competitive Behaviour: The Rail Act 1993 would contain provision for the Regulator to take *Concurrent Powers and Duties* under Sections 44, 45, 50, 52, 53, 86 and 88 of the Fair Trading Act 1973 and

Sections 2-10 and 16 of the Competition Act 1980. This would confer on the Director General Railway Services (DGRS) powers to initiate investigations of *Anti-Competitive* behaviour and, if necessary, refer them to the Monopolies and Mergers Commission (MMC).

Private Companies:

In addition to general conditions in the licence there should be provision for the *Full Business and Regulatory Accounts*. Provisions for Cross Subsidy and Predatory Pricing should automatically come into force once the *Licensee* controls more than 15 per cent of services in his operating area.

Support Services: The nature of "Support Services" is such that they would not necessarily have any significant affect on the competitive operations of Rail Services. Also, since they are not directly concerned with the Provision of the Facilities for, and the operation of, Railway services, any Restrictive Practice or Anti-Competitive practice, would be an OFT affair.

PROMOTION OF COMPETITION:

The promotion of Competition in all practical aspects of the provision and operation of Railway services, is the prime objective and is totally inter-linked with the protection of the customer and the provision of services to cover all reasonable demands for those services. The incorporation of the Restrictive Trades Practices Act 1976; The Fair Trade Act 1973 and the Competition Act 1980, reinforce the point that the Railway System is capable of supporting a wide variety of existing routes and of developing new ones. The following sections develop the Legislative themes further.

Restrictive Trades Practice

Registration of Restrictive Agreements—Section 21(2) RTP Act 1976. Cover the need to control Restrictive Trade Practices which commonly occurred prior to 1976. Usually these practices were agreements between existing parties which act to prevent "New comers" to a market becoming established, or, if established, to act in such a way as to exclude them from access to goods and services enjoyed by other similar, but established industries.

Under the 1976 RTP Act agreements that could be considered restrictive can be registered under the ATPA 76 Section 21 and if the registration is accepted, will be deemed never to have been restrictive. One of the key considerations under this heading is whether an agreement is accessible to any party who wishes to be a party to the agreement, *on terms no more or less favourable than the original parties*. This procedure exists in the Electricity Act 1989 under Section 100 of that Act.

In regulatory terms this Act provides a method of controlling Merger Activity and the Abuse of Dominant Market position, especially with respect to existing Companies/licensees in the market. Traditionally the operation of this piece of legislation is indirectly via the Office of Fair Trading (OFT) because of the complicated nature of the legislation.

Anti-Competition Act 1973-1980

The employment of these items of legislation would be beneficially operated on a "Concurrent" powers basis between the Director General of Fair Trading (DGFT) and the Director General of Railway Services (DGRS). This would allow for the speeding up of investigations into any Anti-Competitive practices that were indentified during the operation of the Rail Network. A bi-lateral agreement (Concordat) between the DGFT and the DGRS would be sufficient for the flexible cooperation between the two appropriate bodies. This system works well between the DGFT and the DGES (Director General Electricity Supply).

Role of OFT/MMC

From the previous paragraphs on restrictive trade practices and anti-competitive practices, it can be seen that there is a well-established body of legislation which protects the consumer from Monopolistic exploitation of the providers of services. Also on anti-competitive issues it has been shown how the Regulator can initiate actions without directly involving the OFT (although the OFT will have been notified and will have offered advice to the Regulator in the matter) and that these actions can be placed with the Monopolies and Mergers Commission (MMC) for their resolution.

The MMC is an impartial body and decisions from it can sometimes be not quite what was expected.

Civil Emergency Procedures

The operation of the UK Network in the event of Industrial Action; weather; natural disaster etc, needs to be considered. The extent to which it is felt that the Railway System is considered to be strategically important will depend on the level of action taken under this heading. Now is not the time to evaluate the effects of problems under this category.

Inter-Modal Ownership (Monopolist Tendencies)

No operating Company shall have an interest (Ownership of Shares; Financial; Managerial etc) in the IA and its subsidiaries

No part of the IA shall have an interest (Ownership of Shares; Financial; Managerial etc) in any operating company.

TUCCs & Consumer Affairs

The other major aspect of the Regulator's responsibility is the protection of the consumers' interests and rights. To some extent the fact that the Railway industry is in the Private Sector as a series of Plcs will serve to protect the interest of the consumers *via* the protection of the interests of the shareholders.

However, the consumers need a body that they can turn to when inefficiency, poor service or sheer exploitation exists. The Transport Users Consultative Committee is just such a structure which both exists and has a well-defined regional structure. This organisation could best be grafted on to the Railway regulatory regime and its activities further strengthened to provide significant protection for Rail Service users.

Consumer Committees

The Consumer Committee structure can conveniently be based on the TUCC Regions, including Scotland. However the boundaries may need to be reconsidered as the Network develops.

The activities of the Committees has been outlined above but would have investigative powers to examine issues relating to the rights of the Consumer including the conduct of the operators and the quality of the services provided which would be measured against a declared "Code of Practice" to be created and operated by each company. This would develop the themes currently on offer in the Rail Charter.

The Consumer Committees would *not* be involved in the Main Regulatory issues although they would be given sufficient relevant data to examine Consumer Affairs problems in the light of relevant Regulatory controls.

Role of Railway inspectorate—located in the regulatory body as part of a larger "Technical/Engineering" Division. Its current functions would transfer to the regulatory body and its impartiality and objectivity would be safeguarded.

Inter-connectors: UK & EC

In the context of the privatised railway industry, the **Inter-connectors** are the interfaces between one Track Authority (or comparable organisation) and another. An example would be the **IA & the Channel Tunnel IA.** The interaction could be both at Strategic as well as Tactical (Day to Day) level. The exact relationship between the relevant parties would be assumed to be "Commercial" with the Regulator having an overview and monitoring role to enable the unencumbered "Transit" of licensed operators across the various systems. This idea of "Transit" is enshrined in the relevant EC Directives, and together with the "Single Market" directives, requires the concept of "Third Party Access" to be applied to the operation of Rail services within and across the European Community. In broad terms the key areas of consideration concerning Regulation and Europe are summarised below:

RELATIONSHIP TO THIRD PARTY ACCESS AND REGULATION:

EC/UK Freedom of entry onto system; involving a "Connection & Use of Network" charging policy with the duty on the IA to quote charges.

The IA could be the medium for Franchising or selling "Slots"; Routes or "Time Banding" on an open competition basis.

Transit and Single Market Directives and the need to identify possible "Constraints" on the network, especially at and around the inter-connectors (eg: Channel Tunnel).

EC Transparency of Costs to Industry and Public Utility Tendering Directives will apply and will require that close attention will be paid to "Standards" as applied to "Construction & Use" of infrastructure and operating equipment.

There will be a need for a monitoring body (either a Regulator or the application of the current anti-competitive and restrictive Trade Practices legislation *via* the OFT).

CHARACTERISTICS OF AN INFRASTRUCTURE AUTHORITY (IA):

INTRODUCTION:

Railway Infrastructure, that is the "Essence" of a Railway undertaking, has been defined as the "Track, Signalling and Terminals" associated with that undertaking. Looking back to an early example, the Liverpool and Manchester Railway (1835) represented the structure defined above upon which its own services were run. This established the conventional view when looking at Railways as a Transport mode. The relationship between Track, Signalling and Terminals has been seen as one of an indivisible partnership with no clear delineation between them and seen in the light of the early Railway development in the United Kingdom there was no real incentive to find an alternative since the Railway Companies were looking at Railway Construction and Development to create Monopoly Profits and Monopoly interests. (M R Bonavia—The Organisation of British Railways.)

Today this relationship can be set aside because the view of the needs and requirements of a railway system have changed from the concept of a Utility operation (both in the "Private Company" phase and in the Nationalised period), in the prospects of Commercial and Operational efficiency through "Competition" for the provision of services (Passenger and Freight). This is the first occasion in which access to the Track can be given to all legitimate parties who wish to provide services, and it can most easily be achieved by dismantling totally the "One to One" relationship that currently exists between operator of the service and the operator of the way.

Once that relationship has gone then the re-examination of the relationship between the operation of the Track, the Signalling and the Stations can be redefined.

The consideration of the concept of *"Infrastructure Authority"* allows for a certain amount of lateral thinking as well as the re-evaluation of the older, main railway traditions, and, as will soon become apparent, this paper stresses the need to lift the "Thinking" about the structure and form of the rail industry out of the 140 years of collective tradition. This is not to say that tradition is invalid as a "Check" and "Balance" on the introduction of new thinking, but that it tends to constrain useful "Conceptualisation" ie productive "Brain Storming".

This paper owes its very existence to the march of Technology which is capable of transforming, and has transformed, the Transport Operational Infrastructure across all modes. The application of this technology has been somewhat hindered by inertia, poor management and vested interest supporting the status quo. The privatisation of the Railways presents a golden opportunity to rectify this situation.

The "Way" and Associated "Metals"

There is an overwhelming argument to retain strategic control over the "Track, Signalling and Terminal Infrastructure" in the hands of an Infrastructure Authority. The investment policy criteria alone requires a close working relationship between the three entities. However, the day-to-day management of each segment can be franchised out to operating companies. This concept has already expressed itself in an implied way in the Adam Smith paper by John Hibbs and Gabriel Roth, "Tomorrow's Way", which looks at the possibility of giving Highways and "Economic and Financial" value which would satisfy the needs of Private Sector investment criteria in the construction and operation of the "Highways" as "Plc". By looking at the provision and creation of Roads in this way it reinforces the concepts applied both here and later in the Chapter on *Highway and Railway Track Similarities and Differences.*

The Track and "Way" can stand on its own as an operating company; it provides the required quality of "Product" in the most cost effective manner. For example:—

> Track maintenance programmes could be tendered regionally or on a "Highway Authority" boundary basis, by the franchiser so that costs would be controlled by the competition process and the quality standards could be monitored by the franchiser and the removal of a firm for poor work etc could be swift and minimise disruption. Under this strategy both the System, ie the railway system and the Consumer, ie passengers and freight users, will benefit.

The IA would be a single strategic entity for the UK mainland Rail system, including the Passenger Transport Authority Networks but excluding Independent Rail Companies such as the Severn Valley Railway, Dart Valley Railway etc, where the greater part of their revenue earning services are within their own boundaries, and self sufficient non revenue earning networks, eg, internal Steel works systems etc could remain outside the registration requirements of the IA, unless there was Revenue Earning traffic originating/terminating within the Industry complex. (Some form of Capacity Exemption Orders could be devised for this eventuality.)

The ownership of the "Way" also presents significant non-rail user benefits, especially in the Telecommunications and other industries with trunking requirements, where wayleaves could be secured by the existence of the track bed.

Control Systems

Again, the Infrastructure Authority must retain strategic control over the method and type of control required in global terms. However, in franchising this facility the Infrastructure Authority could encourage the "Economic and Commercial" development of control systems by the franchisee through general Strategic Guide lines and, perhaps, could reinforce the quest for "Safety with Efficiency" through financial incentives. The most obvious way of ensuring the development of Efficiency and Technological progress is to split the UK system into zones and tender the signalling and telecommunications system in each zone to the Signals and Telecommunications specialists, both in the UK and EEC, thus achieving competition between suppliers and ensuring rapid technological development on maintenance of the "system" as a whole and the most advanced new capital developments on new projects.

The opportunities to promote technological development in signalling and control systems, are wide ranging. The concept of splitting the UK rail network into a series of operational zones and tendering those zones to "expert" companies in the private sector opens up this whole area to genuine "Private Sector" funding. The idea of a "Test Bed" for different (but compatible) Hi-tech Signalling and Control proposals would have great attraction to companies with an eye to export sales and comparable market spin-offs. Since these "Zones" would be franchised by the Infrastructure Authority, there would be significant protential for Revenue Generation into the IA.

The other important feature would be to ensure that developments in this very critical area were designed to meet the needs of the Operating Companies which is, of course, vital.

Here the aim is to achieve a greater occupation rate of a given length of track to increase available capacity, especially in areas of high congestion, whilst at the same time keeping the needs of all the many Private Operating Companies fully in mind.

Here the current developments in technology could be fully exploited, for example:

— Rapid automated redirection of services in the event of a mishap or train failure, together with full "Real Time" customer information updates. The concept of *"Real Time System Following"* is not new and has been in the Airline business for some years. In this context it would be essential to be able to monitor the entire operation within the UK. This would undoubtedly be an Infrastructure Authority strategic function as well as a "Zonal" tactical function, thus communications between the two bodies, as well as between the three elements of the IA operation and, most importantly, between the IA and the operating companies and their customers, would be essential requirement commanding a top priority at all times.

— Higher train flows with fully automated train control. The ability to operate Safely and Efficiently at "Close" headway requires the "Real Time Train Following" facility already referred to. The system requirements would obviate the need for conventional signalling and by the same token, the need for "Full Time" drivers as a "Class" of Rail person. There are risks in the heavy reliance on technology over human control but these risks are minimal compared to the increased safety which would stem from "Fail Safe" computer controls which would not only release further "Track Capacity" but also re-direct trains in the event of breakdown or ther operational difficulties. The savings to both the operators and the *customers* could be significant. This ability to increase track utilisation would also create a better pattern of timetable slots for trains under the categories of Speed and/or Axle weights. The advantages to the appropriate operators would be reflected in the "Charges" for the "Use of the Network" and thus Pricing Strategy would be an important tool to maximise the use of all infrastructure under the control of the IA.

— The development and adoption of efficient and low cost signalling and line side controls for the more lightly used, mostly Rural services, with the encouragement of sound basic automation for the running of State supported local services via Franchising or direct sale.

Again, this is fully possible with a *"Real Time Train Following"* system in place.

— Driverless trains, (with the staffing resource released to the operating companies being redirected into, for example, increased customer care).

Station Infrastructure:

Stations have been traditionally an integral part of the "Infrastructure". There is no operating reason why this should be so, and there is every commercial reasons why it should *not* be. However, with the development of the Signalling and Control technology described above a definite "Communication" link (Requirement) will exist for the dissemination of information from "Real Time Train Following" to customers, via the independent operating companies that are providing the services. This will also have a Commercial Value together with the development of Hi-Tech booking and Customer redirecting at times of crisis (Including through booking of customers to their destinations by alternative modes of transport if necessary). The potential for the "Complete Customer Service" eg: Limousine from Home to station; First Class Rail Journey and Transport to destination could be absorbed into this relationship between the "Control" system and the "Station Infrastructure", but led and initiated by the "Operating Companies".

Passenger Stations represent actual "Property" interests, that is they are (Usually) town centre sites with a "Re-development" value. This value can be realised in most cases, without compromising the operational requirements of the rail system. A station is simply a place for the Interchange of Passengers from one mode to another (eg: Rail to Bus or Rail to Car) and on that basis it is a facility which should be a net generator of funds. These funds can be derived from the additional use availability (eg: Offices; Shops built above/around it (New Street Station; Charing Cross etc.) as well as from the Franchising of the Customer Services resources which the individual operating companies may wish to employ eg: First Class Lounges—Airline style,; Ticket Booking services which could be provided by the individual companies at the major stations and by "Handling Agents" at intermediate and other key stations, and by the on-train Steward/Stewardess at the lightly used stations.

In relation to the more efficient and effective use of the Fixed Assets, the splitting of the *Station Infrastructure* from the Track and Signalling organisations offers significant opportunities for Third Party

Property Developers and enterprising Rail Service operators, to develop office space both at strategically important sites for the prestige sector of business and to develop "Less Valuable" sites for the functional backup sectors of those businesses with a Rail Transport/Telecommunications deal incorporated into the master agreement. Such proposals would help to ensure that Office Location/Relocation was spread across a wider range of suitable sites.

Another aspect of control is the Policing and Security of the system. Currently the British Transport Police are the dedicated force for the Railway system. It may be possible to incorporate this force into the general police force and to utilise the "Real Time Train Following" facilities to detect "Intruders" on to the system. These are not costed options but the introduction of Real Time Monitoring on to the system provides the basis for more comprehensive surveillance.

Policing and security provisions at Stations is an area in which the basic security policing could be provided by the local police force, and supplemented at the larger stations by security guards provided by the individual operating company organizations. The mix of the two systems is a detail to be worked out by the parties involved.

Freight Terminals: represent a different approach, although they can also be considered as "Property" assets which can be developed "Beyond" the direct Rail Freight use without compromising the operational requirements of the particular facility. It would not be unreasonable to suppose that Multi-modal, all purpose facilities could be developed which, *via commercial pressures and decisions* provide the essential Road/Rail interworking which was never really achieved under the Central Planning concepts of the Governments of the 1960's and 70's. The reason for this apparent break through would be that Hauliers/Freight Forwarders could maximise their commercial and operating efficiencies by providing both Road and Rail haulage themselves on an equal basis [see Tomorrow's Way – Hibbs & Roth] and with the same company thus enabling service planning of trunking and feeder routes to be dovetailed into available resources. The potential economies of scale from such a prospect could be very significant.

Security and Policing here is likely to reflect the needs of the passenger Terminal requirements, but with the addition of different level and styles of security for normal and "Bonded" cargoes.

The Infrastructure Authority:

It now becomes easier to see that commercial pressures can be brought to bear on an Infrastructure Authority when the Strategic planning is removed from the day to day commercial and operating requirements, and that the commercial pressures are further encouraged where competitive comparisons can be highlighted and monitored (By a Regulation Authority – the National Grid Company in the Electricity Industry is an interesting comparison, especially as it is recognised as a "Private Monopoly" and that its commercial functions are achieved by a **Price Capping** concept [RPI – X] and that its Strategic and Day to Day functions have *not* been separated in the way described above.).

The terms "Private Monopoly" and "RPI – X" need some explanation:-

  Private Monopoly: this is the term used for the transfer of a single entity eg: British Telecom; from being a Corporation owned, funded and controlled by the State, even down to its tariff charging policy, into the Private Sector where it is owned by a large number of share holders, and where its Corporate Plan is based on creating Shareholder dividends via profit. In both cases there is no significant competition and therefore there is no incentive or pressure for the company to be efficient. Its profits come from its position to charge prices for its services which are significantly above the charges which could be sustained under competition, there is no reason therefore why any structural change in management or manning levels should be contemplated. The tendency, therefore is for the company concerned to carry on with the worst aspects of its life in the Public Sector ie under State ownership.

  One of the possible (and proven ways) of dealing with this problem is to create competition possibilities in as many sector of the industry as possible. The Electricity Supply Industry illustrates this point very well.

  Where competition cannot be achieved then the intervention of the Regulator is perhaps the next best thing.

  RPI – X: is the "Short Hand" for the control of the increase in prices year on year. This control is applied on the *Private Monopoly* sector of a privatized industry such as Electricty. The Regulator controls the way this technique is applied, but in essence the *RPI* = Retail Price index, which is published monthly and the "X" is the adjustment factor decided by the Regulator when considering the overall performance of the Regulated sector of the particular company in the Industry concerned. The concept, when "Fine Tuned" can provide the necessary stimulus to a company to become efficient and shed "Avoidable" Costs and make other efficiencies, and even develop the new business strategies to improve the ratio of Cost to Turnover.

Clearing House & Registration of Licensed Railway Services:

With the facility of "Real Time Rail Service Following" in place the IA. becomes the natural focus for the registration of services operated (Passenger & Freight) over the network. A number of functions can be satisfied by this arrangement:-

A full list of operators, together with their timetables; service characteristics (eg. Maximum Speed constraint; Axle Loading Constraint; Banking engine requirements eg. Lickey Incline .... etc. .) can be controlled both centrally in the IA. for strategic planning purposes and in the "Operating Zones" for the Tactical day to day, hour by hour "System Requirements".

Such an arrangement would allow the examination of new applications to operate services in such a way that IA. **"System Constraints"** could be identified, and consequently new applications to run could be refused or modified in the light of the constraints identified. Part of the arrangement would be the introduction of "Slot Pricing" ie. additional charges for operating to or through areas of Capacity Constraint and this, as with the Aviation Industry would require "Slot" bids for arrival as well as departure from an area of congestion (Note: Aviation practice as well as WSI NGC Settlements practice with Generator bids).

The "Real Time Train following" ability would have a number of essential uses, the main one being "Punctuality Analysis" and with it, Performance Analysis which could be a) linked to the Citizens Charter requirements and b) any "Delay" payments/refunds between the IA. and the specific operating companies. The "Delay" payment concept would ensure a) that time table bids by operating companies were realistic and that b) poor performance by a specific operator could be spotted and remedial action taken by the IA.

In addition the "System Constraint" analysis procedure would identify capacity bottlenecks and constraints and act as an "Investment Indicator" to the Private Sector to provide funding to increase the flexibility, as well as the capacity, of the system to the mutual benefit of IA.; service operators and customers alike.

The IA. could be the central recording agency for "Leasing" purposes for the operating companies; the Tactical Companies associated with the IA Holding Company and the "Sundries" element such as station "Handling Agents", "Rail Service Caterers" etc. All the information under this heading would be passed to the "Regulator" for Licence Fee calculation purposes and would form the basis of the Regulators subsequent entitlement to information which would need to be provided in accordance with the Licence Conditions applying to the appropriate licensee. (Note: paper on "Regulation of Private Railway Services" is due shortly.)

Prohibition as to the Operation of Services:

The Infrastructure Authority would be prohibited from running its own revenue earning services. The prime requirement is that the IA. is the medium upon which the operating companies run and that the IA. is totally neutral with regard to who runs what.

Provision of Emergency Facilities:

The IA. as the Holding Company would be *Duty Bound by Statute* to set up a "Rescue and Operating Support" service which would be controlled by the "Track", "Signalling" and "Stations" companies via a Joint Rescue Operating Committee. The key, but not exclusive, functions would include agreed "Banking Engine" facilities based (a) on long term tabled operations and (b) on the more immediate "One Off" or limited period requirements which would be licensed and covered on an as and when required basis. Also "Rescue" facilities for a break down on the track, of the Operating Company's stock and the provision of heavy engineering facilities for major accidents. (This last category could be seen as part of the Track Maintenance Franchise because it would provide a swifter response time and would already be strategically placed on the Network.)

Charges for this service would be allocated to the licence fee of each individual operator, initially, possibly on a mileage/time incurred per annum based, but then loaded by a "Failure and Delay Incurred" factor for each licensee based on actual results.

FINANCIAL IMPLICATIONS OF AN IA

Cost & Revenue structure of an IA:

Structure of the "Charging" package, ie: Two/Three part charge structure one of the elements at least being related to Route Miles "Bid" for in the licence, another element perhaps being related to the level of "High Attraction" or "Congestion Factor" of a group of routes, ie. popular stations such as Birmingham New Street, Paddington etc. where congestion is high and the fixed assets are heavily used. A third element could be related to a "Contribution" in the form of a fixed charge which would represent the "Minimum Network" required to be in place to satisfy "Core Demand" over the network as a whole. (Note: NGC principle.) It would be necessary to decide the number of Nodes (Stations) that would comprise the network. (This could be based on current Inter-City services or Inter-City plus the Regional "Express Services" and network Southeast.) and to identify a single (mostly the heaviest used) link between "Pairs" of nodes which would give the skeletal service across the Network. The cost of this network would represent the "Minimum Network

Contribution". An example could be "Birmingham–London" which, say, could be Euston but ignoring the Paddington link. (A paper on this issue will be produced as part of a general "Use of Infrastructure" charging proposal in the Autumn [1992].)

Traction Committee: A policy forum made up of user companies and the I.A. which would have a remit to examine issues such as Electrification, applications of new technology etc. (Very loosely modelled on the ESI PSA.) The "Committee" would be made up of the IA. Holding Company and its subsidiary companies, the operating companies individually or collectively via trading associations (But mindful of the risk of anti-competitive activity which could result from such associations), and the Regulator. The Traction Committee remit would include:—

Agreements on "Cost Effective" Common Standards, eg: for Motive Power equipment and all associated equipment to operate and run services eg: uniform fittings for Air Breaking connections to run multi company equipment, *especially* under emergency conditions.

Adoption of the Current Rail Codes of Practice ie. the "Track Code" (based on the principle of the ESI "Grid Code") including the requirement to "Offer Terms" for connecting new operators to the network and publish "Use of Track" charges.

Price control of IA's and their subsidiary companies may need to be considered. The argument for the use of price controls is strongest where the operation to be controlled is a"Natural Monopoly" (In either the Public or Private sectors). Where competition can be achieved then the need for price controls reduces. In line with other privatized utilities the development of competition is paramount and the inclusion of powers in a Regulatory Authority to Combat Predatory Pricing; Cross Subsidy, General Anti-competitive behaviour under the Fair Trading Act 1973 and Competition Act 1980, and any Restrictive Trade Practices under the Restrictive Trade Practices Act 1976 and the appropriate EC legislation and Directives is essential.

One of the problems that has been common to all the "Privatized" industries has been the need to create a competitive environment in which new-comers were not forced out or even prevented, from competing in the industry. In the Privatization of the Bus Industry the dismantling of the public monopoly ie the National Bus Company, led within a short period of intense competitive activity, to a series of Private Monopolies. (A Monopoly position can be considered to exist where a single company owns or controls more than 25 per cent of the market in a particular area.) The three or four main private Bus groupings have done just that. The problem has been how to break the State Monopoly but not allow the Private Monopoly to develop. The answer seems to lie in the way in which the Electricity Supply Industry (ESI) was set up.

The ESI was split into three distinct and physically separate groupings; The Generators; The National Grid and the Distribution Companies. All companies that came into a separate existence on 31 March 1990 (from the old Central Electricity Generating Board) were licensed and in those licences are specific Conditions designed to Prevent both "Cross-Subsidy" and "Predatory Pricing". These conditions effectively prevent the existing "Players" in the ESI from using their vastly superior resources to undertake "Loss Leader" campaigns against new-comers or pass significant costs/revenues through from one part of their corporate function to another with the sole purpose of distorting the market price to such an extent that new-comers would either "Fail" or would choose not to enter the market. This sort of protection of "Fledgling" companies is one of the roles best suited to the Regulator and is essential in the short term (up to 10 years).

The perceived problem of the "lack of competitiveness" of the *IA* can also be mitigated by the establishing of a separate **operating company as a holding company which is there to franchise an Ex BR services** that have not been sold to private operators. The pressure for commercial efficiency will put pressure on the IA. To make rapid, commercial decisions about investment and the employment of new technology. The IA would have no connection or links with Ex BR operating services.

November 1992

APPENDIX 52

THE BRITISH INSTITUTE OF MANAGEMENT

The Future Prospects for the Railway System in the light of the Government's Proposals for Privatisation

EXECUTIVE SUMMARY

— Rail privatisation should be embedded in a national transport strategy.   [Sect 1.2]

— The proposed structure of regulatory bodies should be simplified, and the roles of the Department of Transport and Railtrack enhanced.   [Sect 1.3]

— Railtrack should have the key role in strategic planning for the rail network.   [Sect 5]

— The sourcing of investment funds should be unrestricted. Cost-benefit analysis and other techniques used in road planning should be used to justify schemes.   [Sect 6]

— The attractions of all but a very few operating franchises to the private sector may prove low.   [Sect 3]

— Viewed as commercial sites similar to airports and motorway service areas, stations could prove attractive to the private sector.   [Sect 10]

— Three kinds of franchises should be offered; regular, supplementary and special.   [Sect 7]

— Charges for track use should be made on a cost-plus basis, related to average costs of route category, train mileage and vehicles per train.   [Sect 8]

— The principle of open access for international operators may be reconcilable with the three-fold category of franchises.   [Sects 4 and 7]

— Rolling stock could be leased from a pool held initially by BR and later by a private business.   [Sect 9]

— Monitoring of rail performance is discriminatory unless applied to transport operators by all modes. It could be best achieved internally by a TQM initiative.   [Sect 1.4]

CONTENTS

INTRODUCTION

The British Institute of Management is the leading management institute in the UK. It is a professional body representing over 65,000 individual managers and with 770 subscribing organisations. Its membership embraces all levels of management and organisations in all sectors, both public and private.

In February 1992 the Institute surveyed its members' views on a range of transport issues. The results were published in July 1992 as a widely-circulated report: *Making Tracks for the Future* written by the present author.

The survey produced a number of clear indications. Respondents wished to see additional investment in transport infrastructure, and overwhelmingly wished that such investment should be directed to rail. A small majority favoured rail privatisation, and a rather larger majority felt this would improve services. The setting up of a track authority, as proposed in the White Paper, was the approach preferred by the majority. An integrated approach to public transport was strongly favoured.

Members' views about the White Paper on rail privatisation have not been specifically sought. Whilst, therefore, the opinions expressed in the following submission are broadly based on those expressed in the survey, they are in other respects those of the author—(Mr M. Peel).

1. THE PROPOSALS IN THE WHITE PAPER

1.1 Competition

Competition has been demonstrated to bring real benefits in the provision of public services. However, the proposed arrangements seem likely to generate, at best, only very limited competition.

There was aggressive competition between railways in the period from 1830 until 1922, usually on the basis of geographically competing routes. It was terminated by Parliament as not in the public interest. The very limited competition over a few routes between 1923 and 1948 is generally agreed to have achieved little.

The statement that the industry is "more insulated from the demands of the market" than its competitors [5] seems hard to justify [with the exception of some London commuter services]. The rail network has in fact suffered immense inroads by its competitors into its market position during the last 50 years. So far from being "insulated", it has for the most part been completely exposed to competitors who in some cases have themselves been insulated.

The real competition in passenger transport is between modes and between public transport and the private car. There is no need to stimulate such competition, which at its existing level can already be seen as damaging.

If this view is accepted, the benefits of the proposed privatisation must be sought in other areas.

1.2 A national transport strategy

There is need for a move towards, rather than away from, the nation-wide co-ordination of transport strategy. The proposals as they stand must lead to further fragmentation not only of rail transport, but of public transport as a whole. The role of central government in establishing the national strategy is inescapable.

A body that can play its part in this strategy at national level on behalf of the rail system seems essential; Railtrack could, with the changes proposed in the next Section [1.3], fulfil this role.

1.3 The proposed authorities

The arrangements proposed suggest the involvement of a large number of new or existing authorities. They appear to include:

— The Department of Transport
— The Regulator
— The Franchising Authority
— Railtrack
— British Rail [until all operations are privatised]
— PTAs/PTEs
— The Health and Safety Executive [facing "additional demands": Para 84]
— The Technical Standards Authority [? Para 96]
— The Staff Certifying Authority [? Para 82]
— The Transport Users' Consultative Committees [? Para 74]
— The franchise holders

This appears to call for up to five new public bodies. Finding appropriate skilled staff would be difficult. The costs of separate infrastructures for each would be a burden on the industry and the taxpayer.

The interrelationships and channels of communication between all bodies involved would be complex. The amount of cross-checking and monitoring would be demotivating and the existence of the structure would form a deterrent to potential franchise holders.

The track record of regulatory bodies for other privatised industries is open to question.

There seem to be strong arguments for a simplified structure such as:

The Department of Transport

Overall national transport policy. Negotiating, awarding and overall monitoring of rail franchises. Overseeing right of access to the rail network.

This enhanced role would have the important benefit of lessening the current imbalance between the Department's rail and road involvements.

Railtrack

National rail transport strategic planning, including network considerations and service integration. Market research for new lines. Developing and maintaining track and infrastructure to meet economic, social and environmental needs. Establishing and monitoring technical standards. Safe operation. Timetabling. Licensing operating companies. Control of operational areas of stations. Oversight of through-ticketing, railcard and staff concessionary travel arrangements. British Transport Police. Certifying operating staff.

British Rail

Continuing to operate until privatisation is complete, as proposed. Under overall control of Railtrack when it becomes operational.

PTAs/PTEs

[as a present]

The Health and Safety Executive

No additional role.

The Transport Users' Consultative Committees

　　[as a present]

The franchise holders

　　[As proposed]

The considerably enhanced role of Railtrack should do much to integrate the network and the services it does and could offer to customers. It would offer a strong presence able to represent rail views at national level and to help counter-balance the road lobby. It would facilitate the effective contribution of franchisees within their specific areas and services. To be effective, it would need an independent and authoritative Chief Executive backed by high calibre staff.

1.4 The monitoring of rail performance

The suggestion that rail transport alone [as contrasted with bus, coach and air transport] requires the detailed performance monitoring apparently envisaged in the White Paper [19(d), 28 and elsewhere] is surprising.

This view appears unjust, and its promulgation can only act as a disincentive to potential franchise holders.

Monitoring applied equally to all public transport services may be beneficial, and in accordance with the intentions of the Citizens' Charter. However, there must be a danger, as touched on above [Sect 1.3] that this would involve extensive and expensive record-keeping. It is presumably not the wish either of the Government or the electorate to saddle public transport with additional bureaucratic procedures. Occasional inspection or sampling could produce good control more cheaply.

The widely accepted concept of Total Quality Management [TQM] places responsibility for monitoring and improving performance on the individuals who actually produce the goods or services. This approach has the major added advantage of strengthening rather than weakening motivation. It may prove the most effective and cheapest within public transport.

2. THE AIMS AND OBJECTIVES OF A PRIVATISED RAILWAY

What should be the aims and objectives of a privatised railway?

　　— To provide an attractive and cost-efficient rail passenger and freight service.

　　— To play its part in the national transport strategy and to co-ordinate with other providers of public transport in order to maximise the benefits of an efficient system.

　　— To contribute to the environmental and economic wellbeing of the country through the fullest exploitation of the environmental benefits of rail transport.

3. ATTRACTIONS FOR THE PRIVATE SECTOR

What are the attractions for the private sector?

Public passenger transport is not an area in which fortunes are made. It may be that, with the exception of a very small number of high-profile services (with major airports, London–Scotland, London–Birmingham), few potential franchise holders will come forward. If the proposed cumbersome and demanding regulatory structure were put in place, this reluctance seems likely to be exacerbated; the problems already experienced by Charterail and the Virgin Group may be indicative.

Such attractions as there may be will obviously include opportunities for profit and the strengthening or protection of a market position by complementing existing operations (ie in road, air or water transport). It is possible that a specific interest in railway operation in its own right might bring a small number of operators into the market, perhaps including one or two currently involved in private railway operations.

The attractions of the ownership or leasing of stations may prove much greater. [See Section 10 below]

4. THE PRINCIPLE OF OPEN ACCESS

Is there any conflict between the principle of open access and the granting of exclusive franchises?

A solution may be found if the three kinds of franchise suggested [Section 7 below] are used; "regular" for a full service run to an agreed timetable; "supplementary" for individual timetables trains within the service identifiable from others by the nature or quality of what they offer, and "special" granted only for the running of individual trains for special markets. Operators from other railway administrations wishing to provide international services would normally fall within the "supplementary" category.

5. Strategic Planning and the Co-ordination of Interests

Who should do the strategic planning for our railways and how can different interests be co-ordinated? For example, can freight develop effectively on a primarily passenger network?

As the guardian of the existing network and timetable, Railtrack would be the best body in the proposed structure to undertake strategic planning.

The timetable is the basis of all a railway does; from it flow both customer appeal and the needs for the resources; track, signalling, terminal facilities and rolling stock. Infrastructure should be maintained and provided to meet the needs of the timetable—not the other way round. Railtrack will be best placed to maintain this integrity of timetable and network.

It is essential that interconnections between passenger services are not only maintained at the present standard, but substantially improved. Lack of a national timetable strategy has always been one of the most serious weaknesses in British railway services, and was made much worse by the closures of cross-country and interconnecting routes in the last three decades. Far too much railway strategy has been London-based and centred on routes radiating from London. In fact, a national rail timetable would almost certainly be better based on the north-east/south-west spine.

Electrification is a specific issue with environmental and resource implications stretching far beyond rail users. A national strategy, in which Railtrack would be deeply involved as advisers and implementors, is needed.

There should be no serious obstacle to freight development on what has only become primarily a passenger network in recent years. Heavy freight flows rarely run parallel to or at the same time as heavy passenger flows. Daytime track capacity is only under strain at a small number of points on the existing network; the greater part has space capacity. Spare night-time capacity is almost universal. There are therefore few points at which capacity for any foreseeable flows of freight could not be found either now or with comparatively small capital investment.

6. Investment and Subsidy

What will be the Government's role in subsidy and investment? In what circumstances will cost-benefit appraisal be appropriate, and what criteria should be used for future rail investment?

Investment can only be undertaken on the basis of proper strategic planning. For this reason, investment should be planned by Railtrack as part of the national transport strategy.

The special place of electrification in this investment strategy has been mentioned. [Sect 5 above]

Funding for investment plans should be allowed from any suitable source without restriction: private capital; the EC; PTAs/PTEs; local authorities; national government. Government should not be involved in the assessment of individual schemes unless required to finance them. It will inevitably act as lender of last resort for schemes of national interest otherwise unable to find backers.

Cost-benefit analysis should certainly be adopted for infrastructure investment, as with road and other infrastructure schemes. The aim should be, as far as practicable, to produce a level playing field for all modes of transport.

7. The Operation of Franchises

How should franchises operate so as to maximise the public interest, both for profitable and subsidised services?

Franchises should be of three kinds; regular, supplementary and special. The same franchisee could hold any or all.

Regular franchises should be offered for the operation of year-round, timetabled services. Except as suggested below, they should cover all services on an identifiable route, and provide appropriate speed and frequency standards to meet the need identified by Railtrack. They should be subject to a minimum notice of withdrawal by the franchisee of six months, to expire at one of the two timetable changeover dates. Holders of regular franchises should be required to participate in full through-ticketing arrangements, and to supply and honour railcards.

Supplementary franchises should be awarded for trains within regular timetabled services which are clearly distinguishable by virtue, usually, of type of rolling stock or standard of on-train service [eg sleeping, luxury or special facility stock or services] from other trains operating on the route. International services, especially if using purpose-built stock, could be seen as falling in this category.

Special franchises should be offered for the right to operate special, non-regular trains such as excursions, services in connection with all kinds of special events, private charter, tourist and land cruise trains etc. The franchises may be restricted to limited routes, areas or dates, or cover a longer period or the full network under appropriate terms.

8. Charges for Track Use

Railtrack, the track authority, will charge all operators "commercial" rates for track use. What principles should be used to set these charges?

Whatever regime is adopted should be simple. Until sound commercial data is built up, a cost-plus basis seems the best. However, exact costing of track usage is difficult, and any attempt to meet all possible variations of train operation would produce nightmarish complexities that would be a serious commercial disincentive.

Overall, a train mileage/vehicle number rate by route category has much to recommend it. Track costs depend partly on the speed standard of the route, and partly on the passage of vehicles producing wear and tear; signalling costs depend largely on the passage of trains as units. The formula would thus be;

$$m*vn*rc$$

where   m = train mileage run

vn = number of vehicles per train

rc = route category

The weights would initially be based on current overall costing information and adjusted as changes or refinements occurred.

9. Rolling Stock Investment and Leasing

What argumemts are there for switching immediately to a regime of rolling stock leasing for all operators, including BR? What are the White Paper's implications for BR's on-going inmvestment programme?

Rolling stock, particularly locomotives, need not be specific to individual services. In the past, BR and its constituent parts have tended to proliferate a wider range of stock than could be justified. The implications of this are that adequate passenger stock of the four or five categories needed for railway operation could readily be held [initially by BR, subsequently by a private company] as a pool for hire by those franchise holders who did not wish to buy. In some cases it may be practicable to share stock operation between franchise operators on an agreed basis to maximise utilisation and minimise costs.

Operators would presumably be keen to use individual liveries, but repainting is comparatively cheap and easy.

It seems essential that nothing should be done to hold back BR's already inadequate programme of investment in passenger rolling stock. There does not seem to be a need for an immediate switch to leasing.

The White Paper proposals do not seem to offer any problems in regard to freight rolling stock.

10. The Operation of Private Stations

How is the value of stations to be assessed and what will be the relationship between a privately owned station and BR's operation of trains therefrom?

Stations have a value as commercial sites analogous to motorway service areas and airports. Their value will therefore lie in the possibilities for all kinds of retailing, catering, hotel services, hospitality, conference and meeting facilities. There may be options for office development. Arrangements for ticket sales may be made on an agency basis. Accommodation could also be leased to staff of franchise holders for ticket sales, enquiry facilities and for parcels services.

It is to be hoped that planning permissions will be readily available to maximise that value of the sites, which will not only be profitable to their owners/lessees, but also beneficial as centres of the communities of which they form part.

The platforms and related operational areas [bridges and subways] would best be regarded as separate and part of the infrastructure in the control of Railtrack. Staffing of operational areas, which will include train arrival and departure display boards at major stations and public address systems, should be the responsibility of Railtrack. Most of the latter will, in any case, be serviced through the Railtrack telecommunications network.

Even small stations may be found attractive under this regime; one or two already exist.

September 1992

APPENDIX 53

RAILWAY DEVELOPMENT SOCIETY (SCOTLAND)

I refer to the Transport Committee's investigation into Railway privatisation. You will receive a submission from RDS on this matter specifically answering the questions posed in the press statement. This letter is by way of a supplement. (In the event of any contradictions between this letter and enclosures and the RDS submission, the latter should be given precedence.)

I enclose a copy of our branch newsletter which contains an article on privatisation.* I would be grateful if you could copy this letter and the newsletter, to the members of the committee.

If we have to have privatisation in the form proposed I would be grateful if your committee would look at the specific proposals for ScotRail. While the break up of the BR network would be regretable, to say the least, the break up of ScotRail, would be disastrous. The entire ScotRail network should be franchised as a whole.

I hope your committee will look at the disastrous affect of bus deregulation as an example which should on no account be repeated.

My greatest fear is that the same chaos and uncertainty which now pervades the bus industry will be repeated with the railways if we have dozens of franchisees operating on the rail lines.

As may be clear from other submissions, RDS do not take an idealogical line on privatisation. We simply look at the practical effect it could have on passengers.

I hope your committee will take a strong line that any scheme must not make the network more difficult for the passenger to use. The early indications of the Stagecoach operation, with nine pages of instructions to BR ticket staff does not bode well.

The following conditions must be a fundamental part of any scheme.

There must be only one ticket office at each station.

All operators must accept all rail cards, rover tickets season tickets etc. All tickets must be valid on all trains on any routes between stations. The all-line timetable must continue with ALL services contained in it. All timetables must contain an expiry date. (This may seem elementary but it is the very lack of such expiry dates on bus timetables which has contributed to the chaos and reduction in use of buses.) For example in response to my complaint to Highlands and Islands Enterprises that the former HIDB comprehensive timetable an essential publication for tourists had been dropped their reason was that the accuracy of the timetable could not be guaranteed because of bus deregulation.

It is vital therefore that the stability and network advantages of the railways should be maintained. Your committee may wish to look at the Swiss system where a mixture of public and private railways, substantially subsidised provide a very efficient and well used transport system, totally coordinated and without duplication and competition.

I hope all this is of use to your committee.

21 September 1992

Privatisation of BR

I am grateful to you for forwarding to me relevant documentation regarding the Committee's work. I am delighted with the way in which the Committee are beavering away, to put it mildly, and I look forward to the committee's interim report which I trust will be trenchent and will receive proper media cover.

In the mean time there is another aspect which your committee may pursue. You will be aware that there has been considerable disruption to transport in Scotland from blizzards and I get the impression that ScotRail have coped reasonably well compared with chaos on many roads.

It is not difficult to imagine all sorts of problems if the Government's idiotic ideas are implemented if similar conditions prevail. If we have a track authority and numerous private train operators will there not be endless arguments about who is responsible for snow clearing? I have no doubt that BR have a dedicated band of workers skilled in clearing snow etc. Will this work force be broken up? Even if responsibility for this thankless but vital task is clear there may well still be arguments about whether it was done properly in the same way that motorists complain if there is any failure on the equally skilled and dedicated road clearing gangs.

It may well be that this is only one aspect of many potentially disastrous arguments and excuses for buck-passing if ever BR is broken up which will already have occurred to your committee.

It will also no doubt occur to you that people like Richard Branson simply do not have a clue as to how a railway is operated and I suspect that Stagecoach have already found out that the economics of running buses on roads paid for by taxpayers is very different from running trains on tracks paid for by passengers.

I hope all this is of help to you.

14 January 1993

*Not printed.

APPENDIX 54

ROAD HAULAGE ASSOCIATION (RHA)

INTRODUCTION

1. This submission examines and comments upon the potential for maximising the transfer of freight from road to rail in the light of the Government's White Paper proposals.

THE BASIC REQUIREMENTS

2. *Customer Satisfaction* The basic requirement for a successful rail freight operation is customer satisfaction. This has little to do with privatisation, access to rail networks or intermodal technology. Those matters only affect how successfully customer satisfaction may be achieved. In general, customers want their goods to be delivered in the right place, in correct quantities, on time, without damage and for a competitive charge. A successful rail freight or road/rail freight operation must consistently meet those requirements if it is to succeed.

3. *Understanding of the Customer's Needs* Customers will differ in the degree of importance that they place upon each of their requirements. For example, reliability of timings will be crucial for a customer servicing a just-in-time contract, whereas quality control en route will be a major concern for one moving chilled foods. Rail operators will have to satisfy the customer's specific requirements. Customers will not accept the railways' historic operating conditions and will wish to deal with a movement operator who understands fully the special service, legislative, safety and competitive conditions that prevail in his particular market sector. The success of a privatised railway network in attracting freight from road to rail will stand or fall according to the extent of this understanding.

THE CURRENT POSITION

4. *Trainload Freight* Currently, customer's basic requirements are met best by the operators of Trainload Freight. Quantities, times, conditions, prices and other specific matters are agreed between the customer and British Rail and it works well. The regularity of Trainload Freight movements helps to ensure consistent service quality and a detailed understanding of the specific market sector. The only threat to its continued success lies in the cost of the service in comparison with road transport and other non-rail movement means.

5. *Railfreight Distribution* Railfreight Distribution provides a less satisfactory service. Utilised freight must be consolidated into train loads or moved very long distances, a minimum of 200 miles, say, in order to obtain a competitive quote. Otherwise, haulage and distribution by road is cheaper, more flexible and provides better consignment care en route. Futhermore, when Eurotunnel opens, road freight will become even more competitive on the shorter international journeys as trucks use "Le Shuttle" as a roll-on, roll-off underground ferry.

6. *Intermodal Freight Movement* In an attempt to attract more business from road to rail a small but growing number of intermodal distribution companies have been formed. These include such companies as Charterail, Combined Transport Limited, Allied Continental Intermodal Ltd. and MAT. The pioneer in this field in the UK is Charterail. It runs trailers "piggyback" on special wagons together with other trailers that can be formed into trains using railway bogies as "fifth wheels". It provides a good example of private enterprise and a national railway working together to satisfy customers. Unfortunately, its current difficulties may result in a loss of confidence in potential customers for, or potential providers of, intermodal services. They may perceive the Charterail experience as an indication of the problems associated with operating in a competitive marketplace while dependent upon monopolistic supplier subject to strict regulation.

PRIVATISATION—FREIGHT ASPECTS

7. *Price* The Government proposals place rail infrastructure in the hands of Railtrack and it is assumed that initially, at least, some other residual part of British Rail will provide traction, staff and wagons on hire to private operators who do not have their own. It is claimed that such arrangements will provide the choice and competition that customers require and realise the full potential of the railways. In practice, this full potential will only be realised if the price is right. This is fundamental for both trainload freight and wagon or intermodel services. A figure of 8 per cent return on assets employed by Railtrack has been mentioned. This level of return would almost certainly prevent the movement of more freight from road to rail. There are, however, a number of quantifiable benefits arising from such movement of freight from road to rail. These include:

(a.) The relief of road congestion.

(b.) The reduction of road maintenance expenditure.

(c.) The reduction of the need for new roads.

(d.) Saving of the cost of health care for traffic related illnesses.

Also, the protection and enhancement of the environment would be assisted. Quantifiable benefits could be offset by Government against the return on capital employed required of Railtrack. Such an arrangement could both encourage and acknowledge the benefits of movement of freight from road to rail.

8. *Access & Speed* It is generally accepted that unitised rail freight should only be considered if the distribution plan involves movements of at least 200 miles. This distance is determined from considerations of the journey time by road, the time lost in transhipment and the fact that the train must be loaded in good time to be able to use its allotted path. Hence the degree of time criticality of the load sets a limit to the use of an intermodal system and an important element in attracting more freight traffic must be the improvement of ease of access to the railway. This can be achieved by locating freight terminals in the right places and by loading and unloading containers or swap bodies from trains very quickly.

9. *Relationship Between Customer, Provider and Government* The potential for movement of more freight by rail is affected by inter-relationships between the intermodal customer, Railtrack and Government. It is in the interests of all that the use of rail should be developed to its full commercially profitable potential. The end customer is not going to change from a well understood working system to an intermodal one without a trial, a sight of a similar operation or a most attractive financial incentive. The price of the service has been dealt with earlier in this submission and this consideration is limited to the once only start up, or transfer, costs. These would be for the purchase of the necessary equipment, possibly the installation of a rail siding and probably the cost of making drivers and some traffic staff redundant. The financial burden would be significant and there will be a very positive incentive to do nothing. This is particularly the case during the current recession and it is certain that the effects of the economic downturn will still be felt when the Channel Tunnel opens in Autumn 1993. It is considered, therefore, that there is a requirement for incentives in addition to the existing improved Section 8 Freight Facility Grants for installing rail sidings. The most effectve additional incentive could be to allow the value of all intermodal equipment to be written off against tax in the first year instead of the present 25 per cent on the balance remaining. This would provide a clear demonstration of support and recognition of the contribution made to the environment. A further incentive could be assistance in meeting redundancy payments arising from increased movement of freight by road. Finally, where a service can be shown to be new and experimental in some degree there could be a grant for its development. This could include a grant to Railtrack to assist in sharing the risks of introducing the service. The greatest risk to the customer and the operator lies in the start up phase and Government commitment and financial support could result in many more company directors agreeing to give rail a try.

SUMMARY

10. In summary:

(a) The key condition for increasing the amount of freight moved by rail is customer satisfaction. Goods must be delivered to the right place, in the correct quantities, on time, without damage and for agreeable delivery charges. Furthermore, the customer needs to be confident that the service will continue to be provided by someone who understands his business.

(b) Trainload and long haul international freight generally meet with customer satisfaction. Unitised freight and intermodal services do not. In addition, confidence needs to be restored following the demise of Speedlink and the Charterail problems.

(c) Privatisation will work if the price is right. Railtrack must negotiate competitive prices for use of its lines whilst making a reasonable rate of return on its assets. That rate should take into account the contribution made by its activities to environmental and road infrastructure savings.

(d) The full potential for rail freight will only be achieved if it is made attractive to unitised moving within the UK and on short cross Channel journeys. This requires:

(1) Minimising loading and unloading times at terminals.

(2) Siting the rail terminals at key motorway/trunk road intersections in order to integrate rail with existing road distribution patterns.

(3) Swift transfer of goods at intermediate stations in order to operate fast freight trains as close to passenger train timings as possible.

(4) Encouraging customers to change from road to intermodal through financial incentives eg tax incentives tied to intermodal equipment, etc.

(5) The provision of starting up assistance that would allow Railtrack to set charges that will encourage company directors to change their distribution channels.

29 September 1992

APPENDIX 55

CONSUMERS' ASSOCIATION

INTRODUCTION

Consumers' Association (CA), publishers of Which? and other consumer magazines, is an independent, non-profit making consumer organisation established over 35 years ago and currently with 880,000 members. CA relies on research conducted by its parent organisation, the Association for Consumer Research, a registered charity.

Rail services are not a new subject for CA. The price, range, quality and safety of rail travel provided for consumers in the UK have been the subject of a series of customer surveys undertaken by CA since 1977. More recently CA has taken an interest in the legal relationship between transport providers and their customers. CA does not take a viewpoint on the principles of private versus public ownership but acknowledges that particular market structures may cause problems for consumers.

CA's main comments of the Government's proposals for rail privatisation are, in summary:

> *Separate passenger representation.* The views of passengers must be taken into account in the complex debates that will surround franchising and regulation. In order to ensure that those views are heard a well-funded independent passenger representation body is vital to ensure that passengers' views are canvassed and put forward.

> *Regulation.* Quality and efficacy of regulation, and the input of passengers' views into the regulatory and franchising processes, are vital if the improvements in rail services to passengers are to become a reality.

MAIN POINTS

1. *Aims of the White Paper*

1.1 We applaud the aims of the White Paper and if franchising of services achieves them, all well and good. However, much of the detail necessary to arrive at firm conclusions on the Government's proposals is not present in the White Paper and therefore CA's comments are more in the nature of questions and requests. We recognise and agree with the Essential Requirements detailed at para 8.

2. *Separate Passenger Representation*

2.1 Given the range of roles which the Regulator and the Franchising Authority are being posed by the White Paper it is absolutely vital that, in efforts to turn any final proposals into reality, the voice of the passenger is heard. Franchises are to be 'organised to meet the best interests of the passenger' (para 25.). But what are the best interests of the passenger and who is qualified to speak on their behalf? CA's concern is that it will be all too easy for these interests to be sidelined as the complex negotiations on franchising get underway, with neither the regulator nor the franchising authority championing the passenger interest:

> 2.1.1 The role of a regulator is very different from that of passenger advocate. The Rail Regulator is charged with overseeing track access and promoting competition as well as promoting the interests of consumers. In addition the Regulator is to arbitrate between parties in the event of disagreement.

> 2.1.2 The Franchising Authority has responsibility for 'negotiating, awarding, and monitoring franchises' within a flexible framework built around possible private sector interest.

2.2 To ensure that passengers' views are not overlooked it is vital that a separate well-funded consumer representation body ensures that they are both canvassed and put forward. The present passenger representative body, the Transport Users Consultative Committees, might form a starting point but their role requires enhancement to ensure that they are listened to and have a real role in the process of decision making and the awarding of franchises. The Gas Consumers Council could well be looked at as a model for representative bodies in privatised industries.

2.3 It is quite easy to envisage that in the future a cross country journey might involve travelling on services run by BR as well as franchised operators. It might not always be obvious to whom complaints should be addressed and matters might well be complicated by operators blaming Railtrack for particular delays or incidents. A single point of entry for complaints after they have been taken up with the operator(s) concerned is vital. Again a separate consumer body would answer the need.

3. *The Role of the Regulator*

3.1 As the White Paper states at paragraph 59 regulation 'raises complex issues'. If the benefits of the private sector involvement in the running of the railways are to be felt by passengers then effective competition is vital to raise and maintain standards. The commissioning of a major consultancy study into this area (para. 59) by the Government will only allay public fears about the feasibility of the private/public mix of the Government's plans if it is made public and appropriate consultation takes place concerning its findings.

3.2 Review of regulatory and franchising arrangements should be built into the system. Given the complexity of the proposed arrangements a review, by the Monopolies and Mergers commission, of how regulation is working after say 2-3 years seems vital to ensure that the aims of the White Paper are being met.

4. *Franchising Arrangements*

4.1 We are concerned that when the Franchising Authority franchises services on the Government's behalf the grants will first be decided and then the objectives for service levels set. While this would point to the Government's desire to reduce levels of expenditure, we would argue that the necessary level of service should be set *first,* after consultation with passengers, and then the budget set to meet that level of service. The possible impact on fares caused by franchisees being expected to make payments to the Government for running profitable routes, and Railtrack's expected return on capital and consequent lack of subsidy, need to be examined carefully.

Checks also need to be built into the arrangements to take account of the fact that the highest bidder for a particular franchise may not always be offering the best deal for passengers.

4.2 In the setting of standards and establishment of complaints mechanisms, consumer consultation is crucial if the system is to suit passengers rather than service providers. Clear, binding, commitments to consult passengers and passenger representatives are needed to be supplemented by survey work among individual passengers wherever possible. This is in keeping with the principle elucidated in the Citizen's Charter which demands "evidence that the views of those who most use the service have been taken into account when setting standards".

4.3 The research CA has carried out on passengers views on rail services show that they have strong opinions about the level of service they currently receive. A copy of our summary data on British Rail is attached in Annex A.*

4.4 The franchising authority must have sufficient resources, as well as the necessary powers, to conduct its own research, either on a systematic basis or by random spot checks, to ensure that the performance data produced by operators is in line with their figures. As a minimum, the methodology of operator monitoring must be agreed by the franchising authority.

4.5 We agree with Government that there can be no standard franchise arrangement. However certain ground rules need to be established to deal with the following:—

4.5.1 Acceptance of liability for service failures.

The White Paper states that 'the franchisee will. . . have to meet the requirements of the Passenger's Charter and so provide compensation for passengers when standards are not met (para 29.).

In itself, this is an empty commitment as the Charter's refund provisions are ex-gratia. BR's Conditions of Carriage, despite the Citizen's Charter year old promise of revision, still contain their notorious exclusion clause, Condition 25, used to deny liability for failure to run services. Any re-write of these Conditions should adopt the approach of London Underground in accepting legal lability for the refund provisions of their Customer's Charter.

If these Conditions are not re-written before privatisation all franchisees should anyway adopt legally binding refund provisions. If not, our research shows that the terms and conditions of other private sector transport operators often include exclusion clauses as bad as BR's—the Franchising Authority will need to act on this, otherwise passengers will be at the mercy of operators when it comes to complaining.

4.5.2 Quality of service.

The White Paper states that "standards such as punctuality, reliability and overcrowding will be written into the contracts" (para 19(d)). This does not go far enough. BR for years has been set standards for cleaning, call response from telephone enquiry bureaux and queuing times at ticket offices. Why should these standards also not be written in, alongside others the passengers deem important? And if network benefits are to be ensured, standards should likewise be built into the franchises for the availability of timetable and other information, ticket buying facility, non-availability of reserved seat refunds, catering and complaints system requirements.

The Charter's introduction of performance targets was welcome but the inadequate level they were set at was not. In many cases they are lower than previously agreed targets. If these are the levels of standards which franchisees are to meet then there is little hope that passengers will see tangible improvements in service. Much more challenging standards must be set for franchisees to meet.

4.5.3 Fares.

"Broad objectives" will be set for fares (para 28). This is not enough. Once a franchise has been awarded then it will in effect give a monopoly to whoever wins the franchise for a particular area. Effective price control will be necessary for the duration of the franchise. Attention must also be given to the balance of prices eg peaks vs off-peak fares, discounted vs standard fares to ensure that passengers are not exploited by the market power of the franchisee. Given that not all services will

---

* Not printed.

be franchised straight away then this argument also applies to powers that the Regulator must have over BR's continuing operations.

4.5.4 Failure of franchisee to meet standards.

There must be mechanisms for dealing with situations where the amount of subsidy granted to a franchisee at the beginning of a franchise proves insufficient. And passengers will need to be reassured that their interests will be protected when a franchisee fails financially: will they be stranded whilst the conflicting claims in a liquidation are sorted out or alternative arrangements made? If a franchisee fails to meet standards imposed by a franchise there will presumably be contractual arrangements whereby they will have to pay penalties, much as BR now has to pay penalties to Passenger Transport Executives when standards slip. But on a much larger scale this could lead to widespread disruption especially if a franchise is taken away from an operator who is performing badly—there will not necessarily be anyone waiting to step into the gap. And towards the end of a franchise period when a franchise might suspect that they are not going to win the franchise next time there might be a temptation to let standards drop—there must be effective sanction against this type of problem.

4.5.5 BR's Future.

In areas where there are initially no takers for the franchises, arrangements must be made to ensure that the "rump" BR operation is left with incentive to deliver a quality service.

As "BR's role as an operator diminishes over time" (para 22) it is vital that its demise is not hastened by the taking away and leasing of rolling stock which may bring benefits to one line but a consequent lower level of service on another line.

4.5.6 Elderly and disabled passengers.

CA's surveys conducted amongst disadvantaged passengers indicate varying degrees of difficulty with public transport but in particular access to stations and trains, reliability of information and efficiency of staff appear as problems. Two thirds of those surveyed gave these difficulties as reasons why they do not travel further or more often.

Franchises should specify that trains, stations and information services will be accessible to passengers with mobility or sensory handicaps and where franchisees inherit inaccessible services they should provide a schedule of improvements which they will undertake to carry out. Effective consultation with passengers with disabilities and their representatives are vital to this process.

5. Safety—the need for an independent public transport safety agency

5.1 The right of passengers to an acceptable level of safety when using rail services is essential. The safety system must operate openly in full public view. There is a need for safety to be regulated and to be seen to be regulated at arm's length from those responsible for providing or funding services. Several major accident enquiries, including those into the Marchioness and Clapham railway disasters, have voiced concern that the system of maintaining safety standards is not always working as well as it should.

5.2 CA sees a clear need for an independent public transport safety agency, which would assume the functions of the various bodies responsible for investigating accidents and which would act as a watchdog over the regulatory authorities. The agency would have powers to investigate accidents, make recommendations, and to promote safety standards generally.

12 October 1992

APPENDIX 56

TRAFALGAR HOUSE PLC

New Opportunities for the Railways

The Privatisation of British Rail

INTRODUCTION

Trafalgar House is the UK's largest construction and engineering company. It has extensive involvement in the provision of privately financed transport infrastructure and has probably acquired more experience in this field than any comparable company. Trafalgar House formed Dartford River Crossing Limited which designed, financed, built and now operates the Queen Elizabeth II Bridge across the River Thames at Dartford. Trafalgar House and its Italian partner, Iritecna, have won the concession to design, finance, build and operate the Birmingham Northern Relief Road, which is scheduled to open towards the end of the decade and will be Britain's first privately owned and tolled motorway. Trafalgar House and Iritecna are also bidding for the Western Orbital Route, the private sector motorway which will complete the ring motorway around Birmingham. In 1989 Trafalgar House and BICC formed Eurorail, a private sector company, which was chosen by BR as its partner for the development of a high speed rail link between London and the Channel Tunnel. This project did not proceed because of the unwillingness of the Government to help fund the necessary investment.

Trafalgar House is currently helping bring private sector disciplines and management to BR's operations: through the secondment of individuals to the Channel Rail Link project team; and by providing the project management for Phase I of the Channel Tunnel Rail Link, the upgrading of existing track. An extremely good working relationship with BR has been established on this project, which is proceeding on time and within budget.

Our own experience leads us to conclude that the Government is right in setting the objective of bringing increasing private sector discipline to the operation of the railways. We believe improved services should result from this. Generally speaking we see merit in the methods chosen by the Government and set out in the White Paper. But they raise many questions as regards putting them into practice and we offer below a number of comments on aspects of the proposals for (a) bringing the private sector into the operation of services, (b) the maintenance and development of the railway infrastructure, and (c) investment in rolling stock.

OPERATION OF RAIL SERVICES

The private sector will need to be convinced that franchises offered by the Government are commercially attractive. The White Paper provides no evidence that they will be and much fuller information is needed before the Government can contemplate offering franchises.

We believe there will be particular concern among potential franchisees about the implications of the policy of freedom of access described in Chapter 4 of the White Paper. The analogy is not perfect, but it is fair to point out that we would never have entertained accepting the concession for the Birmingham Northern Relief Road or the Queen Elizabeth II Bridge if we had faced the possibility, as a matter of Government policy, of having to allow a rival operator a degree of involvement in utilising the asset. Another area of likely concern will be the interface between a franchisee's own service and services which are operated by others, whether BR or another franchisee. A third point of significance is that the White Paper is silent on the possibility of franchises being offered in packages, for example an InterCity route plus some supporting local network. The White Paper states that InterCity franchises will as far as possible be kept distinct from other services. This seems to us unnecessarily constricting. It may be that a franchise for services in Network South East or Regional Railways might be more attractive if accompanied by a franchise for an InterCity route. We recognise that there would probably be nothing to stop an operator bidding for a number of franchises as they become available, in order to build his own network. But the Government should recognise the possibility that there will be greater attraction in acquiring those franchises in one transaction.

We highlight these as examples of the sorts of commercial considerations that we believe the Government will have to give much greater attention to if there is to be a realistic chance of significant transfer of services into the hands of the private sector. Our own experience in Eurorail suggests that the Government and private sector, perhaps not surprisingly, have different perceptions of the balance between risk and reward. The Government must be ready to accept the private sector's terms for involvement if it is to achieve its objectives. The White Paper provides no real evidence that it will do so.

MAINTENANCE AND DEVELOPMENT OF THE RAILWAY INFRASTRUCTURE

The particular interest of Trafalgar House lies not in the operation of railway services but in the maintenance and development of infrastructure. The introduction above briefly mentions our involvement in privately financed infrastructure projects. In addition, we of course undertake numerous infrastructure works in a traditional contractor role, including for BR.

We consider that the White Paper gives inadequate assurance that Railtrack, the future track authority, will be able to take the investment decisions necessary for the proper maintenance and development of the railway infrastructure. The White Paper states that investment "will largely be financed from charges to operators, including supported operators." Railtrack's charges to operators are to be subject to the oversight of the Regulator, whose duty is to ensure that such charges are "fair". There is a risk that Railtrack's investment needs will take second place to the needs of operators as a result of the understandable political desire to secure as much private sector involvement as possible in the provision of services. Our concern in this respect is underlined by the fact that the Regulator will apparently have only a very limited role in relation to decisions on investment in infrastructure.

We consider that what is required is a full statement by BR and the Government of what investment is planned and needed—and the cost of that investment—for railway infrastructure over the next 25 years. Only with proper information of this sort about Railtrack's investment programme can decisions about what constitutes "fair" in terms of track charges be made adequately.

It will inevitably be the case, once a degree of private sector involvement has been achieved, that many of Railtrack's investment decisions will affect the current and future activities of several operators. The interests of operators so affected may be very different. Those interests may also be different from those of Railtrack. For example an operator's needs might be driven by relatively short term commercial considerations, particularly near the end of the lifetime of a franchise. We understand the intention is that franchises will typically be of 5-10 years duration. This is a short period compared to the investment cycle for railway infrastructure and it would seem unlikely that operators will have much incentive to take an interest in investment in infrastructure. Reconciling these diverse interests will not be easy. The White Paper is unclear as to who will be responsible for doing so and our concern is that in such a situation the expedient course will be the postponement or shelving of an investment decision by Railtrack.

In the long run, the success of railways in the private sector will be dependent on the quality of the infrastructure available. If it does not benefit from proper investment, perhaps for the reasons described above, the Government will find its long term objective of moving railways into the private sector increasingly difficult to achieve.

INVESTMENT IN ROLLING STOCK

Trafalgar House is no longer involved in manufacture of rolling stock. However the concerns identified above in relation to investment in infrastructure probably apply equally to rolling stock. The White Paper does not make it clear who would be expected to initiate and implement investment in new rolling stock. The short life of franchises makes it unlikely that franchisees will have an interest in doing so. There is no body identified that would. We would leave detailed comment on this to others more directly involved in the field, but plainly it is an aspect of the Government's proposals requiring further careful thought.

25 September 1992

APPENDIX 57

RAILWAY DEVELOPMENT SOCIETY

Memorandum of Observations on the future of the Rail System in the light of the Government's Proposals for Privatisation

1.0 INTRODUCTION:

1.1 The Railway Development Society, the national voice for rail users, welcomes the opportunity to submit evidence to the Transport Committee as it has serious reservations as to the practicality, or even the desirability, of the Government's proposals for the Privatisation of British Rail.

1.2 Firstly it sees the proposals as a recipe for chaos and confusion with a heavy dose of bureaucracy such that it could actually add to the cost of running the railways by as much as 30 per cent. If so, at the end of the day we are convinced that these extra costs can only be reflected in the fares paid by passengers.

1.3 As a prime representative of the consumer it is significant that of the 70 affiliated Rail Users Groups we have consulted, and whose comments form part of this evidence, we have yet to find one that is in favour of the Government's proposals.

1.4 One of our main concerns is that the Government will maintain continuity in the programme of investment in the re-equipment of British Rail without which we would raise serious doubts for the future of railway manufacturers in this country. Any uncertainty over who will be operating particular services and the equipment they will need can only serve to undermine their position.

1.5 Whilst we do not disagree with the principle of separating Infrastructure from Operating, based as it is on EC Directive 91/440 of 29 July 1991, we are concerned that only the *Operators* will receive financial support from Government which could lead to ossification, rather than development, of the rail network and possibly even be contrary to the principles of the Directive.

1.6 Our understanding of its provisions is that rail infrastructure should remain the responsibility of the State *and be adequately funded**. We would therefore suggest that any proposal to dispose of track and signalling, in part or *in toto,* to a private operator could well contravene these provisions and possibly lead to further conflict between Westminster and Brussels.

1.7 We shall also suggest (in answer to specific questions) that the proposals in the White Paper, based as they are upon the assumption that BR is a monopoly, start from a false assumption and that whilst the provisions of the Directive were intended to create a more level playing field there is still a long way to go before road and rail are competing on equal terms.

1.8 We are also not convinced that the Citizen's Charter will safeguard the interests of the *User* and consider that any regulatory body would of necessity need to be invested with much stronger powers than those at present residing in the Transport Users Consultative Committees. Such powers would need to be sufficient to guard against rail closures by default—including *Bustitution.*

1.9 In structuring our response we have tried as far as possible to concentrate on the issues identified by the Committee in its Press Notice of 16 July 1992.

* Our emphasis

2.0 AIMS AND OBJECTIVES:

2.1 In seeking to answer this first question we suggest "to whom" should be added after the first part and "to invest" after the second. On this assumption we consider that the first question should be approached from the point of view of the consumer ie the passengers who are going to have to pay the price of Privatisation at the end of the day.

2.2 What are the aims of all Privatised Industries? The most important is surely to make profits but we feel that the average Essex man (or woman) on the London Tilbury and Southend Railway is not going to be impressed with huge profits, such as have accrued in some recently-privatised industries, if there is not a significant and measurable improvement in the standard of service provided.

2.3 One of our associated Groups has suggested the following definition which we feel adequately answers the question:

"To operate, within an integrated national transport strategy, safe, efficient and economical passenger and freight rail services which can meet public needs and demands and can thereby compete effectively with, and complement, other transport modes—notably road."

Our main fear is that the Government's aim is to provide "the minimum tolerable service at lowest possible cost."

2.4 We are also concerned that Privatisation could lead to certain elements of the community being denied access to the rail system such as the Disabled. The recent commercial decision by British Rail to reduce from one-half to one-third the day return discounts on the Disabled Persons Railcard does not augur well for this section of society and the costs thereby avoided could merely add to the present burdens of Local Authorities.

2.5 We consider that the railways constitute an important part of the social and economic infrastructure of the country and that any diminution in their importance in an effort to reduce costs could stunt economic revival.

2.6 As to the prospects for Private Sector investment whilst we accept the proposed split between Operating and Infrastructure we are doubtful that the support provided by Government in the form of PSO Grant and other "Sweeteners" will be sufficient to encourage Development of the rail network given that no such support will be forthcoming for Railtrack.

2.7. Some of the attractions to the Private Sector could be negative from the point of view of the consumer and examples are quoted below:

(a) to exploit those routes, at those times, calculated to prove the most profitable (colloquially referred to as "cherry picking");

(b) to purchase or lease rights over railway premises capable of profitable development for other commercial purposes (ie other than railways);

(c) to take over a going concern along with staff possessing a vast body of operational expertise and experience.

2.8 Certainly removing the constraints of the External Financing Limit will, in theory, place greater capital at the railways' disposal but will the rates of return be sufficient to actually release it?

3.0 OPEN ACCESS TO RAILTRACK

3.1 Our first thoughts on this aspect were that "Open Access" seemed entirely incompatible with "exclusive" franchising as one is virtually a contradiction of the other and it could be argued that the latter could lead to the very monopoly that the Government is trying to avoid. Pronouncements from Marsham Street, however, seem to assert that competition will occur at the "bidding" stage and that such a situation would not occur but what if the franchisee were to be taken over by another competitor?

3.2 In fact, discussion of Monopolies could be an irrelevent side issue as we would question the whole tenor of the Government's proposals in the White Paper, based as they surely are on the premise that British Rail enjoys a privileged position. Its share of the nation's passenger and freight markets, a mere six per cent in each case, hardly constitutes a monopoly when viewed against the transport industry as a whole. The argument appears to concentrate purely on the fact that it owns its own track and infrastructure in addition to its rolling stock and motive power.

3.3 The owner of a small business would be astonished if someone were to enter his premises with the intention of setting up in competition, and would be enraged if told that the ownership of his floorspace was a "monopoly". If the Citizen's Charter enshrines the principle that a citizen's home is his castle, why should this principle not apply to a specialised transport operator?

3.4 Turning to the position of the Board itself we understand that BR will not be allowed to apply for franchises but that the Government has not ruled out "Management Buy-outs". We consider that these would be at the most a "second best" solution but are more concerned that the situation would create a totally negative management culture in what was left of BR and more importantly could lead to a HIATUS IN INVESTMENT (at least during the Privatisation process).

3.5 Whilst any system, given goodwill and unlimited access to computers, can be made to work, nevertheless when profits, shareholders' interests and the possibility of bankruptcy replace the simple concept of "Public Service" the whole idea could end in total chaos.

4.0 STRATEGIC PLANNING

4.1 Again our first reaction was that this ought to be the responsibility of the Department of Transport, as it is for roads. Nevertheless, given the Department's relative lack of interest in and possible lack of knowledge on operational and commercial rail planning, in view of the relatively small number of staff involved in this field, there is a strong case for saying that another PUBLIC body should do so. If British Rail is not to undertake this task the only alternative would be RAILTRACK given the principle enshrined in the EC Directive.

4.2 At this point it is considered that BR's own performance on this front, given the restraints under which it has been operating, should at least be acknowledged. In the last few years it has electrified routes to places like Edinburgh, Leeds, Newcastle, Norwich, King's Lynn and Weymouth; added scores of new and reopened stations to the network; gained new business by cross-country Sprinter trains, and reopened more than 100 miles of passenger line, especially in Scotland, Yorkshire, the Midlands and Wales. It has done this despite having received less Government support than any comparable rail network in Europe.

4.3 In principle, Strategic Planning should be in the hands of one Public Body. The problems between the existing Sectors of BR are probably already known to the Committee from its own previous studies and it is significant that the operation of market forces was largely responsible for the demise of CHARTERAIL. We would suggest that the inherent presumption that the Private Sector can always manage things better needs to be severely questioned.

4.4 With regard to Freight our main concern is that rail will be competing on a level playing field with road. To quote from a well-known railway expert (Richard Hope) "The White Paper poses another threat to freight. At present, freight trains only pay marginal wear-and-tear charge for using passenger lines, most of which are subsidised. Railtrack will receive no subsidy, and will be required to charge users impartially. With track charges for freight set to rise, millions of tons could switch to roads."

4.5 Freight is also by its nature inherently slower than passenger traffic and seems unlikely to be able to compete on mainly passenger route paths, with daytime passenger Inter-City or commuter services. Furthermore one important difference between road and rail is that train drivers need to have route knowledge before they can travel over a particular route. If an operator has to pay large training costs before he starts or extends a service he will continue to send his goods by road, as a lorry driver can use any road in this country. The rules regarding route training need to be checked and, if new signalling technology, such as ATP, will reduce the need for route knowledge this should be reflected in the charges made to the user. We will have more to say on this aspect in answer to a later question.

5.0 SUBSIDY AND INVESTMENT:

5.1 In response to this question we would reiterate our view that the Privatisation of British Rail should NOT lead to a hiatus in the programme of investment in the re-equipment of the railways and would again question the ability of RAILTRACK to maintain and develop the network if it is under a strict requirement to make an 8 per cent return on investment with no direct funding from Government. We would therefore prefer the Swedish model where both Operation and Infrastructure are entitled to financial support from the State a principle we understand to be enshrined in EC Directive 91/440.

5.2 As to how projects should be appraised, whilst some doubts have been cast on aspects of COBA to validate the cost effectiveness of road and rail schemes, the principle must be applied to both if the Government is genuine in its desire to effect a transfer of freight traffic from road to rail and a prime example which comes to mind is the Wensleydale Line in North Yorkshire.

5.3 With roads "free at the point of use" and rail infrastructure which the customer must pay for (particularly with the requirement for an 8 per cent return on investment) there appears to be little incentive for private operators (especially freight) to switch from road to rail when they are to be financially penalised for doing so.

5.4 Whilst we welcome the Government's acceptance that Grant should be paid in urban situations where development of rail can provide a "consumer surplus" in terms of easing congestion we feel that if road and rail are to compete on equal terms, as the EC Directive is intended to encourage, then this particular anomaly should be resolved at the earliest opportunity.

6.0 RAILTRACK CHARGES:

6.1 Again our first reaction to the methods of charging for the use of RAILTRACK raised the spectre of complete and utter chaos with interminable arguments between the parties as to who should pay how much and for what. Nevertheless one of our affiliated Groups has produced a fairly simple charging regime which we would recommend for consideration viz.

6.2 The basic assumptions would be that:

(a) RAILTRACK will need both to cover all its costs and to plough back profits into infrastructure investment;

(b) all scheduled passenger and freight movements would, as now, be timetabled nationally and processed by TOPS;

(c) operators must themselves meet all costs of either diversions or special bus services occasioned by engineering possessions (whether planned or emergency).

Subject to these assumptions every path allocated should be charged at a basic rate per unit distance but with surcharges added in respect of:

(i) low speed running (ie, prolongation of track occupancy);

(ii) high speed running (causing heavier wear and tear) and;

(iii) heavy weight, such as freight (leading, again, to heavier wear and tear).

6.3 To this regime we would add that such rates should be based on an agreed standard of maintenance ie, either for passenger or freight, with an added factor for the complexity of the layout and possibly the addition of a Premium for use during times of high demand.

6.4 However, serious consideration would need to be given to the effects this would have on the viability of freight services and in view of the problems that have been experienced by CHARTERAIL it is doubtful whether a significant transfer of road freight could be achieved on the basis of outright sale and/or without financial support from Government, both of which the White Paper appears to exclude.

6.5 Whatever the outcome of these deliberations it is quite clear that, as with timetabling, the need to resolve these issues between a multiplicity of operators is likely to add to the overall costs of running the railways, possibly by as much as 30 per cent.

7.0 MAXIMISING THE PUBLIC INTEREST:

7.1 As a representative of the consumer we want to see as much as possible built into the Franchise Specification with a guarantee of minimum levels of service—including early morning and late-night running. Added to this should be the obvious requirement for through ticketing; ticket inter-availability; facilities for the disabled; capacity for luggage; prams, bikes and dogs and in appropriate urban situations the validity of Railcards if chaos is not to ensue. The experience of the recently Privatised Metro in Manchester does not give cause for optimism on this front.

7.2 To be effective and of least cost to the public purse it is considered that all franchises should be for at least five years although 10 would probably be the most cost effective. There would also need to be some safeguard that if an operator "ceased trading" for whatever reason, the service would revert to BR with appropriate compensation therefore through the Public Service Obligation Grant.

7.3 Furthermore there would need to be strong safeguards for the consumer via the TUCCs; OFFRAIL or the Regulator with a requirement for significant consumer input via Local Users Groups or organisations such as our own Society. Such bodies should automatically contain representatives of users who could, for example, be selected by season-ticket and Railcard holders.

7.4 The Regulator would also need to have power to ensure that different operators co-operated satisfactorily in relation to the areas described in Para. 7.1 above and also in the retention of "Park and Ride" facilities where appropriate.

7.5 Consumers should also have ready access to information relating to tenders. It is important that service standards should be made public before franchise bids are sought to reduce the possibility of standards being reduced to attract more franchise bids if there is little interest in running some services. The need to maintain connections with other services should be included in this package.

7.6 In short such powers, under a Privatised system, would, to guarantee a minimum of long intervals between services and to prevent closure "by default" eg Stockport–Stalybridge, need to be much tougher than those at present vested in the Transport Users Consultative Committees.

8.0 ROLLING STOCK LEASING:

8.1 The main argument for leasing rolling stock is that it would free British Rail from the current constraints on new investment therein but with the future role of BR seen as the operator of trains that nobody else wants to run unless a firm procurement policy is established the prospects for any further investment in this field appears grim.

8.2 Given the threat to the British railway manufacturing industry this would pose it could be argued that all BR rolling stock should be transferred at the earliest opportunity to a holding company and leased-back to BR (or whoever). This would certainly be better than the uncertainty which would prevail whilst the how and wherefore of Sale and Franchising was worked out. Nevertheless the prime question is who would pay for the rolling stock initially. If not the Government (or a government appointed body) what Finance houses or other investors would be interested?

8.3 As BR is the only owner of passenger rolling stock, some of which is tailored to particular routes and systems, there is not, as such, a second-hand market, unless one includes the type of clapped-out equipment that is sometimes sold to private operators or railway preservation societies. Any comparison with the lease-car system would therefore be very misleading.

8.4 In any event who would finance the leasing of rolling stock that is over 10 years old? Experience with this method of procurement in connection with the Bradford electrification has proved that there are pitfalls unless there is a guarantee (or guarantor) as to user and term. The leasing of Class 50 locomotives by BR was only possible because the Board guaranteed to use them for at least 15 years. What prospects for a Franchisee with only a five-year term.

8.5 There is also the issue as to who would be responsible for setting the standards for new stock and the fact that some of a specialised nature could not easily be transferred to another location without expensive modifications.

8.6 If, as the Government envisages, there are to be numerous individual operators of routes future orders of rolling stock are likely to be in small quantities. This could also have an adverse effect on the future of the British Rail manufacturing industry. (It is significant that the tramcars for Manchester were built in Italy as no British firm was interested in such a small build of vehicles or indeed had recent experience of their manufacture.)

8.7 It is therefore considered that whilst there is a role for leasing it should not be the general rule. Furthermore whilst companies are entitled to tax relief for the procurement of assets, whether they make profits or not, there is a fear that where profit margins are tight there will be a general deterioration in the age and quality of rolling stock as has occurred in the Privatised bus industry. In the end therefore it will be the consumer who pays the price of Privatisation.

9.0 VALUATION OF STATIONS:

9.1 The initial response of many of the Society's affiliated Rail User Groups was that it would be in the best interests on the travelling public for stations to remain with RAILTRACK as part of the Infrastructure and that they should be valued at their existing use. If operators had to pay stopping fees to private station owners, as has been suggested in certain academic circles, this could lead to the abandonment of certain stops to the detriment of the travelling public.

9.2 If however development value is to be allowed there needs to be a guarantee in any sale for the minimum basic rail facilities to be retained, including car parking provision where essential to the commercial demands of the service. The minimum standards required of service franchisees should be mirrored in those for station owners. These can include a basic minimum amount of seating and shelter according to the average daily usage of the station plus disabled access; cycle storage and information facilities.

9.3 We would also seek to ensure that valuable downtown sites are not sold off for development, as has occurred in the USA, and to a lesser extent in the UK, with the facility moved to a less convenient location with the possible loss of valuable bus interchange.

9.4 Paras. 17 and 44 of the White Paper go some way to meet these needs, the latter declaring the objects of sale or leasing of stations to be "better use of the commercial opportunities" and "improving the usefulness of stations to the community by re-development and other means".

9.5 The corollary to this should surely be that:

(a) a purchaser or lessee must be under a legal obligation not to interfere in any way with the equipment or operation of Railtrack, nor with the running of trains by franchisees or by BR;

(b) sale or rental values must therefore be assessed on the basis that such obligations would inevitably reduce the development value of the premises.

9.6 We have seen the price that has to be paid by the travelling public to realise development value in the case of Broad Street in the City of London but if Privatisation is seen as the only way of achieving this we must at least place on record what has already been achieved by BR itself, not only at Liverpool Street, but at Cannon Street, Blackfriars, Ludgate, Charing Cross etc, the profits from which have accrued to BR as a whole and not just to an individual owner. Is this not just an exercise in re-inventing the wheel?

10.0 CONCLUSIONS:

10.1 Consumers, remain unconvinced that the Government's plans, as set out in the White Paper, will lead to better rail services. Many of the proposals display naivete, vagueness or wishful thinking and lead one to question its real purpose in putting them forward.

10.2 The only way in which such proposals would be acceptable would be by the retention of a PUBLIC track authority, a PUBLIC operating company or the most robust conditions for any PRIVATE operators or owners who might be allowed on to the national network.

19 September 1992

Supplementary Memorandum from the Railway Development Society

As a member of the Railway Development Society, I am writing to you as a Vice-President, to draw your attention to the widespread concern there is over the Channel Tunnel Rail Link as to whether provision is being made for the adequate transport of classic or conventional freight (excluding aggregates) as well as passenger traffic.

The Link is now to have a capability to carry "some freight". The eastern section, having been designed, and chosen, as a passenger route, in a corridor which precludes expansion to four track, would need to be re-engineered to take classic freight.

It is now being re-engineered, but with gradients steepened to 1 in 40. The passenger 'supertrains' for which it is being designed may be able to negotiate these at or near the postulated speed of 140 mph.

But are we seriously to believe that there are magical freight trains which can haul classic freight over these gradients, allied with the tight curves which are always conveniently overlooked, at speeds sufficient to avoid problems with cant incompatibility?

If the alignment chosen precludes a fully shared passenger/freight railway, such as the Neubaustrecke or the Rail-Europe proposal, the freight capability of the Link will be constrained to the limited amounts which can be carried on trains with performance characteristics similar to the passenger train, such as the French La Poste. Franchisees would find carrying classic freight unviable and inpracticable.

If the link is to have a genuine classic freight capability, it should be possible to explain, at least in principle, how this is to be achieved. Three years of equivocation on the subject suggest it is not practicable, and the deeply shocking Union Railways "Briefing for MPs and Councillors— No. 1" (below) indicate that the Link will not carry conventional freight trains for the reasons given in the "Comparison of Routes", page 19; and that "consultation" will, once again, be cosmetic.

8 December 1992

Union Railways: Briefing for MPs and Councillors—No. 1.

In this profoundly disturbing paper, many of the terms used are ambiguous, almost childishly imprecise, perpetuating the ambivalence over what, if any, freight is to be carried on the link, and infering that consultation will again not transcend the peripheral.

1. The Link will be designed to carry fast freight, i.e. parcel type and the limited amounts which can be carried on passenger only alignment.

2. On BR scheme, "slow" freight, meaning classic or conventional freight, would require four tracks, which is precluded by the constraints of the corridor, let alone the cost. This is generalising from the particular, the Neubaustrecke provides a fully shared system on two tracks, so would the Rail-Europe scheme. It is possible; but would not be practicable on BR scheme as presently known.

3. Public consultation, far from being "full" as in DTp paper, will be limited as before to environmental impacts and mitigation; the horizontal and vertical alignments will again not be negotiable, neither will the function.

4. Consultations with MPs, County, District and parish Members, have not been on the route, details of which have only been disclosed, in part, to Officers in strict confidence. Ashford B.C. have stated that the meeting which had taken place did not constitute consultation with the Council on a corporate basis, and that the confidential nature of such meetings with Officers precluded such consultation taking place. Maidstone B.C. have withdrawn from such meetings.

5. Sir Keith Speed and Andrew Rowe, MPs, are calling for publication of the reference route when it is put to Government. As this would show whether the reference route is passenger only, unsuitable for freight as BR have said, it will be resisted. Consultation would then be whitewashed over a fait accompli.

6. A classic or conventional freight capability will be presented to Government as an operational extra, hideously expensive and therefore not researched. See final para of p.1, from what data are these figures derived, given that the route was merely a concept?

7. There is a danger that a route will be railroaded through, having been revealed only in the Spring announcement, with immutable vertical and horizontal alignments, and track geometry which closes for ever the practicable option of carrying classic freight since, even if normally feasible, this would result in an incurable limitation on the capacity, and therefore viability, of the Link.

8. It is essential that MPs, MEPs and Councillors are fully consulted prior to any route decision, not merely issued with limited and onesided information which becomes misleading because of its inadequacy. If an

optimum solution has been found, it should speak for itself, and not need to be veiled in secrecy and obfuscation, leading to premonitions that it may prove chimerical, and, worse, still to be imposed.

9th November 1992

Union Railways, launched officially on July 27, is taking forward at Government's request the work on the Channel Tunnel high speed railway project, the first main line to be built in Britain for over 100 years and one of the largest construction projects in Europe.

Union Railways, headed by Dr John Prideaux, is a subsidiary of the British Railways Board. With responsibilities covering both the Channel railway and Heathrow Express, the company brings together BR and private sector engineering, planning, environmental and consulting staff.

The need for the high speed railway

International passenger services through the Channel Tunnel to Waterloo will start in late 1993–early 1994. International trains will share the heavily congested commuter network south of London. Substantial increases in commuter traffic must also be catered for, and British Rail estimates that by 2000 the capacity of existing lines into Waterloo to handle international traffic will be exhausted.

The railway will be the principal rail connection between Britain and Europe. For domestic travellers, it offers scope for a reduction in journey times from Kent, for example cutting the journey time from London to Ashford from 73 to under 40 minutes. Domestic links to the line could take up to an hour off the Canterbury–London time. At present, it takes as long to reach Ramsgate from London as to get to Darlington, Cardiff, Exeter or Crewe. Remedying this, which will release capacity within the existing network to run an additional 12 trains per hour into London, will be a major boost for the economy of north and east Kent. The eastern approach to London will also enable the railway to play its part in the economic regeneration of the East Thames corridor.

Freight

Union was asked to take into account projected needs for freight and passengers. The two-track high speed railway will be designed to carry fast freight. Studies by BR, DoE, the Department of Transport and the Treasury concluded that there was no economic or commercial case for building another freight track alongside the passenger line. The 43 freight paths per day to the tunnel available on the existing network where BR, in conjunction with Kent County Council, is mitigating noise impacts, will be sufficient until well into the next century. We and French Railways expect a maximum of 60 freight trains a day through the tunnel, but not until 2020.

Developing the route as a main line for slow freight would have required a fully four-tracked railway, a wider area of land to be acquired and more extensive engineering work. Costs for the 1991 outline proposal would have risen from about £4.5 billion to £7 billion with an estimated marginal return of only £10 million annually. It would have been necessary to restart planning work on the Cheriton to Detling section, and construction would have taken two further years.

Current state of work

In October 1991 the then Secretary of State for Transport, Malcolm Rifkind, announced the Government's preference for a route corridor based on a concept produced by Ove Arup for an easterly approach to Kings Cross. In March 1992, Union Railways was given clarification on a scope for the railway. It was asked to start design work on a two-track railway, with options to introduce some four-tracking, using passing loops, near London. The project team, including Ove Arup, was asked to define a route to a point where it could be safeguarded for planning purposes. The Secretary of State also said that he expected the project to be carried forward by the private sector, and advisors were appointed to examine funding options. Total cost will depend on the number of stations, extent of environmental protection and linkage to other transport systems— decisions which will be made by Ministers.

The corridor from Folkestone runs through the following local authority areas:

Kent: Shepway, Ashford, Maidstone, Tonbridge and Malling, Rochester-upon-Medway, Gravesham and Dartford.

Essex: Thurrock.

London: Havering, Barking and Dagenham, Newham, Hackney, Islington and Camden.

Since March, we have held two series of technical consultation meetings with all affected authorities. We also sit with the local authorities on the three Channel Tunnel Rail Link Fora and working groups convened by DTp. Dr Prideaux has initiated a programme of meetings with MPs and leading councillors from affected areas. During the autumn, we will hold further rounds to assess the views of MPs, councillors, Chief Executives and technical officers. MPs and councillors are representatives of local opinion and we will ensure they are fully consulted.

We have thus far spent over 1300 staff hours in consultation and held some 98 meetings with MPs, County, District and parish council officers and members. Route proposals, which have involved the preparation of a large number of costed options and variations (for example for stations) and assessment of environmental or economic considerations, should be submitted to Ministers by the end of 1992. We hope that Government will then rapidly make its choices so that a route can be safeguarded.

Safeguarding is often misunderstood. It is a process by which Ministers, acting under the Town and Country General Development Order 1988, may define a zone within which planning applications must be referred by planning authorities to developers for advice. Some areas in Kent have been safeguarded. Of 46 planning applications submitted to BR in the year following initial safeguarding, 90 per cent were approved or not commented upon.

Following route announcement, which is expected next spring, there will be a period of public consultation on environmental impacts and mitigation (an environmental impact assessment will be prepared). We hope that a route will then be suggested and a hybrid Bill to provide for construction period could be deposited in Autumn 1993 for passage by 1995. A five-year construction period would follow, and the railway could be opened by the year 2000.

16 October 1992

APPENDIX 58

CENTRE FOR LOCAL ECONOMIC STRATEGIES

The Future Prospects for the Railway System in the light of the Government's Proposals for Privatisation

The response of the Centre for Local Economic Strategies [CLES] to the specific questions posed by the House of Commons Transport Committee is set out in this Paper. To assist the Committee (but not at present for publication) the Paper is supported by a CLES working document, "A critique of the White Paper".

The Centre works with and for local authorities and seeks to contribute to policy debates on economic issues. It is committed to the development of public services, to regeneration strategies, to acting on environmental imperatives, to regional democracy and to collaboration across Europe.

Both texts have been prepared by Jonathan Tyler, a Principal Research Officer. He has been involved with the railway industry for thirty years, as an operator, planner and market researcher with British Rail [BR], as a University Lecturer in Rail Transport and Transport Policy, and latterly as an independent consultant developing Geographic Information Systems for BR. He is currently evaluating the opportunities for increasing rail's share of the freight business generated by the Humber Ports.

1. What should be the aims and objectives of a privatised railway?

The characteristics of railway technology inherently create a high-capacity mode of transport, both in terms of the unit of movement and the total throughput. Those same characteristics generate costs that are substantially invariant with volume, however efficiently the system is managed. In order to justify the expensive resources which have gone into creating the capacity it is essential to devise a regime which maximises the return on those assets.

The problem lies in the definition of "return". In theory a company driven solely by profit objectives might achieve an adequate financial return by charging a high margin over variable costs on traffic volumes that did not fully use the available capacity. That tactic is however unlikely to be pursued because competition from road transport generally precludes large margins. This would remain the case even if pricing structures for the use of roads and railways were made similar and even if external costs were more equitably levied (both of which are essential to the operation of a market in transport), especially since road transport has a potential advantage over rail in that its units of movement are smaller and hence more flexible.

Profit-maximisation is therefore inappropriate for the infrastructure and for the generality of train services. "Return" must instead be conceived in terms of the *use* of assets, for three reasons.

—First, rail can only remain competitive if its overhead costs are spread across the largest practicable number of users.

—Second, if rail is to fulfill its potential in relieving congestion—the increasingly unacceptable corollary to road's advantages—its capacity needs to be more than marginally exploited.

—And third, as environmental and resource constraints bite, it is becoming unacceptable *not* to utilise the system to the full.

It is no exaggeration to say that, *if the nation wishes to have a railway network at all,* then it must accept this volume-maximising objective. Any other policy will lead to inexorably to permanent financial instability, with all its consequences in deteriorating services and organisational turmoil. This fundamental decision is of vastly greater importance than any question of ownership. If taken positively, however, it does not have a critical implication for the relationship between the state and private companies contemplating entering the railway business.

In respect of *infrastructure,* whatever the extent of private involvement, it will be necessary for the foreseeable future to charge less than allocated costs in order to reverse the present spiral of decline caused by spreading overheads across falling volumes. That means state support, in order to achieve for the greater good the three benefits described above.

In respect of *operations* private companies might be allowed to maximise profits rather than volume on their trains if they so wished (a choice between a cheap, crowded train and a pricier but more comfortable train might benefit consumers), but the freedom must be limited to prevent lower-volume trains taking up disproportionate track capacity.

Moreover, our argument necessarily implies that the proposal in the White Paper to require Railtrack to be self-financing and to channel grants to service-operators must be changed. It is wrong in logic, and it is quite clear that in practice it will mean unacceptable overhead charges to private operators (even threatening existing freight traffic) and acute problems in the distribution of grants. It is essential to adopt the policy already being followed in Sweden and likely to be followed in Germany whereby the infrastructure is regarded as a national asset. Where appropriate private capital and private-sector styles of management can then be introduced into the provision of services. That philosophy would also appear to underlie the European Directive on Railways [91/440].

What are the attractions for the private sector?

CLES is committed to asserting the proper and positive role of the public sector. This question must therefore be addressed chiefly by the private sector. For many reasons we believe that a combination of the difficult nature of the railway business with the constraints imposed by the Government's awareness of popular concern will severely curtail private interest. The danger is that during the period while that becomes apparent British Rail will be wracked with indecision, to add to already plummeting morale and the huge handicap of continuous reorganisation.

2. *Is there any conflict between the principle of open access and the granting of exclusive franchises?*

There is no conceptual or legal conflict, but the proposed mix of policies is flawed economically. If a franchisee constrained by certain obligations can at any time be challenged by an operator not so constrained, one of three outcomes will occur.

— Many potential operators will not accept a franchise in the first place, thus diminishing competition.

— Or, having signed a contract, a franchisee may demand compensation and/or surrender the franchise if competition materialises: this has already contributed to instability in the deregulated bus industry and would do even more serious damage in rail transport.

— Alternatively, a franchisee could fight back by concentrating resources, marketing, special offers and managers' time on the directly-challenged services but at the expense of other services and customers (any attempt to limit the scope for this would make non-entry even more likely).

It is improbable that any one of these outcomes would help to deliver a better service to existing travellers or to attract new customers to the railways. For the generality of the passenger business the Government must choose between competition for *protected* franchises or wholly open access. Since the latter is recognised to be unworkable it must accept the former. That does not rule out open access for some marginal, specialised markets such as Cruise Trains (the glamour of which has had a disproportionate effect on thinking about the mundane realities of ordinary passenger services).

3. *Who should do the strategic planning for our railways and how can different interests be coordinated?*

Two issues are of particular importance, namely investment (and hence technological development) and timetabling.

Because of the inherent characteristics of railways, as referred to above, many projects are substantial in scale and of their nature involve more than one traffic. This effect is reinforced by the fact that the technical relationship between infrastructure and vehicles is closer than that in any other mode. It is thus inevitable that the planning and implementation of the majority of investment must be the responsibility of a single body (however much management may be decentralised).

The sum of any separate decisions cannot possibly produce an optimum solution, and may be corporately detrimental, as has happened in Japan and to some extent between the Sectors of BR. Since the system as a whole cannot attract a profit-maximiser it follows that a strong state body is essential, though the private sector can no doubt undertake some tasks on an agency basis.

In respect of timetabling the complexity of the network is such that problems in managing the interaction of different services can only be resolved by a strong planning body. The number of space-time permutations is so great that no effective market can be established (the analogy of "slots" is highly misleading), while a committee procedure, though valuable for consultation, would be certain to produce sub-optimal compromises. Furthermore, in order to stand any chance of attracting significant numbers of people from private cars the future passenger network will need to be modelled on that in the Netherlands (where services are extensive, frequent, fast and above all coordinated nationally), and that will not materialise simply as the sum of independent initiatives. However worthy each one may be.

For example, can freight develop effectively on a primarily passenger network?

There is no intrinsic reason why freight cannot develop effectively on a primarily passenger network. While the integrity of that network must be paramount, only a strong planning authority can make proper provision for freight paths within the timetable structure. A weaker authority, more vulnerable to both political pressures and to the influence of high-profile private passenger operators, is less likely to find paths commercially acceptable to freight customers. (One example of this process is that the Dutch model and the national interest point to day-long regular-interval services, into which freight paths can be incorporated by careful planning, whereas less structured timetables meeting fragmented private objectives will necessarily diminish the capacity and quality of the system for freight.)

4. *What will be the Government's role in subsidy and investment?*

The response to this question is implicit in the arguments already presented. To summarise, the case for retaining a national railway network is strong, but since it rests on immediate and longer-term benefits to the nation rather than on any conceivable profitability in private-sector terms, only the state can take ultimate responsibility for the system. The search for viability has failed, and there is no evidence that private-sector disciplines (market disciplines have applied for many years) would make any significant difference, however valuable they might be at a secondary level.

It should be noted that most improvements both in Britain and abroad, some of them spectacular, have taken place with state funds and under public-sector managers. Where state funds are used to achieve wider benefits they should be referred to as "grants" or "payments under community contracts". They are *not* subsidies.

To the greatest possible extent responsibility for support and investment should be decentralised to democratically-accountable bodies. The Passenger Transport Authorities have achieved notable improvements in conurbation services in collaboration wth BR, and many Counties have been instrumental in shielding their residents from the negative aspects of bus deregulation as well as contributing to rail projects.

In what circumstances will cost-benefit appraisal be appropriate, and what criteria should be used for future rail investment?

It is a natural extension of these arguments that cost-benefit appraisal is appropriate for any railway project and should be undertaken as a matter of course. Even in the case of an operation with a basic profit objective, such as a private freight train, it is desirable to introduce wider appraisal criteria and hence to extend the qualifying criteria for Section 8 grant if the community would benefit from, say, reduced road investment, eased congestion and ecological gains—as would seem likely with combined (intermodal) transport.

5. *Railtrack, the track authority, will charge all operators "commercial" rates for track use. What principles should be used to set these charges?*

We have argued above that the financial objective proposed for Railtrack is fundamentally wrong. Most of the present infrastructure is underutilised, British Rail having attempted, valiantly but unsuccessfully, to pursue the surplus-maximising objectives imposed by successive governments. Rates that would retain existing traffic cannot therefore achieve the stated aim of enabling Railtrack to break even.

If 'commercial' means either rates based on some system of cost-allocation that would, if they were obtained in all cases, cover all costs or discriminatory pricing that yielded the same amount in total, then most existing railfreight will transfer to the roads, many low-density passenger lines (both rural and conurbation) will become candidates for closure, and the resultant spreading of inescapable overheads ever more thinly will lead to the final collapse of the system.

To avoid that catastrophe (and it would be damaging to reach the brink and then reverse the policy) it is essential to recognise now that it is Railtrack which should receive State support. Once that is done Railtrack should be directed to levy such charges on operators as will maximise the use of capacity. The aim should be to cover costs where possible. On some well-used lines that may be achieved. Elsewhere, below-cost charges will be necessary as an inducement to operators and thus to customers.

Subject to appropriate managerial procedures being put in place to discourage laxity in cost-control or technological extravagance that is more likely to be in the national interest than narrow financial disciplines. The annual planned grant to cover the shortfall should be viewed as a positive investment in a communal asset.

This scheme is also to be preferred in terms of the Government's objectives for introducing the skills of the private sector. Though we consider these to be over-rated we concede that they could lead to improvements in some secondary aspects of the passenger service, in service delivery and in the freight sector. Under the existing proposals that may never be put to the test because a combination of lethal prices for using the track, the tight constraints on the pricing and timetabling of services and the administrative problems of paying huge state grants to franchisees will deter most private operators. The response would be very different if they were to be given a clear remit to make a commercial success of the operation of trains.

6. *How should franchises operate so as to maximise the public interest, both for profitable and subsidised services?*

The general answer to this question has already been given in terms of seeking to maximise volume (and particularly growth by attracting car-users) and of providing a service that whould achieve that. We make three particular points.

First, going for volume does not mean 'at all costs': crowded trains will deter business, and quality cannot be neglected in a sophisticated market. Striking the right balance is something that can mostly be left to professional managers, whether public or private, but both contract provisions and democratic oversight are essential to provide a framework.

Second, the national network will lose creditability if similar disciplines and appropriate coordination are not imposed on the ralationships *between* franchisees. There are damaging frictions now in the interaction between the three passenger businesses of British Rail, and they must not be perpetuated and extended by a plethora of franchisees.

Third, it is essential that the franchising of regional and local services should be undertaken by an authority accountable to the people of the area. In the conurbations with an existing Passenger Transport Authority that should become the Franchising Authority. Elsewhere the task might be entrusted to consortia of Councils.

7. *What arguments are there for switching immediately to a regime of rolling stock leasing for all operators, including BR?*

Given the (necessarily) high cost but long life of railway locomotives, coaches and wagons, coupled with the uncertainties in the market and the comparatively modest commitments required for road operations, there will be few, if any, companies strong enough financially and sure enough about the business to invest their own capital. That makes an active leasing market critical, for which there are three prerequisites.

First, stability. Companies must feel that the rules are not going to be casually changed (which means that the track regime must be transparent and reasonable with respect to access and prices), that they are not vulnerable to maverick operators (which means strict control of standards), and that the leasing market itself is secure enough not to face disruption from company failures.

Second, critical mass. Investment in rolling stock for leasing will itself not occur unless sufficient customers are forthcoming for the risks to be spread and for a balanced profile of first-time, mid-life and final users to build up. And third, the risks must be further reduced by greater standardisation, so that stock can be moved from one user or one route to another without difficulty—this may well conflict with the ambitions of innovative operators, and in the passenger business it is another reason to focus private operation on the secondary factors, in this case the *interior* design within a standard shell.

Against that background the idea of moving at once to leasing could be beneficial if it gave the establishment of a leasing market the momentum it may otherwise lack, with consequential damage if few private companies are entering the business but British Rail are constrained from taking any initiatives of their own.

At least one safeguard is essential. It would be unacceptable for BR to be outbid in seeking to lease stock for a particular service by a financially powerful new operator who then introduced changes which either proved unpopular or left BR with residual burdens, and still worse if the new firm soon pulled out because they found running trains was not quite as easy as they had thought (some of Richard Branson's plans for the East Coast Main Line threaten to bring about this scenario).

What are the White Paper's implications for BR's on-goiing rolling stock investment programme?

In addition to the points made above it is important to stress a fundamental problem in the proposals. In the present organisation of British Rail as a group of vertically-integrated businesses investment decisions are increasingly based on market requirements. Plans recognise both technical opportunities and the technical constraints (including the close track-vehicle symbiosis) but are no longer technology-led. That is as it should be. Under the proposed structure the link will be broken (before its benefits have come to fruition), and it is not clear how the alternative scheme will function.

In any future project in which rolling stock and infrastructure works are conjoint an operator and Railtrack will have to develop a singularly close and trusting relationship, which would be at once soured if anti-competitive practices were alleged or if the operator felt the charging rules worked against him. If more than one operator were involved, as could well be the case, the scope for differences between independent, profit-seeking parties is considerable, not least because some operators might actually be disadvantaged (for example if a passenger acceleration reduced the number of freight paths). This could lead to the collapse of projects unless strong authority is vested in the Regulator—thus further confirming that on a railway individual unco-ordinated initiatives are unlikely to deliver a coherent system.

For this reason, as well as because of potential failure of the leasing market and acute uncertainty, the proposals seem likely to undermine an already inadequate rolling stock programme and may destroy what is left of the railway manufacturing industry in the process.

8. *How is the value of stations to be assessed and what will be the relationship between a privately owned station and BR's operation of trains therefrom?*

We cannot comment on the technicalities of valuation, but we are profoundly concerned about the philosophy that appears to lie behind the proposal. The land on which a station stands is not simply a parcel which can as well serve purpose A as purpose B as purpose C and between which consumers are more or less indifferent. It is rather a site dedicated to the purposes of a railway station (we assume that the context is the consensus in favour of more use of rail). That station is locked into the network of other activities and linked transport services that collectively serve the economic and social life of the area. Any redevelopment following sale that enhances the attractiveness of the station to travellers (through physical improvement or additional facilities) would therefore be legitimate and welcome, but anything which marginalised rail customers would be unacceptable to the community.

The precedents are not good. In North America development of real estate pushed stations out of city centres with most damaging consequences for the visibility and accessibility of passenger services. Several towns in Britian have lost convenient rail and bus stations because short-term land values took precedence. And some station concourses have become so cluttered with retailing activities that passenger movement is hindered and the presentation of the service has degenerated because it is no longer the-obviously dominant function.

It is essential that Railtrack and the train operators have final authority over design and certain technical matters (for reasons of safety and operational integrity) and that quality provision for travellers remains the primary function of the site. This may mean that outright sales are impossible, and that leasing of non-operational areas is a better option.

30 September 1992

New Threats to the Railways: the Fragmentation of British Rail

A CRITIQUE OF THE WHITE PAPER

Jonathan Tyler
Principal Research Officer,
Centre for Local Economic Strategies

1. OBJECTIVES AND ASSUMPTIONS

1.1 Two questions must be asked in considering the Government's proposals for the future of British Rail [BR], as set out in the White Paper[1].

— Will they increase the railways' share of the transport of people and freight—given the virtual unanimity that that must be achieved?

— And, even if doubts exist on that score, are the proposals credible on their own terms?

The short answers are that the outcome could be disastrous for passengers, that the prospects for freight are rather better, but that the scheme could collapse under the weight of its inherent contradictions.

1.2 In the first paragraph the Government says that it "is determined to see better use made of the railways" [¶1], and one of the "essential requirements" is that "The Government wishes to continue developing the environmental benefits of rail" [¶8f]. If those objectives are of paramount importance one might expect that they would find expression in measures of achievement set out by an administration so keen to impose targets on other sectors. In fact, the White Paper is devoid of any statement about existing and targeted shares of the market and contains no specific plans for securing environmental improvements.

1.3 Instead the argument rests wholly on the belief that attainment of the general objectives, as well as more particular benefits to customers, will flow naturally from the very fact of involving the private sector. Because the White Paper has been so long in coming, so surrounded by rumour and lobbying, so patently unable to prepare for a simple sell-off, the idea has got about that the proposals are less ideological than earlier privatisations. On the contrary, the document is richly infused with ideology.

1.4 It is repeatedly assumed that only

"The introduction of competition through greater involvement of the private sector [can] be instrumental in achieving [high quality services]" [¶2].

No other option is mentioned, and no evidence supports innumerable assertions of this 'truth'. As to other examples of private railways, the statistic relating to Japan is mendacious, the reference to Sweden is misleading, and the claimed "success" of the American freight railways is ludicrously irrelevent to Britain

---

[1]New Opportunities for the railways: The Privatisation of British Rail. Cm 2012, July 1992.

[¶7]. One might expect that a policy of privatising railways that is unique in the European Community might be argued more forcefully[1].

1.5 Similarly, one does not have to be a fan of state-owned enterprises to regard as gross simplification the statement that

> "Management and employees in the private sector have greater incentives to provide the services which the consumer wants. The profitability of their company—and at the end of the day their jobs— depend on providing a service which attracts custom. Nationalised industries do not face such acute pressures" [¶19a].

It is in passing insulting to the thousands of dedicated railwaymen who have lost their jobs as unsympathetic governments have enforced contraction—and to hundreds of hard-working bus-drivers who have been summarily dismissed as a result of the power-politics of their privatised industry.

1.6 This prejudice comes through particularly when the Paper has to admit that some railway businesses are actually successful. Thus

> "InterCity has been *one of* BR's successes . . . It has proved increasingly popular with the public . . . [and] has made profits since 1988–89 . . . The *first priority* is to improve the service to customers by introducing private sector management, culture, disciplines and incentives" [¶34, 35; our italics].

The effortless flow of the argument through this *non sequitur* is breathtaking.

1.7 InterCity is far from perfect, but it is not self-evident that private managers could achieve a quantum advance. Specifically, one should allow for the shortcomings which are the consequence of Government policy[2] and for alleged defects which are, if anything, the outcome of too rigorous an adoption of private-sector disciplines, such as the text-book striving for market discrimination which generates public antipathy to the fares structure.

1.8 There is a further manifestation of the abandonment of objective discourse by this Government. Most references to the public funds currently paid to BR for running financially-unremunerative though socially-necessary passenger services use the word *subsidy* [for example, ¶8c]. All references to money to be paid in identical circumstances to future franchisees use the word *grant* [for example, ¶14]. The former is loaded with (unfair) implications of ineffieiency, the latter accurately reflects what the community has willed[3]. Even the Secretary of State himself seems confused, since in his Foreword he misleadingly refers to BR's "large losses".

1.9 Part of the problem is that the Government (and their cheer-leaders in the think-tanks and the press) have trouble in comprehending the true nature of the railways' "monopoly". Thus the technically-correct phrase "monopoly in the operation of [rail] services" is used in the Introduction [¶2], but the inference that BR does not have a monopoly in any effective sense is never drawn out. Instead there soon follows the claim that

> "The industry is more insulated from the demands of the market than its private sector airline, coach and road haulage competitors" [¶5—*what happened to buses and cars?!*].

It may be that the railways have not responded sufficiently vigorously to the challenge of these modes, and that state ownership partly explains that, but staff who have been fighting for the very survival of the railways for a generation hardly feel they have been "more insulated".

1.10. Given this calibre of argument and the absence of any measurable objectives it is impossible to judge whether the proposals will increase rail's market share, unless one accepts unreservedly that privatisation will of itself secure that result. One is therefore forced to focus on the internal coherence of the proposals. And it has to be said that even on its own terms the White Paper is a curious document[4].

---

[1]Obfuscation is going on. Separating track from operations is the important aspect of what Sweden has done, private ventures are as yet limited and problems are reported. Separation, not privatisation, is the dominant factor in Germany. France continues with an increasingly market-oriented vertical structure, which borrowed ideas from BR's sectorisation. The European Community Directive which establishes a "right of access for certain international services" [91/440; ¶58] does not apply to domestic services and has nothing to do with ownership as such, despite the impression given by discussing them in the same paragraph (the EC right for *private* operators is limited to 'combined transport' *freight*).

[2]For example, one of the new Mark IV sets on the East Coast Main Line was recently damaged in an accident. BR issued a public apology for having to substitute older and slower trains while it was repaired. What they could not say was that the lack of a sensible reserve of Mark IV sets was directly attributable to Government stringency—in the guise of profit objectives—which the French or German Railways would never have had to face. Recognition of the undesirability of "Government involvement in managerial issues" [¶19c] is a self-serving, not logical justification for privatisation.

[3]The Paper says that "Both Network SouthEast and Regional Railways are *heavily* dependent on subsidy. In 1991–92 . . . Of Regional Railways" turnover of £905m, *no less than* £629m came from grant . . . there is *no prospect whatsoever* of financial viability" [¶38, our emphasis]. This statement not only uses unworthily prejudiced language but makes no attempt to discuss the reasons for paying grant and begs the question of why financial viability should be an objective in the first place, despite an earlier acknowledgement that "social and other benefits [justify] continuing subsidy" [¶8c]. The issue is also put more neutrally in the description of BR contracts with the PTEs [¶39].

[4]There was no preceding Green Paper of public consultation, only the spectacle of right-wing "analysts" vying in public for ministerial attention and the British Railways Board lobbying in private. This was neither edifying nor democratic nor constructive.

2. CONTRADICTIONS AND IGNORANCE

2.1 The White Paper is self-contradictory and displays ignorance about the railways. Many detailed examples are discussed below, two general ones should be given at once.

"Services must not be disrupted by organisational change" [¶9].

"BR, with the Government's agreement, has, over the last ten years, regorganised the railways in business sectors based on different markets—InterCity, Regional Railways, Trainload Freight etc.. . . . BR currently operates as a vertically integrated railway, with track and train operations under its control. The Government believes that track and train operations should be separated . . . The Government recognises the challenge which this restructuring will pose for BR following the recent organisational changes introduced under the Organising for Quality initiative. It will work closely with BR management to ensure a smooth transition to the new structure" [¶11, 12].

There could hardly be any greater insouciance, and only their professionalism will prevent the tangible disillusion and cynicism among railwaymen from corroding their everday performance

2.2 It is astonishing that the White Paper does not argue its case for abandoning the vertically-integrated railway, other than it being deemed expedient if privatisation is to work. The debate is not new, there *are* merits as well as disadantages in both alternative structures. Yet no evidence is presented that sectorisation has failed. On the contrary, a tentative judgment might be that, while it has its raw edges in terms of effective interaction between marketing staff, train operators and infrastructure engineers it is showing promise in replacing a technically-driven culture with sharpened cost-awareness and customer-led product-mangement. Instead, all we have is "The Government believes . . .".

2.3 Equally, "An single railway network is convenient and flexible for passengers. These benefits include a national timetable and through ticketing" [¶8d]. This commitment is repeated later [¶88] though with the qualifiction "so far as possible". Nevertheless the whole thrust of the proposals is to break up the network. "Smaller operating companies" [¶19f], diversity [¶26], innovation [¶6] and choice [¶19b] are valued more highly than the benefits of an integrated system.

2.4 Sustaining the network commitment will be at best immensely and counter-productively complicated, at worst possible. A particular contradiction is that at one moment the scheduling scheme depends on a glib misconception about the practicality of dispersed responsibility, at another on a dirigiste view of the need for "a unified timetable for the entire network" [¶90]. Nor is anything said about the future of crucial network-wide attributes such as the computer reservation system, access standards for the disabled or the instantly-recognised double-arrow symbol on street signs.

2.5 Nevertheless the Government is clearly sensitive since yet more paragraphs are devoted to ticketing:

"Rail passengers now benefit . . . from being able to deal with a single railway operator. They can buy through tickets . . . they can generally turn up at the station and catch the next train [or] change the route of their journeys. The Government wishes to retain these advantages . . . It will be for train service operators to make arrangements to accept each others' tickets . . . . The Government believes that, as now, passenger service operators will find it in their commercial interest to offer a range of discounted fares and travelcards" [¶91–94].

This is arrant nonsense. If something like the present regime is to survive (and its rules are hardly popular on account of their simplicity or perceived fairness) then dozens of entrepreneurs will find that they have no freedom of manoeuvre in the key area of pricing. Conversely, if they have that freedom then the attempt to preserve some semblance of a common scheme will be overwhelmed by an avalanche of rubrics and an accounting nightmare which will render it unworkable—while passengers unable to comprehend or aggravated by officious restrictions will just fade away.

2.6 After all, why should a company agree to let "its" customer return on another company's train, with no penalty? Why should it give the same discount to, say, a Senior Citizen that its competitor gives—it might want to offer more, or less? Again, if a traveller turning up at a station is not allowed on the next train for some pettifogging reason to do with who runs it, then frequency and hence flexibility has been diminished in a real and possible very damaging manner. And hanging over all this is the threat of the Regulator, who must "prevent anti-competitive practices" [¶93] *and* maintain network benefits—tasks that are mutually incompatible.

---

[1] The hugh reorganisation was completed on 1 April 1992. The implications of abandoning it for something entirely different have received virtually no attention in the press. The BR Board has accepted its fate, complaisantly doing its shareholder's bidding, even though it must know that the drive for quality, staff morale, the integrity of the network and critical investment are all under threat. It is neither willing to defend the role of public enterprise nor to tell the Government that its scheme cannot work.

[2] For example, lack of co-operation between InterCity and Regional Railways over timetabling of connections, publicity and assistance to each other when services are disrupted.

3. THE FRANCHISING OF PASSENGER SERVICES

The proposals

3.1 Chapter 2 sets out a scheme for franchising passenger services in *geographic* units. Nowhere is there any reference to running services only at certain times of the day or week or year: it is apparently to involve taking on a whole territory or line of route, peaks and troughs, warts and all. This is quite different from how deregulation works in the bus industry—and from the much-hyped schemes to take over the profitable trains and niche markets.

3.2 In itself it is an improvement on earlier ideas, since it would discourage cherry-picking and, if the Franchising Authority were tough, fragmentation. However, units large enough to make geographic and economic sense are mostly going to be substantial businesses. It is doubtful whether any existing private companies have the resources to run them successfully: even the White Paper acknowledges that "The railway is a very large, complex and specialised operations" [¶9]. They would have to rely on recruiting the current staff or those staff could form a company to acquire the franchise (the Government intends to encourage this [¶85]). In either event the infusion of private-sector attitudes would be substantially diluted.

3.3 The Government's answer to this presumably lies in the statement that the franchise areas "will be designed, wherever possible, to provide scope for competition" [¶25]. So effective, and ruthless, has rationalisation been that it is difficult to identify a single pair of places in Britain which could be offered meaningfully-comparable services by two routes operated by different franchisees. The only exception of any substance is between London and places in Scotland, but that would depend on expensive rebuilding of the West Coast Main Line—and the Scottish routes are of course those on which BR already faces the toughest air competition.

3.4 The cynical explanation for this naivety is that Ministers and their advisers really do believe that the customer has a choice between the 07.40 from York to London and the 08.30 from Birmingham to Bristol. Reports of the outstanding performance of the franchisee running the former might, one supposes, spur the incompetent franchisee running the latter to greater efforts for fear of losing the contract next time round, although that is a somewhat tenuous mechanism of consumer power

3.5 A more accurate, but no more reassuring explanation may be that the Government has committed itself to geographic units that make "operational sense" because of its enthusiasm for franchises that "will reflect a regional or local identity" [¶25]. Provided these were based on contemporary realities rather than on heritage-industry legends this could indeed be a valuable motivating force and one which local governments should actively encourage if the many other matters of concern are resolved. It would nonetheless be foolish to think that it could create within-mode competition. The real competition will come, as now and just as insistently, from other modes.

Timetable planning

3.6 Competition is not the only issue on which the White Paper is less than coherent. The timetable of services, inter-connecting where necessary, is the core of the offer to the potential customer. Unless a train runs at a time that is acceptable for the journey concerned the offer will be of little interest at any price, though obviously people differ in their trading-off of journey-timings against price. Less tangible qualities of the service, including its reliability, play a greater or lesser part in each consumer's final choice, but they are essentially secondary. This distinctive feature of the transport market has a corollary on the producer's side: the 'output' has to be carefully planned in advance (because of the complexities) yet cannot be stored if insufficient demand materialises. Maintaining load-factors, on which the financial outcome crucially turns, is the key task of management.

3.7 It is not therefore surprising that the White Paper should emphasise the scheduling function. No less than eight public bodies are to be involved, directly or indirectly.

- The Government itself will "set broad objectives for service levels" [¶28], not least through the Citizen's Charter [¶73].

- "Railtrack [the Track Authority] will be responsible for timetabling" [¶23].

- The Franchising Authority "will specify the minimum services a franchisee will provide" [¶28]; this includes "minimum frequencies" [¶29], although an earlier paragraph talks of "required standards. . .of frequency" [¶21].

---

[1] Because of the age-profile of operating staff the retirement rate will be high during the 1990s. New private operators will either face acute shortages or the additional challenge of a substantial recruitment and training programme.

[2] This must be what is meant by "the opportunity for new operators to run services [will] give customers wider choice and rail operators the stimulus of competition to provide better service quality and value for money" [¶57]—if that is anything more than cant. In truth, the Government must know that choice between two trains running in similar timings over the same route (which is the only substantive choice) is likely to be a rare phenomenon.

— The Regulator will oversee "arrangements for track access", promote competition and ensure that "network benefits are maintained" [¶64] and will require "best environmental practice" [¶75]: if these phrases mean anything they imply a powerful coordinating function

— In the large conurbations the Passenger Transport Authorities [PTAs] and Executives "will continue to be responsible for specifying the services to be provided" [¶39]; London, it should be noted, will have to persevere without an equivalent democratic input.

— By determining and assuring compliance with safety standards the Health & Safety Executive will exercise influence [¶78b]: recent flexing of their powers suggests it could be more than marginal

— Similarly, by determining the capabilities of locomotives and the running characteristics of coaches the "industry-wide body" which is to coordinate technical standards [¶96] will affect the parameters of timetable design.

— The Transport Users' Consultative Committees [TUCCs] will continue to be allowed to comment from the sidelines [¶74].

And finally, enter the operators.

3.8   This is absurd. First, it owes much to a prevalent misconception that train paths are discrete entities that exist in manageable numbers: for example, "allocation of train paths will be overseen by the Regulator" [¶23]. In fact, both in planning and in real time, there is a virtually infinite number of space-time permutations through block sections and across junctions. Paths cannot therefore be traded in the simplistic manner implied by the analogue of 'slots' for take-off and landing at airports. The Government's ambition to "set out clear and unambiguous rules" [¶65] will crumble as disputatious parties challenge the unavoidably arbitrary allocation of paths—and of their associated costs.

3.9   Moreover the scheme is so obviously cumbersome and bureaucratic in institutional terms and has so many sources of conflict that the Government may be forced to amend it. For example, in Manchester the PTE, instead of negotiating a service timetable as now with BR (which can be fraught), will have to negotiate initially with the Franchising Authority [¶39], which will then have to go to Railtrack. Railtrack, having been approached by the InterCity desk of the Franchising Authority and by various freight operators, may be unable to agree the specification, and a tripartite debate will begin.

When it has been resolved the franchise will be advertised, and the winner will start quadripartite negotiations

3.10 Or again, how is the "national timetable" [¶8d], which the Government says is essential, to be achieved?

"Railtrack will need to liaise closely with the Franchising Authority and with the operating companies through regualar timetabling conferences, before producing a unified timetable for the entire network" [¶90].

Good, but such conferences were notoriously unwieldy and incapable of producing anything other than lowest-denominator compromises when private companies previously ran Britain's railways These habits survived well into BR days, until the 1960s some enlightened managers, imbued with both commercial acumen and a sense of public service, began a comprehensive restructuring, including accelerations and increased frequencies.

3.11 Under the recent reorganisation the process has continued. The significant point, nonetheless, is that the many enhanced features of the current BR timetable are offset by cut-backs at the margin, both geographically and temporally, as a consequence of commercial disciplines, and by silly failures of coordination between quasi-independent sectors. How much worse this must become when responsibility is fragmented still further! And what a lawyer' paradise it will be apportioning blame for the hundreds of minor,

---

[1] He is also injuncted to ensure "that cooperation between operators to provide such benefits does not give rise to anti-competitive practices" [¶69]. Balancing these aims sounds innocuous, but the fact that in some circumstances they are mutually exclusive portends a legal minefield. The precedent of the bus industry is that clumsy interventions by the Office of Fair Trading have frightened off operators contemplating joint working and publicity.

[2] In the event of a serious accident which the Railway Inspectorate's Inquiry found to be the result of patent incompetence by a private operator or of a failure of coordination between the numerous parties, the Health & Safety Executive would be under immense political pressure to intervene. Those who respect the longstanding safety culture of the railways based on a simple and well understood division of responsibility between the Inspectorate and railway managers know that intervention in such circumstances is not necessarily well considered.

[3] Creating a system with many cross-boundary flows is to take huge risks. That may not have been appreciated since the scheme shackles itself with gratuitous boundary problems: for example, franchise areas delineated according to private-sector interest with making "operational sense" only a secondary consideration [¶25]; a break-up of InterCity that "so far as possible" keeps the services "distinct from other services" [¶36] and disregards its Cross-Country profit centre which interworks with all four of the main London radials [¶36] (this break-up may render later sale of the whole impossible!); the possibility that franchise areas may not match PTE areas [¶39]; and the potential conflict, also unrecognised, at multi-user stations [¶44].

[4] Criticism of timetables—speeds, frequencies, connections—is almost as old as the railways. The record is mostly one of complacency, even when the twentieth century brought competition. And the 'fliers' of the 1930s which so captivate public (and prime-ministerial) imagination, were significant only as froth on top of otherwise mediocre services.

and some major, hiccups each day which, because this is an organic system, will necessarily affect the operations of more than the perpetrating or unlucky franchisee! The wording of the threat of losing a franchise for poor performance [¶19d] suggests that these interactions are not understood.

Commercial constraints

3.12 A further absurdity is that the scheme cannot deliver what the Government says it wants if a franchisee is bound by practical constraints and administrative hurdles in respect of the key attributes of the product. As well as having limited scope on scheduling, few private operators will be able to impress the market with radical innovation in vehicles: most franchisees will be unable to afford new or substantially refurbished rolling stock, much of which will have to be leased or purchased second-hand [¶33]. In any case, "technical standards will be co-ordianted through an industry-wide body" [¶96].

3.13 Moreover, the Government will "set objectives for . . . fares" [¶28], and "Franchises will . . . specify . . . maximum fares" [¶29], while the retention of network ticketing will act as a commercial straightjacket. The timetable, vehicles, maintenance facilities and necessary staffing will dominate the cost structure and make markedly lower fares unlikely. Claims that "Smaller operating companies will bring . . . greater opportunities to cut out waste . . . without sacrificing quality" [¶19f] are unsubstantiated. Though there are undoubtedly always savings to be made they could not transform railway economics, as BR have painfully found, and they would be offset by the payment of private-sector salaries and of profits. In particular, since "The productivity of the BR workforce is among the highest of any European railway [¶3], it is an irresponsible myth that great savings can be made by further reductions in staff

3.14 It follows that the franchisees' "freedom to provide the extent, type and quality of service which they believe best meet passenger demands" [¶30] will be severely limited, bordering on illusory. In that event little may happen, with BR left to run the show as potential bidders recognise the limitations. Alternatively, a flurry of private companies will enter the market, but be forced by the rules to concentrate their innovations on the secondary or even trivial aspects of the package—the hostesses' uniforms and the contents of the sandwiches. Some franchisee will garner the rewards of recent public investment, others will leach a gold mine of government grants.

3.15 This outcome is unlikely to have much impact on rail's share of the market. It is instructive to look at the ideas that have surfaced so far. One is for up-market trains for 'executives'. People who propose this have clearly not travelled recently on an InterCity business-peak train: it is difficult to imagine anything more up-market without it becoming gross, and if the objective is to improve the delivery of what is promised then people are going to find that that is not so easy. Similarly, there has been talk of videos and free meals. Many existing passengers would abhor the former (BR has asked them), while the popularity of the upgraded catering (some BR, some contracted-in) does not suggest a major failing in the present facilities Above all, if either or both were to be included in the fare then customers would be deprived of choice, not assured of more.

3.16 In sum, without for one moment defending every detail of what BR presently either offers or delivers— and at times it is dreadful—we know of no evidence of a vast market waiting to be tapped by this sort of superficial tinkering Were the Government proposing to allow entrepreneurs to run some experimental services with features aimed at niches either up- or down-market, then that might make sense and introduce some genuine choice. The successful ideas could then be taken further. Instead, what is now in prospect is an enormous upheaval based on ideological theorising.

Morale, finances and closures

3.17 Several other features of the plans are disturbing. One part of BR (ie that separated from Railtrack) "will become a residual operating company responsible for operating passenger services until these are all franchised" [¶16]. For the reasons explained above this may be for an extended period. And the Government recognises that "individual services will continue to be provided by BR only if no satisfactory private sector

---

[1]If the Government hopes to achieve savings through the private sector cutting wages (which is how significant 'economies' have been made in the bus industry) then, quite apart from social justice, it will find quality of service deteriorating. Some of BR's failures to deliver reliable quality (and some safety lapses) are attributable to what is historically a long-hours/low wage system. Certain quality enhancements so lauded by supporters of free-enterprise buccaneers will be staff-intensive and therefore costly. Some modest savings may be made by the compulsory contracting out of maintenance [¶24].

[2]A *Financial Times* correspondent commented, apropos of an InterCity waitress who (wrongly) thought she already worked for a private company, that "privatisation is a state of mind", Videos, incidentally, hardly seem appropriate on trains for hard-working executives. Of Sea Containers' reported bid for large parts of the former Southern Region, the practicality of double-deck coaches within the British loading guage is questionable, the idea of transporting commuters' cars into central London is mad, and the acceptability of the big fare increases necessary is politically zero.

[3]The authors of the White Paper are muddled about the relative importance of the attributes of the 'product'. The distinction between its essence (departure and arrival times, price and primary design features), its secondary frills and its actual performance is not clearly made. Thus choice is promised [¶19b and 57] with no definition of what will be available, the Passenger's Charter is said to make "commitments about improving services" [¶4] without it being specified what is to be improved,and the Franchising Authority will "monitor the level of services" [¶19d], the word 'level' being totally ambiguous. Given the constraints outlined it is also not clear whether franchises' "freedom with respect to the extent, type and quality of services" [¶30] refers to the essence or the frills.

bid is received" [¶28]. It has not occurred to them that the morale of staff expected to perform this despised, fragmented role will plummet, if they can be retained at all.

3.18 Next, the document categorically states that Railtrack will not be 'subsidised', it "will be expected to make a return on its assets and to charge operators for the use of its track" [¶23]. that is not necessarily an exceptional objective, although if the Government is so ready to impose on railways a concept of separate responsibility for tracks and vehicles borrowed from road transport, one wishes that it were moving more vigorously to the self-evidently justified direct charging of cars and lorries for their use of infrastructure.

3.19 The implications of this policy for Railtrack have not however been thought through: there is certainly no commentary in the White Paper. At present, where services do not cover their expenses (which is the case on much of Regional Railways and Network South East) the shortfall, including the infrastructure element, is met as a block item through the Public Service Obligation grant, ie the money voted by Parliament because the community is considered to benefit from retaining those routes. Its allocation to specific services may be undertaken as a management exercise and be discussed with government, but this has not been a statutory requirement since 1974.

3.20 Grants per passenger-kilometre vary considerably, reflecting both disparate circumstances and the fact that fares have been capped (on certain lines there is some recoupment of high costs). Something now has to give.

— If Railtrack is to subsume high-cost lines in a national pool, as now, its intended profit-maximising objective will have to be modified, charges on (relatively) profitable routes will be higher than they would otherwise be, and the company will be drawn into operating issues from which it is supposed to remain aloof.

— If costs are to be spread not across the whole network but across franchise areas then private companies will fight shy of situations where they face a wide range of financial performance but constraints on their managerial freedom of actions, such as Government commitments to control fares [¶29] and only to permit closures if *demand* changes [¶8c and ¶71][1].

— If infrastructure charges are precisely allocated to each line, and especially to the long stretches in sparsely-populated areas and the surviving branches remote from London which the Government thinks local consortia may take on, then either the huge cost will force closure onto the agenda, or enormous grants will be paid out by a quango (the Franchising Authority) to private companies, without any democratic control. It was this prospect which deterred the Government from outright sale of geographic units [¶10].

3.21 It is also not clear whether the high cost but long life of railway equipment is compatible with fairly short-term franchises. The White Paper itself does not sound too confident:

"having to purchase rolling stock outright before commencing operations could prove a *formidable* barrier to entry for operators entirely new to the market. That barrier *should be* lowered *if* they are able to lease new rolling stock from private sector leasing companies or *if* a healthy second hand market *can be* developed" [¶33, our italics].

The situation might be eased, and British manufacturing industry aided, if long runs of standardised stock were built, yet the very principal of breaking up the system into entrepreneurial units will militate against that. Transitional problems when a franchise changes hands are ignored altogether.

3.22 This discussion of the franchising proposals has drawn attention to a great many weaknesses. They may become so manifest that the Bill will be amended during its Parliamentary progress. However, unless a full-scale Tory revolt occurs the concept of franchising will be enacted. We have argued that the constraints may nevertheless deter the new entrants who alone can demonstrate whether privatisation *per se* can dramatically enhance services.

Liberalised access

3.23 Against this background it is extraordinary to find that Chapter 4 introduces still another dimension, namely freedom of access:

"to encourage the greatest possible development of commercial rail services [the Government will] establish a framework and procedures through which companies wishing to provide new railway services . . . will have a right of access to the railway network" [¶56].

This is another idea which may have some merit, especially for freight, but its appearance alongside franchising suggests either political spatchcocking or ideology run riot.

3.24 The Government again seems unsure of its ground, since the White Paper says

"provision will need to be made to reconcile the requirements for franchised services with the opportunities to be provided for liberalised commercial services. The Government has commissioned a major consultancy study to address these issues" [¶59].

---

[1] One potential bidder is reported to want the freedom to close—quite understandably, since that is what he would do if one of his bus routes were no longer viable. Area management of buses and trains together might of course yield long-sought benefits of coordination, but a private area monopoly is neither desirable nor one imagines what the Government intends.

In other words it has published what it knows to be a complex plan before its consultants have demonstated how, or even whether, it can be made to work. Most professional railwaymen remain highly sceptical[1], and the consultants are reported to be somewhat perplexed. Even if some mechanism is found the prospect of a new entrant able to run only when it is profitable and to target only selected markets will further weaken the interest of potential franchisees, who will have no such luxuries.

3.25 It is illuminating that all the flavour-of-the-month entrepreneurs quoted at every opportunity by Ministers and the press have *not* talked about taking on a whole service. Private cruise-trains (not just *James Sherwood's* "Orient Express") already operate with BR approval. More could do so, but they are pure entertainment and have nothing to do with Britain's transport crisis. BR were probably unwise to give *Brian Souter* (of Stagecoach Buses) the opening to operate seating coaches on one Anglo-Scottish night train, though it may have been a cunning move to introduce him to the sharp realities of railways. Whatever, this tiny scheme has already created a jungle of ticket anomalies of precisely the kind which the Government says must be avoided [¶88][2].

3.26 *Richard Branson* proposes to run high-quality trains between Edinburgh, Newcastle and London. Very well, though BR are not making a bad job of that now. It is time that the media took a more critical look at this too. He has the effrontery to demand that BR hand over some of *their* trains, since he is not prepared to risk building his own. If his train ran in lieu of a BR train passengers would transfer simply on account of the timing—a classic case of creaming. If the two ran close together, fares and the quality of on-board service would no doubt decide the division of passengers, but the overall economics would probably be worsened since Branson could not offer sufficiently superior a service to attract enough customers from the airlines or the roads to cover the increased costs. And he would expect BR to carry the passengers to and from the intermediate stations his trains would not deign to call at—a recipe for timetable fragmentation.

3.27 Finally, the Government has tossed in the proposal to sell or lease stations to parties other than franchisees because it "believes that the private sector would make better use of the commercial opportunities at stations" [¶44]. This blithely ignores both the extensive, cash-generating activities over many years of the British Rail Property Board in partnership with the private sector[3] and the problem of co-ordinating many different interests. The Paper adds the qualification "provided that the interests of operators and passengers . . . are protected", but, in view of some recent projects where the needs of passengers and the *marketing* of rail travel have been sacrificed to the priorities of developers and retailers, some scepticism is in order[4]. At worst the proposals could be the *coup-de-grâce* to any hope of retaining that coherent image so vital to confidence in rail passenger services[5].

4. THE FREIGHT BUSINESS

4.1. Consideration of the proposals for freight traffic [in Chapter 3] can be briefer, since they are inherently more straightforward and probably less contentious. "The Government's policy is . . . to establish a competitive and privately owned rail freight industry in the course of this Parliament" [¶46], That is unequivocal. So too, on the surface, is the argument that

> "Individual freight operations, even within the two existing businesses, may, in any case, have little in common . . . little would be gained by maintaining a monolithic structure for privatisation. Dividing the current businesses and activities where appropriate would increase the opportunities for competition, lower entry barriers, and focus operations more closely on the needs of the customers and localities served" [¶49].

4.2. However, if the Government had wanted to be really frank, that paragraph would have read:

> "The Trainload business will be broken up and sold to its customers, who will internalise each operation and have no requirement for competitive services, through they may hire-in the rolling stock and skilled staff. Its profits will no longer be available to cover the large losses of Railfreight Distribution, which will therefore be valueless and can be given away. Instead they will be used to increase the surplus

---

[1]When the response is "they would, wouldn't they?" It should be remembered (a) that the technical relationship between infrastructure and vehicles is more integrated than for any other mode of transport (consider for example what is required in preparing track, signalling and stations for the Networker trains in Kent), and (b) that railwaymen *know* from their everyday responsibilities how the effect of incidents ripples across the system in ways which *must* be made more difficult to manage if multiple competing parties are involved.

[2]The Manchester *Metrolink* has, inexcusably, done likewise—as a result in part of the semi-private institutional structure insisted on by the Government.

[3]Some sales of land have been detrimental to the future ability of rail-freight to exploit its strengths.

[4]London Liverpool Street is a triumph of good design from which everyone has gained; the cluttered concourse at Manchester Piccadilly shows how not to do it. Property developers' freedom has naturally ensured that the richest pickings have already been taken, while their overshoot in supplying office space and retail units seems likely to depress the market for some time. It is difficult to see much interest in a business park at Cilmeri or a Sock Shop at Achnashellach.

[5]The post-deregulation disintegration of bus networks is commonly accepted as a principal reason for the decline in ridership. Fares have risen rather than fallen. In many areas a private monopoly has replaced a public monopoly. The model is hardly a good one for the Government to apply to the railways.

of private companies such as the electricity generators, the oil majors, aggregates suppliers and British Steel."

A clue is in fact given: "The different parts of BR's freight operations are likely to attract different purchasers. Where a current service is entirely geared to meeting a particular customer's needs, that customer may wish to take a stake in that service" [¶50].

4.3 In the cast of Trainload, then, nothing much will change beyond ownership. Innovative operators may somewhat reduce costs, but given BR's own cost-trimming over may years[1], the proposed charging regime of Railtrack and rail's advantage in moving bulk freight, it is unlikely that many substantial new flows will thereby materialise. Neither will there be any transfer to road unless further sub-division of operations beyond what BR have already carried out leads to a serious loss of scale-economies—it, for example, the leasing market fails to achieve the critical mass which enables lessors to buy locomotives in worthwhile numbers and to offer flexible contracts.

4.4 More interesting is what could happen in the general freight market. Railfreight Distribution [RfD] has an insignificant market share, having comprehensively lost out to the lorry in the transformation of distribution patterns in recent years. Even where it has a rather higher share, as in inland movement of deepsea containers, it is believed that profit margins are slim. The cash loss overall is huge and has not been reduced as much as was hoped by the abandonment of the *Speedlink* system. Many doubt whether the Channel Tunnel opportunities, important though they are, can yield the turnround expected. The similarly ailing parcels business is also proposed for sale and liberalised access [¶54, 55].

4.5 Yet despite a gloomy scenario there is a real prospect of change and an air of excitement among potential private-sector players. Several factors appear to be at work. The first is that by opening up the business to many different players, a burden of history can be swept away. The BR operation has been dogged for years by its managers' preoccupation with retreat in the fact of an unfavourable structure of relative costs and quality, rendered progressively even more so by government actions such as permitting higher lorry weights and building untolled motorways. To that should be added undoubted elements of incompetence, bureaucracy and lack of vision, and the unwisdom of not challenging the refusal of successive governments to face up to the fundamental issue of whether Britain should have a general-purpose freight railway at all.

4.6 The second factor is that external events are rekindling interest in rail, so that the moment is opportune. Congestion, together with measures (many inspired by the European Community) being introduced for safety and environment reasons, may at last be bringing to an end the widening of the rail/road cost-gap. Meanwhile concern to be seen to be "green" is making manufacturers, forwarders and even road-hauliers look again at the advantages of rail for trunk and bulk hauls. New wagon technologies and combined intermodal operations are facilitating this trend.

4.7 And a third factor is that a single operator, however well managed, is perhaps not best-suited to cope with the variegated and rapidly-changing demands of the freight market. Whatever may be said about the environmental damage lorries have been allowed to wreak, the sheer flexibility of road transport accounts for much of their success. By encouraging the entry of a range of players to the rail business that too could become more responsive.

4.8 It appears that many are waiting in the wings, notably those who are aware of pro-rail attitudes in mainland Europe. They could being to the railways substantial volumes of traffic now passing by road. Those who devoutly wish that outcome should not waste effort deploring privatisation on principle: the "cherry-picking" riposte is here a nonsense, for all the cherries were plucked long ago. In this sector private companies may afford the only hope of radical benefits to the environment, though there should be no illusions that the transition will be easy.

4.9 Firstly, the rail-freight industry will have to make plain to the Government that, unless the administrative structure is simplified, RfD's rump of non-trainload traffic will be smothered in bureaucracy. All of it is vulnerable to a predatory haulage industry. Secondly, Railtrack will have to continue marginal pricing of freight use of passenger lines, since otherwise the industry will face insupportable increases in costs. Thirdly, highly competitive firms will have to learn to work together in order to build up the common systems, shared maintenance facilities and total volumes without which viable wagonload and unitload operation is improbable. And fourthly, since high entry costs for individual parties make joint schemes necessary and plainly in the public interest, it is essential that the Office of Fair Trading takes a more relaxed view than it has so far done in respect of sensible agreements in the deregulated bus industry[2].

4.10 Local governments have no direct locus on freight, and only limited indirect role. Realistically, that is unlikely to change. The momentum will mostly come from the entrepreneurs. Nonetheless, given their economic development and planning powers, they need not adopt a purely reactive stance. The could seek to encourage and assist innovating players, facilitate Section 8 Grants (which the Government is committed to retain [¶53]), or even act as catalyst where a consortium could put together a freight-plan for mutual benefit—

---

[1]The two greatest economies probably lie in increasing the size of trains and in raising the proportion of drivers' time spent driving, but the investment implications of the former and the safety issues implicit in the latter (concerning route knowledge for example) are more problematic than some would like to think.

[2]The capricious intervention of the European Commission—in the name of competition—in the case of the European Overnight Sleepers is not a reassuring precedent either.

and that of the local environment. Examples might be shared trains for blocks of wagons, collaboration between a port and freight forwarders in running unit-load services between conurbations and ports, or provision of multiple private sidings on a trading estate.

5. TROPICS UNMENTIONED

5.1 It is important finally to comment on what the White Paper does not say, or deals with quite inadequately. These points will mostly be familiar to those who follow the transport debate, and it is amazing (or alarming or depressing) that they should be treated so.

5.2 Two paragraphs [¶8 and ¶19] are headed respectively "The Essential Requirements" and "The Benefits of Private Sector Involvement and Liberalisation". All the sub-headings are concerned with *internal* objectives. Apart from a platitudinous reference to the environment nothing whatever puts the railways in any national transport context. That might be contrasted, for example, with the plans of Nederlandse Spoorwegen, which have been developed as an integral component of Dutch National Transport Plan that is itself organically linked with land-use and pollution-control plans. In Britain the ecological, resource, health and quality-of-life arguments for developing public transport do not impress the Government—unless, that is, they believe that Bransonesque gimmicks will do the trick.

5.3 Similarly, investment is effectively dismissed as an issue. Standard Government claims about high absolute levels are made [¶4], without any discussion of whether these are sufficient relative to identifiable needs for sustaining the present network, let alone expanding its capabilities. Nor even is there anything more than piety about the infusion of private capital.

> "The Government is committed to continuing investment in rolling stock but *hopes* to pass as much of this as possible to the private sector ..." [¶33, our italics].

> "The Government wants to ensure that Railtrack continues to invest . . . [It] will *look* for contributions from the private sector. Indeed, the private sector *might wish* to finance certain investments ... without any recourse to public funds" [¶43, our italics].

5.4 In view of the tight-fisted response of private businesses to repeated Government pleading to invest in public transport, the little-better response in regard to roads except for profit-generating estuarial crossings and the hazards of developer-led projects demonstrated by the Jubilee Line fiasco, a rather more convincing argument was called for. The danger now is that precious years will be lost while the Government discovers that *public* schemes need more *public* commitment than this, both for their sound planning and to encourage private capital—as Britain's competitors in Europe know. Nor is anything said about future arrangements for contributions from local authorities, despite the role they have played in promoting a number of initiatives in recent years.

5.5 It is only fair to acknowledge here one unexpected proposal: the Government is

> "ready to provide direct support ... for schemes which, although not earning an adequate financial return, provide a satisfactory cost-benefit return when wider benefits are taken into account" [¶43].

For years Whitehall has maintained that cost-benefit analysis is largely irrelevant to public transport because benefits to users can be captured through pricing and because externalities are too limited or to intangible to be capable of assessment. It has had to be dragged into permitting non-cash items to be considered in certain restricted circumstances, despite the routine and controversial use of cost-benefit techniques to justify road building. This new statement is therefore astonishing. Taken literally it could mean the application of far wider criteria than hitherto for judging development plans for *any* part of the railway business *and*—what has not been the case—the consequential release of capital funds for schemes showing a positive return. Is that what the department of Transport really meant[1]?

5.6 Several references have been made to the critical issue of charges for the use of infrastructure, on which the Government awaits a report from consultants. It is astonishing that the White Paper does not discuss a fundamental matter of *policy*, which needs to be resolved before the technicalities are tackled. Simplifed for the present purpose the agrument is this.

5.7 Railways are inherently a high-cost, high-capacity technology. That truth certainly applies to a trunk main line, and remains important even for a pared-down branch. There are two ways in which such a system can be priced:

— either its operator can attempt to maximise the surplus over train-runing costs, even if high prices reduce volume and hence leave the tracks underutilised, or

— the aim can be to maximise system-throughput, costs being recovered whenever possible but with state funds making up any deficit that may (but need not) arise as a result of the necessarily lower prices in return for the benefits of exploiting a national asset to the full.

5.8 Now BR has been called upon by successive governments to pursue the first option. This is the principal explanation for fares that are exceptionally high by European standards, for the constant triming of marginal services (paradoxically), for both overcrowding and spare capacity, and for timidity when it comes to market

---

[1]The Parliamentary answer of 3 July 1992 which purported to widen the application of cost-benefit methods only referred to their use for assessing "relative priorities" in *urban* situations.

opportunities that involve radical thinking and some risk. The requirement has also crippled a freight business already in a weak competitive situation as a relentless search for a viable core has led to the deliberate shedding of traffics, leaving overheads which cannot be proportionately reduced to be spread over a fast-reducing base.

5.9 To be blunt, the policy has failed, BR's precarious financial record makes that clear. In any rational context one might have expected that a Government concerned to address "the railway problem" would at least have contemplated the possibility that, *if the country is to have a railway at all,* then the alternative strategy might better serve its interests, especially in a scenario of gathering ecological and congestion crises for the rival modes and of remarkable consensus about rail's untapped potential. Volume-maximising is after all broadly speaking the aim in mainland Europe and has not been unsuccessful in delivering quality systems and environmental benefits[1]. Instead the Government's consummate obsession with privatisation is the beginning and end of all argument. Ultimately, *ownership* matters little, the *purpose* of having a railway matters greatly.

5.10 A futher concern here is the contrast between the Government's approaches to railway policy and to other transport policy issues. It is bad enough that there is scant official recognition of the well-documented case that a combination of misleading price signals, inequitable tax structures between modes and substantial uncharged-for externalities varying dramatically in their incidence render the transport market hopelessly imperfect[2]. It is worse that the treatment of the modes continues to be so different.

5.11 Contrast, for example, the abrupt imposition of an ideological solution on the railways, without an attempt to evaluate the outcome and with a fair smattering of saloon-bar rhetoric, and the simultaneous caution on two items of roads policy, namely environmental impact assessement and user-charging. Seemingly unlimited *public* money continues to pour into the road-building programme whilst these two matters, whose implications might undermine that programme, are painstakingly investigated over stretching years.

5.12 Finally it must be recorded, though it is a forlorn hope that the point will register in the current climate, that the White Paper says nothing at all about any democratic participation in determining the future of the railways (apart from passing acknowledgement of the existing functions of the PTAs and TUCCs). As everywhere people are reduced to the status of individual consumers making "choices" between what commercial organisations offer them. The fact that any decisions concerning an essentially *collective* system can only be made effectively by people acting *collectively*—and conversely that fragmented choices may not add up to very much and might lead to unstable fragmentation—has naturally passed this myopic Government by.

6. THE NEED TO OPPOSE—AND A COMPROMISE

6.1 It is difficult to know how to respond to the challenge of the forthcoming Bill. It merits full-frontal opposition to its irrelevant nostrums and daft constructs[3], but neither its parliamentary critics nor the railway and environment lobbies may be able to mount a sustained campaign. Nor does this Government have a good record of listening to reasoned objections to its plans. There must be a real danger that, as the manifold inconsistencies become apparent, the Government will retreat further into dogma and inflict its scheme on BR, with calamitous consequences. That could be avoided by having ready an alteranative that is more practical while still meeting the Government's key objective of involving the private sector. This should also recognise the fact that rail-freight interests stand to gain most from that yet could find themselves mired by the unworkable mechanisms proposed for the passenger business.

6.2 The starting point should be the scheduling procedure. We have argued that the White Paper's proposals are at best hopelessly cumbersome, at worst fatally flawed. Indeed in places it appears that the authors simply do not understand the fundamentals. For example, timetabling is said to be "of critical importance for the safe and efficient operation of the railway" [¶89]. Now operating plans do not arrange for two trains to be on the same section of track simultaneously because it would not be sensible to have to vary them day-by-day to avoid that happening. Only in that indirect sense does timetabling contribute to *safety*. In real time responsibility rests unequivocally with signalling staff and train crews. It is *efficiency* with which timetable planning is concerned.

6.3 In the next paragraph, after all the talk about new services, innovation and open access comes the commitment to conferences "producing a unified timetable for the entire network" [¶90]. Unless that is to be dismissed as mere obeisance to "network benefits" [the Chapter heading], this suggests a final realisation that Railtrack will actually have to be not only a most powerful regulator but also a planning body with clout.

6.4 A virtue should be made of this. The Government should recognise that no coherent timetable can emerge from innumerable diverse initiatives. It should acknowledge that public confidence in the railways, and their ability to contribute real environmental gains by attracting substantial numbers of new customers

---

[1] We record a personal view that British Rail has, in general and for all its faults, run as good a railway as it could, *given the constraints of government policy,* and in parts an excellent one.

[2] The only possible inference, that individual and corporate decision-making has been so distorted for decades that *no* current transport behaviour can be presumed to be economically rational, would give the mandarins apoplexy.

[3] So daft that some see in it the final conspiracy of the road lobby to destroy the railways.

away from their cars depends, first and foremost, on a timetable which is stable, logical and integrated. Moreover, given British geography, trains must be fast, frequent and available from early morning to late at night, every day. They must operate over a dense network and be coordinated with other modes[1]. The system must be physically and economically acessible to everyone in the community, and simple to understand and to use.

6.5 Railtrack (or British Rail!) should be charged with designing such a national timetable, quite explicitly as a function of the state[2]. It would conduct demand research, and it would seek advice from users, local governments and operators, but its ultimately authority for the greater good would be established. Private companies would then be invited by the Franchising Authority to bid for the *operation* of particular trains, services or groups of services. They would be judged on their performance in terms of reliability and punctuality and on the quality of the on-board services. They would be expected to accept network ticketing arrangements but could offer loyalty bonuses to travellers who regularly patronised their trains in preference to those of competitors (where more than one franchisee shared a route)[3].

6.6 Planning of the timetable would have to presume train characteristics on each route, since variations in running speed reduce capacity, another technicality overlooked by proponents of unconstrained access. Again this should be picked up as an opportunity by Government. A scheduling process with a continuity of its own is likely to promote a stable leasing market for rolling stock, which will both facilitate market entry and stand a chance of securing a baseload of work for British manufacturers who otherwise face a collapse of orders. Potential franchisees could be involved in the planning process, perhaps with competitive bids for the type of stock they would recommend.

6.7 Paths for freight trains would form an integral part of the timetable, whether at slack passenger hours or by careful plotting where they could be accommodated without detriment to the passenger market. The busier a route, the more it would be necessary to specify acceptable speeds in order to maximise the number of paths. Operators would then select from the notional freight paths on each route-segment and through each junction that combination which would produce the best available end-to-end trajectory for each of their trains. Where demand outstripped supply an auction procedure would be used, although in general the price would be determined by reference to marginal costs, since a market in paths for parts of journeys cannot exist.

6.8 This comprise is proposed partly as a device to enable the Government to pursue its main aim in introducing an entrepreneurial outlook and private funds, both of which may have some merit in themselves, without hazarding the very existence of the railway by insisting on market processes in a system that intrinsically requires planning. However it also seizes the opportunity to develop an approach to timetable construction which is desirable in its own right and could dramatically enhance the perception of the passenger service.

6.9 In that way the Government could both pursue its ideology and gain plaudits for an improvement of real substance. If it were to choose that course local governments should offer their support in return for participation in the scheme. If it chooses otherwise they will, sadly, need to consider a tactic of implacable opposition to a policy which will assuredly destroy everything that is good about British Rail and fail to put right what is wrong.

September 1992

APPENDIX 59

BRITISH TRANSPORT POLICE

The Future Prospects for the Railway Systems in the light of the Governments Prospects for Privatisation

Submission of Evidence by Desmond O'Brien O.B.E., Chief Constable, British Transport Police

EXECUTIVE SUMMARY

1. The British Transport Police is the national police force for the railways. The Force has been re-organised into a two-tier command structure and its senior officers have performance related contracts. These developments have put the Force well in advance of the British Police Service. (Paragraphs 4.1 to 4.10).

2. Throughout the history of the railways Government has recognised the need of a dedicated police service for the railways, be they in private or public ownership. (Paragraphs 2.1 and 2.2).

---

[1]Ideally there should be a well-defined *hierarchy* of services, both between modes and within each mode, with the services of each "order" feeding in and out of the services of a higher or lower rank—the Dutch and Belgian public transport systems offer a model.

[2]In Switzerland the numerous local railways, funiculars, bus companies and ferries run by independent operators accept the framework of a national timetable determined by the Swiss Federal Railways—and they share a single timetable book.

[3]This is of course modelled on the scheme put forward by many parties as preferable to full-scale deregulation of buses and on that actually being implemented by London Transport through tendering of bus routes. The Government's wilful rejection of the proposed national scheme and their determination to impose deregulation on London despite the patent benefits of tendering does not, admittedly, augur well.

3. The British Transport Police perform the full range of policing activities in both its 'public duty' and 'railway specific' roles. (Paragraph 2.5).

4. The Force has identified nine core activities in the management of the security of public space. The approach is one of partnership with passengers, Railway Businesses and the whole community. (Paragraph 5.1 to 5.4).

5. The Force has developed considerable expertise in the management of major incidents and multi-agency training in this field. (Paragraph 5.6).

6. The Force has played a key role in minimising the disruption caused to public transport by terrorism. (Paragraph 5.7 and 6.4).

7. A dedicated national police force for the railways helps meet the essential requirements set out in the Government White Paper "New Opportunities for the Railways". (Paragraph 7.3).

8. A secure and clear-cut source of funding for the British Transport Police is the crucial issue, rather than the number of operators within the network. (Paragraph 7.5).

9. The question of who assumes responsibility for the 'public duty' costs currently met by British Railways Board corporately must be addressed. (Paragraph 7.8).

10. There must be appropriate legislation in place to enable a 'post-privatisation' Police Committee to raise a budget and effectively discharge its statutory duties. (Paragraph 7.9).

11. There may be a case for direct involvement of a Secretary of State in appointing the Police Committee and becoming accountable for British Transport Police to Parliament. (Paragraph 7.10).

12. The jurisdiction of British Transport Police officers will require widening if it is to discharge its duties where assets such as track and stations are transferred into private hands. This will require legislation. The preferred option is to give British Transport Police officers the same jurisdiction as all police officers working in the public arena. (Paragraphs 7.12 and 7.13).

1. INTRODUCTION

1.1 The British Transport Police is the national police for the railways, policing British Rail and London Underground.

1.2 The Force has a strength of 2,053 police officers and 377 civilian support staff, operating from 90 police stations nationwide and Force Headquarters, which is located in London. Of the 51 police forces in England, Wales and Scotland, 21 have more officers, 30 fewer officers.

1.3 The railway network operates in every police force area. The British Transport Police has at least one police station in all but six of them. Excluding London Underground there are almost 25,000 miles of rail, 3,000 miles of which are electrified. (See Appendix A for details of passenger volumes, numbers of staff etc).

2. HISTORY

2.1 Britain's railways have been policed by dedicated police forces from their inception. Parliament required that Railway Statutes incorporated powers to raise and maintain police forces to ensure that railway companies provided adequate policing of their works and operations.

2.2 Government has maintained this policy throughout periods of private ownership, Government control in wartime and nationalisation.

2.3 Under Section 69, Transport Act 1962, the Secretary (then Minister) of State for Transport approved a scheme for the organisation of the British Transport Police.This required the British Railways Board to ensure that a single, unified police force serves British Rail and other transport undertakings wishing to use its services.

2.4 Currently the users of the BTP are:—

(i) British Rail

(ii) London Underground

(iii) Docklands Light Railway

(iv) Strathclyde P.T.E.*

(v) West Yorkshire P.T.E.*

(vi) South Yorkshire P.T.E.*

(vii) Merseyside P.T.A.*

(viii) West Midlands P.T.E. (Centro)*

*Costs are recovered by ScotRail/Regional Railways from the PTE/PTA concerned.

2.5 Following agreement with the Department of Transport, 80 per cent of the budget of the British Rail element is provided by British Rail Corporate and 20 per cent by the British Rail Businesses. This reflects the work of the Force as 80 per cent public duty and 20 per cent railway specific. The Force undertakes the full range of policing activities required of any police force in the 1990's and is essentially about policing people.

3. CONSTITUTION

3.1 The jurisdiction of the Force is set out in Section 53 of the British Transport Commission Act 1949 as amended by Section 25 of the British Railways Act 1978 and Section 3 of the Briitsh Railways Order 1980. In summary British Transport Police Officers may exercise their police powers on premises, lands or property owned by, leased to, leased by or operated by the British Railways Board, London Underground Limited or their wholly owned subsidiaries.

3.2 The Force has a statutory Police Committee appointed by the British Railways Board, which includes representatives of British Rail, London Underground and rail users. The responsibilities and duties of the Police Committee were amended by the Secertary of State for Transport in March 1992. These responsibilities and duties are the same as those of a Police Committee for a Home Department Police Force, which includes the provision of an adequate and efficient police force. The Chief Constable has a statutory duty to control and direct the force, this includes a requirement to follow any guidance or instructions on police matters given by the Home Secretary and the Director of Public Prosecutions (and their counter-parts in Scotland).

3.3 The British Transport Police Complaints and Discipline procedure complies fully with Part IX of the Police and Criminal Evidence Act. The Force has a legal agreement with the Police Complaints Authority to enable it to discharge its duties in respect of complaints against British Transport Police Officers.

4. FORCE STRUCTURE

4.1 On 5 April 1992 a new Force Structure was introduced. The Force is now organised in eight operational areas operating on a two-tier command structure. (See Appendix "B"). This was the result of a wide ranging review during 1990–91 which involved discussions with and contrubitions from the widest possible range of people and organisations. This consultation process took place both within the Force and externally with the railway industry, other police forces and the public.

4.2 The five divisions and nine sub-divisions were replaced by eight territorial areas, each headed by an Area Commander. Each Area Commander reports to the Chief Constable. (See Appendix "C" map of Areas*)

4.3 Area Commanders hold the rank of Superintendent, Chief Superintendent or Assistant Chief Constable dependent upon the factors that prevail in any particular area. These include:—

(i) Geography;

(ii) Demography and

(iii) Staffing levels.

4.4 Area Commanders have responsibility for negotiating budgets with the Railway Businesses, within prescribed guidelines and subject to ratification by the Chief Constable, the Police Budget Group and the Police Committee. Area Commanders have control of expenditure within police policies and responsiblity for financial management.

4.5 The new Force Structure has a number of key principles at its core:—

(i) Emphasis on community needs and aspirations.

(ii) Increased individual responsibility for each police officer and civilian member of staff.

(iii) Local accountability for policing plans and operations.

(iv) The devolution of decision making to the lowest appropriate level.

(v) The relocation of the maximum amount of resources to a level consistent with effective and efficient working practices.

(vi) The police station as the key service provider.

4.6 Police stations fall into three categories:—

(i) Purely community stations which do not have officers administratively posted.

(ii) Police stations which provide police cover commensurate with local needs.

(iii) Police stations which provide 24 hour cover.

Each staffed police station is headed by an Officer in Charge who reports to and is responsible to the Area Commander. Each Officer in Charge must consult with their community and agree output with the Area Commander.

---

*Not printed

4.7 Officers in charge of police stations hold various ranks from Constable to Chief Inspector. Similar factors which determine the rank of Area Commanders are taken into account when deciding upon the appropriate rank to head a police station.

4.8 The Force is managed on a two-tier basis:—

(i) *Force Management Team*—which assists the Chief Constable in deciding Force Policy. It consists of the Chief Constable, Deputy Chief Constable, the Headquarters heads of Operations, Support Services, Communications and Technology, the Detective Chief Superintendent and all Area Commanders.

(ii) *Area Management Team*—which carries out Force policy and establishes Area Strategies. It consists of the Area Commander, Area heads of Operations and Support Services and each of the Officers in Charge of Police Stations in that Area.

4.9 There has been a positive response to the new Force Structure, Roger Freeman MP, the Minister for Public Transport said:—

"... I believe that the British Transport Police have something to teach the Home Department Forces about structure, efficiency and flexibility of operations ..." (Extract from Hansard 18 June 1992)

Sir John Woodcock, HM Chief Inspector of Constabularly said:—

"I do commend you for everything you have done. I would feel delighted if every Force had grasped this nettle in the same way that you have. I am quite certain that the new structure will serve the needs of the Force that much better and there is little doubt that you have got ahead of the game which is most praiseworthy".

Chief Officers, for example, are on fixed term contracts with performance related pay.

4.10 This structure is a framework on which a national transport policing system could be established.

5. CURRENT ROLE

5.1 British Transport Police operate in an environment of people on the move. Mass transit systems are the lifeblood of a modern complex economy and users need and demand a safe and reliable transport system.

5.2 In order to meet this need the British Transport Police has identified nine principle areas which define its core activities:

(i) To enhance the perception of safety and security in public places, thereby making public transport attractive and saleable to the consumer and safe for operating staff.

(ii) To maintain control of public space in order to avoid the creation of "no-go" areas and costly efforts to regain that control.

(iii) To follow an integrated approach with railway operators to ensure that results are not diluted by independent actions.

(iv) To work with all agencies concerned with public safety and security in the wider community to ensure that activities complement and enhance each other.

(v) To offer a wide range of police expertise in particular:

(a) Crime prevention;

(b) Effective detection methods ensuring the apprehension of offenders and

(c) Providing an effective deterrent by using high profile policing techniques.

(vi) To seek out those factors which impair a user's sense of security on the railways and provide measures to overcome those fears.

(vii) To ensure that problems of security and safety enjoy the "ownership" and commitment of all involved.

(viii) To promote the commercial benefits that can accrue to railway operators from having a dedicated, specialist policing service.

(ix) To emphasise that security and safety of public space is a pre-condition to the implementation of other commercial processes which adds quality to the service.

5.3 The increasingly technical nature of the railway requires British Transport Police Officers to have safety and industrial skills, as well as a knowledge of specialist legislation, for example the new Transport and Works Act 1992. These requirements are above and beyond the knowledge of general legislation and basic policing skills demanded of any police officer. In addition an awareness of the commercial aspirations of the railway businesses is required.

5.4 It cannot be emphasised too strongly that the London Underground system provides unique policing problems not shared by any other police force. The service provided by police is an essential element in the operators marketing policy that states that the purchase of a ticket to travel includes the purchase of a safe journey. Such a policy requires the commitment of both police and railway managers. A similar philosophy exists within British Rail which places much emphasis on both system and personal safety. This will still exist within the twin doctrines of service and profit contained in the White Paper, "New Opportunities for the Railways".

In a debate on the White Paper in the House of Commons, the Secretary of State for Transport said:

"I am well aware of my Hon Friend's interest in the matter, and I am grateful to him for raising it: he has enabled me to pay tribute to the work of the British Transport Police. In the White Paper, we have made it clear that the Government has no plans to end the arrangement whereby the British Transport Police are responsible for security and the enforcement of law and order on the railway. We have also said that we shall consult interested parties about appropriate future arrangements. I think that the talks are scheduled for September."

5.5 Currently British Transport Police Officers investigate approximately 85,000 crimes annually. There has been notable successes in recent years in reducing the reported levels of violent crime. (See Appendix "D" for details of recorded crime).

5.6 The Force has a vital role to play in the management of major incidents. Of recent memory are the tragedies at Clapham and Purley. Following the report on the Kings Cross Fire by Desmond Fennell OBE, QC, the Force has taken a lead role in multi-agency training for major incidents within the railway environment.

5.7 Since the terrorist bomb attacks at Victoria and Paddington Railway Stations in February 1991, the British Transport Police has played a vital and developing role in the categorisation of bomb threats nationwide (See paragraph 6.4).

5.8 The skills and expertise gained in this field have wider application throughout industry. In the oil business, for example, in the safety of oil rigs and off-shore installations.

6. ADVANTAGES OF A NATIONAL POLICING ARRANGEMENT

6.1 Public transport customers have a number of expectations which determine their use of the system:

(i) The journey will be safe.

(ii) They will be unhindered by anti-social behaviour.

(iii) The train and environs will be clean and free from graffiti.

(iv) Single system safety/security includes policing.

The British Transport police are an essential and integral factor in meeting these expectations.

6.2 Moving across police force boundaries one will see and experience different policing needs and priorities. This is inevitable as local police forces seek to address local needs. This is not a relevant consideration to the rail traveller who has consistent needs, from start to finish of a journey. Trespass on main lines of railway or smoking on the Underground system have a high priority within the railway environment. Local forces cannot attach the same degree of significance to such matters.

6.3 Within the railway environment actions taken at one location can have a significant effect on railway operations for many miles. The closure of a station or stopping a train will have a "ripple effect". Train services can be halted, severely delayed or terminated. Thousands of people may suffer serious disruption stuck in trains, perhaps in tunnels. At best this causes annoyance, at worst physical distress or physical injury.

The knowledge of the railway system and safety demands, coupled with professional police knowledge, give the British Transport Police the ability to advise or take the best course of action.

6.4 Examples of the importance of this expertise are best illustrated in the current terrorist situation where the existence of a national police force for the railways prevents a far higher number of closures and delays than would otherwise be the case. This amounts to risk management within the law, whereas territorial forces might err too much on the side of caution. Such an increase in stoppages would lead to the loss of public confidence and financial costs of millions of pounds. (See Appendix "E" for details of bomb threats and suspect packages currently dealt with*).

6.5 Recent changes in policing have pointed the way forward as being an "optimum mix" of national and local policing arrangements as appropriate. Existing examples of bodies to deal with problems include the National Criminal Intelligence Service (NCIS); the National Identification Bureau (NIB) and the National Planning Unit. The policing problems of the railway provides a prime example of a network requiring a unified response. A response that is sufficiently flexible to tackle locally based problems that may have very much wider implications to the safety and security of the system as a whole.

6.6 Attempts to deal with inter-force policing problems have traditionally been dealt with by *ad hoc* arrangements. In the 1970s, for example, a more formal system to police the Midlands Motorway "Box" through a combined unit of four forces proved problematic.

6.7 To maintain the standard of policing currently employed on the national railway network would involve extensive co-ordination between 51 police forces, together with the substantial costs that would ensue.

* Not printed

6.8 The separate railway Businesses need to relate to each other and to identifiable police officers at all levels and in all areas of activity if they are to discharge their legal duties in respect of safety. This will be even more complex with privatisation.

6.9 Common standards, objectives and priorities can only be set and measured if one force manages the policing requirements. (See Appendix "F"—copy of Force Statement*).

6.10 A Joint Objectives Group consisting of British Transport Police and senior executives of each of the railway Businesses and London Underground Limited, agree measurable key operational objectives which allow results to be measured by the Police Budget Group (consisting of Managing Directors of all the Businesses and London Underground Limited, and the Chief Constable). This in turn influences their budget review and decisions by the Police Committee on the Forces' Annual Budget.

6.11 A crucial element in this process is police officers thinking in business terms and business managers thinking of crime prevention as an everyday management role.

6.12 The current process by which joint objectives are agreed in key areas of Business/Policing activity would be seriously undermined without clearly identified people and procedures to turn needs into action which produce desired results.

7. FUTURE DEVELOPMENTS

7.1 The case for and desirability of a national, dedicated, specialist police service for the railway network, composed of people who volunteer to police the railways, has been outlined in some detail.

7.2 The Force has undergone a fundamental re-structuring applying the most up-to-date thinking on the delivery of police services, encompassing the need for cost-effectiveness, efficiency, local accountability and flexibility. It has done so in order to ensure that it is equipped to police the railways whatever the shape of organisational changes that occur within the public transport system.

7.3 The government White Paper "New Opportunities for the Railways" sets out as essential requirements:—

   (i) Safety.

   (ii) Quality of Service.

   (iii) Network Benefits.

   (iv) Environmental Benefits.

Clearly if operators are able to deliver the required level of service a high quality dedicated policing service will be of significant importance. The British Transport Police provide this service currently and appear best placed to continue to do so.

7.4 The number of operators within the railway system does not in itself alter the needs of policing a "network". In London and the South East, for example, distinct Businesses, London Underground Limited, Network SouthEast and InterCity serve the public in what is essentially an integrated urban mass transit system. The sphere of operation covers an area policed by thirteen separate police forces. Account has to be taken not only of the unique problems of each operator but the needs of the whole system. Significantly plans are well in hand for a single police control room for this area.

7.5 If the British Transport Police is to continue to build on its success in reducing the incidence of violent crime and its holistic approach to managing the security of public space, the key is not the number of operators but a secure and clear-cut source of funding.

7.6 Currently the British Transport Police Committee agrees a budget which is determined at ground level by operators and police in informed discussion. The British Transport Police Committee takes cognisance of its statutory responsibilities to secure the maintenance of an adequate and efficient police service.

7.7 As stated in paragraph 2.5, British Transport Police resources are split between "public duty" (80 per cent) and "railway specific" (20 per cent). All resources are used in a law and order role, the "railway specific" proportion is more sharply focused on the policing requirements of the Railway Businesses. It must be stressed, however, that even in this instance it is the publlic who use the system who ultimately derive the benefit.

7.8 A significant increase in the number of operators would make the process of agreeing requirements more complex, but not necessarily more difficult. It is vital that operators are clear as to the proportion of costs that they would be required to meet and how the 80 per cent "public duty" costs currently met by British Railways Board corporately, was to be funded

7.9 It will be essential that a post-privatisation Police Committee has the statutory powers to set a budget and discharge its responsibilities regarding the efficiency of the Force.

7.10 In considering the role and powers of the Police Committee in a "privatised" railway it may be appropriate to examine whether there should be more direct involvement of a Secretary of State. The

* Not printed

Secretary of State could appoint members to the Police Committee and be accountable for the Force to Parliament.

7.11 The balance to be sought is one where the British Transport Police are able to offer a cost-effective policing service that meets the needs of the operators and the demands of the public to travel safely and in comfort, knowing that they enjoy adequate levels of safety and security.

7.12 The only question that arises from private ownership of railway stations and property from the policing perspective is one of jurisdiction. The present jurisdiction of British Transport Police officers would preclude them from policing property not belonging to, leased or worked by British Railways Board, London Underground Limited, or their wholly-owned subsidiaries. Given the desirability of maintaining the benefits of "network policing" this issue would have to be addressed through legislation.

7.13 The most effective solution would possibly be the most simple, that is for British Transport Police officers to be given the same jurisdiction as all other police officers working in the public arena. Such a proposal avoids the need to construct legislation to encompass all eventualities within the railway system and at the same time has other positive benefits. Currently the ability of the Force to exchange officers with other Forces in order to gain experience is inhibited by differences in jurisdiction and pension regulations. By removing this barrier to the development of officers it would enable British Transport Police to lay a greater role in mainstream policing and increase the knowledge base within the Force.

8. CONCLUSION

8.1 As an organisation the British Transport Police Force is well equipped to meet any policing challenge that the privatisation of the railways brings. It has developed a flexible organisation with a devolved management structure able to respond both nationally and locally. It has developed proven expertise in contingency planning, the handling of major incidents and countering the terrorist threat to the railways. Provided that appropriate legislation is put in place there is no reason it cannot continue to provide a cost-effective innovative policing service to its communities. The key areas which have been highlighted are:

(i) Funding;

(ii) Jurisdiction and

(iii) Constitution.

LIST OF APPENDICES

'A'—Details of Passenger Volumes etc.

'B'—Force Command Structure

'C'—Territorial Areas and Police Stations (not printed)

'D'—Crime Statistics

'E'—Number of Bomb Threats/Suspect Packages Dealt with Forcewide (not printed)

'F'—Force Statement (not printed)

APPENDIX 'A'

POPULATION STATISTICS ON THE RAILWAY NETWORK

1. *Population per day*

   ie., passenger volumes, numbers of staff etc.

1.1.	Daily British Rail Total	2.03m
1.2.	Daily LU/DLR Total	2.11m
1.3.	Number of BR staff	138,001
1.4.	Number of LU/DLR staff	21,213
1.5.	Grand Total	4,299,214

1.6. This does not include—

(a) Tenants/Shop—staff in retail units

(b) Users of these facilities "not travelling"

2. *Comparison with Home Office Force*

2.1. Compare this with the West Midlands Force policing, a population of 2,648,939 with a Force strength of 6,818.

- APPENDIX 'B'

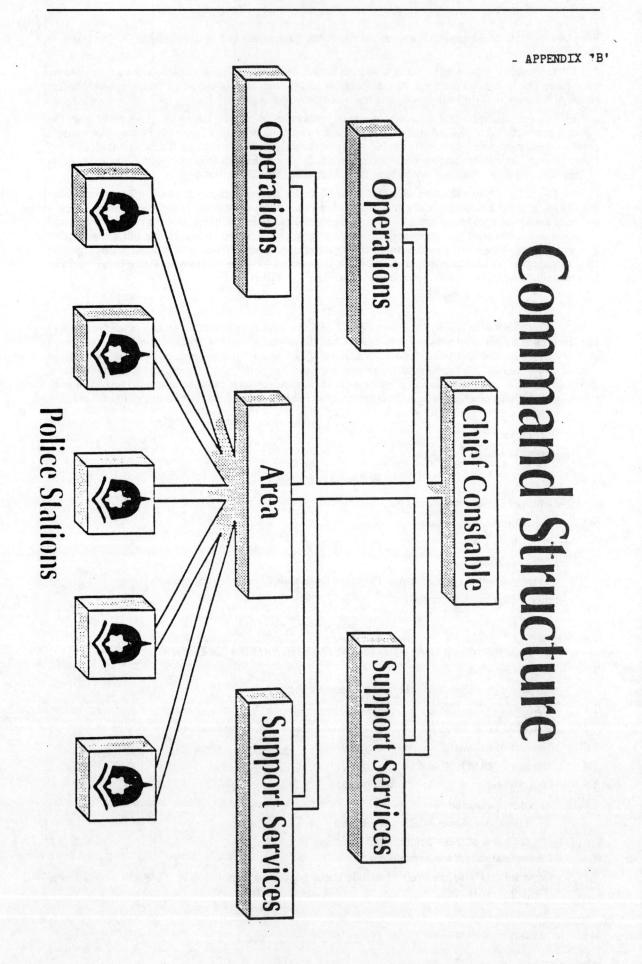

Command Structure

APPENDIX 'D'

CRIME STATISTICS FOR 1991–1992

1. *Total Crimes for 1991*

BR Areas	71,642
LUL Areas	15,185
Force Total	86,827

2. *First Half Trends:* January-June 1991 and January-June 1992

REPORTED	JAN-JUNE 1992	JAN-JUNE 1991	PER CENT CHANGE
BR Areas	34,571	38,506	− 10.2
LUL Areas	7,023	8,230	− 11.0
Force Total	41,594	46,736	− 11.0

A decrease of 5,142 crimes (11.0 per cent)

3. *First Half Trends: Re Crimes of Violence*

ASSAULTS	JAN-JUNE 1991	JAN-JUNE 1992	REDUCTION
Public	648	582	66
Rail Staff	216	201	15
Police	126	103	23

6 November 1992

APPENDIX 60

Supplementary Memorandum from Mr T. Hart, Department of Economic History: University of Glasgow

RAIL FRANCHISING AND SUSTAINABLE MOBILITY

A Response to the Consultation Document on the Franchising of Rail Passenger Services

POLICY OBJECTIVES

1. The Consultation Document must be assessed against the overall aims of present government policies affecting transport. These aims can be summarised as:—

(1) to promote sustainable mobility and a sustainable economy through a "level playing field" approach taking full account of environmental objectives and the need for a sound and stable economy

(2) to lessen the pressures on general taxation and public borrowing arising from transport and to shift towards larger elements of private sector finance in transport

(3) to strengthen business confidence in transport programmes as part of policies for short and longer-term economic revival

(4) to increase localised responsibility and "subsidiarity" in transport and environmental decisions

(5) to reduce bureaucracy and increase opportunities for enterprise and innovation

(6) to improve efficiency via operational competition either directly or through competition for franchises.

2. The Consultation Document (CD) is fundamentally flawed because of a focus on (6) without reference to the other five policy objectives; particularly, objective (1) to which the UK committed itself at the Brazil Earth Summit, 1992, and in the regular annual reviews of the Environment White Paper of 1990.

3. With respect to objective (1), the CD contradicts this objective by requiring a hard financial return from rail track while making no mention of the treatment of road track (1.5). Without a radical reform and commercialisation of road track, this approach provides added incentives to increase total costs by shifting movement from rail to road. It also places rail in a non-equal position compared to local bus operators who, through the bus fuel duty rebate, are virtually exempt from contributing to road track costs. Para 1.5 of the CD fails to create the level playing field needed to optimise the use of existing infrastructure and to guide decisions on future investments.

4. With respect to objective (2), the administrative costs and uncertainties introduced by the CD seem likely to increase pressures for government expenditure—especially short-term pressure on current expenditure to create new regulatory frameworks and sustain further management restructures without adverse impacts on quality of service to existing users.

5. With respect to objective (3), it is evident that—even if the CD proposals have longer-term value—their immediate effect will be to increase rail uncertainty and reduce investment to unacceptably low levels. The immediate need is for increased investment related to sustainability objectives.

6. With respect to objective (4), the main drift of the CD is to continue and intensify centralisation—as in the proposals for an all-embracing Rail Track Company (including both trunk and local routes) and for a centralised Franchising Authority.

7. With respect to objective (5), the proposed arrangements amount to increased bureaucracy, more likely to stifle than encourage innovation and holding little real prospect of any substantial increase in private sector financing for major infrastructure schemes.

8. The other serious flaw of the CD is perpetuation of a rail focus when it is apparent that organising for sustainable improvements in transport and the environment requires distinctive treatment of longer-distance and more localised transport. A road/rail division hampers, rather than promotes, efficiency.

9. However, this criticism of the CD does not mean that the status quo is preferable. The status quo is itself poorly related to objective (1) and to the other subsidiary objectives. Change is clearly desirable but it needs to be managed in a way which builds confidence by providing a stable framework for future decisions affecting movement, the environment and the economy as a whole.

10. The essentials of this new framework need to be established over the next three years, forming a base from which the transport decisions and transport patterns relevant for next century can evolve.

TRACK COSTS AND INVESTMENT

11. The concept of negotiating rail track charges, inevitably involving delays and uncertainty in dealings between Railtrack and franchisees, should be abandoned and replaced by a straightforward guideline that, in normal circumstances, rail freight and passenger operators should contribute, say, 10 per cent of income towards track costs. Exceptions to normal circumstances are dealt with at 15.

12. This system should be introduced at the earliest possible date, i.e. in 1993. Track charges could be payable direct to the Department of Transport (or arguably, to the Secretaries of State for Scotland and Wales with respect to their areas of responsibility) with rail track investment becoming incorporated in present programmes for road investment. A combined road/rail investment programme for 1993/98 should be announced within the next six months. Knowledge of this programme, and of the track charge guidelines, will be vital information for the business calculations of potential railway operating companies.

13. Five-year rolling programmes for infrastructure investment should replace present compartmentalised plans for road and rail infrastructure investment. For the first five years, national funding should include provision for grants towards rail passenger rolling stock (allowing rolling stock orders to be maintained in the transitional period while new operating companies firmed up their own investment programmes).

14. The five-year programme should indicate that, while total public investment in transport will be maintained around present levels, the balance would shift towards rail investment.

Departures from 10 per cent Track Charge Guideline

15. Three variations from this guideline should be introduced:—

    (1) power to central government to raise track charges above 10 per cent where this is essential because of severe pressure on track capacity or available rolling stock i.e. a type of congestion charge

    (2) an obligation to remove charge where a rail service was non-congested and competing with local bus services enjoying Fuel Duty Rebate (or, alternatively, retain charge but remove Bus Fuel Duty Rebate)

    (3) power to raise charges above 10 per cent on sections of route (both road and rail) where a Franchise for New Infrastructure had been granted either totally reliant on private sector funding or on a mix of public and private funding—i.e. these franchises could introduce standardised forms of road and rail pricing for major commercial projects of the type previously funded entirely from public sources.

16. Rail track accounts should be separated from other aspects of rail accounts from April, 1993, with full "shadow" accounts for road and rail track from the 1993–94 financial year.

17. Government should indicate its preference for a trunk rail track network by April, 1993. After responses, an agreed network and trunk investment programme should be finalised by April, 1994, with provision for regular reviews.

18. By an April, 1995, target date, rail track and road track should be reconstituted as free-standing publicly owned companies for trunk route (BritRail and BritRoad) with remaining track and powers over local land use planning and the environment passing to Regional Boards. This reform would be compatible with the setting up of additional Infrastructure Franchise Companies related to specific major improvements and increases in private funding.

19. Also timed for April, 1995, motor taxation should be split into "pure tax" and a majority element available to meet transport costs. Regional Boards would receive the portions of motor taxation (and of rail track charges) related to non-trunk movement together with direct responsibility for funding support for local public passenger transport. This would provide a realistic and workable basis for decentralised decision-taking.

OPERATIONAL ISSUES

20. Between 1993 and 1995, motor tax policy should be reformed to:—

(a) replace Car Licence Duties with tax-neutral increases in Road Fuel Tax

(b) increase Road Fuel Taxation by 5 per cent a year in real terms until road traffic growth is stabilised or electronic road pricing introduced

(c) replace Heavy Lorry Licences with metered charges (including the rebate of possible "excess" payments of Fuel Duty)

(d) introduce Yearly, Weekly of Daily Licence Discs for cars using city roads at peak periods (income from such licences could be directly available to Regional Boards in advance of electronic road pricing)

21. The CD does not resolve the tension between flexible franchising and the need for the synchronisation of principal timetable changes in public transport with suitable provision of advance publicity and reliable timetables. This tension should be resolved by requiring all scheduled service operators (rail, ferry, bus, etc) to register proposed changes in timetables at two or three fixed points in the year. This would remedy one of the most serious deficiencies arising from bus deregulation while applying similar standards to other public transport services. Rail registrations would be made with BritRail and the Regional Boards as track authorities—these authorities would have power to deal with track slot allocation issues subject to a right of appeal to a Civil Transport Authority.

22. To replace distorting monetary incentives to use cars when rail or bus use is more cost-effective, the fiscal changes listed at 20 should be accompanied by a legal requirement that maximum standard fares for rail and bus travel should not exceed the marginal costs of single occupant car use and should include standard nationwide concessions for pensioners, child, student and group travel—always subject to government authorisation of higher fares in conditions of congestion.

23. A realistic guideline might be a maximum standard fare of 8p per mile subject ot a zonecard fare structure for trips below 20 miles and with a 50 per cent discount for concession groups (children under 3 travelling free). Legal maximum fares could be reviewed yearly in the light of motoring costs. Outwith areas of local congestion, operators could be free to introduce lower fares at their commercial discretion. Higher non-standard fares could also be permissible provided that at least 50 per cent of capacity on individual routes was always available at standard fares or lower.

Railway Passenger Operating Companies

Trunk Services

24. The franchise proposals of the CD are too complex, managing to combine centralising tendencies with uncertainty. Simpler proposals are required especially in the present context of national recession, removing the need for a National Authority for passenger service franchising and providing a direct impetus to rail expansion.

25. Part of this impetus should come from government initiatives to establish the Track Charge Guideline and the Five-year Investment Programme outlined at 11 and 13 of this document. Additionally, a distinction should be made between the treatment of trunk and other services.

26. Shadow companies for trunk operations should be established by BR from April, 1993, becoming publicly-owned PLCs from April, 1994. Initially, these companies should have defined spheres of operation and should be asked to register services which they could operate without public subsidy by April, 1994. They could be precluded from registering services of less than 100 miles in length. Other companies should be given the opportunity to register trunk services to commence from April, 1955—from which date the ex-BR PLC companies would also have freedom to vary services.

27. This would establish a competitive framework for trunk operations without the requirement for franchising. Disputes over train slot allocation would be handled as proposed at 21.

28. Using information from existing cost centres, six trunk companies could be formed from existing trunk BR operations. These could be expected to show at least a five per cent return on captial with the possibility that two of the six could form the basis for outright sales as from April 1995.

29. Though mainly operated on the trunk network of BritRail, through trunk services could also be extended over other parts of the route network:

(a) where companies saw this as being in their commercial interest

(b) as part of freely concluded contracts with enterprise companies, tourist boards and local authorities where such bodies saw advantages in the extension of trunk services not otherwise provided.

30. Possible ex-BR companies could initially be based on:

— East Coast route   — Midland Cross-country
— West Coast route   — BR International
— Western

31. From a date to be decided (probably in the late 1990s) local and Regional Companies could be allowed to enter the trunk market but legislation should require their initial focus to be on their specialist market.

Local and Regional Services

32. As with trunk services, shadow zonal companies could be set up by April 1993, converting to PLCs in April 1994. Unlike trunk companies, however, regional companies could have a five year guarantee of being the sole provider of passenger rail services in their operating zones subject only to:

— the operation by other companies of trunk services not offering significant local competition

— specified extensions of through service by adjacent regional companies to suitable terminal points, eg, a "Central Company" could be allowed to operate an hourly service from Sheffield to Manchester through to Liverpool in the operating zone of a "Northern Company"

— the terms of local franchises within conurbations.

33. Para. 4.4 of the CD argues that the first of these conditions would not be necessary since it would be unlikely that commercial companies would wish to compete with subsidisd companies. However, given the Track Charge Guideline and the relief of regional companies from the present burden of track costs, regional companies should be able to achieve a "break-even" position accommodating a certain degree of cross-subsidy within their operating zones. Their net earnings could be adversely affected if other companies were permitted unrestricted and selective competition within their operating zones. This would also be a significant potential danger even for a regional company with a subsidised franchise.

34. Provided that the Track Charge Guideline was introduced and supplemented by a special Train Mile payment (itself an inducement to improve frequency of service) of perhaps £1 per mile for more sparsely populated areas served by branches more than 20 miles long, there is reason for believing that—under level playing field conditions—Zonal Companies could provide train mileage at least as great as present mileage without a requirement for operational support.

35. Complex franchising arrangements would therefore be unnecessary though the operating zones of companies would come up for review every five years. This should provide a sufficient stimulus for maintaining, and improving, efficiency. As at present, local authorities would have powers to improve on the level of services registered by the Zonal Companies while Regional Boards would have an increasing role in providing investment grants (principally for infrastructure and stations but not precluding some assistance towards rolling stock purchase).

36. Zonal Companies could be geared to convenient operational groupings of services with Regional Boards providing the main mechanism for co-ordination of public transport, road and land use planning over wider areas. The proposed National Rolling Programme for Investment would also have a specially important role in the first years of operating a system of zonal companies. Thereafter, the policies and investment programmes of the Regional Boards would become dominant.

37. Possible Zonal Companies might be:

1. **Thameslink** (including investment grants for added capacity).

2. **London Crossrail** (integrating services west from Paddington/Marylebone and east from Liverpool Street/Fenchchurch Street with outer terminals up to 30 miles from London).

3. **London Express Crossrail** (serving key interchanges at Willesden, Kings Cross (North London Line) and Stratford and offering through services such as Northampton-Ashford, Oxford-Norwich, Heathrow-Stansted and Bristol-Ipswich—this route could also accommodate InterCity and continental services proceeding through London and replacing present plans for an expensive Stratford-Kings Cross (South) tunnel increasing congestion in an already congested part of London.

4. **Essex/Anglia.**

5. **Brighton** (zone south from central London).

6. **Kent** (zone south-east from central London).

7. **Wessex** (including access to London, Cardiff, Gloucester and Oxford).

8. **Wales and Marches** (including access to Mancheser, Birmingham and Oxford).

9. **Central** (access from Birmingham to Liverpool, Manchester, Sheffield, Grimsby, Norwich and Ipswich).

10. **Pennine** (zone from Newcastle to Preston, Liverpool, Manchester, Sheffield and Hull).

11. **Devon and Cornwall.**

12. **Cumbria** (zone from Carlisle to Barrow, Preston and Leeds with access to Manchester and Liverpool).

13. **ScotRail** (either in one company including routes to Newcastle via Carlisle and via Berwick or in three units based on.

    (a) **Highland Lines** (including access to Edinburgh and Glasgow).

    (b) **Glasgow-Aberdeen-Edinburgh** triangle plus East Borders.

    (c) **Glasgow suburban and south-west** (including route to Newcastle via Carlisle).

38. Companies 11, 12 and 13A would have substantially smaller turnovers than any of the other companies but offer special geographical and political circumstances meriting consideration in any plans for the creation of zonal companies. They would benefit from localised management and promotion in areas with particular tourist and leisure potential.

Conurbations and Supplementary Suburban Services

39. While it has been suggested at 34 that zonal companies with a breakeven remit would be likely to register a wide range of services capable of being operated without external subsidy (with evidence of extensive registration becoming an important part of the case for extending the proposed five year operating periods), there would be problems of service contraction on certain urban routes where income still failed to reflect the external benefits of expanded rail operations. These will be specially apparent in the years before the more extensive application of road pricing.

40. In such cases, there is scope for more detailed planning and co-ordination of rail and bus services improvements, including the possibility of converting certain sections of route to Light Rail operation integrated with street operation and the provision of new routes more economically and beneficially than through heavy rail engineering.

41. In such cases, Regional Boards should have powers to propose **Franchise Zones** as mentioned at 32 and as part of schemes for improvement (including possibilities for private financing). Because these special zones would affect the rights and net earnings of zonal companies, they would require a public inquiry process and governmental approval. This could be incorporated in reformed procedures modifying bus deregulation and laying down a framework for the creation of Franchise Zones incorporating localised regulation of services and the possible creation of busways and Light Rail routes within designated urban segments.

42. After designation, both existing and new public transport companies (with safety validation) would be able to bid for these special franchises.

43. Rather than having separate bodies for rail and other services, a regulatory overview of the whole range of transport could be provided by setting up a **Civil Transport Authority** (incorporating functions presently undertaken by the Civil Aviation Authority and by the Traffic Commissioners) and by **creation of a separate Transport Division within the Health and Safety Executive** to deal with transport safety.

CONCLUSIONS

44. The changes proposed accept the view of the CD that the status quo is no longer acceptable with respect to rail organisation and financing but they relate possible changes to the wider objectives of transport policy within a simplified, yet radical, framework.

45. The proposals highlight the unsatisfactory treatment of track costs in the CD and the pitfalls of added bureaucracy and added uncertainty in the midst of a general recession. They emphasise the urgency for more fundamental change to establish a stable, coherent and readily understood framework for future decisions.

46. This framework has been designed to avoid the complexities and uncertainties of extensive franchising. It provides an immediate stimulus to modal shift towards rail usage, and more generally towards public transport. It avoids any general increase in tax burdens, minimises bureaucracy and opens up significant

opportunities for the beneficial introduction of private finance into transport projects. This is the challenge, and the prize, to which government policy and early legislation must be seen to be responding.

10 November 1992

APPENDIX 61

BRITISH TRANSPORT POLICE FEDERATION

Submission to the Transport Select Committee inquiring into "The future prospects for the railway system in the light of the Governments' proposals for privatisation".

1.0 INTRODUCTION

1.1 The British Transport Police Federation welcomes the the opportunity to present evidence to the Transport Select Committee in order that we can best represent the views of our members.

1.2 Our aim in this document it to inform the Committee of:

(i) the role and responsibilities of the British Transport Police

(ii) the role of the British Transport Police Federation

(iii) our position following publication of the Government's White Paper

(iv) the complications for policing that could arise—post privatisation

(v) the implications for policing post privatisation with:

(a) different operators running railway services and

(b) the sale of land and property.

1.3 It is not for a police employee representative body to oppose on ideological grounds the Government's proposals for the railways. The Federation's concern about the prospect of privatisation is purely pragmatic. We aim to reflect the very real worries of our members, both with regard to the safeguarding of their current conditions of pay, service and benefits and their concern that the vital role they perform as the national police for the transport system is not devalued to the public detriment.

2.0 THE BRITISH TRANSPORT POLICE

2.1 Britain's transport industry has been policed by dedicated police forces since it's inception. Upon nationalisation of the railways in 1947 the British Transport Police (formerly British Transport Commission Police) was formed.

2.2 The British Transport Police is a dedicated, specialist Force providing a highly skilled service to British Railways and London Underground. We consider ourselves an integral part of mainstream policing throughout the United Kingdom. British Transport Police officers have the same pay, training, discipline and promotion examinations as Home Department Police Forces.

2.3 Officers of the British Transport Police are Crown Officers, having sworn allegiance to Her Majesty The Queen. They are also employees of the British Railways Board. This hybrid situation is unique amongst United Kingdom Police Forces with no other Force having a commercially led employer. Officers of the British Transport Police are appointed Constables under Section 69 of the 1969 Transport Act and Section 53 of the British Transport Commission.

2.4 All of the work of the British Transport Police is law and order related. It has been acknowledged by Government that 80 per cent or more of that work is to the benefit of the public; the remainder, while still in the public arena, benefits the transport industry. Accordingly the budget of the Force is apportioned in that ratio, with 80 per cent provided by British Rail Corporate and 20 per cent by British Railways Businesses.

3.0 THE ROLE OF THE BRITISH TRANSPORT POLICE FEDERATION

3.1 The British Transport Police Federation was formed over 70 years ago and is the second oldest among United Kingdom Police Federations.

3.2 The Federation represents the ranks from Constable to Chief Inspector, having over 2,000 voluntary members in a Force of 2,050.

3.3 The Federation has collective responsibility for negotiating all Conditions of Services on behalf of its members.

3.4 We acknowledge that the Federation has a role to play in the management and efficiency of the British Transport Police. We are keen to play that role and have fulfilled it by supporting the recent changes to the Force and its structure and through our Machinery of Negotiation have secured agreements that enhances the Force as well as being beneficial to our members. We have therefore taken the opportunity to submit evidence to Sir Patrick Sheehy and his Inquiry into Police Rewards and Responsibilities.

4.0 POSITION POST—PUBLICATION OF WHITE PAPER

4.1 At a meeting between the Minister for Public Transport Roger Freeman, MP, with the Chairman and General Secretary of the Federation 3rd June 1992 the Minister stated that some reference would be made to British Transport Police in the Government's White Paper.

4.2 When published, the document "New Opportunities for the Railways" made just a single reference to the British Transport Police. Paragraph 98 acknowledges our role as having *"responsibility for security and the enforcement of law and order of the railways. The Government has no plans to end this arrangement but will be consulting interested parties on appropriate future arrangements for ensuring security and law and order."* This paragraph offers comfort in its opening lines and then makes it conditional on the interested parties sharing view to that there is no need for change.

4.3 At a subsequent meeting with the Minister on 10 September we voiced the fears and concerns of our members that the future of the Force was not assured. More than anything else we sought from the Minister a message of confidence in the future shape and responsibilites of British Transport Police.

4.4 We were pleased that the Minister gave us a categorical assurance that our future was secure. He said that British Transport Police would remain as a separate, independent, unified Force, dealing with law and order issues on the railway. The future of the British Transport Police was assured, it would not be broken up; it would not be merged and it would not be privatised.

He gave further assurances regarding the Appointment of Constables; Jurisdiction; Negotiation Rights; Contracts of Employment; Superannuation Fund; and Travel Concessions.

4.5 The Minister addressed the funding of British Transport Police and indicated that there would need to be a formula established to raise money for the Policing from the private sector operations. A Financial system would have to be devised where a passenger franchisee will contribute to the running of the Force. The object would be to ensure that the cost of British Transport Police is included in the franchise. The British Transport Police must not find itself in the situation where there is an annual budgeting exercise with individual franchisees. This would lead only to conflict between the Force and the Franchisee because of their different priorities.

4.6 The Franchisee would not be the decider of the cost or the level of policing but that they should have some input into that decision (excluding operational matters). He stressed that the franchises on offer would show a policing cost.

5.0 THE POSSIBLE COMPLICATIONS FOR POLICING—POST PRIVATISATION

5.1 It is our view that unless the Government resolves the matter now then funding could become one of the main complications following the allowance of different operators for running railway services. As stated in 4.5 a system is to be devised whereby a franchisee will contribute to the cost of running the Force. This cost may not be agreeable to the franchisee and any commercial regulator, left to his own judgement would surely seek to waive this cost to attract the franchisee. Only primary legislation would ensure that the franchisee could not abstain from his responsibility to provide a meaningful contribution towards policing costs.

5.2 Private ownership of land and property and different operators running services could, unless there were proper safeguards included in primary legislation, introduce a variety of complications for policing.

5.3 A major one is that of access. A private owner or operator could dictate who they allow access to and when. If an operator/owner suddenly decided that they would not allow police access to, say, football supporters, it could put the police in a position where they would be unable properly to supervise such rail passengers. One could also envisage great difficulties if an operator/owner decided not to heed police advice relating to a terrorist threat.

5.4 Equally important is the jurisdiction of British Transport Police. At present British Transport Police officers can operate *"in, on or in the vicinity of any of the Board's premises, or anywhere on any matter relating to any of the Boards."* The Minister has acknowledged that changes must be made to this definition of jurisdiction. It must be got right and of necessity will have to give British Transport Police adequate access to all operators'/owners' property.

5.5 The British Transport Police must also be protected from operators/owners who would seek to exceed their authorised input into the Force by interfering in operational matters—and they will. British Transport Police must remain an operationally independent Force primarily accountable to the public it serves.

6.0 IMPLICATIONS FOR POLICING POST PRIVATISATION

6.1 The Ministers assurance that British Transport Police would continue was received well. We are a very public service as our fight against terrorism shows. Yet we can envisage resistance from the newly privatised services to paying for a police service which is largely for the benefit of the public and is acknowledged as such.

6.2 The question of a formula to raise money to fund the British Transport Police must therefore be resolved quickly. The British Railways Board are planning that Railtrack will go live by April 1994. We envisage a situation where British Rail Corporate will no longer be in a position to meet its 80 per cent of the Force's budget. A clear statement on funding is needed.

6.3 The British Transport Police is the only United Kingdom police force which is funded directly by a commercially driven organisation even though that organisation is in turn publicly owned. The Federation is concerned that a police service should not be influenced by the undeniable commercial pressures on the host company which would have responsibility for the British Transport Police after privatisation. It would be our view that it would be preferable if the British Transport Police were taken outside of the privatisation considerations altogether and its role as a police service properly acknowledged by associating the Force directly with a Government Department in the same way as the Ministy of Defence Police and the London Metropolitan Police are with the Ministry of Defence and the Home Office respectively.

6.4 At present no Secretary or Minister of State has formal responsibility for British Transport Police. (Other than for Appeals under the Discipline Regulations). Informal arrangements have existed for many years whereby the Secretary of State for Transport and the Minister for Public Transport adopt and monitor British Transport Police.

6.5 We would request that the Secretary of State for Transport amend the British Transport Police Force Scheme to make this arrangement formal. This should take place now and remain permanently or at least until all 'privatisation' issues are resolved. This would ensure a continuing and accountable service to the public.

6.6 The British Transport Police Force Scheme is likely to require further amendment to expand representation on the Police Committee. Membership was restricted to participating Boards (British Rail and London Underground Limited), the Minister supported by this Federation altered the Scheme in 1991 to allow consumer representation, a post currently held by the Chaiman of the Transport Users' Consultative Committee.

7.0 CONCULUSION

7.1 Having flagged up these initial concerns, some of which are fundemantal, the Federation wishes therefore to reserve its position on the final form that privatisation might take. We would particularly wish to be consulted on any issue which might lead to the increased exposure of the public to crime or to any compromise in safety standards.

7.2 We acknowledge that the British Transport Police and this Federation must continue to adapt to changing circumstances. As an independent national Police Force we have the skills and expertise to police the transport industry in the United Kingdom as part of mainstream policing. We submit that our role should be expanded and enhanced to benefit both the industry and the public.

7.3 We are pleased to submit this report to the Transport Select Committee and will be available and willing to appear to give oral evidence if so required.

12 November 1992

APPENDIX 62

GEEST NORTH SEA LINE B.V.

Thank you for your invitation to respond to your questions on the privatisation of the Railway System, as set out in the White Paper "New Opportunities for the Railways". I apologise for not being able to get this submission to you by the requested date but I hope the response to your questions are of some assistance to you and the Transport Committee.

Q. *What should be the aims and objectives of a privatised railway? What are the attractions for the private sector?*

A. The aims and objectives of a privatised railway should be to have improved efficiency by injecting into the system the benefit of the best commercial interest obtainable and prepared to work in this demanding and essential service industry. The attractions for the private sector would be long term cost stability which will enable companies to predict future cost changes more accurately and be able to control increases better than they otherwise would. Therefore, the attractions for a privatised railway activity is self evident with long term benefits being general overall efficiency, reducing the impact of providing this vital service to the tax payer. The more railway borne freight traffic that is possible will undoubtedly have an environmentally improved impact. To summarise, therefore, efficiency, long term attractions especially over longer routes.

Q. *How can freight traffic develop effectively in a primary passenger network?*

A. Utilising the infrastructure to an enhanced degree and being able to provide synergy in the passenger network. If the correct freight paths could be secured it would be possible to construct a quality service within and alongside the primary passenger network providing good access to the commercial user. The short haul rates especially around the major cities, ie London, will prove difficult but on through routes and on long distances then freight can be developed effectively and to the general good of all users within the primary passenger rail network.

Q. *What principles should Railtrack, the track authority, use in charging freight operators for the track infrastructure?*

A. The short answer is market rate must be the principle which Railtrack applies. If the charging structure is wrong, simply said little if any business will be attracted. Therefore, at the end of the day the Railway will be used only where it is seen to be competing favourably with its competitors. It has its own strengths and weaknesses, ie it is a more structured operation and has various elements which are not normally needed in road movements but it can provide a commercially environmental answer where the rating structure is so constructed.

Q. *Under what circumstances might it be sensible for track and related infrastructure used only for freight to pass into private hands along with the operational part of the freight business? Could open access and effective competition be maintained in such circumstances?*

A. The related infrastructure should be separated from Railtrack and they should be open to general user access. If not there will be a conflict of interests, loss of efficiency and undoubtedly the development of the freight movements in rail will be severely disadvantaged. It is, therefore, essential in simplistic terms for the track to remain under a public or neutral body control and for the terminals to be allocated to separate private companies who should be required to provide not just inhouse services but general commercial access.

Q. *How can rail compete effectively with road transport in carrying freight? Under what circumstances is the privatisation of freight services likely to increase the attractiveness of transporting freight by rail?*

A. Again it can be simply boiled down to price and efficiency where the structure of the routing gives the Rail network a fair chance to succeed. Normally this is on the longest terminal to terminal distance possible within the main commercial centres of operation. It is not fair to expect Rail to compete effectively with road transport distances of say less than 100 miles. Privatisation of the freight services is likely to lead to competition, cost control and that accompanied with commercial awareness and efficiency should lead to an improved attractive proposition of transporting freight by rail.

Q. *Would you prefer to lease or own your own rolling stock and/or locomotives if you were to operate freight services?*

A. The answer must be lease.

Q. *Will private freight operators be better able to take advantage of the opportunities offered by the Channel Tunnel than BR?*

A. The broad answer would be yes because the opportunities offered by the Channel Tunnel could be structured in such a way as to remove the BR effect which can be seen as only hindering and adding to the over manning of the service. The private freight operators, therefore, would be able to make quicker more simplistic direct comparisons of freight costings which would lead to enhanced possibilities for use of the Channel Tunnel.

11 November 1992

APPENDIX 63

Memorandum from Mr P W B Semmens

"The Future Prospects for the Railway System in the Light of the Government's Proposals for Privatisation"

Having studied—and used—our railways prior to 1948, I am sure there are ways in which a privatised network could enable the country to benefit to a greater extent than we do at present from the vast investments in our railway system. There are, however, many hazards in the privatisation process, and I would like to bring a number of general points to the Committee's notice that are pertinent to their current inquiry.

1. OPEN ACCESS

It should not be overlooked that this concept is virtually as old as the railways, but had to be abandoned at a very early stage. When the Stockton & Darlington Railway was authorised in 1821, it was to be the railway equivalent of a toll road, and anyone with suitable rolling-stock would be able to use it on payment of the specified tolls. For the first eight years after the opening in 1825, when a banner on the inaugural train proclaimed "Public Benefit at Private Risk", it operated in this way. During this period the railway company took virtually no direct part in the conveyance of passengers (who were all hauled by horses), and shared the operation of the mineral traffic with various operators.

By the early 1830s the operational problems resulting from this method of working were becoming too great, and, with plans to improve the railway's infrastructure and introduce more steam locomotives, the company took over the working of all the trains themselves, buying out the other users. (Jeans, J.S., *Jubilee Memorial of the Railway System* (1875), page 88.) This did not prevent nearby users of rail transport connecting their own lines with those of the railway company to their mutual advantage. Such a process has continued nationally ever since, involving "Private Sidings" agreements, as well as quite extensive private railway systems, which represent a large proportion of the massive current investment by the private sector in rail freight operations.

To be able to use the Stockton & Darlington Railway in the early days, the would-be outside transport contractor had to have a vehicle with the requisite technical features to operate on that particular railway line. The same applies today, and this presents a very different state of affairs to the airline business, which, it must be remembered, is also a form of *Public Transport*. There is nothing to prevent an airline buying—or hiring from the world-wide aircraft-leasing business—a faster or bigger aircraft, powered by whatever type of engine is required, to operate an alternative service over most routes. The only physical restrictions are the facilities at the terminal airports.

Not only is there no international leasing market for railway vehicles, other than a few specialised freight wagons, but there cannot be one for passenger locomotives and stock, as far as this country is concerned, for many decades to come. This results from the different national loading gauges and other requirements, including methods of traction, as well as signalling and other safety systems. To standardise these internationally as a specific project would involve great expense. It can only effectively be done in an evolutionary way, as happened during the development of the international air transport industry during the last four decades. On the other hand, having a single railway authority in this country enables that to act as a leasing body for its motive-power and rolling-stock fleet, which it deploys to the different routes to achieve the largest overall return.

2. TIMETABLING

One of the all-important aspects of having more than one operator for the railway network is the question of a Network Timetable. To take an example from Bus Deregulation, the writer wanted to use the local buses in Newport, Gwent in May this year, to see something of the area. He tried to obtain a timetable, only to be told that they now just published *Timetable Alterations*. Already the private owners of the Metrolink system in Manchester have not made timetables for the former railway lines to Bury and Altrincham available for the national timetables. The "White Paper" (Cm 2012) referred to the benefits of a single railway network. It is thus vital to stop the Manchester experience from spreading after privatisation, or the use of the railways will fall dramatically, as bus ridership has done since deregulation.

3. THROUGH TICKETING AND INNER TICKETING

Cm 2012 also referred to the benefits of Through Ticketing, and this is again something which has disappeared for long-distance passengers with Manchester Metrolink. The question of how this feature is to be maintained for passengers after more general privatisation thus needs careful study.

If a second operator is franchised to use a particular route, the number of trains can only increase marginally, because, even if there are no track capacity limitations, the overall demand will not rise overnight. As a result, unless tickets are interchangeable, the user is bound to be offered a more restricted choice of trains. With modern revenue management systems, the leisure traveller is going to be offered "own-line" returns, so immediately there will be less trains available to chose from, and the full-fare business traveller (first- or standard-class) will similarly lose flexibility if return tickets are not available by both companies' trains.

In his November 1991 lecture to the Railway Study Association, Professor W Bradshaw commented, "I say to those who want to privatise the system, be very, very careful before you let loose a number of competing operators on the same track." (*RSA Bulletin* No. 41, page 16.) As every traveller knows, from their point of view any service is fragile, and every perturbation is likely to diminish passenger confidence, and hence usage. It must not be overlooked that users of public transport require an extra degree of discipline which they do not have to adopt if they use private transport.

4. FRANCHISING

Civil Service experience of franchising includes that of the catering operations at our National Museums, which are for periods of 3-5 years. In the writer's experience at such an establishment, a change-over from one contractor to another, complete with change of staff, can take place quickly and without difficulty. However, while that is possible with a small static catering operation, it cannot be done with a railway, since it takes a long time to introduce new stock, drivers, train crews and other operational staff.

Merely to change the management and leave the existing staff to operate the services will not improve morale or company loyalty, which are both vital to the success—and safety—of such a complex and specialised system.

It is possible to switch airlines on a particular route virtually instantaneously. This is because aircraft do not have to be specifically tailored to the routes they operate, and the fact that there is a pool of them available to lease. That industry is, in any case, well used to coping with the unplanned diversion of aircraft to another airport for weather and other "operational reasons".

5. STATION SALES

If any railway stations are sold off to private companies, it is vital to ensure that this does not permit the new owners to asset-strip the site. This has occurred with recent bus take-overs in this country, when the new owner has more than recouped its outlay by selling the city-centre bus depot, and operating from nearby streets. (Morris, S, *Railway World,* November 1992, page 35.) Many of our Victorian stations would make magnificent sports centres or shopping malls, and the railway operation could then be switched to a few open platforms, with minimal facilities, situated several miles away on the outskirts of the city. This has happened extensively in North America, but they are now, thankfully, in process of reversing the process in a number of places.

THE WAY FORWARD

The way forward for our railways must be to follow the basic principle being adopted in Japan and Germany for the ultimate privatisation of their railways, but not necessarily the details of either. In both those countries privatisation is seen as a *long term* aim, and neither is seeking to achieve an overnight "fix". I know that the Committee has taken steps to get evidence from German Rail, but in both those countries the process is seen as an evolutionary one. Instantaneous solutions are not being sought, in spite of the fact that the original level of losses on both systems make the present day grants to British Rail and London Transport seem minor by comparison. Such a process also requires a greater commitment to a national transport policy by the Government, which is, in any case, vital for the longer-term prosperity of this country, with its limited land resources and the constraints which will have to be imposed for world environmental reasons.

14 November 1992

APPENDIX 64

TIPHOOK RAIL LIMITED

The Future Prospects for the Railway System in the light of the Government's Proposals for Privatisation.

Thank you for your letter dated 15th October encouraging views on the Government's plans for privatisation as set out in the White Paper "New Opportunities for the Railways".

(a) Formal submission from the Association of Private Railway Wagon Owners.

As Chairman of the Association of Private Railway Wagon Owners (APRO) I have previously presented the Association's views on the White Paper in our letter dated 24th September.*

(b) Specific questions detailed in your letter.

The aims and objectives of a privatised railway are to move the maximum amount of bulk freight products on railways profitably. The attraction for the private sector is profitable return on the utilisation of their assets whether they be rail wagons, terminals or management operations etc. The Government must be aware that commercial private ambitions are not wholly compatible with environmental or ecological aims of society as a whole.

(c) Freight traffic can develop effectively in a primarily passenger network by better management of slot allocation and greater use of "antisocial" hours when passengers do not require track, ie night/early morning rates.

(d) Railtrack must be aware that costing for freight is already highly sensitive, considering the easy option of freight customers to use road haulage facilities. Costing should be on the basis of the market price deducting operating costs; maintenance and safety related costs, marginal infrastructure costs, leaving the residual balance as a contribution to the infrastructure.

(e) If there is no actual or foreseen demand for track and related infrastructure, except freight, such track and infrastructure could be offered to private sector for outright ownership and management. Guarantees to maintain freight services from private owners would require underlying guarantees from the freight customer. Outright private ownership to track would preclude open access, as with any other use of private property.

(f) Rail competes effectively with road transport for voluminous bulk movements between specially constructed rail terminals. Privatisation of freight services will only attract further freight on the basis of more competitive door to door pricing.

(g) Tiphook Rail would prefer to own or lease it's own rolling stock or locomotives if we were to operate freight services.

(h) Private side operators will undoubtedly be able to take better advantage of the opportunities offered by the Channel Tunnel than BR because of more commercial and widespread relationships with European customers and European railways.

---

* Printed Appendix 25.

I hope this submission is of interest to the Committee. Tiphook will naturally be pleased to make it views known in greater depth if the Committee so requires.

11 November 1992

APPENDIX 65

NFC INTERNATIONAL DIVISION

1. *Aims and objectives of a privatised railway*

The key aim and objective is that a privatised railway should be customer focused and should operate on commercial principles. In particular it should provide a reliable service—the single most important feature.

2. *Developing freight effectively in a primary passenger network*

This is a difficult issue and it is recognised that no easy solution exists—such as speeding up freight trains since this would inflict unacceptable wear and tear on the track.

Wherever possible perhaps passengers could be given priority by day and freight by night. However the only satisfactory solution appears to be to use separate tracks for passenger and freight traffic. Although it is recognised that building a second infrastructure would be commercially impractical, wherever possible, existing non-high speed lines could be used for freight. Such a scheme is suggested by Central Railway Group in the UK. In France, existing lower-speed track is reported to be used by freight when new, high speed TGV tracks become operational for passenger traffic.

In general we recognise that reliability is more important than speed for freight.

3. *Charging principles of the track authority*

This is a very difficult question. Currently we use road exclusively and this is satisfactory. We would therefore be looking for a rail alternative which costs no more and is as reliable. We recognise the environmental implications of road transport and would welcome the chance to put freight on the rail wherever possible and would therefore not necessarily be looking for a cheaper alternative to road.

4. *Circumstances under which it might be sensible for track and related infrastructure used only for freight to pass into private hands along with operational parts of the freight business*

This would be very acceptable, providing a mechanism to prevent abuse of monopoly power was introduced, such as OFTEL.

5. *Rail competing effectively with road for freight transport*

Road and rail are usually not in competition for freight traffic. They are complementary modes of transport with rail suitable for long haul and road for short haul, pick up and delivery.

Transporting freight by rail will become more attractive when the length of haul becomes longer—when the Channel Tunnel opens—and when reliability improves. Also improvements need to be made in flexibility and user friendliness with regard to rail.

6. *Leased or own rolling stock*

We would prefer to lease rather than own rolling stock.

7. *Private operators versus BR's ability to take advantage of opportunities offered by the Channel Tunnel*

This is a difficult question. A private operator would probably be able to move in a faster, more entrepreneurial way and perhaps be more in touch with customers.

16 November 1992

APPENDIX 66

Copy of a letter to the Secretary of State for Transport from Mr J A Evans,
Darwin College, University of Kent, Canterbury

I am writing to you because I believe that your plans for the privatisation of British Rail will make the rail system much worse than it already is. Your statement in the House of Commons in July that more competition is needed is wrong. British Rail has not got a monopoly: it has to compete all time against other forms of transport; be they cars, coaches, lorries, buses, aircraft and shipping services etc.

In any case, the rail system needs unity so that timetables can be arranged to provide connections between different services at interchange stations, to encourage more passengers to use these services. (I know that there are a few blunders on this front at the moment!)

The same applies to ticketing. Leaving local variations aside, e.g. in the Network SouthEast area with longer distance cheap day returns, you should be able to buy the same kind of ticket to say, Blackpool from Crewe and Penzance. Having said this, the mileage in which cheap day return tickets are valid should be extended. They are available throughout Network SouthEast area (approx 250 miles from Kings Lynn to Weymouth), but are only valid for 50 miles outside the NSE area. (e.g. they are not available between Leeds and Manchester.) Another point on ticketing: should privatisation go ahead with more than one operator running train services between any 2 stations, then all tickets should be valid on all trains between those points, subject of course to the present time restrictions (and of course Network Card discounted tickets only being valid on Network SouthEast trains.) Otherwise, a very limited service will be available to, say, season ticket holders between Reading and London, where there are 2 Network SouthEast routes and the Inter City services to London Paddington/Waterloo. People would find that their season ticket is only valid on one type of service, leading to a reduction in service frequency and an increase in overcrowding.

Through ticketing is vital to Britain's railways in attracting new passengers, and in retaining existing ones. It could add quite a lot of extra time, money and inconvenience to a journey if another ticket has to be purchased if changing trains en-route.

Railcards are another necessity that must be retained on all routes. The Disabled, Young Person's and Senior Citizen railcards for obvious reasons. and the others like family railcard and Network Card in order to encourage more off-peak leisure travel by rail. However, the prices of these railcards must also be held roughly to the reasonable levels that they are at the moment.

A large investment is needed in the railway system **NOW,** not in a few year's time. It will take a few years for major projects to get from the design stage to completion, especially on the order of new trains - which are urgently needed on many routes. Also, unless new orders are made soon, we will see the present train manufacturers going out of business because they have no work on their books. Their present orders will be delivered to British Rail by 1994. This is like many of the bus manufacturers, which have gone out of business since the buses were deregulated. This was because the private companies did not want to pay out lots of money to build new buses. Instead, they kept old buses running past their useful life, and services suffered as a result. At the same time, many bus fares went up. Once British train manufacturers have been allowed to go out of business, then any new order will have to go abroad to foreign companies. This helps the economies of other countries, whilst doing nothing to help the employment situation here. It also will not help our balance of payments deficit.

Types of investment needed are: more new lines and stations; new and longer trains, more electrification and replacement of life-expired equipment, especially signalling, after the recent news over the safety concerns of certain types of relay signals.

The government claims that it is committed to helping the environment. How can it be if it is spending billions of pounds on building new roads that destroy the environment (e.g. Tywford Down) and encourage more cars that put exhaust gases into the atmosphere? What is needed is a major cut in road spending, and the money put into building new railway lines and trains instead. This will help the economy, by creating more jobs in the manufacturing industries associated with new rail projects. It will also help the environment by attracting new custom onto the railways form the roads. This will also help the motorway system, because it will mean less traffic on the roads. This is especialy so if **tax relief is given to companies transporting freight by rail** in any form: either in whole train wagons, or the new intermodal system in which rail wagons convert into lorries. This would take many lorries off our road network, reducing traffic volumes and also cutting wear on the road surfaces.

By implementing the suggestions in the last paragraph, you could avoid having to destroy the environment even further by widening the M25 yet again.

I also have a list of other proposals which you should seriously consider as ways of improving the transport network of the United Kingdom.

1. Build an **outer London Circle line** by extending the North London line over/under the River Thames at Woolwich and completing the circle by linking the major stopping places in South London; namely Bromley South, East Croydon, West Croydon, Clapham Junction and Richmond. A new station is also needed on the north London Line to interchange with Kings Cross and St. Pancras stations, both with Inter City, Thameslink and Underground lines. This will make Cross London services much easier by avoiding the need to cross central London. All mainline services, however, should stop at the new interchange stations to encourage this.

2. Another major project which will help cross-London journeys is one that ought to be very familiar to you by now, namely **THAMESLINK 2000.** This project needs to be completed as soon as possible. The Scheme is fairly cheap, with the benefits far outweighing the costs. The scheme will allow a far wider range of cross London services than there are at the moment. It would also take much pressure from London Underground, by removing the need for many people, especially commuters, to change from the train onto the Underground system when travelling into London.

It is simply madness not to carry ahead with this project just because the treasury object over the cost. This project is likely to make money within a few years, whereas a costly road scheme is readily paid for by the treasury—but is surely cannot recover any of the money spent, let alone make a profit!

3. The above also applies to the **Cross-Rail** project, linking Paddington to Liverpool Street stations.

4. Another simple project in London that would benefit many commuters to the city of London would be an extension of the line from Finsbury to Moorgate. I understand that there is a disused section of this tunnel running from Moorgate to Bank. If this were to be restored and the line connected to the Waterloo & City Line at Bank, this would enable trains to take commuters from Hertfordshire right into the heart of the city, and throught to Waterloo. Connections are now in place at Bank to make travel to DOCKLANDS easier by means of the Dockland light railway. Also, if a new station were to be opened a Blackfriars, it would provide good connections with Thameslink services and the District/Circle Underground lines. Another part of this project, but I don't know whether it is now possible due to the new Channel Tunnel rail terminal at Waterloo, is a connection from Waterloo & City line with the mainline rail network at Clapham Junction. Completion of both of these elements would enable through train services to run from Stevenage/Hertford/Welwyn Garden City to Hampton Court and Windsor. These services would attract much leisure traffic, especially so as there is no direct link from Kings Cross to Waterloo, which is the London terminus of the trains to Bournemouth. Also, the new Channel tunnel terminal will open there next year. (Although one ought to open at Kings Cross before too long...). Longer distance service would also be possible between Cambridge and Reading (Via Staines) or Southampton.

5. The building of a rail link from Luton via Luton Airport to Stevenage. Connected with a re-opening of the line to Dunstable, a regular hourly service can run between Dunstable and Cambridge. Also, another service can connect Luton and the airport with Stevenage, Hertford, Bishops Stortford and Stansted Airport.

6. The building of an electrified rail link between Hitchin and Ampthill. Also involved is the electrification of the Bedford to Bletchley line and the current freight only link to Oxford from Bletchley. This would allow hourly Network Express services to run between Kings Lynn, Ely, **Cambridge,** Letchworth, Shefford, Bletchley and **Oxford.** Also, a stoping Cambridge to Northampton service could run, giving a link from North Hertfordshire to Milton Keynes. Parallel bus services are poor. A Great Northern train service to Bedford can also be introduced to serve the new stations on the link between Hitchin and the Midland Main Line. These links in proposals 5 and 6 would improve connections to Inter city services at Stevenage, Luton, Bedford, Milton Keynes and Oxford. This would avoid the need for many people to travel via London, therefore reducing the number of people having to change stations by underground. They would also be useful as diversionary and freight routes.

7. The electrification of the Midland Main Line from Bedford to Leeds/Doncaster via Nottingham, Derby and Sheffield. This would boost the services on this line. also, with a short electrified link from Derby to Birmingham, Inter City cross country services could run electrically propelled on the northern leg of the journey on both the East and West Coast routes. By also electrifying from Manchester to Sheffield, and from Norwich to Birmingham, then the regional Railways cross country services from Norwich/Stansted to Birmingham/Liverpool can also be electrically propelled.

8. The Building of the **High Speed Rail Link to Channel Tunnel.** This is urgently required **NOW.** The sooner that building starts on this project, the sooner that the Thameslink 2000 project can go ahead by the redevelopment of Kings Cross. The high speed line would also help to carry commuters from Kent to London. The service between Kent and London at the moment is very poor. **New trains are urgently needed on all routes in Kent.** (I appreciate that trains are in the process of delivery for inner suburban services.)

9. The electrification of the trans-pennine routes from Liverpool to York, Hull, Middlesborough and Scarborough are required to improve the standard of service on these routes.

10. Electrification of Birmingham commuter lines to Dorridge and Leamington. If this was extended to Banbury, and met by an extension of Network South East's planned electrification to Reading, (in connection with Cross rail) then there would be an alternative electrified route from London to Birmingham. It would also give Oxford an electric service. Also, by using dual-voltage locomotives, then the Inter City cross Country services from Poole, Bournemouth, Dover, Brighton, Reading, Oxford, Birmingham to the North could be electrically operated throughout: provided the midland main line was also electrified to Leeds and Doncaster.

11. The building of the **Jubilee line extension** as soon as possible. This would give much better connections to the Greenwich and Docklands areas, besides giving a link between Stratford and Waterloo (2 of London's future 3 Channel tunnel stations) and the West End and Baker Street.

12. The building of the proposed **extension to the Docklands Light Railway** from Island Gardens to Greenwich and Lewisham, giving better connections from South East London/Northern Kent and Docklands and the City. Also, possible extension of the DLR from Bank onto Moorgate and Farringdon, using the Stretch of track from Moorgate to Farringdon that is due to close when the full Thameslink project goes ahead.

13. Urgent approval of the IC250 project to upgrade the West Coast Main Line.

14. Building of the **Heathrow Rail link.** This should be built as soon as possible. This would allow through trains from Heathrow to London (and Stansted once Cross-Rail is complete). There would be connections available on Cross Rail at Farringdon for Gatwick (and Luton....) and also at Stratford for the continent.

15. General investment in providing new trains for more reliable service that are more frequent, and longer trains as well.

10 November 1992.

APPENDIX 67

Letter from Mr D A Prior

Congratulations on your appointment as Chairman of the Transport Select Committee. It is good to see someone appointed who has a committed interest in railways.

Having a deep interest in railways—my father and both grandfathers were railwaymen all their lives—and using the railways myself quite often, I have very many doubts about the privatisation of Britsh Rail as proposed in the recent White Paper.

Basic problem

We are geographically a small country with most of the population located in the southern half. We need an efficient rail system to complement and ease the road system (at present costing millions in traffic jams) at the most economical cost to tax payers and users. We cannot afford to waste vast sums of money.(Some mistakes will, of course, always be made.) However, as you said in a recent speech, "We do not want a Poll Tax on wheels".

Doubts about proposals in the White Paper

1. Will a national timetable, through ticketing, standard fares structure and railcards be retained? (I myself am a Senior Citizen).

2. Fares—Fares are to rise in January way above inflation (some more than others). Putting up fares so much at the present time is economic madness. Everyone else seems to be reducing the cost of both goods and services. Presumably these fare rises are due to the current policy that the user pays for all railway improvements. Road users only pay part of road costs.

Would the franchisees increase fares even more than B.R. after privatisation as they would have to make profits on top of operating costs?

If so, people will be driven off the railways onto the roads causing congestion, more road building, greater environmental damage, increased costs to industry and commerce, greater stress and accidents (20 people are killed on the roads for every one on the railways and a good many people who survive accidents become severely incapacitated and unable to work).

I enclose a few recent letters from our local paper—*The Kentish Gazette*—relating to some of the above.*

3. The proposed bureaucracy for running the railway. It strikes me as a recipe for arguments galore over access to track, fares and charges by Railtrack. I have also seen in the railway press that there may have to be another body to discuss revenue collection—back to the Railway Clearing House!

4. Who is to be responsible for the provision of new rolling stock? The current stock on the Kent Coast Line is about thirty years old and in urgent need of replacement. A Networker costs a quarter of a million pounds. Is the franchisee going to find the money to buy or lease these new units, or will the railway soldier on with old stock?

There is a lot more I could say about the privatisation proposals, but no doubt you will be receiving representations from various groups and individuals both for and against.

My main concern is that the changes as proposed will lead to another Beeching era and loss of a national network. Can we afford to let this happen? B.R. could be improved—at the moment it is like the curate's egg—good in parts. It needs investment—both public and private. If lack of funding does not kill the railway, I have a feeling the present D.O.T. ideas will. I see the dead hand of the Treasury behnd the proposals.

I sincerely hope that the Select Committee will look long and hard at the Bill before it and that the outcome will be a user-friendly railway not, as has happened with bus de-regulation, far fewer miles, older buses, fewer passengers and higher fares. (My wife and I travelled on a Cambus from a camp site just outside Cambridge into the city whilst on holiday. The fare was high for the length of journey and the bus extremely old. At one point my wife was very scared for, when the driver turned the wheel of the bus one way, the bus went the other!)

In the present financial situation we can no longer afford to follow the dogmas of the 80s. We must watch costs and increase efficiency but pursue policies to maintain jobs and skills for the sake of our children. No rushed, badly-thought out dash for growth though. Oh that we still had the cash spent to support the £ on Black Wednesday; it would certainly have paid for the Jubilee Line, the improvement of the West Coast Main

*Not printed

Line and a number of by-passes and, possibly the EFA in the next few years, the Channel Tunnel Link and Cross-Rail.

24 October 1992

APPENDIX 68

HUDDERSFIELD–PENISTONE–SHEFFIELD RAIL USERS' ASSOCIATION

Impending Railway Privatisation

I am writing to you on behalf of this association about the impending progressive privatisation of British Rail. We are concerned to ensure, as far as we are able, that any changes are beneficial to our members and fellow-passengers. Since your committee is involved in this and related issues, I am bringing the following to your attention.

(a) There should be an improving quality of service in all its aspects: safety, reliability, punctuality, frequency, speed, timetabling, connection, information, seat availability, security, cleanliness, ticketing, fares, etc. Prospective franchisees should be judged in this light, as should any changes in the organisational structure of the railways.

(b) Our line is part of a regional and national rail system. It is essential that a national timetable and fare structure be maintained, with through tickets and railcards recognised by all operators, both regional and national. Frequent, sudden and sometimes secretive changes of the type now imposed on bus users should not be permitted. We are dismayed at reports (eg The Independent 15 July 1992) that future rail operators will not be required to accept each other's tickets, that "smaller stations" would not have to provide the full range of tickets (The Independent 13 October 1992) and that franchisees would be free to "reduce services" apparently without further reference (ibid).

(c) We welcome the indications that the Government now recognises the vital importance of public transport. However, we are concerned that government support is much lower than in almost all other EC countries. Without adequate investment, it seems unlikely that privatisation, in itself, will effect the dramatic improvements we really need. Thus, any major changes in railway organisation should be judged, at least in part, by the investment they generate.

(d) We believe that public transport should provide an integrated and effective service as in many EC countries with governments of various political hues. Though the two local PTEs strive to retain a degree of integration in our area, they are having an uphill struggle. We are concerned that the franchising of rail services will, if not properly regulated, lead to further fragmentation.

(e) We wish to see the assessment and funding of rail investment (and that for public transport in general) placed on the same basis as that used for roads. Full account should be taken of such factors as users' time, accidents, congestion and pollution.

(f) We would like to see rail user groups strongly represented on any panel which selects franchisees to operate their services.

We are a non-party-political association and I would like to make it quite clear that we are not against railway privatisation in itself. We are deeply concerned, though, that some of the ideas now being aired will, if implemented, leave us in an even worse position than at present. We have discussed this with the Central Transport Consultative Committee which is in broad agreement with us, but we are not convinced that it carries sufficient political clout to protect rail users in this forthcoming upheaval. It is possible that you and your committee are the passengers' last hope for avoiding, at best, a continuing decline or, at worst, an utter disaster.

We are relying on you!

27 October 1992.

APPENDIX 69

Letter from Mr J Nicholas

I write to you as Chairman of the Commons Select Committee on Transport.

Like yourself I would like to see more passenger and freight traffic travel by rail. I have very strong reservations about the government's policy of railway privatisation, but inadvertently they have highlighted the cost of railway infrastructure, in comparison to road, to any new railway users.

Might I ask that you ask the Select Committee to press the government to produce a "level playing field" between road and rail. If the government pays the full cost of the rail infrastructure it could then charge each user an annual rail fund licence. If each freight locomotive paid at the HGV rate, and each multiple unit passenger train at the coach rate then I am sure we would have little difficulty in attracting much more traffic on to the railway, be it BR or new operator services.

The misadventures of Tiger Rail, Charterrail and Stagecoach must surely give us the evidence of massive hidden subsidies to road transport not enjoyed by railways.

29 October 1992

APPENDIX 70

EDENBRIDGE AND DISTRICT RAIL TRAVELLERS'S ASSOCIATION

The Privatisation of British Rail

BACKGROUND

In the early part of this Century there were about 100 different companies operating rail services. In 1923 the railways were grouped into four large companies (Great Western Railway, London Midland and Scottish Railway, London and North Eastern Railway, and Southern Railway); In 1948, the railways were nationalised and became 'British Railways'.

THE WHITE PAPER

On 14th July, 1992, the Government White Paper on the Privatisation of British Rail, entitled 'New Opportunities for the Railways' was published.

The foreword to the White Paper by the Secretary of State for Transport, John MacGregor, states:

"Privatisation is one of the great success stories of this Government. It has taken different forms in different industries. But common to all privatisation has been the harnessing of the management skills, flair and entrepeneurial spirit of the private sector to provide better services for the public.

The time has come to extend these benefits to the railways. This calls for a new approach. British Rail makes large losses. It cannot therefore be sold as a complete concern in the same way as other industries which we have privatised and there will not be substantial proceeds to the Exchequer. Our objective is to improve the quality of railway services by creating many new opportunities for private sector involement. This will mean more competition, greater efficiency and a wider choice of services more closely tailored to what customers want.

This White Paper explains how we are going to achieve these objectives."

However, despite what the foreword says, most people have said that the White Paper is vague and poses more questions than what it provides answers for.

INFORMED COMMENT

The railway press over the past few weeks has contained numerous articles about the privatisation of British Rail and none of those articles appear to come out in favour of privatisation of the break up of British Rail as proposed in the White Paper.

The following views cannot be ignored—

Howard Davies, Director-General of the Confederation of British Industry

"It is absolutely essential that privatisation is not used as an alibi for cutbacks on much-needed investment in the rail system."

How is rolling stock to be treated (purchased, leased, maintained, developed, etc.)? A Report by Steer Davies Gleave warns of 'radical cut-backs' unless the Government immediately steps up public investment to keep the railway manufacturing industry going during the handover to private operators. At the moment there are no orders for new trains after 1995.

What happens if a franchisee fails to meet targets? Also, what happens if a franchisee goes bankrupt. Does the line go to a new operator overnight or is it closed overnight?

If Stations are sold will the new owners charge so much for use of those stations by the train operators that less trains will call at those Stations? Will access be guaranteed?

When a line is closed for engineering works, who will pay for any replacement bus service, the Track Authority or the train operator? Perhaps no replacement bus service is provided and there is no service for a period of time.

There could be different companies running trains (doubtful on both of our local lines, but could be the situation nationally). This situation could lead to no reliable timetable, through ticketing or fares structure. It could lead to many problems at major stations as to which operator has priority—would the Orient Express be allowed to leave before one of Roger Freeman's Typist trains? If each franchisee is allowed to set his own timetable the implication of this is that the 'All Britain Rail Timetable' will be abolished. How will Station and Travel Centre Staff be able to tell customers about trains in other parts of the country?

Will the various Railcards still be available? (senior Citizens, Families, Disabled National Cards and Network SouthEast Card). If not, there will be an increase in fares for many rail users, which could lead less people to use rail.

Will fares continue to rise annually at double the rate of inflation as has been the case in recent years? Fares could even rise at more regular intervals. It is understood that each franchisee will be allowed to set his own fares which could lead to higher fares.

Would privatisation lead to further rationalisation of servicing and maintenance depots? The Association is all too well aware of the deterioration of services on the Uckfield Line following closure of Tunbridge Wells Depot in 1985. Also, will further rationalisation of servicing and maintenance depots affect possible reopenings in the future (e.g. Uckfield-Lewes, where the existence of Brighton and Eastbourne Depots is crucial to the success of the Uckfield Line following reinstatement of this section). Where would possible new operators service stock? Would there be Depot sharing? What about local authority planning permission for new Depots?

The Government intends to maintain an effective voice for consumers' interests and to ensure that none of the benefits of the existing system of Transport Users' Consultative Committees is lost. Would franchisees be prepared to have dialogue with those Consultative Committees and would they be prepared to have dialogue with Rail Travellers Associations?

11 November 1992

APPENDIX 71

NORFOLK RAIL POLICY GROUP

The Privatisation of British Rail

1. INTRODUCTION

1.1 The long-awaited White Paper "New Opportunities for the Railways" was published in July and sets out the Government's plans for privatisation of British Rail. A number of options have been examined, but the Government has chosen to adopt a flexible approach under which each of the existing rail businesses will be treated differently. British Rail will retain responsibility for track and infrastructure and will continue to operate passenger services until such time as they are franchised to private operators.

1.2 It is difficult to assess the implications for rail services in Norfolk as the proposals involve change on a massive scale, but are short on detail. There are clearly potential benefits to be gained from a more competitive ethos, the relaxation of investment rules and identification of the support requirements of groups of services. There is great uncertainty, however, as to the future of rural services, the levels of investment and support and the possible loss of network benefits.

1.3 This report seeks to identify those issues which will be of greatest concern to the Rail Policy Group. At a strategic level, the Group has put forward policies which seek to develop the role of local rail services by:

— Retention and development of the rail network in Norfolk to meet present and future demand for rail transport;

— Wider recognition of the role of the railway in meeting social need and minimizing road traffic congestion.

1.4 Achievement of these aims could be greatly assisted by equality of treatment in the provision of road and rail infrastructure. The Group believes that Government must play a role in providing a modern rail infrastructure for the nation. The White Paper proposes, however, that operators of rail services will pay the full cost of track and infrastructure. This would not provide the "level playing field" which could help to redress the balance in modal choice between rail and road transport.

1.5 The White Paper "This Common Inheritance – Britain's Environmental Strategy" states (Para 5.61) that "there is an important place for public transport in Britain's strategy on CO_2. In combination with other measures, modern and cost-effective public transport can draw traffic at the margin from the roads and contribute to overall reductions in CO_2." It is not clear where the responsibility will rest for ensuring optimisation of the role of the privatised railway with regard to global warming.

The Group seeks assurances from the Secretary of State that the Government accepts the wider role of the railway in minimizing road traffic and will ensure that this is reflected in legislation brought forward to implement the White Paper proposals;

The Group asks the Secretary of State to explain:

— The reasoning behind the proposal not to take the opportunity to establish a "level playing field" between road and rail transport;

— Who will be responsible for monitoring the role of the privatised railway with regard to global warming.

2. INFRASTRUCTURE

2.1 Railtrack is expected to be financed largely from charges to operators, including those in receipt of subsidy. The Government is apparently willing to provide some direct support for railway investment in projects which provide a satisfactory cost-benefit return, but do not meet current requirements regarding the first year financial return. No further details are given.

2.2 If the aspirations of the Rail Policy Group are to be met, it will be necessary for Railtrack to invest in renewal of Norfolk's railway infrastructure, improvements in track capacity, electrification and strategic developments such as Thameslink 2000. Initiatives such as electrification raise particular concerns as they will require co-ordinated investment between Railtrack and each of the operators using the route in question.

2.3 An alternative approach to track and infrastructure would be for the Government to provide and maintain it in the same way as it does for the trunk road network. It would then be possible for payments made to the Government for profitable franchises to be used to cross-subsidise un-profitable franchises. Provision of a "level playing field" in this way could encourage greater competition and facilitate the transfer of traffic from road to rail. It would also avoid potential difficulties in complying with the draft EC directive requiring a non-discriminatory charging regime for use of rail infrastructure.

2.4 Railtrack will have responsibility for timetabling under rules laid down by the regulator. Sectorisation has already given rise to some erosion of the network approach to timetabling. This can only get worse as timetable input comes from more than the existing three operators of passenger services. It is not clear what arrangements will be made for consultation with rail users or local authorities. A mechanism is needed for local authorities to make their views known on the level of service required and to react to any significant changes to timetables. The Group has called for rail businesses to give at least six weeks written notice of changes to timetables in line with the obligations imposed on bus operators under the Transport Act 1985.

2.5 The possible sale or lease of stations raises the possibility that future owners may develop sites in such a way as to prejudice the main function of stations in providing adequate facilities for passengers.

The Group seeks assurances from the Secretary of State as follows:

— *That Railtrack will develop an investment plan for each line taking into account the need for renewal of existing infrastructure, the provision of additional track capacity, strategic developments such as Thameslink 2000 and further electrification;*

— *That a full assessment will be made of the alternative of Railtrack being funded by the Government rather than by charges to operators;*

— *That the Franchise Authority will be required to ensure that timetables are fully co-ordinated with particular regard to different franchises covering the same line of route;*

— *That provision will be made in legislation for the local authorities to be consulted on timetables by rail operators and an obligation placed on Railtrack to give at least six weeks written notice to County Councils of timetable changes;*

— *That local authorities will be consulted before stations are sold to the private sector;*

3. REGULATION

3.1 It is not clear from the White Paper how the Regulator will allocate train paths to operators at "pinch points" such as the approach to London from Norwich. This problem will become particularly acute in relation to freight services, which may be able to demand a higher priority than they have at present, and competing passenger services operating under "open access".

3.2 The Regular will be charged with promoting the interests of consumers. The White Paper does not explain how this role will be exercised in relation to the combined effects of the pace and scale of change on the quality of service delivered to the passenger.

3.3 The White Paper states the intention of not losing the benefits of TUCCs, but does not spell out how the voice of the rail user will be heard in future. It is important to recognise that the TUCCs are not simply consumer lobbies, but do work very closely with B.R. officials to address issues raised by users.

3.4 Reference is made in the White Paper to a study by the Health and Safety Executive of the implications of privatisation. The resulting recommendations will be published, but no mention is made of consultation.

The Group seeks assurances from the Secretary of State as follows:

— *That the Government will undertake wide consultation on the outcome of the consultancy study being undertaken on freedom of access;*

— *That the Regulator will be required to make an annual report to parliament covering, inter alia, the extent to which quality of service has been affected by the changes proposed;*

—*That the Regulator will be required regularly to consult with regional planning forums on the extent to which local delivery of rail services is affected by implementation of the White Paper proposals;*

—*That the Health and Safety Executive will consult rail users before making recommendations to the Government regarding the safety implications of privatisation;*

The Group asks the Secretary of State:—

— To enlarge on the arrangements which will be made for representation of users interests to British Rail, Railtrack, the Franchise Authority, the Regulator and the passenger railway operators;

— To clarify the future role of TUCCs.

4. FRANCHISING

4.1 Franchises are likely to reflect a regional identity. This suggests that East Anglia local services may be packaged into a single franchise. The Franchise Authority will set a minimum service and quality standards within broad objectives set by the Government. If the aspirations of the Group regarding maintenance of existing service levels are to be met, it will clearly be necessary for there to be some local authority input before the Franchising Authority draws up specifications. These will need to be more detailed than the White Paper suggests if they are to cover such issues as the extent to which trains call at intermediate stations.

4.2 The Group has a policy of seeking improvements to Network SouthEast services including the development of Thameslink 2000. If franchises are based on the current Network SouthEast divisions, it is difficult to see how Thameslink Express services will be provided across London. The Group also wishes to see the continued operation of Summer Saturday trains from London and the Midlands to Great Yarmouth. It is not clear how these will be incorporated into a franchise or whether they can remain as a residual BR operation.

4.3 The White Paper says the Government is concerned to ensure that so far as possible, customers retain the benefits of a national rail system but goes on to state that it will be for train operators to make arrangements to accept each others' tickets. Experience of bus deregulation suggests that this will not happen on a comprehensive basis. If the quality of service delivery to the passenger is to be maintained and improved, there is a clear case for franchises to specify ticket interavailability to include not only standard fares, but also discounted tickets and national railcards. Specifications could also be expected to insist upon maintenance of published connections, provision of information on both timetabled services and disruptions and the provision of adequate facilities for disabled passengers and cyclists.

4.4 The Group has policies seeking improved rolling stock on the Norwich to London and King's Lynn to London lines. It is not clear how this will be achieved. The White Paper suggests that most operators of franchises will start by renting existing rolling stock from BR to provide a level playing field, it would appear necessary for franchises to be limited in duration to the expected life of existing stock or to be long enough to ensure the capability of the franchisee to invest in new rolling stock. Further potential difficulties arise with regard to electrification projects where the timing may be uncertain when franchises are awarded, yet a substantial investment will be needed in rolling stock if the benefits are to be obtained.

4.5 There is no clear indication in the White Paper of what will happen if the holder of a franchise ceases to operate, fails to operate profitably or consistently fails to meet quality of service targets. There would appear to be a need for a mechanism to defray the costs which would fall upon BR in providing a replacement service for safeguards against reductions in service levels or increases in fares to compensate for operating losses and for some form of financial penalty for failure to meet contractual obligations.

4.6 Freedom of access gives rise to a fundamental problem with regard to franchises. If bids are based on the expectation of competition which does not arise, the cost to the Franchise Authority, and hence to the taxpayer, will be inflated. If bids ignore possible competition which does not arise, there are serious implications for the quality of service.

4.7 A key factor in maintaining a high quality of service to the passenger will be the ability of new passenger railway operators to generate a common sense of purpose among their staff. This will be difficult to achieve if core activities are subcontracted.

The Group seeks assurances from the Secretary of State as follows:

— That the Franchising Authority will be required to consult local authorities before drawing up specifications, which should be sufficiently detailed to define the extent of the service provided and the frequency at each station;

— That the Franchising Authority will be required to draw up franchises in such a way as to ensure continuing investment in renewal of rolling stock;

— That Network SouthEast franchises will make provision for the development of through services under Thameslink 2000;

— That the Franchise Authority will require successful operators to maintain ticket interavailability for standard fares, discounted tickets and national railcards and that service specifications will insist upon maintenance of published connections, provision of information on both timetabled services and disruptions and the provision of adequate facilities for disabled passengers and cyclists;

— That franchise operators will be required to put up a surety with BR against default and that financial penalties will be imposed for failure to meet contractual obligations;

The Group asks the Secretary of State for clarification as to how the White Paper proposals will facilitate:

— The continued operation of seasonal trains such as those currently operating from London and the Midlands to Great Yarmouth;

— The replacement of rolling stock currently in use on the Norwich-London and King's Lynn-London lines and the electrification of the Norwich-Great Yarmouth and Norwich-Peterborough lines;

The Group asks the Secretary of State to explain:

— What arrangements will be made for franchises to be renegotiated in the event of competition under "open access";

— What controls the Franchise Authority will exercise over subcontracting on the part of franchise operators.

5. SUPPORT FOR PASSENGER SERVICES

5.1 The Group has taken the view that support for the social railway is a Government responsibility. Constituent authorities have, nevertheless, been prepared to provide financial support to prevent loss of existing services and to facilitate electrification. The policies adopted by the Group are to lobby Government for an adequate level of PSO grant and to press for a coherent framework of financial support to maintain an acceptable level of service.

5.2 There would appear to be a strong possibility that the level of PSO support required will increase as a result of the White Paper proposals and, in particular, the loss of cross-subsidy between profitable and non-profitable routes.

5.3 If Norfolk's rural rail services are to be retained, the Government may need to increase the level of subsidy. If the Group is to be able to expand the role of rail to meet the wider transport objectives of local authorities in Norfolk, there is a further issue of funding to be addressed. The White Paper simply states that local authorities will continue to have powers to make additional contributions to cover the cost of enhancements to rail services and infrastructure. Local authorities are not in a position to develop rail services or infrastructure unless this is taken into account in public spending provisions.

5.4 Similar considerations will apply if franchising results in the provision of an unacceptable level of service. In these circumstances, there will be a "prima facie" case for local authority intervention. The duty of County Councils under the Transport Act 1985 to secure public passenger transport services extends to rail as well as bus services. If they are unable to persuade either the Franchise Authority or the franchise operator to maintain the level of service required, local authorities may wish to consider support for journeys to replace those to be withdrawn.

5.5 If replacement journeys are by rail, there will need to be a mechanism for negotiations to be completed in a timely manner so as to maintain continuity of service. Whether bus or rail replacements are provided, there will be a need for Government to recognize that local authorities will not be in a position to fund such expenditure on any scale without this being reflected in public spending provisions.

The Group seeks assurances from the Secretary of State as follows:

— That the amount of PSO grant paid by the Government will not limit the ability of the Franchise Authority to maintain Norfolk's rail services at their current level;

— That PSO grant will be made available to facilitate development of the rail network in Norfolk to meet future demand;

— That the involvement of local authorities in general and the duty of County Councils in particular in relation to the provision of public transport will not be ignored;

— That a mechanism will be established for timely action by local authorities to ensure the continued operation of socially necessary railway journeys;

— That the Government will ensure that expenditure on the part of local authorities to maintain or develop rail services is covered by Revenue Support Grant.

6. FREIGHT

6.1 The White Paper envisages the progressive transfer of BR freight business to the private sector. It also states that the existing grant scheme for the establishment of private freight facilities will continue in a modified form. Much depends on the basis chosen by Railtrack for the allocation of costs to freight services.

6.2 If freight services are called upon to meet the full proportionate cost of track and infrastructure rather than being marginally costed—as are those currently sharing track with passenger services—viability may be difficult to achieve. This could result in transfer of traffic from rail to road.

6.3 The absence of regulation of tariffs may result in mail and parcels traffic being priced off rail by operators of passenger franchises.

The Group asks the Secretary of State to clarify how the risk of increased carriage by road of mail, freight and parcels traffic in Norfolk will be avoided.

The Group seeks an assurance from the Secretary of State that an embargo will be placed on sales by British Rail Property Board of land which may be suitable for the development of freight depots until circumstances in relation to privatisation are clearer.

10 November 1992

APPENDIX 72

Letter from the Chancellor of the Exchequer to the Chairman Select Committee on Transport

Thank you for your letter of 22 October. I am sorry that I was not able to reply by 2 November as you requested. I hope, however, that this letter will be the more informative because of the delay. As you know, I announced in the Autumn Statement the results of my review into the scope for involving the private sector more fully in providing infrastructure for this country. My announcement also included an important measure specifically directed at British Rail.

In your letter, you asked first about the use of cost-benefit analysis in evaluating policies and about the costs and benefits of BR privatisation. All policy proposals are, of course, analysed very carefully before they are decided on. That analysis includes quantification, if robust estimates of the effects can be made.

The Government's proposals for privatising BR were set out in the Manifesto on which we fought the last Election. Before deciding on those proposals we looked at the merits of different approaches. The conclusions that we reached reflect one of the lessons that this country has learned under Conservative Government in the years since 1979: the best way to make state-owned businesses responsive to the consumer is through competition and privatisation.

For my part, I look forward to the day when passengers and freight customers will be able to benefit from this policy directly by using trains run by private sector companies—with private sector standards of service and efficiency.

Regarding your second question on the rules on BR's use of the private capital markets, I can assure you that the Government has never had any objections to private investment in railway projects, where it is worthwhile. However, it is usually not worthwhile to use private finance if there is no accompanying transfer of risk to the private sector. It is only where the private sector takes an appropriate share of the risks of an investment project, that gains in efficiency overall are made. This is why the proposals in the White Paper are aimed at transferring the responsibility for investment to the private sector wherever possible, including responsibility for the commercial risks.

The proposals which I announced in the Autumn Statement point a new way forward for partnership between public and private sectors in infrastructure projects (including railways), through the use of competitive joint ventures. This should allow projects to proceed with the benefits of the contribution which the private sector can make, even if the project overall cannot make a fully commercial return. As an additional measure in the run up to BR privatisation I have announced that BR will be allowed to lease some £150 million of new rolling stock. This should help the development of a rolling stock leasing market in advance of franchising, benefiting the economy as a whole and the railways in particular.

18 November 1992

APPENDIX 73

THE BADGERLINE GROUP

The Future Prospects for the Railway System in the light of the Government's Proposals for Privatisation

BACKGROUND

The Badgerline Group is one of the major bus operators in the UK, having its origins in the privatisation of the National Bus Company. The group has a proven track record of good quality service and investment, and it believes that an opportunity for further expansion might be available from the Government's proposals for the railway.

Badgerline had no particular expertise in respect or railway operation, but it does have a background of providing public passenger transport with buses and coaches. The Group is happy to carefully consider the proposals which the Government is bringing forward, but it will be concerned to ensure that any involvement is both commercially sensible and allows sufficient degree of control to ensure a quality service.

POSSIBLE AREAS OF INTEREST

The Group takes the view that it is sensible to look primarily at potential railway franchises which relate most closely to its bus operations. This suggests the more local type of railway service rather than InterCity, and leads us to look at areas where we are already major bus operators. A typical example is therefore the London, Tilbury, and Southend line, which operates through much of the territory covered by our Thamesway bus company.

We are also substantial bus operators in the West Country, although here it is less easy to identify obvious local rail networks which both make a sensible potential franchise and relate to our present areas of operation.

We are not interested in freight operations, but we do believe that there are benefits in being involved with as many aspects as possible of any passenger services with which we come to be associated. We may therefore be interested in the operation of stations, at least in terms of information and ticketing for passengers.

We also recognise that we will be seen as the service provider, and before any commitment we will want to be absolutely clear on how the other parties, such as Railtrack, will work and be accountable for providing the necessary standard of performance so that a good quality rail service is provided.

FRANCHISES

We were somewhat disappointed by the lack of specific detail in the recent consultation document. It is appreciated that there is an intention to give scope for considerable flexibility in designing franchises, and we agree with that thinking. However, we had expected to see more detail, particularly in terms of the costs and revenues of present railway services.

Leaving aside the question of investment there are two broad areas on which we need to be satisfied in order to assess whether we are interested in particular franchises, and at what sort of price. The first of these areas is that covering existing costs, revenues, resource commitments, and demand patterns. The second area is the question of just what is covered by the franchise, how it relates to the other bodies involved, and the extent to which our business is exposed to matters outside our control. Basically we understand that this second area covers many matters for debate, but there does not seem to be any reason why we cannot be given the necessary detail information to get on with considering the existing situation.

In terms of the specifics of any franchise agreement, our opening position would be that we would wish to have as much control as possible over the quality of the total service we were involved in providing. This has implications in terms of how bodies such as Railtrack carry out their functions, and how matters such as station facilities and ticketing arrangemants are dealt with.

We believe that if any major investment is to be justified, then the period of the relevant franchise will have to reflect the life of that investment, or provide guaranteed recompense in some other way. Further, there will clearly have to be explicit commitments within the franchise agreement to protect the franchisee. These will need to apply for the life of the franchise, and cover such matters as the level of subsidy or other ongoing payments, and major variations in cost imposed on the franchisee by parties outside his control. These might include, for example, action by Railtrack in respect of train path or other essential infrastructure charges, or the imposition by the Regulator of safety requirements additional to those known at the time of the franchise agreement being concluded.

To put it simply there are significant risks to a franchisee in terms of passenger demand and revenue, and in ongoing direct operating costs. Franchise agreements and associated arrangements will very clearly need to minimise uncertainties in other respects if potential franhisees are to be encouraged to proceed.

OPEN ACCESS AND COMPETITION

We appreciate the principles behind the introduction of competitive elements into railway operation. However, we are concerned that there is a clear conflict between the principle of open access and the granting of franchises.

As we see it the granting of a franchise will come as the result of a competition for that particular package of railway services. The successful franchisee will have been involved in that competitive process before he commences operations, and will in any case be likely to be involved in some degree of competition with sections of other franchises or the remaining operations of British Rail. His principal competitor will, as ever, be the private car.

Most franchises are likely to be loss-making, so that a competition on the basis of price will arrive at the lowest level of payment from the franchising authority to the franchisee. Within his assessment of the position before arriving at his bid the franchisee will have taken into account a mixture of reasonably viable and decidedly loss-making journeys. Clearly any competition under open access arrangements is most likely to target the most remunerative operations, and thus significantly undermine the basis of the franchisee's business. The possibility of this type of situation will undermine the confidence of potential franchisees without any clear likelihood of long-term benefit to the passenger.

Equally we would accept that there are "niche" markets or other particular circumstances where the open access principle seems absolutely appropriate. It is not easy to see how to resolve this with the concerns of potential franchisees about "cherry-pickers", but we would emphasise that the more uncertainties there appear to be for a potential franchisee, the less likelihood there is of him proceeding to get involved.

RAILTRACK

We feel that there are a number of substantial aspects concerning the proposed track authority which are of major significance, and which will need to be resolved before franchises can be agreed.

The most obvious area is the question of charges. A prospective franchisee will need to know the level of charges, or at the very least the range of acceptable movement, for the period of his franchise. This will obviously be one of the fundamentals to build into the equation in any agreement with the franchising authority. A franchisee may well vary the level of service during the lifetime of a franchise. As well as being clear on the level of charges, it may also be appropriate for the charging system to encourage service improvements—perhaps where appropriate by some charges being based on marginal costs.

We see the design of the service we offer as being an essential part of attracting users; an important area of design is the timetable, and we are concerned about the extent to which this comes under Railtrack control.

Railtrack will be allocating train paths to various users, then controlling the day-to-day train operations, and sorting out various difficulties which arise virtually as a matter of daily routine. We are concerned as to how Railtrack, as a subsidiary of BR, will act fairly between a number of operators, one of whom is also a section of BR.

We are concerned about the quality of response we can expect from Railtrack in times of difficulty. For example, if there are adverse weather conditions, or a signalling or points failure, will Railtrack's reaction be speedy and efficient? There are cost implications to Railtrack if it ensures an excellent response, whilst the passengers adversely affected by a poor response are those of the operator who has no control of the required remedial action. Railtrack must be accountable in some way, and some sort of standard of response may need to be laid down.

Railtrack is required to make an appropriate return on assets, and thereby finance investment and, presumably, ongoing operational and maintenance costs. We would be concerned that if this return is not made, or if Railtrack is inefficient in other ways, that this will have a consequential effect on operators outside their control. This could obviously disrupt services and adversely affect costs and revenues. Operators like ourselves will want to be reassured that there will be established standards and monitoring so that our interests are protected.

TICKETING ARRANGEMENTS

We support the retention of through tickets, network tickets, and, where appropriate, the interavailability of return tickets.

However, we are concerned about certain aspects, which can basically be summarised in our need to control our own business.

Essentially the various ticketing arrangements which involve more than one operator must involve a fair allocation of revenue. Operators like ourselves will want to know how any allocation system works, and what revenue will be forthcoming in respect of the various passengers carried on our services. The detail of arrangements will need to be incorporated in franchise agreements.

We are also concerned about ticket sales, and the question of dealing with passenger enquiries. We see this as a very important point of contact with our customers, and this therefore needs to be very carefully considered when the arrangements for stations and ticket offices are finalised. As a general rule these matters are amongst those over which we would seek to have reasonable control—this is a critical area of our business.

THE RELATIONSHIP WITH OUR BUS OPERATIONS

We do not believe that any significant conflicts arise from our Group's involvement in both rail and bus services in an area. There is not a great amount of competition in general between bus and rail services. There are obvious localised exceptions to this, but it is important to realise that both public transport modes are competing primarily with the private car.

There is a wide range of benefits which may be able to be achieved by co-operation between the rail and bus sections of our Group if we become franchisees. These include connectional facilities, bus/rail feeders, through ticketing, interavailability of returns, network tickets, common information and ticket sales points, and joint publicity arrangements.

Additionally, there may well be economies and efficiencies of various kinds arising from our involvement in both rail and bus operations.

INVESTMENT

We are not yet in a position to take a firm view on the question of investment in major items such as rolling stock. There are, however, a number of points of relevance.

Firstly, the length of any franchise agreement will be fundamental in assessing the case for capital investment. Also, the timescales in connection with obtaining any new stock are quite lengthy. Franchise agreements may need to involve differing conditions for before and after significant investments are put into place.

We will need to feel much more knowledgeable about the business before any commitment. To some extent this relates to present cost and revenue information which ought to be available from BR, but there are also numerous risks and uncertainties thrown up by the range of matters to be resolved concerning how the railway is to be run in the future.

CONCLUDING POINTS

It is essential that any potential franchisee is able to be absolutely clear about each and every detail if a franchise agreement is to be satisfactorily concluded. The Badgerline Group view is that it is most likely to make a success of any franchise by an involvement with every aspect directly affecting the customers of that franchise, and thereby ensuring that a high quality service is provided.

November 1992

Supplementary Memorandum from the Badgerline Group

RAIL FRANCHISING PROPOSALS

As you know we are a major bus operator who has expressed interest in the rail franchising proposals being brought forward by the Government.

Obviously it is of fundamental importance to us that any involvement we have makes commercial sense for our organisation, but we are also concerned that the end result is a good quality service for the passenger. This is an essential if our business is to be able to develop.

In connection with our recent discussions with Department of Transport Officials and others, I was most interested to read of some of your recent comments. We have been developing our view on how best to proceed as we have learnt more about the proposals. We are convinced that a franchisee will need to take on a fairly sizeable amount of passenger railway operation if he is to be able to justify acquiring the necessary railway expertise, marketing and back-up to make a success of his operation.

We are also convinced that a successful franchisee will need to control as much as possible of all the various aspects affecting the service provided for the passenger. This encompasses station information and ticketing arrangements, on-train facilities and day-to-day control of track, signalling and so on, in addition to the basic function of train service operation.

We believe that these areas of concern imply the need for a somewhat different approach in respect of rail passenger service franchising than has been indicated in recent Department of Transport comments. Our view is that the quality of service for passengers is likely to be better where franchisees are large enough to employ the best skills and back-up, and where they can control the complete customer service. This clearly will reduce some of the largely theoretical competitive elements, with competition being for the market or franchise, rather than within it.

I thought it worthwhile to acquaint you with our views and if you feel that we can be of assistance with more detailed comments, then please do not hesitate to contact me.

7 January 1993

APPENDIX 74

W H Smith Group plc

Our responses to your questions, in brief, are as follows:

Q. *Do you believe that private owners would be better able to take advantage of the commercial opportunities at stations?*

A. In principle, yes. As long as BR's expenditure is subject to tight Treasury control, it is obvious that private owners would have more funds at their disposal for investment. If this was not so, there would be no point in privatisation.

Q. *Would you prefer rail services franchisees to be responsible for stations or should they be sold or leased to private developers?*

A. Franchisees should run stations as a total package, including the dormant surrounding land which is currently in the BR Property Board portfolio. This means that franchisees should have the necessary financial resources. Unless they can develop station property as a whole—for example, along the lines of the Broadgate development—they will add little value to the overall business. Allowing franchisees to "cherry pick" those activities within stations which will yield the highest short-term gain would be the wrong way to proceed.

We also recognise that this approach raises two potential difficulties:

(i) Smaller provincial stations which may not be of interest to potential operators and will therefore suffer from lack of investment and passenger traffic.

(ii) Larger urban stations where one operator gains a monopoly and imposes excessive rents on sub-franchisees.

Q. *What should be the relationship between a privately-owned station and the train operators who use it?*

A. This should be one of partnership. It is important that the contractual arrangements with new operators should provide a climate of certainty in which retailers will be encouraged to invest for the longer term. Existing contractual arrangements achieve this objective.

Q. *What sort of protection should be given to the interests of passengers and train operators?*

A. Our main concern is to achieve a balance between the needs of operators, passengers and retailers, particularly in respect of trading hours. Passengers and retailers alike need access to station facilities at reasonable times during a 24 hour period. The potential area of dispute would obviously be at the extremities of each day. Most retailers would not normally wish to open their outlets very early in the morning or very late at night when passenger traffic is very light. A reasonable balance would, therefore, have to be achieved, which would vary with the location.

I hope you will find these responses helpful. If we can be of any further assistance, please let me know.

24 November 1992

APPENDIX 75

PUBLIC TRANSPORT CONSORTIUM OF NON-METROPOLITAN COUNTIES

An all-party group representing counties with a particular interest in public transport

RAIL PRIVATISATION

At a recent meeting, Consortium members again considered the Government's proposals for rail privatisation set out in the White Paper "New opportunities for the Railways", in the light of a discussion between Consortium officers and the Minister of State.

Members attention was drawn to your suggestion that the Government should delay publishing a Bill to enable the very complex issues involved to be further examined and debated. I was directed to write in support of your review.

As you know, the Consortium has been a contributing party to the Joint Local Authority Associations' submission to your Committee's inquiry into the proposals. I was asked to let you have in addition a copy of a recent letter from the Department of Transport concerning disposal of disused lines. It is interesting to note that, since the letter was written, BR have reintroduced the use of the line in question as a diversionary route. In the light of this, the Consortium would ask your Committee to consider this question, with a view to recommending that a moratorium be placed on disposal of such lines, at least until the franchising regime is in effect.

2 November 1992

Copy of the letter from the Department of Transport

Thank you for your letter of 3 July to the Secretary of State about BR's decision to close three freight railway lines in Cheshire.

There were only two freight trains a day on the Northwich to Middlewich section and no trains at all on the Helsby to Mouldsworth line. The limited freight traffic on the Northwich to Sandbach line has been rerouted, so existing customers located at Sandbach and Middlewich will continue to be served by rail. The closure of the lines will not affect potential Channel Tunnel traffic as alternative routes are available.

The Northwich to Sandbach line has been used in the past as a diversionary route for the West Coast Main Line between Crewe and Acton Bridge. The value of the line in this role is limited because it is only a single track, non-electrified line, with a slow line speed. BR's passenger businesses have said that they do not foresee a role for this line as a diversionary route.

Your views about the regime for the disposal of railway land after privatisation have been noted. Although the precise arrangements for the treatment of disused land have yet to be finalised, a regime facilitating easier disposal is *not* envisaged.

7 August 1992

APPENDIX 76

Letter from Mr J Towers

I attended the public session of your inquiry into rail privatisation last Wednesday and wondered if I might make a few observations that might be pertinent to your deliberations. I was there in my capacity as assistant editor of the road transport weekly "Motor Transport".

My first point refers to the evidence given on container haulage by Marion Ward of P&O Containers. Under a long standing agreement, from which the shipping lines are currently trying to extricate themselves, inland container haulage is subsidised by the shippers so that customers far away from ports are not penalised on delivery charges.

That is one of the reasons P&O and others are able to put most of their containers through such a small number of ports. I would also slightly take issue with Alan Jones of TNT, on the grounds that TNT's operations worldwide are losing a great deal of money at present.

Privatisation has been challenged on safety grounds. You might already be aware that a series of new level crossings between Chichester and Havant have been fitted with the kind of half barriers that attracted so much criticism, and which I thought had been outlawed, following the dreadful Hixon train crash in 1968.

I am most concerned that the Government has got its wires crossed over the railways. I have to say that I am not impressed by the calibre of senior management at BR, which as several witnesses implied will not disclose costings, will not co-operate in furthering relationships with customers and is not at all customer-focussed.

Under the current scheme that management will remain in overall charge because it will control the "Railtrack" authority. Might not a better option be to allow private sector companies with an interest in rail-related civil engineering, such as Pirelli or Costain, to bid for design, build and operation contracts to control the rail infrastructure?

It would provide a private sector fillip to encourage much needed rail infrastructure investment and would also bring in urgently needed commercial acumen to that side of the business. My main concern is to keep network identity, particularly for passenger services.

I am sure many MPs share my concern that intensive local train services could fall apart under the current drive for piecemeal franchising. If it is the duty of Government to provide the framework in which the economy and enterprise can operate then surely it is their duty to allow people to get to work as quickly, cheaply and reliably as possible.

I see nothing in current proposals, either regulatory or fiscal, that even approaches that.

My qualifications for writing to you, as well as being a transport writer, are membership of the Chartered Institute of Transport and the Institute of Logistics & Distribution Management, I was also one of the authors of the Confederation of British Industry's 1992 book on transport in the Single European Market.

19 November 1992

APPENDIX 77

SCOTTISH ASSOCIATION FOR PUBLIC TRANSPORT

Rail Privatisation

The Scottish Association for Public Transport (SAPT) has prepared the enclosed summary paper on Rail Privatisation. The Minister for Public Transport, Mr Roger Freeman, has given a response to some of the points made in our summary paper. But some of our concerns remain.

We are assured by Mr Freeman that subsidised passenger rail services will continue, with the minimum frequency and quality of service specified by the Franchising Authority for each service. Nevertheless, the concept of a single Franchising Authority for Britain is over-centralised and too remote to be entrusted with specifying local rail services in Scotland. Instead, a number of Scottish Transport Boards or PTEs should be established comprising representatives from local authorities and Enterprise companies. These would administer budgets and service levels for rail franchises within their areas (similar to the successful Strathclyde PTE), and could be incorporated in the local government reorganisation proposals.

Privatised InterCity Anglo-Scottish services would run a serious risk of severe contraction. To improve the prospects of viability, the Government must earmark capital, from the proceeds of rail privatisation, to invest in a strategic 140 mph Railtrack network, increasing the competitiveness and long-term profitability of InterCity trains which have fallen far behind European speed standards due to comparative lack of investment. Mr Freeman confirms in his reply to SAPT that the Government are willing to consider direct support for Railtrack investment schemes which, although not earning an adequate financial return, provide a satisfactory cost-benfit return when wider benefits are taken into account. It is important that this ruling is applied to help upgrade InterCity speeds northwards from London to Edinburgh, Glasgow, Aberdeen and Inverness, to improve InterCity's market share, viability, and long-term prospects in Scotland.

Railfreight currently is charged only marginal costs for use of track and signalling. Mr Freeman reaffirms that the proposed Railtrack Authority will not be subsidised, and will be expected to earn a return on assets. As coal and steel traffic fall, Railtrack charges will increase for the surviving freight trains. Much of Railfreight could follow "Tigerail" and "Charterail" into liquidation, while heavy goods traffic will rise still further on Britain's congested road system. To create a fair competitive framework for freight, a fixed licence charging system must be introduced for railfreight wagons, similar to HGV licensing. Otherwise the Government will be faced with the senseless situation of having to increase public expenditure on new or rebuilt "free" motorways, to accommodate freight traffic priced of the under-utilised rail network by an unsubsidised Railtrack Authority required to make a return on capital.

New Opportunities for the Travelling Public

SAPT's response to the White Paper on Rail Privatisation

1. OVERVIEW: The Government's objective in privatising British Rail is to help to control costs, encourage innovation and competition, and attract private investment at higher levels than the current public sector limits. However, success will depend critically on how the Government proposals develop in detail, particularly with regard to rail track charges, revenue support, and investment relative to road.

The White Paper leaves many relevant questions unanswered. Many of the current proposals in the White Paper are liable to increase uncertainty and centralised bureaucracy. There is a need for a strategy and policy objectives for transport in general, and the railway's role within it. There are four major areas of concern which SAPT believes need more clarification by the Government:

GUARANTEED SUPPORT: The Government should ensure that rail privatisation will genuinely benefit the travelling public, and will not be used by the Treasury as a means of producing a windfall from the sell-off, while cutting on-going Government revenue support for the rail network.

LOCAL CONTROL: Instead of a centralised U.K. rail Franchise Authority, there should be greater local responsibility for administering franchising for local rail services, including a commitment to maintain and develop the unprofitable but vital lines in the Highlands.

GREATER INVESTMENT: Priority Government investment is needed to modernise the InterCity Railtrack infrastructure which is being left far behind by TGV technology in France and other European countries. After decades of under-investment, Government funds from the proceeds of privatisation should be invested back into Railtrack to create a 140 mph-plus network between Britain's main cities, including the East Coast route from Glasgow and Edinburgh to London. Without modern standards of infra-structure, privatised inter city rail companies will be less competitive with road and air with little chance of long-term viability.

LEVEL PLAYING FIELD: The White Paper proposes a further move towards market forces for rail transport, with the Railtrack authority expected to recover full track costs from train operators. But the competing road network remains untouched by financial disciplines. The nation now needs a complementary review of road costs and funding to ensure direct comparability with rail, with road funding transferred from taxation to toll charges or electronic metering charges related directly to road use (including vehicle weight) and enviromental costs. Without this, the White Paper will accelerate the decline of fail freight, and undermine the viability of privatised passenger trains which have to compete with a road system funded within a completely different financial framework.

These issues are analysed in the following sections. SAPT hope that the Government will give full consideration to these issues so that the rail privatisation Parliamentary Bill can be framed to bring genuine progress towards a better future for transport in Britain.

2. GUARANTEED SUPPORT

ScotRail has improved its performance remarkably recently. Passenger figures have increased on many lines, while radio signalling and Sprinter trains have cut operating costs. Nevertheless revenue covers only 50 per cent of costs, with the Highland and West Highland lines well below this average. There can be no doubt that Scottish rail routes will continue to require Government support, irrespective of ownership.

But there is a danger that privatisation and franchising of services will lead to further pressure to cut costs, losing sight of the more important objectives of rail transport which include to provide an efficient public transport network, an alternative to growing road congestion around the cities, and a catalyst for the development of tourism, Scotland's biggest industry.

The Government should guarantee financial support for Scottish rail services at a level sufficient to sustain or increase service levels, and to fund replacement of assets and route modernisation where needed.

Sustained long-term growth of rail passenger traffic on all Scottish lines must be a major policy objective of the Government. This contrasts with bus deregulation where the cheapest tenders are normally accepted: but bus passenger figures have continued to fall while lack of investment in new buses is causing the average age of the bus fleet to rise.

In addition to financial support, the Government needs to safeguard a number of important features of the current rail network:

— comprehensive through ticketing with continued nationwide availability of family and group discounts, and tourist tickets including "Britrail" and "Freedom of Scotland"

— national rail timetable, with timetable alterations synchronised to commerce on predefined dates

The considerable improvements made by ScotRail in modernising the rail network and attracting more passengers, while simultaneously cutting costs, could well suggest that a privatised ScotRail, formed by an employee/management buy-out, would be an advisable approach which would safeguard many of the "network" benefits of the current rail system and maintain the pace of progress.

3. LOCAL TRANSPORT BOARDS

The White Paper proposes that minimum train service frequency, quality and fares will be defined for each franchised service by a Franchise Authority and the Government.

A guarantee that service levels will be maintained is certainly needed, particularly on the Highland and West Highland lines. However, the proposed National Franchising Authority would be over-centralised to satisfy local transport needs. Control of local train service frequencies by a centralised U.K. Authority would be a quite unnecessary increase in central government control, ironically being proposed by an administration that generally believes in less government!

An alternative to this remote centralised control would be to transfer franchising of Scottish lines to the Scottish Office, or to establish regional transport boards to administer the budgets for each area. The overall budget level could still be controlled by central Government, but service level details would be agreed locally. The Strathclyde Passenger Transport Executive is an example of how such a structure can operate successfully.

Scottish Transport Boards could be formed with representatives from local authorities and local Enterprise companies. Perhaps four areas would be logical in Scotland:

— Lothian/ Fife/ Central/ Borders

— Tayside/ Grampian

— Highland and Islands

— Strathclyde/ South-West.

These would administer budgets and service levels for rail franchises.

Financial support for local bus services could also be channeled through these Transport Boards, creating an opportunity to coordinate timetables where practical to improve connections between train, ferry and local bus services. Better connections would be of particular benefit to tourists but would also stimulate use of public transport by local residents. This could go a long way towards improving public transport while retaining Government control of overall budget levels.

4. INTERCITY INVESTMENT

4.1 *Inter-City Viability*

For long term viability, fully privatised interCity rail companies will need to earn much higher profit levels than British Rail's InterCity sector which achieved an operating surplus of £50 million in 1990-91 falling to only £2 million in 1991-92.

Insufficient profit is generated to reinvest in the faster trains and infrastructure that are needed to bridge the widening technology gap between British and continental railways.

Construction of high-speed route in most European countries will ensure a rapid growth of rail revenue in Europe, with high speed trains capturing traffic from both road and short-distance flights, usefully cutting traffic congestion on the roads and in the air. "TGV" results in France already show their can be achieve, albeit at high capital cost in constructuring new lines.

In Britain, postponment of the InterCity 250 project means that 20-year old trains limited to 110 mph will continue on the premier line linking Britain's biggest four cities, while France, Germany, Spain and Italy forge ahead with train speeds up to 186 mph.

The Department of Transport decision to increase state spending on motorways can only reduce the future potential and profitability of inter city rail transport and will undoubtedly undermine the Government's efforts to privatise InterCity successfully.

There is a serious risk that privatising the marginally profitable InterCity to operate on rail infastructure suffering from years of underinvestment could send inter city rail transport in Britain into terminal decline, with a vicious circle of low speeds leading to low market share and poor profitability which in turn generates insufficient investment.

How will the British electorate react if an InterCity company should follow Chaterail or Tigerail towards liquidation?

It is therefore vital that a strategic high speed 140 mph-plus Rail track in the city network is created to increase the potential competitivness and long-term viability of privatised inter city train operators. Out with the high speed network, less profitable InterCity Trains (eg to Aberdeen, Inverness and Fort William) would continue, and could if necessary be financially assisted and expanded from the local transport budget.

4.2 *"Fast Track" Investment*

Establishing a stable profitable inter city rail, operation will depend on achieving more competitive journey times against road and the main "Shuttle" routes from London to Manchester, Glasgow and Edinburgh. Track realigment, elimination of level crossings, installation of Automatic Train Protection, and maximum speeds of at least 140 mph are pre-requisites for continuing profitability on the main inter city routes.

Upgrading and realigning the East Coast Main Line to 140 mph, with high speed bypasses for speed bottlenecks, could reduce London-Edinburgh journey times to a highly competitive 3 hours 15 minutes, with Glasgow reached in 3 hours 55 minutes. This scheme would be likely to cost around £400 million but could be phased to achieve a quick return. Viability of daytime European train services from Glasgow and Edinburgh via the Channel Tunnel to Paris and Brussels would also benefit from upgrading the East Coast route.

On the West Coast route, top priority will be to upgrade the West Coast Main Line from London to Birmingham, Manchester and Liverpool to 140 mph or faster (InterCity's recently postponed £750 million scheme). This would shorten journey times from London to Carlisle and south-west Scotland.

Under the Government privatisation plans, the state Railtrack Authority would be responsible for capital investment schemes of the type outlined above. SAPT strongly recommends that, after decades of rail under investment, the Government should launch Railtrack with a "FAST TRACK" investment programme using resources from the proceeds of privatisation, plus a shift of some funding from the state-funded motorway programme. Raising line speeds towards European standards on main InterCity routes would give the privatised inter city companies a better chance of long-term survival.

5. ROAD AND RAIL FINANCING

While the Rail White Paper proposes a move towards market forces and franchising, the road sector will remain untouched by direct financial disciplines.

At a time of increasing pressure on public spending, and environmental concerns over growing pollution, the level of state spending on roads is ironically being increased, without any attempt by the Government to introduce equivalent pricing and investment criteria for both road and rail. Indeed it is likely that the Rail White Paper, without any corresponding changes to road policies, will tip the scales more heavily towards increased road usage.

The disparity in the treatment of road and rail track costs will be aggravated by the White Paper's requirement that the Rail Track Authority should maximise financial contributions to track costs by franchise holders. This will increase the pressure to raise fares and trim services when the opposite incentives apply in the road sector, where fixed road taxation applies.

The country now needs a complementary set of Government proposals for financial accountability for road usage and construction. Without realistic charges for road usage, it is quite clear that the Rail White Paper is likely to accelerate the decline of a rail freight and prejudice investment on InterCity rail projects, with traffic moving to Britain's "free" roads, creating a massive congestion and pollution legacy for the 21st century.

SAPT therefore recommends that the Government should, as a matter of urgency, set up a steering group to produce a ROADS WHITE PAPER which could contain a number of fundamental changes to the organisation and funding of roads in Britain.

The road system is the greatest remaining bastion of state spending, cross-subsidisation, and Government control in Britain. The Government now needs to face up to the challenge of introducing usage-related charges and bringing financial discipline to Britain's motorways and urban roads systems, starting with some of the issues below.

5.1 *Road Organisation*

The close involvement of the Department of Transport and the Scottish Office with road schemes is an unhealthy relationship which has distorted transport policy for decades.

By analogy with the Rail White Paper, a quasi-independent Road Authority ("BRITISH ROADS") could be formed, with responsibility for trunk road and motorway construction and maintenance, British Roads could be financed from electronically collected tolls, and would be obliged to pay for indirect road costs including policing, pollution, health service charges for roads accident victims, in addition to construction and maintenance costs for trunk roads and motorways.

5.2 *Freight*

Electronically metered pricing for heavy lorries would take account of increased road construction and maintenance costs due to the axle-loads of heavy vehicles, and pollution, accident and congestion costs caused by HGVs. Road hauliers should not be cross-subsidised by motorists. Proceeds of this charging system for the road haulage industry would be paid to the Road Authority.

Realistic charging would clearly increase the cost of road haulage to industry and commmerce. If the Government decides, from industrial development considerations, to continue with the existing hidden subsidies to the road haulage industry, then the same approach should be taken with rail freight. Freight wagons and locomotives would pay an annual licence to the proposed Rail Track Authority, similar to an HGV licence fee, with no additional mileage-related charge for track usage. Otherwise, private rail freight companies have little hope of competing effectively against road hauliers.

5.3 *Car Charging*

Motorway tolls, long accepted in France, could be levied by the Roads Authority, with charges recorded electronically.

Congestion on city centre roads should similarly be tackled by electronic road charging, as currently being considered for Edinburgh and other cities.

6. CONCLUSION

SAPT believes that the rail privatisation proposals could be considerably improved if the Government and Parliament incorporate our suggestions in the final rail privatisation programme.

Only by adopting these suggestions can the programme become in fact one of "New Opportunities for the Travelling Public".

10 November 1992

APPENDIX 78

Letter from Mr A J Wilkinson, to the Secretary of State of Transport

White Paper—"New Opportunities for the Railways"

I am employed by British Rail as Train Plan Validation Officer for Inter City West Coast and I have 24 years railway operating experience. With this background, I feel impelled to hereby give you the benefit of my opinions and raise some pertinent questions in respect of your proposed privatisation measures for our railways.

I have no political allegiance or bias and my only interest is as a dedicated, time-served railwayman.

In common with a substantial proportion of railway employees, I have a fundamental belief in the logical correctness of our railway system as being the most efficient, cost-effective form of mass-passenger and bulk-freight transport ever devised.

The challenge for Government should be to provide the political and business climate for the full potential of our railways to be realised. To achieve massive extra investment in the railway infrastructure and additional rolling stock to provide the capacity for railways to take most of the long-distance and much of the shorter distance traffic (passenger and freight) off the roads over the next 40 years.

Don't forget, that the burning of fossil fuels is an ecological "time bomb" and because of this, future Governments will be forced to bite the "bitter pill" of regulating road transport in favour of more fuel efficient transport (ie, railways and canals).

Logically, our Railways are the only realistic future for inter-urban transport. This is why the steps taken by you at the current "crossroads" for Britain's railways must be thoroughly and positively thought-out.

WAYS IN WHICH PRIVATISATION COULD BE MADE TO WORK

1. Franchises should only be allocated to private operators on the specific understanding that, in the event of a disruption to services which is outside the Franchisee's control (ie, under the jurisdiction of the "Railway Regulator"/"Track Authority"), then the "Railway Regulator" could commandeer a Franchisees' resources to maintain the service of another Franchisee in the short-term, until the cause of disruption was resoloved. In other words to maintain a flexible common-user approach to the deployment of resources in a crisis.

2. By the abolition of all "tax advantages" for the "company car" user. In the short term, this would no doubt cause problems for the motor industry. However, it would greatly increase revenue from passengers,

using the railway for business and commuting instead of motor cars and would transform many passenger lines from loss into profit.

It would also be a wonderful "anti-pollution" gesture and reduce the balance of payments deficit by a reduction in the volume of imported motor cars. Moreover, funds saved by the Exchequer could be ploughed into much-needed railway infrastructure investment.

3. By applying the same safety disciplines to our roads, as those which already apply to our railways a start could be made with the strict observance of speed limits. The main reason that such trunk roads as the A74 (Carlisle-Glasgow), A1 (Newcastle-Edinburgh) and A417/A419 (Gloucester-Swindon) have such a poor safety record is that commercial vehicles and company cars are allowed to flout the law, by often grossly, exceeding their permitted speed limits for the type of road.

The only way to deter this will be to increase the penalties (ie, a 10 fold increase in fines for speeding by "professional" drivers). Again, revenue derived from these heavy fines should be put into Railway infrastructure investment.

4. By halting future Government investment in Motorway and Trunk Road development where there is a viable existing parallel rail route. (ie "A45" West Midlands-Felixstowe, A74 Carlisle-Glasgow and A1 Newcastle-Edinburgh.) You may then say these developments are essential on safety grounds, in which case I say there is nothing basically unsafe which cannot be cured by the rigorous enforcement of speed limits (see item 3).

The funds thus withheld should be directly diverted into railway infrastructure investment.

SOME PERTINENT QUESTIONS

1. As you will know, one of the fundamental economic "laws" involves the "economies of scale".

After 44 years our National Railway has achieved superb economies of scale and together with far-sighted productivity agreements this has made it one of the most efficiently run railway operations in the world. How will the privatised fragmentation of these economies of scale in the national railway industry benefit the railway user?

2. When a franchisee runs a passenger service, will the Citizens Charter still apply to him in respect of train punctuality and cancellation targets?

If it does, who will refund the passenger when services fail to meet their "Charter" targets for punctuality or cancellations? Will it be the Franchisee, the Track Authority or the Railway Regulator? It is not inconceivable that that a proportion of blame attaches to all three, plus even an "Act of God" element. In such cases who is to be the final arbiter amongst this dubious selection of bureaucracy?

3. The Government has stated that BR Staff will be encouraged to bid for franchises or to mount a "buy out" for parts of the freight or parcels business. Railway employees are not among the better paid workers in the country and a considerable proportion are entitled to claim low income support. Where do you expect such people to find the capital to stage a successful bid?

How will it be possible for railway employees to invest small amounts in private railway services if the franchisees are all fully subscribed existing private limited companies?

4. The White Paper says that BR Staff, their dependants and retired staff will have their free and concessionary travel safeguarded. However, when "Sealink" was privatised in the 1970s, we were given similar reassurances but in recent years some "Sealink" routes have been re-sold to other operators who refuse to honour the "Sealink" agreement on travel concessions (the Isle of Wight ferries operated by "Wightlink" is an example).

So, if franchisees change hands after privatisation will the old BR staff travel concessions still be honoured?

5. I understand that it is proposed that BR employees who are transferred to new companies will take their existing terms and conditions of employment with them. However, any subsequent changes will be a matter between them and their new employer.

   (a) A profit-motivated employer will surely try to hire cheaper, less experienced operators to run his trains, rather then pay the going rate to experienced railwaymen by honouring existing terms and conditions. For working all the hours God sends railwaymen are not overpaid now, so will this give us a safer railway? (Refer also to the "Social Chapter" of the Maastricht Treaty.)

   (b) If, after a period of time a private operator relinquishes his franchise for a service to another operator, will the terms and conditions of service of employees still be the same or is there to be a "loophole" allowing subsequent holders of a franchise to impose their own terms and conditions?

6. I have contributed a proportion of 24 years very hard-earned salary to the BR Staff pension scheme.

A Government Minister has said that "individuals pension rights will be safeguarded" but "the mechanism that is used to achieve that has not yet been decided upon". What does this mean?

How safe is my pension?

The word "mechanism" when related to pension funds smacks of "Maxwellian claptrap". Why cannot the BR Pension fund be left alone for the benefit of the contributors. After all, the old pre-nationalisation company pension schemes (pre 1948) still exist, so why does the BR scheme have to have "mechanisms" to safeguard it?

7. On the Nationalised Railway all profit is ploughed back into re-investment in rolling stock and infrastructure. On BR, all productivity measures which can be made, without impinging on safety issues, have been taken, so it is fair to say that, without further large-scale investment, our railways cannot be run more effeciently than they are currently.

When services are taken over by private franchises, an element of any profit will have to be withheld to pay a dividend to shareholders, thus bleeding what profit there is, out of the industry.

Also, if franchises are only to lease rolling stock from the track authority, who will be funding investment in new rolling stock? Or by painting old stock in new colours does this defer re-investment and halt the depreciation of hard-worked assets?

8. What happens when a mishap or a Track Authority failure of equipment causes a franchisees rolling stock to be trapped at an inaccessible location?

A typical scenario would be:

A points failure occurs at the only exit from the carriage sidings at 0430 in the morning and it is not put right until 0730 the same morning. During this time several sets of empty coaches, which should have run from the sidings to the main terminal station for passenger trains, are marooned.

However, in the main station there are several sets of coaches stabled overnight for other morning services and by expert manipulation of the accessible rolling stock by supervisors and controllers, the transposition of the "common user", nationalised rolling stock results in few, if any, of the booked services being cancelled.

However, what will happen in such cases when several different franchisees are involved in an identical situation?

I would fear that many more cancellations would arise as the booked rolling stock will have to work the franchisee's own services only. If not available the train is cancelled! This is why I implore you to give final decision-making authority to the Railway Regulator on all cases of service disruption—however it is caused.

9. What measures are you taking to ensure that the Railway Regulator is not tempted by bribes from unscrupulous franchisees?

10. If several different passenger service operators hold franchises to run trains into one station and each employs their own drivers and guards, this will surely result in a gross loss of productivity from staff will it not?

To maintain the existing level of service, more staff will be required to cover for holidays, sickness, late running trains etc. owing to the loss of flexibility and economies of scale formerly enjoyed by BR.

CONCLUSION

In 20 years time, if the oil is not running out, the use of the internal combustion road motor vehicle will be coming to an end on environmental grounds. We will then need our Railways as the principal means of transport in most parts of Britain.

I greatly fear that the current railway privatisation proposals, as set out in the White Paper, could provide for the Railways a mirror image of the current plight of the coal industry in the closure of many unremunerative routes. Moreover, the costs of re-instatement of such routes in 20 years time will be monumentally greater than those of retention.

I wrote this as a very concerned, experienced, practical Railwayman.

In my experience, the railway will always produce unforeseen disruptive incidents every day somewhere or other (there are too many external influences to be otherwise). However, the skill and commitment of railway staff is never far away in restoring things back to normal. The loyalty of railway staff is not something to be jeopardised; however by fragmenting services and stations amongst a myriad number of independent operators you risk doing just that.

2nd November 1992

APPENDIX 79

Letter from Mr J Gilbert

Having read the article in the Times on Monday 26th October 1992, (page 3), in which I whole heartedly agree with your quoted observations and Michael Dynes analysis of scepticisms, etc, I would like to add my comments as follows:

I am very concerned at the Government's proposals to privatise British Rail as indicated in an enclosed copy of my letter to the Prime Minister, dated 27 February 1992. I was not impressed by the Prime Minister's reply of 19 March 1992 enclosing the Tory manifesto on railway privatisation and therefore changed my allegiance to the Labour Party at the General Election.

Having been retired 10 years, but previously serving 45 years in railway signal engineering and associated interdepartmental functions initially on the LMS and then on a number of railway Regions and eventually at Board HQ, I think I know something of the problems which would arise should a privatised strategy be implemented and it deeply worries me, as I tried to explain to the Prime Minister in my letter.

I am not associated with railway activities in my retirement, but reference in my letter to the business sector implementations would now appear to be a red herring, although there must have been Government backing. I am sure you know more of the present state of affairs. In addition, I am unaware of what the Railway Board's response to the White Paper will be (they have, I understand been asked for comments!) and I trust they will be worth digesting.

You quite rightly commented on the possibility of a "poll tax on wheels" and one could also include the apparent short comings and lack of foresight and indifference to expert advice concerning privatisation of electricity which is now being uncovered. Your observation "There are 16,000 trains a day . . . the risk of a ghastly mash up" is absolutely true—evolution not revolution!

There are many other modern disciplines not quoted in my letter to the Prime Minister, for the efficient running of railways, but I am sure you are receiving such information from many professional people who know what they are talking about as opposed to the non-professional "quick fix" types and no doubt some "Yes" men of the Tory Party and whose aims are completely different from those of running a public transport system.

I am sure you will be able to present a very well thought out case for an efficient, solid and progressive non-privatised railway system in the future—I would have thought closely based on the principles of the existing business sectors, if they are beginning to show promise and able to expose a gamble of great magnitude with a National Asset, without due regard to the consequences, if privatisation was implemented.

11 November 1992

Copy of the Letter from Mr J Gilbert to the Prime Minister, 10 Downing Street

Privatisation of British Rail

I have been following the media for some time now on the Government's intention to privatise British Rail and your realisation of it's complexity in implementation.

It is noted that one of the favoured options is the revival of the regional railway companies (as before Nationalisation in 1948).

British Rail has advanced a long way since that era, thanks to modern technology and nationalisation, which has made possible a modern integrated railway system by the coordination of interdisciplinary functions throughout the railway, eg., modern communication systems, standardisation of track, signalling and rolling stock equipment. Improved operational functions in safety, higher speeds and track capacity for both trunk routes and suburban services and in which could be added the many "environmentally friendly" electrification systems.

These overall disciplines would be needed if privatised regional railway companies were formed, but who is to guarantee that under this arrangement the disciplines and standards would not be impaired? In this age of fast developing technology it is essential there be a centralised authority to oversee continuity in the application of such developments.

Separate railway companies would be an overburden in the execution of such disciplines in modern railway operation.

British Rail has made tremendous strides in modernisation and productivity and fully aware of its commitment to break even, but the fact that one sector—Intercity—has only just recently made a marginal profit does not appear a logical argument for en mass privatisation. One gets the impression that Government considered privatisation an easy task until it really concentrated it's mind to the problem.

How can British Rail be privatised when only one sector has shown a marginal profit. Network South East (the Government's nightmare) has not. Who is going to buy out a loss making concern? What happens if it still did not make a profit when privatised? Higher fares, less trains, unsafe railway, a different owner, demoralised staff and no money to modernise the rolling programmes (track, signalling, rolling stock, etc) into the 21st century. Roads even more congested. The unfortunate Network South East commuters would be in a more sorry state than today and Mr Major's charter would be working overtime.

It would appear that continental governments have faced up to these scenarios and their electorates support them in the continuation of modern flexible nationalised systems. In this country one has the impression of continuous friction between Government and railway, which goes a long way to the engendered love/hate of the general public towards railways.

A modern railway cannot be run on a shoe string. Neither can it be run on privatisation methods where profit at all costs is paramount and if not achieved, services, safety and operational efficiency decline into a state where an increasing National Asset recedes because there is no custodian—the Government.

Very shortly, thanks to the Channel Tunnel, British Rail will have the facility to become an intercontinental railway (as are it's European neighbours). For the purpose of expanding continental traffic into the 21st century, the railway system in Britain will require a flexible streamlined operational and administrative organisation capable of promoting freight and passenger services in which it would be hoped that freight would be a prominent cornerstone.

In April 1992, it is understood that British rail plan to implement in full their new organisation of business sector accountability for InterCity, regional railways (provincial), freight, Network South East, etc., which it is assumed has received Government support. This organisation has the ingredients of a privatised model (under BR direction) which could surely be used for identifying the pros and cons of any future privatisation. It offers an evolutionary stepping stone rather than revolutionary—with all its attendant complexities and unknowns of implementation.

Having developed this organisation at considerable time and cost, logic surely dictates that this model be given time to be evaluated in day to day operation, rather than any revolutionary alternative, because I do not consider it is in the long term national interest to privatise such as complex and valuable National Asset until first gaining field experience with the model described above. I feel that an electorate would endorse such an approach.

In the meantime, the country awaits the Government's proclamation of it's intentions on the privatisation of British Rail, prior to the General Election and which will also determine how my vote is cast, having been a Tory supporter all my life.

27 February 1992

APPENDIX 80

Letter from Mr J W Roy

I note with interest your comments on Rail Privatisation, as quoted in today's Daily Telegraph.

"The Government's proposals have never been tried anywhere else and neither have they been costed. There will be no experiment before full privatisation is implemented."

As a former employee of Charterail Ltd., I must qualify my agreement with your view.

Charterail was by its nature an experiment, which showed that the concept of moving freight by road was an attractive proposition for FMGC organisations, who would take some convincing.

It succeeded in attracting a number of household names, eg Coca Cola, Safeway, RHM, Tate & Lyle and others. However the concept proved economically unviable in the present climate vis a vis road transport, largely because the company was unable to obtain a realistic cost for the use of the rail network from BR.

BR provided the locomotives, and ran them and the network, but not the rolling stock.

On the basis that the locomotives provided were obsolete, and fully depreciated, my estimates of BR direct costs for the running of the service from London to Glasgow and back are:

1. Maintenance costs per locomotive	... ...	£50,000
Cost per trip	... ...	200
2. Fuel costs per trip	... ...	500
3. Labour costs per trip	... ...	200
Total marginal cost per trip	... ...	900
Rate per mile	... ...	£2.00

A reasonable rate for the use of BR facilities to move trains on the route might be, say, 4 times the direct cost, given the off-peak use of the network, and the desire to encourage the operation, giving a rate of approximately £8 per mile.

In reality, BR were expecting and charged a rate well in excess of £10, which killed the Charterail operation, despite it having the stated approval of the Government, and active encouragement from John MacGregor and Roger Freeman, and previously Malcolm Rifkind. Government were not prepared to intervene in the dispute between Charterail (of which BR are a major shareholder) and BR, neither were BR willing (or able?) to provide a breakdown of their costs, to justify their charging rate.

I do wonder if even at this late stage, when Charterail is on the verge of liquidation, a concerted effort, and a good wind from the government, might achieve salvation for what has been a brave experiment, and provide an early qualifier for investment in the freight sector of a privatised railway?

5 November 1992

APPENDIX 81

Memorandum from Mr D Scott Hellewell

For public transport to be successful it must reflect the needs of the market it seeks to serve. Success can be measured in many ways, for example, profits earned, number of passengers carried or ton-miles of freight moved. Its social/economic value can be assessed using cost-benefit techniques. The market is not one market but a multi-faceted market. It may be analysed in many ways—by reason for travelling, by type of journey, by time of travel, etc.

Railways are a special form of public transport in that they alone provide a complete system-track, signals, power supply, rolling stock, stations, depots, etc,—unlike road-based systems—let alone airlines, airports, ports, canals and such-like. This is just one of the many reasons why railways appear "expensive" compared with other modes. When considering road-based alternatives all the elements referred to above come under different ownership, management and accounts. The whole is not grouped together.

Nevertheless, the opening statement about public transport needing to react to the market is just as valid for railways as for other modes. One of the great achievements of the Sectorisation of BR has been to make BR more responsive to customer needs, albeit at the risk of friction with other sectors at the margins. For the first time, the technical support—infrastructure and rolling stock—reflected the needs of the operator, who, in turn reflects the demands of the customers—passengers or freight. They are all identified with a common business, with accountability for their performance.

Separate the functions—marketing, operating and technical—and you return to the functionalised, pre-Sectorisation railway. However good the Regional/Divisional structure practiced by BR from 1948 until the 1980's, it was too "general" to reflect market needs. It did, or at least could, reflect geographical needs which are important and should not be lightly ignored. It is significant that the smaller Regions and more localised pre-Grouping Companies were more successful than the bigger ones.

As a mode "rail" is a one with a great deal going for it both as a transporter of passengers and freight. Britain's rail network is desperately in need of investments [as is much of the nation's transportation infrastructure]. To be a successful mode, numerous ingrained attitudes and practices within BR and LUL will have to be removed.

It has been said that BR management is "structurally conservative" in its attitude to the service it provides. It is true that most railway managers "joined as lads" and have experience of no other industries, let alone other forms of public transport. In many senses railways are a "world within a world" and this accentuates in-breeding. There is no doubt that management and staff attitudes and motivation must change since they are just as important to the well-being of the transport organisation and the perception of the users as are the more obvious investments in infrastructure and trains. The one should interact with the other—new investments, new thinking and new working practices.

The Consultations Document's proposals create three new bodies: Franchising Authority, the Regulator and Railtrack. These bureaucratic institutions—never normally known for their market-awareness—with their costs, are yet another overhead on an already overburdened mode. Those costs will either have to be met from the fares and charges or by the franchisees in their bids. Increases in productivity and in effciency will be unlikely to be sufficient to absorb these additional [and unnecessary] cost increases since BR is well-up in the International Productivity stakes.

These new institutions break the essential link between the market-led railway and the necessary levels of infrastructure required to provide the service the market wants and is prepared to pay for. It will be to turn the clock back a very long way to either an engineer-led railway which, whilst being perfection to some people, is likely to be unaffordably expensive.

British Railways are a system—a National [and shortly to be an International] network. Networks have their own strengths. The "network effect"—long understood by our continental colleagues—is either not understood or not accepted by the DTp in particular, and the Government is general. One of the effects of Bus Deregulation has been to fragment the regional and area networks, through ticketing and publicity, with the consequent 15 per cent drop in passengers and loss of facility as a public transport carrier.

Public transport systems—and railways are no exception—exhibit a fundamental organisational conflict. Many of their markets cover wide geographical areas and thus marketing, publicity and information and planning require an overall view, ie a view from the top downwards. However, the provision and operation of those services [frequently man-power intensive even after investment] needs to be done at the lowest level, so that it can react quickly to changes in demand whether spontaneous or pre-planned. It is at the lower level where costs arise and can thus be best controlled.

In Regional Railways, BR has very nearly got the structure right. It is a national business from Penzance to Thurso, supporting the InterCity "trunk" but with very strong connections and important markets, which are Regional or area based. Accordingly it is divided up into five Regions, each with its own Director. Each Region is then sub-divided into Service Groups or Areas. Those other businesses serving National markets—InterCity, freight and parcels—are harder to organise, but on the freight side the individual customers can be identified. Network South-East is, like Regional Railways, clearly focused on a Region—albeit a large one—but sub-divided into a logical nine line structure. It makes operational sense, has clearly accountable units and has features with which staff can identify.

It is suggested, therefore, that the Business-led structure of BR is today very near the mark of the ideal in organisational terms. An area where it is having difficulty relating to staff attitudes and motivations, which all-too-frequently lag behind the public's reasonable expectations. From an internal BR point-of-view there are still far too many "old Spanish customs" which affect staff attitudes, morale/inflate costs and pull down reliability. In a word, BR's staff require to become "flexible railway people" able and required to carry out any job for which they are trained and qualified. This is extremely difficult to achieve with a strong unionised workforce, commanding greater loyalty than the management. It is very hard to obtain loyalty to the business let alone to BR corporately. A step in this direction would be for each of the businesses to employ the staff. A natural extension would then be for their pay and conditions to be determined by each business, initially nationally and eventually locally.

The problems of BR are basically two: lack of investment and a structurally conservative management. The investment problem—shared with all transport—reflects the on-off policies of successive Governments and the inate conservatism of the Treasury. Both these attitudes are in stark contrast to the position in Continental Europe where there have been consistent policies for several decades and where a more positive attitude is taken to public expenditure. The Government, rather than learn from this, and to force change upon the Treasury, propose to break-up BR as the easier option.

I have suggested that the present structure of BR is very nearly right—but attitudes need changing from top-to-bottom. Attitudes are notoriously difficult to change, but surely it is a goal worth pursuing. This will require promotion of first-class railwaymen [and women] and an injection of "new-blood"—possibly bringing some people in from Europe. The BR attitude of "we know best" must be stamped out.

One place to start this attitudinal revolution would be with the BR Board itself. In line with normal commercial practice, the Board should have a number of non-executive directors in addition to the usual functional directors and the five Sector Directors. They would represent the wider interests of business, commerce and users. They would assist in relating BR to its markets, whilst at the same time, bringing in new ideas.

The only good reasons for privatising the railways would be to break the link with the Treasury, to remove them from Political interference and thus to allow the BR management to manage. As has been argued above, the Treasury must change its ways if GB Ltd, if it is to survive, let alone BR. It would be naive to think that Political interference could be got rid of—Privatisation is a high price to pay to change attitudes. If there was an obvious privatisation scenario, then the gamble might be justified. Dogma alone is not sufficient justification.

To those who know and understand the complexities of railways and/or who have studied them world-wide, it was known that there was no easy solution. It is now becoming obvious that the lack of solutions is at last dawning on Whitehall and Westminster. The civil servants are "waiting for private enterprise" to come up with their ideas. Two who have tried—Stagecoach and Charterail—would appear to be having second thoughts or going bust. Recently Richard Branson was quoted as saying "He believed the Government's proposals could work providing the operation is on a more regional basis". He went on to say "the price of entry into the market must be right" and surely that is the opening point for any entrepreneur.

30 November 1992.

APPENDIX 82

Letter from Mr P J Lynch

Although I have not read the White Paper on BR Privatisation I have a copy of the summaries issued to BR staff. The proposals give me considerable cause for worry.

1. The mechanism seems unduly cumbersome—the responsibilities of the franchising and regulatory bodies surely could be embraced by one body so that those responsible for awarding the franchises are also charged with subsequently ensuring that the franchisees comply with all the terms and conditions.

2. Nowhere have I read how franchisees can be made to fully carry out their contract, whether for 5 years, 10 years or whatever. When Clarkson's suddenly folded the rest of the holiday travel business was large enough to absorb most of their commitments. When DanAir folded BA were able to do likewise. But suppose a major franchisee finds itself in difficulty, who will step in to pick up the pieces on, say, the East or West Coast Main Line? I have in mind that there are, according to present forecasts, likely to be 30-40 franchisees so it seems unlikely that there will be any one in a really major league.

3. I am concerned at the potential loss of flexibility in the use of trains. To take a simple example, on the old Western Region the HSTs are in common use on services to Devon/Cornwall, Bristol/Western Super

Mare and to South/West Wales, plus one or two less intensive services. The sets are diagrammed to ensure programmed maintenance and fuelling; they can also be switched, eg at Paddington (by agreement with control at Swindon) at very short notice to cover emergencies. This is purely within InterCity but short-term adjustments can also be made to keep the services going if certain Network South East failures occur. Thus if it is not possible to find an NSE set for the 12.20 Paddington-Oxford the 12.15 HST to Bristol can be held back for 5 minutes to get Oxford passengers to Reading or Didcot for onward connections.

Unless one franchisee assumed responsibility for all HST services on the Western I can see a great loss of flexibility which now makes it possible to keep things going when things go awry. The same applies, I am sure, on other trunk routes. If privatisation *must* go ahead there is something to be said for the "old companies" basis espoused by the PM.

I have several other grave misgivings about the proposals as I now understand them, mainly arising from the prospect of a proliferation of franchisees, but I think I have said enough to be going on with.

19 November 1992

APPENDIX 83

Memorandum from Mr J M Chamney

Railway Privatisation

Government proposals have been published to transfer the railway industry in whole or in part to the private sector, in the belief that by so doing, a better service could be provided, and hopefully at less cost to the taxpayer. Is such a concept correct? To arrive at an informed opinion, it is necessary to study a little of the history, and then consider the role of railways in relation to other forms of transport, and any other relevant factors.

When the provision of railways was initially considered, Parliament was faced with the first examples of the compulsory acquisition of land on a major scale. This inevitably would cause alteration and damage to private property, invasion of privacy, interference with rights of way etc. So in granting the extensive powers that the railways sought, Parliament only did so on the basis that it was in the national interest, that it was for the public good and that the system had to serve the communities through which it passed. It also required that all reasonable facilities had to be provided for passengers, and for the despatch and receipt of goods and merchandise—this concept remaining for over 100 years until after nationalisation. So important was it considered by Parliament that the emerging railway system should be safely and correctly regulated there was a considerable number of Acts passed up at the end of the 19th century. Concurrently it was realised that the railways were enjoying monopolistic powers over charges. So here again Parliament stepped in again to control them, and by 1888 there were over 900 Acts on the subject. In effect this control existed until after nationalisation. In addition to all this, the railways were in general, required to conform to the common carriers' legal obligations to carry anything presented to them, without discrimination, at rates not related to the specific cost, and to be legally liable for loss or damage. This is in stark contrast to, say road transport, which only had to conform to the private carriers' obligation to compensate a customer, if he, the customer could prove the carrier had been negligent. Furthermore the private carrier was free to choose what he wished to carry and to fix his own charges. To attempt to run a business under these uncompetitive and unrealistic conditions would be enough to make a modern accountant's hair stand on end.

But how far did this matter? Until the first World War, there was no competition, and the railways made a profit. Between the wars the increase in road competition reduced the railways' profit to the point where they had considerable difficulty in breaking even. True the Government had instituted a system for licensing for road vehicles to inhibit manifestly wasteful competition, but this had little effect in redressing the imbalance of the conditions under which the two systems operated. However the railways still carried a large enough volume of freight to off set the costs of unremunerative services, such as those for commuters and those in rural areas. To let matters drift was culpable, (as Parliament's attention was drawn to it), but in a sense understandable. The railway system did not cost the taxpayer anything, the passenger service was good, and much of the parcels and goods were moved as fast as the first class post of today. Furthermore the system was reputed to be the best in the world, and it was certainly the safest. It was fundamentally reliable, and was very much an all weather system. It operated for 365 days and nights of the year, and provided broadly, a country wide facility for passengers and freight at fares and charges which could be reasonably afforded. Stations were adequately staffed, and the business well managed, and the whole organisation respected, and held in public esteem. It is therefore quite understandable that politicians and others, hankering after those halcyon days, see privatisation as a means of returning to them, but nothing is less likely. The railways have an identifiable high infrastructure cost, and unless a high volume of traffic is carried there on, there is no way in which the system can be made to cover its costs, by conventional methods of accounting. Privatisation as such as a mechanism to restore matters to what they used to be is a non runner.

Could the private sector run and manage the railways better than the present incumbents? This is unlikely and three examples illustrate this point.

An investigation into the management teams of the nationalised industries was carried out some years ago, and this revealed that in terms of calibre and ability, the management was the equal to anything in private industry. However the benefit conferred was greater in nationalised industries as the corporate effort was overlaid by a strong sense of public duty and responsibility.

Some year into his chairmanship of British Railways, Dr Beeching was discussing, with a group of managers, the difficulties the industry faced, I remember him saying that to help his understanding of the problems, and to check whether the management was on the alert, he had caused to have investigated, all the suggestions and ideas submitted to the Board on how the Service could be improved. These were understood to include those from MPs, the Civil Service, Industry, local authorities, and the travelling public. Less than 1 per cent were found to be of any practical use. This confirmed his opinion that his managers were not allowing potential for improvements to go unexplored.

The third example is to take a look at the rail system of Switzerland. Both the main and subsidiary lines are a mixture of state ownership and management, and private ownership and management. Apart from the different liveries of the rolling stock, it is impossible to tell which undertaking is responsible for what. The same standard of excellence, professionalism and efficiency prevails throughout the system.

To imply that the management of BR is perfect is absurd, but there is no evidence to support the notion that anyone else would do it any better.

If the railway system was to be transferred to the private sector, could the service be made more reliable and efficient? Here again we run into problems. As the railway is a guided system of transport, it is vulnerable to a delay caused to one train impacting on others. In the past the infrastructure contained a reasonable measure of flexibility with in effect, alternative methods of routeing. When these facilities came up for renewal, they failed to meet the Treasury's requirements for return on investment, and were taken out. Concurrently with this has been the widespread introduction of modern technology for signalling and running the rail system. Unfortunately this is susceptible to periodic failure, and that coupled with the reduced degree of flexibility causes widespread disruption and delay,—a feature virtually unknown in the past. To put these matters right, would need expenditure of £ millions for which no financial justification in the orthodox way can be shown. It has been suggested that if the railways were in private ownership, money for investment could be borrowed on the financial markets. True enough. But only if a return is forthcoming. Privatisation for this reason is thus irrelevant.

The whole question of financing public transport to give a thoroughly good and efficient service has to be reviewed in depth, with particular reference to those who must use it daily to get to and from work. Road congestion in the inner cities is now a matter of concern, and various ideas have been floated, such as supplementary taxation, on fuel and road pricing, to discourage unnecessary car usage. None of these ideas will work, as the cost of provision and running the large majority of cars is defrayed wholly, or in part by the users' employers, and supplementary costs would simply be passed on. A strategy to encourage the more rational use of scarce road space will only work, when everyone without exception, who sits behind the wheel of a car, paying for the full cost of its provision, maintenance and running out of their own pocket. The alternative is the progressive growth of areas into which cars are prohibited from going and in principle this should be avoided, as it interferes with convenience and individual choice of transport. If as one can predict, a point is reached when a greater shift to the use of public transport becomes inevitable, so will the pressure mount for adequate investment in it, almost certainly for the resources which cannot show a financial return. Taking this particular area of transport, it is important, even to the extent of some repetition to review it further. Too frequently the rail service fails to meet the aspirations of its users. Passengers arrive at work late, frustrated and weary, and the same situation may prevail on their return. Under investment has contributed to much of the difficulty. In the past there were problems, but not on the scale of today. The specification should be that those travelling to their jobs should arrive on time and fresh to start the day's work, and at its close, to be afforded, when they are tired, decent and punctual service home, so as to be able to enjoy their leisure time properly. The dictum of the Lord Justice Cameron, when reviewing railway finances, is very much to the point, "If the nation has willed the end, then it must will the means".

Could this be funded within reason? The answer may be yes. More than a decade ago, one of the universities made a study of the costs to society of the company car. Among the findings were, if my memory is correct, that the arrangement deprived the Treasury of about £3 bn p.a. in revenue. With the considerable growth of the arrangement in recent years, this figure could be now about £6 bn, or say £7.5 bn allowing for the falling value of money—a figure roughly equivalent, every year to the cost of construction of the Channel Tunnel. These figures should not be taken too seriously at this stage, as it is not known what assumptions were made in the first place, but it is an indication of the scale of the subvention, and the possible amount of money which would become available if all car users paid their costs, as a financial discipline to discourage excessive use.

It could be argued that a return to something like the pre-war arrangement of requiring a far greater proportion of freight to be carried by rail rather than by road would be a solution to the financial difficulties, as well as road congestion. In the short term this would be impracticable, if not impossible though it may need consideration in the longer term. A recent study by the EEC demonstrated that for motorway construction the cost would be only a fraction of what it is, if only built to cover the needs of the private car, and that the tax paid for the lorries though not insubstantial nowhere near pays the true cost. This is probably correct as the movement of heavy loads needs a robust and expensive structure for the purpose, no matter what actual form of transport is employed. The study is understood to have been confined to motorways, but that is only part of the exercise. Heavy vehicles have access to the bulk of the whole road network, and thus the calculations must be made on the basis of the difference in total cost of provision and maintenance for a network required to carry loads of no more than 1 ton (the private car), and that which is currently spent. The shortfall between what the system costs, and the tax already paid for freight vehicles can be determined. The final item which needs to be considered is that of environmental pollution. If the assumptions which have been made on the effects of CO^2 emmissions are broadly correct, and the need to stabilise them on a global basis are authenticated, the report by the O.E.C.D. on the subject is relevant. It is reported that to reach the desired objective, road transport (which is one of the two principal causes of the problem) would need to be reduced by about half. State intervention would become unavoidable. It is fair to assume that society will resist measures to constrain the use of their cars, so the only alternative would seem to be to transfer the bulk of freight now on the roads, back onto the railways, and hope that this will be enough to stave off further measures like permanent petrol rationing. If the O.E.C.D. findings are to be questioned, the Government must say what alternative strategy will bring about the desired result.

In drawing this review to a close, the following points can be made: 1. There is no identifiable case for privatisation of any or all of the railway system. Tinkering about with it will solve none of the underlying problems, and most likely lead to uncertainty, and inferior service. It might even be construed as an attempt to abnegate state responsibility. 2. The major rail systems of Europe are State owned and managed and it would be difficult to argue that there was much wrong with them. True, they cost their respective taxpayers more, but that is largely acceptable in view of the quality of the service. 3. No one should be tempted to try to franchise or purchase any part of the railway system. The infrastructure costs are too great an incubus, as will be the need for investment in resources to make the system more reliable, for which normal investment criteria are inapplicable. 4. The contribution that public transport could make to the solution of environmental issues requires assessment. This needs a comprehensive review in itself. For example, internal air flights no doubt produce more pollution for passenger carried than anything else. 5. Currently there is being conducted an investigation into the energy policy of the nation. The same is needed for transport, and in fact the two may be linked. Dogma, notions and opinions (including mine) are all very well, but there is no substitute for an in-depth study, and the establishment of facts. If it can be given sufficient time, the Commons Select Committee on Transport is no doubt the best forum for conducting this review. 6. If it can be arranged, an agenda or remit that is agreed on an all-party basis is likely to produce the best data on which future policy can be formulated, and hopefully with which political parties will agree, as long-term stability is essential.

And, finally, Britain probably had the best railway system in the world—it could do again. Political gerrymandering has done untold damage and it is time this miserable chapter was closed. Once again, we should have a system that meets public aspirations and in which society can take justifiable pride.

16 November 1992.

APPENDIX 84

Memorandum from Transport 2000 Derbyshire & Peak District Group

Rail Privatisation

NATIONAL THROUGH TICKETING

There are encouraging words in the Privatisation proposals about through ticketing but no details of how it would work in practice. All too often when you arrive at Derby on your late running Regional Railways train, you see the back end of your InterCity connection disappearing round the corner. That is bad enough in itself but at least you know that your ticket is valid on the next train going your way, be it Regional Railways or InterCity. We do not want a situation where you have to wait hours for one of the right colour to come along. If private operators under open access agreements have the effect of displacing franchisee's trains then we want to be able to use those trains as if they were part of the national network.

We want to be able to purchase the cheapest combination of tickets for the journey at our local sales outlet, station, train conductor, shop, travel agent etc:, and not be forced to join a queue at an intermediate train changing point to take advantage of the Super Saver or what ever. We do not want further encouragement for people to motor to their nearest "main line" railhead rather than use local connecting services.

RAILCARDS

We fear that the national system of Railcards could be a casualty of the proposals or could become so restricted in use that they become worthless. They must achieve the objective of increasing revenue or the Passenger sectors would have discontinued them.

The present differences in ticket types and Railcards between Network South East and the rest of the country is a source of annoyance, We would like to see some harmonisation here, but fear the present proposals will take us further away from that goal.

REGIONAL TICKETING—DERBYSHIRE WAYFARER

In our area we have the Derbyshire Wayfarer ticket, valid on all public transport in Derbyshire, and to and from one or two key cities outside, for the day. This is of immense value to us, and is a most useful addition over and above the standard ticketing arrangements. It gives the public transport user a certain amount of the freedom of the motorist and is particularly useful in the Peak National Park. We fear that negotiating this with different rail franchisee's could be difficult and costly for the local authority. It only needs one significant operator to refuse to take part and the whole scheme becomes devalued. (This facility could also be under threat from the unitary authorities proposal).

SERVICE SPECIFICATION

The idea of a service specification is something which we welcome; We were most disappointed therefore to see how little was said about this in the Franchising Document. Just specifying the present frequency of operation is far from adequate. Our major concern is what is to happen to evening services. We have seen the gradual erosion of these over the years. What other Western European country would tolerate the last train service from its second largest city, on a major axis to neighbouring conurbation, being at 20.56 on a Saturday! This has been the approximate time of the last Saturday service from Birmingham to Derby for years. It is in fact the last service to anywhere in Derbyshire, Nottinghamshire or Leicestershire.

Every winter our railway closes down at approximately 22.00 on Saturdays to allow the Engineers unhindered access to the tracks. Sunday morning services are almost non-existent. This situation was much better 30 years ago. We believe that the specification should give starting and finishing times, including weekends, state if withdrawal of service for engineering work will be permitted and whether alternative services, eg replacement buses should be provided.

We are also concerned about who is going to specify the service to be provided. We would like to see local authorities and possibly other elected bodies have an input to the service specification. Failing that a requirement for the Franchising Authority to consult with the local authorities a certain time before the introduction of a timetable would give them the opportunity to buy in additional services.

INVESTMENT

Infrastructure—There have been promises of new equipment and methods, which might speed up the maintenance of the railway, but it is a long time coming. How will Railtrack raise the capital for such equipment?

We want to see not only quicker ways of repairing the infrastructure, but improvements made to reduce journey times eliminate bottlenecks which are apparent even in this time of recession. This means investment in additional track space. We would like to see Railtrack be able to use Cost Benefit analysis as part of the justification for its schemes so that their merits could truly be judged alongside those of road schemes. In the meantime ways must be found of maintaining the investment in the infrastructure.

Rolling Stock—A large proportion of our local train services are operated by diesel multiple units built 30 to 35 years ago. They breakdown at frequent intervals. We know of no plans at all which will allow the them to be replaced. There needs to be a programme of electrification of inter-urban routes, which would allow modern diesel stock to be cascaded.

Many of our Sprinter operated services load to levels way above Network South East guidelines at peak times, It is clear that there is considerable unsatisfied demand at peak times. Again there are no plans for British Rail to provide desperately needed additional rolling stock. The only hope is for local authorities, which themselves are under threat, to cobble together schemes and fight for almost non-existent grants.

InterCity services also need the decisions taking now as to whether diesel High Speed Trains are to be replaced by Electric traction when the diesels are life expired.

It is not clear at all how the franchising of services will lead to an improvement in the situation. By the time somebody unlocks the key to rolling stock investment, we will be lucky if there is any rolling stock building industry left in this country.

FREIGHT

We view with alarm the present shifting of Freight from Rail to Road, contrary to the Secretary of State's declared aims. Surely in this time of recession, Railfreight could be released from its obligation to make an 8 per cent rate of return on its assets. Could not ways be found of bringing further private investment into Railfreight ahead of more complete Privatisation. There will soon be no role left for Private Railfreight.

CONCLUSION

We can find little in the proposals so far to allay our concern for the future of our rail services. Regardless of how the Privatisation proposal progresses, for the sake of the nation, as well as the future operators and owners of the railway, private or public, the present hiatus in placing orders for the future (other than in the channel tunnel services) must not be allowed to continue.

How different the situation is for road infrastructure, where we are bombarded with multi-million pound scheme after multi-million pound scheme.

22 November 1992

APPENDIX 85

THE INSTITUTE OF FISCAL STUDIES

Setting the Fiscal Balance between Road and Rail

The first section of this note sets out some general principles that might be used to guide fiscal policy in the area of road and rail transport. The second section considers the possible effects on private road transport of changes in the taxation of motor fuels.

1. GENERAL PRINCIPLES

(a) The social costs of different modes of transport

The reason for considering fiscal incentives to change the balance between road and rail use is that there are various social costs of road use which are not reflected in the cost of road use borne by road users. Although some of these social costs may also arise in the case of rail use, the argument that fiscal policy might encourage greater rail use reflects a view that the social costs are lower for rail use than for road use.

These social costs are of four main types:

— *environmental costs*—pollution of various forms, including the contribution of vehicles to emissions of carbon dioxide and other green house gases, nitrogen oxides which contribute to acid rain, and particulates (soot, etc) which can cause health problems. Other relevant forms of pollution include noise pollution, and aesthetic "pollution" in terms of the impact of roads, traffic and parking on the rural landscape and the urban environment.

— *accident costs*—the costs of injury and accident fatalities caused to pedestrians and other road users; the damage to physical property; the costs of treating accident victims in the National Health Service.

— *consumption of the road infrastructure*—in the form of "marginal road damage costs"; the physical wear and tear caused by vehicles using the roads.

— *congestion costs*—the costs in terms of extra journey time which road users impose on each other when road become congested.

It is desirable that these social costs should be reflected in the costs of road use faced by individual road users. The tax system may have an important role to play in achieving this.

A starting point for considering how the social costs of road use should be reflected in taxation is to begin by considering how road use should be taxed in the absence of any social costs. In this case, the notion of neutrality in consumption taxation suggests how private motoring should be taxed: basically, taxes on consumer spending should aim at raising public revenue requirements, whilst causing the minimum disturbance to individual consumption patterns. It is often suggested that a uniform consumption tax is the best way of achieving this—all items of consumer spending should bear the same rate of tax. This rule may need to be tempered by concerns about the effect of a uniform consumption tax on income distribution—the UK zero-rates VAT on certain "necessities". But, apart from this, the taxes on most goods and services are levied at the same rate. Considerations of general revenue-raising would therefore imply that the standard VAT rate should apply to the purchase of motor vehicles, petrol, etc. In the absence of considerations of social cost and income distribution, the same would in principle apply to public transport, too.

Where taxes on transport are simply intended to raise revenues, they should not be levied on "productive" road use—by businesses. This a reflection of the more general rule that intermediate goods should not be subject to taxation—a rule that is, for example, reflected in the arrangements for refund of VAT to VAT-registered businesses, so that their purchases are, effectively, free of VAT.

The appropriate structure of additional charges over and above this level to reflect the social costs of road transport will be complex. A number of the social costs vary greatly between different categories of road user (eg a very high proportion of the damage to the road surface is caused by the heaviest lorries), and between different locations and different times of day.

It is unlikely that changes to the existing structure of taxes on the purchase, registration and use of motor vehicles can adequately reflect the pattern of social costs. This suggests that new initiatives such as road pricing may be necessary.

In the absence of road pricing, it may be necessary to make the best of the situation by making use of the scope for restructuring existing taxes. In this "second best" situation, it will generally be appropriate to reflect the social costs of road use not merely in the taxation of vehicles and petrol, but also in the taxation of complementary goods and services and in subsidies or reduced taxation on substitutes for road transport. An efficient package of taxation measures (in the absence of scope for direct road pricing) to reflect the social costs of road use might therefore levy higher taxes on parking places, on employment or housing in areas with poor public transport facilities, etc. It might also include reduced taxes, or direct subsidy, to public transport facilities.

(b) The level of tax revenues, and infrastructure spending

The above principles of taxation have two implications for the level of revenues that should be obtained from taxes on transport. Firstly, some part of the tax on private motoring should be regarded as general revenue-raising taxation, and does not need any justification in terms of the costs of supplying the road infrastructure, or the social costs of road transport. Secondly, over and above this contribution to general revenues, however, the appropriate taxes on road transport depend on the costs that road users impose on the rest of society. The correct level of tax on road users will not, therefore, be calculated to cover the costs of building and maintaining the road network—the correct taxes may yield more (or possibly less) revenue than road spending, and the level of total road spending by government is irrelevant in determining the level of taxes that road users should pay.

It is sometimes suggested that there is some "unfairness" in the fiscal treatment of road and rail, since rail users are required to pay for the infrastructure costs of the rail system, whilst the road infrastructure is provided out of public spending. This "unfairness" may indeed be a source of inefficiency in the econcomy (even if, in fact, aggregate revenues from road users exceed the costs of providing the road infrastructure), but the problem lies in the rules by which the railway network is required to price its services. Requiring the rail network to break even may lead to inefficiently-high prices, if there are economies of scale in providing the rail network. In these cases, efficient pricing for the rail network would require that the rail network prices its services below the break even level. Efficient pricing may thus be reflected in financial losses from the rail system's operation, or in subsidies targeted to aspects of the railway system's operation.

2. *The taxation of motor fuels.*

Environmental issues are likely to become increasingly important influences on the taxation of road transport. Vehicle emissions are responsible for significant amounts of carbon monoxide, carbon dioxide, nitrogen oxides, lead and various other forms of pollution. Over the next 30 years the Department of Transport projects a doubling or more of road usage in the UK from current levels. Hence even to maintain total emissions at their current level it would be necessary to halve the current rate of emissions per mile travelled. Another trend which makes such an offsetting strategy more difficult to achieve is that towards larger engine sizes. Whilst it is not true that a larger engine *necessarily* burns more fuel than a smaller car, it is generally so. Department of Transport figures show that between 1983 and 1988, the 20 per cent rise in new car registrations was entirely accounted for by cars with an engine size in excess of 1,500 cc.

Environmental considerations might be reflected in the structure of road taxes in a number of different ways. Certain specific environmental problems might be best tackled by specifically-targeted fiscal measures—such as incentives to use lead-free petrol, or to fit catalytic converters.

Encouraging use of lead-free petrol by introducing a differential tax rate seems to have been relatively successful—the marginal saving when buying lead-free petrol rather than leaded petrol outweighing the fixed costs of converting cars to run on lead-free petrol for all except those who do very few miles per year[1]. In this case, the absolute value of the duty rates is less important than the duty *differential*.

A similar differential could be introduced to the car tax on new cars to encourage the purchase of cars fitted with a catalytic converter. The incentive should take the form of a lump-sum amount, rather than a reduction in the percentage rate of car tax. It would not be appropriate to have a different *percentage* rate—this would give too large an incentive to buyers of expensive cars, and too small an incentive to small car purchasers.

More general environmental problems associated with petrol consumption could be tackled by fiscal measures to encourage reduced petrol consumption, so long as the environmental problems are broadly-speaking proportiqnal to fuel use. Greenhouse gas emissions from road transport broadly fit this requirement, and might justify higher petrol taxes.

It is unlikely, however, that problems of vehicle congestion will be appropriately dealt with by measures acting on fuel consumption—congestion costs are not closely related to fuel consumption, since many journeys are in rural areas, or at off-peak times, involve negligible impact on congestion, whilst peak-hour journeys in urban areas may impose very high congestion costs indeed. Thus, measures targeted at peak-hour urban journeys alone would be a much more efficient way of dealing with congestion problems than fuel taxes.

There are two ways in which taxes can be used to encourage reduced fuel use. Increasing the marginal cost of fuel will reduce the number of miles travelled, and give an incentive to increase miles travelled per gallon. Alternatively, more direct tax incentives could be used to increase vehicle fuel efficiency.

Simply raising the price of petrol will increase the cost of each journey. Some potential motorists may be encouraged not to make a particular journey, or to do so by an alternative means of transport rather than by

---

[1] Some car-owners may have converted not for financial reasons, but because they are concerned about the environmental consequences of their behaviour. People may have altruistic, "pro-green" preferences which shape their behaviour. Tax differentiation may encourage such behaviour by signalling which goods have lowest environmental cost.

car. Road-pricing, aimed primarily at curbing congestion, would have a similar effect. However, in addition to this effect, taxing petrol also encourages new car purchasers to take fuel-efficiency into account in order to cut their transport bills, and give manufacturers an incentive to develop fuel-efficient engines to satisfy consumer demand.

Some estimates, derived from the IFS Simulation Programme for Indirect Taxes, of the distributional effects on household incomes and private petrol use of an increase in the duty on petrol of 55 pence per gallon are illustrated in the Table. This shows the effects that a duty increase of this magnitude would be expected to have on motor fuel expenditure by households, assuming that the current pattern of car ownership remained unchanged. This is based on a sample of about 7,000 households drawn from the UK Family Expenditure Survey, and an estimated demand system, based on data from the same survey over the period 1970-86, which allows for a full range of own-price and cross-price substitution effects on the pattern of consumer-spending. The estimates are based on data from the 1986 Survey, and are expressed in 1986 prices; the distributional picture presented is still likely to be a broadly accurate guide to the current situation, although the figures in money terms will, of course, have risen subsequently as a result of inflation. Overall an increase in the duty on petrol of 55 pence per gallon would lead to a reduction of household expenditure on motor fuel of some 8 per cent, and additional tax reveunes, in 1986 price terms, of £2.1 billion.

Petrol spending to increase with income at lower income levels, because the density of car ownership is much lower amongst lower income households. In addition, the richer the household, generally the greater the quantity of petrol purchased. Petrol duty therefore has a "progressive" incidence across income groups, and the changes in the distribution of additional tax payments shown in the Table raise few serious distributional problems.

Nevertheless, high taxes on petrol may, in the short term at least, be unacceptable for their impact on rural dwellers. One purpose of environmental taxation is to induce substitution between more and less environmentally damaging products (in addition to simply reducing consumption in total). Where there is no possibility of making such switches, the burden of the tax will be unavoidable. Higher petrol duty may make households in sparsely-populated areas, who are poorly served by public transport and have little option but to run a car, worse off without inducing any reduction in their petrol consumption.

Effects of an increase in petrol duty of 55 pence per gallon

(by quintile of gross household income)

1986 incomes and prices

Quintile of income	Poorest	2	3	4	Richest
All households					
Household income (£ pw)	53.70	112.65	196.10	291.70	520.35
Spending on petrol before tax change (£ pw)	0.92	3.19	6.64	9.14	14.86
Increase in tax paid (£ pw)	0.21	0.76	1.64	2.34	3.96
Change in petrol comsumption (%)	−12.1	−11.05	−9.8	−9.2	−8.3
Percentage with use of a car	*14%*	*46%*	*71%*	*86%*	*95%*
Households with use of a car					
Household income (£ pw)	104.75	196.15	271.43	353.39	596.33
Spending on petrol before tax change (£ pw)	6.96	9.26	9.86	12.85	16.64
Increase in tax paid (£ pw)	1.63	2.28	2.56	3.26	4.51
Change in petrol comsumption (%)	−11.3	−10.1	−10.2	−9.0	−7.8

Source: M Pearson and S Smith, Taxation and Environmental Police: Some Initial Evidence, IFS Commentary 1990, pp 30-31.

In contrast to petrol duty, VED, as a lump sum tax, does little to discourage car use and emission of pollutants. The *marginal* cost per mile travelled is unaffected by the tax, and VED acts, in a sense, like an admission price, having little impact on subsequent use for those who decide to pay the admission price. It might have an effect, if set high enough, of persuading some that it is not worth paying the initial fee in order to be able to drive, but raising the same amount of revenue by increasing the tax on petrol would normally have a more favourable environmental impact. One option which has been extensively discussed in the Netherlands, for example, would be to abolish VED, and replace it with higher petrol duty yielding the same revenue.

Alternatively, instead of keeping it as a lump sum tax, VED could be restructured to vary according to engine size, to encourage smaller cars.

Such a strategy is inferior to simply raising petrol prices if the only objectives are environmental. Raising petrol prices discourages those with small cars from undertaking journeys where there is an alternative, as well as encouraging fuel-efficient engines, whereas a differentiated VED can only do the latter. In addition, VED is rather a blunt instrument. On *average* a 1000cc car is likely to be more fuel-efficient than a 1500cc car, but for some models the converse is true. Petrol duty again seems targeted rather more closely on the production of pollutants than is a tax on engine size. Nevertheless, one reason why VED differentiation might be useful, albeit very much as a second best policy, is that differentiation of VED to discourage large engines would encourage rural drivers to switch to smaller cars, without penalising them for living in areas with a poor public transport system.

In the long term, policy might seek to discourage people from commuting long distances, or living in remote areas where car ownership was essential, and in these circumstances, higher petrol taxes would be appropriate. In the short term it may be necessary to acknowledge that people may have made commitments to live in particular areas that cannot be costlessly changed, and VED differentiation may be a useful part of an overall policy package, perhaps including an announced, phased, increase in fuel taxes, but which avoided imposing the severe adjustment costs that would follow an abrupt change in fuel taxes.

4 December 1992

APPENDIX 86

Memorandum from Mr D St. John Thomas

In responding to your invitation to submit evidence to the enquiry The Future Prospects for the Railway System in the Light of the Government's Proposals for Privatisation, I should like to state that I am a best-selling railway author with a history as a railway journalist and broadcaster as well as a consultant directing a number of enquiries such as The Lake District Transport Enquiry, over a period of forty years. My views have always been respected for their common-sense, practical approach.

1. There is overwhelming dismay about some aspects of the government's privatisation proposals, though it should be noted mainly from people who would not wish to return to the all-union position of yesteryear and who feel that the private sector does have a role to play.

2. It is worth noting how much things have changed. Once if BR's own Travellers Fare did not find it economic to provide an on-board refreshment service, private enterprise was not allowed to fill the gap. And if a refreshment room were closed by BR as uneconomic, it had to remain closed for a full year before private enterprise could set up a replacement. Part of the huge improvement in catering has been brought about by a more commercial and less protected approach.

3. But when it comes to the overall running of services, those with knowledge of the problems and potentialities do not feel that the way forward is through the franchising of all or even numerous services, and that private enterprise can be better implemented in other ways.

4. There are several reasons why running railways is so much more complicated than operating road or air services. Economic opportunities for overtaking are limited; signalling is much more expensive and sophisticated; and while many routes might have slack capacity, there are inevitably "pinch" points where an overall view has to be taken which may well conflict with the economic opportunities for individual services.

5. In particular I feel that the railway system here as in any Continental country stands or falls as a whole. It has, for example, a single timetable, and it is interesting to note that even when the Manchester super tram takes over BR to Bury, its service immediately ceases to be included. It is worth emphasising that the railways benefited from deregulation of bus services because substantial parts of the population no longer has a reliable bus timetable and turned to the railways which kept to their timetable.

6. There is also the vital point that ten trains a day in one service is much more valuable than two separate services with separate timetables and tickets of five each. King's Cross-Newcastle upon Tyne now has a basically half-hourly service, should one start franchising slots out of that inevitable flexibility would decline, and with that decline of course, the railway becomes less competitive. Had Virgin taken four prime King's Cross-Edinburgh slots, the loss to the remaining service would have been noticeable.

7. I passionately believe that a foundation stone should be sufficient central planning to enable the continuance of a national railway timetable such as, again, you can get for any European country, and that much of the present fear surrounds the danger that Britian will be the only EEC country in which it is very hard to discover who runs what trains and when.

8. So I would establish a railway commissioner (if not called Ofrail!) charged with ensuring proper integration and with the power to ensure that any franchisee is obligated to adopt standard timetable change dates and to pay for his part of the national timetable uniformly presented. That could well reduce the attraction to some potential bidders, but at some stage social responsibility has to come before pure commercial motives. If it did not, much of BR would shut shop today.

9. This so far, like nearly all comment, concentrates on the passenger side. But those with knowledge of the industry have nearly all stated that the consequence of privatisation is almost bound to be the further removal of freight from the system. Transparency of cost is desirable up to a certain point, but, when it leads to further traffic being switched away from rail, one has to question practical as opposed to theoretical value.

10. While sectorisation has been the vehicle that has enabled BR to become much more commercial, it has also involved greater bureaucracy and extra costs and has itself led to loss of freight traffic. And that is on the basis that one sector is in theory not allowed to include a profit element in its charges to another.

11. Some freight and passenger services are only economically possible with goodwill and co-operation between sectors even if there is not positive cross-fertilisation. Put two private businesses in opposition, or just determined to pursue their own commercial interests above all other, and inevitably traffic (and especially freight traffic) walk away. Again, only with strong central control, such as by a railway commissioner, is there a chance of adequate co-operation being forced.

12. I do not believe that the principle of open access is practical, and moreover believe that if it is attempted the results will be so confusing and give such bad value as to cause serious public outcry. I therefore propose that private involvement should be encouraged in other ways.

13. Those other ways could include the privatisation of a complete unit of services, and there might be a few examples of self-contained lines, like the London Tilbury & Southend system, where this may indeed make sense subject to the timetable and other provisions noted above. But it has to be added that people are eternaly optimistic about transport and that the level of failures has always been high. The much-publicised Stagecoach involvement in the Scottish overnight services has substantially failed and is probably only continuing at all through political expendiency. The failure of the freight scene has been much more serious. In both cases the operators blamed BR for being too expensive and similar complaints come from Virgin on the proposed Edinburgh service, and from BAA concerning the proposed high-speed link from Paddington to Heathrow. Again only a strong central control could make such future involvements possible. Lobbying by the government simply destroys the economic independence that is supposed to be the basic purpose.

14. Moreover without strong central control the track authority will still be seen as imposing unrealistic charges and have no incentive to cut costs and indeed an ever-tougher safety standard to meet till services will be closed and passengers transferred to more dangerous roads in the effort to make the railways watertight safe.

15. There are many other ways in which private enterprise could be involved. An excellent example is not merely the rolling stock by locomotives provided by Yeomans for the Somerset quarry traffic. Restaurant car, sleeping car, station services (indeed the entire management and running of stations) could be franchised without affecting the integrity of the overall service. BR no longer has to build its own trains. Is should be encouraged to do what it does best and needs to do itself and sub-contract whatever can be sub-contracted.

16. The move toward privatisation is probably caused as much by frustration at BR's own management record as by pure political motive. But because BR have not always made the best job of running themselves does not mean that splitting up the services into numerous operations will or indeed can do as well. In passing, much of the frustration with BR arises from its autocratic policy making and statements such as that made by the former Intercity director that there never could be a case for electrifying between Glasgow and Edinburgh when it was clear to many people that with electrification already completed at both ends and heavy traffic in between, there existed a classic electrification potential. Stronger central control as applied by the watchdogs on privatised industries can surely also be applied to BR in an effort to generate more openness of debate and commercial opportunity.

17. So far as the franchising of individual services are concerned, everything suggests a high failure and continuing turnover rate, implying chaos if franchising was done on a scale that could not be taken over again easily by BR. At least until some successful franchisees are well established, it would be foolish to go too far down the avenue.

18. Planning the future of the railways is already excessively difficult taking government policy and changing financial constraints into account. With large-scale franchising, there would be a danger of total instability.

19. The best possible solution would be to accept that BR basically provides the railway services but is charged with using private enterprise where better value can be obtained and is controlled by a railway commissioner somewhat along the lines of the privatised utility controllers. This may mean back-tracking on stated aims, but better to do this orderly and get good value from the system than endanger stability and see traffic transferred to the roads in considerable volumes.

20. BR should be charged with running profitably and it should be the railway commissioner who decides what degree of small service should be applied. There should again be more openness, ideally with public enquiries where appropriate, certainly with the rights of submission which does not exist now in practical terms. The current Transport Users Consultative Committee system is out-dated, is not treated seriously by BR and has lost what teeth it used to have (BR by-pass it by withdrawing all but one daily train one way only

and so technically do not close the service or have to consult) while, at the same time, it is difficult for the public to make their views known about the value of subsidised services through the transport minister.

27 November 1992.

APPENDIX 87

Letter from Mr R F J Turtle

Railway Privatisation

I write as a Member of the Chartered Institute of Transport, a retired railway officer, and the Secretary of two Associations for retired railway people.

For one of the latter, I edit periodically a Newsletter, in which, inter alia, I include a "Commentary" on the current scene, and for information I enclose a copy* of one such which went to members in September last. This particular Association however does not wish at the moment to be associated with my submission to you since any comments on the White Paper and expected Bill will be made through its "umbrella" organisation, which incidentally directly represents nearly 20,000 retired railwaymen and women.

It was felt by some members however that my "Commentary" was worth wider publicity, and I therefore hope that it may be of use to you in your capacity as Chairman of the Select Committee on Transport.

Retired railway people have two main fears, as outlined: (1) pensions and (2) travel facilities. In regard to the first, it would appear that there are already so many safeguards in regard to the BR Pension schemes that those already in receipt of a pension have little to worry about. Whether the same can be said of those not yet retired is less clear. The main concern therefore is with travel facilities.

You are no doubt aware that all railway workers are entitled to certain free travel and unlimited reduced-rate travel, the extent of which depends on length of service and status achieved. These privileges are carried into retirement. You will see that I make the point in my article that unless gold-plated assurances are built into any Act which may follow whereby all franchisees and any to whom to franchise may be passed on that travel facilities will be granted equal to those currently being received, there can be no guarantee on this score.

It is not simply the potential loss of travel facilities as such which retired people would regard as a betrayal—for many years, these privileges have been held by "management" to be part of staff remuneration, especially at times of wage or salary negotiations, and thus have a monetary value. Taking this argument further, it can also be said that pension levels, being based on final wage or salary, are to that extent depressed in perpetuity from what they might have been but for the notional value of travel. From the experience so far to hand from such privatisations as Hotels, NCL, BREL and Sealink, we know that facilities have been degraded, reduced or lost. I am sure that there is no need here to repeat the Sealink saga!

On the question of the merits or otherwise of the privatisation proposals in the White Paper, you will observe that I come down heavily on the side of the "plc" solution—this is simply that the management structure is now in place with the three businesses, that this is working well (enabling InterCity for example to make a profit last year), and that any further damaging re-organisations should be avoided. You will be well aware of Gerry Fiennes' comments on that subject!

What so many ordinary travellers want is a rail system that works, where they can identify management clearly. For it to work efficiently, investment is required, and, as we have seen with the SNCF for example, if investment is permitted outside of the Treasury (with its civil service cum accountant's approach to all questions) there is no doubt that much more will be achieved, and quickly. Nobody knows better than the present railway management what needs to be done, and British Industry would be only too glad to supply the goods—before it is too late!

I hope the foregoing will be of use to you—I am well aware of your vast knowledge of the structure and operation of railways, but if what I have written is superfluous perhaps you will forgive me, but the subject is so important to so many people that I feel an effort must be made. It is of little comfort to say, too late, that one wishes one had said something.

APPENDIX 88

Letter from Ipswich Buses Ltd

TRANSPORT POLICY

I had intended to write to you earlier to congratulate you on your appointment to the Chairmanship of the Commons Transport Select Committee, as well as for sadly commemorating the 25th anniversary of the closure of the Somerset & Dorset joint line last year by your reference to it in the House of Commons. Both my parents grew up near this railway and it played an important part in their earlier life. However, attending the Pindar Transport Seminar at the National Railway Museum, York last Thursday I heard you speak on

* Not printed.

aspects of transport policy which gave a good number of us in the audience the feeling that there were some Conservative politicians who understood and care about transport policy.

Certainly the warnings which you sounded in your speech about the possible damage to the rail network if a hastily conceived fragmentation of the passenger rail network is applied were felt to be true. Equally concerning is the lack of any action by government to encourage freight movement by rail following the closure of the Speedlink wagon load service and the financial failure of Charterail. The Railtrack authority proposal does give the opportunity to treat the rail network financially on the same basis as the road system, as I understand the Swedish rail system is now being financed. I have a feeling that there is a widespread concern about the future of the rail system by the public—including non-users, who wish to see better use of the system for freight and a nationwide high frequency passenger network making it possible to travel between most places in the UK at reasonable fares.

I turn to another proposal in the government's transport policy. This is the intended compulsory privatisation of the municipal bus companies. Unlike the former National Bus Company subsidiaries which were privately developed and owned until 1948 (the old Tilling/Railway owned companies such as Wilts & Dorset) or 1969 (the B E T group companies such as Southdown), the municipal companies have much older roots going back mainly to the 1883-1910 period when private companies could not finance local tramway development.

The 1985 Transport Act, although a failure in several respects, did achieve a very logical reorganisation of the municipal transport departments into council owned private companies with transparent financial arrangements. Generally their standards of service higher than most company operators and they have helped retain greater bus usage in those towns that they serve. Your own constituency is partially served by the Bournemouth "Yellow Bus" municipal company which provides a high quality service. Enforcing the sales of these companies will mean that the purchaser will have to recoup the price by making economies— probably in marginal services in the evening, at weekends particularly. At present in the Ipswich area over 99 per cent of our company's mileage is provided on a commercial basis including a provision of a reasonable Sunday service.

Not only is the government proposing to enforce sales to the highest bidder, reducing the likelihood of staff being able to purchase the company, but all existing staff will have to leave the Local Government Superannuation Scheme regardless of length of service. This is despite the fact that a number of privatised companies have retained membership of the LGSS. You can imagine the effect on the morale of my more senior staff of this proposal!

In Ipswich most Conservative councillors appear to be against the sale of our company and my information from colleagues is that opinions are similar elsewhere in the other district councils which own bus companies.

To conclude, I wish you every good fortune in your effort to realise the benefits of a high quality and comprehensive rail system as the foundation of a proper public transport system. I would also ask for you and possibly your committee, to consider whether there is any advantage in compelling the privatisation of the 35 or so efficiently run municipal bus companies against local feeling.

In closing, I do hope that you are able to give this matter your consideration.

23 November 1992

APPENDIX 89

Memorandum from Mr D J Caldwell

Great Yarmouth Rail Freight Re-Development

I refer to your letter of November 6 in relation to my previous enquiry regarding submission of evidence to the Committee in support of rail freight development.

I am pleased to submit my Marketing Survey conducted specifically for the Great Yarmouth Borough Council* and of my response to the seven questions set out in your letter. May I hasten to point out that *all* the information and opinions expressed both in the Survey and in the replies to the questions are purely of my own origin, and no other outside stimulus or influence is represented thereby.

In presenting this information to the Committee, I trust that the broad basis and outline of what I am attempting to do to assist the Great Yarmouth Borough Council in its quest to generate more prosperity for the town and its immediate area, will be recognised and appreciated for what it represents. My input to date is

* Not printed.

completely independent and self-funded; my ultimate objective within this appraisal and enquiry is to possibly secure tenure and be party to any franchisee or consortium authorised to operate such a rail-freight business in conjunction with the Great Yarmouth Borough Council.

What should be the aims and objectives of a privatised railway? What are the attractions for the private sector?

A privatised railway system in the true sense of the word is probably an impossibility. This fact has been long established, as no railway in the world is entirely profitable in all its aspects. What a privatised, or to be more specific non-State operated railway needs to achieve is of course some degree of return on any investment made in it, be it Directors', Venture or Shareholders' capital, and this must be at least in the medium to long term, an attractive proposition vs. the degree of risk compared with other industrial investments that are available.

The second objective, and indeed one could argue the most important objective of a privatised railway should be that of providing the SERVICE which customers need. Passengers must be catered for and attracted back to the railway instead of being driven from it as has been the case up until now, with all but a few parts of the BR network actually appealing to travellers. Privatised freight operators will need to generate their own business through properly targeted marketing and then to maintain and build further in that business by providing the efficiency and *reliability* expected of them by their customers. The Railtrack Authority would similarly have the responsibility delegated to it to provide the correct pathing and infrastructure to allow the franchised trains to operate. The two must work hand-in-glove otherwise the end-user will cease to be a customer, with all the implications that would precipitate.

The attractions for the private sector therefore lie in the areas of safety, reliability and environment, provided the private operators/franchisees are given a "level playing field" to be able to cost-effectively compete with road transport, in terms of government subsidies.

Private operators and franchisees will be able to come into the railway scene with new ideas, techology and marketing capability which in the main it would appear that the State-run industry has either had its hands tied or has failed to respond to potential demand over the years, thus exacerbating the run-down of much of the system over the last 10 to 15 years. Additionally, it is probably correct to say that until the White Paper on "New Opportunities for the Railways" was produced, succeeding governments' policies have never really been pro-railway, and in truth have favoured road transportation to the point of all-but killing-off freight service and severely running down certain areas and types of passenger services. Many local rail passenger journeys are out of necessity, subsidised by local government from Community Charge payers' pockets, and this could surely be turned round with a proper balanced input of privatised skill and expertise in attracting customers back to a "user friendly" railway which must retain a sufficient degree of State Government subsidy in order to make it viable.

How can freight traffic develop effectively in a primarily passenger network?

The obvious first answer to this is to run as much freight traffic as possible outside of peak-passenger traffic time, eg at night and secondly, not in conflict with heavily-used commuter trains at peak times. Modern air-braked bogie rail freight vehicles can run at speeds that to all intents and purposes will allow point-to-point freight trains to operate fairly integrally with all but the very fastest paths of HST's (High Speed Trains), and on major trunk routes where HST path density is such (eg ECML, WCML) the freight trains can in many cases be diverted into "slow" running lines or if necessary halted momentarily on existing newly constructed refuge loops, which has always been practised anyway. A classic case in example to increase track capacity in this way exists on the Great Eastern Colchester main line just east of Chelmsford, where New Hall Sidings (up and down) were taken out of use several years ago now and yet urban development in this area points to a dire need to build a double-loop "parkway" type commuter station to relieve the ridiculous and un-necessary congestion caused by London-bound commuters having to use the town-centre station in Chelmsford. Such a scheme, as indicated, would increase both passenger track capacity, and allow refuge for freight trains where at present, none exists between Witham and Shenfield.

Thirdly, and unless an insurmountable technical reason exists why modern passenger and freight vehicles cannot be hauled in the same consist, certain long distance trains could be passenger and freight combined particularly in night services where a lesser passenger demand very often precludes the running of a full passenger train. Again, a specific example, of this can be offered within the scope of the attached Marketing Survey executed for the Great Yarmouth Borough Council's proposed Rail Freight Re-development wherein a definite need for overnight passenger transportation between Great Yarmouth and Aberdeen is virtually assured, and a properly targetted service based on standards in excess of First Class air transportation could prove to be a suitable partner to the suggested rail freight operation between these two points. The idea could of course be repeated elsewhere within the U.K. or even to the continent once the Channel Tunnel is open.

Lastly, "Motorail" type services (but not however using covered vehicle accommodation) could and should be integrated particularly with the mixed freight-passenger idea, and with the emphasis again towards Continental Services. What Principles should Railtrack, the track authority, use in charging freight operators for the track infrastructure?

As touched on in the first question, the whole of this aspect of railway operation and economics depends on a "level, playing field" being developed to allow rail transportation to compete fairly and squarely with road haulage, and the degree of subsidy offered to the latter, in whatever shape or form, should be the first co-efficient to be dialled into any pricing equation appertaining to the railways. Once this level is set, then a fairly straightforward change structure can be developed from existing unit weight-distance-time parameters with possibly a pre-set charge applicable to an operating contract whether the train runs or not. This would then at least cover Railtrack's fixed costs in terms of personnel, providing motive power, etc., Modern weighing and tachometer readouts would quickly provide the track authority and franchised operator with indisputable evidence on which to calculate charges.

In addition, it may be perceived in the not too-distant future that a "pollution penalty" could be imposed on motive power, and in this instance as mentioned in the answer in the fifth question, rail traction however generated ie locomotive diesel-electric plant, power station oil/gas or nuclear generated electricity would surely win hands-down over road haulage in terms of harmful emissions per unit-load-distance.

Under what circumstances might it be sensible for track and related infrastructure used only for freight to pass into private hands along with the operational part of the freight business? Could open access and effective competition be maintained in such circumstances?

I would imagine that it would only be sensible, and indeed mutually beneficial, for privatised freight-only track to be permitted within the legal physical boundaries of a franchisee/operator's property or premises. Outside of that, and with the exception of privately operated bona-fide museum railways, the track should be available to all operators otherwise true competition is likely to be stifled. It would not, for instance, be healthy if say the whole of the Settle—Carlisle line were bought by a private operator to the exclusion of all others, or even selected other parties. To this end, not much mileage of track in the UK is specifically turned—over to freight—only traffic at the present time, and I don't think that this would raise too-large an issue as regards to having privatised freight-only operators using it. Rail networks within ports eg Felixstowe, Southampton etc., that are currently owned by dock authorities should be integrated into the National Track Network, but still maintaining their autonomous position and levying charges appropriate to usage.

How can rail compete effectively with road transport in carrying freight? Under what circumstances is the privatisation of freight services likely to increase the attractiveness of transporting freight by rail?

The very obvious answer to this question is one of sheer bulk load. The bulk liner train carrying a single commodity from one point to another over long distance (ie probably in excess of 300 kilometres in the UK) represents the most cost-effective means of transportation for most heavy commodities (disregarding of course gas and oil pipeline transmission, and water-borne transport where the time factor is not critical).

The railway to all intents and purposes is an extremely safe method of land transportation for both passengers and freight. Coupled with the increasing need for ecologically "friendly" human activity on this planet before certainly the precious gaseous envelope surrounding it is irrevocably destroyed in the main by poisonous emissions from internal combustion engines which power road-based transport, the railway can be shown in terms of pollutant emission per unit-load-distance and in terms of lives/property destroyed, to present a far superior overall picture and track-record compared with road transport.

The privatisation of freight services will increase the attractiveness of transporting freight by rail particularly in the area of customer dependency and trust. Without casting too many stones, I think it is fair to say that although the political will has not been present, the aggressive marketing tactics and strategy needed to secure and keep such business has also been lacking (or appears to have been) on the part of BR. I hasten to add at this juncture that I have no intention within this discourse to criticise or condemn BR in any way.

British Rail unfortunately suffers from an almost universal and appalling public image, and it is this which needs to be transformed through the marketing awareness and conscientious customer care of the right people within the private sector whose livelihoods depend upon results. My Marketing Survey shows that even now, people are prepared to consider using railway freight services despite the abandonment by BR of potentially very lucrative business. The introductory passage of the Survey I think covers and strengthens all salient points with particular relevance to the Great Yarmouth—Aberdeen potential and at the same time, is applicable to other long-distance situations including Continental destinations.

Similarly, rolling efficiency is far greater on rail than on road, and therefore less energy needs to be expended in terms of kW motive power to move the same load. Speeds are higher by rail, and point-to-point times for trains over long distances can be significantly less than by road. EC rules governing road transport drivers' hours and indeed maximum speed limits will almost certainly place much of the long-haul road transport at a disadvantage. Lastly, in terms of fuel efficiency, some electric locomotives are fitted with regenerative braking which means that electrical energy is actually fed back into the conductor system under braking conditions instead of all being dissipated as wasted heat in the case of friction brakes.

Would you prefer to lease or own rolling stock and/or locomotives if you were to operate freight services?

It is more than likely that in the outset, any freight operation based on the Great Yarmouth–Aberdeen connection would use leased rolling stock and locomotives. Depending on the amount of business generated within a set time-scale, it could of course be envisaged for the service to eventually purchase its own dedicated fleet of ro-ro flat-beds and certainly electric locomotives, should the Peterborough–Norwich–Yarmouth and Edinburgh–Aberdeen rail sections be electrified. Passenger vehicles (as indicated in my answer to question 2) may also come into our scheme, and suitably modified Mk 111 first class sleepers and lounge cars would probably be what we have in mind, together with a 100 mph-rated parcels/brake for each train.

It would also be proposed to run the trains in dedicated livery consistent with a corporate marketing strategy, this in itself distancing the operation from the traditional BR image and thus making it more attractive to its customers.

Maintenance of course would come into this, and I feel that every consideration would be given to BR to routinely service stock and locomotives at Norwich Crown Point, Edinburgh Haymarket and Aberdeen Clayhills depots.

Will private freight operators be better able to take advantage of the opportunities offered by the Channel Tunnel, than BR?

Having attended the Freightconnection 92 Exhibition at Birmingham NEC in September I understand that BR are themselves setting-up as a private enterprise concern in competition with other prospective operators. Given that this new company has the marketing capability to go out and get the business (or at least its share of it) then I see no reason why BR cannot be as successful as anybody else. They must however take on the challenge in the same way as will the truly privatised franchisees, otherwise the bottom line answer to the question is "yes". Personally, I would like to see BR actively competing and indeed getting business on the strength of its own capabilities which do exist, if only they can be stimulated and encouraged in the open market.

23 November 1992

APPENDIX 90

Letter from Mr F H Jaekel

In his 80th year, the writer, LMSR trained, Nigerian Railway appointments to the rank of acting general manager, cannot be associated with any interests other than pro bono publico.

Against nationalisation in 1948, the whole now being greater than the sum of its parts, the clock cannot be put back and the writer must be against privatisation. It is not just the simple privatisation of the single axis Fenchurch Street to Shoeburyness but the privatisation of a dense network of alternative routes and the Minister would be well advised to seek guidance from railway chief executives and not from the lobby of the Ministry's civil servants if the complexities of the issue are not to be brought properly to his understanding.

The population of the Lincolnshire/Norfolk territory remember Dr Beeching and the government supported axe that robbed main lines of their feeder services and will not wish to see steps taken that will encourage investment in profitable trunk routes at the expense of regional routes destined slowly to disappear from the face of the map.

British Rail has reorganised from a regional basis to a business orientated one, a departure copied on the continent and elsewhere, and staff already low in morale will not welcome a further change whereby the passage of a train is multi-controlled by regulator/signalman, franchisee, railtrack, leasing company, competitor and the Health and Safety Executive. And what of train failure? Which party will clear a disabled train and after what time interval? Has this been thought through?

Does the Minister contemplate a return to the Railway Clearing House (RCH) and are franchisee drivers not to be subject to one common discipline (like the regulators)?

Is Party political dogma to persist whilst remedial works continue to be postponed and British manufacture continues to be run down to paralysis, in keeping with inept moves by other departments of government!

Is integration of all-transport modes to be akin to the integration of all-energy modes, ie, a non-starter!

What of pronouncements of "green" issues, the environment, relief to congested roads in urban areas and the transfer of freight from road to rail! Is this to be considered under the heading of lip service.

Will an all-system timetable remain available and will there be guidelines on connecting services by different operators at junctions? Will through fares be available, published and honoured? Will seat reservations where journey breaks have become essential be honoured?

Station architecture diversification may be welcomed but will accounts, statistics, audit, be standardised? Will legal issues be protracted and subject to different interpretations? Can there continue to be an overall directing policy? How many parties will fund research? Will there arise complaints of varying standards of staff health and welfare? Stock maintenance, lineside and shop, will add to complications and therefore induce price rises.

Will buffet and restaurant car facilities be further hived off! How will British Transport Police operate under hived off elements of the system? And complaints; will the Transport Users Consultative Committee become an overlord! And lastly, the event of withdrawal of labour on a selected leg; have the repercussions been thought through?

BR is efficient per manpower in many parameters. The White Paper is short in specification; has there been a cost/benefit exercise? Can this government contemplate still further rises in unemployment, direct and associated? Should it not turn to the lessons learnt from bus deregulation.

What a railway requires is freedom to act and an ability to set a tariff that takes cognizance of a motor vehicle's support to the cost of its own infrastructure maintenance.

The continued delays in announcement of the Bill's particulars is evidence of the government's awareness that all is not well. It is to be hoped that the Royal Assent timed for late July 1993 will not meet with the favour of the House.

10 December 1992

APPENDIX 91

HULL CITY COUNCIL

Threat to Regional Intercity Services

This authority wishes to express its support for Grimsby Borough Council in its campaign to save the InterCity service between South Humberside and London. North Humberside is similarly threatened, with the proposed withdrawal of the daytime InterCity service between Hull and London from May 1993.

For places such as Hull and Grimsby, a direct train service to and from London is of great importance in attracting investment and promoting economic development. Their removal from the InterCity network would reduce awareness of these places, increase their perceived isolation, and deter investment from taking place in areas with already higher than average unemployment. It would undermine much of the hard work that has been done by local authorities in promoting their areas, particularly for economic development.

It is hoped that the decision will be reconsidered, with account taken of wider social and economic factors and not solely narrow financial considerations.

11 December 1992

APPENDIX 92

CLEETHORPES BOROUGH COUNCIL

The proposed withdrawal of the Cleethorpes to King's Cross InterCity Service

In June 1992, the Borough Council learnt with great concern of the proposal by InterCity to withdraw the daily direct service between Cleethorpes and London King's Cross. The news of the proposed withdrawal brought a quick response from local businesses. Copies of those letters received from local businesses are attached for the Committee's information*.

At the present time, despite the recession, the level of investment in the area has been maintained at a relatively high level. It has to be said that much of that investment has been made following detailed consideration of the advantages of this area relative to alternative locations, and a key factor has been the level of accessibility. There can be no doubt that the loss of the direct InterCity service will have a severe and damaging effect on efforts to attract further investment in the area with potential consequential effects upon employment levels.

In addition, the Borough Council is making tremendous efforts to revitalise the tourist industry and a major bonus has been the fact that there is a main line station in the heart of the resort. The provision of a Regional Railway's 158 link to Manchester has been warmly welcomed and support given to British Rail in its plans to refurbish Cleethorpes Station, in an effort to further improve the potential for holiday traffic. It is known that the operators of the Pleasure Island Theme Park, which is currently under development, are looking at encouraging visitors to the theme park by rail.

The loss of the London service is seen as having serious repercussions and the effect would be felt in all locations along the line from Cleethorpes to Newark. Thus, the impact would be felt by communities, industries and other rail users located within the administrative areas of Humberside and Lincolnshire.

The Borough Council is most concerned that, based upon the findings of consultants[1], (appointed by a consortium of local authorities along the route) the withdrawal has been based upon questionable savings.

---

* Not printed.
[1] Steer Davies Gleave, September 1992.

These savings not only relating to the withdrawal of the service from the Newark to Cleethorpes line, but also the re-use of the train set on an alternative route. Whilst independent consultants have indicated the financial case for withdrawal is marginal, InterCity is confident that alternative Regional Rail services will adequately fill the gap left by the loss of the high speed train on this route. This confidence by British Rail is displayed despite the known reluctance of passengers to change trains at Newark.

In summary, the Borough Council considers that the withdrawal of the InterCity service would be a significant loss to one of Britain's most buoyant industrial and commercial areas. If the 'green shoots' of recovery are to sprout, then potential growth areas such as South Humberside should be given the right climate for growth. A good transportation network is an important element in creating this climate. In turn the InterCity train is the flag ship of the railway passenger service and of considerable importance to the transportation network.

8 December 1992

APPENDIX 93

Letter from Mr P G Rayner

I write again to personally put some more items before you which I sincerely hope are of interest and assistance. They are somewhat random for I write, much as I speak, and it comes out in bursts!

Modern Railways were good enought to offer me some space to write an article about Privatisation, and the different ways in which it might work. After much thought I declined for I did not wish to publicly explain to any would be privatisers or franchisers ideas which could be construed as being supportive to the concept. It became known within BR that I was writing this article and a number of senior people put items to me hoping I would air them. Some of these managers are pro- privatisers and others anti. The views are from some people who have given evidence before your committee but cannot say all they would like in view of the "open culture" that exists within BR at the present.

I list the views without comment:

1. InterCity is a national network of Express trains, it strives for a consistent quality across the UK. It also has a connecting timetable which is actively promoted and improved (i.e. an opportunity not a regulators restraint.)

2. The InterCity product is well regarded and is considered as a BR success, most people will be dismayed to find it broken up. UK gave InterCity to the world; first to break it up.

3. There is a core to a national timetable structure is difficult to comprehend. I know from another source you have visited my beloved Crewe Planning Machine which does understand the problems of Timetabling. InterCity Cross country is a 115 million pound business which criss crosses all routes, Plymouth to Newcastle, Bournemouth to Glasgow etc. Takes 18 months of in house professional debate to produce it now. The InterCity Timetable is a good example of co-ordinated hub and spoke link with Regional Railways and Network South East. The view which I know has been expressed by the Minister about Timetables demonstrates a total ignorance of the procedures. The professional advisers, Coopers & Lybrand, suggested by Mr Freeman as being able to contribute valuable specialist expertise on timetables is laughable were it not so sad. I will at the end of this comment debate the York situation and the Crewe situation the better to clarify the issues for you.

4. InterCity has a marketing resource and as it is in competition with air, coach, and car it needs a strong central brand to do this. Apex national promotions, Senior citizens railcards is impossible to co-ordinate quickly between disaggregation groups.

5. The high cost of smaller operations is not understood. The East Coast has ten HST's of which nine are in traffic and one is spare. If two operators owned five HST's each in their own colours only eight HST's would be diagrammed and they would each need a spare. There is no pool of spare trains and this example would multiply round the country.

6. InterCity also pools its specialist activities to ensure experts at an affordable cost. Central procurement saves tens of millions of pounds annually.

7. There is a spread of best practise in a national organisation which has safety implications. Safety is a subject on its own and could be the key to proving how foolish privatisation is, but that is not the purpose of this document.

8. Short term unavailability or extraordinary demand can be met with stock from other routes.

9. Medium and long term modifications can be contained with a larger fleet. i.e. Door Locks.

10. A larger fleet is more robust against major disruption.

11. A National fleet cascade strategy is possible without an enormous wrangle with intermediaries.

12. It does not shut the door to open access for there are advantages in the stability of a host network. (A view I have to say I disagree with but pass it on).

13. Railtrack is a window of opportunity for its key objective ought to be to maximise the use of infrastructure to provide maximum number of train paths.

14. It will focus the need for sensible and efficient operation of signalling control centres to the overall benefit of train running.

15. It will require provision of signalling headways that are capable of handling increased taffic without costly re-signalling whenever demand changes.

16. It will enable efficent use of operating and engineering resources dedicated to the total spectrum with the ability to provide a service to all users of the infrastructure.

17. It will enable scarce expertise to be properly employed.

18. It should ensure a minimising of short term solutions that are aimed at solving a particular problem for a particular type of service whilst posing many more problems to the total operation.

19. It will greatly enhance safety by providing simple geographical allocation of responsibilities.

20. Railtrack will be able to take responsibility for safety and engineering standards.

I hope this letter is not too long nor that it covers too many subjects that you already know about. The belief by Roger Freeman that Coopers and Lybrand can actually advise on timetables is indeed a worry for it indicates a complete lack of understanding of how a railway works. Coopers in my view should stick to making marmalade and not get involved!

The reference to York is also a worry to me for it is being run at the moment by arch privatisers within the industry, not that I don't respect their views, it is the operating performing conforming nonentities that surround them that are the danger. The Timetable on the East Coast is easy to design and operate for two reasons:

1. There are only a handful of trains, The West Coast route runs more trains north of Weaver Junction than the East Coast runs south of Hitchin. The two are not comparable. Liverpool, Manchester, Preston, Birmingham all generate a workload that on the East is generated solely by Leeds.

2. The second and most important factor which makes the East Coast easy to timetable and even easier to operate is the fact that the two Up roads are side by side in the direction of travel, as indeed are the two Down roads. Thus if you want to go from fast to slow line on the East Coast in either direction you do not conflict with the trains in the opposite direction. Euston to Crewe was designed with the Up and Down Fast and Slow in Pairs and the reverse is the case.

It is this sort of detail that is so easily not understood, and ignored. It is sad that half knowledge is so dangerous but I suppose it exists everywhere and is only annoying when it assumes knowledge in ones own area of expertise. I was Timetable Production Officer for the total timetable in the seventies and, believe me, it's the timetable that decides productivity and efficiency, and not the day to day matters, and it is in timetable production that today's business managers on BR don't even understand, let alone a team of consultants with hired help.

I think that covers all I had to tell you, I do hope by various methods you are getting the answers to the key questions that need asking, from my own feedback from friends, and from looking at TV and reading the papers I get a reasonable amount of information down here and can see how very well your inquiries are going. I do hope they listen to your eventual conclusions. Some of the utterances, like saving money on the SE Divisional track which Sea Container hoped to do annoy me more than others, but I am a peaceful man at heart.

3 December 1992

APPENDIX 94

Memorandum from Professor L Lesley

British Railways Privatisation Proposals

These comments are intended to stimulate debate rather than necessarily defending one policy over another. If the present British Railways system is to be returned to private ownership and operation, a number of pre-requisites need to be demonstrated.

(a) That the likely revenues exceed reasonable operating and capital costs. (Profit).

(b) That the profit generated is sufficient to service the purchase price, which then becomes the equity base against which to make investment judgements.

(c) The risks involved—political, technological, social, workforce and market—are manageable.

Given that the existing BR operation involves revenue support from central government of the order of £700 million per annum, then potential buyers would have to satisfy themselves that either operating costs could be reduced by £700 million (on a total of £4,000 million: 12 per cent) or that revenues can be increased by £700 million (from an existing total of £3,000 million: 14 per cent).

The evidence to date suggests that neither of these in themselves are possible separately, and that the chance of achieving half of either (operating cost reductions of £350 million and revenue increase of £350 million) is only slightly higher.

If it is not possible to operate a privatised BR profitably using the existing financial framework, then the Government can only achieve its privatisation objective of giving BR away with an endowment (either as a dowry or a guaranteed annual commission payment). A single payment dowry would have to be of the order of £5,000 million. This recognises the fact that the value of an unprofitable enterprise (like BR.) on the open market is essentially zero or perhaps its scrapping value. This is not to say that some of BR's assets have no value, for example land holdings, but (in this scenario) that the totality of BR is valueless. The current liabilities having to be offset against the assets which have a realisable value.

However for BR to be given away with a dowry then fails to meet another objective of reducing public expenditure, at least in the short term. This raises a further question of the way in which BR could be made more cost effective, so that it might be privatisable.

For any new private railway company to remain cost efficient there must be competitive forces and the possibility of other companies entering the market, which means a low cost of entry both in terms of finance and regulations. With Britain's railways currently having less than a 10 per cent market share in both passenger and freight traffic, then clearly there are already many competitors. It is thus the second area which needs consideration, the ease of entry of new companies to ensure that existing operations remain efficient. Clearly in the present framework for transport financing, there are few if any scenarios where a straight commercial investment is possible. This was clearly demonstrated by the failure of the private sector to promote a new high speed rail line between the Channel Tunnel and London.

We therefore arrive at the notion of privatisation of the operation of the railways, rather than the totality of the whole system. In this case the infrastructure would continue to be owned by the public sector, like the public highway network. In the short to medium term, rolling stock would also remain publically owned. This would enable private companies to operate parts or all of British Railways, leasing equipment from a public body and having access to the network at a nominal charge, like road haulage and bus companies enjoy with the highway network.

This separation of infrastructure and operation is also close to the EC July 91 Directive, which has at its aim the equalisation of competition between road and rail transport. The EC argues that with rail transport a minority mode, it is now no longer possible to change the economic framework of road transport to match that of rail transport. Therefore, the economics of rail transport must be changed to match road transport. If the rail infrastructure network was a direct Central Government responsibility, as roads are, then the cost of maintaining, renewing and extending the rail system could be justified on the same (cost benefit) basis as roads. Given an annual total of about £6,000 million to transport, if it were divided on the basis of network size then rail infrastructure would enjoy an annual expenditure of about £1,000 million, twice the present figure given to the whole Rail system. Such a figure would certainly pay for electrification, new lines, increasing the loading gauge to UIC standards, etc.

This division of publically owned infrastructure and privately operated services is the model which Sweden has adopted, and Switzerland is considering. The entry cost to the operating market is low, new companies can compete, either directly (as in the UK bus deregulation)—or indirectly (by tendering individual or groups of services in London). If private operators inspite of low or no cost track access, are not forthcoming, then operating subsidies might be included as part of the tendering process (like UK Social bus service, filling the gaps left by Commercial operations).

Here there is a way in which the privatisation of operations might be possible, whereas the present proposals clearly are unworkable. On the other hand if HMG put up BR lock, stock and barrel, there might be circumstances where SNCF could be a willing buyer, with BR as a region of SNCF. Alternatively, SNCF, DB and some other European railways might form a consortium to buy BR so that access could be guaranteed to British Rail tracks in the future, when restrictions on road haulage in those European countries make rail transport the only practical solution for the increase of exports to the UK.

Finally, in my opinion, BR should remain in public ownership, perhaps with private management of operations for the following reasons.

(a) To ensure the continuity of a nationally coherent rail network providing an alternative to road transport.

(b) That network synergy remains. The example of air transport, where the trend is to fewer but larger companies, rather than a multiplicity of small operations. Passengers need a user friendly system, with a single access and homogenuity of service. The hotch potch of services may have worked pre-1923, but only because railways had virtual monopolies. Had private cars been a mass form of transport then, there would not have been 120 companies left to amalgamate into the Big Four.

(c) There is a minimum size needed for economies of scale in operation. Irish Railways are too small for those economies to be achieved, yet the present HMG proposals would create maybe 20 "Irish Railways" in Britain. These economices of scale were amply demonstrated in two world wars when the railways achieved substantial increases of traffic with fewer resources.

(d) Railways provide a public service in many areas. The exact definition and specification of public service has and will change. Without a public rail system, in increasing areas of the country many people would suffer immobility by virtue of not being able to afford or not be able to drive a car.

(e) Motor traffic on UK roads is now a major cause of air pollution. Nearly 80 per cent of Carbon Monoxide, 50 per cent of Oxides of Nitrogen, 30 per cent of organic solvents and 20 per cent of Carbon Dioxide originate from UK road traffic. Railways pro rata produce less pollution and by virtue of electrification can significantly reduce air pollution.

(f) Transport in the UK is an oil dependent industry. Over 99 per cent of transport energy comes from oil. Road transport is 100 per cent oil dependent. North sea oil production is now declining. Within 10 years the UK will not produce enough oil to power its own transport system. With the world demand for oil growing, the UK will have to compete for its oil supplies. Electrified railways can be powered from coal generation, and because steel wheel on rail is an order of magnitude more energy efficient than rubber tyre on road, then energy demand would fall.

As an indication of the magnitudes involved an increase in the tax on petrol and DERV of about 35 pence per gallon would yield a revenue of about £4,000 million, enough for BR. to operate free of charge for passenger and freight services.

1 December 1992

Air Pollution in UK caused by Transport.

Carbon Dioxide pollution from Transport in UK.

Carbon Dioxide pollution from Transport in UK.

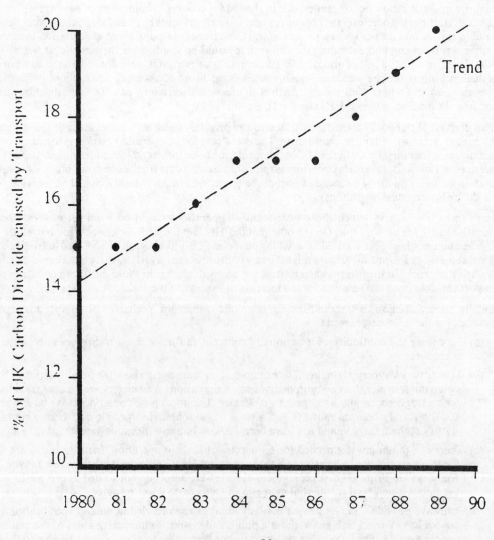

Carbon Dioxide pollution from Transport in UK.

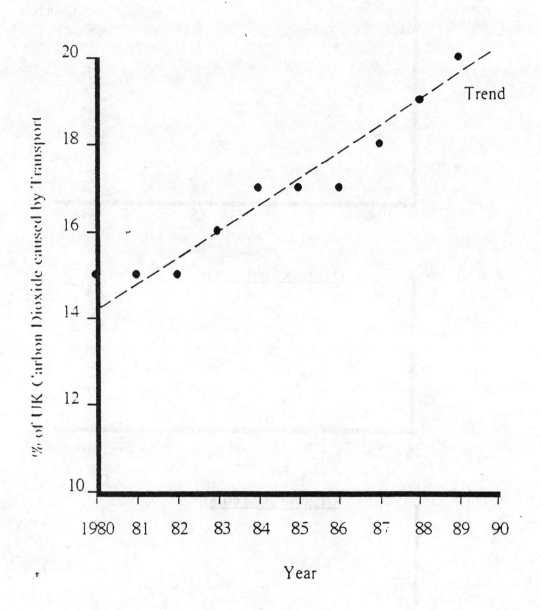

Air Pollution in UK caused by Transport.

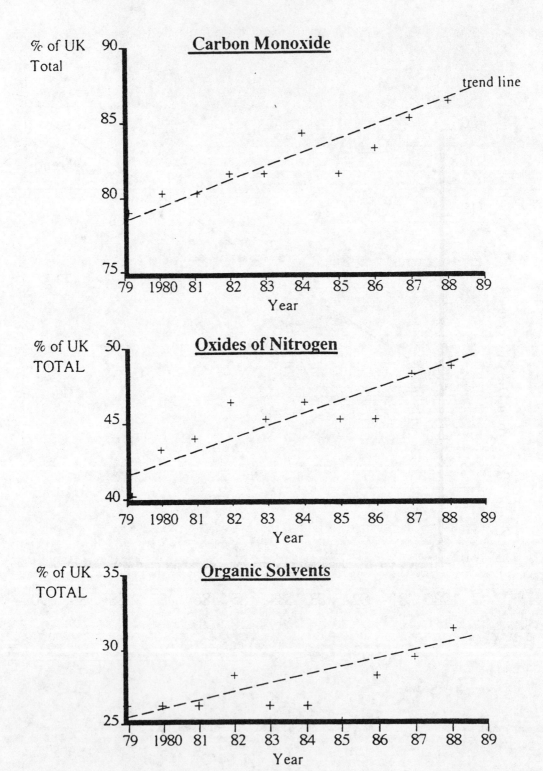

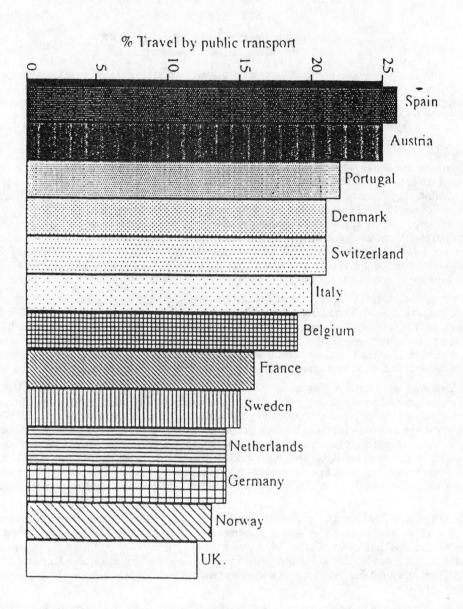

Source: HMSO, Transport Statistics 1991.

UK and European Modal Split Comparisons (1989)

APPENDIX 95

Memorandum from Professor John Hibbs OBE
Privatising Railway Transport

1. *Summary* This paper looks afresh at the case for private ownership of railways in Great Britain, criticises certain of the policies currently developed by the government, and concludes that there is an urgent and pragmatic case for privatisation which, while based firmly in free market economics, sees competition as a function of the whole transport sector, including the place of the private car.

2. THE CASE FOR PRIVATE OWNERSHIP

2.1 *Capitalisation* Britain's railway system (including the London Transport railways) has been starved of capital since it was taken into state ownership under the Transport Act 1947. When funds have been relatively freely available, they have not always been wisely used, as in the case of the disastrous 'modernisation programme' of the 1950s. There is a link here with para 2.2, in that the system has lacked an autonomous board with responsibility for strategic planning, able to assess its future capital needs and go to the international capital markets accordingly. This function has been interdicted by the Treasury, which however has not taken on the responsibility itself. A railway undertaking, or undertakings, outwith the PSBR, free to take long-term investment decisions in the way that the utilities (Gas, Water, Electricity &c) can now do, could be expected to rejuvenate the system in response to competition from other modes of transport.

2.2 Such an undertaking could expect some degree of investment, in its infrastructure, from public funds, at least so long as the nation's roads remain in public ownership. (On this, see Hibbs & Roth, 1992). But such funding should be subject to the same cost/benefit calculations that apply to investment in roads. In this way the severe and pressing problems that are currently not being faced, in terms of both overdue replacement (West Coast Main Line track) and new construction (freight access to the Channel Tunnel), could be tackled in a more rational and more economical manner than the present dispensation permits.

2.3 *Managerial Autonomy* A Commons Committee chaired by Sir Toby Low (Low Report, 1960), recommended some 32 years ago that railway managers should be instructed to be 'more commercial', and leave social issues to the government, advised by the Statutory Consultative Committee. This policy, which was welcomed by many railway officers at the time, failed to achieve its objective, because it is not possible to act truly commercially if your hands are tied as to investment policy. As successive Chairmen of the British Railways Board have discovered, because the responsibility for finance lies above them, they do not have the power that a company board assumes to pursue a policy geared to the satisfaction of the shareholders and of the customers. As a result, the people of Britain, who are both 'shareholders' and customers, continue to lose out both ways.

2.4 Only a genuine free enterprise dispensation can provide the pressure necessary to customer satisfaction, combined with the economic use of scarce resources. For financial and managerial autonomy bring an effective 'bottom line' into every calculation, whereas the unspoken belief that the state will always pick up the tab leads, as it has often done over the past 45 years, to waste and inefficiency. To adapt Dr Johnson's remark: "Depend upon it, Sir, When a man knows his business is to collapse in a fortnight, it concentrates his mind wonderfully".

2.5 It is no criticism of innumerable conscientious and capable railway managers, including most of those known to the author, to stress the inefficiency of the railway business during the period of state ownership. If I may draw upon my own experience in the former Eastern Region in the early 1960s, I believe we were a management team that, under the leadership of our Chairman, Major-General Russell, and our General Manager, Mr (later Sir) Henry Johnson, could have moved successfully into the private sector, and flourished there.

3. RAILWAYS AND COMPETITION

3.1 It will be noticed that the foregoing argument has not mentioned competition. Railways exist in a highly competitive market; to the extent that they once had a degree of monopoly power, its demise must have been plain to see when the nation survived the General Strike in 1926, largely due to the development of commercial road transport. It sometimes seems that the lesson has yet to penetrate the state of public knowledge, but the fact should by now be well-known, that British Rail is very much a minority carrier. Their position in the passenger market is to some extent protected by the low cross-elasticity of demand as against the car and the express coach. It is this market situation that demands the aggressive response of management, if rail passenger transport is to remain viable. In the freight sector, the internal movement of traffic suitable for rail appears to be likely to shrink still further in the foreseeable future, but the potential for new traffic from the opening of the Channel Tunnel, and from the use of rail for the "stem" element of distribution, each cry out for exploitation.

3.2 *Internal competition—is it needed?* There is a school of thought which subscribes to an image of competition between many small entrepreneurs as the objective of privatisation. Ironically, this is as likely to prove disastrous for the economic health of the railways as were the consequences of the "grouping" in 1923. The Railways Act 1921 not only forced a major re-organisation upon three-quarters of the industry (the Great Western Railway apart), but it also required the re-classification of freight rates (which were then controlled under statute). The consequences were the diversion of managerial effort away from the need to respond to the rising growth of commercial road transport. Neither is it too much to say that the over-frequent re-organisations that have taken place since 1945 have diverted attention from the changes in the industrial base of the country, and from the growth of popular and commercial car ownership. Another drastic re-organisation is not what the railways need today, though an element of re-structuring in terms of scale is certainly desirable.

3.3 Railway companies, like bus companies in a controlled market, will tend to combine, notionally in pursuit of economies of scale. Without going into the theory, it may be said that there is a limit to such growth, as managerial dis-economies (rigidity, remoteness etc) tend to set in; but there are benefits to the firm that arise from "economies of scope". These probably tend to the creation of area companies, such as were anathema to Parliament in the 19th century, but that are no longer an economic problem now that they do not amount to a transport monopoly. None the less, it is easier to manage a smaller rather than a larger railway, and the real problem that faces us in seeking the optimum form of privatisation is how to get the balance about right. It is very unlikely to be found in a plenitude of small firms, but neither is it very promising in the shape of British Rail PLC.

3.4 *Viable companies* One's instinctive leaning, which I believe to be supported by theory, is toward the existence of a number of companies, each with a fairly clearly defined system, and all of them *owning their own track*. "Running powers" over sectors of each others' system would be accounted for by a re-established Railway Clearing House, and "boundary problems" would be overseen by a public Regulator. The scale of these operators would be nearer to that of the major pre-grouping companies than to the "four main lines" of 1923-1947, but there is no reason to build them upon past history; and they should certainly be smaller than the old Great Western or London & Northern Western companies. (Nostalgia, that great burden upon efficient management, should not be pandered to.)

3.5 Such companies would be subject to an element of inter-firm competition—Anglo-Scottish traffic, London-Birmingham services, and the trans-Pennine lines, for example. Because of their manageable scale they should be able to innovate; we are already seeing the way this can happen, in the case of Regional Railways. Such internal competition and innovation would provide an immediate advantage in meeting and challenging the competition of other modes; including the forecast threat from Information Technology. Neither should the existence of minor railways, with low fixed costs, be rule out; in the USA there have been many examples of large companies selling "unremunerative" branches to staff or local entrepreneurs, to be run cheaply, often with a guarantee of some connecting traffic.

3.6 *New entry* Such a system should permit the entry of new capital where the market justifies it; Channel Tunnel links would seem to be an opening, with perhaps the use of the former Greater Central rights-of-way. Hybrid companies should be able to innovate, as for example in the case of the Heathrow link. The removal of Treasury control would enable a range of new possibilities to be explored. Equally, in line with the point made in para 3.5, bus companies might invest in minor lines, and Conurbation Transport Executives might face their own "bottom line" in maintaining passenger sevices in cities.

3.7 *Diversification* Just as bus companies might buy railway lines, to operate or to convert into busways, so also should the railway companies be empowered to operate buses, in connection with their train services. (Being no longer statutory companies, this could be provided for in their Memorandum and Articles). One of the great mistakes now seems to have been the railway companies' investment in the area bus companies after 1929, which failed to provide the kind of co-ordination that might have been expected. It did not develop even after the companies were brought into the public sector, between 1947 and 1968. There are however operational reasons that account for this, for whereas a "railway bus" can await a delayed train, another firm's bus may have to leave so as to cater for other passengers along the route.

3.8 *Publicity and through booking* One of the manifest weaknesses in the current proposals is the lack of provision for common functions that must be at risk if they are not allowed for. The division of BR into business sectors is already making for difficulties in obtaining information, and one of the disappointments in the outcome of bus deregulation has been the overall failure of the bus industry to recognise the need for market information to be widely available. The new Railway Clearing House (see para 3.4) should have the additional function of securing through booking facilities, and the publicity required to make them available; it might indeed have the useful function of operating the station booking offices, and authorising the high street travel agencies to sell railway tickets. It should, needless to say, be jointly owned by the companies, much as the bus firms at Newcastle-upon-Tyne own their joint ticketing company.

4. Conclusions and Recommendations

4.1 *Franchise no solution* The main purpose of railway privatisation is to return the railways to the freedom of the commercial world, within the discipline of the markets. This has been partly achieved in the case of the bus and coach industry, with significant advantages. If the railway companies envisaged in this paper wished to franchise certain activities, as air terminal companies do, that would be their business, but if train services themselves were to be franchised separately, any equity in them would be retained in the ownership of the franchising authority. If this were to be, as is most likely, a public sector agency, then the objectives of the legislation would be compromised; and if it were not, then there would be an unnecessary intermediate level of commercial responsibility, having an ambiguous relationship with the railway companies. Proposals for franchising on bus services on any scale have come up against the vested interest of the franchisee at re-tendering, with the commercial distortions that have recently been observed in the television industry.

4.2 *Track Authority not needed* The case for separating railway operation from railway infrastructure rests solely upon the perceived desirability of commercial competition for "paths" in the track diagrams. It is argued here that the emergence of competition *per se* is not the real objective of privatisation. The argument for retaining the unified ownership of track and trains is powerful, and well illustrated by the costs imposed upon motorway users by track authorities with no incentive to provide for efficient movement of goods and passengers. Direct ownership of "track, terminals and signalling" is far more effective than any alternative in providing for the efficient movement of trains, and enabling railway companies to exploit their inherent advantage of track discipline.

4.3 *Cross-subsidy no problem* Parliament in the 1870s required the then monopolistic railway companies to provide for the maintenance of loss-making sectors out of profits made elsewhere. After 1930 the policy was extended to the bus companies. The result in both cases was disastrous, as the spread of car ownership after 1960 enabled people to opt out of this enforced bargain. The policy was also disastrous for the railways' competition with the road freight companies, and contributed to the late development and frequent misuse of sophisticated traffic costing skills.

4.4 The issue of "unremunerative" business should be the responsibility of the Regulator. To define cross-subsidy as arising where recipients are less than average total costs is a nonsense; no retailer expects the same margin on every line in the store. But where the Regulator is satisfied that a given quantum of service fails to earn enough to cover its "out-of-pocket" (marginal, or escapable) costs, then there may be a need for it to be "bought in" by subsidy; the cost to the public purse being minimised through the efficiency of private enterprise. This, it will be noted, is to carry the policy of the Low Report (see para 2.3) to its logical conclusion.

4.5 *A framework for policy* To achieve the objectives outlined in this paper, a possible process might be as follows:

4.5.1 The Department of Transport to take the advice of a suitable consultancy and of senior railway managers, and to identify portions of the system that would make commercial sense as independent railway companies. These should not be unduly influenced by existing or historic boundaries.

4.5.2 A second process of this kind should then identify the initial haulage and rolling stock requirements of these companies, and arrive at an initial allocation of assets. This should allow for the emergence of inter-working agreements, such as the former East Coast Main Line Committee.

4.5.3 A Bill should provide for [1] the establishment of a Regulator (OFFRAIL); [2] the definition of the new companies and the allocation of assets; [3] the process of tender for sale; and [4] the continuing regime, including the powers and duties of the Regulator, the establishment of the Clearing House, with its powers and duties, and the procedure for authorising new railway construction (without the need for a Private Bill).

4.6 *Concluding remarks* Since this paper attempts no more that an outline policy, there would of course be various issues to be addressed which have not been included here. It is hoped, though, that the Committee will find the ideas put forward of some interest. There is just one point, however, that needs to be stressed.

4.7 Because the recommendations provide for intergration of the infrastructure and movement aspects of the railways in the ownership of the independent companies, it is implicit that they will be freight as well as passenger carriers. This should not be allowed to inhibit the emergence of new kinds of entreprenurial activity, not least in terms of the opportunities offered by the opening of the Channel Tunnel. One of the duties of the Regulator must always be to ensure that the companies do not act, singly or in collusion, to inhibit innovation in the provision of new kinds of service. The experience of bus deregulation has shown that not all managers can be relied upon to abandon the traditions inherited from years of public control when they find themselves in the unfamiliar world of the market.

REFERENCES

Hibbs & Roth 1992: *Tomorrow's Way—Managing Roads in a Free Society*. Adam Smith Institute.

Low Report 1960: Report from the Select Committee on Nationalised Industries upon British Railways. HMSO.

4 December 1992

APPENDIX 96

MEMORANDUM FROM THE RAILWAY CONSULTANCY

We were interested to read in the *"Financial Times"* of various submissions made to the Transport Select Committee by potential private-sector rail operators. We have been carrying out extensive analysis for clients also interested in railway operation in a privatised environment, and, as Richard Branson suggested, we also believe that the charging mechanism for access to infrastructure is the key issue. However, we have also been able to derive a costing mechanism, which incorporates all the Government's desired objectives, as well as other objectives which we consider important (for instance, that the rate charged to an operator will not vary significantly over time according to changes in the sevices operated by others). We are pleased to include the draft of an article submitted to the *"Transport Economist"* journal setting out our method and the rationale behind it. We recommend it to you, and would be happy to discuss it further if required.

A Theoretical Basis for Apportioning Railway Costs—Nigel G Harris

INTRODUCTION

The British Government has set out in a recent White Paper (Cmnd 2012, HMSO, 1992) its intention to allow private operators onto the mainline railway network in Britain, whether to tender for existing services, or to provide wholly new ones. However, the White Paper did not set out the details of one key element of the Government's proposals—namely, the costing mechanism through which operators will be charged for the expenses the infrastructure authority (Railtrack) incurs in maintaining the network. These costing details are to be published towards the end of the year but, in the meantime, it is interesting to add to the debate on the subject which included a TEG meeting in June. What criteria should be used as the basis for costing? How will such criteria be measured? And by whom? How much cost is involved? This paper endeavours to provide some answers to these and other questions.

Criteria for Costing Mechanism:

The White Paper itself sets out a number of objectives which it is hoped the costing regime should achieve. They are:

"(a) to promote efficient operation;

(b) to promote competition and innovation;

(c) to encourage the efficient use of infrastructure and other resources;

(d) not to discriminate unfairly between competing operators and services; and

(e) to provide the means for financing investment in Railtrack's infrastructure."

To these one might add two others:

(f) to avoid large changes in the costs to operators which are due to changes in the operating practices of others; and

(g) to reflect as accurately as possible the actual costs incurred by the operation concerned, subject to some necessary simplifications.

The Economic Rationale

Briefly, the standard economic arguments for pricing in such a situation may be categorised as either marginal (suitable for short-run policy, when capacity is already in existence) or average (suitable when construction costs are also to be taken into account). The Government is unlikely to follow a marginal cost approach, since this certainly does not guarantee Railtrack an income which will enable it to cover its costs, let alone gain a return on investment, even if it would stimulate rail service provision. On the other hand, the standard average cost approach calculated on a line-by-line basis also has its disadvantages. For instance, two operators running the same level of service with identical vehicles but on different lines could be paying vastly different charges, depending on whether the route was shared with other traffic. This problem is particularly acute with passenger traffic, since it is in the majority in Britain but imposes far lower costs than freight traffic. Competition would therefore only be stimulated on mainlines, where individual operators could expect to be sharing the track costs with a number of other operators. Congestion effects would mean that the efficient use of infrastructure would also not be encouraged. There would also be political difficulties due to the closure pressures on less-used lines.

Therefore we must return to the criteria set out above, the last of which most nearly relates a charging mechanism to the underlying economic rationale for permanent way-related expenditure.

Theoretical Background:

Engineering theory states that the damage inflicted by trains on the permanent way and its associated structures is a function of three variables, thus:

Damage = f (total annual tonnage *axle load* speed^2)

This simple relationship could provide an excellent mechanism for determining the payments due from train operators to the infrastructure authority, provided it is also understood that the above equation only holds for a constant track quality; should one wish to improve the ride on a particular route, then additional costs would arise, and these are also thought to increase with the square of the ride quality index (which is the sum of the standard deviations of three measurements within a specified distance of track:

(i) the gauge;

(ii) the height of the left-hand running rail; and

(iii) the height of the right-hand running rail.)

Calculation of Payments:

Broadly-speaking, calibration of the above equation provides the basis for an efficient, fair and simple charging mechanism for over one-third of total railway costs (but nearly three-quarters of Railtrack's). Calibration is easily carried out using data from BR's Annual Report and Accounts, thus:

In 1991-92, BR spent approx £1.3 billion on track, structures, signalling and telecommunications, all of which are largely dependent on train mileage. They also ran approx 330 million train miles on this infrastructure, on which the damage caused is estimated at:

Damage $= 330m * 200$ tonnes/train $* 12$ tonnes/axle $* 70$ mph^2

$\qquad = 3.38 * 10^{15}$ units,

(if 300M tms of passenger trains are assumed to weigh 200 tonnes each, and 30M tms of freight trains 1000 tonnes each)

or nearly 3M units per £ spent.

(In fact, this figure may be low, as BR have been investing heavily in permanent way for Channel Tunnel services which have not yet begun, but similar calculations can be made in future).

As an example, an operator wishing to run one million train miles pa of trains weighing 40 tonnes, with a 10-tonne axle-load, and travelling at 70 m.p.h. maximum speed would therefore accrue

$1,000,000 * 40 * 10 * 70^2 = 1.96 * 10^{12}$ damage units, which should cost $2.234 * 10^{12} / 3M = £0.75M$ in track expenditure to repair.

Advantages of the Method:

There are a number of reasons why this method is to be recommended; these may be classified according to the criteria set out above:

(a,b,c) it is a fair and efficient system which guarantees that operators make the correct market response—if they run more, faster or heavier trains, which increase track wear and tear, then they will cause the infrastructure authority more expenditure but also become liable for more payments;

(e) it guarantees the infrastructure authority its return on investment—if an 8 per cent profit margin is required, then an 8 per cent markup can be introduced (also, pricing can be geared to include the costs of damage incurred by engineers' trains and equipment, which can be substantial on lines with low-frequency multiple-unit-operated services);

(f) it avoids large swings in annual payments, which make budgetting difficult for both train operator and infrastructure provider (the train operator will be faced with a huge increase in payment if another operator on the same line ceases to operate services, whilst the infrastructure authority are unlikely to see all operators simultaneously withdraw services without corresponding savings in expenditure).

(d,g) it is simple—train weights, speeds and annual mileages are all well-known; and

As the method satisfied all the criteria set out in paragraph 60 of the White Paper, as well as another key objective, it is to be firmly recommended.

To account for variations in quality, one could require Railtrack to maintain a base quality level (say a particular ride quality at 70 mph), with any additional quality required for higher speeds being funded from operators cogniscent of increases in speed (hence patronage) and reductions in vehicle requirement.

Terminals

The remaining one-quarter of Railtrack's costs will initially be station costs, pending the sale of terminals to the private sector. It is less easy to see how these costs can be allocated whilst retaining all the criteria set out above for permanent way costs. An analogous method, for instance, would be to attempt to calculate the number of station stops by all operators throughout the whole country, and to divide the station costs on this basis. However, unlike the input data requirements for the permanent way method, this is not a statistic that operators use for management purposes, and the huge numbers involved make it very unwieldy.

One could, of course, merely deal with each station separately, leaving operators to split any costs between them, but this could involve a great deal of bureaucracy unless stations with the same level of service were grouped together, as well as being ripe for legal debate. One operator might well take the lead, and any others might attempt to use a marginal cost argument for the costs that they impose, whilst the first operator would argue for average costs. This might well discriminate unfairly between competing operators and services, as the cost of calling at similar stations could vary very widely depending upon the other services provided, whilst individual operators will deliberately concentrate services at particular stations, in order to reduce costs. It also assumes that current management accounting practices are able to identify costs to individual stations.

There is, however, a significant possible improvement to the average cost approach for terminals. Although it would be theoretically-ideal to treat each station separately, this is unworkable in practice; nevertheless, given the vastly-varying size, complexity and structure of railway stations, some categorisation by type is vital. For instance, whilst new stations in West Yorkshire are being constructed at a cost of £300,000 or so, £4M has recently been spent at London's Paddington station on roof repairs alone. Not only in terms of expenditure do stations differ vastly—so do their development potentials and station trading levels. Isolated rural stations have few station trading possibilities, and development may be limited to converting the premises into residential property. On the other hand, city-centre stations have great trading potential, and sites may also give opportunities for lucrative office or retail development.

As far as categorisation goes, there seem to be no hard-and-fast rules, but one might suggest six categories, in decreasing order of cost:

1. Very large heritage stations with trading and development potential limited by architectural considerations (eg London St. Pancras, York, Edinburgh Waverley). (typically 8-15 platforms).

2. Very large urban stations with large trading and development potential (eg London Victoria, Birmingham New Street) (10-20).

3. Large stations with some trading and development potential (eg Doncaster, Birmingham International, Crewe, Inverness) (4-8).

4. Medium stations with limited trading and development potential (eg Durham, Oxford, Bridgend) (2-4).

5. Small stations with railway buildings (e.g. most of London's suburban stations) (2).

6. Very small unstaffed rural or urban halts without any buildings (1-2).

It is not clear whether the Government (either through Railtrack or even an non-transport body such as English Heritage) will contribute towards the upkeep of stations in the first category; if they do not, operators are likely to avoid them, which could have serious consequences for urban planning as well as transport provision.

A pragmatic cost allocation method would entail the allocation of every station in the country to one of the above categories, and the average station cost for each category to be computed. For each station, the (averaged) cost could be divided between operators on the basis of estimated passenger usage or the number of station stops, as already happens between London Underground and British Rail for the stations that they share. By using a category average, the volatility of costs arising from serving particular stations are reduced, as compared to dealing with the actual figures for each station.

However, the method still does not fully meet criterion (f) from above. Operators must therefore hope to improve their financial position as regards stations through trading and development, although the significantly-smaller sums of money involved in respect of stations relative to permanent way may mean that operators are less worried about apparent injustices.

CONCLUSIONS

Neither the average, nor the marginal, approach for infrastructure costing is without its problems if applied at the line-by-line level. However, this paper has showed how the largest category (of permanent way and related costs) could be apportioned by a system-wide average approach based on the actual damage caused by individual operations, and this method fulfils all the Government's criteria whilst also satisfying other important criteria. On the station cost side, though, the equivalent method is unworkable, but again a modification to the average cost approach involving the categorisation of stations is sensible. Here, costs representative of a particular category could be used, which would at least mean that operators were charged similar amounts for serving similar stations in different parts of the country, and large variations in payments between stations and years reduced in magnitude.

26 November 1992

APPENDIX 97

Letter from Mr G Smith

As you will of course know, there was a train collision at London Bridge on 25 November. Whilst everyone will be pleased it was not too serious, it does raise some vital issues in the privatisation debate.

At present BR has total responsibility for *all aspects* of such an incident (unless vandalism is involved) and there is no dubiety as to who should take particular courses of action. However, if we consider the situation that could exist under the government's proposals, I believe there is great cause for concern on safety and customer service issues. For example:

(i) The infrastructure would be owned by Railtrack;

(ii) The signalling maintenance may be contracted out;

(iii) The permanent way maintenance may be contracted out;

(iv) The trains involved may belong to different operators;

(v) The train crews involved may belong to a third party;

(vi) The nearest stations may be franchised to different operators;

(vii) The alternative diversionary transport systems, whether they be rail, underground or bus, may belong to further operators.

This scenario then begs answers to the following questions:

(i) Who is responsible for calling the emergency services?

(ii) Who is responsible for evacuation of casualties?

(iii) Who is responsible for recovery of vehicles?

(iv) Who is responsible for repair of the infrastructure?

(v) Who will *insist* that other transport operators assist with free passage for the thousands of delayed travellers—and how will they recover all the costs involved?

(vi) Who will be responsible for the customer service to injured and, possibly bereaved, people? At present BR do this very well from their customer service departments, but will these exist in a franchised situation of diverse operators?

(vii) Who will admit liability and thus passengers' legal problems to a minimum?

I am sure there are easy answers to some questions but, indeed, there may be even further questions to ask.

May I please request that your Committee considers these issues.

27 November 1992

APPENDIX 98

Memorandum from Messrs P B Whitehouse and C M Whitehouse

(A) WHITE PAPER

1. *General*

The Government's objective is to improve the quality of railway services by creating many new opportunities for private sector involvement. By creating a competitive environment rather than the current monopolistic one, improvements are likely and the private sector environment should be well placed to provide a higher quality of service and better value for money for the public who travel by rail, as the private sector method of operation is perhaps more accountable and better able to provide incentives for shareholders, management and staff than the public sector. By operating franchises for profit (or reduced subsidy) there is always the incentive to do better.

However, there are several hurdles created by the White Paper which need to be overcome and the Government's approach in granting franchises and agreeing sales within the ambit of the White Paper will depend on flexible solutions being adopted as envisaged by paragraph 12 of the White Paper if all the Government's objectives are to be achieved.

2. *Specific Issues*

(a) If quality of service is to be maintained and enhanced, as is the Government's stated objective, this will be dependent on the approach taken to the quality of the infrastructure, trains and staff. Dealing with each of these in turn: the infrastructure involves several critical dependencies, pathing, timetable, planning and capital improvements. If these are not carefully examined and planned for, then difficulties will arise. The recent announcement by Chris Green, Director of InterCity that there is unlikely to be any investment on the WCML except for safety purposes pre to 1998 is an example of how the Government need to re-think their attitude to infrastructure investment. Further, the capital investment in the construction of new trains needs to be re-thought as there is likely to be a stop on such new building from 1994 which, if not remedied, can hardly help the provision of quality of service by franchisees. As far as staff are concerned, whilst BR has many good people, if care is not taken in the implementation of the privatisation proposals, there will be a significant downturn in motivation as the proposals overturn the "operation for quality" initiative recently established, rather than build on the work which has been achieved. This will require extremely careful handling.

Furthermore, the essence of the privatisation proposals produce several layers of contractual obligations and requirements in addition to the command led business structure and this will increase the bureaucracy required and also increase the costs of operation which also tend to militate against quality.

The Government needs to consider its approach to infrastructure and trains and also to minimise the contractual obligations on the implementation of the White Paper in order to enhance quality of service.

(b) *Infrastructure Separation:* As the operation of trains and the maintenance and development of the track on which they run are to be separated, there needs to be a clear relationship between the Government, Railtrack and the franchisees (as well as the other relevant regulatory authorities) to provide an incentive to develop the infrastructure. This is particularly important as control of the infrastructure will be divorced from operation of trains and a clear dialogue through the Rail Regulator not only in law or contract but in practice will be imperative if benefits are to be achieved.

(c) *Open Access:* Generally speaking, we think that franchisees will require to operate the whole service pattern of trains on lines included within their franchise and will not be happy for predators to cream off profitable elements pursuant to the open access regime suggested.

The principle of open access is sound for different products or services but provides unrealistic competitive opportunities over many routes. To take two examples: first, open access has already been proven to work in the USA where the private companies own the infrastructure and operate freight trains but allow Amtrack to operate passenger trains on an open access basis. Second, some routes (especially rural and suburban routes) offer no real room for open access involvement as the trains operated are often on minimum requirements and subsidised by public grants anyway. Any further competition would be likely to increase costs and require additional grants without increasing the public benefit.

(d) *Charges:* The Government's attitude to charges is critical to the process of privatisation and this is duscussed in more detail in answering the specific questions set out in the press notice.

If Railtrack is not to qualify for any subsidies and operate at a profit then it appears that the cost of operating trains can only increase which may not help the Government's requirement for the quality of service to be enhanced as either private operators will be looking at ways to minimise costs or grant providers will need to increase their subsidy as a result.

An announcement on behalf of the Government as to how the costs of sharing the track will be worked out will be critical to the success of the privatisation process. If the cost is to be shared out equally across the train paths, than the operation of trains on an incremental basis (as for freight now) could spell either the end or a much reduced operation of such activities.

(B) SPECIFIC QUESTIONS

1. *What should be the aims and objectives of a privatised railway? What are the attractions for the private sector?*

A private operator should aim to run an efficient transport system for profit, improving the quality of service and, where applicable, requiring lower grants.

The private sector may well be interested in providing lease finance for rolling stock. It will also be interested in operating the profitable routes (subject to track charges and open access requirements) and it may also be interested in operating those services for which a 100 per cent PSO grant is available, together with the operation of maintenance and repair facilities. Subject to determining costs of operation, a significant part of the network (expected to be Regional Railways) may well fall to be operated by BR for some considerable time unless incentives are provided.

2. *Is there any conflict between the principle of open access and the granting of exclusive franchises?*

In essence, these two concepts are almost impossible to reconcile. Anyone seeking to operate on the open access principle would be likely to seek train paths at the times most attractive to the market, thus abstracting the prime business from a franchisee who has to operate to a carefully regulated standard and level of service.

The only area where open access seems to be a practical proposition is when it is applied for by an operator in a completely different market area from the franchisee, eg, a freight operator running trains over an InterCity network. However, this would still require careful control of track access and timetabling.

If exclusive franchises are to be granted, care will need to be taken to deal with the private operations currently authorised, for example, certain trainload freight and passenger charter operations.

3. *Who should do the strategic planning for our railways and how can different interests be co-ordinated? For example, can freight develop effectively on a primarily passenger network?*

The Government appears to have no current strategic transport policy in this country, which it should have. Strategic planning for railways should not be taken in isolation to strategic planning for transport generally, in particular roads.

The privatisation proposals in effect seek to turn the railways into something more akin to roads and care must be taken to ensure that any decoupling of infrastructure planning from service planning and operation does not resolve in a mis-match. Consequently, the establishment of the independent regulatory is likely to be crucial in this field.

As far as the concept of developing freight on a primary passenger network is concerned, this can certainly be done as history shows us. Except in the most intense urban or suburban situations, the marginal addition of facilities required for effective freight traffic movement must be more economical than providing comparable enhancement to a road network and it also adds to the earning power of the basic railway infrastructure by broadening its market base. Every day examples from British Rail and European operations clearly demonstrate this as a basic fact. The regulated nature of rail traffic make it ideal for such mixing of traffic. More so, in many instances, than road where mixing often reduces the overall levels of safety to the public.

4. *What will be the Government's role in subsidy and investment? In what circumstances will cost-benefit appraisal be appropriate, and what criteria should be used for future rail investment?*

The Government's role in subsidy and investment will be crucial and this seems to be an area where, so far, no conclusions have been reached, partly because it has not yet been decided whether road and rail are to operate on a "level playing field" or not.

The Government should consider the costs of the proposed road building plans and the proportion of the costs which relate to the movement of commercial freight. It is suggested that the costs of maintaining and, to some extent, enhancing the current rail network to encourage the movement of freight by rail would be much less than the costs of developing the road network and would also have a great social benefit.

The criteria to be used for future rail investment will depend on whether or not the Government adopt a strategy policy as a whole, taking into account the quality of service, social benefis and subsidy/investment required for the country's transport services and then deciding how best they may be met.

The same cost benefit criteria and measures of theoretical rates of return should be used for all transportation methods.

5. *Railtrack, the track authority, will charge all operators "commercial" rates for track use. What principles should be used to set these charges?*

Until the answer to the preceding question has been determined, it is not possible to answer this question. The alternatives are to set charges relating to direct costs or to subsidise charges (on a similar basis to the way road are subsidised) taking into account political/social values.

At present, it is clear that the infrastructure costs are subsidised by the Government and if subsidy is not continued then the costs to franchisees and potential train operators will increase over and above the current cost in the public sector. This is likely to make privatisation unattractive generally speaking.

In any event, if the Government wishes to proceed with the privatisation of the railways, it will need to disclose its intended price structure in order that potential franchisees and operators can see what they will need to deal with and establish their business plans.

It seems inevitable that the privatisation proposals will require the total Government subsidy to increase not only because Railtrack is to operate without subsidy thus increasing the costs of a potential franchisee which is unlikely to be met by increasing ticket charges, but also because currently the operation of one national network allows cash savings by British Rail through economies of scale which may well not be open to individual franchisees.

6. *How should franchises operate so as to maximise the public interest, both for profitable and subsidised services?*

Franchisees should seek to improve quality of service, provide value for money, liaise with other public and private services and consider the social benefit of the provision of their services to the community. These objectives should apply to both profitable and subsidised services.

The public interest in the operation of rail transport must be to have the highest quality of service measured by providing a service easy to use at an affordable cost which is safe, reliable and comfortable.

7. *What arguments are there for switching immediately to a regime of rolling stock leasing for all operators, including BR? What are the White Paper's implications for BR's on-going rolling stock investment programme?*

There seems to be much in favour of a regime for rolling stock leasing from almost every viewpoint. Apart from financial advantages to the operator (including BR) the consumer will also benefit because rolling stock would be available to every potential operator and not necessarily be tied to the fortunes of any particular franchisee or operator. A leasing regime is likely to maintain and probably increase the quality of rolling stock, both in concept and maintenance requirements. Looking at what has happened to some bus fleets following de-regulation of bus operation provides a salutary lesson which it is hoped will be avoided with railways.

It seems that the White Paper has blighted investment, particulary in rolling stock but also in relation to local authority funded developments. The effect of this hiatus on Britain's railway industry base is almost as disastrous in the medium term as its effect on the rolling stock fleet. In the long term, the effect on the industry is likely to shrink our national industrial capacity further and adversely affect our balance of payments and potential for adding value in the economy, as successful franchisees and operators may well have to seek rolling stock from overseas.

8. *How is the value of stations be be assessed and what will be the relationship between a privately owned station and BR's operation of trains therefrom?*

We believe this part of the White Paper has now been dropped and that stations will not be sold. Consequently, it is probably not necessary to assess how the value of stations is to be arrived at.

If the Government seeks to make Railtrack "commercial" then it must be given the maximum earning power, including potential to gain income and capital from BR's present property assets. The alternative is merely a form of asset stripping where any income would not be re-invested in the railway infrastructure.

Unlike the massive task of safety validating huge numbers of property owners, it would be a simpler task to safety validate Railtrack as station owner which would then lease certain areas and facilities to operators (possibly as part of any track assess/franchise arrangements) and to third parties as normal commercial arrangements (as now). This approach would prevent operators entering the market solely to strip assets or direct activities away from their prime main of operating a rail service.

9 December 1992

APPENDIX 99

CENTRE FOR POLICY STUDIES LTD

Thank you for inviting the Centre for Policy Studies to submit evidence to the Select Committee's inquiry into the future prospects for the railway system in the light of the Government's proposals for privatisation.

This submission aims to highlight some of the gains which might be expected to be achieved from the disaggregation of British Rail, the introduction of private capital into the industry and the fostering of a competitive market in rail services. In preparing this short paper I have benefited from the helpful advice of various members of the Centre's Privatisation Study Group. In my role as a Research Fellow of the Centre, I act as Secretary to this Group.

The privatisation of British Rail is going to be a major and complicated task. Inevitably there may be some difficult transitional problems encountered along the way. Nevertheless, we believe these difficulties are worth tackling in order to gain the expected benefits which we outline in this submission. Our evidence focuses on what we believe to be the most compelling arguments in favour of privatising British Rail. These are listed below under ten headings:

(1) *A New Spirit of Enterprise and Innovation*

Freeing the railways from state ownership is likely to provide the opportunity to harness a new spirit of enterprise and innovation in the industry. The involvement of private capital should lead to a new "can do" private enterprise culture which can be expected to transform employee morale. Opening up what has hitherto been a statutory state monopoly to a range of competing companies will provide the opportunity to try out a range of new services, pricing structures and working practices.

For the first time, customers will be able to choose between competing services and their differing requirements will be signalled through the market to a range of rival rail operators. Private operators' profits will be determined by their ability to satisfy consumer needs.

(2) *A New Management Freedom to Manage*

Private rail companies, unshackled from the debilitating effects of government intervention, will have a new freedom to manage. In common with many nationalised industries, one of the major problems besetting British Rail is that it has been over-managed. Since the railways were nationalised in 1947, management has steadily grown top heavy. Part of the reason for this was the attempt to integrate an additional layer of business management on to the existing regional tiers of management, inherited from the former railway companies such as GWR. Attempts to mesh together these two management structures have never proved satisfactory.

New railway operators can be expected to streamline management and focus it on the operational management function. This should produce substantial efficiency gains in comparison with the layers of bureaucratic management and administration which so typify British Rail.

(3) *New Working Practices*

Many talented people currently work for British Rail. However, it remains questionable whether their talents are fully utilised. One of the main advantages of privatising British Rail will be the ability of the new private operators to introduce new working practices such as split shifts and part-time working, tailored to the peaks and troughs of consumer demand. Private operators are also likely to devote more attention to staff training because the profitability of their companies will depend on the quality of staff they employ and the service they provide to customers. In vivid contrast with the position since 1947, where there has only been one monopoly employer, the splintering of the rail industry into a number of competing companies should provide greater career choice for those people working in the industry. For example, this might lead to more women train drivers.

(4) *Greater Access*

In pursuing its policy of privatisation the Government is taking the approach underpinning the European Community Directive 91/440 a logical step further. Directive 91/440, which comes into force on 1 January 1993, allows operators of international services access onto other countries' national rail networks.

The Government is seeking to extend the logic of this approach to domestic services within the UK. For the first time in at least half a century we can look forward to the emergence of a contestable market in rail transport. These much-needed reforms to the supply side of the industry will generate a further benefit, namely greater consumer choice.

(5) *Greater Consumer Choice*

The customer will benefit from a competitive private industry both for freight and passenger services. For the first time, the customer will be able to exercise choice. Competing operators will offer different combinations of prices, seating arrangements, entertainment, catering, and other passenger services. For freight users, privatisation will encourage substantial new investment in rail freight, exploiting the new opportunities which will be presented by the channel tunnel link. As the Government consultation paper, "New Opportunities for the Railway" (Cm 2012), points out, the disaggregation and sale of BR's freight operations, serving a wide range of business markets, would encourage greater specialisation and the exploitation of new intermodal technologies, allowing the transfer of freight between road and rail.

(6) *Access to International Capital Markets*

As a public corporation, British Rail is precluded from raising capital on the international capital markets. At the moment it must borrow from the government, through the National Loans Fund and similar government sources.

Private companies will be able to draw on far more flexible sources of capital, including the euro-capital markets. Banks and other financial institutions can be expected to devise specifically tailored packages to meet the requirements of rail operators and those companies involved in the rail freight market. Financial engineering for new road and rail infrastructure projects is likely to become an increasingly important aspect of international project finance. For example, the proposed high speed link between Madrid and Barcelona will be funded through a combination of public and private finance, the Dutch are planning to franchise a new rail link between Rotterdam and the German border, and the German government announced in July 1992 that it plans to privatise the German rail system.

A further aspect of this more sophisticated approach to rail finance will be the likely emergence of a new industry in the shape of railway leasing companies, providing locomotives and rolling stock to new entrants into the industry. A parallel can be drawn with specialist aircraft leasing companies which facilitate improved access into the airline industry.

(7) *Ability to Exploit Economies of Density*

Whereas there are few economies of scale or scope in the railway industry the academic literature does suggest that there are significant economies of density to be exploited. Economies of density refer to potential savings achieved through a more intensive use of fixed assets. In the case of rail, such economies can be expected to be achieved from several rail operators running competing services on the same piece of track. On reflection, this can be seen to be sheer common sense: the greater the number of passenger trains or freight services using a particular line of route, the lower the charges borne by each individual operator using the rail track and associated infrastructure. In turn, consumers can expect to benefit from these economies of density through lower prices.

(8) *More Accurate Identification of Costs*

In the press notice announcing the Committee's inquiry into rail privatisation the Committee ask whether there is any conflict between the principle of open access and the granting of exclusive franchises? Initially, it might be felt that there was a danger of new entrants "cherry picking" the most profitable rail services operated by the incumbent franchisee, for example, peak hour commuter services.

However, on closer consideration it can be argued that "cherry picking" abnormal profits or monopoly rents earned on certain rail services, is no bad thing. As the moment, profitable rail services tend to cross subsidise other loss making services which might be run for social reasons, for example, those rural services with very few passengers. In the past governments have tended to encourage this practice as politicians often find the identification of the true cost of subsides embarrassing. Consequently, there is a tendency towards obfuscation.

Free market competition exposes the true costs of operating a service. Futhermore, competition encourages downward pressure on prices as new entrants apply new thinking, whether it be new technology, new working practices or better design to the satisfaction of customer demand. In reality, this is how all industries improve and customers gain a better deal. Unfortunately, statutory state monopolies tend to safeguard existing practises and inhibit new thinking on the development of a product or service.

(9) *Competition for Subsidy*

Taxpayers currently fund blanket subsidies to a range of rail services through what is referred to as the Public Service Obligation (PSO) grant. In 1991–92 this subsidy totalled £892 million, a substantial increase on the year before when the PSO grant amounted to £642 million.

As emphasised above, the introduction of a competitive rail industry will expose the costs of running specific rail services to the public gaze.

Under the Government's privatisation plans, private operators will have the opportunity to bid competitively for subsidy, where it is needed. On the evidence provided by competitive tendering in the bus industry, this approach should reduce the level of subsidy required. For example, in a study of bus deregulation in the United Kingdom, Dr Stephen Glaister, Reader in Transport Economics at the London School of Economics, has concluded that "The primary objective of the (Government's) bus policy was to greatly reduce subsidies to local bus services rapidly, without undue fares increases and without cutting service levels. In this it was successful: competition led to cost and subsidy reductions, and bus kilometres run substantially increased" (see Dr S Glaister, *Bus Deregulation in the UK,* a paper presented to the World Bank Transport Regulation Seminar, Baltimore, June 1990).

Accordingly, the adoption of a system of competitive tendering for loss making rail services is likely to reduce the level of support currently provided by the taxpayer. This will be achieved through harnessing the entrepeneurial skills and energies of the private sector to explore whether loss making services can be provided more efficiently, as has been shown in the bus industry. Prices will be aligned more closely to true costs, and cross subsidisation is likely to be replaced by explicit subsidy.

(10) *Clearer Articulation of Government Transport Policy*

The disaggregation and sale of British Rail can also be expected to lead to a clearer articulation of Government transport policy, particularly with regard to public policy towards competing modes of transport, ie road, rail, air, etc. Currently, the Government adopts a covert transport policy—the sum of its policies on taxation, subsidy, licensing and investment on trunk roads, rail, airports, and so on. These policies are enshrined in the Department of Transport annual expenditure plans (for example, see *Department of Transport Report,* Cm. 1907).

Privatising the railways is likely to bring into sharper focus the relationship between road and rail. For instance, if the Government genuinely wishes to encourage more freight on to rail, it must examine the total cost of providing a highway system for the road haulage industry. Road pricing and tolled motorways are both means towards achieving a more economically rational method of allocating freight traffic between road and rail. At present road hauliers pay an annual fixed road licence; there is no marginal charge for each journey. In this regard, rail is seriously disadvantaged, since freight customers are charged for each individual journey.

Similarly, for the private motorist, the introduction of road pricing and tolled highways is likely to lead to a more economically efficient use of the road system, whilst at the same time easing congestion problems. The introduction of charges for the marginal use of motor vehicles is also likely to make the alternative of rail travel more attractive.

The introduction of private capital into the railways is likely to encourage a more explicit articulation of Government policy on how the various modes of transport should inter-relate. Private investors will want to know about the policy considerations influencing how rail is allowed to compete against road and airline services. Thus, the Government will need to explain the reasoning behind the regulatory rules and fiscal policy which it formulates since these will determine the ways in which the different modes of transport compete against one another.

Conclusion

In this short submission we have sought to identify a number of the reasons why the Government's plan to introduce private capital and competition into the railways can be expected to generate real consumer benefits. The proper aims and objectives of a privatised railway can be summed up as providing a competitive, efficient service tailored to meet customer requirements. Where there are compelling social reasons for doing so, certain rail services can be supported through subsidy, but on a competitive tendered basis. The Government's role should be to act as a specifier of standards, not as a provider. This specifier role can be performed most appropriately at arm's length through the regulatory institutions outlined in the Government's consultation paper, *"New Opportunities for the Railways"* (Cm. 2012).

I trust this evidence proves helpful and illuminates certain points. Please let me know whether the Committee has any further queries on this submission.

14 December 1992

APPENDIX 100

Letter from Railstore Ltd to The Secretary of State for Transport

We refer to the letter to you dated 2 December 1992 from Robert Adley MP, regarding the loss of freight business by British Rail.

Today we have been informed by British Rail that they are about to reduce the level of their freight services to 'Anglia', in our case from daily service to a twice a week service. Similar levels of service are to be implemented for the three other freight depots included in the loosely described area of 'Anglia'. We thought at first that they had come to see us so that a study could be made of the likely impact upon their freight business in the area, but it is obvious that this aspect has not been studied at all.

There appears to be some vague hope that not too much traffic will revert to road but BR freely admits that some will.

When most of the business world is attempting to improve its levels of service (we have attained BS 5750) BR choose to reduce theirs and so put in jeopardy most of their business in this area.

We keep reading that the Government's policy is to take lorries off the road by encouraging the transfer of the freight to rail. We are sure we will be forgiven for not believing this so called 'policy' when the Government does nothing to stop British Rail doing exactly the opposite.

The correct course is for a proper study to be made of all aspects of this proposal including the business aspect (ie what view do our customers have) and hence how much traffic will be lost to set against the so called 'savings'. To enable this to take place early in 1993 BR should maintain its present level of service until it is complete, and we ask you to intervene immediately to ensure that they do not put this partly studied proposal into effect from 25 January 1993 which is the date they have arbitrarily imposed.

15 December 1992

APPENDIX 101

Letter from Mr J Andrews

Only a few months ago, the then Transport Secretary announced that he favoured an increase in the carriage of freight on the railways, and that the appropriate grant would be offered to new rail customers, where appropriate. If that is indeed Government policy, it seems unfortunate to say the least, that the decline in the amount of freight carried by BR is accelerating with near break-neck speed, now. First, there was the abolition of "Speedlink" followed by the sad collapse of both Charterrail and Tiger Rail. Now, the latest issues of "Rail" and "Railway Magazine" report the loss or cessation of the following freight flows:

(1) Two "Castle Cement" block trains from Lancashire to Glasgow and Tyneside.

(2) Closure of the Eastgate terminal of "Blue Circle" cement and an end to the Northfleet-Theale cement traffic.

(3) No more cars between Longbridge and the Bathgate (Glasgow) terminal.

(4) No more traffic to two Metal Box Co. factories at Wisbech and Westhoughton.

(5) No more bulk fuel on the West Highland line.

(6) An end to the bulk cider from Taunton Cider Co.'s works, at Taunton; this shared freight working with:

(7) Fitzgerald Lighting wagon load traffic from Bodmin, now to cease.

As if that was not bad news enough, in *one week,* there is news of the closure of three rail-served steel terminals in the West Midlands; the closure of the BR works at Cardiff (Cathays); the closure of the Powell-Duffryn wagon works near Cardiff.

I confess that I am but a mere rail enthusiast and occasional rail user, and thus would never claim to comment with any degree of professional competency. However, it is surely the case that BR's pricing policy, when negotiating contracts with customers, is hindered by the requirement that BR shows a profit (8 per cent?) on all investment, capital outlay and operational costs. When passed on to customers, this inevitably must make the road haulage option ever more attractive to them, a totally unfair advantage.

With the rail privatisation Bill attracting more and more media coverage, may I ask you, as a staunch advocate and supporter of the many advantages of railways, to use your influence and office to highlight this appalling run-down of the rail freight network, on BR. If, indeed, we see BR sold off, piece meal, to the private sector one can easily envisage the total end of rail-borne freight, apart from maybe a few bulk loads, such as coal, petroleum, aggregates and some metals. Perhaps some good will come from the projected freight flows from Europe, through the Channel Tunnel, but that is still a long way off yet. Meanwhile, we seem about to lose more railway-related jobs, and the number of heavy lorries on the roads looks set to increase, without end.

12 December 1992

APPENDIX 102

FITZGERALD LIGHTING LTD

As we will lose our rail freight service in mid-December, I feel now is the appropriate time to write to you personally. I have followed closely your support for railways over the years and I note particularly your involvement on the Rail Transport Committee and the report circulated from yesterday's meeting.

It is very important to try to obtain an overall view as to what HMG is pushing BR into, with reduction of traffic and the effects of the general downturn in manufacturing, coal and Ravenscraig closures.

I note particularly the comments made by Sir Bob Reid, concerning train load freight. However, that benefit may be steadily eroded. The situation with Taunton Cider and Charterail is indicative of BR trying to get maximum revenue for the infrastructure. In many cases, traffic does not go from private siding to private siding, but to centralised operations so it may run in semi-train load traffic between centres. This means an onerous handling cost has to be added, that cost "kills" the economies of the whole movement.

Our economies in sending two wagons per week to each of three destinations have now finally petered out. There will be very little system ability left with BR to allow for the growth of traffic, only an excellent system for reduction.

I have kept my own MP, Mr Paul Taylor, informed on this and I am certain that you do read the technical journals, giving the greater detail. It is interesting that the Swedes are now stating that BR and the Government are not necessarily correct in what they are trying to achieve with the separate track authority and the method they are using for charging.

4 December 1992

APPENDIX 103

Letter from Mr G Q Simpson

I have taken the liberty, as a member of British Rail staff, to write to you in your capacity as Chairman of the committee on rail privatisation. I feel you should be aware of the rapidly growing demoralisation of my colleagues as we see our industry cease to invest, freight traffic taking to the roads (despite the Government's "hopes"), our supply industry running out of orders, and all the benefits of a unified, national network about to be thrown away.

May I urge you to press the Government to act quickly so that the damaging uncertainty is ended and sensible investment decisions can be taken. May I also urge that the following be adopted as Government policy:

1. A strategic transport policy, including provision for renewal of railway infrastructure and assets.
2. Continuity of rail investment in the transfer to privatised operation.
3. Positive action to transfer freight from road to rail.
4. Fair treatment for existing rail staff including real protection for conditions of service and travel concessions.
5. Protection for present and future rail pensioners.
6. Preservation of the existing national rail passenger timetable.
7. Continuation of existing national railcard schemes.

3 December 1992

APPENDIX 104

Letter from Mr J R Wilber

PRIVATISATION OF BRITISH RAIL

I am writing to express my extreme concern and grave reservations over the Government's proposals to privatise British Rail. As a regular traveller, I feel the whole concept is flawed. Should the privatisation proceed, the country will experience reduced services overall, with few improvements and considerable detriment.

At present British Rail offers an integrated service between its various types of passenger train services. But already, as a result of a major reorganisation of the railway's businesses into Network SouthEast, InterCity and Regional Railways, together with the Government policy that they should be as profitable as possible in order to reduce the demand on subsidy, the passenger is seeing unrealistic high fares, service reductions, shorter train lengths leading to crowding, and investment programmes being cut. As a daily passenger, I am also seeing the other side to the railway operation which will be magnified if privatisation takes place viz: InterCity, Network SouthEast and Regional Railways trains do not necessarily make convenient connections into or out of each others services, nor do they help each other out in times of problems.

I am convinced that, for people who travel by rail, the Government's proposals represent a real threat to the continued existence of an integrated system, availability of the various Railcards and Saver tickets as well as the ability to continue the "walk on" facility that has always been one of the best features of our railway system. New companies taking over our railway services are certain to have their own views on the fares they want to charge and are certain to insist on a pre-booking and reservation system. Suppose one has a ticket for the John Smith express and is delayed and miss it; you most certainly will not be permitted to just walk onto the next Fred Bloggs train as you can onto the next BR service irrespective of the "owning" business.

If privatisation proposals are proceeded with some passengers may experience service improvements but I fear the majority will see no change or a worsening of service. This will lead to people deciding to reject rail in favour of their cars. All the evidence from abroad suggests that improved public transport leads to less acute problems of road traffic congestion and this, in turn, improves the ecology of the country through less car emissions.

Britain's railways receive less Government support than those of any other country in Europe. Privatisation is not the answer. It will lead to even higher fares, more service cuts and the probable closure of unprofitable lines, particularly in rural areas where the railway represents an important lifeline. What is needed is Government commitment to public transport and the railway in particular. The railway is a national asset and as such should remain in national ownership. Perhaps though, it should be released from the straightjacket of Treasury funding and the Railway's Board permitted to seek extra investment from the Private Sector.

Please do not allow the Government's privatisation proposals to be fact.

8 December 1992

APPENDIX 105

Letter from Mr P B Doggett

I am writing to you as a concerned railway user and because I know that you both understand the industry and are chairman of the Transport Select Committee. I have just purchased my December copy of Modern Railways. In it I read that as a result of privatisation the following things may or are happening:

(1) investment tails off rapidly in two to three years leaving BR underfunded and the rail industry very short on orders. Yet orders from new franchise operators may not arrive in time to fill the gap;

(2) that railfreight is in sharp decline as it attempts to meet an eight per cent return on assets policy, yet without any consideration on the effect that this will have on future operators;

(3) that privatisation plans are delayed because of parliamentary time, further increasing uncertainty;

(4) that present privatisation plans require a complete restructure of BR just after they have completed a restructure. The cost of the new changes in morale and money are probably unknown;

(5) that the National Timetable will cease to exist, meaning that it will become harder to plan a journey and as different operators may not talk to each other that journeys may become more difficult as connections vanish;

(6) that cheap through fares may well disappear, in fact, many through fares may vanish when franchise operators refuse to accept each others tickets;

(7) that the successful and very useful travelcard in London (which I use to travel to work from SE to NW London) may vanish or have limited application as operators opt out.

I am not against privatisation in principle but at the moment the benefits of it seem somewhat illusory in comparison to the potential losses. I am not sure what your opinion is of the privatisation plans but is there nothing that can be done to bring the Government more to account for its plans? Any private company proposing a major change without having analysed it first would be given a massive vote of no confidence by the shareholders, but governments seem to be able to get away with murder!

I would ask you in whatever way you can to press ministers on these and other issues so that rail users may be protected and better informed about the changes that are to occur. I believe that careful planning and policy changes could make out railways play a more effective role in the nations economy.

I am not sure if party loyalty allows you to express your thoughts to me on the privation plans, but I do thank you for reading this letter and letting a concerned rail user express his anxiety.

1 December 1992

APPENDIX 106

THE NATIONAL COUNCIL OF WOMEN OF GREAT BRITAIN

RAILWAY TRANSPORT

I have pleasure in notifying you of a resolution passed and ratified at our Annual Conference/Annual General Meeting held in Harrogate in November 1992.

> The National Council of Women in Conference assembled calls upon Her Majesty's Government to retain overall responsibility for the expansion and development of British Railway Services (both passenger and freight), as an environmentally necessary alternative to increased reliance on road transport with its heavy cost in terms of road building, road accidents and air pollution.

The National Council of Women appreciates that much had already been done to modernise and promote Britain's railways, but we attach great importance to its continued expansion and development.

Whatever the outcome of the privatisation debate, we are anxious that the Government should maintain overall responsibility for the future of the railways, to ensure that the network is not reduced or allowed to deteriorate.

The high cost of road maintenance, increasing numbers of road accidents, health hazards from pollution, increasing consumption of finite resources and economic damage to industry from traffic congestion all indicates that road transport is not an acceptable alternative.

The National Council of Women, therefore, calls upon you to use your efforts and influence to bring about an improved and more efficient rail system, both passenger and freight.

7 December 1992

APPENDIX 107

Letter from Mr D R Smith

RAIL PRIVATISATION

I must express my very real concern that BR is on the verge of losing a large amount of its freight traffic. This would have severe knock-on effects for the viability of other freight services, and some knock-on effect to passenger services. Many rail routes are in danger of closing.

Privatisation, particularly if it is accompanied by a charging structure for the use of the infrastructure which bears no relation to the taxes levied on road users, will only make matters worse.

It is therefore important that

(1) Rail lines are not allowed to be closed and tracks be ripped up, or land sold

(2) Rail users pay a tax/licence fee for use of the network which is comparable to road users.

(3) Surplus coaches/freight vehicles which are modern and in good condition must be retained rather than scrapped.

25 November 1992

APPENDIX 108

GREAT GRIMSBY BOROUGH COUNCIL

From May 1993 the Cleethorpes to Kings Cross InterCity daily service (via Grimsby) is to be withdrawn. The service runs once a day in each direction and it is our only direct rail link with the capital. The decision to remove it is ill-timed and will have a significant impact on the local economy of Grimsby.

The population of the urban centre of Grimsby and Cleethorpes is about 150,000. One in three of the workforce is directly employed in the food, chemical, tourism and port sectors of the local economy, with many more jobs indirectly dependent upon them. Since the dramatic overnight collapse of the deep-sea fishing industry in the mid-1970's it might appear to the outsider that the area has little to offer the business community. Indeed, over the last 15 years unemployment has consistently been above the UK average.

Over the last 10 years, however, there has been a notable diversification of the local economy away from fishing-related employment towards the four principal sectors mentioned above. Grimsby is now known as "Europe's Food Town" thanks to its expertise in this field, and business, the Local Authority and the community have combined to make the best of the Humber Bank, the port (particularly in relation to the Single European Market) and the potential for tourism.

Nevertheless, the area's peripherality in relation to the rest of the UK, and particularly London, remains a substantial disadvantage. Every firm in the area is likely to need to attend business meetings in London, and medium and large sized firms will need to do so on a regular basis. Indeed, our direct InterCity service has been used as a means of encouraging businesses to set up in the area.

Tourists, too, are an important factor in the local economy. Cleethorpes is a popular seaside resort with enormous potential for the private leisure market. In Grimsby itself, we recently opened the National Fishing Heritage Centre which has attracted over 100,000 visitors in its first 12 months, many of whom travelled by train.

In all of our discussions with British Rail, it has been argued that Regional Railways will compensate for the InterCity withdrawal. The need to change trains, however, has a significant impact on demand, as BR's own market models readily acknowledge. It will clearly be a deterrent for business people to have to collect all of their papers together, or for a mother to carry young children from platform to platform. And, of course, there is no guarantee that the connecting train will be on time.

InterCity have argued that their decision to withdraw the Cleethorpes service has been made purely on financial grounds. Despite this, they have been wary of providing a full access to their financial data. This led Great Grimsby Borough Council (together with a consortium of Local Authorities along the route) to appoint transport consultants (1) to assess InterCity's case. The findings suggest that the withdrawal has been made upon questionable savings.

South Humberside has the highest concentration of railfreight in the UK. In recognition of this, and as part of the promotion of the Humber Ports, a consortium of Local Authorities from Ireland to Northern Germany has been formed under the title "Green Links to Europe" with the aim of transferring freight from road to rail. We believe that any reduction to services in South Humberside could have longer-term effects on this desirable shift.

Perhaps most pertinently, it should be noted that the reduction in demand for InterCity services has coincided with the recession. This has had a particularly severe effect upon tourist/leisure demand. As Steer, Davies, Gleave concluded: "A relatively high proportion of leisure travellers suggest a scenario whereby the onset of recession, the adverse timings of the early morning departure (from South Humberside) and the increasing restrictions on Saver tickets will have contributed to patronage decline."

CONCLUSION

There are two sides to our conclusions. The first relates directly to the current situation, where InterCity has a remit to provide its services at a profit, with no Government subsidy. Given this scenario, it must be recognised that all of the factors listed—an economy with substantial potential, a growing tourism market, the temporary effects of recession and the promotion of railfreight potential through the Humber Ports— point to a *temporary* down-turn in demand. It is also clear that at least one direct daily InterCity link with the capital is crucial for the economic development of an urban area the size of Grimsby. InterCity's decision is based on short-term considerations which will have long-term detrimental effects on our prosperity and quality of life.

There is, however, a different scenario which sees rail services as being fundamental to regional policy. British Rail is a service not an industry, and as such its duty should be to ensure a level of mobility which in part redresses regional imbalances. This concept is already acknowledged by the Government in its subsidies to Regional Railways, and Great Grimsby Borough Council believes that the same principle should be extended to all InterCity routes currently under threat. We urge you to consider our case very carefully.

16 December 1992

APPENDIX 109

NATIONAL COUNCIL ON INLAND TRANSPORT

We note from your chairman's letter (Railway Gazette International, December 1992), that your committee is still open to evidence from organisations without a direct commercial interest.

We are, as you know, greatly concerned by the Government's proposals, which, although apparently intended to improve our railway system, are, we feel, likely to have precisely the opposite effect. We have been following closely the evidence given to your committee, and have noted that only one or two witnesses have stated that, under certain conditions, the proposed changes might offer a chance of improving the system; the vast majority have been openly opposed to the proposals, and none have had answers to several of the very serious questions which your committee members have put to them.

We have been particularly concerned with the proposed splitting up of the network, the loss of through ticketing (except at full fare), the loss of interavailability of tickets (important in the event of change of journey plans and especially for return journeys) both in respect of different routes and different operators, the almost certain loss of travel inducement arrangements, designed to sell spare capacity, such as network, senior citizen, family and young persons cards, the consequences of bankruptcy of a franchisee, and the danger of the system becoming set in a rigid mould, development being almost impossible because of dismemberment between different franchisees and authorities.

We have also been very worried by two matters already apparent:

(1)   the diversion of freight traffic to the roads, presumably the result of instructions from the BRB to managers that all traffic must be charged sufficiently to yield an 8 per cent profit, regardless of whether this renders rail uncompetitive with road;

(2)   the uncertainty caused by the privatisation proposals, which has led to cessation of orders for the railway manufacturing industry.

The effects of (1) will soon be apparent in further loads on our already overloaded road system, leading to more accidents and higher maintenance costs, borne by the taxpayer, and to higher rail rates and fares. (2) will lead, not only to up to 30,000 more direct job losses, but, perhaps of even greater importance, to the destruction of a significant British industry, and, for perhaps a decade, great difficulty in obtaining new equipment. You will remember that to circumvent the EC requirement that as from 1993, all European rail equipment contracts should be open to bidders in all EC countries, most European manufacturers now have order books full for at least the next five years. Moreover, owing to the British loading gauge, British orders for locomotives and rolling stock will be for non-standard sized equipment, will therefore not be able to be ordered as extensions of Continental orders, and will cost more.

We feel that whatever may be the possible theoretical benefits of privatising the railway system, the one thing which is clear is that *now is not the right time* to attempt this upheaval. To overcome the effects of inadequate investment and errors of judgment in recent years, the Government must allow the railway system to invest adequately—either from private sources or if necessary from public sources—to produce a level playing field on which rail can compete effectively with road. It is equally important for such fair competition that road traffic pays as it goes—this requires some form of road pricing, eg, increased fuel tax replacing vehicle excise duty and possibly third party insurance.

When, with due payment from the community for external benefits provided by rail to the community, rail becomes financially profitable, privatisation, in the form of partial share ownership by individuals, will be easily promoted—even then the railway system is so important to the user and to the nation that any change should be introduced cautiously. We would suggest that if any part of the network is to be managed separately from the main system, this must be on a pilot scheme basis, and in any case there must be provision for the section to continue to function in the event of bankruptcy of the operator.

We feel that there may well be a case for certain lines of local, and possibly of regional, importance to be operated by or on behalf of a consortium of local or regional authorities, in much the same way as certain so-called private lines in Switzerland are operated by cantonal and municipal authorities, but the operator must be a responsible one, and preferably under some degree of public control, and there must be co-ordination with the main network.

We would point out that, while it is true that EC Directive 91/440 requires "that the accounts for business relating to the provision of transport services and those for business relating to the management of railway infrastructure are kept separate", it permits, but does not insist, "that this separation shall require the organisation of distinct divisions within a single undertaking", or "that the infrastructure shall be managed by a separate entity". We are worried that the setting up of Railtrack may produce an organisation not sufficiently responsive to the needs of the travelling public and of the operating bodies, nor indeed to market forces. We understand that problems of this sort have already arisen in the only country (Sweden) which has set up a separate infrastructure organisation (Banverket), and prefer that Swiss system which separates accounts only.

27 December 1992

APPENDIX 110

Letter from Mr J C Natzio

I am writing to you on the subject of railway privatisation because I believe that my own MP (who appears to be Mr MacGregor) may be inhibited in his response by reason of his Ministerial responsibilities.

I have to say that I have been dismayed by all that I have read and heard on the subject, and can envisage no scenario which does not involve a widespread reduction in services, and/or a continuing large public investment—the latter being in my view by far the lesser of the two evils. Given the present situation, and the work and achievement of the past years in development of the business Sectors, privatisation by Sectors seems the only sensible course (accepting the need for continuing subsidy) if the whole enterprise is indeed to go ahead. Franchising seems a real recipe for disaster, with the ill-effects of bus deregulation doubled in spades.

It does seem an act in defiance of common sense, and incidentally politically suicidal, to privatise a consistently loss-making, non-manufacturing, high-profile public utility, and it is hard to believe that the

Government is as indifferent to the results as it appears. I do very much hope that the Select Committee will be able to use its expertise to try to ensure an outcome which will be in the public interest.

7 December 1992

APPENDIX 111

Supplementary Memoranda British Transport Police

Response to the Department of Transport Consultation Document

"The Future Status of the British Transport Police"

EXECUTIVE SUMMARY

1. The British Transport Police is the national police force for the railways. The Force reorganisation took account of possible changes as a result of privatisation. Changes will be catered for in the flexibility of the Force Structure (paragraphs 1.4 and 1.5).

2. Control of the public space, of which the railway is part, is essential if people using the railway are to travel free of incident, nuisance and crime (paragraphs 2.2, 2.4 and 2.5).

3. London Underground and Network SouthEast are an integrated mass transit system which should be policed by one agency (paragraphs 2.9–2.11).

4. The Channel Tunnel will greatly increase the numbers of people entering the domestic railway network, both underground and surface (paragraph 2.12).

5. Policing the railways requires additional safety and major incident training, and a knowledge of specialist legislation (paragraphs 2.14 and 2.15).

6. Minimising the disruption caused to public transport by terrorism is vital (paragraphs 2.16 and 4.3).

7. The Force carries out only those functions which could accurately be described as policing activity (paragraphs 4.1 and 7.1).

8. Railway dedicated policing allows Railway Businesses to set priorities, but is still performed in the law and order rôle (paragraph 6.1).

9. The Force has identified nine core activities to manage the security of public space (paragraphs 6.2 and 6.3).

10. Effective public duty policing is the responsibility of Government; this can only be provided by bona fide police forces (paragraphs 8.1 and 8.2).

11. Jurisdiction and responsibilities will need to be widened if the Force is to discharge its duties where assets such as track and stations are transferred into private hands (paragraphs 9.1 and 9.3).

12. There is now an unequalled opportunity to regularise the ambiguous constitution of the Force to put it on a firm statutory footing. This requires primary legislation (paragraphs 10.1 to 10.5).

13. Such legislation must enable a 'post-privatisation' Police Committee to raise a budget and effectively discharge its statutory duties (paragraph 10.5).

14. There should be Ministerial responsibility for the Force (paragraph 10.5).

15. The cost of public-duty policing should be met by the Government (paragraph 12.2).

16. The four options as set out do not adequately deal with policing the railways 'post-privatisation' (paragraphs 11.1–11.7).

17. A recommended option is outlined (paragraphs 12.1 and 12.2) which encompasses:

(i) Funding;

(ii) Rôle of the Secretary of State;

(iii) Rôle of the Police Committee;

(iv) Independence of the Chief Constable.

"THE FUTURE STATUS OF THE BRITISH TRANSPORT POLICE"

1. INTRODUCTION

1.1 The Chief Constable of the British Transport Police welcomes the opportunity to comment on the Department of Transport Document "The Future Status of the British Transport Police".

1.2 The commitment of the Government to the retention of the British Transport Police as the national police force for the railways is acknowledged, as are the recent tributes that have been paid to the Force by the Secretary of State for Transport and the Minister for Public Transport.

1.3 The British Transport Police is sensitive to the question of enforcing law and order in a busy, vulnerable public and commercial environment that is not confined by geographical borders or localities.

1.4 The Force is a pace setter in the British Police Service, introducing devolved decision making, streamlined management systems and performance-related pay for Chief Officers. The reorganisation of the Force in April 1992 was radical and far-sighted. It is in advance of other police forces in this country.

1.5 In the planning stage for the reorganisation, as well as catering for the new business structure of British Rail it was anticipated that changes would result from privatisation. These will be catered for in the flexibility of the Force Structure. (Map of Force Structure at Appendix "A".)

1.6 The reputation of the Force is also spreading internationally with visitors this year from:
  (i) Switzerland;
  (ii) France;
  (iii) Hong Kong;
  (iv) Poland;
  (v) Russia;
  (vi) Bangladesh;
  (vii) Australia;
  (viii) USA;
  (ix) Hungary;
  (x) The Netherlands;
  (xi) Sweden.

Paragraphs 2.1 to 2.19 which follow describe the task of policing British Rail and London Underground Limited.

2. POLICING BRITISH RAIL AND LONDON UNDERGROUND LIMITED

2.1 The task of policing British Rail and London Underground Limited is a diverse and complex one. It ranges from busy urban areas in Scotland, the North and Midlands, the mass transit system of Network SouthEast and London Underground Limited, to quiet rural lines in sparsely populated areas of the country. Whilst some of the policing problems are common to all areas, others are located within specific areas of the system.

2.2 The one task common to the entire railway system is control of the public space which is the railway environment. People using the railways have little personal control over that space and rely upon operators, police and others to provide journeys which are free of:

(i) incident;

(ii) nuisance; and

(iii) crime.

In short, an environment in which they feel secure. This is best guaranteed by a dedicated railway police service *whose members have volunteered to police the railways*.

2.3 The size of the system is immense. British Rail and London Underground Limited together cover 10,603 route miles with 2,720 railway stations. In 1991–92, 739.7 million passenger journeys were made on British Rail, 758.9 million on London Underground and the Docklands Light Railway. 135.8 million tonnes of freight were also carried by rail.

2.4 The railway environment presents opportunities to the criminal in many ways. Crowds can be guaranteed at certain times of the day in places such as mainline termini and underground stations in the rush-hours, presenting opportunities for crimes such as theft from the person (pickpocketing). Conversely, fewer people can be expected at other times, which presents opportunities for violent crime such as robbery and sexual assault.

2.5 The millions who travel daily on the railway need to be confident that their personal safety and protection of their property is safeguarded. This not only requires the safe operation of the railway itself, but the existence of an environment which is free of crime and the fear of crime against either themselves or their property.

2.6 In 1991, 160,978 offences were reported to the police. They included:

Crimes of Violence	2,249
Sexual Offences	717
Robbery	1,401
Theft	54,190
Public Order	405
Drugs	562
Burglary	3,969
Criminal Damage	13,859
Fraud	3,587
Forgery	1,219

2.7 Summary offences also threaten public tranquillity and require firm police action if passengers are to have journeys which are nuisance-free. Included in the safety-related category of offences are such things as stonethrowing and trespass, both of which can be potentially life-threatening. In 1991 the offences included:

Trespass	18,504
Stonethrowing	3,962
Drunkenness	4,679
Begging	1,126
Indecent Exposure	532
Common Assault	403

2.8 In addition to trains and the line of route, railway stations must be effectively policed if they are not to become a magnet for criminal activity which reduces safety and increases the fear of crime.

2.9 In London there are no less than 42 interchange stations between British Rail and London Underground, and the flow of passengers between the surface and underground is high in both volume and frequency. Network SouthEast run 8,000 trains per day and London Underground approximately 9,000. Network SouthEast and London Underground Limited carry in excess of four million passengers daily. A high proportion of the people travelling by Network SouthEast and the other mainline train services terminating in London transfer to the Underground system and *vice versa*. Incidents on one system can and do have major implications on other systems in terms of crowd control, safety and train delays.

2.10 London Underground and Network SouthEast is an integrated urban mass transit system for Greater London and the South East, which covers an area policed by 13 separate police forces. This system must be policed by one agency. The benefits of policing this system as an entity include:

(i) The interchange of expertise in railway policing;

(ii) Countering a terrorist threat which does not discriminate between the two modes of transport;

(iii) Clear lines of communication and co-ordination of response in coping with large flows of people between the two systems.

2.11 Crime committed in the environment of the railways, especially in transit, does not recognise county or force boundaries and neither can the policing.

2.12 The Channel Tunnel will bring more travellers into the domestic system. In the first year of opening it is estimated that 6-9 million passengers will pass through Waterloo International Terminal, many entering the London Underground system on arrival in London. By the year 2000, 20 million passengers will be using the train services that pass through the Tunnel.

2.13 It is the nature of these types of problems—the high volume of passengers flowing from one system to another, the international dimension and a co-ordinated response to disruption caused by crime or terrorism—that makes law and order on the railway system important.

2.14 The increasingly technical nature of the railway requires police officers to have safety and industrial skills in order to protect life and prevent danger. These included search and recovery, first aid, fire safety, track safety and major incident training. A broad knowledge of specialist legislation (for example the new Transport and Works Act 1992) is also essential.

2.15 Officers must be certificated and fully conversant with safety actions in respect of:
  (i) working on lines;
  (ii) overhead power;
  (iii) live rail power;
  (iv) signalling equipment;
  (v) restricted areas;
  (vi) signalmen;
  (vii) track protection devices.

2.16 The railway network has proved to be a target for PIRA terrorist attacks during the periodic waves of activity in mainland Britain. Since the commencement of the current campaign in February 1991 there have been 3,170 bomb threats issued against the railway and 4,245 suspect packages to be dealt with nationally. There have been 10 live explosive devices either found or detonated, and 10 incidents involving incendiary devices. Since it is the intention of those planting devices and/or issuing threats to cause a maximum amount of disruption, a co-ordinated response by a national police force dedicated to the railways and able to manage risk within the law is essential. This is what the British Transport Police does for British Rail and London Underground Limited by threat categorisation.

2.17 In other EC countries which have specialist railway police forces, these are being strengthened to combat crime. In a number of countries where such a force does not exist, an examination on how to establish a railway police force to regain control of public space is under way. Once control of public space on the railways is lost, it is difficult, if not impossible, to regain, and is costly in the extreme.

2.18 The New York Underground system, which is one-third larger than the London Underground, has a specialist force 10 times larger than the number used to police the Underground system in London. Despite that, there is a campaign to regain control under the slogan "Taking Back the Subway for the People of New York", which says it all.

2.19 The general picture is that railway systems do require dedicated, specialist policing. Where this is not the case, instances of serious anti-social behaviour and crime have increased, in some cases dramatically. For example:

> **Portugal**—A security department with no police powers has been unable to counter an upsurge in crime on suburban trains including drug abuse, vandalism, theft of property and assaults on railway staff. National Police are being utilised whilst consideration is given to establishing a specialist police force.

> **Switzerland**—A working party involving the Federal Railways, Police, Ministries of the Interior and Transport are examining how to provide specialist railway policing to deal with an upsurge of crime on the railway network. Swiss officials recently visited British Transport Police Headquarters in connection with this project.

Paragraphs 3.1 to 10.4 which follow clarify statements contained in the Consultation Document.

3. THE STATUS OF THE CHIEF CONSTABLE

3.1 Paragraph 7, on page 7 of the Consultation Document, states that the Chief Constable is responsible for the administration of the Force. The British Transport Police Force Scheme (Amendment) Order 1992 has amended the position and makes the Chief Constable responsible for the direction and control of the Force.

4. MEANING OF SECURITY DUTIES

4.1 Paragraph 36 on page 11 of the Consultation Document refers to the British Transport Police having a "general security rôle". This is incorrect. British Transport Police are a national police force dedicated to *policing* the Railways. The activities of the Force are 100 per cent law and order policing in exactly the same way as Home Department forces.

4.2 As stated, all British Transport Police activity is policing. With one exception the Force does not undertake duties which would normally be undertaken by commercial security firms. The reference at paragraph 26 of the Document to security guards on London Underground releasing police officers is incorrect.

4.3 The exception is the escort of vulnerable container goods from railheads. Financial arrangements outside the normal budgetary system pay for the time spent on these escort duties. There are no other duties which could be described as "security" in the narrow meaning of the word.

4.4 Security, in the British Transport Police context, is used to describe three functions:

  (i) security in the sense of preventative high profile policing patrols to alleviate the fear of crime and enhance the opportunities to detect and apprehend offenders;

  (ii) crime prevention advice;

  (iii) security in the sense of general and specific measures to counter the terrorist threat. This embraces a wide spectrum of activity including advice and support to the railway industry to implement their own systems; liaison with other police forces and the security service in relation to the threat; high profile policing to deter terrorists and reassure the public and high speed response by specially trained police officers to minimise station closures and disruption to train services.

5. SEALINK AND ASSOCIATED BRITISH PORTS

5.1 At paragraph 16 on page 8 of the Consultation Document, reference is made to Sealink and Associated British Ports withdrawing from using British Transport Police. Almost all the activities carried out by British Transport Police officers at these locations were 'private security' type duties (for example, guarding premises and entrances gates). It follows that it was cost-effective not to continue to use trained police officers.

5.2 These locations are also self-contained in many respects. In effect, these ports did no more than join their peers who were already buying in or employing their own private security organisations.

6. CORE FUNCTIONS

6.1 Paragraph 36 of the Consultation Document draws a distinction in the allocation of resources between general security and law and order policing. As explained in paragraph 4.1, this is incorrect. British Transport Police resources are split between 'public duty' (80 per cent) and 'railway dedicated' (20 per cent). All resources are used in a law and order role, the 'railway dedicated' proportion is more sharply focused on the policing requirement of the Railway Businesses who set priorities. It must be stressed, however, that even in this instance it is the public who use the system who ultimately derive the benefit. Preventing trains from being obstructed, managing the threat of terrorism or dealing with vandalism to the railway infrastructure are of direct but not exclusive benefit to the railway operator.

6.2 The British Transport Police, together with the operators, have examined mass transit systems throughout the world and have identified three fundamental requirements for the railway system to be commercially attractive. It must be:

> *Safe*
>
> *Clean*
>
> *Secure.*

6.3 To achieve this objective requires the involvement of the police, railway operators and wider community in a number of key areas:

(i) Enhancing the perception of safety and security for people whilst in public space;

(ii) Retaining control to prevent the creation of 'no-go' areas;

(iii) Pursuing an integrated approach to the problem with railway operators;

(iv) Obtaining maximum use of resources through inter-agency and community co-operation;

(v) Using police expertise;

(vi) Ensuring that all parties share ownership of the problem;

(vii) Promoting the commercial benefits that can accrue to railway operators through marketing the services offered by the British Transport Police;

(viii) Realisation that enhanced perceptions lead to a better quality of service.

Experience of systems where this approach has not been pursued shows that regaining control is costly.

6.4 It is through the pursuit of these aims that the British Transport Police seeks to carry out the following functions:

(i) Prevention of crime;

(ii) Maintenance of The Queen's Peace;

(iii) Detection and apprehension of offenders.

7. CONTRACTING OUT BTP FUNCTIONS

7.1 The British Transport Police (with the exception stated at paragraph 4.2) do not undertake non-police functions. Any functions which do not require the exercise of police powers should be contracted out, for example:

(i) The escort of cash or high value loads;

(ii) Static guarding of premises;

(iii) Supervision of car parks.

8. ALTERNATIVE POLICING ARRANGEMENTS

8.1 Whether the railways are in public or private ownership, the Government has a responsibility to provide effective public duty policing. No operator should be allowed to make alternative policing arrangements unless using a bona fide police force.

8.2 The Government White Paper "New Opportunities for the Railways" sets out as essential requirements:

(i) Safety;

(ii) Quality of service;

(iii) Network benefits;

(vi) Environmental benefits.

A single unified police force with specialist responsibility for the railways is the most effective way of ensuring that these requirements can be met.

9. JURISDICTION

9.1 At the present time, British Transprt Police officers have powers of the office of Constable whilst:

(i) Acting on or in the vicinity of property owned or used by the British Railways Board or London Underground Limited;

(ii) Anywhere else **provided** it is a matter affecting these two bodies.

9.2 It follows that if (for example) a railway station were to be sold into private ownership, without an extension of powers this Force would automatically lose policing jurisdiction of that station. Hence it is possible that by doing nothing British Transport Police could be allowed to "wither on the vine". This should not be allowed to happen. It would not be in the public interest to provide a piecemeal service to millions of people.

9.3 The onset of privatisation creates another fundamental problem. The jurisdiction of the Force is defined in terms which relate to bodies that will not exist after privatisation. Legislation will need to be put in place to enable British Transport Police officers to discharge their law and order function throughout the network. The simplest and preferred option would be for jurisdiction to fall in line with all other police officers policing in the public area. This would avoid the necessity of attempting to encompass new railways or new ownership as and when they occur.

10. CONSTITUTIONAL POSITION OF THE BRITISH TRANSPORT POLICE

10.1 The constitution of the British Transport Police is an ambigious compromise. It has been altered, added to and amended in a piecemeal fashion over the last 28 years. Now is an unequalled opportunity to regularise it by correcting these anomalies.

10.2 Primary legislation would enable this situation to be rectified. Such legislation might take the form of an extension to the Police Act 1964 and the Police (Scotland) Act 1967, or the enactment of a British Transport Police Act clarifying the constitutional anomalies and putting the Force, its officers and their work on a firm statutory footing.

10.3 Access to PNC, the development of effective criminal intelligence flows (particularly with New Scotland Yard and the Security Services to counter the terrorist threat) has been hard fought because of the uncertain constitutional position vis à vis every other police force serving the public.

10.4 The access to the information and intelligence freely shared by Home Office forces would not be made available if Chief officers were uncertain as to the control and public duty rôle of the British Transport Police. There is a real danger that unless the official position is clarified prior to changes to the railway organisation, access will be withdrawn.

10.5 Primary legislation should be introduced which:

(i) Gives responsibility for policing transport networks which are, or were, formerly worked, owned or leased by the Boards, to the Chief Constable of the British Transport Police;

(ii) Makes all officers of the British Transport Police Constables within the definition of the respective Police Acts;

(iii) Gives the Police Committee the statutory authority to maintain the British Transport Police, together with the necessary powers to discharge this duty;

(iv) Creates Ministerial responsibility for the Force;

(v) Makes the Force subject to HMIC Inspections;

(vi) Confirms the statutory position of the Chief Constable.

11. OPTIONS

11.1 The options contained in the Consultation Document have been considered.

11.2 **OPTION ONE—British Transport Police Retained—direct funding by DoT/Home Office**

This option contains elements which are considered essential, namely:

(i) It identifies the responsibility for law and order costs falling to Government;

(ii) It allows for direct Ministerial responsibility to safeguard the public interest.

However it fails to address:

(i) Appropriate inputs from other interested parties—operators and users through a Police Committee;

(ii) How British Transport Police responsibilities would be defined.

11.3 OPTION TWO—British Transport Police Retained—Responsible to the Track Authority.

This option is fundamentally flawed:

(i) It assumes British Transport Police provide security guard services;

(ii) It does nothing to alleviate the current constitutional difficulties;

(iii) It fails to address the problem of law and order costs, unrealistically expecting commercial undertakings to pay for a public service.

11.4 OPTION THREE—British Transport Police Retained—Responsible to the Regulator

It is not clear precisely what is proposed.

(i) In paragraph 28 it is suggested that the Secretary of State could appoint a Police Committee, but does not explain what rôle the Secretary of State would have vis à vis the Force;

(ii) In paragraph 29 it is suggested that the Regulator would appoint the Police Committee who would be "accountable" to the Secretary of State, it is further suggested that the Department of Transport and Home Office could be represented on the Committee. If the Government has no defined responsibility for the Force, what would be the purpose of the Home Office or Department of Transport representative sitting on the Committee? What authority would the Police Committee have to secure a budget?

Option three again fails to address the basic issues, in particular law and order policing and its funding.

11.5 OPTION FOUR—British Transport Police Retained—Responsible to the Secretary of State

Option four is similar to option one, save reference is made here to the appointment of a Police Committee and the word "responsible" as opposed to "funding" is used. It is similar to option three as outlined in paragraph 29.

This option does cater for Ministerial responsibility.

11.6 Each of the options contains elements that would be constituent parts of the 'best option', but because they fail to address the fundamental issues none in the present form offers the means of safeguarding an effective policing service for the railways. It follows therefore that the preliminary conclusions at Paragraphs 31 to 33 suffer accordingly. The following statements made in the Document are important:

(i) **"Direct funding of British Transport Police by the Government should be rejected"—(Paragraph 31).**

The Government already partly funds British Transport Police through the PSO Grant; the issue is the degree and process of such funding.

(ii) **"The Option cuts across the general privatisation philosophy and in particular, does not give private companies full control of their costs" (Paragraph 31).**

The British Transport Police are primarily engaged in law and order policing. This does not conflict with general privatisation philosophy. There is a need to distinguish between the optional area of Government involvement (commercial) and a principal purpose of Government, the provision of effective law and order services.

It is unrealistic to ask a private commercial company to pay for public law and order policing.

(iii) **"Option four implies a close 'hands-on' involvement by the Department which conflicts with the general ethos of Privatisation" (Paragraph 33).**

The reality is that Department of Transport involvement with the British Transport Police has developed at many levels. It is opportune to formalise what already exists.

(iv) **"Offical consensus therefore favours an evolutionary approach" (Paragaph 33).**

This option could be potentially damaging to the ability of the Force to sustain an acceptable standard of service. Police officers acquire the necessary skills and expertise over a long term. To attract and retain the services of the people with the right qualities takes much effort. This option prolongs uncertainty amongst the Force with adverse effects on morale.

11.7 A merging of options two and three does nothing to tackle constitutional issues or the question of funding. In the short term, the disadvantages of option two remain and in the long term the picture is unclear as to option three.

12. RECOMMENDED OPTION

12.1 It is recommended that the option best likely to secure a national police for all the railway systems, operating as an integrated part of mainstream British policing, with Government funding for all its law and order activities, is on the following model:

(i) Direct Government funding through the Department of Transport for law and order activities on a ratio of 80 per cent and 20 per cent, as at present;

(ii) Controlled through a representative Police Committee answering to the Secretary of State for Transport;

(iii) The Police Committee to have a funding mechanism which allows it to provide an effective policing service free of uncertainty, ambiguity or complexity in respect of funding;

(iv) The Chief Constable with operational independence under the law, to be answerable to the Police Committee for the efficient administration of the Force;

(v) The British Transport Police to provide the national police service for the railway including London Underground Limited with parity to Home Office police forces.

12.2 The Police Committee should represent the operators, users and the public interest. A secure system of funding would enable the Chief Constable to forward plan effectively to ensure policing needs are met. The representation on the Police Committee of all interested parties would ensure that cost effectiveness and efficiency were not compromised.

12.3 The recommended option provides a way forward now for the British Transport Police to meet the challenge of policing the railways on a national basis into the next century not subject to delay and uncertainty while rail privatisation is defined.

8 January 1992

APPENDIX 112

Memorandum from Dame Elizabeth Chesterton DBE

Architectural and Design Standards for the Future Railway System in the Light of the Government's Proposals for Privatisation

In 1956 a design panel was set up to advise the British Transport Commission (now the British Railways Board) "to advise on the best means of obtaining a high standard of appearance and amenity in the design of its equipment". This was followed in 1977 by the appointment of a Director of Environment and the establishment of an environmental panel, later to become the Architecture Panel. Chaired by Board members, other members were chosen from outside BR for their particular expertise and experience in the relevant fields.

Joint partnership ventures with local authorities were set up to effect station improvements and the employment of local youth was undertaken through youth opportunity schemes.

The two panels worked with the BR establishment to encourage a climate of understanding about the importance of high standards in architcture and design as a fundamental business resource and as part of an overall strategy—customers increasingly expecting a first class and safe environment and an image of quality.

In 1985 this approach was strengthened by the appointment of a Director of Architecture and Design and though, through the reorganisation of British Rail's structure into separate businesses, this post was dropped, its influence in the improvement of standards was and is still being felt in major projects recently completed eg, Liverpool Street and, still under construction, Waterloo (Channel Tunnel terminal). Also in a number of smaller stations and in recent rolling stock.

In 1991 the two panels were brought together as the British Rail Architecture and Design Panel, chaired by a board member and, apart from the Director of Public Affairs, with a membership as before, drawn from outside BR, other directors attending by invitation.

The panel's role was redefined, not as an auditing body, but to add value for the railway businesses through the encouragement of best practice in architecture and design, its aim being to help guide policy and, through its advice at an early stage on relevant projects, to promote continuous improvement in the quality of the rail experience in relation to international standards.

Its terms of reference were restated as to review overall business policies in architecture and design, the quality of the output and the need for consistency across the businesses; and to convey through its chairman, to the Chief Executive or directly to the Board, such views and opinions as it thinks fit on major building and rolling stock projects and other projects involving particular sensitivity in architecture and design.

The Panel, set up by BR and chaired by a board member, cannot by its nature contribute evidence to the Transport Committee Inquiry on the Government's proposals for privatisation.

However, the outside membership has felt it right to make sure that in the evidence the Select Committee has been considering, proper emphasis has been given to promoting for Britain's railway system a high quality environment for rail travel and, because the railway undertaking has a nationwide impact on life in towns and cities, an equally high quality contribution to their fabric at points of contact.

This leads to three important questions:

> In the light of the proposals for privatisation, by what management means can consistently high standards in architecture, design—embracing uniform signage—and all else that contributes to a high quality and safe environment, be guaranteed for the benefit and convenience of customers and the smooth running of the system?

> How can similar high standards be achieved in urban contexts where the local environment is affected?

> How can the accumulated wisdom and worthwhile relationships with local authorities, born of experience in the present organisation, be carried forward into any new one?

12 January 1993

APPENDIX 113

CYMDEITHAS RHEILFFORDD DYFFRYN AMAN (AMMAN VALLEY RAILWAY SOCIETY)

The Role of Preserved Railways in the National Railway Network.

1. INTRODUCTION.

1.1 The purpose of this memorandum is to draw the attention of the Transport Committee to the opportunities offered by the restoration of railway branch lines, which are remote and peripheral to the national network. Many have been abandoned as uneconomic, and will never be commercially viable or profitable, but in the care of the railway preservation movement, with its expertise, dedication and experience freely given, can be restored and operated to the social and economic benefit of the local communities which they serve and in the interest of the nation in general when integrated to the main line network.

1.2 The recently formed Amman Valley Railway Society has carried out an extensive study of the role of a restored branch line in the regeneration of a typical Welsh valley in industrial decline. As a result it has committed itself to a momentous community initiative to save and care for its valley branch line network. It is grateful to the House of Commons Transport Committee for this opportunity to put forward its findings and views on opportunities for restored railways, as it considers that they may be worthy of further study and more general application.

2. THE CASE FOR PRESERVED RAILWAYS.

2.1 The main and initial objective of a railway preservation project is to restore a line and equip it for the purpose of enjoyment and recreation. If this were the sole purpose then there would be no case for putting forward its benefit for the public at large other than that it provides a local amenity for exercise and amusement.

2.1 It is but a small step to extend the role from that of a leisure facility to a public service. Every sport requires outside support in order to provide the necessary funds to prosper. Thus one finds that the natural course of development of a preserved railway follows a progression from "fun runs" to a revenue producing passenger transportation service. This is a role that makes railway preservation a key initiative. It is for this reason that the importance of such projects deserves to be recogised and encouraged.

2.3 The benefits of standard gauge preserved railways are realised when they can provide a connecting service to the national railway system. The natural habitat of the railway preservationist is the abandoned remote and peripheral branch line or the rural cross country interconnecting line. Many of these lines have long since been abandoned and even dismantled as uneconomical. They are not financially viable and never will be, whether under public, private or franchisee management control. The only way under which they will ever be revived is through a railway preservation society. The number of such lines throughout the country is considerable. Yet only a fraction of the total have been adopted by the railway preservation movement. These lines at one time made a considerable contribution to the economy and life style of the country. This potential benefit may still be restored. They form an important class of their own in the opportunities they provide for the future. If the Government, as stated in the White Paper, wishes to involve the private sector, then it cannot afford to ignore proposals for the regeneration of what may be described as the forgotten tertiary railways.

2.4 Apart from their potential for direct benefit to the community and to the country the tertiary lines are the source of a number of indirect benefits. These must be taken into consideration if one is to make a fair assessment of their true value. Many branch lines are over 150 years old and their histories remain unknown. The inevitable consequence of the adoption of a line for restoration is that it provides a link in the form of a living memorial to the past. It preserves the local heritage in that it promotes a revival of interest in the history of the line and the area which it serves. Hence the demand for definitive histories derived from primary source material, and the mysterious emergence from the woodwork of railwayana, industrial memorabilia, nostalgic souvenirs and various other relics of the past—enough to form a pay-on-entry museum.

2.5 A working railway becomes a tourist attraction in its own right. It may attract visitors to areas where there is no indigenous tourist industry. It opens up the tourist potential of the area in that it provides a gateway to its attractions. It promotes a new found interest in the environment and restores civic pride and social commitment in areas that have suffered high levels of deprivation.

2.6 The activities imposed by a railway preservation project cover a multitude of disciplines. These disciplines extend beyond the limits of formal curriculum orientated education and may only be acquired by on-the-job training. Its worth to the Community, in academic terms is equivalent to the establishment of a field unit of a College of Technology. It preserves the skills of the work force. Often it provides work experience in a community where there is no gainful employment.

3. THE STRENGTH OF THE PRESERVATION MOVEMENT.

3.1 No apology is made for the use of the word "Movement" in the Memorandum. For how else can one describe the achievements of the preservation world other than that they are the creation of a growing force in motion more aptly described as a "Movement". If one is to advocate confidence in its projects one must understand the underlying strength and permanence of the movement.

3.2 A common perception of the railway preservation movement is that it is confined to a few railway enthusiasts motivated by sheer nostalgia. This does not explain the progressive and steady growth in the membership and wide public support over the past forty years and the interest it generates in people of all ages and inclinations. The appeal of the railway preservation movement is not a passing fashion, it is here to stay and there appears to be no end to its prospect for widespread growth.

3.3 At present its geographical distribution is admittedly patchy. It cannot be described as a truly national movement. Many areas of the country are deserts in railway preservation terms. This applies particularly to the regions where the traditional heavy industries, such as coal and steel are in decline and where the social benefits could be of great importance. There are countless numbers of redundant branch lines. Not all, but a significant proportion are suitable for restoration and integration. This would be possible without saturating the system and without fear of drying up enthusiasts support. Given the necessary encouragement the barriers to regeneration can be removed and opportunities presented for significant expansion.

4. BARRIERS TO GROWTH

4.1 Despite the underlying strength and appeal of the movement there are barriers to its potential growth especially during the formative period. One of the main problems arises out of the high start-up capital necesary to acquire and up-grade the basic element of a railway system—that is the track bed and its infrastructure. The track must be acquired as one integral lot within a short time scale, set by a competitive bidder in the form of the scrap merchant, and is in most cases the highest single item of capital expenditure. The purchase price is well beyond the internal resources of the average society and it must seek outside financing. If this important hurdle cannot be negotiated then the prospects for survival are not good. Other options for track access are not appropriate to the underlying economy of preservation projects as their viability is based on a significant injection of voluntary effort into the equation. Thus outright purchase appears to be the only feasible option.

4.2 A second barrier is presented by the cost of acquisition and restoration of rolling stock and other operational equipment. This type of material may be acquired item by item over a long period of time determined by the fund raising capacity of the society. It is therefore not a critical barrier to success but it does determine the lead time for the introduction of a fare paying service. In a typical case this time scale may extend over 8 years and more when dependant on internal resources. Inward investment by outside investors may reduce this time to four years.

4.3 A third commitment that must be respected falls into the field of regulatory measures which are at present in place and which may be imposed in the future by the Health and Safety Board. These may require the training and validation of maintenance and operational staff, the inspection and certification of track equipment and rolling stock and the granting of operating licences. These measures may attract heavy if not prohibitive fees. In addition, the very nature of preservation as a hobby requires that training is done on the job and in house and the result is to set a minimum lead time for the introduction of an operational service. In an average case the minimum time scale may not be less than four years.

5. PROPOSALS FOR NEW OPPORTUNITIES

5.1 The preservation movement will not be able to exploit the new opportunities for the railways unless the problems set by the barriers to growth and expansion are addressed. The need to provide grants towards start-up capital in the formative stage of development must be recognised. The present system whereby societies seek assistance from local, county and regional authorities is unsatisfactory in that it amounts to a lottery. These authorities are faced with competitive calls on limited resources, and cut-backs on existing services. Although they are generally supportive, in these circumstances the prospects for new capital ventures, unless they have high job creating capability, hang on uncertainty. A factor that must be taken into account is that a railway line by its very nature, may serve the administrative area of more than one authority, a situation which compounds the complexity of the funding procedure.

5.2 A railway society is a voluntary non-profit making organisation. Even in the consolidation stages of its development availability of funds for improvements and expansion is scanty. Its income could be significantly improved through tax exemptions. It would be a significant advantage if it could operate as a Charitable Trust, with tax benefits from covenants and exemption from VAT yet remain subject to the controls of a

Public Company. Certain European countries provide the statutory framework for such organisations, such as the in case of the "Association Sans But Lucrative" (ASBL) which is in essence a "Charitable Company". It is realised that this proposal has far reaching implications in that this type of structure could be justified in many other worthy causes and may take many years to legislate. It may in the goodness of time feature in the harmonisation programme of the European Communities.

5.4 Finally, great fears have been expressed regarding the implications of the White Paper proposals for validation, certification and licencing. These fears do not arise from recognition of the need in the interests of safety but on the costs and drain on limited resources. These fears must be overcome if initiatives are to be encouraged and stimulated.

6. CONCLUSION

6.1 The Government in "Opportunities for the Railways" has made proposals for the privatisation of parts of British Rail with the object of stimulating more competition. This Memorandum makes out the case for the preservation of a part of British Rail. If this were made the object of competition then two parties would be involved. The one would have the vision and ambition to secure the future of the railway for posterity; the other would consign it to the scrap yard and hence to the steel furnace thus wiping out a national asset from the face of the land forever. For the alternative to preservation is incineration.

6.2 If new opportunities are to be created for privatisation then they should be made equally for preservation, but it can do without the competition of the scrap merchant!

15 January 1993

APPENDIX 114

STANHOPE PROPERTIES PLC

British Rail Privatisation: Realising Property Asset Values

CONTENTS

Conclusion

1.0 Introduction

2.0 Key Features of Railhead Redevelopment Projects

3.0 Learning from Experience

— Broadgate and Ludgate Achievements

— Past Performance—Collaborative Development between British Rail and the Private Sector

— Development Needs—the Role of Infrastructure

— The Future

4.0 Conclusion

CONCLUSION

In the context of the present proposals contained within the White Paper, I conclude that major stations should remain with the Track Authority as the unifying body able to draw together the wide variety of issues and complex functions in the operation of a modern railway environment. The further that the division of operational responsibilities is taken, the more likely there is to be gross disparity of interests which will eventually lead to the mistakes of the 1960s and 1970s which materially detracted from the built environment within and around great stations.

1.0 INTRODUCTION

1.1 I have been involved in property development, and the London market in particular, for 25 years. Between 1976 and 1983, I was joint Chief Executive of Greycoat Plc. In 1983, I established Stanhope Properties Plc, where I am Chief Executive. My experience in development involves the creation of over 10 million square feet of commercial office space and associated retail and leisure space. The projects in which I have been involved are characterised by their scale, complexity and frequent association with rail infrastructure. They have also been typified by masterplanning and the creation of new "places". Principal projects are:—

Project	Development Period	Commercial Office Space
Victoria Station	1979–1983	0.325m sq ft built
Broadgate (Liverpool Street)	1984–1992	4.0m sq ft built
Ludgate (Holborn Viaduct)	1989–1992	0.6m sq ft built

Stockley Park (Heathrow)	1984–1991	1.5m sq ft built
Chiswick Park	1989–present	1.5m sq ft proposed
King's Cross	1989–present	5.0m sq ft proposed

1.2 These projects involved new and radical approaches to the management of construction and public/private sector partnerships as well as demonstrating the scale of commercial gains to be realised from British Rail-owned land assets. This new approach enabled the projects and buildings to be delivered within costs and times which average about 70 per cent of UK industry norms. A large proportion of the projects has been constructed over tracks rather than on redundant railway property with no operational requirement.

1.3 I have prepared this paper in response to the Government's plans for privatisation of the railway system as set out in the White Paper. "New Opportunities for the Railways". My comments and views are restricted to those issues relating to the commercial opportunities at privatised stations and the relationships between privately-owned stations and train operators. My comments are based on the experience of the projects outlined above, all of which required a detailed understanding of British Rail's operational imperatives.

2.0 KEY FEATURES OF RAILHEAD REDEVELOPMENT PROJECTS

2.1 The 3 completed projects in which I have been involved at Victoria (Victoria Plaza), Liverpool Street (Broadgate) and Holborn Viaduct (Ludgate) over the last 12 years were made possible by a fresh commitment to public/private partnership. They achieved substantially improved rail facilities and the development of a new breed of office buildings. The latter now places London in the forefront of development and construction technology in Europe. The projects demonstrate the value of creating successful places and the lessons learned from earlier railhead developments.

2.2 British Rail have generated in excess of £500 million from Broadgate and Ludgate alone, either directly by rents/land payments or indirectly by developer provision of station works. This is the most successful railway redevelopment programme in Europe.

2.3 The swift and cost effective implementation of these projects would not have been possible without a comprehensive, co-ordinated approach from British Rail Project Manager, supported directly by the Manager Director of Network SouthEast, co-ordinated the numerous departments of the railway to provide in each case a seamless process, strategy and implementation. Without ownerships of all of the land, and without the safety, passenger service, control processes, Parliamentary Bill process and Town Planning applications all being under one direction, it would not have been possible to develop the projects with such efficiency and effectiveness.

2.4 Anything more than one major landowner/lessee would have enabled ransom strips to be exploited by lessees. The redevelopment process would have been slow and the substantial profits threatened.

2.5 The rail stations which have resulted are architecturally distinguished and of a very high quality. Furthermore, the integration of land development and infrastructure improvements is helping to serve London's broader objectives of managing commuting patterns and reducing congestion.

2.6 All of the rail-based projects in which I have been involved have had a common set of objectives.

—*Improved railway services;*

—*Development opportunity and profit;*

—*Improved quality of environment for rail users and the general public, and*

—*Enchance the rail business by generating increased passenger demand from the developments themselves.*

2.7 During this period, British Rail has developed in joint venture with a variety of partners, a total of 6 major London stations, and as a consequence their knowledge and expertise now represents the most efficient development team undertaking railhead projects in Europe.

2.8 Interestingly, few over-track commercial office developments of any scale have taken place in continental Europe. The only one which compares to the London projects is Montparnasse, Paris. I believe that British Rail's expertise is in itself marketable within the member states.

3.0 LEARNING FROM EXPERIENCE

3.1 It is with these specific experiences drawn in the broader context of urban renewal and development as a whole that I now turn to the main body of my evidence. This comprises the lessons to be learned from my experience in railhead developments for the current privatisation proposals. The comments fall into 4 areas:—

—*Broadgate and Ludgate achievement*

—*Past performance—collaborative development between British Rail and the private sector*

—*Development needs—the role of infrastructure*

—*The future*

3.2. *Broadgate and Ludgate Achievements*

3.2.1 To illustrate the scale and complexity of these redevelopment projects, Appendix I* contains aerial photographs taken at the start and completion of each project, and illustrating the complexity of construction activity at London's Liverpool Street Station.

3.2.2 Development of these projects revolved around 3 principal headings, namely: (a) Management of the Process, (b) Design and (c) Construction.

3.2.3 **(a) Management of the Process** One of the keys to success was the close management of the interface between railway and development activity, and therefore the balance to be struck between the operational aspects of running rail services and development activity. This led to maximum operational safety and minimal disruption to the travelling public. At the same time there was a need to protect a wide variety of operational and management interests.

3.2.4 *The Issues* Railway development is a complex undertaking requiring the co-operation of many parties. Time available for development construction (possession in railway terms) is always limited. Current safety requirements for both railway staff and passengers, and the need to generate temporary space for construction and relocate station facilities, demand that large areas of the concourse and track area be available. The following major participants were involved:

British Rail

— Property Board Development—UK Property Operations
— Property Board Station Trading—non-BR concourse retail and advertising
— Divisional Operations—operation of timetabling of railway
— Divisional Retail Manager—BR concourse retail
— Architects' Department
— Civil Engineering—track and infrastructure
— Electric Power—railway traction system
— Signals
— Telecommunications
— Etc.

Independent Interests

— Railway Inspectorate
— London Fire Brigade
— District Surveyor
— English Heritage
— Non-statutory, special interest groups
— The local community
— Etc.

3.2.5 The problem was one of co-ordinating and unifying a large variety of differing and sometimes conflicting minority interests towards a common purpose.

3.2.6 *The Solution* Through this plethora of highly specialist interests, the common link both in terms of direct management involvement, expertise and contractual relationship, was British Rail. A critical decision was therefore made early on to draw these diverse activities and interests together via a British Rail Project Director. This appointment was mirrored by an equivalent appointment within the development team. The result was the creation of an efficient core team with clear responsibilities and which was understandable to others.

3.2.7 It is my view that without the unifying effect of this core team, made possible by the singular interest of British Rail, the costs, quality and time targets set for the respective projects would not have been achieved.

3.2.8 Without the overriding control of the concourse and track vested in British Rail the ability to create such a small tightly-knit team would have been impossible given the breadth of representation illustrated above. Furthermore, the absence of powers vested in British Rail as operator would have given rise to additional obstacles such as:-

— Property ransom positions by non-British Rail concourse retail users and advertisers as well as operational franchises, ticketing sales and accommodating operations.
— Extensive and complex negotiations with franchised railway operators to achieve platform, concourse and track down time to permit concourse level construction activity.

---

* Not printed.

3.2.9 In summary, the existence of a unifying body controlling and managing land usage and rail operations and leasing back concourse and air rights space is an essential vehicle in permitting the design and construction flexibility necessary for optimum value creation.

3.2.10 *(b) Design* The influence of the core team approach was a key to success. It allows design and construction activities for rail and development to be considered simultaneously giving rise to solutions which consistently accommodated the necessary parameters for sound commercial development whilst preserving operational flexibility and improving railway passenger environment. Additionally, it enables the development of innovative solutions; for example, the reconstructed platforms 11-18 at Liverpool Street also from the foundations for 1,500,000 sq ft of commercial office space above. The costs and time saved alone are enormous in addition to the reduction in passenger service disruption achieved compared with a more conventional approach.

3.2.11 The principle was to ensure that no commercial development would cause unnecessary restraint to future operational changes, and at the same time, to avoid unco-ordinated railway works that would prejudice sensitive future developments. To achieve this, a long-term masterplan for both operational and commercial development improvements had to be co-ordinated throughout. A comprehensive design approach emerged and "piecemeal", increment improvement was avoided.

3.2.12 (c) *Construction* Whilst the core team was highly important to the design process, the construction activity was even more critical to success.

3.2.13 The list of organisations referred to earlier in this text includes: overhead power; signalling and communications; timetabling; station trading, and station operations. Restrictions to construction activity imposed as a consequence of special safety requirements and timetabling in a live railway environment introduced restrictive working disciplines including night and weekend operations.

3.2.14 Perhaps the best example of the close working relationship needed is illustrated by the Ludgate Project where, in 17 days from 12–29 May 1990, in a continuous 24-hour working operation by contractors employed by Rosehaugh Stanhope Developments, and working in conjunction with British Rail, the 600 metre long viaduct and 3 bridges were removed. An existing bridge was lowered over Queen Victoria Street and 600 metres of new running track and associated signalling power services were installed.

3.2.15 This was achieved only as a result of the closest co-ordination of activities between British Rail operations and the development team acting in reality as joint clients defining and managing a singular objective and single construction team. Anything less than this system would have resulted in a confrontation attitude which would have been wasteful and costly in the project.

3.3 Past Performance—Collaborative Development Between British Rail and the Private Sector

3.3.1 Taken together, the Broadgate and Ludgate projects have generated over £500 million of actual or realisable capital to the benefit of British Rail. British Rail have also retained ground rent interests which will enable them to benefit from future growth in rental revenue. At Broadgate the commercial development was undertaken as part of an integrated renewal of Liverpool Street Station and resulted in major improvements to the passenger environment.

3.3.2 In addition, both projects have provided major benefits to the wider community. At Broadgate, the ownerships of the Dalston Viaduct was transferred to the local authority (enabling a reserve for the future East London Line Extension to be preserved as well as creating light industrial space to provide new employment to the area).

3.3.3. At Ludgate land ownership between the City Corporation and British Rail were rationalised to provide the opportunity for the redevelopment of the last of the derelict Second World War bomb sites. The removal of the Victorian Bridge blocking views of St Paul's from Ludgate Circus, together with the removal of the associated viaduct has allowed the removal of the psychological divide in the City fabric which as existed for over 100 years.

3.3.4 All this has been achieved at no cost or risk to the public purse and at the same time the first new railway station for 100 years in the City of London has been constructed which would otherwise have cost the public sector £100 million.

3.3.6 In each instance it has been possible to achieve these results, raise the necessary finance and let and dispose of the resulting property whilst the freehold interest remains with British Rail.

3.4 Development Needs—the Role of Infrastructure

3.4.1 In any market conditions railway stations have a noble status within the fabric of our society and as such stand as key building blocks in any pattern of social and economic growth and regeneration. The integration of land development and transport opportunities must be regarded as having a critical role to play.

3.4.2 Our cities and suburban centres must be lively, dynamic locations and therefore more people must live nearer these centres. Existing run-down communities must be improved. Degraded lives make a degraded location. My direct experience has demonstrated how successful places can be created at rail stations which contribute to the more general objective of urban regeneration.

3.4.3 London and our large cities have marvellous transport systems and with the cost and timescales involved in the creation of new infrastructure there is an overwhelming economic argument to bring jobs and housing to this, rather than adopt the policy of decentralisation. The implications for generating additional passenger traffic and fares are obvious.

3.4.4 To take one example, the new use and upgrading of the existing North London Line could allow greater density of development for housing and jobs. Adopting a more general policy this could help to provide up to 200,000 extra housing units in London.

3.4.5 Given the significance of railway stations in such a strategy, why give away the profit benefits of these strategic land holdings to a few minority owners?

3.5 The Future

3.5.1 Railway stations act as nodal points for housing, retail and commercial property, and with the advent of new infrastucture projects (such as Crossrail, Channel Tunnel, Chelsea-Hackney and King's Cross), international stations within an integrated transport strategy will grow in importance.

3.5.2 The complexities of the interrelated activity of railway operations and commercial development, design and construction require the closest co-ordination of activities via a small team with the powers to control and direct the process. Without this discipline cost and timescales will rise, quality will be reduced and customer service suffer.

3.5.3 The value of a station as an asset is optimised by design integrating every element from the transport and retail functions at the concourse through the introduction of feeder services and highways to the commercial development itself whch benefits from the nodal location. The integrated approach necessary to achieve this end leads to the conclusion that the sale of a stream of income generated from the concourse and station avoids ransom positions and provides flexibility for the future.

3.5.4 Few developers possess the experience and expertise to undertake railway related developments. Its inherent complexities suggest that it is not something to be tendered. In consideration of the privatisation proposals, therefore, cognizance should be taken of the need to safeguard and maximise development opportunities at stations, and the procedures by which this will be achieved.

3.5.5 The air rights sale arrangements over railway station lands already provide a successful public/private solution. Introducing third parties would lead to values accruing to them, when their rationale for involvement was unclear. Moreover, they would benefit from "ransom strips", ie land ownerships sold to them unnecessarily and which enabled them to obtain additional payment.

4.0 CONCLUSION

4.1 In the context of the present proposals contained within the White Paper, I conclude that major stations should remain with the Track Authority as the unifying body able to draw together the wide variety of issues and complex functions in the operation of a modern railway environment. The further that the division of operational responsibilities is taken, the more likely there is to be gross disparity of interests which will eventually lead to the mistakes of the 1960s and 1970s which materially detracted from the built environment within and around our great stations.

11 January 1993

APPENDIX 115

SUPPLEMENTARY MEMORANDUM FROM THE CLYDESDALE RAIL ACTON GROUP

Assurances of Rural Train Services?

I provide the following information for your perusal although I can well understand that the Committee does not have spare time at present!

We do not wish you to consider our local problems as such but provide it as an example which gives grave doubts about the assurances recently given by Government Ministers about safeguarding rail services from complete or effective closure.

The example is at Carstairs where the 58,000 people of Clydesdale have lost their only return train services to Edinburgh and the South. Trains still run, the station has not been closed but hardly any trains now stop at the station and THE ONLY RETURN TRAIN (from either direction) LEAVES EDINBURGH OR THE SOUTH BEFORE THE FIRST OUTWARD BOUND TRAIN ARRIVES effectively making the service unuseable.

The Transport Users' Consultative Committee have recommended reinstatement of the service in two consecutive annual reports to the Secretary of State for Transport and the Secretary of State for Scotland. The reports have been ignored by British Rail and the ministers. I enclose copies of the replies to our letters to the ministers and copies of replies by the ministers to our Member of Parliament.* The replies are extremely disappointing.

I am afraid to say that the assurances given recently to Parliament and the British People can only be regarded as false for the following reasons:

The Ministers ignore the recommendations of the TUCC's and CTCC, the very statutory bodies appointed under Act of Parliament to make recommendations on safeguarding rail services.

The Ministers say that the level of service is entirely up to British Rail which again, almost by definition, means particular services cannot be safeguarded.

They refer to "precise level of service" even though that service may be effectively unuseable and therefore not a "service" in the normal meaning of the English Language.

The Ministers say that Regional Railways provide socially necessary services even though they know full well that Regional Railways do not provide any services in Clydesdale and in fact are prevented from doing so by ministerial directive. It would be the obvious answer should the Minister care to direct Regional Railways to provide these socially necessary services.

In any case the Minister goes on to say that subsidy is only given in block and that it is up to British Rail to decide where to spend it which again means that assurances safeguarding services can only be considered as false.

Needless to say I am not only concerned about safeguarding rail services but also what comes close to contempt of Parliament and the English Language.

I thought these letters may be of interest to the Transport Committee.

16 January 1993

APPENDIX 116

Memorandum from Mr G McKechnie

The Observer column the *"Financial Times"* of 23rd November posed the following question "Is there anybody, anywhere, with a good word to say about the government's plans for the privatisation of British Rail?" albeit belatedly, as I have been abroad, I should like to respond to this challenge with a few comments.

1. Spotlight on land transport infrastructure

To the nation's detriment, road and rail infrastructure in Britain has suffered from neglect for some years. In part, this neglect stems from the fact that roads and railways have not been readily amenable to the government's approach to dealing with the oversized public sector. Until recently the only politically acceptable approach appears to have been restrict funding. This approach clearly has had its effect on British Rail. Some of the results have been beneficial but its limits appear close to being reached. The July 1992 White Paper "New Opportunities for the Railways" remedies this problem by introducing an acceptable framework (acceptable to the Government) either in which awkward but fundamental questions can be asked, policy debate conducted and, eventually, the railways restored to what I believe to be their rightful place in Britain's industrial firmament.

This spotlight on land transport seems to me to be a clear benefit of the Government's privatisation plans for British Rail.

As an example of the type of transport issue in need of a spotlight, consider the question whether, over a longish distance, freight should travel by rail or road. As a percentage of total freight carried, that transported by road has long been growing at the expense of rail-carried freight. This is because of the shippers' considerations of relative cost and convenience between the two modes. Today, even though it is enjoying only a declining market share, British Rail freight business is profitable. But this is because freight is charged by British Rail on a marginal basis. If this charging policy were to be changed and freight were to bear a proportionate share of railway infrastructure costs, it is likely that much of today's rail freight traffic would find that the cost advantage had shifted in favour of road. However, such an analysis is explicitly based on the costs borne by the shipper. If the full cost of road transport—including congestion pollution and the vastly disproportionate contribution of heavy lorries to road deterioration—is taken into the equation, it is far from clear that a steel wheel on a steel track is not the cheaper mode of transport. I expect this will become even clearer as intra modal technology develops and the opening of Eurotunnel shows advantages to loading trains at locations remote from the tunnel mouth.

The proposals to franchise passenger rail services mean that consideration of issues such as this cannot be deferred. Before charges to be made by Railtrack for the use of infrastructure by passenger services can be set, and thus the franchising scheme established, the formulae for costs to be borne by freight need to be known. One hopes that the much-awaited study by Coopers and Lybrand on Railtrack's pricing policy will have been prepared to a brief adequately broad to address these issues.

---

*Not printed

It does seem likely that attention given to issues related indirectly to rail privatisation, such as recent statements on the future of road pricing schemes, originate at least in part in the debate stimulated by this spotlight.

I am irresistibly tempted to digress here to another issue raised by subsidising road-carried freight through the E.C. Does this subsidy to road distort the efficient allocation of resources in such a way as to favour the location of industry in the E.C.'s golden core at the expense of the periphery? With renewed focus on transport infrastructure through UK (Autumn Statement) and E.C. (European Investment Fund) investment initiatives, this question would seem now to bear particular investigation. If the distortion does indeed exist, this subsidy to road freight contributes to the need for another equally well discussed, but offsetting, subsidy: the Cohesion Fund. It is perhaps, then, ironic that one of the chief intended uses of the Cohesion Fund is transportation infrastructure in the periphery with its apparent advantage of immobility. Or is this another deliberately offsetting element of the package to allow manufacturers in the golden core better access to the peripheries of the Single Market? Under another regime a Scot might have to pay more for his lemon—and a Greek more for his haggis—but if it were considered a problem it is likely that a better remedy than general freight-by-road subsidies could be found.

2. Transparency

The railways today receive subsidy. This is granted in recognition of the socially desirable benefits (positive externalities) they generate. The quantum of positive externalities generated is generally regarded as higher in other E.C. countries than in Britain. Nonetheless, the White Paper does recognise the benefit and the proposed franchising structure is based on the continuing payment of subsidy. One may or may not believe that the Government wishes to continue to pay subsidies to rail, but the statement is clear and the radical structures proposed rest on that premise.

Today, except on the broadest basis, which may itself be misleading because of British Rail's accounting practices, the detailed use of these subsidies is opaque. The fear has been expressed that, if the application of the subsidies on a line-by-line basis became transparent, there would be irresistible pressure for the closure of certain regional lines. Is closure under these circumstances such a bad thing? If the social benefit (not commercial profit) is clearly less than the cost of providing it, should the service not legitimately be closed? Might some of the regions involved not even welcome railway closure if an equivalent amount to the closed line's subsidy were redirected to a demonstrably better value-for-money activity in the region?

The closure problem seems to lie not in the closure of a line per se, but in the quite legitimate fear that the government would not fund on alternative activity in the region which was better value for money and hence that the region would be the net loser. If the result of closure were to be the liberation of funds for the local communities, perhaps even giving the people of the region a voice in their alternative use, the horrified chorus that greats rumours of closure might just be muted. Indeed a rational use of the funds and the prerequisite closure of a branch line might find local encouragement.

The Government, and the opposition parties, believe in open government and in giving consumers of a Government services a voice in their provision. The openness and transparency that could result from implementing the railway privatisation, and a contribution in a small way to the openness and responsiveness of the governmental process, is a benefit of the plans.

3. Efficiency of Asset Usage

The Government's railway privatisation proposals envisage the corporate separation of Railtrack, which will own track and associated infrastructure (why not other long life assets such as stations as well?), from the provision of service. Railtrack is to charge the franchised providers of service for the use of its infrastructure. The details of this charging regime are immensely important to the success of the privatisation programme as well as to the future direction of transport in Britain.

A properly conceived infrastructure authority and charging regime can encourage the efficient use of assets. I quote from Mr. Per Andersson of the Swedish State Railways reflecting in May 1991 on the experience in Sweden after a similar separation between rolling stock related activities and the infrastructure authorities:

> "The Real Estate Division is the landlord of all land and buildings. All use free of cost is banned from the enterprise. All other divisions have to rent localities and land from the Real Estate Division and pay market prices. In their way every unit of SJ gives an account for costs and revenues and shows its real result. Earlier the different divisions had an insatiable desire for localities. Nowadays they have decreased their desires and minimized the localities and costs. The Real Estate Division has got increased resources to rent out on the external market."

In Sweden, although consideration is being given to introducing the private sector into the railways, both arms of the railway industry remain for the time being within the public sector. Based on wide-spread evidence one can safely expect that the private sector would be even more driven to efficient asset utilisation if the correct incentives were provided. These will have to be carefully built into the contracts between Railtrack and the franchisees and should probably deal with Railtrack assets on as small a unit basis as is practicable.

4. *Contracts and Role Definition*

The Government aims, in the introductory words of the White Paper, for "greater responsiveness to the consumer, and a higher quality of service and better value for money for the public who travel by rail." Extremely laudable aims! The dynamics of awarding the contracts to franchisees hold out the opportunity of these aims being met in the proposed industry structure.

British Rail has achieved much over the past decade in an environment of tight operating and financial contraints imposed by Government. These achievements have not had much positive impact on public opinion: consumer surveys consistently rank British Rail as the least satisfactory among public sector services. Muddled roles and objectives have contributed to the industry's problems. The proposed new structures separating purchase (the Government through the Franchising Authority on behalf of users) and provider (franchisee) provides the opportunity for greater clarity as to roles and objectives and for better service—as demonstrated in local authority compulsory tendering.

The relationship between purchaser and provider is to become one of contract. If the agreed contractor standards are not met, the franchisee will suffer financially. He will have a commercial incentive to meet standards in a way which BR, however well managed, has never had. If, prior to contract award, the prospective contract service standards are judged by potential bidders to be unattainable within the financial parameters, no franchisee will sign up. Or he will only sign up on a basis where the subsidy enables standards to be met, always taking projected improvements in efficiency into account. Higher subsidy levels may well prove to be the requirement lines (eg LTS or Kent Coast) that have suffered from lack of maintenance investment. The likely result of these pressures will be to the benefit of the railways and their users. Assuming that it is not politically acceptable to see rail service standards run down immediately following privatisation, I suspect H.M. Treasury is already having to contemplate a possible increase, at least initially, in its outlay of rail subsidy.

There are, clearly, a number of interests that will require balancing here. A on-rail competition, at least where the subsidised services run, seems remote (and the Consultation Document seems implicitly to recognise this). This balancing will need to be done mainly through the contract mechanism by the Regulator. The Regulator will have a duty to promote the interest of consumers (White Paper para 64; Consultation Document para 2.8). Clearly it is essential that the Regulator (and the Franchising Authority) be given, or be able to establish, positions that permit them to discharge this duty not only viz-à-viz franchisees but also under some circumstances viz-à-viz government.

The very process of role definition and the rebalancing of interests in this way provides an opportunity despite the eventually acknowledged absence of on-rail competition, for rail service improvement.

5. *Regional Railway Companies*

The proposal for companies more closely associated with their particular region, providing an avenue for local voice, seems to me to offer an unquantifiable benefit and a contribution to the distribution of power and to democracy.

6. *A Privatisation Different from Previous Ones: A New Industrial Space*

The proposed railway privatisation differs structurally from previous privatisations in other industries including those such as British Airways in the transport sector. In earlier privatisations a company was, after being tidied up, simply (though the process was costly to the taxpayer) transferred from one ownership to another with the railways, a basic restructuring of an industry is taking place. A new industrial space is being created. New entrants (not only franchisees, but also others such as operating lessors of rolling stock) will bring new ideas and dynamism. This is potentially much more exciting than past privatisations. From the process, lessons will be provided as to how the role of the state might be redefined in areas hitherto impervious to the Government's treatment.

One of these areas, topical and not unrelated to the privatisation of BR, is transport infrastructure investment. Here what "The Economist" called "an intelligent alliance between state and market" (11 September 1992) is needed. The alliance, if it is to operate broadly, cannot be based simply on funding criteria or total risk-shifting. This appears to have been amply demonstrated over recent years. Rather, it will have to involve an intelligent assessment and allocation of risks between the various parties (including the state) willing, and able most cost-effectively, to bear them. This will require thought, debate and experimentation. The state will not be able to opt out of this process given the long term nature of the assets. At a minimum it must set the rules and provide a coherent context as it is striving to do with the railways. The proposals for railway privatisation, with many questions yet to be answered "flexible solutions will be needed", White Paper para 12 offer the prospect of encouraging the process.

4 December 1992

APPENDIX 117

SUPPLEMENTARY EVIDENCE FROM THE RAILWAY DEVELOPMENT SOCIETY

As a member of the Railway Development Society, I am writing to you as a Vice-President, to draw your attention to the widespread concern there is over the Channel Tunnel Rail Link as to whether provision is being made for the adequate transport of classic or conventional freight (excluding aggregates) as well as passenger traffic.

The Link is now to have a capability to carry "some freight". The eastern section, having been designed, and chosen, as a passenger route, in a corridor which precludes expansion to four track, would need to be re-engineered to take classic freight.

It is now being re-engineered, but with gradients steepened to 1 in 40. The passenger "supertrains" for which it is being designed may be able to negotiate these at or near the postulated speed of 140 mph.

But are we seriously to believe that there are magical freight trains which can haul classic freight over these gradients, allied with the tight curves which are always conveniently overlooked, at speeds sufficient to avoid problems with cant incompatibility?

If the alignment chosen precludes a fully shared passenger/freight railway, such as the Neubaustrecke or the Rail-Europe proposal, the freight capability of the Link will be constrained to the limited amounts which can be carried on trains with performance characteristics similar to the passenger trains, such as the French La Poste. Franchisees would find carrying classic freight unviable and impracticable.

If the Link is to have a genuine classic freight capability, it should be possible to explain, at least in principle, how this is to be achieved. Three years of equivocation on the subject suggest it is not practicable, and the deeply shocking Union Railways "Briefing for MPs and Councillors—No.1" indicate that the Link will not carry conventional freight trains for the reasons given in the "Comparison of Routes", page 19; and that "consultation" will, once again, be cosmetic.

8 December 1992

APPENDIX 118

Memorandum from Mr R Smith to Mr Robert Adley MP, Chairman, Transport Committee

The Future of British Rail

I hope that you will spare a few moments to consider some constructive views on this pressing matter. I feel that almost alone among those at Westminster you have a sound knowledge of railways, share my anxieties at the way that rail transport in this country is going rapidly downhill, and take a thoroughly realistic approach to the debate on how matters can be improved.

My credentials are as a former rail commuter for over 14 years; as a former chief official in local government town planning, one-time regional planner and lecturer in the same field; as a long-term reader of *Modern Railways;* as a Eurotunnel shareholder; as a senior railcard holder who with my wife still regularly travels 450 miles by rail when visiting our daughters and grandchildren; and as a builder and operator of extensive model railways!

I am not a supporter of rail privatisation, because I believe in the virtues of a unified system, something that rail operators worldwide have recognised over the past 150 years as being better than early Stockton and Darlington methods. (If we must have a track authority, it should embrace the whole system). Even so, I should welcome a climate in which potential major customers of rail freight (such as pulpwood producers and shippers) who are prepared to operate their own trains over BR metals should have rights of access to do so. I also recognise the virtues of private enterprise in such fields as on-board catering, where many Scotrail passengers are very well served.

So much for background. To me the nub is that we should be trying to ensure the *maximum transfer of passenger and freight movements from road to rail,* in the interests of the environment, of the high-tech railway manufacturing industry and its valuable exports, of passenger safety, and to make better use of our magnificent system of rail rights of way.

I therefore believe that *the government must set out to create not merely a level playing field, but one designed to achieve a road to rail transfer largely through market forces.* At the moment all the portents in Britain most regrettably point the other way, due to the extreme financial and safety discrimination long levied against rail. Carelessly applied, privatisation threatens to destroy our valuable rail manufacturing industry just as it has already ruined our bus manufacturers and coal industry, and leave us with a rump rail system that does not do justice to our historic role as railway innovators.

To avoid this will require fresh and fair thinking and an urgent new legislative approach such as seems unlikely ever to emanate from either the Department of Transport or the Treasury, given their dismal past records and general lack of constructive thought on this fundamental problem. I have tried to summarise on the attached sheets some measures towards achieving these aims, which match those of the EC and which if critically applied should bring great benefits.

POINTS TOWARDS A BETTER RAIL SYSTEM

1. Consideration of all proposed central and local government transport infrastructure investments using the same formula, whether for road or rail; this formula to take into account all the environmental and safety benefits of rail, i.e. lower land take, lower calls on all emergency services, lower fuel consumption, less air pollution, etc.

2. Funding of all infrastructure improvements in road and rail in exactly the same way, by grant not loan since these remain national assets and should be open to all to use.

3. Immediate cessation of Treasury interference in BR rolling stock investment decisions (no such interference and consequent delay and loss of revenue as BR has endured since nationalisation has been placed in the way of road operators since 1953).

4. Relative rates of taxation of fuel for road and rail use for both passenger and freight services to reflect in inverse proportion the numbers of accidents per passenger-km and per tonne-km moved by road compared with rail. This should virtually free rail users of fuel taxes.

5. The transfer of all costs of providing and maintaining intersections between road and rail (bridges and level crossings) to road funds instead of the railways, which have borne most of these costs since their inception.

6. Adoption of the same system of inquiries into the causes of individual road accidents causing multiple deaths and serious injuries as are applied to rail, and identical concern for proper remedial measures. If as seems likely this proved too costly, in view of the disproportionately high number of road accidents, then government should cease to concern itself with rail safety problems, leave this to the HSE and concentrate all available resources on solving road safety problems, such as by imposing automatic guidance and speed regulation systems in road vehicles. This would force road users to carry the true but currently hidden costs of their operations.

7. The funding of the British Transport Police, if such a separate body has to be retained, to be identical with that of other police forces.

8. The transfer of all railway fencing renewal costs to adjoining proprietors, as in the case of highways; except that where trespass is a major problem, the state should contribute to the costs in order to protect rail users.

9. Transfer of all costs of maintaining historic railway structures no longer in use or usable for rail purposes, to other public or private funds.

I suggest that if these principles were immediately applied to the British rail and road systems there would be no need to denationalise either the rail tracks or the operation of most passenger trains; that much traffic would return to rail, BR's financial losses would rapidly disappear, and investment in rail rolling stock would rapidly rise.

FURTHER POINTS IF PRIVATISATION IS IMPOSED THROUGH A TRACK AUTHORITY:

10. *The state, not rail users, should assume financial responsibility for the infrastructure,* as it does for roads.

11. Consequently *no charge should be made for access to any uncongested rail route* either for BR operating sectors or duly licensed private operators. Even greater freedom of access is currently allowed to ALL British roads for licensed (and some unlicensed!) vehicle operators, the taxpayer already footing the bill. When applied to the railways this principle would encourage the use of less-used routes, but would of course require proper regulation of access times and movement arrangements by a Rail Track Authority (RTA).

12. To pay for this system of regulation and top up public rail route investment where most necessary, *charges should be levied on operators by the RTA for the use of congested sections* of rail routes, or for *preferential times of access* to generally uncongested routes. At the same time *road pricing* in congested locations should be introduced. For both modes the charges would be on an economic, ie competitive basis; those users both road and rail most likely to benefit being prepared to pay most.

13. Any net proceeds from road pricing would be required to be spent by the RTA on *improving the capacity of congested rail routes* by such measures as would enable the raising of speed limits, by new flyover or diveunder junctions, selective multiple tracking, resignalling with state of the art equipment to minimise headways, by electrification (or re-electrification using overhead catenary) and *by constructing entirely new routes* where all other measures fail.

14. Since the state owns the motorway system, a track authority should be able to obtain *the right to lay rail tracks in motorway central reservations,* subject to principle (1) above and to providing appropriate safety barriers. On their completion, such schemes would actually raise the carrying capacity of eg the congested M25 and provide an orbital rail system for London, creating opportunities for trains on such presently unserved routes as

(a) Poole—Woking—Heathrow—Stevenage

(b) Birmingham International—Milton Keynes—Hemel Hempstead—Basildon—Southend

(c) Ipswich—Brentwood—Dartford—Gatwick—Brighton

and so on.

18 December 1992

APPENDIX 119

Letter to Roger Freeman, Esq., MP, Minister of Transport, from the Railway Heritage Trust

Government Proposals for the Privatisation of British Rail

In response to the Government's privatisation proposals for British Rail, the Railway Heritage Trust on 30th September submitted its comments to the Transport Committee, chaired by Robert Adley, MP. A copy of my letter and submission is enclosed for ready reference.

On P7 para 4 "The Future", issues to be addressed were highlighted and observations on each option were made.

Of prime importance is para 4.1 where the future of the RHT and its funding is considered.

I appreciate the magnitude of your task in evaluating the numerous major issues involved in privatising British Rail, but the work and role of the RHT is seen as being as important to the future well-being of the railway heritage as it has been over the past seven years in the schemes it has sponsored.

Are you now able to give any guidance as to the future of the RHT and its work, which has always been given your valuable support.

23 December 1992

APPENDIX 120

Letter from Mr R Avery

Reduction in Freight Traffic by Rail

I am writing to you in your capacity as Chairman of the Commons Select Committee on Transport.

You may possibly have heard of me, as my photographs of rail subjects occasionally appear in various railway magazines. I know you are interested in railway photography yourself. However my reasons for writing are rather more fundamental.

I am extremely concerned about the reduction in the amount of freight traffic by rail in the last few months. I am employed by BR's Trainload Freight division and can state with authority as well as the traffic loss associated with the closure of Ravenscraig, the following flows of traffic have either ceased altogether within the last six months or are about to be lost to road transport:

Transport of new cars; Washwood Heath-Bathgate.

Movement of Grain Traffic, East Anglia-Burghead (Morayshire); 1 train per week.

A considerable amount of cement traffic from the Blue Circle plant at Oxwellmains, near Dunbar.

The much publicised collapse of the Charterail intitiative serving Deanside (Glasgow) and the proposed extension to Aberdeen.

A considerable reduction in petroleum traffic from Grangemouth, including the recently announced proposed discontinuance of rail-borne petroleum traffic to Oban, Connel Ferry, Fort William and Mallaig.

The very recently announced discontinuance of cement traffic between Clitheroe (Lancs) and Gunnie (Coatbridge). This was a daily very heavy flow, surely just the sort of traffic Trainload Freight are looking for.

The movement of steel from Tees-side and elsewhere to Stockton Haulage at Stranraer, en-route, presumably, to Ulster.

The end of a twice-weekly train from Exter to Mossend for Messrs Taunton Cider.

The above represents a very large amount of Railfreight's total Scottish tonnage, and I understand the picture is much the same over the whole country.

A number of my colleagues have friends/family who work in the industries affected, and certain disturbing similarities between each firm have come to light.

The common factor is large price increases (up to 80 per cent has been quoted to me) imposed by BR, who have displayed little or no willingness to negotiate or manoeuvre. Not surprisingly, existing and potential railfreight customers are being driven away. It seems very odd to me, a mere middle manager involved in everyday operations, that in an economic climate where most organisations are having to bend over backwards to retain business or find new customers, BR is doing its best to drive its customers away, indeed it seems to be succeeding admirably. One would of course expect a certain reduction of traffic in a recession but what is occurring is far in excess of what would be expected. My own enquiries within the industry have confirmed that a review of existing freight flows has indeed taken place, within substantial rate increases.

One does not need a great deal of imagination to realise that the whole thing is being orchestrated; that the present Government, hell-bent on privatisation, wants rid of all but the most profitable traffic flows as quickly as possible, irrespective of the consequences, so that potential entrepreneurs will be attracted to the idea of buying the freight business, or at least part of it.

My suspicions are fuelled by the recent article in The Independent which purported to show that the Department of Transport would be happy to see the end of Rail Freight altogether unless it was profitable.

It is with regret that I should have to write to point out what should be the blindingly obvious—that this policy flies in the face of common sense, for the following reasons:

(1) The British Railway System in its present form the capacity, through conveyance of freight traffic, and its removal from roads, to greatly increase the quality of life for many millions of people, both directly (people using and living near roads) and indirectly, by reducing overcrowding, increasing safety, reducing noise and atmospheric pollution and reduction of accidents. Yes, it would cost more, and it may not always be profitable, but it would be worth every penny. Try sitting at 45 mph on a wet day on the A74 near Lockerbie behind a stream of juggernauts, alongside the empty rails of the West Coast Main Line. Is this really what the Government wants? Apparently yes, and if this is the case, it will be the end of my support for them when the next ballot box comes round. Furthermore, surely what is happening flies in the face of stated Government Policy concerning safeguarding the environment.

(2) The opening of the Channel Tunnel in 1994 will present, hopefully, opportunities for Railfreight, but the Government seems determined to rid Railfreight of the means to handle any increased traffic on offer.

I have yet to meet anybody, in any walk of life or from any political persuasion (with the apparent exception of the present Department of Transport), who does not believe that most of the country's heavy freight should go by rail; I feel strongly that this is one area where your party's dogma about profits must be abandoned. It must be said, too, that the Conservative Party's apparent disregard of public opinion in matters of this nature is, sadly, only to be expected these days.

What I have said is practised in almost every other European country, but, same old story, not in Britain.

It is also most regrettable that I must ask you to keep this letter under wraps, and the fact that I have written to you confidential, as there is a school of thought within the industry which disapproves of people writing to Members of Parliament about matters which concern them, and I have a wife, two kids and a mortgage to pay off, and require to stay in employment.

29 December 1992

APPENDIX 121

Letter from Mr Robert Adley, MP to the Chancellor of the Exchequer

At the moment, I am withholding judgement on the practical effect of the Autumn Statement on British Rail insofar as the new arrangements for leasing are concerned.

The purpose of this letter, Norman, is to draw your attention to the Development (Loan Guarantees and Grants) Act of 1929. Under said Act, the railways undertook a considerable number of major capital improvement schemes; Government grants being available, up to maximum period of fifteen years, representing interest on the capital outlay incurred on the approved works.

The effect of the legislation was dramatic. Numerous major infrastructure schemes were undertaken, most of which were labour-intensive.

I wonder whether the Treasury would like to have a look at this particular piece of legislation and contemplate what effect might be achieved, at what price, in today's world.

14 December 1992

Reply from Mr S Dorrell to Mr Robert Adley's Letter

Thank you for your letter of 14 December to Norman Lamont. I was very interested to read your comments on the effects of the Development (Loan Guarantees and Grants) Act 1929 in attracting private finance into public infrastructure projects.

I very much share your interest in this area. As you may know, the Prime Minister has asked me to take forward the Government's private finance initiative.

Our aim, where possible, is to maximise the involvement of private finance in projects which have hitherto been the preserve of the public sector. The changes Norman announced in his Autumn Statement are a major step forward in achieving this objective. The end result should be that more investment can take place, freed from the inevitable constraints of the PSBR.

In the specific context of the railways, the proposals set out in last July's White Paper are, I think, clear evidence of our determination to attract private sector finance and skills into an industry which has long been deprived of them.

One point worth underlining in this context, however, is that we are not in the business of attracting private finance in order to break our own public expenditure controls. Naturally the private sector is keen to finance projects where the risk remains with the Government. I must say that I am very doubtful about the attractiveness of this sort of financing: to my mind, if the private sector is to take on responsibility for financing projects, it must also take on responsibility for risk. Not least among the benefits of this is the private sector's considerable skill at managing risk.

8 January 1993

APPENDIX 122

Supplementary evidence from Barclays de Zoete Wedd

Thank you for your letter of 11 February. I apologise for not replying earlier but I have been out of the country.

Your letter raises some interesting points. As a general principle it is not impossible for the private sector to enter into contracts with Government Agencies for a period in excess of the three year Public Expenditure Planning Cycle. In these circumstances the private sector investors would pay particular attention to the legal powers including the statutory duties and powers of enforcement, that the Franchising Authority would have. If the Authority were empowered to enter into long term contracts we think it is most likely that franchises would take the view that funds would be allocated to honour the contractual responsibility. The private sector would undoubtedly be cautious if the magnitude of the contract was large and the profitability of franchisees was unduly dependent on this subsidy.

I trust this information is useful in the on-going debate and please contact me if you require further information.

22 February 1993

APPENDIX 123

Supplementary Note from Central Railway

May we take this opportunity to make a number of points which may not have been clear during our hearing?

1. Many firms have committed time and resources to developing all aspects of Central Railway as a genuinely commercial railway project which could create a great deal of value for the taxpayer and indeed the country as a whole. Our approach to promoting our project is inevitably unfamiliar and different from that of subsidy-seeking projects. We are trying to bring to bear in the railways market private sector skills, management and finance. The company could only attract steadily growing support from serious firms, as it has, if they thought the project a serious attempt to establish a new railway business.

2. Lest there be any confusion on the matter, can we make it clear that the track gauge of the railway we propose is standard to BR, Eurotunnel and SNCF and other major European Railways outside the Iberian Peninsula. Any train operating on existing British railways could run over the new railway (apart from purely third rail electrified stock). We also propose links into other parts of the British railway system. Three are planned in particular:

— with the *Midland* main line at Leicester for access to the north of England;

— in West London for access to the *Western, West Coast and East Coast* main lines;

— to Waterloo International Station, and other London stations.

By building a railway entirely compatible with UK and Continental systems—both existing railways and new lines now being planned by *SNCF* and others—and of course compatible with Eurotunnel, CRG's railway would be a link between the European railway system and the UK's. British and Continental railway companies will be able to use access to Central Railway to provide rapid and reliable passenger and freight services to London and beyond.

3. Substantial work already done by our consulting engineers shows that the engineering is feasible. Our design enables any disruption caused by our upgrading work to be kept to the standard BR maintenance schedules.

4. CRG is not "cherry picking". On the contrary, we have made proposals to the Government to complete our route in an environmentally sensible way by acquiring discrete loss-making elements of the existing rail system and, by investing, improve services on them. We propose to remove the burden of subsidy for these lines from the taxpayer entirely.

CENTRAL RAILWAY

List of companies with which we are formally working on the project:

Financial Advisers

　　Robert Fleming & Co

　　Panmure Gordon

Lawyers

    McKenna & Co

    Slaughter & May

    Reynolds Porter Chamberlain

Project Managers/Engineering Design

    The Parsons Corporation

    Mott MacDonald

    Spie Batignolles

Market Research

    SNCF

    Higginson & Partners

Land Services

    Parkman Land Services

Auditors

    KPMG Peat Marwick

Insurance Advisers

    Alexander Stenhouse

22 February 1993

APPENDIX 124

Railway Heritage Trust's comments to the Transport Committee Inquiry—House of Commons, on the White Paper Proposals

1. *Background to RHT Formation*

1.1 Both the public & Government expressed growing concern re Environmental/Heritage issues post war

1.2 This led to legislation re Listing procedures to ensure retention of the nation's heritage buildings which were fast being demolished

1.3 Railway modernisation—the Beeching era of 50's and 60's—set out to change BR's image by sweeping away the old "steam" associations and introducing modern trains and stations

1.4 Criticism of BR's attitude to its rich heritage reached its zenith when the "Doric Arch" at Euston was demolished to make way for the new station

1.5 BR policy changed to a pro-active role towards Heritage and the Environment and offering funding for a new Trust—*independent* of BR—to focus on heritage buildings and structures

1.6 Following RSA conference in November 1984, the RHT was formed on 1st April 1985 whose two main aims were:—

    (1) The conservation of listed buildings and structures of historic interest which still form part of the operational railway.

    (2) To act as a catalyst between outside parties and BR Property Board on the conservation of non-operational listed buildings and structures with a view to their transfer to local trusts or other interested parties.

2. *Formation of Trust*

2.1 With strong support from BR, RHT was formed as an independent "company limited by guarantee" with a Chairman and three directors.

The Chairman was William McAlpine, later to become Sir William McAlpine, Bt, and the three Directors were Simon Jenkins, Marcus Binney and Leslie Soane. An "Advisory Panel" of 35 members who are enthusiastic about the environment and railway heritage give invaluable advice and support to the Trust. They represent a wide range of interests and are experts or influential in their professions.

2.2 Funding was provided by BR, initially with £1 million to be used on operational buildings.

BR Property Board quickly recognised the value of the Trust's role and provided a further £200,000 for non-operational property.

The BR sum has since been increased annually by inflation adjustments until the budget for 1991–92 was £1.7 million with BRPB providing £300,000.

2.3 A key role of the Trust has been to act as a catalyst with other parties in attracting financial support for schemes of value and interest to the local community. This has enabled BR's own funding for schemes to be enhanced and work carried out that would otherwise not be done. Heritage buildings—and BR had 1,073 in January 1992—frequently require a higher standard of repairs/restoration than would be affordable in BR's financial position. Thus BR's emphasis is on structural stability and safety rather than the quality of renovation a listed building warrants. The additional funding provided by other parties and the Trust has ensured more appropriatre standards are attained or work effected that would otherwise be neglected.

3. *Work of the Trust*

3.1 Historically, most of BR's infrastructure of bridges, viaducts, stations, signal boxes, warehouses, goods sheds, locomotive and carriage repair depots and a host of other ancillary buildings, were built in the 1825–1890 period. Many are over 150 years old and an even greater number are more than 100 years of age and increasingly need more extensive maintenance.

In the seven years since the Trust was formed, arising from the Department of the Environment's pressure for the completion of the national survey of buildings for listing purposes, the number of listed buildings in BR's portfolio has risen from 630 in 1965 to 1,073 in 1992—an increase of approximately 60 per cent. Additionally, it owns 49 scheduled Ancient Monuments.

These figures demonstrate the increasing demands on BR's finances and the importance of supplementing its conservation work by involving other organisations.

The Trust's role in focusing attention on railway heritage, both within BR and externally, has gained wide approval. BR's financial support for the Trust—some £8 million in seven years—and importantly, the attraction of a further £7.5 million from external parties, has meant over £15 million being spent on this work in addition to the considerably larger sums directed by BR to their heritage portfolio.

3.2 The Trust performs an important liaison role between BR and many other organisations with Heritage and Environmental interests.

Through RHT's involvement, links have been forged with official agencies, eg English Heritage, Historic Scotland and CADW and an improved relationship between BR and them now exists.

By working with the Association of Railway Preservation Societies (ARPS), it has been possible to benefit both BR and ARPS in disposing of redundant BR buildings for re-use on enthusiasts' railways—to the satisfaction of all parties.

Similarly, from membership of the English & Welsh Viaducts Committee and the Scottish Viaducts Committee, the Trust has assisted in disused viaducts being sold or handed over to local Trusts who then own and maintain them. The local community and BR gain from these joint activities.

This enabling role by providing "seed corn" funding for schemes has ensured the implementation of renovation work which could otherwise have foundered for want of an initial grant offer.

3.3 In April 1993, BR was re-organised into businesses, each with "bottom-line" financing responsibility. Despite pressure to improve their results there has been full support from the Chairman, BR Board and the businesses for the Trust to continue its work with BR's financial support. The Trust has this year been given a further £1.8 million for its work to continue.

3.4 Restored stations have become showpieces for the railway business as a whole, whether small country stations like Downham Market and Beverley, or major city stations such as Bristol Temple Meads. Dirty, decaying stations are a discouragement to potential passengers: one of the Trust's major achievements has been to show just how dramatically a run-down station can be transformed, becoming a landmark that is a source of pride to the whole community.

3.5 Since 1985, some 300 stations, bridges etc, have been given Trust grants and this represents less than one third of BR's listed structures.

There are many more needing similar attention.

4. *The Future*

The foregoing briefly portrays how the Trust was formed, its objectives, and progress to date.

From expressions of interest and support by the public, it is clear that the railway heritage must be conserved but how is this best to be achieved under the Government's privatisation proposals?

Issues to be addressed are:

4.1 Is the Railway Heritage Trust to be retained and, if so, how is it to be funded? The work could be seen as complementary to that of the proposed track authority—RAILTRACK, with its responsibility for infrastructure. A "ring-fenced" allocation of funding from track tolls could be provided to safeguard the future of the railway heritage, similar to the Trust's present work.

4.2 The proposal—paragraph 17 of the White Paper "New Opportunities for the Railways"—for the private sector to lease/purchase stations could transfer all responsibilities for those listed to the new lessee/owner. Short-term leases for buildings would not be conducive to the maintenance and repairs being to adequate standards—leading to a degradation over time.

If the Trust is retained, its scope could be widened to cover grants to any "eligible" tenant/owner of historic railway buildings.

4.3 Per paragraph 18, the long-term future of railway heritage could be dealt with either by a Trust funded by the private sector or as a division of the Government agencies in this field, eg English Heritage. Funding support from external agencies, if the latter course is pursued, would probably cease.

4.4 A key feature of any success achieved by the Railway Heritage Trust has been its *independent* role as perceived by all parties involved with the Trust.

5. *Conclusion*

The Railway Heritage Trust has been successful in its objectives to help BR to conserve the rich and diverse railway heritage of buildings and structures which more and more are seen as an important and attractive part of Britain's environment. This is reflected in the interest of the public in the work of the Trust and from the interest and support of the Tourist industry both at home and from overseas. Britain is seen as the leader in the field of industrial archeology with its railway heritage and other countries are now recognising its importance to their built environment.

With Britain being the birthplace of the railway-led Industrial Revolution, there is increasing interest, both from home and overseas, in all aspects of the railways' impact on the environment. None more so than in the bridges, viaducts, stations, hotels, goods sheds, locomotive depots, signal boxes and a host of other buildings built by the Stephensons and Brunels of history.

The proposals for the privatisation of BR must reflect the importance of the railway heritage and make specific provision for its future.

30 September 1992

APPENDIX 125

Memorandum from Mr. P. K. Else: Sheffield University Management School

SOME IMPLICATIONS OF THE PROPOSED RESTRUCTURING OF BRITISH RAIL

1. An important feature of the Government's plans for privatising British Rail, as set out in the White Paper, is the proposal to split British Rail's current activities between a number of different concerns. One potential advantage of this is that it facilitates the introduction of competition by separating out those activities where competition is potentially possible, such as the provision of actual train services, from those which are naturally monopolistic, such as the provision of track and signalling (infrastructure). When both activities are combined within the same organisation the tendency to natural monopoly in the provision of infrastructure tends to dominate. The separation of functions makes it easier for competition in the provision of services to be introduced and maintained. However, there are a number of disadvantages which could arise with a less integrated structure than currently exists. The purpose of this memorandum is to point out a number of them. Some arise directly from the proposed separation of responsibility for providing track from that for providing services (see paras 2 to 6 below) whilst others stem from the division of responsibility for operating different services between separate independent concerns, which will follow from the proposals to allow such concerns to bid for the right to operate services or groups of services (see paras 7 to 11 below).

2. Considering first the separation of responsibility for providing services from that of providing infrastructure, the government's proposals envisage that the track authority, Railtrack, will set its charges at a level sufficient to cover its costs and provide an adequate return on its capital. A particular problem here is that such an arrangement could price some traffic, which would be profitable to a unitary organisation, out of the railway market.

3. It has long been established in the management accounting literature, that, if one branch or division of a company sells materials or services to another branch, which are used in the provision of some final product, the appropriate *transfer price* is equal to the marginal cost of producing those materials or services. That is, basically, the cost the branch would avoid by not producing it. This then allows the buying branch to set its price for the final product at a level which is most beneficial to the company as a whole, taking account of all relevant costs. If it is charged a higher transfer price, then it would tend to set a higher price for its final product, to the detriment of sales volumes and also to the profits of the organisation as a whole.

4. A particular problem with railways is that the marginal cost arising from one train's use of a particular section of track is relatively low, amounting to little more than the extra wear and tear involved and the costs of operating the signalling system. In fact, the bulk of railway infrastructure costs are fixed costs which don't vary with track use, particularly in the short run. This means that it would be impossible for Railtrack to cover its costs with marginal cost based pricing, let alone earn a satisfactory return on its capital. As a separate company, it would thus feel obliged to charge prices for track use well above marginal cost. The problem is that such prices could deter low margin traffic which is, nevertheless, potentially profitable to the railway system as a whole, in that it is capable of generating revenue greater than the additional costs imposed on the system by accepting it. Moreover deterring such low margin traffic could reduce the viability of some higher margin traffic because it would then have to bear a larger proportion of the fixed costs of the system (see Appendix 1 for a simple numerical example).

5. The traditional approach of railway concerns to this kind of problem has been to develop a system of charging what the traffic will bear, so that the bulk of fixed costs are recovered from high charges on traffic for which rail travel has particular advantages, whilst other traffic, for which other modes of transport are more competitive, is carried at relatively low prices and makes a smaller contribution to fixed costs.

6. In principle, such a discriminatory approach could be adopted by Railtrack but it would face two problems in attempting to implement it. The first is that it would not be dealing directly with the final users of the services, and so would be less close to the market. Its information on what the traffic could bear would, therefore, inevitably be more fragmentary than that available to whose fixing charges under present arrangements. Secondly, there is the problem of the extent to which the regulator would allow such discriminatory pricing, given that it would involve Railtrack exploiting its monopoly powers in certain markets.

7. Turning to the problems arising from the provision of different services by different operators, any individual train service provides a service for passengers between stations served on its route, but is also likely, to a greater or lesser extent, to be used by passengers travelling to and from destinations requiring the use of other services as well. Thus, for example, the current local services from Leeds and Huddersfield to Sheffield via Barnsley, are used by passengers travelling to and from stations on its route to London, Birmingham, Newcastle, Glasgow and a host of other destinations as well as the stations directly served by these services. In the absence of these local services, some of the longer distance passengers would no doubt find their way to the nearest convenient rail head and travel on by train from there, but others would undoubtedly transfer to other modes of transport for their entire journeys. The existence of one service thus helps to sustain demand and revenue on a number of others, and a curtailment of one service may have an adverse effect on the profitability of others.

8. A single undertaking responsible for the provision of all services should, as a matter of course, take these wider effects into account in deciding on the level of service to offer. If, however, in the example quoted above, one organisation was responsible for the local services and others for connecting services to a range of other destinations, the local operator's decisions would be based on the revenue arising from journeys on the local service alone, to the exclusion of revenue generated for other rail services. This would mean that any benefits, in terms of improved profitability, to that operator of, for example, an improvement in the local services would be less than the benefits to the railway network as a whole. Such improvements, therefore, which might appear to be unprofitable for an independent operator, could be profitable for a more integrated concern. Moreover, in more extreme circumstances, an integrated concern may find a marginal service financially viable, whereas an independent concern trying to run it would not.

9. It might be argued that if the providers of any service benefited sufficiently from the existence of an unprofitable connecting service, then it could compensate the operator of the latter to keep it going. However, whilst that might be a possible solution if there were only one operator benefiting, it would be much more difficult for satisfactory compensation payments to be arranged when a number of other operators were involved, because of the problems involved in assessing what should be paid by each individual operator. (See Appendix 2 for another simple numerical example). There might, therefore, be a tendency for a set of independent concerns to run fewer and less frequent services than a more integrated concern. An obvious corollary of this would seem to be that the maintenance of the existing range of unprofitable, but presumably socially desirable services, currently operated by Briitsih Rail would require rather greater subsidies than at present.

10. These tendencies could be accentuated if the break-up of British Rail made it more difficult for its customers to plan more complicated journeys involving the use of several trains because of the lack of a national time-table, fare-tables and through booking facilities. This in itself could reduce the demand for rail travel relative to other forms of transport by raising the real cost to passengers of rail journeys, and also raise the cost of organising freight movements.

11. Again, therefore, there are reasons for suggesting that services which would be accepted as profitable on an integrated rail system might be seen to be less viable under the less integrated organisation proposed for the railway system in Britain. It might, of course, be argued, that opening up the rail system to competition from new operators will generate sufficient efficiency gains to make marginal services more viable and hence offset these tendencies. It may also be observed, however, that, in the nature of things, such competition is likely to be fairly limited. The restrictions on infrastructure capacity and the need to pre-plan the use of it must inevitably mean that the market for rail travel is less contestable than other transport markets. In addition, the negotiation of appropriate contracts between Railtrack and operators and between operators of related services is likely to involve transactions costs which could absorb at least some of the efficiency gains.

Peter K Else, Senior Lecturer in Economics Sheffield University Management School

Appendix 1

1. Consider an individual railway route on which there are two distinct traffics, F and G, which can perhaps best be considered as two types of freight traffic with, say five trainloads of freight each week. Suppose the monthly costs directly attributable to each traffic are the same and as indicated in Table 1 below, and, in

addition, that there are fixed costs associated with maintaining the route of £52,000 per month. The maximum prices chargeable are assumed to be £60,000 and £100,000 per month for F and G respectively, determined by the costs of using some alternative mode of transport. Higher rail charges would thus mean that the traffic transfers to that alternative mode. However, it would be possible for an integrated railway company, providing both track and services to keep the charges for each traffic below their maximum levels and still cover its costs. For example, if the charge for F was set at £57,000 and that for G at £95,000 total costs would just be covered and there would be some scope for raising prices a little to generate some modest profits.

Table 1

	Costs and Revenues (£'000 per month)	
	F	G
Service cost	40	40
Attributable track cost	10	10
Maximum price chargeable	60	100
Maximum surplus over attributable costs	10	50
Possible cost covering charges	57	95
Minimum charge with equal allocation of fixed costs	76	76

2. Under a system with independent track and service providers, the track concern, less aware of the different choices open to F and G, might attempt to charge the same price for both uses of the track. To cover its costs, it would have to set a charge of at least £26,000 to each for the use of its tracks,which would mean the total charge to both F and G for the use of rail transport would have to be at least £76,000 if all costs were to be covered. With the charge at this level, rail would remain the best option for G, but F would seek to transfer to its alternative mode of transport. Moreover, with no traffic F and unchanged fixed costs, the costs to be covered by traffic G would rise to £102,000 which would then be above G's maximum price. Both traffics could thus be lost to rail, even though they could, taken together be carried profitably.

Appendix 2

1. Consider now a highly simplified railway system in which there are two connecting lines. Line 1 carries passengers from A to B and line 2 from B to C, with some passengers from A changing at B and travelling on to C and *vice versa*. The traffic flows across the network are summarised in Table 2.

Table 2

	Journeys per day ('000)		
To	A	B	C
From A		60	40
B	60	—	60
C	40	60	—

2. If Passengers all pay £1 per trip between A and B and B and C and £2 for the combined trips, the revenues on each line are as indicated in Table 3. Further with costs as indicated in the third column of Table 3, the net surpluses are as indicated in the final column.

Table 3   £'000 per day

	Revenue	Costs	Net Surplus
Line 1	200	230	−30
Line 2	200	160	40

3. With these figures it can be seen that, taken as a whole, the network is profitable, but by itself, line 1 appears to be unprofitable. Under separate ownership, therefore it might appear to be a candidate for closure. Moreover, under extreme assumptions, in which all users of line 1, irrespective of whether they travel on to C, transfer to other modes of transport when line 1 is closed, line 2 is left with only 120 passengers per day and, assuming no further cost savings were possible, would also become unprofitable.

4. Under these circumstances it would be worthwhile for the operator of line 2 to offer a subsidy of £30,000 per day to the operator of line 1 to keep it in operation, but with more operators in the network the problems of negotiating appropriate subsidy arrangements become greater, as can be seen if a third line from B to D is added to the network and traffic flows are as in Table 4.

Table 4

	Journeys per day ('000)			
to	A	B	C	D
From A	—	60	20	20
B	60	—	70	60
C	20	70	—	10
D	20	60	10	—

5. In this case, with the same fare structure as in the previous example, the revenues, costs and net surpluses are as indicated in Table 5.

Table 5 £'000 per day

	Revenue	Costs	Net Surplus
Line 1	200	230	−30
Line 2	200	170	30
Line 3	180	170	10
Total	580	570	10

6. Again the network as a whole appears profitable, but line 1, taken in isolation, does not. Again, however, lines 2 and 3 benefit from keeping line 1 open, because without the traffic using that line, they would both be £40,000 per day worse off. Once more, therefore, they would have some incentive to pay to ensure the service on line 1 was kept open, but this time there is scope for disagreement on who pays what. Since both stand to gain the same amount, it could be argued that they should pay equal amounts. On the other hand, it might be argued that the operator of line 2 should pay more because it has the greater profits and thus a greater ability to pay. But even if that point was conceded, there would be scope for considerable disagreement on how much more that operator should pay.

7. Clearly, as the number of affected operators increases, the problems of securing agreement between operators on the payments to be made to keep the parts of any network in a similar position to line 1 in our simple example increase. The fact that any operator is unlikely to have access to full information about the financial position of its potential partners is an additional problem which adds further to the difficulties of reaching a satisfactory agreement. In contrast, a unitary organisation running all services should, as long as it was sufficiently aware of the interdependencies between its services, find it much easier to identify the optimal arrangements.

4 January 1993

APPENDIX 126

THE INSTITUTION OF ELECTRICAL ENGINEERS

Future of the Railways

I should be grateful if you would draw the following comments to the attention of the Chairman and Members of the Select Committee.

The Institution does not propose to comment on the principle of privatisation, but on the credibility of the proposed methods. It is essential for the future maintenance and development of the railway system in the UK that there exists a vertically integrated organisation of sufficient size and authority to achieve the necessary economies of scale, which are essential in research, development, design and procurement.

Privatisation of British Rail

The White Paper "New Opportunities for Railways" has been studied with interest and this letter embodies the major issues and concerns identified by members, particularly those who have expert knowledge of railways, their equipment and operation.

The White Paper

The White Paper fails to adequately reflect the complexities of all aspects of the railway system. Its treatment of management, operations, maintenance and procurement is superficial, and so lacking in form that specific criticism is difficult. One area of particular concern is the section entitled Technical Standards and Research where these vitally important subjects are dismissed in three short paragraphs (95 to 97), no attempt is made to set research and development into the context of the proposed structure following privatisation.

Not only does the White Paper fail to adequately address matters relating to the organisation and operation of the railways subsequent to privatisation, but it also largely ignores issues which need to be resolved prior to privatisation.

The following list serves to identify not only these elements but also illustrates the detail in which they need to be considered:

— The definition of technical standards for equipment and system interfaces to ensure that in the event of fragmented regional operation, the various subsystems will nevertheless operate as an engineering integrated system of high integrity.

— An economics of operation framework including R&D estimates based on target measures of performance relating to customer need eg, viable fare structures, including those for low population areas, based upon fully itemised cost headings.

— If the infrastructure is to be run and maintained by a single technical management with franchises being used for the regional commercial operations, then a clear definition of the technical, engineering and operational responsibilities of each party are needed.

— The definition of a shared well founded support R&D infrastructure eg, a shared technical centre within which projects persecuted by operators and British equipment supplies can be carried out making use of shared equipment and facilities and an assessment of the likely cost structure. This will help ensure collaborative working and the maintenance of strong technical support to high standards.

— Definition of the arrangements to be made for ensuring high standards of maintenance and repair of infrastructure and systems.

System Requirements

Modern railways are complex systems and all aspects must be effectively integrated and controlled in order to achieve safe and efficient operation. It is not possible to effect changes in one area without considering their impact elsewhere in the system.

This applies irrespective of whether the subject being considered is short-term, for example, today's operating schedule, or involves longer-term proposals, such as new types of track, signals and/or rolling stock. The individual railway passenger is made all too easily aware of the integrated nature of the railway system by the delays and difficulties which he or she experiences as a result of unrelated failures, often remote from the chosen route.

New technological developments can only be introduced through a system which has the means to integrate and control both the new and the existing system. Developments leading to increased speed and other improvements can only be successful if the operation of these new faster trains is compatible with all aspects of the existing system, and furthermore can only be effectively exploited if the existing system is flexible enough to accommodate any new requirements. There is particular concern because of the continuing high rate of innovation, and the resulting lack of technological maturity. These in turn give rise to significant problems which make substantial demands on management. Examples include the problems of achieving electromagnetic compatibility (EC Directive) and other related problems associated with electrical noise and the limits imposed by the electricity supply companies (RECs).

It cannot be over-emphasised that a modern railway, most particularly an electric railway, is technically a system in itself and the trains, track and power supply are in a continuous, close and intimate inter-relationship which requires that they be designed together. The latest signalling and control systems, for example, are physically partly on the track and lineside, and partly on the trains.

Safety

The achievement and maintenance of the highest possible level of safety must be the first consideration of railway operation. Satisfactory safety standards will not be attained merely by close supervision and control of daily operations, but must be present at all levels, and at all stages, including those associated with research and development. This will only be achieved if this requirement is designed into the overall organisation from the outset.

Although it may be possible to attain acceptable standards by imposing a regime based on strict management, in turn monitored and supervised by an external body such as the HSE, as is proposed in the White Paper, this type of arrangement can never provide the same assurance as the fully integrated arrangement referred to above.

The need for safety inevitably limits the discretion which can be given to any group participating at a subordinate level. Furthermore, the existence of an increased number of interfaces subject to commercial pressures, themselves generate further cause for concern, not least because of the additional load imposed by their supervision and control.

Management and Structure

In any enterprise it is essential that all participants are similarly motivated and share a commitment in the achievement of a common goal. For the railways this might be expressed in its simplest terms as the safe operation of the system with all trains running at, or very close to their scheduled times.

This need for a common aim appears to have been given little consideration in the White Paper, and indeed the division proposed with train operation separated from the provision of the track and signalling system illustrates this point. It is not clear what will motivate the track providers who may well have different priorities, for example, giving lower track maintenance costs greater importance than increased train speeds, whereas train operators will surely wish to pursue higher speeds and improved journey times.

Industrial Considerations

The growing costs associated with the development, design and manufacture, together with the drive for increased efficiency have resulted in continuing rationalisation of the railway equipment supply industry. Industrial re-organisation in Europe has now led to the grouping of suppliers in a few major firms. These companies now compete for major contracts worldwide and without the countervailing power of a large customer it is unlikely that the suppliers will be willing to supply equipment particular to the needs of the UK at economic prices. Furthermore, the fragmentation of the home market will make the survival of the remaining UK railway equipment manufacturers more doubtful, and will certainly affect their ability to undertake sufficient research and development in order to secure overseas markets.

Research Development

As noted previously the White Paper deals with research and development in a superficial manner. No proposals are made for the future of the research and development facilities currently operated by British Rail, and indeed the only reference to this matter is a statement that the Government is considering how best to involve the private sector in railway research.

Under existing public sector arrangements it is unfortunately the case that a number of initiatives involving significant advances in railway technology have not received the funding required to enable them to be implemented. Under the White Paper proposals, however, it is not clear how even the initial research is to be funded. Any fragmentation of responsibility and the introduction of greater diversity of commercial interests correspondingly increases the difficulty of achieving the concentration of resources and interests required for success in high technology. The Institution has previously drawn attention to the need to facilitate all steps in the process of innovation, and it is noted with regret that the current White Paper proposals appear totally to ignore this matter.

At best, if implemented, the White Paper's proposals would stifle innovation with the result that the development of railway technology in the UK would be dramatically slowed, and the UK railway equipment industry would be further weakened. Ultimately our railways would be based on imported technology, and equipment.

If the Institution can be of further assistance we would be pleased to provide it.

22 January 1993

APPENDIX 127

BRITISH RAILWAYS BOARD

Please find attached the information that was requested by the Committee during their visit on 26 January.

Unfortunately, we no longer produce line loading diagrams of the type requested. However, I have provided a list of the average loading figures for Borough Market Junction.

The figures for Thameslink journey statistics account for the number of journeys for the most recent 13 periods, and include all classes of travel, in both directions.

Borough Market Junction

| | Charing Cross | | Cannon Street | |
	Up	Down	Up	Down
Design Capacity	30	30	30	30
Off-peak "standard hour"	21*	21*	4	4
Busiest hour:				
a.m.	29	29	27	23
p.m.	26	26	22	26

* two of these trains are Thameslink services, and two are South Central services.

At Cannon Street it is possible to route a small number of trains away round the 3rd side of the Borough Market triangle to the carriage sidings at Stewarts Lane.

THAMESLINK STATISTICS

Interstation Flows

Bedford to Brighton	10,681
Luton to Gatwick Airport	25,186
St Albans to Croydon (East and West)	11,417
St Albans to Brighton	16,030
St Albans to Gatwick Airport	31,333
St Albans to Sutton	1,813
West Hampstead to Tulse Hill	90
West Hampstead to Croydon (East and West)	337
Cricklewood to Streatham	66

Operational Statistics

Customers carried every weekday	*70,000*
Customers travelling in morning peak	*24,400*
Trains every weekday	*261*
Total carriages owned	*344*
Total train miles every year	*5,300,000*
Stations served daily	*82*
Passenger Revenue budgeted (1992–93)	*54,300,000*
Staff directly employed	*610*

Customer Statistics (per cent)

Origin of travellers 1991:	
London	35
Outside London	65
Journey Purpose:	
To/from work	42
To/from school/college	6
Employer's business	11
Personal business	18
Visiting friends/relatives	18
Sports/entertainment	6
Shopping	3
Holiday	5
Other	3
Average age of customers:	
Under 24	18
24–59	72
60 +	10

COST AND REVENUE SHARING BETWEEN BR AND LONDON TRANSPORT

There is extensive and long standing integration between the services of BR (Network SouthEast) and London Underground in both the provision of services and facilities and the sharing of revenue.

Cost sharing relates to the operation of joint lines and stations. There are four joint lines, three owned by BR and one by LT, where both parties run trains, and 26 joint stations, where one party sells tickets and provides retail services on behalf of the other but train operation remains separate.

Joint lines are the responsibility of the owning administration, to whom all revenue is allocated. The owner is responsible for stations and safety, the other operator runs trains and is reimbursed costs by agreement. Joint station costs are charged by the owner on an agreed formula related to use. The gross charges for joint lines and stations amount to about £6m per year, or a net payment of £1m by BR to LT.

Through ticketing between BR and LT is well established and reflects not just the need to provide for joint lines and stations, but the extensive interavailability and through booking that is offered on one ticket between the separate railway administrations, including the facility to cross London between BR termini by Underground.

Effectively the two railways provide a common structure of through fares and have compatible ticketing. Present requirements include encoded tickets in a special format for the automatic gates. It is also necessary to coordinate pricing decisions and the timing of changes, and agree procedures for the divison of revenue.

The largest single item of joint revenue is the Travelcard, sold in both season ticket and one day off-peak form, which now caters for much of the London journey-to-work and leisure markets. This product is priced and promoted by agreement between NSE and LT, but subject to Government regulation. Unlike ordinary single and return tickets, because of its Zonal mulit-modal nature, Travelcard revenue cannot be indentified to particular lines or stations. Instead surveys are undertaken of actual use, from which factors can be derived to allocate revenue to BR and LT, using passenger miles as a measure. Travelcards issued are then split between revenue retained and revenue transferred, by an appropriate "apportionment factor".

The gross annual value of Travelcard revenue is £788m with a net transfer from BR to LT of £86m, and a further net transfer of £15m for other tickets. In practice there is a complex settlement of net costs and revenues made between BR and LT, with payments, from BR to LT, made 4 weekly in arrears.

12 February 1993

APPENDIX 128

BRITISH RAILWAYS BOARD

Evidence by Castle Cement

Thank you for the opportunity to comment on the evidence given to the Committee by Castle Cement on 27 January.

We would like to make the following points:

1. Locomotives

Trains from Clitheroe were worked by Class 37 locomotives, not Class 47. It is common for Class 37s to be operated in pairs to maximise train size and trains from Clitheroe were operated on this basis. Only in exceptional circumstances would more than two locomotives be needed—for example to rescue a failed train.

Class 37 locomotives are between 28 and 33 years old and this obviously impacted on their reliability. Plans were developed, and were about to be implemented prior to Castle Cement's decision to cease using rail, to use brand new Class 60 locomotives on trains from Clitheroe.

2. Continuity of Management

The account manager for Castle Cement's business was seconded for 4 months on a project to develop new business. The covering arrangements involved an experienced senior manager and were advised to Castle Cement in advance. Normal, regular liaison was maintained during the period of secondment.

3. Service Quality

Trainload Freight would not claim that service quality on these traffics was perfect and has, on occasion, fallen to unacceptable standards. Given that the nature of the evidence presented to the Committee was anecdotal and had no statistical backing it is impossible to comment on specific instances. However, considerable managerial effort has been devoted to improving service quality for Castle Cement's trains.

Trainload Freight is committed to a high quality of service and other witnesses to the Committee paid tribute to this. Over 75 per cent of Trainload Freight's business is now accredited to quality standard ISO 9000.

12 February 1993

APPENDIX 129

BRITISH RAILWAYS BOARD

During the session on 27 January, Sir Bob Reid undertook to write to the Committee concerning the future of the line between Blackburn and Hellifield.

This line, although previously used solely in connection with the Castle Cement works at Clitheroe, is in fact "owned" by our Regional Railways' passenger business—only the section between Blackburn and Clitheroe was used for freight traffic.

The future of the line is not in danger because of the transfer of Castle Cement traffic onto the roads—the contribution this provided towards the maintenance of the line was marginal, and there are other possibilities for the lines future.

It is currently used by Regional Railways "Dalesrail" services, operating at weekends since 1972, which run from Manchester and Blackpool to Carlisle via Blackburn, Hellifield and the Settle and Carlisle line.

This line has also seen the recent introduction of a Saturday-only service between Blackburn and Clitheroe, and proposals are currently being examined for the introduction of a regular passenger service from May

1994. This would involve the opening of three new stations at Whalley, Langho and Wilpshire, and the rebuilding of Clitheroe.

The services currently in operation are included in our timetables and, as such, are regarded by the North West England Transport Users Consultative Committee as fulfilling our statutory obligation to run passenger services over the line.

The line also has strategic importance as it enables the diversion of services from the West Coast Main Line to allow engineering work.

16 February 1993

APPENDIX 130

Thank you for your letter of 7 December to William Waldegrave about the Citizen's Charter and BR privatisation. I am replying on William's behalf.

You asked whether identical obligations would apply to private sector train operators in future as apply to BR now. It is, of course, important to recognise that the Citizen's Charter is not about us imposing obligations. It is about those organisations which provide a service to the public—such as BR—making clear the standards they aim to meet, and their code of practice for dealing with their customers when, for whatever reason, they fail.

The British Rail Passenger's Charter is *BR's* document—BR's own code of practice for dealing with railway passengers. We do not expect private sector rail operators running services under franchises to adopt BR's Charter verbatim. Rather, franchisee's will generally be expected to publish their own codes of practice for dealing with passengers if standards of service fall below a certain level. Each franchisee's charter should thus be regarded as complementary to the minimum service standards and quality levels that will be written into the franchise contract and monitored by the new Franchising Authority.

We believe that private sector operators will be able to offer better quality to the passenger, in terms of punctuality and reliability, than BR currently offers.

21 January 1993

APPENDIX 131

Letter from the Department of Transport

Thank you for your letter of 1 December about subsidy for franchised services.

The franchise contract will specify the service and quality levels that the franchisee is to deliver in return for the subsidy that the Franchising Authority will make available to support those services. Competitive tendering in the franchising process will ensure that the successful bid for subsidy provides the best value for money. (If none of the bids received by the Authority represents value for money then it will require BR to continue to run the services.)

Provided that the franchisee meets his contractual obligations, he will be free to apply any profits as he sees fit. However, regular financial returns to the Franchising Authority will reveal if "excess" profits are being made (perhaps because of greater than expected efficiency improvements), and will inform the Invitation to Tender put out for subsequent franchises, so helping ensure that in the subsequent franchise better value for money is achieved for the general taxpayer.

John MacGregor

23 December 1992

APPENDIX 132

Letter from the Department of Transport

I refer to your letter of 18 January 1993 about capital investment in BR over the next three years and about BR's Outline Plan.

Figures for future capital investment can only be broad estimates at this stage. They will be refined further by BR as they develop their budget for 1993–94 and their Corporate Plan for subsequent years. Figures for 1994–95 and 1995–96 will, or course, be subject to further consideration in forthcoming public expenditure rounds.

Nevertheless, current estimates by both the Government and by BR are consistent with the *broad* estimates for likely capital investment which I gave at the Select Committee Hearing. These estimates reflect definitions and price bases used for the public expenditure round. The broad estimates which I gave you also included the arrangement, announced at the time of the Autumn Statement, for leasing of an additional £150 million of new rolling stock by BR over the next three years.

You question the consistency of such broad estimates for capital investment with the EFL figure set for 1995–96. Income for investment purposes is not limited to that covered by the EFL. The EFL relates to grant payments by central Government, primarily PSO grant, and borrowing by BR. Investment is also funded by income from revenues (fares and charges), asset sales and grants by PTEs.

You ask me to supply you with a copy of British Rail's Outline Plan. The Outline Plan is a working document, produced by British Rail in consultation with officials in my Department, and it is subject to regular up-dating and revision both during and after the annual public expenditure round. The latest version is no more than a draft, and much of it has already been overtaken by events. It would therefore be inappropriate and perhaps misleading to make the Outline Plan public.

The appropriate document will be the Board's budget. We will of course be happy to give the Committee a clearer view on BR's plans for 1993–94 once that has been finalised.

I am copying this letter to Sir Bob Reid.

John MacGregor

27 January 1993

APPENDIX 133

Letter from the Department of Transport

Thank you for your letter of 10 November about what might happen if a franchisee went into liquidation.

The Railways Bill will contain specific provisions to ensure the continuity of services in the event of a franchisee going into liquidation.

John MacGregor

4 January 1993

APPENDIX 134

Letter from the Department of Transport

Thank you for your letter of 26 January about railway infrastructure investment under the Government's privatisation proposals.

The fundamentals of the new regime are clear. Railtrack will be responsible for ensuring that the basic railway infrastructure is maintained at an appropriate level. Railtrack will be a Government-owned company. Improvements to the infrastructure should be in response to the demands and needs of operators; so far as possible and appropriate, operators should pay for the improvements which they want, and the Government will, of course, encourage and facilitate a regime which encourages this.

The rest of this letter deals with the more detailed application of these principles and the procedures to be adopted.

Under current arrangements, most infrastructure investment decisions on individual projects—from inclusion in the Rail Plan, to authorisation and funding—are for BR. Decisions on the overall level of investment are made in the annual Investment and Financial Review (IFR) during public expenditure rounds. But in future, Railtrack will take lead responsibility for investment in infrastructure. I will be looking to Bob Horton and his future top management team to develop their own proposals for investment plans and procedures. I certainly do not wish to tie Railtrack down at this stage. So what I say must be treated as indicative only at this stage, so far as Railtrack's own detailed approach is concerned.

Subject to that essential qualification, I would expect Railtrack to develop medium-and long-term plans. A corporate plan (similar to the present BR corporate plan) would take forward the financial planning of Railtrack, including its planned investment, for five years into the future. In recognition of the time required to initiate and plan investment in railway infrastructure, there should be a long-term plan for the following five years (a procedure not currently undertaken by BR), setting out in broad terms the future investment which Railtrack access contracts with operators. Railtrack's corporate and investment plans will be considered during the annual IFR discussions with Government. My aim will be to keep to a minimum Government consideration of individual projects.

Railtrack will need to hold discussions with others in the industry in order to form a view of the likely demand for investment. The Franchising Director will need to be involved in these discussions, as will franchisees. Investment of this kind may take many years to plan and execute, so the Franchising Director may need to act, in a sense, as a proxy for future franchisees, as well as needing to take account of the changes to service patterns which major investment projects might facilitate when looking at passenger demand and the specification of franchised services. However, I would expect investment in Railtrack to be commercially driven: this means that if it is Railtrack which is bearing the financial risk associated with investment decisions and income from access charges, it is Railtrack which must have the final say.

Railtrack will be self-financing: it will need to recover through charges its day to day operating costs and a return on assets. Railtrack's investment decisions will be influenced by the charges it expects to receive from operators, although the Government may provide direct grant support for investment for schemes which cannot earn an adequate financial return, but provide a satisfactory cost-benefit return when wider benefits are taken into account. Where operators of franchised passenger services are unable to pay the charges, the necessary subsidy will be provided. Where investment can be attributed to a particular operator, the costs of investment will be reflected in that operator's access charge, subject to the term of existing access agreements. Investment will be funded by Railtrack partly from its internally generated funds and partly from borrowings (from the National Loans Fund while it remains in the public sector).

Railtrack's role will be that of supplier of infrastructure services to operators of rail services: open access freight and passenger operators, and franchisees. Investment decisions must be customer-led. They may follow from performance standards agreed in access contracts between Railtrack and operators. It is for Railtrack to determine whether it needs to invest in order to meet the standards required, and whether it is in a position to recoup the cost of any investment from access charges. Railtrack will need to be satisfied that it will be possible to secure sufficient income to pay for the investment and achieve a return on the assets.

Railway infrastructure assets are long lived, and it may take many years to plan investment in and construct such assets. Operators may have access agreements which terminate before investment is completed. This maturity mismatch is significant because of the specific nature of the assets involved and the high sunk costs associated with the investment. Railtrack will be expected to take a commercial view of the maturity mismatch, seeking to maximise up-front contributions from operators where possible but otherwise financing investment costs from revenue.

In 1994, Railtrack will inherit an investment plan and the associated projects from BR. Beyond 1994, and for the medium-term, Railtrack must build into its investment plans the requirements of operators. In the early years, whilst the franchising market is developing, the public sector will clearly have a more prominent role in the investment process that in the longer term, when the role of private sector operators will increase.

You asked me to use the Thameslink 2000 project as an illustration. The rationale for Thameslink 2000 is to develop the north/south axis of which the central part is the Snow Hill tunnel. There are infrastructure pinch points, especially at Borough Market junction, which operates more trains in the peak from using the route. BR's operators would like to run a Bedford/Gatwick/Brighton service through the day but they cannot. Existing paths are used for essential services (commuter routes into Charing Cross, Waterloo East and Cannon Street). In future I would expect this sort of project to arise in the same way from a demand for additional capacity by operators, who over time will increasingly be in the private sector. Railtrack would have lead responsibility for examining ways of meeting that demand. It would discuss the precise demands with operators and the Franchising Director, and the arrangements—where appropriate—for any specific contributions towards investment. The Franchising Director and the operators would take the lead in ensuring that any rolling stock was acquired and that its characteristics were known to the Railtrack planners. That has to happen now, of course.

These arrangements will ensure that investment in infrastructure improvements is customer-driven with Railtrack balancing the risks and rewards associated with investment decisions. This will put in place the right incentives for the development of a healthy and efficient industry which responds to the needs of customers. As you can see from the Thameslink example, the planning which Railtrack and its customers will have to undertake in a major investment are in principle no different to those which happen now within BR.

John MacGregor

5 February 1993

APPENDIX 135

Letter from the Department of Transport

Thank you for your letter of 11 February asking for answers to a number of questions which owing to time constraints it was not possible to cover when I appeared before the Committee on 10 February. As requested, my answers are set out below.

(1) What is the Department's rough estimate of the eventual total number of franchises?

I would not even want to make a rough estimate at this stage. I have promised to provide within the next few months a "map" of possible franchises for the whole network.

(2) Will the Government guarantee the residual value of leased railway assets?

The Government wants the private sector to take key decisions on the procurement and management of rolling stock as soon as possible, and accept the risks and rewards which flow from them. As the franchised railway becomes established, a second-hand market in rolling stock will develop. An effective second-hand market should allay concerns about the residual value risk of leased assets. However, the Government recognises that such a market does not exist at present and that transitional measures may be required until it does. The consultation paper issued on 27 January identified a number of possible transitional measures, including public sector acceptance of some of the residual value risk. We are currently exploring these in detail with potential lessors, financiers and rolling stock manufacturers. We expect to conclude these discussions by Easter to enable an announcement to be made on the way forward.

(3) You have guaranteed the publication of a national timetable. Which body will perform this task? Will you ensure that it is widely on sale at an affordable price?

We intend to ensure that a national timetable is published. Railtrack, as track authority, will have responsibility for planning and producing a working timetable for the railway. That information will be available for reproduction in printed form. We expect that the private sector will see opportunities to publish a national timetable on a commercial basis. But we are proposing to insert a condition in Railtrack's licence which will require arrangements to be made for the publication of a national timetable if it would not otherwise be published by another party. We would expect the price of a printed timetable to be governed by commercial considerations.

(4) How much more will the HSE's proposed safety regime cost than the existing one? Can you break this down between the cost of setting up the regulatory framework, the cost of enforcement and the cost of compliance by operators?

It is too early to say what the costs of the safety regime will be and how those costs will be broken down, and therefore how the costs of the new safety regime will compare with current costs of ensuring safety.

However, the HSC's Report recognises that the safety regime will have resource implications for the railway industry eg in the production and validation of railway safety cases (RSC). The production of RSCs in practice will simply reflect the commitments and arrangements which a railway undertaking will anyway need to have in place for safe operation. The Report considers that the additional effort required to document and provide evidence to support a claim of proficiency should not be too onerous if managment systems are right. The Report also considers that the additional resources needed specifically because of the validation system are not a simple matter to predict but will not be unreasonable. The Health and Safety Executive (HSE) will also need additional resources for its activities under the new safety regime. The Report notes that there may be compensations with HSE guidance possibly representing a considerable saving in time and effort and with recognised schemes of assessment avoiding the burden of individual systems which would otherwise be required.

One of the fundamental principles governing the work of the HSC in drawing up their recommendations was that any system which emerged must not lead to any diminution of current safety standards. As far as possible, it should facilitate any necessary improvements of those standards. A further governing principle of the Report was that the degree of statutory control should be the minimum consistent with the need to ensure adequate and cost effective levels of control of risk and to secure public confidence.

The Government endorsed the principles of the Report. In particular we are concerned not to place any unnecessary regulatory burden or costs on the industry while ensuring we continue to have a safe railway.

(5) What incentive will Railtrack have to refrain from specifying over-rigorous safety standards or costly maintenance procedures?

Railtrack has every incentive to reach agreement on an equitable basis with potential operators in order to secure income through charges for access. It would not therefore be in Railtrack's commercial interests to specify over-rigorous safety standards or maintenance procedures.

Nevertheless, the Report recognises the dominant position of the validating body in the new safety regime and the scope for disagreements over the safety related terms of access or the assessment regime applied to the railway safety case. The Government has accepted the Report's recommendation for a dispute resolution procedure where the Secretary of State would be the adjudicator subject to the advice of the HSE. However we would wish to see recourse to arbitration as exceptional with the parties seeking HSE's views informally on any disputed issues involving safety before seeking formal, legally binding remedies.

(6) Which aspects of railway operating costs currently borne by your Department and BR will in future be the responsibility of the Franchising Authority and individual operators?

The Franchising Director will be responsible for providing continuing subsidy to support socially necessary services.

The intention under franchising is to transfer to the private sector the financial risks associated with operating costs. That is payroll costs, leasing or other financial charges for rolling stock or other assets and the costs of maintenance of these assets. Franchisees will also be expected to take on risk associated with fares revenue and risk related to performance specification.

John MacGregor

22 February 1993

Printed in the United Kingdom by HMSO
C8   4/93   000316 PP

ISBN 0-10-020013-3